ANCIENT CIVILIZATIONS
AND RUINS OF TURKEY

FROM PREHISTORIC TIMES UNTIL
THE END OF THE ROMAN EMPIRE

by

EKREM AKURGAL

ISTANBUL 1973

Translated
by
JOHN WHYBROW, M. A.
(pp. 3-36)
and
MOLLIE EMRE, B. A.
(pp. 38-230, 290-351)

First published 1969
Second edition 1970
by
MOBIL OIL TÜRK A. Ş.

Third edition 1973
by
HAŞET KİTABEVİ
469 İstiklal Cad. Istanbul

Printed in Turkey
Türk Tarih Kurumu Basımevi, Ankara 1973

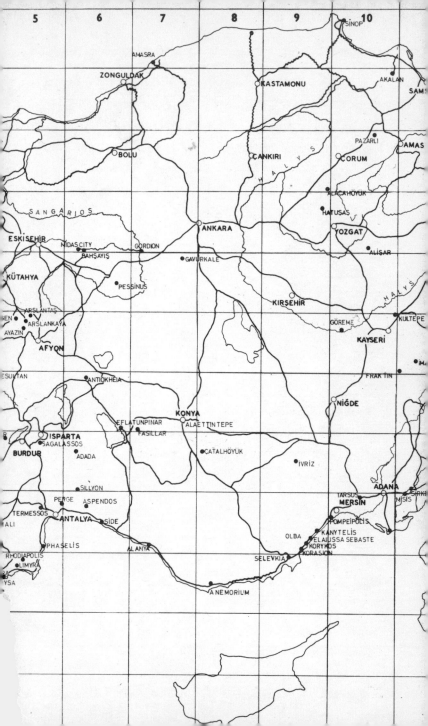

ANCIENT CIVILISATIONS
AND RUINS OF TURKEY

CONTENTS

(In alphabetic order)

V

FOREWORD

The present book is a revised and enlarged edition of the archaeological guide to the ruins of Turkey, which was first published in 1969. It covers the period from prehistoric times to the end of the Roman era.

The book has been written for those interested in archaeology and ancient history, as well as for the specialist. Detailed information about the ruins is presented in the main text, which is intended to be read before the sites are visited. The plans and photographs are provided with concise captions so that basic information concerning each site can be read on the spot.

The first part of the book (pp. 3 - 36) presents an outline of the successive civilizations which existed in Anatolia from the 7th millenium B. C. until the fall of the Roman Empire. A study of these pages will reveal that Anatolia was the birthplace of some of the most important ancient civilizations. This section, which I originally wrote in German, was translated by Mr. John Whybrow, M. A., formerly Head of the English Department, Faculty of Political Science, Ankara University.

The main part of the book (see P. IV), which deals with descriptions of the sites, was translated from my Turkish manuscript by Mrs. Mollie Emre, B. A., Assistant Director in the English Preparatory School of the Middle East Technical University, Ankara. The part of the text relating to Pergamon (pp. 74 - 82) was translated from my Turkish manuscript by Miss L. Alpers (now Mrs. Bordaz). The additions to the second edition (pp. 231 - 278) were written in English by myself.

Because of the extensive additions and revisions required for the second edition, a new stylistic redaction of the text was necessary. For their valuable assistance in this matter, I am greatly indebted to Mr. Norman Bissett, M. A., M. Phil., of the British Council, Ankara, Head of the English Department, Faculty of Political Science, Ankara University, and Mrs. Joanna Preston.

For their invaluable aid in the proof-reading of the text, I would like to thank Associate Professor Dr. Cevdet Bayburtluoğlu, Mr. Richard Harper, Deputy Director of the British Institute of Archaeology, Ankara, Mr. Norman Bissett, Mrs. Faith Bissett, B. S., M. A., Mrs. Preston and Miss Kathy Faulkner.

The plans and most of the line-drawings of human and animal figures were executed by Mr. Murat Erdim, after my sketches. Mr. Emre Madran was kind enough to draw the plans of Troy (Figs. 14, 15). The bulk of the figures on Hittite statues and reliefs, already published in my previous books, were prepared by Mr. Refik Epikman, according to my drafts.

The maps and plans which appear in the additional part of this edition were prepared by Associate Professor Dr. Cevdet Bayburtluoğlu, Associate Professor Dr. Ümit Serdaroğlu and Archaeologist Orhan Bingöl. The plan of Alabanda (Fig. 91) was drawn by Architect Mustafa Uz and that of Herakleia (Fig. 90) by Archaeologişt Nurettin Çelem.

I would like to thank my assistants, Mr. Coşkun Özgünel and Mr. Vedat İdil, who helped me greatly in the preparation of this book. I am also deeply indebted to the archaeologists Mr. Orhan Bingöl and Miss Gülgûn Kızılgüneş, who assisted me in the preparation of the bibliography, and Mr. Sabahattin Kulaklı, who prepared the index.

Permission to reproduce many of the black-and-white illustrations was granted by the Turkish Ministry of Tourism. I should like to extend my warmest thanks to Director Adnan Yarar, Archaeologist Mrs. Ayşe Bülent Erdem, and to Chief Photographer, Mr. Hayri Tuncer, for the excellent pictures. The majority of the coloured and black-and-white plates were taken by Mr. Mehmet Ali Düğenci, Photographer of the Turkish Historical Society. Others were taken by the Turkish and foreign photographers whose names are listed at the back of the book. Some new Photographs, taken at Side and Perge (Pls. 97, 99), are published in this book by courtesy of Professor Arif Müfid Mansel. Other Photographs, included for the first time in this edition were taken by Associate Professor Dr. Ümit Serdaroğlu (Pl. 93), by Coşkun Özgünel (Pl. 55) and by my son, Ali Akurgal (Pls. 96 b, 98).

I wish to express my appreciation to Mobil Oil Türk A. Ş., who first conceived the idea of producing a book of this kind, and who spared no expense in its publication.

Finally, I extend my thanks to Mr. Gökmen İğdemir, Director of the printing house of the Turkish Historical Society, and to his able and industrious staff, for their care in making this new edition of the book as nearly perfect as possible.

Ankara, November 1970   **Ekrem AKURGAL**

FOREWORD TO THE THIRD EDITION

The first two editions of this book which were published by Mobil Oil Türk enjoyed great popularity among specialists and tourists. The second edition became out of print in its first year.

In the present edition, which is now published by the Hachette Library in Istanbul, I have brought the bibliography up to date and revised the text, where necessary, in the light of new discoveries made in the last two years.

Ankara, 30 March 1973   **Ekrem AKURGAL**

PART ONE

ANCIENT CIVILIZATIONS

THE PREHISTORIC PERIOD (7000 - 2000 B.C.)

The excavations carried out in the last thirty years have revealed that civilizations of very great importance flourished in Anatolia during the prehistoric age. Years ago, Şevket Aziz Kansu was the first to discover the most ancient remains of civilization on the peninsula. In recent years, in the Antalya region, Kılıç Kökten and Enver Bostancı have brought to light cave sites at Karain, Belbaşı and Beldibi, some of which date back to the Upper Palaeolithic era. The next most ancient settlements in Anatolia are the mound at Mersin excavated by John Garstang and habitation levels at the Hacılar and Çatal Höyük sites, which James Mellaart uncovered. The fascinating wall paintings of Çatal Höyük represent the summit of all known Neolithic art (Ankara Museum).

The earliest evidences of agriculture were found in aceramic Hacılar, ca. 7040 B.C. according to Carbon 14 dating. Considerable quantities of food, such as wheat, barley and lentils, were found in the houses there. The bones of goats, sheep and horned cattle are visible among the remains of meals. The only household animals appear to have been dogs.

The Çatal Höyük settlement, where twelve different habitation levels have been distinguished, dating from approximately 6500 to 5650 B.C., stands out as an incomparable prehistoric centre of culture. It was here that man created one of his first great works of art.

The most important works are the mural paintings and painted relief sculptures which adorned the walls of the houses and domestic shrines. Some of these are now exhibited in the Ankara Museum. The shrines were located in the centre of a complex of four to five houses, usually consisting of one large room. Neither the houses nor the shrines had doors. Access was from the roof by means of wooden ladders. Both types of building have the same ground plan; they were built of mudbrick and had small windows set high up under the eaves. Every living room was provided with at least two additional raised floors. The main floor was reinforced at the edges with wood and coated with plaster and red paint. At one end was a bench which served as a divan, work-table and bed. Beneath this bench the dead were buried after the flesh had been removed from their bodies. These graves contained beautiful burial gifts, such as the magnificent obsidian mirror found in a woman's grave. In one of the shrines at Level VII, a mural painting, ca. 6200 by Carbon dating, was found which apparently represents the eruption of a volcano, supposedly the nearby Hasan Dağ. This is the earliest known landscape painting in history. Particularly favoured among the myriad themes of these polychrome mural paintings were hunting scenes, dancers and acrobats and above all paintings of a religious and funerary character.

The rites of some fertility cult were probably held in these domestic shrines. They contained a strikingly large number of bulls' heads or horns, mounted in rows along the walls or attached to the sides of the bench or to raised platforms. These no doubt represented the male deity; for the husbandmen of Anatolia the bull was not only a symbol of fertility and strength but, more important still, the genitor of the horned cattle without which they could not cultivate their land. This explains why, after agriculture first began in Anatolia, the male god was depicted in the shape of a bull and seldom in human form. This practice, as we shall see, persisted until the Hittite era (see Pl. 88a).

Only the great Mother Goddess appears in human form on the painted stucco reliefs of Çatal Höyük. However, she too is sometimes represented by her wild beasts. The beautiful, richly-coloured stucco relief of two leopards which adorned the wall of one of the shrines in Level VI, ca. 6000 B. C., may be assumed to represent the mighty goddess. A statuette depicting the goddess seated on a throne supported by two felines indicates that leopards were in fact her attributive animals. The goddess is about to give birth to a child — a typical posture and frequent motif of the Hacılar clay figurines. Statuettes have also been found at Çatal Höyük depicting the goddess giving birth to a bull's or ram's head. There is another mural relief from Level VII at Çatal Höyük which most probably represents a pregnant goddess, since her navel is more emphasized than usual by two engraved concentric circles. Childbirth, the bull and the bull's head are typical symbols of fertility. Characteristically, fertility symbols are the dominating feature of these places of worship in which the dead are buried. A consolation in death, they stand for rebirth or even life after death.

The clay figurines from Çatal Höyük and Hacılar are particularly expressive (Fig. 121). A favourite motif is the naked female body in various attitudes : reclining, kneeling, sleeping, and above all giving birth. The portrayal of male figures in isolation is rare : for instance, the god riding on a bull from Çatal Höyük — the oldest example of a motif which survived in Anatolia up to Roman times. On the other hand, male and female figures frequently appear together in hierogamic scenes closely entwined in a loving embrace.

The earliest earthenware vessels in Anatolia were made in the first Çatal Höyük period, ca. 6500 B. C. Beginning with the simple monochrome articles of the early Neolithic period, they gradually evolved into the magnificent pottery of the late Neolithic and early Chalcolithic era. In the upper two habitation levels at Hacılar, ca. 5400 to 5250 B. C. by radio carbon dating, superbly painted earthenware of unrivalled beauty has been brought to light. It may be claimed together with the finds from Çatal Höyük as the first great creative achievement of man (Ankara Museum).

In Anatolia, both stone and metal tools and artifacts occur in the Chalcolithic period which begins at Level V in Hacılar, ca. 5500 by radio carbon dating. This is the golden age of Hacılar, whose art works have already been mentioned. The important finds of Can Hasan, excavated by David French, belong to the same period (Ankara Museum).

In the late Chalcolithic age in Anatolia a period of stagnation set in which lasted through the fifth and fourth millennia. Practically 2000 years of retarded development had serious consequences. Anatolia, which had played a dominant role in the 7th and 6th millennia, fell far behind Mesopotamia until well into the 2nd millennium in cultural and political matters. While writing was invented in the Near East around 3000 B. C. and the peoples of that area attained a very high cultural level, the whole of Anatolia was sunk in a primitive, prehistoric village culture. Hamit Koşay discovered several major centres of this straggling late Chalcolithic civilization in central and eastern Anatolia. He unearthed some beautiful, highly polished mono-chrome pottery, in elegant forms, which possesses a remarkable artistic value in spite of the primitive level of life in those small settlements where it was produced (Ankara Museum). Some other important works were found at Alişar, excavated by the Americans under the direction of von der Osten.

In the first phase of the Anatolian Bronze Age, from roughly 3000 to 2500 B. C., no remarkable developments from the preceding late Chalcolithic era are noticeable in the central and eastern towns of the peninsula. In fact, this period in Anatolia should also be considered late Chalcolithic.

The foundation of the first settlement at Troy is notable, for it shows a close affinity with the early Bronze Age culture of the Aegean and Cyclades and has scarcely anything in common with the old established culture of the Anatolian centres. House 102 uncovered at Troy has all the typical features of a megaron, as Blegen pointed out, and an obvious connection with the west (see Fig. 14).

The buildings and works of art excavated by Seton Lloyd at Beyce Sultan (Ankara Museum) deserve special attention.

THE PERIOD OF HATTIAN CULTURE (2500 - 2000 B. C.)

It is not until the middle of the third millennium that a change begins to take place in the Anatolian peninsula. This is the point at which the Bronze Age really starts. At this time, there lived in central Anatolia a race of people, the Hatti, whose name has come to us through Hittite sources. The Hatti gave their name to the Anatolian peninsula, which was known in Mesopotamia as the Land of the Hatti from the beginning of the Akkadian Dynasty, 2350 to 2150 B. C., until the time of the Assyrian kings in the 8th century. Even the Hittites called their kingdom the Land of the Hatti; thus, though their language was called Nesian, they were known as the people of the Hatti Land. In the few existing fragments, the Hattic language is chiefly recognizable by its extensive use of prefixes. Hattic is different from all other Asian and Near Eastern languages. The influence of the Hattic civilization is also apparent in Hittite religious rites, state and court ceremonies and in their mythology. As the name implies, Hattusa, the Hittite capital, was originally a Hattic settlement. The pronounced Hattic elements in Hittite culture show clearly that this protohistoric people had reached an advanced intellectual level. Outside the Mesopotamian area, they are the earliest civilized nation of that age which we know by name and of whose language and religion we have some knowledge. The finest works of art of the period originated from the very heart of the old Hattic civilization. Thirty years ago, in the royal tombs at Alaca Höyük near Hattusa, Turkish archaeologists Remzi Oğuz Arık and Hamit Koşay discovered bronze, gold and silver objects of extraordinary beauty and value. These works of art even overshadowed Schliemann's "Treasure of Priam", and placed the Anatolian Bronze Age in the forefront of historical research. They include mysterious, unfamiliar objects, which cast a strange and powerful spell on the beholder (Pls. 84b, 85).

Troy II. The history of another Anatolian Bronze Age culture is reflected in the ruins of the second settlement of Troy (Fig. 15).

Troy II signifies a development of the previous settlement. The essential character of the new period is early Aegean and early Cycladic, as in Troy I. Blegen rightly emphasized the western character of this culture. Early Helladic "Urfirnis" pottery, already found in the upper levels of Troy I, was again imported and also manufactured in the local workshops. The connection with the cultural centres of Central Asia Minor and the east is clearly recognizable. Matz is right in saying that the rulers of Troy were no mere peasant-kings. They knew how to exploit their hold over the international trade-routes in order to maintain their dominion and extend their territory. All the metals like gold, silver, copper and tin must have been imported from the central or eastern parts of Anatolia and from the east. Trojan artists learned various methods of metal-working, including the granulation process, a sophisticated goldsmith's technique, from oriental jewellers who had 500 years of such toreutic experience behind them. Their tubular earrings, for instance, are based on an ancient eastern model. The finest examples of the Trojan goldsmith's art belong to a hoard which was uncovered by Heinrich Schliemann. Besides bronze vessels and weapons, this long-lost treasure contained goblets of solid gold and silver, gold jewellery and bars of silver. The bars must have been intended for barter purposes. One gold vessel belonging to the hoard, the so-called "saucière", 7.5 cms. high and 600 grams in weight, is Aegean in style. The twin handles bear a close resemblance to the "depas", a specifically Trojan vessel. The two beak-like spouts are identical in form to the elegant, beak-spouted Helladic bowls of the same period which are made of clay and coated with "Urfirnis".

The potters of Troy II were already conversant with the two major technical innovations of the time, the kiln and the potter's wheel. At the first cultural level at Troy, the vessels were made by hand and fired on an open fire. In both Troy I and II, the links with inner Asia Minor are plainly visible. The second walled city of Troy suffered a fearful catastrophe between 2200 and 2100 B. C. The destruction of the stronghold may have been due to the incursions of the Indo-European tribes into Asia Minor which began just at this time. However, in the succeeding unimportant early Bronze Age building periods III - V, there are no traces of a new population. A cultural change does not appear to occur until the foundation of the new city of Troy VI, ca. 1800 B. C.

THE EARLY HITTITE PERIOD (2000-1750 B. C.)

The influx of the Indo-European tribes into Asia Minor towards the end of the 3rd millennium now halted the impressive growth of the Hattic civilization. There is an exact parallel for this period of stagnation in Troy, where the unimportant building phases III - V follow the golden age of the second settlement. The break in development which occurred in both regions of the peninsula at the same time suggests that there is a causal relation between the cultural impoverishment and the disorder which probably resulted from the Indo-European invasions.

We have records of a number of Central Anatolian city-states in the first quarter of the 2nd millennium which were ruled by minor potentates : Kanesh (Nesa), Kussara, Hattusa, Zalpa and Puruskhanda. Like many other, so far undiscovered cities, they began life as principalities of the native peoples, i.e. Hattic minor states. Then, following the Indo-European immigrations, they fell gradually into the hands of the Hittite rulers.

At first, the most important of these towns was Kanesh, identical with present-day Kültepe, near Kayseri. The excavations directed by Tahsin and Nimet Özgüç, with Kemal Balkan in charge of philological research, have yielded excellent results. It is in Kültepe that we can discern the first concrete traces of the Hittites, whose presence there was established by Sedat Alp. He demonstrated convincingly that the suffixes ala, ili, ula, found in native proper names mentioned in the Kültepe writings, are Hittite transformations of the Hattic suffixes al, il, and ul. Recently, moreover, continuing the work of H. G. Güterbock and using new arguments, he has virtually proved that Kanesh and Nesa were one and the same. Since the Hittites called their tongue Nesian, Nesa (now Kültepe) was most probably their capital. A large building of the megaron type uncovered on the main mound at Kültepe dating ca. 2000 B. C. is also clear evidence proving the arrival of the Indo-European Hittites in this formerly Hattian city.

Writing was first employed in Anatolia in the days of the city-states. Thousands of Assyrian cuneiform tablets have been found in the Assyrian colony of Kültepe which throw light on many contemporary matters. Even early Hittite rulers like Anitta, king of Kussara, seem to have been already using Assyrian cuneiform in the 18th century B. C.

The unique art of the Hittites developed from a happy cross-fertilization of the cultures of the indigenous Hattic and immigrant Indo-European peoples. In the main, the conquerors respected the religion and customs of the natives and adapted themselves to local conditions. The Hittites' adoption of Hattic place names and proper names shows clearly how the two ethnic elements fused together.

The advanced artistic level of this early period can best be judged by its monochrome pottery (Pl. 86), which exemplifies the native development of an old trend. The hallmark of the period is the longspouted jug. (Pl. 86c). The abrupt inversion of form below the belly of the jug and the hard contours display an attractive tectonic structure. The burnished red-brown surface enhances the plain, severe design. The harmonious line of the handle and the boldly elongated spout have a controlled energy and a compelling attraction. The pair of sharp-edged nipples at the shoulder of the jug and the sharply profiled tip of the spout have not only a decorative effect but also a specific function. The tip of the spout is a drip-catcher, and the nipples provide a grip for one hand while the other holds the handle. The burnished slip attempts to reproduce the effect of metal. The well-proportioned design is in fact modelled on metal vessels. This jug represents the apex of a long evolutionary process, and its classic form. After this, there is no further evolution – only imitation and, finally, decadence.

Other vessels of this period display similar sharp inversions of form, hard contours, and boldly elongated spouts. These features persist in the ceramic art of the succeeding Old Hittite Kingdom (Pl. 86).

The advanced cultural level of this early historical period is also evident in other artistic activities. At the Kültepe and Karahöyük excavations, impressive buildings have been discovered which indicate the presence of palaces and temples at that time.

THE OLD HITTITE KINGDOM (1750 - 1450 B. C.)

The dominant role in shaping the new Hattic – Indo-European culture in Anatolia was played by the Nesians, i.e. those who spoke the Nesian language, but were called the "People of Hatti" because they inhabited the land of the Hattians. The term "Hittites" is of modern use and derives from the Old Testament. From the outset, the new state was so strong that a few generations later Mursili I (ca. 1620 - 1590 B. C.) was able to conquer first Aleppo and then Babylon, thus causing the downfall of the Hammurabi dynasty. The Hittites used the cuneiform script imported from Mesopotamia in the 18th and 17th centuries. They also had a picture-writing which can be seen on their seals and public monuments and is related to the hieroglyphs found in Crete.

The art of the Old Hittite Kingdom is closely linked with that of the earlier age. Some of the artistic pottery from Alaca imitates the design and the tall arched spouts of the burnished monochrome vessels of the preceding period. However, we can trace the beginnings of a new aesthetic concept in the slender proportions of many vessels from Alaca, Alişar and Acem Höyük (Pls. 86 a-d). The high standard of living in the Old Kingdom is reflected in the numerous handsome earthenware hip-baths discovered at Alişar and elsewhere. The somewhat abstract lions and bulls of the previous age take on a more naturalistic form in the art of the Old Hittite Kingdom.

Old Kingdom architecture continued in the native Anatolian tradition; nevertheless there are unmistakably original features, both technical and formal. One example is the appearance of the Cyclopean wall system, which was hitherto unknown in Anatolia. On the citadel of Hattusa, the seat of the Hittite rulers, there must have been palaces similar to those recently discovered in the cities of the early historical age. The latest German excavations at Boğazköy have revealed that the stone-vaulted subterranean passages which were used for defensive sorties in the Empire period were also known in the Old Hittite Kingdom.

THE HITTITE EMPIRE (1450 - 1200 B. C.)

In the 15th and 14th centuries, the Hittites established one of the three most important states in the Near East. In the 13th century, they shared with the Egyptians the hegemony of the eastern world and created a civilization of great originality and distinction.

Hittite art reached its peak during the Empire. Monumental sculpture and architecture began to flourish at this time. The representational art fostered by the building of the huge temples and palaces of the Hittites held an eminent position in the eastern world. The Hittites created the best military architecture of the Near East. Their system of offensive defence-works, handed down from the Old Kingdom, grew into a unique type of fortification under the Empire. The impressive Cyclopean walls at Hattusa and Alaca display a high level of craftsmanship. From the point of view of their strategic contouring in a very difficult terrain and in the layout of their offensive defence-works, the walls of ancient Hattusa are an unrivalled masterpiece (Fig. 139).

At the German excavations in Hattusa (Boğazköy), five temples have been uncovered whose size and architectural design place them among the finest monuments of their time (2nd millennium). The largest of them, the temple of the local weather god, is reasonably well-preserved and still gives a vivid impression of its time. The whole complex, storerooms included, is 160 m. long and 135 m. wide. The temple itself is a rectangular building with an inner court. On the north-eastern side there is an additional wing containing nine rooms; here the actual places of worship were located. In the largest of these stood the statue of the weather god. This, unfortunately, is no longer in existence (for new discoveries see the chapter on Boğazköy).

The major characteristic of Hittite architecture is its completely asymmetrical ground plan. The Hittites employed square piers as supports and had neither columns nor capitals. Unique and typical are the large windows with low parapets which were set not into the walls of the courtyard but into the outer walls of the temple. The statue of the god stood in a projecting section of the room so that it was illuminated from three sides. This desire for light suggests that Hittite religious worship once took place in the open air, as was still the custom in the Yazılıkaya sanctuary (Fig. 144).

It is unfortunate that not a single cult statue has survived; in fact, we have no free-standing sculpture at all from the Empire period. On the other hand, a great number of impressive-looking reliefs have been preserved. The outstanding reliefs of the period are carved on the face of a rock formation at Yazılıkaya, the holy place 2 km. to the north-east of Hattusa. The large open gallery with its reliefs of male and female deities formed the shrine of the adjacent temple, whose foundations have since been uncovered. Whereas in Hattusa the religious rites were carried out in closed rooms in front of the cult statue, in Yazılıkaya they were performed in the open air before the reliefs of deities. These reliefs present a collective picture of all the Hittite gods.

In the side-chamber, king-worship took place, and the statue of King Tudhaliya IV once stood at the north-east end. The pedestal of this statue and a cartouche relief on the wall have been preserved. The remaining reliefs in the chamber represent King Tudhaliya being embraced by the god Şarruma, and also the sword god and a procession of twelve other gods. Like the mountain god represented on the king's cartouche, all these reliefs face north, i.e. towards the statue. Anyone entering the now inaccessible south entrance to the side-chamber would be faced with the dominating presence of the king's statue at the north end.

The lions of the Lion Gate at Boğazköy and the sphinxes of Alaca can still be seen in situ. The museums of Istanbul and Berlin each preserve one of the sphinxes of the Boğazköy Sphinx Gate.

The relief sculpture of a god from the door jamb of the King's Gate at Boğazköy is now in the Ankara Museum, together with the orthostat reliefs from the walls of Alaca. The iconographic details of the Hittite reliefs indicate that the sculptors worked to a fixed plan and rules. Not only the individual details of the headdress, hairstyle and dress, but also the modelling of the limbs invariably followed a set scheme. The facial features, eyes, eyebrows, mouth and ears were always drawn in the same way. Characteristically, the Hittite male figure is invariably depicted wearing an earring, sometimes a beard, but never a moustache. The position of the arms is always the same whether or not the figure is holding anything. In male figures, the arm nearest the observer is always sharply flexed and pressed against the body, while the other arm is slightly flexed and a little outstretched. In female figures, both arms are always flexed and outstretched (Fig. 51).

Ceramic art of the Empire period is insignificant compared with sculpture, although there is some evidence that one type of polychrome technique was perfected. From Bitik, there is a very beautiful vessel with figures in relief whose facial features have much in common with the Alaca Höyük relief sculptures. This distinguished example of court pottery is dated around 1400 B.C.

The second German excavations at Boğazköy, which began under Kurt Bittel in 1931, were successfully continued under his direction after the Second World War. Each dig yielded new finds of first-rate artistic quality and importance; for instance, two splendid clay bulls were unearthed during excavations on the citadel called Büyük Kale (Pl. 84 a).

During the Hittite period, there were also other states in Anatolia. In the east and south-east lay the Mitanni Kingdom, the most powerful of the Hurrian lands, which was of major importance around the middle of the 2nd millennium (ca. 1650 - 1450). Hurrian is one of the strangest languages of the east. It has an agglutinative character and is unlike Semitic, Indo-European and the prefixing Hattic language. In the spheres of religion and literature, the Hurrian civilization exercised a strong influence on the Hittites. During the Empire, the Hittites adopted the Hurrian conception of the deities. The rock reliefs of the Yazılıkaya sanctuary embody this concept in plastic form. The Gilgamesh epic, the Kumarbi myth and Kikkuli's treatise on horse-training are derived from Hurrian originals. The Hurrian culture reveals Indo-Aryan and Luwian influences. All the rulers of Mitanni had Indian names. Thus the Hurrians were ruled by an aristocracy of Indo-Aryan origin. The members of this apparently very sparse line of nobles were charioteers and mounted knights. They were called Marianni and it was certainly through them that horse-breeding and the use of war-chariots became widespread in the Near East. According to the research carried out so far, the only evidence of a Hurrian art is in their stone-engraving and pottery. The most typical motifs on their seals are hybrid animals, the pillars of heaven and the sacred tree. On some seals Cretan and Mycenaean influences can be detected in the portrayal of chariots and the rendering of the flying gallop. Most typically Hurrian are the large, cup-shaped vessels with their decorative patterns on a black background. This type of pottery appears during the reign of Shaushattar in the middle of the 15th century and continues in the more refined examples at Alalakh. Other works which can be considered as products of Mitannian art are the mural paintings of Nuzi that include frontal views of cows' heads and heads of women with cows' ears.

In the south of the Anatolian peninsula lived the Luwians, an Indo-European race whose existence can only be inferred from their linguistic heritage. The same is true of the Palaians, likewise Indo-Europeans, who lived in the region of Paphlagonia. The countries of Arzawa and Kizzuwadna were situated in the south of Anatolia. Ahhiyawa, which is mentioned in the Hittite texts, was probably located somewhere in the south-west of the peninsula.

The Middle Bronze Age foundation of Troy VI, which followed the Early Bronze Age Trojan civilization, occurred at about the same time as the foundation of the first city-states by the immigrant Indo-European tribes. It is perhaps no mere accident that the Early Bronze Age ends and the Middle Bronze Age begins in Hellas at exactly the same time. The rise of these new and contemporaneous civilizations in three neighbouring areas of the ancient world must be connected with the great Indo-European immigrations which began towards the end of the 3rd millennium and probably continued until the beginning of the 2nd millennium. Blegen has already demonstrated the original relationship between the people of Troy VI and the Middle Helladic states of the Greek mainland. A similar but much less obvious affinity originating from the same source can be discerned between the Hittite and Troy VI civilizations. Although the Hittites had always been under a strong oriental influence, their civilization has certain basic features in common with Mycenae and Troy VI, especially in architecture and town planning. However, there seems to have been very little direct contact between Troy and Hattusa. Not even the minutest fragment of Hittite pottery has been found at Troy. The similar traits which can be observed in the architecture and pottery of the two cultures do not imply any direct contact. They are more probably due to local Anatolian influences which reached Troy by various circuitous routes. Overland communications were unsafe and Troy was linked to the west by tradition and by her geopolitical position. Matt pottery, of Helladic and Cycladic origin, and Mycenaean ware figure predominantly among the imported ceramics. Moreover, Cretan works of art and Cypriot ceramic fragments have been found, which are further indications that Troy VI had established relations with the outside world via maritime routes. The local pottery of Troy VI is monochrome, modest, and has little attraction. The best products are the Minyan ware found in large quantities in the older habitation levels of the sixth settlement. Like their contemporaries who lived on the Greek mainland, the Trojans had brought this type of pottery with them from their common homeland.

The topmost habitation level of the sixth layer (ca. 1325 - 1275 B. C.) and the level VIIa (ca. 1275 - 1240) are Homer's Troy. It was the city's important strategic position and the rising economic ambitions of the Mycenaeans that led to the Trojan war. Possibly the Iliad is the story of the unsuccessful attempts of the Achaeans to take Troy VI. As we first read in the Odyssey, it was only through the stratagem of the Wooden Horse that the impregnable fortress was eventually conquered. It is this mythical episode of the great epic that proves the historical truth of the Trojan War. A poet's imagination is of course highly inventive, but how would Homer or his predecessors have managed to invent the Trojan Horse legend if the Achaeans had not actually erected the wooden statue of a horse in Troy as an expression of thanks to Poseidon the Earth-Shaker for destroying by earthquake the mighty citadel they could not conquer? Today, thanks to Blegen's keen eye, we know that Troy first fell victim to a severe earthquake in 1275 and afterwards to the Achaean attack in 1240. However, no one could maintain that the epic poets were aware of this act of nature. There are no references to it in the poetry of the time. Thus, the idea of the Wooden Horse is the historical core of the legend. Success was granted the Achaeans only after the terrible disaster had befallen the city. The Trojans scarcely had time to repair the city walls, renovate a few of the old buildings and erect some new houses before the crafty and ruthless Achaeans came and set fire to the town.

The power of the Trojans, which had been a bulwark of Anatolia against the west and the Balkans throughout the 2nd millennium, ended unhappily with this blow they suffered at the hands of their aggressive cousins. Soon after, the city was destroyed, about 1180 B. C., the Thracians, who had long had designs on the fertile regions of north-west Asia Minor, stormed the Hittite Empire in huge waves.

ANATOLIA'S DARK AGE (1180 - 750 B. C.)

The presence of the Thracians in Troy VII b 2 is proved by the large quantities of "Buckelkeramik" found in that level. This is a specific type of pottery of Eastern European peoples. In Hattusa, written sources cease around 1180. This date also accords well with the assumption that Hattusa fell victim to attacks by the Thracians. The annals of the Assyrian king Tiglath-Pileser I, who reigned between 1112 and 1074, form an important document concerning the immigrations of the East European tribes into Asia Minor. From them we learn that he waged war against the Mushki, who first appeared fifty years before his reign began on the north frontier of Assyria in the region of the Upper Tigris. Thus these Mushki (possibly the Moesians of south-east Europe) and many other Balkan tribes had stood since about 1170 before the Assyrian

borders, after overrunning Troy and Hattusa. Egyptian sources also agree
entirely with these dates. It is true that Rameses III (1200 - 1168) uses the
name "Sea or Island Peoples" for the tribes who had penetrated the borders
and coast of his kingdom; however, since he says that they destroyed among
others Arzawa and Carchemish, we can take his records as a confirmation of
the Assyrian annals, for Carchemish lies precisely on the upper Euphrates,
not far from the frontiers of the Assyrian Empire. The Egyptian sources tell us
that not only the Thracian and South-East European tribes, but also the Sea
and Island Peoples took part in this huge migration. Another current in this
immense human tidal wave was the Dorian migration to the Greek mainland.

The consequences of this merciless aggression were catastrophic. The
invaders destroyed the civilizations of Asia Minor with such cruelty and
violence that a dark age resulted which lasted for two hundred years in western
Anatolia and at least 400 years in the rest of the peninsula. Years ago I pointed
out that from 1180 - 775 Central Anatolia was very thinly populated and
occupied by nomadic tribes who presumably left no material traces in mound
settlements. So great was the catastrophe that even the Hittite tradition
disappeared completely in Central Anatolia. One thing is certain : there were
no urban settlements in the heart of the Hittite lands until the birth of the
Phrygian state. Thus none of the present town names of Central Asia Minor
like Gordion, Ankara, Yozgat, Çorum, Tokat, Boğazköy or Kırşehir is of
Hittite origin, though centres south of the Halys bend and southern Anatolian
towns like Niğde, Adana, Malatya, Maraş and Carchemish all have names of
Hittite origin and date back at least as far as Hittite times.

NEO - HITTITE ART (1200-700 B.C.)

In South-East Anatolia and North Syria, where there appears to have
been no dark age, the late Hittite principalities became remarkably active
after the fall of the Empire. Late Hittite art can be divided into three distinct
styles, namely, Old Neo-Hittite, Middle Neo-Hittite and Late Neo-Hittite.

The Old Neo-Hittite style is a continuation of the art of the Empire
and is found exclusively in Malatya. The great relief of Malatya (Ankara
Museum) is a typical example of this artistic trend (Fig. 123). Two consecutive
scenes are portrayed. On the left is the weather god in a chariot drawn by
two bulls called Seri and Hurri. On the right he is seen receiving the libation
offered by King Sulumeli, after the god has alighted from his chariot. In his
right hand the god holds a boomerang and in his left a thunderbolt. In the
background on a level with his head there are two hieroglyphs representing
divinity and the weather god symbol, both indicating his identity. Both
stylistically and iconographically the Malatya relief is a late descendant of the
Yazılıkaya and Alaca schools, which produced outstanding sculpture during
the Empire period.

The Middle Neo-Hittite style (900-750 B. C.), unlike the Old Neo-Hittite,
is not an immediate continuation of the Anatolian-Hittite tradition. Although
the art forms of the Empire period persisted, Middle Neo-Hittite developed

its own individual features. Its best and most characteristic examples were found in Carchemish and Zincirli (Pls. 88 b, 89 b, 91). The former are now in the Ankara Museum, and the latter in Istanbul and Berlin.

The Late Neo-Hittite style (750 - 700 B. C.) embraces three special artistic currents: the Assyrian Hittite style, the Aramaean Hittite style and the Phoenician Hittite style. To the first trend belong the Araras reliefs from Carchemish (Fig. 133), to the second the sculptures from Zincirli, (Pls. 17, 18) Sakçegözü (Fig. 129), and Maraş and to the third the majority of the Karatepe sculptures (Pl. 105). There were active schools of sculpture which produced outstanding artistic work in the second half of the 8th century, particularly in Zincirli and Sakçegözü. The works of art they produced exercised a significant influence on Greek and Etruscan art. The lions and griffins of Greek sculpture are faithful imitations of those produced in these centres. Greek art was also influenced in many other ways by Late Neo-Hittite art. Two decisive factors were the key position of the individual principalities as the gateway to the Near East, and the favourable historical circumstances of the 8th century. Thus the common culture of the Hittites, Luwians and Aramaeans, created throughout years of peaceful co-existence, enabled them to become worthy representatives of the eastern world.

URARTIAN ART (900 - 600 B. C.)

In the extreme east of Anatolia on the plateau surrounding Lake Van lived the Urartians, descendants of the Hurrians. They built an empire and a civilization of strongly Assyrian stamp. Their works of art enjoyed great favour in their day. In particular, bronze cauldrons embellished with human heads or animal foreparts were exported to Phyrgia, Greece and Etruria. Some excellent examples of Urartian art now in the Ankara Museum are the bronze cauldrons adorned with human and bulls' heads and dating from the end of the 8th century B. C.

Our knowledge of the Urartian civilization is steadily increasing. The Soviet scholars Piotrovski and Oganesyan have discovered Urartian building levels containing outstanding works of art at Karmir Blur and Arin Berd. Now there is a series of excavations at several Urartian sites under the direction of the Turkish philologists, historians and archaeologists Balkan, Bilgiç, Erzen, Özgüç and Temizer who have unearthed rich new finds of exceptional quality.

PHRYGIAN ART (750 - 300 B. C.)

In Central Asia Minor, the Phrygians created a great civilization which belonged essentially to the Greek sphere but was also strongly influenced by the Neo-Hittites and Urartians.

The Phrygians were originally a Thracian tribe and probably took part in the destruction of Troy VII a and Hattusa. Their first archaeological traces, however, appear in the middle of the 8th century. Midas founded the Phrygian

Empire, but it was short-lived (ca. 725 - 675 B. C.) and was devastated by the Cimmerian invasion in the first quarter of the 7th century.

The most important finds were made in Gordion, the Phrygian capital, and in other centres of Phrygian civilization such as Alişar, Boğazköy, Alaca, Pazarlı and Ankara. The works of art found during the German excavations at Gordion, which were carried out at the beginning of this century, are now in the Istanbul Museum. The finds from the American excavations, which have been carried out under Rodney S. Young for the last 15 years, are in the Ankara Museum. The works of art recently uncovered in the tumuli of Ankara are now in the Museum of the Middle East Technical University.

The Phrygian language was probably related to Thracian dialects. Their writing was very similar to the Greek, and was already in use before the end of the 8th century. The outstanding works of art of the Phrygians had a noticeable influence on Cycladic vase painting. Phrygian metal artifacts and textile products were very popular in the Hellenic world.

In the first half of the 6th century, after the Cimmerian invasion, the Phrygians experienced a second golden age which blossomed in their new centres between Eskişehir and Afyon. We find there some interesting monumental rock carvings in a good state of preservation (Pls. 81, 82; Figs. 109-115).

Probably the most imposing of these monuments is the so-called Tomb of Midas at Yazılıkaya near Eskişehir (Fig. 111). This relief is 17 m. high and carved in the rock face. It represents the façade of a building and provides an architectural frame for the niche in which the goddess Cybele was displayed at festivals. The outstanding feature of Phrygian rock façades which distinguishes them from all other contemporary rock monuments of Asia Minor is their geometrical design. The terracotta friezes of the same period and even the much older works of art made of wood, mosaic and ceramics, use the same vocabulary of ornamental design. This use of ornamentation expresses an individual national character and creates a delightful contrast to the mighty soaring proportions of these huge monuments. Phrygian rock monuments appear to strain after grandeur, and they tend to reproduce a form of miniature art in gigantic proportions; nevertheless, the transformation is successful. The Yazılıkaya cult monument bears two inscriptions, of which the upper one contains the name Midas. Unfortunately, the name does not help us to give an exact date to the monument, since, according to Herodotus, there were several Phrygian kings called Midas or Gordios. However, the other Phrygian rock façades in the area can be dated somewhere between 575 and 550 B. C. by means of those reliefs which show a strong Greek influence. Thus the Yazılıkaya monument, which conforms to this type of rock façade, cannot date back further than the beginning of the 6th century B. C. (see also the text to Fig. 115 a, b).

THE LYDIAN, LYCIAN AND CARIAN CIVILIZATIONS

The same period saw the rise of the Lycian, Lydian and Carian civilizations in West Central Anatolia. These peoples can be regarded as indigenous. Like Hittite, the Lycian and Lydian languages belong to the Indo-European-

Anatolian group. However, Lycian and Lydian contain many pre-Indo-European elements. These peoples can be regarded, at least partly, as the representatives of the old pre-Hittite civilization in Anatolia. Their descendants survived probably until the first half of the first millennium, but no archaeological traces have as yet been found.

Xanthos, the Lycian capital, is one of the most beautiful ruins of Anatolia (Pl. 78 b). The enchanting, well-preserved Lycian monuments of between 600 and 200 B. C. together with the equally well-preserved Roman ruins, compel our admiration (Pl. 5). Recent French excavations under Pierre Demargne have unearthed some impressive works of art, which are now in the Istanbul Museum.

Extremely important discoveries have also been made at Sardis, capital of the one-time Lydian Kingdom much admired by the Greeks. G. M. A. Hanfmann has carried out systematic excavations there (Fig. 43) since 1958.

Carian has not yet been deciphered, although the script is similar to Lydian, Phrygian, Lycian and Greek. Thus it is not possible to determine which language group it belongs to. Herodotus writes that the Carians were called Lelegians according to Cretan legend, and lived on the islands in Minoan times. However, the Carians themselves disagreed with this view and maintained that they were natives of Anatolia and related to the Lydians and Mysians. Earlier Italian excavations and those now being carried out under Doro Levi in the region occupied by the Carians have brought notable results. The discoveries of the new Italian excavations at Iasos can be seen in the Izmir Museum. The earlier finds of the Swedish digs at Labranda are also in the Izmir Museum. The civilizations of Eastern and Central Anatolia we have so far briefly dealt with were affected by the influence of the Greeks living in Western Anatolia from at least 650 B.C. on. After 600 B.C. the Greek influence is even more evident. Nevertheless, these civilizations retained individual characteristics up to the time of Alexander the Great. It is after 300 B. C. that the Greek style in art becomes completely dominant. From the point of view of subject matter and historical content, of course, the works of art produced in this period derive from the old established Anatolian tradition. This tradition survives as a successful blend through the Roman period up to the spread of Christianity.

THE AGE OF THE GRECO - ANATOLIAN
CIVILIZATION

Recent excavations in Izmir (Smyrna) and Miletos have clearly indicated that the Aeolian and Ionian cities on the west coast of Anatolia were founded around 1000 B. C. With the help of the new material, we are now in a position to assess the true importance of the part played by East Greek art within the Hellenic world. At first, these early Greek settlements in Anatolia were poor and primitive. During the first few centuries from 1050 to 750 B. C. the immigrant Greeks subsisted mainly on the produce of their land. They lived in crudely constructed, one-room houses (Pl.41 b). The Greek motherland

41 a

was the main influence in their art. Their protogeometric and geometric style pottery was produced locally. They copied the models of the Greek mainland in all essentials of technique and style, but new impetus was given by the Ionian cities. Probably as early as the 9th century the Panionion, or Ionian League, was founded - a form of Ionian expansion against the Aeolian cities. The capital of the League lay on the coast at the foot of the Mycale mountains. By means of this political confederation the Ionian cities were enabled to spread as far as north-west Asia Minor. The foundation of the Milesian colony of Cyzicus goes back to the beginning of the 7th century, as the potsherds found there prove.

The East Greek world made its first cultural gains during this early period. Although the motherland had a long lead in economic and artistic matters, spiritual leadership now lay in the hands of the Greeks of Asia Minor. The founding of their oldest cities and the creation of the Homeric Epic won for the Ionians an ascendency in social development and intellectual life which they continued to enjoy in the following period.

When the Milesians began to colonize the Mediterranean and Black Sea coasts about the middle of the 7th century, the East Greek world reached its zenith. The wealth accruing from trade and industrial production was the basis for the prosperity which grew during the 6th century in Anatolia.

The originality of East Greek art and culture owes a considerable debt to its long-standing contact with the indigenous Lydian, Lycian and Carian cultures in Anatolia, not forgetting the Phrygians. For although they originated from Thrace, the Phrygians became so thoroughly assimilated into the native Anatolian civilizations that they were already a true people of Asia Minor by the beginning of the 6th century.

The Ionian civilization was a product of the co-existence of Greek people with the natives of Asia Minor. With the help of many oriental influences, it produced in the 6th century B. C. not only a magnificent body of poetry and a unique art, but also laid the foundations of the exact sciences thus making possible the first achievements of the western mind. The first half of the 6th century saw the beginnings of Ionian architecture and sculpture (Pls. 19,42). The end of the previous century had already seen the development of the Aeolic style of architecture, under the influence of oriental models. The best examples were found in Neandria (Fig. 17) and ancient Smyrna (Fig. 41). In each town were found a temple and several capitals, together with other important architectural fragments of the Aeolic order.

The Ionic capital is a Greek modification of the Aeolic. It was first made in the second quarter of the 6th century in one of the Ionian centres of the Greek world. The superb Ionic buildings are among the most outstanding achievements of mankind. The temple at Ephesus, 55×115 m. in size, is a huge edifice. Built shortly before the middle of the 6th century, it was the first monumental sanctuary in the world to be built entirely of marble. With its 127 impressive columns, it was regarded as one of the wonders of the world. Unfortunately, only fragments remain of these wonderful 6th-century Ionian buildings, and they are now preserved in the museums of London, Berlin, Istanbul, Izmir and Ephesus.

The Greek motherland came under the spell of the exquisite works of Ionian artists as well as of Aeolian and Ionian poets. The new elements in Attic sculpture of the 2nd half of the 6th century — the chiton, the himation, the folds of drapery and the radiant expression on the faces — are specific characteristics of Ionian art.

The Ionian schools of sculpture were centred mainly in Miletos and Samos. The Samian artists worked much more in the style of the Cycladic and Attic craftsmen at first, but, towards the middle of the 6th century, sculpture was produced on the island which reflected the Ionian taste of Asia Minor. One of the masterpieces of this new tendency is a splendid head in the Istanbul Museum, whose body was recognized a few years ago in the Samos Museum (Pl. 19). The finest Ionic sculpture is now in the museums of Berlin, London, Istanbul and Izmir.

In architecture, the Ionian contribution to Greek art was much greater and even more significant than in sculpture. The elegance, charm and originality of Greek architecture are largely due to the creativity and fine sensitivity of the Ionian artists. The slim proportions of the Ionic order lightened the solidity inherited from the Doric style and opened up rich new horizons to Greek architecture. During the classical period, when the already sacrosanct, ponderous Doric temple was in urgent need of fresh inspiration, Ionian elements sprang to its aid. In this way, the monuments on the acropolis in Athens acquired their cheerful gaiety and liveliness.

East Greek vase painting, on the contrary, went through a period of stagnation. While the Athenian craftsmen of 600 B. C. were painting richly figured vases in the new black figure style, East Greek potters had not progressed beyond the conventional style derived from the Orientalising period. In the necropolis of Çandarlı (Pitane), vases have been unearthed which belong to the second quarter of the 6th century, but which were painted in the reserved technique of the 7th century.

The early Greek period in Anatolia, which we have just briefly outlined, has been researched during the last few decades. Carl Weickert, Karl Schefold, Pierre Demargne, Doro Levi, John M. Cook, Pierre Devambez, Gerhard Kleiner and H. Metzger have carried out excavations in Western Anatolia and made significant contributions to the better understanding of this period. The present author has also participated in the field research of this period with his excavations of early Greek cities in Anatolia. Several excavations are still continuing.

Between 546 B. C., when Cyrus conquered the Lydian kingdom, and 334 B. C., when Alexander crossed the Dardanelles, Anatolia was under Persian rule. A number of Persian and Greco-Persian works belonging to this period were found in Pontus, Cappadocia, Lycia, and the Propontis.

Several sculptures in the Greco-Persian style have come to light in the region of Lake Manyas in north-western Asia Minor, especially in Ergili, recently identified as Daskyleion, former seat of the Propontic Satrapy. After the well-known women riders of Ergili, the finest sculptures are the three stelae which were recently found in the same region (Pl. 20). In the 5th century, under Persian rule, Anatolia was unable to play any significant role. Nevertheless, towards the end of the 5th century and the beginning of the 4th, works of outstanding quality were produced in Lycia. The Heroon from Gölbaşı and particularly the Nereid Monument are among the most important works of art of the classical age. Although they betray a marked Phidian influence, their real greatness lies in their native Anatolian features. A particularly important work of creative art, now in the British Museum, is the relief sculpture of the phalanx hastening to battle from the Nereid Monument. The rows of identical figures in the relief have a powerful rhythmical effect. It is unique in the ancient world and represents the first successful attempt at expressionistic sculpture. The creation of such superior works of art as the Nereid Monument in Xanthos encourages one in the belief that the sarcophagus from the royal necropolis of Sidon was actually a Lycian work (Pl. 21).

In the 4th century, the Ionian art and culture of Anatolia played an important if not leading role in the Hellenic world. The most important architectural works of this period are the buildings of Pytheos, the great Greek architect : the temple of Athena at Priene, the prime example of Ionic style, and the Mausoleum at Halicarnassus, one of the Seven Wonders of the World. Other great buildings were built at the same time in several cities of western Asia Minor. Labranda, excavated by Swedish archaeologists, still contains well-preserved ruins which give a vivid impression of the architecture of that time. Especially noteworthy are the excavations at Amyzon and Claros carried out by Louis Robert. The results of these excavations throw important light on the nature of the Doric order in Asia Minor. After Didyma, the temple of Claros was the most important oracle in Anatolia. Thanks to Roland Martin and Kristian Jeppesen, the basic scholarship on the architecture of the period has been carried out.

The Sarcophagus of the Mourning Women, and the so-called Alexander Sarcophagus in the Istanbul Museum are outstanding works of the period (Pls. 9 a, 22, 23). The former is dated about 350 B. C. and the latter is late fourth century.

THE HELLENISTIC AGE (300 - 30 B. C.)

The year 334, when Alexander crossed the Hellespont, heralded a new era in Greek civilization which was of great importance not only for the Hellenic people but also for the whole world. Known since Droysen as the "Hellenistic Age", this historical period, which ended with Augustus, saw the expansion of Greek civilization as far as Asia and Africa. Alexander's cultural policy respected the eastern mentality, but this created a tendency towards syncretism. Through the mingling of the oriental spirit with Greek civilization, a world culture came into being which was Greek in outward appearance but oriental in essence. Alexander was worshipped in Egypt as the son of the god Ammon. In Persia, he wore Persian costume and introduced the practice of proskynesis (prostration) to those approaching his person. This compromise between two radically different mentalities ended in the triumphant advance of oriental religions into Europe.

Hellenistic civilization flourished in Anatolia, where there was already a healthy foundation of Hellenic culture. Under the guiding Anatolian-Ionian spirit, a highly advanced civilization emerged whose remains still impress the whole of mankind deeply.

Several different kings ruled over Anatolia during the Hellenistic period. The kings of Pergamon (283 - 133 B. C.) who ruled in Aeolia and Ionia were eminent representatives and promoters of true Greek civilization. The Bithynian kings (327 - 74 B. C.) encouraged Greek civilization, while the Pontic rulers (302 - 36 B. C.) followed the example of Alexander's cultural policy, which was outwardly Greek but inwardly of a marked oriental character.

The Greek world experienced an economic boom during the Hellenistic period. Through contact with the eastern world, a lively trade activity developed under the leadership of capital cities such as Alexandria, Rhodes, Pergamon and Ephesus. Science also came into its own during this period. Astronomy and geometry, sciences founded by the philosophers of Ionia in the 6th century, were properly formulated for the first time in Alexandria during the Hellenistic period. With its library of 200,000 volumes, Pergamon became the second most important centre of learning of its time.

HELLENISTIC ARCHITECTURE

At the beginning of the Hellenistic period, Ionian architecture revealed no signs of a change in style. In the new Artemision at Ephesus (330 B. C.), the same ground plan as that of the archaic building was used (Fig. 53). The Apollo temple in Didyma (Fig. 84), begun in 310 B. C., had almost the same plan as the old building of 540 B. C. The very fame of the magnificent old buildings became an obstacle to the progress of Greek architecture in the Hellenistic period. The plan of the temple of Athena in Priene, which is actually a prime example of the very best Ionic style of architecture, was unable to start a new school because it was 150 years too late from the point of view of the history of architectural development. Only one feature of Pytheos' layout became traditional in Anatolian architecture : the opisthodomos of only one intercolumnar span which was first encountered in Ionian architecture in the Athena temple of Priene and which reappears afterwards at the beginning of the 3rd century in the Artemis temple at Sardis (Fig. 44). The narrow opisthodomos subsequently became a characteristic feature of Anatolian sanctuaries (Figs. 48, 62). Pytheos' ground plan, however, had only one imitator; Hermogenes alone used it in his temple of Dionysus at Teos (Fig. 48). But the old-fashioned ground plan he had taken from the Doric order was quite out of place in the organic development of the Ionic temple.

This peripteros, with its 6 by 11 columns and colonnades one span in depth on all four sides, is really just a variation of the late archaic ground plan we find in temples such as the Aphaia sanctuary at Aegina, a late 6th century Doric building.

The colonnades formed by the peripteros around the naos differ considerably from the Ionic style. In Ionian art, the tendency had been towards ever greater depth in the disposition of the peristasis. However, in Priene the colonnades have a depth of only one intercolumnar span. The only Ionian feature is the deep pronaos. Otherwise, the plan has a pronounced Doric character.

The Doric temple of Athena at Pergamon (Fig. 24), built during the first quarter of the 3rd century, has almost the same ground-plan as Pytheos' Ionic building. It has a peristasis with 6 by 11 columns, and frontal and lateral colonnades one intercolumnar span in depth. However, it was not to be expected that the architecture of Asia Minor would change over from the Ionic to a Doric ground-plan scheme. Already in 670 in the Hecatompedos II on Samos, a tendency can be observed to emphasize the entrance side of the temple with extra rows of columns. This predilection for prominent frontal sides is apparent in the Hera temples III and IV on Samos and also in the dipteral Ionic temples of the archaic and Hellenistic periods (Figs. 52, 83). The same trend is even more marked in the Artemis temple at Sardis, started at the beginning of the third century, and in its successors. This tendency is exemplified also in seven small prostyle temples, one at Priene, one at Magnesia, and five at Pergamon (Fig. 33, 75).

For these reasons, it was only at the beginning of the 2nd century B.C., after a century's delay, that the true characteristics of Hellenistic architecture appeared.

In the book of Vitruvius, the name of Hermogenes is closely associated with these innovations. He was an outstanding architect and a fine theoretician. According to Vitruvius' account, we learn that Hermogenes, like Pytheos, left writings about his own architectural works and theories. We know from Vitruvius that Hermogenes built the Dionysus temple at Teos and the Artemision at Magnesia. Moreover, he tells us that Hermogenes preferred the eustyle principle, whereby the distance between the centre lines of the columns (interaxial span) measures two and a quarter times the diameter at the base of the shaft. Hermogenes was also the "inventor" of the pseudodipteros (Fig. 63).

The present remains of the Dionysus sanctuary at Teos do in fact conform to the above measurements. The Teos temple is constructed exactly according to Hermogenes' eustyle system. On the other hand, it is not a pseudodipteros but a peripteros, which repeats the old-style design on the Athena temple at Priene. However, there are two other Hellenistic innovations in the architecture of this building which have a connection with Hermogenes, namely the use of the Attic base and the Attic frieze. Both elements are also evident in his temple at Magnesia (Figs. 64, 65).

Since the Dionysus temple at Teos is not a pseudodipteros but follows the Priene ground-plan, we may assume that it is one of Hermogenes' earlier works. The Dionysus temple at Teos, like the Athena temple in Priene, is a peripteros with 6 by 11 columns. It has the same deep pronaos with two columns *in antis* and the same narrow opisthodomos, also with columns between antae. At the same time, the cella of Hermogenes' building is almost as large as the pronaos. However, unlike the Priene temple, its length does not correspond to half the length of the naos.

Besides this, it should be pointed out that the Teos temple observes a strict axiality in its form. All the partition walls of the naos (cf. the Artemision at Magnesia-on-the-Maeander Fig. 63), are in line ewith the corresponding columns of the pteron. In the Athena temple at Priene, the rear wall of the pronaos, however, is not on the same axis as the columns of the peristyle. Hermogenes evidently allowed himself some modifications here although in all other respects he adopted Pytheos' architectural layout.

Not long ago, the small shrine of Zeus Sosipolis in Magnesia (Fig. 62) was perceptively ascribed to Hermogenes by Gottfried Gruben. The stylobate of the shrine measures 7.38 × 15.82 m. and it is probably one of the master's early works, erected before the Dionysus temple at Teos. The ground plan is eustyle with the prescribed eustyle columns $9 \frac{1}{2}$ times the height of the lower shaft diameter; thus the Magnesia temple is a prime example of Hermogenes' architecture as described by Vitruvius. Other architectural features like the Attic frieze and the alternating sequence of Attic profiles (torus-trochilus - torus) at the foot of the walls are innovations of Hellenistic architecture which show a close connection with Hermogenes. We can add to this the richly ornamental doors which are modelled on those of the Erechtheum in Athens. In view of these well-attested common characteristics, the shrine can safely be attributed to Hermogenes, as Gruben has already maintained. The continued use of the Ionic base suggests that the small Zeus temple was built earlier than Hermogenes' two buildings in Teos and Magnesia, where this old-fashioned type of base is no longer seen. The absence of frieze reliefs on the entablature might also be evidence of its early construction. Obviously, Hermogenes would have tried out his innovations gradually. Nevertheless, the new features of Hermogenes, i.e., of Hellenistic architecture, are seen most clearly in the Artemis temple at Magnesia.

The development of the pseudo-dipteros is his greatest achievement (Fig. 63). In the pseudo-dipteros the inner pteron is omitted – an advance of great importance in Greek architecture. For in this way, as H. Drerup has recently demonstrated, a spacious colonnade two spans in width is formed around the actual core of the temple. Since these surrounding colonnades were pleasant halls to walk in, protected from sun and rain, the temple became one of the citizens' most important amenities. Moreover, they produced a pleasing visual effect through the striking contrast between the white columns gleaming in the sun and the deep shadows they formed.

Hermogenes' pseudo-dipteros was a pioneering work; in the succeeding Hellenistic and Roman periods it became the standard temple type. With its spacious colonnades it expressed the taste and genius of its time. In the Hellenistic period, the stoa's shady, well-ventilated space was developed into an impressive architectural form. The fondness for spacious buildings can be seen clearly at Priene. In the middle of the 2nd century B. C., while great building activities were in progress and the Athena temple received a new altar and cult statue, the architects did not hesitate to erect a Doric stoa in front of the south side of the shrine. This hall was open to the south, enabling visitors to enjoy the warmth of the sunshine and the magnificent view over the city and landscape. On the other hand, the view of the temple and altar was impaired. The south colonnade of the temple, only one columnar span in depth and barely 40 m. long, was quite unsuitable for taking a stroll or enjoying the view. For this reason, the Doric stoa, 80 m. × 7 m., was built, whose cool, generous shade offered a pleasant place for walking and an ideal open area with an impressive view of the lively town and the gentle wide plain.

In the Artemis temple, Hermogenes gave up the old Ionic base (Fig. 66), which was probably considered rather delicate and over-detailed. Instead, he introduced the simpler, less delicate-looking Attic base (Fig. 65) and combined it with the old Ionic plinth. This new architectural form of Hermogenes also became standard; his base was the classical model for succeeding periods and was handed on to the architects of the Renaissance through Vitruvius.

In his greatest building, the Artemision at Magnesia, Hermogenes' capital has also lost the elegant and dynamic form of the old Ionic type. In the capitals of the Artemision, the upper edge of the egg - and - tongue pattern, i.e. the lower line of the canalis, runs in a straight, almost hard line, and the scrolls are so contracted that the egg - and - tongue pattern under the cushions can no longer be seen even from below. Hermogenes was not interested in lively dynamic lines, plastic profiling or small details which could be appreciated only from close view. As in the deep surrounding colonnades of his temple, Hermogenes' chief interest lay in the impressive play of light and shadow and in the effect produced from a distance. Thus the egg - and - tongue pattern is more deeply and freely engraved and the palmette, like the folds of the dresses on the figures of the Zeus altar of Pergamon, is deeply cut away for contrast. The bold manner in which the diagonal palmettes encroach upon the ovolo is also a new feature which can only be understood as part of the baroque and emotional character of the Hellenistic period.

In Vitruvius' book we see that Hermogenes' treatise on proportion classifies temples according to the relation of lower shaft diameter to the span between the columnar axes. He distinguishes the following 5 types of temple :

pyknostyle   (close-columned; span : $1 \frac{1}{2} \times$ diameter)
systyle   (narrow-columned; span : $2 \times$ diameter)
eustyle   (well-columned; span : $2 \frac{1}{4} \times$ diameter)
diastyle   (wide-columned; span : $3 \times$ diameter)
araeostyle   (lightly-columned : span : $3 \frac{1}{2} \times$ diameter)

Hermogenes expressed a preference for the eustyle temple where the interaxial span is equivalent to $2 \frac{1}{4}$ times the lower diameter of the shaft. However, as we have already seen, he applied this principle only in his early works (Fig. 48). In his masterpiece, the temple at Magnesia, he abandoned the eustyle principle probably because he felt it produced too crowded an effect. In the Artemision, the lower diameter of the shaft is 1.40 m and the span 3.94 m. Here, the span being $2 \frac{1}{2}$ diameters, Hermogenes was approaching the diastyle principle, in which the span is 3 times the diameter. Had he used the diastyle principle in the Artemision, the span would have had to measure 4.20 m.

The tendency towards buildings with widely-spaced columns which we observe in Hermogenes reflects the general trend of all late Greek architecture. The explanation lies in the Hellenistic conception of architecture; the architects of this period aimed to reduce the massiveness of their constructions and attain the maximum lightness. The architects of the later Hellenistic period developed the principle of widely-spaced columns further in their public buildings and made the distance between columns even greater.

In the temple of Zeus at Magnesia the dentil band has been extended to the sloping geison for the first time. This peculiarity is a sign of the architects' growing inclination to enrich their monuments with decorative designs and enliven a structure by means of contrasting ornament. Hermogenes was no doubt the founder and defender of this new architectural concept.

The tendency to lighten building mass is also seen in the much - discussed three openings in the pediment of the Artemision at Magnesia (Fig. 64). The middle opening is 2.5 m. in height and the two side openings 80 cm. The central opening was supposed to serve as a means of manifesting the presence of the goddess. Similar pediment openings are seen on numismatic representations of the temple at Ephesus. It is possible that Artemis appeared to her credulous congregation at religious festivals through this doorway in the manner of a "deus ex machina". Whether such ceremonies actually took place or not, the three openings in the pediment of the Artemision had a definite purpose from the point of view of Hermogenes' style. A glance at the graphic reconstruction of the temple (Fig. 64) will confirm that the central openings of both pediments are located directly over the central span of the façade (Fig. 64) and that the latter is one third wider than the other spans. With this large opening, the architect possibly wished to relieve part of the pressure of the pediment on the two centre columns, since the distance between them was considerable (5.25 m). Yet the real purpose of this "doorway" and its two "windows" appears to be primarily aesthetic. I believe that the design is determined by the same love of axiality which we have already noticed in the ground plan. In both the breadth and length of the design we know that the walls and columns observe the strictest axiality. Furthermore, it should not be forgotten that these three openings are repeated on the tympanum of the rear (east) pediment. If the opening had served only as a stage for the enactment of miracles, then one opening on the main (west) front would have sufficed. By means of these centre openings in the tympanum, the heavily emphasized middle axis of the ground plan is projected upwards in the elevation of the building. In other words, the two openings at either end of the temple are on the same axis, parallel with the axis of the ground plan.

The three openings should be regarded as a unit. Without the side windows, the middle doorway would lack symmetry and harmony and call too much attention to itself. The single dark space would be too dominant a feature. The smaller windows, therefore, have an animating and at the same time a softening effect on the surface composition of the pediment. Besides this, the three tympanum openings together with the three acroteria form a fine crown over the whole temple façade.

Hermogenes' principle of widely-spaced columns required a reduction in the weight and therefore in the height of the frieze and the supported architec-

tural elements. As the interaxial span increased considerably, the height
of the architrave and frieze decreased in the next period. The architrave was
reduced from three to two fasciae, thus necessitating an increase in the number
of metopes to avoid their becoming too wide. Consequently, in the 2nd
century B. C., there were three metopes per inter-axial span in temples
and four in halls (Fig. 27). Moreover, the use of a triglyph frieze above an
Ionic architrave with two fasciae is probably due to the reduction in the height
of the frieze. In the case of the Athena temple at Pergamon, for instance, if
the very low frieze of the halls had not been vertically designed with 5 metopes
and 6 triglyphs above each interaxial span, this part of the building would
have over-emphasized the horizontality of the temple like a second architrave.

Much has been written about the dates of Hermogenes' buildings. The
most likely period, as A. v. Gerkan suggested, is between 150 and 130 B. C.
From the point of view of the history of art, the 2nd century B. C. is the only
acceptable dating. Datings based on historical incidents, unless they agree
with stylistic considerations, are often misleading.

The great pioneering innovations of Hermogenes cannot possibly have
taken place in the 3rd century. We have seen in Ephesus and Didyma how the
old-fashioned style of the archaic period continued to influence the design
of the ground plan. Even the Artemision at Sardis (Fig. 44), whose initial
construction phase belongs to the first half of the 3rd century, derives largely
from old traditional forms. It is significant that, as late as 175 B. C., Antiochus
IV, King of Syria, had the temple of Zeus Olympios in Athens erected on old
Peisistratic foundations i.e. in the form of an archaic dipteros. This means
that the traditional methods of building still persisted in the Hellenistic
centres in the first quarter of the 2nd century. It is not surprising that the
new architectural concepts, which doubtless sprang from the new philosophy
of the Hellenistic period, should require a considerable time to achieve a
concrete form. Pioneering innovations like those of Hermogenes can certainly
only have occurred during the course of the 2nd century B. C.

In the Dionysus sanctuary at Teos, large fragments of a central acroterium
have been brought to light as a result of excavations carried out in recent
years. The shape of its acanthus leaves suggests that it belongs to the middle
period of Hellenistic art. Thanks to the vigorous building activity of the Hellenistic kings, Hermogenes and his contemporaries were fortunate enough
to finish their works without undue delay. Consequently, there cannot have
been a very long time between the foundation and completion of the Teos
temple. The discovery of the acroterium therefore gives us a valuable clue
to the date of the building's construction. The outside edges of the acanthus
leaves of the acroterium have "eyes" like those of the central acroterium of the
Artemision in Magnesia. With their highly contrasting play of light and shadow
they are very like the ornamented capitals at Magnesia. The temple of Zeus
Sosipolis at Magnesia which, like Gruben, I would classify as an early work
of Hermogenes, has Ionic capitals, however, which still conform to the "classical" style of the Athena temple at Priene. From the stylistic point of view,
Hermogenes must have built his two early works in the second quarter of
the 2nd century, and the Artemision in the third quarter of the same century.

It is only by a thorough examination of architectural ornament, in our opinion, that the question of the chronological order of Hellenistic architecture can be solved. The Hellenistic architects also introduced innovations in the Doric order, with not altogether happy results. The Doric columns of the Hellenistic period are slim and almost without entasis. The flutes were outlined but not executed. Instead of fluting, the columns have prismatic edges. Frequently the lower shaft is left smooth while the remainder is fluted. On the capital, the echinus profile is almost rectilinear; there are no curving lines. Above the architrave, as we have already explained, the number of metopes has increased and the intercolumnar distance has widened. In place of the metope system still used in the third century, we now find, in the second century, a system of 3 metopes per span in temples and 3 or 4 metopes per span in stoas (Fig. 27). The predilection for blending Ionic and Doric elements can best be observed in the small market temple at Pergamon. Although it has triglyphs and its architrave and capitals are Doric in style, the building has columns and bases in Ionic style, as has been pointed out by W. Zschietzschmann. The inner architrave of the building is Ionic, with two fasciae, but the outer architrave is Doric, with a projecting taenia. In the colonnades of the Athena temple at Pergamon, the Ionic columns of the upper storey carry an Ionic architrave under a Doric triglyph frieze with 5 metopes per span. In the bouleuterion (council house) at Miletos, the echinus of the Doric capitals is carved with an egg-and-tongue ornament. This stylisitic mixture goes rather too far, of course, but as we have seen in the colonnades of the Athena temple at Pergamon, it is nevertheless a pleasure to see a delicate Ionic top storey supported by a heavier Doric bottom storey. The Hellenistic peculiarity of distributing the various orders throughout buildings of several storeys is continued in Roman architecture, as we see in the Marcellus theatre and the Colosseum. The Colosseum in Rome has Doric columns in the lower storey, Ionic in the middle storey and Corinthian, at the top. The Corinthian capital first came into its own in the buildings of Asia Minor. The Corinthian capitals of the Mausoleum of Belevi (pl. 73) are an impressive, luxuriant offspring of the canonical prototype of the tholos in Epidaurus, which has beautiful proportions. The oldest existing temple of the Corinthian order is in the ancient city of Olba (Diocaesarea) in Asia Minor. Its well-preserved ruins can be seen at Uzunca Burç, north of Silifke (Pls. 10 a, 102). When we come later to study each individual ruin, we shall see that the Corinthian capital is employed in a large number of buildings in Asia Minor. Its rich plant ornamentation lent itself to distant effects of contrasting light and shadow and suited the aesthetic sensibility of the Hellenistic age. Roman art, with its strong innate tendency to powerful and lively modes of expression, also preferred the fantasy of the Corinthian capital to the elegance of the Ionic capital or the organic structure of the Doric. It is typical that Sulla, the Roman general and dictator, was fascinated by the Corinthian capitals of the Olympieion in Athens. In 85 B. C., while staying in Athens, he had several columns of this no doubt awe-inspiring temple shipped to Rome, where they were used in the construction of the Jupiter temple on the Capitoline. It is quite possible that the magnificent capitals of these columns from the

Athenian Olympieion helped to make the Corinthian order better known and liked, on Italian soil.

The Hellenistic kings also erected splendid works in Athens. About 175 B. C., King Antiochus IV of Syria commissioned the Roman architect Cossutius, who was probably well versed in Greek architecture, to build a Corinthian dipteros over the old Peisistratic foundations of the Athenian Olympieion. The thirteen adjacent columns of the south-east wing of this —even today— impressive-looking temple belong to the Hellenistic building, while the remaining columns were erected mainly in Hadrian's time. In Athens, a colonnade with two aisles 164 m long was erected by Eumenes II, King of Pergamon. This lies between the theatre of Dionysus and the odeion of Herodes Atticus. Another King of Pergamon, Attalos II, built a stoa in the agora of Athens, 117 m in length and 20 m wide. The present building, which stands on the old foundations, has been restored, partly with the original stone but largely with modern materials. It will be remembered that Attalos I had previously built a stoa in Delphi.

One of the great merits of the Hellenistic Age was the increasing secularization of its architecture. This process was made possible by the gradual weakening of the strong religious feeling of the early Greek ages. In the second century B. C., temples decrease noticeably in size, being reduced to smaller proportions (Fig. 33). They were no longer the chief municipal buildings. Stoas, market places, gymnasia, theatres, town halls and other public halls were now regarded as worthy monuments. Greek buildings were no longer "highly revered but useless" memorials, as one Roman engineer towards the end of the second century A. D. described the temples of the classical age; on the contrary, they were impressive, functional buildings erected to serve the community. The monumental altar of Zeus at Pergamon (Pls. 34, 35) was not a religious edifice in the same sense as a temple in preceding periods. It was, in a tactful and measured manner, much more an admonitory symbol of the victory of the Pergamene people over the Galatians. This worldly philosophy of the Hellenistic age extended the Greek architects' horizon and opened up new perspectives. They now turned to other social and cultural tasks and created an original, forward-looking style which was of enormous service to the development of Roman architecture.

Thus the Hellenistic architects became pioneers for Greek and Roman art. We have already seen how Roman art adopted certain "Hermogenic" or Hellenistic advances such as the pseudo-dipteral temple, the Attic base on an Ionic plinth and the deeply incised ornamentation with its strong play of light and shadow.

The development of functional buildings, which has just been mentioned, is also a Hellenistic achievement, significant in that it made possible the great engineering feats of Roman architecture. Characteristic features like axiality and symmetry, the podium temple, the arrangement of flights of steps and buildings of more than one storey go back to Hellenistic beginnings, experiments and models.

The principle of strict axiality, which we have observed in the Artemision at Magnesia, can be seen equally clearly in the emphasis given to the central axis of two other contemporary buildings - the council house and gymnasium at Miletos (Figs. 79, 80). These are the first attempts at an axial plan, and advanced examples will be found much later on in Roman architecture.

As we have pointed out above, the emphasis on the entrance, a predilection unknown in Doric architecture, is an essential element in Ionic architecture from the outset. The continued development of this trend in the Hellenistic period led to the creation of the façades. A prostyle in Priene (Fig. 75), another in Magnesia (Fig. 62) and five in Pergamon (Fig. 33) are buildings with a pronounced "front end". The sanctuary of Zeus Olympios at Priene, which originated in the third century, is the oldest of them. On account of its position against the rear wall of the market, the temple lost its four-sided character, i.e. the most important peculiarity of a Greek temple. By "securing its rear" within the market complex, the temple acquired a dominating, throne-like position exactly like the temple of the Imperial Forum in Rome. The two above-mentioned prostyles at Pergamon occupy a similar position in the complexes of which they form a part.

The tendency to stress the front side is taken a decisive step further in the prostyle at the end of the theatre terrace at Pergamon (Pls. 31, 32). The front of this building was doubly emphasized by a monumental flight of steps. This podium temple with its open flight of steps is the outcome of a long period of development in Asia Minor. Already its form had become canonical; it reappears a short time later in Roman architecture in a slightly different guise. That Roman art owes its podium temple to Hellenistic architecture is proved by the Ara Pacis in Rome, which copies the design of the steps of the Pergamene altar (Pls. 33, 34). Other Roman podium temples were no doubt equally dependent on Hellenistic models (see Pl. 32, Fig. 33).

Imposing, monumental flights of steps like the one in front of the sanctuary on the theatre terrace at Pergamon can also be seen on Cos and at Lindos on Rhodes. The altar of Zeus already mentioned as podium construction is another highly impressive example of a Hellenistic stairway, with an open flight of 28 steps at the front (Pls. 33 - 35). Flights of steps played an extremely important role in Hellenistic architecture and were an important part of the temples and halls. The theatron of the Demeter temenos at Pergamon (Fig. 34), with its 43 metre - wide flight of 10 steps, is an example from the late fourth century. The Apollo temple at Didyma, begun around 310 B. C., has a high base of 7 steps; moreover, there is an open flight of 14 steps leading up to the east front (Pl. 68 a). The later Artemision at Ephesus stood on a mighty base of 13 steps (Fig. 53). These examples are a sufficient indication that the monumental stairway of the temple at the end of the theatre terrace at Pergamon is a form of Hellenistic architecture in the tradition of Asia Minor.

The storeyed building is supposed to have been invented in the third century by Sostratos of Cnidus, who built the Pharos of Alexandria — one of the Seven Wonders cf the World. What is meant, in fact, is the storeyed stoa, which is a major achievement of the Hellenistic age. The Nereid Monument from the end of the fifth century and the Mausoleum at Halicarnassus (Fig. 95) from the middle of the fourth century were already existing examples of splendid monumental storeyed buildings. However, Hellenistic stoas for the first time in architectural history had external superimposed colonnades (Pls. 32, 33). In the Roman age, these were to become particularly attractive and popular. The magnificent façades we see in the library at Ephesus, the market gate at Miletos (Pl. 74 b), numerous theatre stages (Pl. 101) and monumental fountain buildings derive from the two-storeyed stoas of the Hellenistic period. However, the Hellenistic Age never developed the fronts of its buildings into a façade in the real sense.

Hellenistic architects also studied deeply the problem of space. Their attempts in the Miletos bouleuterion (Fig. 80) and in that of Priene resulted in the construction of congress halls 10.5 metres in width. Nevertheless, the actual solution of the space problem was not achieved until the Roman period. Under the influence of Near Eastern models, Roman engineers continued the experiments of their Greek mentors and, by means of new building techniques, succeeded in creating magnificent interior spaces.

Great ages produce great artists. The second century B. C. was the Golden Age of Hellenistic art and the cities of Asia Minor were in fruitful competition. The most important buildings of the period belong to this same century : the altar of Zeus and the halls of Eumenes in Pergamon, the Sacred Hall, the altar of the Athena temple, the bouleuterion, and the gymnasium and stadium at Priene; also the bouleuterion in Miletos. Thus, Hermogenes' pioneering innovations should be included among the achievements of this Golden Age.

The ornamentation of the temple of Apollo Smintheus at Chryse in the Troad (Fig. 2) is closely related to that of the Artemision in the similarity of the acanthus leaves on its capitals. We are indebted to Hans Weber for his illuminating study on the ruins of this temple. His painstaking research on-the-spot has filled a significant gap in classical archaeology. Thanks to the valuable fragments of the building and frieze which he found, we can now confirm the date of the temple's erection. Hans Weber also rightly ascribed to the Apollo Smintheus temple an Ionic capital found by John Cook in the Troad. Before this, he had correctly observed the close similarity between these finds and the ornamentation on the Artemision. His dating of the temple to the end of the third century or 200 B. C., as he stated in a recent letter to me, is close to the dating which general considerations of art history would find acceptable. The Corinthian capitals of the bouleuterion at Miletos, dated 170 B. C. according to its dedicatory inscription, give further support to the dating of Hermogenes' buildings to the second and third quarters of the second century B. C. (Pl. 72).

In the Artemision at Magnesia, the cushions of the Ionic capitals are adorned with the same tall, slim acanthus leaves. We are reminded not only of the capitals of the Apollo Smintheus temple but also of the leaves of the Corinthian capitals belonging to the bouleuterion at Miletos. The similarity of the acanthus leaves on the capitals at Magnesia, Miletos (Pl. 72) and the Troad lies not only in their tall, slim shape, but mainly in the accentuation of the central rib and the completely closed circle formed by the curled edges of their leaves. This form of eye-like foliage is not found anywhere else. On the acroterium of the Dionysus temple at Teos, for instance, the eyes of the acanthus leaves, like those of other similar monuments in Asia Minor, are not completely closed, but have a small opening. It is highly probable that stone masons of the same school and generation worked on the three buildings at Miletos, Magnesia and the Troad. The comparisons made above are sufficient proof of the contemporaneity of the Apollo Smintheus temple, the Artemision in Magnesia and the Miletos bouleuterion. They might all have been built in the same period as the Miletos structure, 170 B. C., or slightly earlier or later. At all events, they belong to the second century B. C.

This conclusion is important, since we now see that the temple of Apollo Smintheus belongs to the same period as the likewise pseudo - dipteral temple at Magnesia. The temple at Messa on Lesbos (Fig. 1) can scarcely be earlier, since the really progressive developments in Hellenistic architecture were taking place in Asia Minor during the 2nd century B. C.

This analysis entitles us to conclude that the concept of the pseudo - dipteral temple has a definite connection with Hermogenes. Of course one cannot credit him with the invention of this form as Vitruvius does, since it was already developed in Italy in the sixth century B. C. Nevertheless, it should be pointed out that the organic development of the Ionic temple, described above, and the new aesthetic sensibility of the Hellenistic Age were the factors which gave rise to the new architectural form. Our stylistic observations strongly suggest that Hermogenes was the leading spirit of the new architecture and the initiator of most of the innovations in Hellenistic architecture.

Temples related to the Artemision in Magnesia were : the Smintheion at Chryse in the Troad (Fig. 2), the Aphrodite temple at Messa on Lesbos (Fig. 1) and the two other broad - colonnaded temples of Hellenistic Asia Minor, the Hekateion at Lagina (Fig. 3) and the Apollo temple at Alabanda (Fig. 4). The ground plans of the latter two sanctuaries are very similar to one another. As Schober has noted, Menesthes, whom Vitruvius mentions as the architect of the Apollo temple at Alabanda, is also the probable author of the Heka-teion. Schober's accurate dating of the frieze reliefs of the Hekateion to the

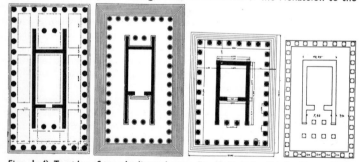

Figs. 1–4) Temples of pseudo-dipteral type: Fig. 1) Temple of Aphrodite at Messa on Lesbos. Pseudo-dipteros of the Ionic order with 8 by 14 columns. Stylobate measuring 23.75 × 41.52 m. Second century B. C. Fig. 2) Temple of Apollo Sminth-

eus at Chryse in the Troad. Pseudo-dipteros of the Ionic order with 8 by 14 columns. Stylobate measuring 24.30 × 43.52 m. Second century B. C. Fig. **3)** *Hekateion at Lagina in Caria. Pseudo-dipteros with 8 by 11 Corinthian columns. Stylobate measuring 21.30 × 28.00 m. Second half of the second century B. C. Fig.* **4)** *Temple of Apollo at Alabanda in Caria. Pseudo-dipteros with 8 by 13 columns probably of the Doric order, designed by the architect Menesthes. Stylobate measuring 21.66 × 34.53 m. Second half of the second century B. C.*

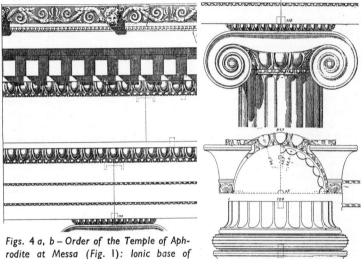

Figs. 4 a, b – Order of the Temple of Aphrodite at Messa (Fig. 1): Ionic base of Pytheos type, Ionic capital of early Hellenistic form and entablature, consisting of an architrave with three fasciae, a frieze and dentils.

final quarter of the second century is a further indication that the pseudo-dipteros appeared just after the middle of the second century and rapidly became widespread.

SCULPTURE

The leading centre of sculptural activity in Asia Minor in the Hellenistic age was Pergamon. Its Golden Age falls in the reign of Eumenes II. In 180 B. C., he built the great altar on the citadel of Pergamon and dedicated it to Zeus and Athena. The sculptures of this great work of antiquity are the finest examples of Hellenistic plastic art. They represent a gigantomachy (struggle of gods and giants) but also symbolize the victory of Pergamon over the Gauls. The style has a baroque note and might be described as an intensified form of the artistic movement of the fourth century. Hair flies loose, and its deeply engraved lines produce a strong contrast of light and shade. Most characteristic is the tragic upward gaze of the deeply sunken eyes, the frowning brows and the half-open mouth. The faces express passionate emotion, agony and anger.

The muscles are exaggeratedly flexed; the clothing is arranged in agitated diagonal folds forming deep shadows. The body movements are violent and wild. New statuary models were created which influenced succeeding periods. Pergamene elements were recently identified by Erika Simon in the frieze of the Villa dei Mysterii near Pompeii.

Besides the faces with their exaggerated expressions of agony, there are also handsome male faces and splendidly characterized male bodies. The female figures are generally quite enchanting. The most beautiful and best preserved are Artemis and Nyx.

The sculptures from the Pergamene altar are now in the Pergamon Museum in Berlin. In the Istanbul Museum there is a single head of a woman. This was identified recently by H. Luschey as the missing head of Aphrodite, in the north frieze of the altar. In the Pergamon Museum there is a bearded head in the most beautiful Pergamene style (Pl. 38), which was found during the recent excavation in the colonnaded street of the Asclepieum in Pergamon. This fine head, larger than life - size, does not in fact belong to the frieze of the altar. At the same time it is an outstanding example of the Pergamene school of sculpture which flourished during the first half of the second century. The head of a young man in the museum at Pergamon was identified by Luschey as the missing head of the sword-bearer in the Telephos frieze of the Pergamon altar.

THE ROMAN AGE (30 B. C. - A. D. 395)

In the first and second centuries A. D., the Anatolian cities were among the richest, most important centres of art and civilization of their age. A large number of them have survived to our own day as impressive ruins in an excellent state of preservation. Many have already been partly excavated and many others are being systematically studied at this moment. The excavations at Pergamon are being continued successfully under Erich Boehringer's direction. The excavations at Ephesus carried out by J. Keil after World War I, and by F. Miltner followed by Fritz Eichler after World War II, are now in progress under H. Vetters and W. Alzinger. Every year they yield important discoveries. In Hierapolis (Pl. 59 a), Italian archaeologists under Paulo Verzone have done distinguished research work. In Aphrodisias, the New York University is sponsoring an excavation directed by Kenan Erim. He has already brought to light highly important buildings and numerous sculptures (Pls. 60 - 63) of outstanding quality belonging to the famous school of Aphrodisias. Side and Perge, located in Pamphylia on the southern coast of Anatolia, have been thoroughly and systematically studied over the last two decades by the Turkish archaeologist Arif Müfid Mansel. There is already a fine museum in Side, where the beautiful finds from the excavations are housed (Pls. 98 - 99).

The Greco - Anatolian tradition continued almost uninterrupted in Roman times. This is primarily reflected in the originality of the local architecture of Asia Minor. Nevertheless, the new building techniques and the engineering methods employed in Anatolian architecture in this period are entirely Roman in character. Even in several large cities like Pergamon, the Hellenistic architects had often executed only the ornamental parts of their monuments in marble, contenting themselves with andesite for the rest. In Roman times, on the contrary, marble became the principal material for building. The newly-invented building material of bricks bound with mortar was then used for the first time in the construction of functional buildings, while marble slabs were used to cover the outer surfaces.

Large monuments were no longer erected on foundations of stone piles or by means of terracing and levelling. They were now built over a substructure of barrel-vaulting or groined-vaulting. Similarly, in Roman times, theatres no longer rested on the slopes of a hill, as was the practice in Greek times, but were supported by a complex of arcades and tunnel vaults. However, most Anatolian architects still preferred to erect their theatres on hillsides (Pl. 39). It is typical that the theatre of Aspendos, although supported by arcades and vaulting, is also built against a hillside (Pls. 100 - 101). Evidently, the architect was most concerned to remain faithful to the old tradition of the hillside theatre.

Other theatres in Asia Minor followed the Roman pattern. Even those theatres built during the Hellenistic period, e.g. at Pergamon and Ephesus, were adapted to suit the prevailing fashion (Pls. 31, 15). The Roman innovations and inventions in building can be listed as follows :

1) The two-storey wall at the back of the stage (scaenae frons) is a Roman architectural feature. The Roman architects had transformed the old Greek theatre with its natural setting, into a regular enclosed space, shut off from the outside world, so that the stage wall had to be the same height as the theatron. Hence the façades of two to three storeys which characterize Roman stages. Asia Minor produced the finest façades of all (Pls. 15, 101). The explanation may possibly be that two-storey colonnades were originally a Hellenistic invention.

2) The podium or pulpitum or proscenium, which had served as the acting area since the second half of the second century B. C., is enlarged by an increase in depth in the Roman period.

3) In Roman times, the side entrances to the theatre (parodoi), instead of being diagonally situated between stage and theatron, as they invariably were in Greek theatres, are at right angles to them (Pl. 39). In addition, they are covered and thus form an architectural link between the theatron and the stage façade. The theatre at Aspendos offers the finest example of this development (Pls. 15, 101).

4) In Hellenistic times, the ground-plan of the orchestra was in the shape of a horseshoe (Fig. 72). In the Roman theatre this becomes a semicircle (Fig. 38). This reduction in size was possible since the orchestra was no longer used as an acting or dancing area. The theatron and the orchestra now conformed to a semicircular plan, thus guaranteeing a good view, even to spectators in the front seats at the extreme edges of the theatron.

5) The theatron (also called cavea or auditorium), which was built against the hillside in Greek times, was later supported by a substructure of barrel-vaulting.

6) In the Roman period, the theatron was crowned by a colonnade, supported by groined-vaulting (Pls. 96 a, 101 b).

7) The most important achievement in Roman theatre architecture was its creation of a self-contained interior. The Greek theatre is characterized by the way it blends with the surrounding town and landscape. In Ephesus, for instance, in Hellenistic times, the spectators in the theatre were also in a sense still in the streets, since the town was visible from every seat, owing to the height of the theatron and the shortness of the rear stage wall. For the same reason, they had a magnificent view beyond the stage to the town and the sea (Pl. 57 b). In the Roman period, on the contrary, after the complete reconstruction which took place in Septimius Severus' reign, spectators in the same theatre found themselves in an interior that was sealed off from the outside world by its three-storey stage wall and the equally high parodoi. No longer distracted by the view of the town and landscape, they could concentrate on the spectacle. With this self-contained enclosure, the Romans attained their ideal of a theatre built in stone. The best example of this perfected type of theatre can be found at Aspendos (Pls. 15, 100 - 101).

The invention of central-heating in Rome, ca. 80 B. C., by means of hot air circulating under the floors and through hollow bricks in the wall, encouraged the erection of huge thermal buildings. Large baths, often combined with gymnasia, were built in all the cities of Asia Minor. The finest examples are the Vedius gymnasium in Ephesus, the Faustina baths in Miletos and the thermal baths of Side, now used as a museum.

As further examples of outstanding functional architecture and engineering, stone bridges and aqueducts should be mentioned. Only a few examples of Greek stone bridges have survived.

The handsome remains of a stone bridge uncovered at Pergamon date from Greek times. However, it is a modest work compared with the imposing examples of the Roman period. Aqueducts are a specifically Roman invention. One of the finest and oldest aqueducts in Anatolia is to be found just outside Ephesus on the Söke road. Amphitheatres, likewise a purely Roman inheritance, were not so common in Anatolia. The gladiatorial contests and animal baiting that took place in them were foreign to the Greek temperament. None of the surviving examples in Anatolia is in good condition. Another typically Roman edifice, the triumphal arch, is very rare in Asia Minor. On the other hand, town gateways were popular in Asia Minor in Roman times. The arched buildings of Antalya (Fig. 160), Patara (Fig. 100) and Perge (Pl. 98 b) are not triumphal arches but rather town-gates which derive from Hellenistic arches. Their earliest prototypes are the single arch leading to the agora in Priene and the double arched entrance to the theatre terrace at Pergamon (see p. 83 and Fig. 24, No. 18).

Other characteristic structures of the Roman period, are the richly ornamented monumental façades of libraries, fountains and rear stage walls

(Pl. 101). The design, consisting of projecting or recessed architectural features such as columns, pediments or niches, is a purely Roman conception. Most typical of all is the symmetrical alternation between rectilinear and curved sections of pediments. This variation and alternation of tectonic elements is a design created by Roman artists in their attempt to develop new architectural ideas from Greek precedents. The most important variation in design between the original Greek and Roman columnar architecture can be seen in the emphatically horizontal lines of Hellenistic stoas, as opposed to the vertical emphasis of Roman façades.

The Roman preference for the vertical emphasis of their façades is best seen in secular structures, especially in their triumphal arches. It is interesting to note that this tendency was the result of a hesitant and gradual development. The earliest attempts to bring the vertical features of a building into prominence were made in the Marcellus theatre and the Colosseum in Rome. The dominating horizontal Greek lines of the façades of these monuments are relieved by placing pedestals beneath the columns of the upper storeys. The horizontal lines are thus broken up at intervals. However, the general impression of horizontality is not completely overcome, since, between each storey, the cornice of the entablatures still forms a continuous horizontal line. The vertical effect is more successfully attained in the arch of Titus in Rome and the arch of Trajan in Ancona. Here the entablature turns outwards at right angles to follow the projection of each column. The strongest vertical effect is achieved in A. D. 312 in Constantine's triumphal arch. Here, the projecting entablature above each column allows the vertical lines to rise without interruption to the top of the arch.

In spite of the widespread use of vertical mouldings based on Roman models, the architects of Asia Minor were to some extent able to preserve the horizontality of their façades. Here the projecting entablatures are not the width of one column, as in Rome, but of a whole intercolumnar span. In addition, horizontal features were always inserted between each storey, so that a well-balanced harmony between the horizontal and the vertical was achieved, as, for instance, in the gateway to the market place in Miletos (Pl. 74 b). The town gateway of Antalya is a good example of Roman influence. (Fig. 160). The prominent sections of entablature of this building are supported, in typically Roman fashion, by columns with tall pedestals. However, since the gateway is only one-storeyed, with a very wide façade, the strongly vertical lines of the columns and the corresponding projecting sections of the entablature do not stand out. The architect has succeeded admirably in establishing a pleasing harmony between the fashionable vertical Roman design and the native horizontal Greek lines.

One of the most important innovations of Roman architecture is the highly impressive development of the arch and the arcade. The use of rows of arches gave an entirely original external appearance to Roman monuments. Arcades were an important element in buildings like the Aspendos theatre, especially in the enlivening and lightening effect they had on the façades (Pls. 15, 101).

The arch had already been used in Asia Minor in the second century B. C. in the construction of market or boundary gates. As we partly stated above, the arch of the market gate at Priene, the gateway in the city wall of Herakleia (Pl. 75b), the gatehouse - tower at Sillyum and the double arched-gate of the theatre terrace at Pergamon seem to represent the first attempts in using this structural element.

By constructing domes and vaults, Roman engineers produced masterpieces of architecture. The Pantheon in Rome is a preeminent achievement of antiquity. The temple of Asclepius in Pergamon which, like the Pantheon, has a cylindrical supporting body, is probably an imitation of the great Roman model.

The colonnaded street, which protected people from sun and rain, was a remarkable invention of Roman architecture. It represented a great advance in town planning, and gave the life of the town a distinctive, ceremonial character. The imposing remains of colonnaded streets have survived in several Anatolian cities (Pl. 96b).

We mentioned above that the Corinthian capital was the main element which Roman architecture adopted from Hellenistic examples (Pl. 73). Actually, the architects of Asia Minor continued their native tradition in Roman times, although they were careful to follow the fashion dictated by Rome. In this way, the composite capital came into use for the first time in the arch of Titus. This reveals a mixture of Corinthian capitals with the volutes of Ionic capitals. Figured capitals decorated with heads, busts and full figures, which were popular in Rome in Caracalla's time, were often seen in Asia Minor. They are Anatolian and Near Eastern in origin.

Roman sepulchral art had little influence in Asia Minor during the Roman period since the Greeks in Anatolia continued to draw on the native tradition.

PART TWO
ANCIENT RUINS

BYZANTIUM

According to ancient writers, Byzantium was founded in the middle of the 7th century B. C. by the people of Megara and Argos under the leadership of Byzas. The finding of late protocorinthian aryballoi during excavations carried out at the Topkapı Palace, i.e. on the acropolis of Byzantium, has more or less confirmed this traditionally-held belief concerning the date of foundation. The city was enlarged by Constantine the Great about A. D. 330, and, from 395 onwards, it was the capital of the Eastern Roman Empire. In 1453 it was captured by the Turks.

The Istanbul Archaeological Museum. The Istanbul Archaeological Museum still contains the best examples of Greek and Roman antiquities in Turkey. The works of art, systematically displayed, are explained in detail on accompanying labels. The section devoted to works of the Ancient Near East consists largely of discoveries made during the time of the Ottoman Empire. It contains collections of sculptures, reliefs and vases belonging to the Babylonian, Sumerian, Assyrian and Hittite periods. The statue base and two reliefs, photographs of which appear in this book (Pls. 17-18), were discovered at Zincirli; they are representative of the Middle Neo-Hittite style. The orthostat relief which depicts a married couple (Pl. 17), and the column base flanked by two sphinxes (Pl. 18 a) date from the second half of the 8th century, whereas the other relief is attributed to the end of the 9th century. Here are reproduced drawings of some other Hittite sculptures and reliefs (Figs. 5 - 10). The explanation of each object is to be found in the corresponding caption.

Figs. 5a,b – Zincirli. Portal lion from inner citadel gate. Early to Middle Neo- Hittite style. 832-810 B.C. Istanbul.

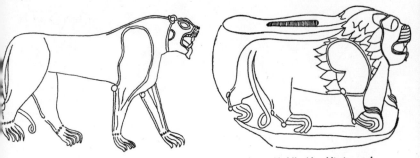

Fig. 6a – Lion relief. Orthostat from Zincirli. Early to Middle Neo-Hittite style
832–810 B. C. Istanbul.
Fig. 6b – Lion base from Zincirli. Middle Neo-Hittite style.
832–810 B. C. Istanbul.

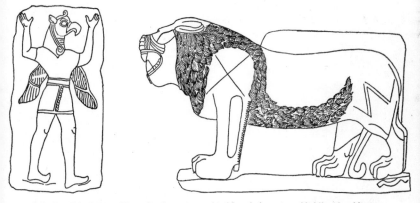

Fig. 7 – Relief from Zincirli, depicting a bird-headed genius. Middle Neo-Hittite
style. 832–810 B. C. Istanbul.
Fig. 8 – Portal lion from Zincirli, Aramaeanising Neo-Hittite style.
Reign of Sargon II (721–705). Istanbul.

The section of the Istanbul Archaeological Museum devoted to the Greek
and Roman periods houses works of inestimable value. In the treasury on
the second floor are kept gold, silver and ivory works of art from various
periods. The two ivory figurines which are seen in the photographs in Pl. 7
were discovered in the foundations of the temple of Artemis at Ephesus.
The statuette of a priestess spinning wool, which dates from the end of the
7th century, depicts a young woman from Lydia. Perhaps she is one of the
ladies who waited on the goddess Artemis, mentioned in Aristophanes' play,

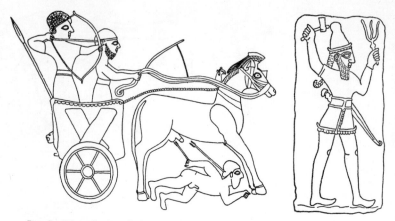

Fig. 9 – War chariot. Orthostat relief from Zincirli, Middle Neo-Hittite style.
832–810 B. C. Istanbul.

Fig. 10 – Orthostat relief depicting a weather god. Found at Zincirli, Middle
Neo-Hittite style. 832–810 B. C. Istanbul.

Fig. 11 – Bust-shaped attachment from a cauldron found at Toprakkale near
Van. Early Urartian style. 710–700 B. C. Istanbul.

Fig. 12 – Gold sheet showing a griffin, found in the foundations of the Artemis
Temple at Ephesus. Greco-Anatolian craftsmanship. Beginning of the
7th century B. C. Istanbul.

Fig. 13 – Portal sphinx from Zincirli. Aramaeanising Hittite style. About 730–720
B. C. Istanbul.

"The Clouds". Her hat, which is decorated with pearls or precious stones, must be of the mitra type that Sappho searched for, in vain, as a gift for her daughter. A similar kind of headgear was worn by King Warpalawas in the Late Hittite period (Pl. 2). The rings hanging from the Lydian girl's bracelets, the heavy necklace, the exotic face, the eyebrows emphasized with deep lines and the ornamental headgear, described above, all point to the influence of Syrian or Late Hittite ivory craftsmanship. On the other hand, the cylindrically shaped body, fashioned like that of a "xoanon" (primitive statue in wood), the way in which the girl is depicted at a definite moment, i.e. in the act of spinning, caught with a lively smile on her face, are indications that the artist who fashioned the statuette was trained in the Greek school of sculpture. The thickened figure, the heavy chaplet and the cowl-like head-covering of the other ivory statuette lead one to conclude that it portrays a castrated Lydian priest (Pl. 7 b.). This figurine does not smile with the lips only but also with the eyes. The lines of the face and body indicate an advance in carving technique. In fact, this work shows comparatively more Ionian influence than the statuette of the young girl, and must have been created at a later date. The statuette of the girl was carved at the end of the 7th century B. C., while that of the priest was fashioned at the beginning of the 6th century.

The statues exhibited in Rooms XI and XII, devoted to the archaic period, are rare and beautiful specimens of East Greek art. The fine archaic head (Pl. 19), which has recently been identified as having originated on Samos, is particularly noteworthy. With its almond-shaped eyes, its enigmatic smile and the delineation of its soft features, this head is an outstandingly fine example of Ionian sculpture. The work shows the hair dressed in sections in front and at the sides, with a fringe covering the forehead. The Samos head is the best example of this type of Ionian hairstyle. The body to which the head belongs was found in a fragmentary condition on Samos a few years ago. This sophisticated work was created by a great sculptor about 550 B. C.

The Greco-Persian burial stelae found at Daskyleion a few years ago are most interesting works of art. Plate 20 shows the best preserved example, which is the tombstone relief of a transporter of goods. This sculptured stele is executed in a style which arose from a combination of the Greek and Achaemenid art forms. For instance, the cart with its many-spoked wheels, the horses with their tails bound tightly in the middle, the crown worn by the seated woman and the top-boots worn by the men are all characteristic features of Achaemenid art. In sharp contrast, the form of the stele, its architectural profile, the tripod and the vessel on it depicted in the lower right-hand corner, the man and wife intimately sitting together, the lifelike attitudes and gestures, and the style in general are all typically Greek. This work dates from about 400 B. C.

The most important pieces of sculpture in the Istanbul Archaeological Museum are the monumental sarcophagi discovered in the Royal Cemetery at Sidon by the famous Turkish archaeologist, Osman Hamdi. These are the Satrap Sarcophagus, the Lycian Sarcophagus, the Sarcophagus of the

Mourning Women and the Alexander Sarcophagus. In the Satrap Sarcophagus lay the body of an unknown king, who lived in the second half of the 4th century, when the city of Sidon was under Persian rule. Scenes from the life of the king are depicted on the tomb. In one scene, the king is discovered seated on his throne. On his head he wears a tiara of Persian style. He is dressed in a long-sleeved chiton-like garment and long trousers (anaxyrides). The tomb is called the Satrap Sarcophagus because of the Persian garb of the main figure, who represents a satrap (a Persian governor) or a king. On the same side of the sarcophagus is depicted a chariot with four horses, which always stood ready at the satrap's command. On the other short side of the sarcophagus, the king is seen on a panther hunt. On one of the long sides are depicted the satrap's chief officers, armed with spears. The other short face shows the king at a banquet, accompanied by his wife. On this sarcophagus, the satrap's robes, the hunting scene and the banquet scene are all eastern motifs. Following the custom of the time, the satrap is dressed like an Achaemenid ruler and, in the manner of such a sovereign, is seen going hunting and seated at a sumptuous table. These scenes which, from the point of view of theme and expression, exhibit eastern features, are wholly Greek with regard to style. The folds of the garments, the stance of the figures, the shape of the sarcophagus together with its architectural ornamentation, are all executed with an innate feeling for Greek classical art. The seated woman, the posture of the satrap on his mount and, on the rear face, the motif of the man being dragged along the ground, are reminiscent of the Greek classical style which held sway during the second half of the 5th century B. C. Consequently, the Satrap Sarcophagus must have been carved at the end of the 5th century.

On one of the two longer sides of the Lycian tomb is depicted a wild boar hunt with the hunters on horseback (Pl. 21 b). The other side shows Amazons in chariots hunting a lion (Pl. 21 a). Fighting centaurs appear on the shorter sides. The pediment at one end of the sarcophagus contains paired sphinxes and that at the other end paired griffins. In contrast to the Satrap Sarcophagus, the Lycian Sarcophagus exhibits no eastern influences and, with regard to its interpretation and expression, bears the stamp of the Greek style. The mounted figures in the boar hunt scene strongly resemble the cavalry in the Parthenon friezes. The broad faces and stocky bodies of the figures are an indication that the sculptor was of Peloponnesian origin. The sculptor has also created magnificent compositions on both of the long faces. In particular, he has successfully achieved depth and the third dimension in his composition by placing the figures one behind the other so that they overlap. The general character of the scenes resembles mural art. The ogival lid of the sarcophagus, the two lion-shaped lugs for raising the lid, the attitude of the lion in the hunting scene and the selection of rather old-fashioned motifs in general such as griffins and sphinxes, indicate that this work conforms to the Lycian tradition. The artist, a skilled sculptor, has very successfully combined the traditional Anatolian Lycian style with an understanding of Peloponnesian art. Judging by the definite classical influences it shows, it would be correct to date the Lycian Sarcophagus to the beginning of the 4th century B. C.

The Mourning Women Sarcophagus is one of the earliest examples of columned sarcophagi, and the finest representation of this type (Pl. 22 a). Like the Nereid Monument and the Mausoleum at Halicarnassus, this sarcophagus is a work in the style of the Ionic temples. However, in one respect, it is unlike the two works mentioned in that it does not possess a high base but rests on a low pedestal, the profile of which is shaped on the Lesbian cyma pattern. A frieze depicting many figures runs around a Lesbian cymatium (cyma reversa). Half-columns rise on Attic bases. The upper structure, as in the case of the Mausoleum and the Priene temple, is composed of an architrave with three fasciae, and above this, a row of dentils. On the attic crowning the sarcophagus is depicted a funeral cortege. The wagons here are of the same type as the transport carriages seen on the Daskyleion reliefs of Greco-Persian style (Pl. 20). On the pediments are hired wailing mourners. The spaces between the half-columns are closed in with a balustrade, on which can be seen the figures of eighteen wailing women, leaning or sitting. These eighteen women are mourning the person who was buried in the casket. It can be assumed that this sarcophagus is a memorial to Straton I, King of Sidon, who died in 360 B. C. It is recorded that Straton was of a flirtatious disposition, and led a dissolute life with the hetaerae he had brought from the Peloponnese. It is surmised that the women depicted on the tomb as mourning the king were members of his harem. From the standpoint of style and in regard to form and interpretation, the Mourning Women Sarcophagus is a work of the classical Greek period. The only traces of Achaemenid and Phoenician influence appear in the long chitons worn by the attendants, and in the chariots depicted on the attic. The posture and clothing of the mourning women point to a close relationship with Attic tomb reliefs, which have been dated to about the middle of the 4th century B. C. In view of this, the sarcophagus must have been made about 350 B. C.

Besides being one of the most famous of archaeological discoveries, the Alexander Sarcophagus is also one of the most important creations of antiquity to come to light. In addition, it is one of the best preserved specimens of Greek art, and, in regard to its vivid polychromy, it is unique. The sarcophagus has been fashioned in the form and style of a building of the Ionic order. The decorative motifs and the architectural ornamentation of the sarcophagus and its cover have been wrought with extreme care and precision. One of the long sides depicts a battle between the Persians and the Greeks, in which Alexander took part (Pls. 9a, 23). It is possible to distinguish the Persians by the tiaras on their heads and their long trousers. Alexander is in the act of hurling a spear, raised in his right hand, at a Persian. The Persian, whose horse has fallen to its knees, is threatening Alexander with a weapon held in his right hand. Alexander can be recognized by the head of a lion's pelt, the symbol of Heracles, which he wears on his own head. On the right, a Persian and a Greek are engaged in foot combat Further to the right, another Persian is about to shoot an arrow at Alexander. Next to this figure is seen a mounted Greek attacking a Persian, who is begging him for mercy. A little further on, a disarmed and naked Greek is throwing himself at the bridle reins of a Persian's rearing horse. In front of this, a kneeling Persian is aiming an arrow at a rider galloping from the right towards the left. Following this comes another group in which one Persian is attempting to save another Persian who is in danger of falling off his horse. The bodies of a naked Greek and, four Persians lie along the entire length of the scene. This vivid scene is framed by the two flanking figures of Alexander on the left and the mounted Macedonian commander, on the right, both of whom dominate the diverse action at their sides.

The subject of the reliefs on the rear side is a lion hunt (Pl. 22 b). Persians can be seen intermingled with the Greeks participating in the hunt. In the centre of the scene, we observe a rider whose horse is being attacked by a lion. This person, wearing a tiara on his head and long trousers, is dressed like a Persian. Five people, three of them on foot, are hurrying from both sides to the aid of the horse placed in this dangerous position. The nearest is a Persian, who is on the point of bringing down his raised axe upon the lion. Two of those on horseback, one on the right, the other on the left, with spears grasped in their hands, are coming to help. The Persian dominating the scene on the left, who is in the act of shooting an arrow, and a naked young Greek, who has a cloak thrown over his arm and who is just in front of the Persian, are rushing to the scene of the event. Three dogs are also included in the scene; one of these is biting one of the lion's hind legs, and the other two are attempting to arrive on the scene with all speed. To the right of the lion hunt a deer hunt is going on. Here a Greek and a Persian are engaged in killing a deer, the former with a spear and the latter with an axe. The central mounted figure has been identified as the Phoenician King Abdalonymos. The fact that he is in the attire of a Persian is in accordance with the custom of the time. After the Battle of Issus (333 B.C.), Abdalonymos was put "on the throne of his fathers" by Hephaistion at the command of Alexander the Great. It is recorded that Abdalonymos once presented Alexander with a very fine perfume. In the light of this knowledge, it is understandable that Abdalonymos' sarcophagus should be decorated with scenes depicting Alexander the Great. Indeed, we need have no doubt that the figure on horseback behind Abdalonymos represents Alexander himself. The fact that the head (Pl. 22 b) does not sufficiently resemble Alexander is of little importance, when we consider that the head (Pl. 23) of the figure depicted on the front face of the tomb does not look like Alexander either. In the latter case, if the head of the mounted figure had not been covered with the head of a lion pelt, it would have been difficult to establish the connection with Alexander by means of the physiognomy alone. The figure in the aforementioned hunting scene is wearing a king's headband and the posture of attack is extremely similar to that of Alexander, as depicted in the mosaic representing the Battle of Issus in the museum at Naples. In any case, many other portrayals of Alexander, like these two, are, in general, idealized representations. The short sides of the sarcophagus give concise versions of the battle and hunting scenes appearing on the long sides (Pl. 9 a). The Alexander Sarcophagus is made of Attic Pentelic marble. The reliefs also definitly show Attic influence. Nevertheless, from the point of view of the battle scene, these reliefs are reminiscent of the friezes carved on the tomb of Mausolus. Whatever is the case, it will be no easy task to discover the identity of the artist responsible for the Alexander Sarcophagus. Originally, he cannot have been a very famous sculptor. A creation that, on completion, would go into an underground burial vault and never more see the light of day would not be expected to be the work of a renowned sculptor. In spite of this, the creator of the Alexander tomb was one of the greatest sculptors of his time; the skill and precision of his marble carving are a source of wonder. This man was not in the avant - garde of artistic trends but a master sculptor who worked in the traditional academic style; the proportions of his figures show restraint and their action is harmonious. The composition, showing an inner feeling for free symmetry, is attractively and successfully realized. The life-like portrayal of figures in action is accentuated by the lavish use of colour. Violet, purple, red, burnt sienna, yellow and blue have all been employed. Hair, eyes, eyelashes, lips and clothing are all painted. In contrast, the bare flesh is uncoloured and only polished with a light lacquer. The Alexander Sarcophagus, with its beautifully preserved colours, is one of the most informative examples of Hellenic sculpture, because polychromy was used extensively by Greek artists. The painting of statues reached an especially high level of skill during the second half of the 4th century B. C. Ancient writers of the period praised the shining effect achieved by the use of paint on the eyes of the statues. A close look at the figures on the Alexander tomb certainly reveals a lifelike brilliance and sparkle. As Abdalonymos was buried in the Alexander Sarcophagus, and as he founded his monarchy during the last third of the 4th century, the sarcophagus must have been made, at the latest, by the end of that century.

The Istanbul Museum possesses the best preserved and finest likeness of Alexander the Great (Room XV). This magnificent head, which, attached to the body, stood as a complete statue in a house overlooking the lower agora at Pergamon (Pl. 25), is a typical example of portrayals of Alexander the Great, with the hair flowing down on either side of the forehead like a lion's mane and in the manner in which the head is inclined towards the left, as described by ancient writers. This work, with its open mouth, the pathetic look in the eyes, the deeply lined forehead and the bouffant hair style, is a typical example of the art of marble carving in Pergamon during the reign of Eumenes II (197 - 159 B. C.) The modelling and general appearance of the head give the impression that the Pergamene sculptor used the Lysippos portraits of Alexander as models.

Another work of the same century, a full-length, idealized statue of Alexander the Great, stands in the same room of the museum (Pl. 24). The statue was found at Magnesia ad Sipylum. The inscription found at the place where the statue was discovered states : "Menas of Pergamon, son of Aias, made (it)". From this, we can conclude that this statue of Alexander is of Pergamene origin. Menas has depicted Alexander the Great in the form of the god Apollo. A row of holes encircling the head reveals that the god was probably crowned with a laurel wreath in metal. The calm expression on the face and the restrained look of pathos in the eyes are sure indications that the statue was meant to represent a god. Moreover, the upper part of the body is bare, in accordance with the custom prevailing in portrayals of the gods in the Hellenistic period. A statue of Zeus, or of Attalos II (159 - 138 B. C.) idealized as Zeus, which was discovered in the temple of Hera at Pergamon and is now housed in the Aphrodisias Room (No. XVII) of the Istanbul Museum (Inv. No. 2767), is similarly attired. The statue of Poseidon originally from Melos but now in the National Museum in Athens is garbed more or less in the same fashion. We can understand that Menas' statue is of Alexander only by the fact that the left hand grasps the hilt of a dagger. For comparison, Alexander appears in a cameo in the Leningrad Museum, holding a dagger in his left hand. From what remains of a statuette of Alexander found at Priene, and now kept in Berlin, it is also apparent that a dagger was held in the left hand.

Menas' statue was leaning on a spear, just like the aforementioned statue of Poseidon in the museum in Athens. It is a fine, valuable work of art, a creation of the middle years of the 2nd century B. C., as is the statue of Poseidon and that of Zeus or Attalos II found in the temple of Hera at Pergamon.

Another of the masterpieces in the Istanbul Museum is the famous Ephebe statue (Room XV, No. 542), which was found at Tralleis, present-day Aydın (Pls. 26 - 28). The statue represents a young athlete leaning for a while against one of the target posts, to recover from the exertions of his athletic training. The "cauliflower" ears, swollen and with the tops flattened like those of a wrestler, show that the athlete has been wrestling from a very early age. Since each wrestler always tries to seize the other's head at ear level during bouts, the ears in time become swollen in appearance like those of the ephebe. Every ancient Greek athlete participated in all forms of sport, and, of these, wrestling in particular was never neglected. The artist has wrapped the cloak around the body in a very attractive manner. The body is hidden beneath thick material and is only suggested by the outline of the left arm bent over the chest and the right arm hanging straight down under the cloak. The impressions left in the surface of the marble by the roots of small plants have given the statue a very charming appearance (Pl.27).In general, the Ephebe statue shows influences of the Polykleitos School. The carriage of the head resembles that of the Westmacott Ephebe in the British Museum, and the hairstyle is reminiscent of copies of the Doryphoros of the Augustan age. Indeed, the arrangement of the hair over the forehead is in accordance with the hair style of the Augustan period. Consequently, this work is understood to have been produced at the beginning of the first century A. D. By means of the original pose and the leaning attitude given to the body, the artist has succeeded in portraying, with great skill, an ephebe resting after strenuous exercise. The charming forward tilt of the head, the childlike expression on the face with its large eyes, characteristic of Mediterranean people, and the relaxed and flowing lines of the body are all in perfect harmony (Pls. 26 - 28). The sculptor of Tralleis has created a work of art which will appeal to people in all ages.

CYZICUS

This city, founded by the people of Miletos, is one of the oldest Ionian establishments in the Propontic region. Judging by fragments of late geometric sherds, which constitute the earliest archaeological finds resulting from excavations carried out by the present author at Cyzicus, the city was founded during the first quarter of the 7th century B. C. Cyzicus was a very important artistic centre throughout the Greek and Roman historical periods. The torso of a man and a relief showing a young woman dancing between two youths, which are housed in the room devoted to the archaic period in the Istanbul Archaeological Museum, were discovered at Cyzicus. Many other works of art from Cyzicus and the neighbourhood are to be found in the same museum. Other artistic treasures unearthed at Cyzicus and in the surrounding area are collected together in the Erdek Open-Air Museum. The ruins of Cyzicus do not greatly attract the interest of those who are not archaeologists. Moreover, since the area is thickly wooded, many of the remains lying on the ground are hidden from view. All that exists today of the temple of Hadrian, which stood in the south-western district of the city, is the subterranean vaulting supporting the platform. The temple was dedicated to the Emperor Hadrian, who was proclaimed the thirteenth Olympian god; in the late Roman era it was accepted as one of the seven wonders of the world. In 1431, Cyriacus of Ancona saw the whole of the upper part of the building with 33 columns intact and produced engravings in proof of his account. With the help of these pictures presented by Cyriacus, it has been possible to identify a beautiful piece of one of the temple columns (Pl. 29), which is now in the Erdek Open - Air Museum. The author of this book has identified ruins in the region of Ergili on the south-eastern shores of Lake Manyas as Daskyleion, the garrison town of the Persian governor Pharnabazos. Bullae unearthed during the excavations at Daskyleion which bear Aramaic inscriptions are housed in the Archaeological Institute of Ankara University. Reliefs which have either been discovered during excavations in 'the same area, or which have been found by chance, are in the Istanbul Museum (Pl. 20). The ruins remaining *in situ* would be of interest only to archaeologists or to those engaged in historical research.

TROY

The discovery and excavation of the Trojan citadel can be considered one of the most important events in archaeological field research. Troy was excavated by Schliemann, Dörpfeld and Blegen. Schliemann was obsessed with the idea of discovering the citadel of Priam and the scene of Homer's epic. In 1870 he made the first spade thrust. Ten metres down, Schliemann's notorious great North-South Trench revealed a burnt layer belonging to the second building period, which convinced him that he had discovered traces of the Trojan war. Thus he assumed that the golden works of art which he found in that layer were Priam's treasure. The excavation of Troy took a fortunate turn in 1882, after Schliemann gained the collaboration of his colleague, Wilhelm Dörpfeld, who had been in the Olympia excavation team and had acquired much valuable experience there. Dörpfeld distinguished nine different layers of civilization. This division was confirmed and further elaborated by the American archaeologists who carried out new excavations at Troy under Carl W. Blegen, from 1932 to 1938. The Americans approached the task with the more specialized techniques which archaeological progress had meanwhile developed. Through detailed observation, they were able to subdivide Dörpfeld's nine layers into no fewer than thirty habitation levels.

Troy I (3000 - 2500 B. C.). This initial settlement, which consisted of ten strata, lying one on top of the other, occupied an extremely small area. At the Ij habitation level, that is, at the time when Troy I was at the height of its development, the diameter of the city was only 90 metres. On the plan published in this book are shown the ruins in their restored condition, based on the various points determined by the German and American expeditions (Fig. 14).

The wall of Troy I (in squares EF - 5/6 on the plan) is still in a very good state of preservation today. The city gate was 2.97 metres wide and was defended by two towers. Of the two, the one on the east has been found in a very good state of preservation, now that the overlying soil has been removed. Its present height is 3.50 metres. The base of the tower was composed of fairly large stones. At the top of the tower, these became smaller and distinctly narrower, and resembled sun-dried bricks or tiles. The American excavators record that this wall, which has a strong batter on its outer face (a receding slope), had been surmounted by a parapet made of sundried brick. Any attack by an enemy trying to force the long corridor-like entrance would be parried from the flanking towers. The American expedition has confirmed the extent of the wall for a distance of 115 metres by opening up wells and tunnels (Fig. 14).

House No. 102, which lies between squares CD - 2/3 on the plan, and was excavated by the American archaeological expedition, constitutes the finest remains belonging to the Troy I level (Fig. 14). This building was erected during the Ib phase at Troy. The building with a round end, which is seen beneath this house, belongs to the Troy Ia phase. The walls of house No. 102 measure 18.75 × 7.00 metres, from the exterior; they are constructed in the herring-bone style. Two fire-places existed in the big room: one in the centre of the room, the other near the east wall. Some portions of the first still remain, but nothing is left of the second. The same room also possessed two benches which could have been used as beds or divans. The one which was placed against the north and east walls, and of which no trace now remains, was 2.00 metres in length, 0.90 metres in width and 0.30 metres in height. On the other hand, that near the north-west corner and still in place is 2.35 metres long, 1.70 metres wide and 0.50 metres high. It was occupied by a double-bed. The "bothros" which was unearthed during excavations, but which does not exist today, was a pit used for setting bread dough to rise. The small platform behind this, which lay against the wall, served as a table for odds and ends, but it too is no longer in existence. The bones of various animals and remains of shellfish found in this corner prove that food was cooked and eaten here. Beneath the paving of the big room, two graves for infants were discovered: one close to the south wall, the other near the east wall. All the six skeletons found have proved to be of new-born babies, or at most, of one or two week - old children. The high death - rate of children during birth at this time is remarkable.

It was necessary to leave long, narrow apertures for light and ventilation in the upper parts of the walls near the roof, which was a flat structure made of wood and sun-baked brick. House No. 102, being a long, narrow, isolated building, with one front room and a fire-place in the middle of the big room, was a typical megaron and is one of the oldest examples known at the present time. To the south of House No. 102, five more parallel walls are visible (Fig. 14). Although no definite plan can be drawn, it may be said that these are the remains of megaron-type dwellings. The south wall of the building, occurring in square 4 D, is constructed in the herring-bone style.

Troy I is a settlement of the Early Bronze Age civilization. Pottery was made by hand. Trojan vessels decorated with portrayals of human faces appear for the first time in this settlement. From the standpoint of culture, Troy I is related to the neighbouring Aegean area. The settlement came to an end as the result of a serious conflagration.

Troy II (2500-2200 B. C.). The II a-g phases of this settlement, composed of seven building strata, played an important role in the history of Troy, despite the fact that it did not exceed a diameter of 110 metres in 2200 B. C. Although Troy I was destroyed catastrophically, there is no break in the time sequence or any change in culture between the two settlements. On the contrary, the culture of Troy I continued to develop in Troy II.

The second settlement gives evidence of a particularly great advance in the sphere of town-planning. Judging by the megarons and the orderly arrangement of the propylons in the II c-g phases, Troy II was the first city in the western world to show signs of a definite planning system (Fig. 15). Troy II, from the standpoint of the originality of its orderly town plan and the success with which it was realized, compares favourably with any of the contemporary towns of the Near East. The specific method of placing megarons side by side to present a continuous front, and of arranging the entrance to this building complex through megaron-like propylons, was faithfully followed seven to eight hundred years later on the acropolis at Tiryns in Greece. The system of passing through another and bigger propylon before entering a building complex made up of serried megarons (Fig. 15) survived also at Tiryns. The acropolis at Athens provides another example of the same type of city planning.

As was the case with Troy I, the main gate of Troy II was in the centre of the south wall (FN). In the 2nd city, however, there were other gateways as well as this. Of these, the remains of the south-west gate (FM, square 6 C) and, in particular, its well-paved ramp, measuring 21 metres in length and 7.5 metres in width, are in a good state of preservation (Fig. 15). The stone portion of the wall, which can still be seen today, has a strong batter, i.e. it slopes inwards towards the top. Above this, a perpendicular section made of sun-dried brick used to extend upwards.

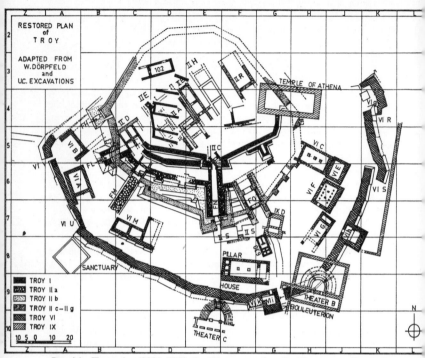

Fig. 14 – **Troy I** *(3000–2500 B. C.) possessed a fortification wall which is greatly restored on the plan (shown in black); however, the east tower of the city gate (squares E–F 5–6) with a sloping outer face is still in a very good state of preservation.* **House No. 102,** *a long, narrow isolated building consisting of a portico (front entrance) and a big room with a fireplace in the middle, is one of the earliest megarons known at the present day. The walls are constructed in the herring-bone style. Five more parallel walls lie to the south, one of which also has herring-bone masonry.* **Troy II** *(2500–2200), composed of seven strata lying one on top of the other, is characterised by three principal periods (II a, II b, II c–g), each possessing a new fortification wall (differently drawn on the plan). From Troy IIa remain two gateways marked FL and FN, each having the form of a fairly long uncovered corridor. These city gates were adjusted to the new wall of Troy IIb and continued to be used. The gateways FM (squares C 5–6) and FO (squares F–G 6–7) were the main entrances (see also Fig. 15). Very little remains of the megarons built side by side on the summit of the city mound. The greater part of the big megaron (marked II A) was destroyed by Schliemann's North-South Trench; only a small part of this building has been preserved; a portion lies buried beneath the pinnacle of earth left after the German excavations. The ruins of* **Troy III-V** *(2200–1800 B. C.) are not shown on the plan. Buildings dating from* **Troy III** *are to be seen to the north-west of the ramp in square C 5. Remains*

of primitive houses of **Troy IV** *have been discovered to the east of house VI A (square B 6). The small wall in the square 5 A dates from* **Troy V.** *For* **Troy VI** *see the caption of Fig. 15.* **Troy VIIa** *and* **VIIb1,2** *are not shown on the plan. The well-preserved houses of* **Troy VIIa** *(1300–1260 B. C.) can be seen between gateways VIT and VIS behind the city wall. Buildings of* **Troy VIIb1** *lie in squares E–F 8–9. A house and some walls dating from* **VIIb2** *are situated in squares A 7 and J–K 5. Remains of* **Troy VIII** *(Greek period) are encountered in squares A–B 7–8. The wall in rustica style lying immediately in front of the city wall of Troy VI and parallel to it dates, together with the altar in the centre of this precinct, from Hellenistic times. Another altar situated to the west and constructed of marble is Augustan in date. Two further altars lie to the south (in squares A·8–9); they were also erected in the Hellenistic period. The Athena Temple (squares G–H 3–4), erected in the Hellenistic age and greatly renovated in Roman times, has been completely dug up. Its place is now marked by a deep hole.* **Troy IX** *(Roman period): the propylon IX D in square G7, the entrance to the temple of Athena, was built in the Augustan age. The wall which partly overlies the south-eastern section of City Wall VI in square K–L 4–8 was also constructed in the Roman period. The Bouleuterion (Theatre B), half of which was built over the city wall to the east of the main entrance to Troy VI (VI T), and also the theatre C (squares E–F 9–10) of which the auditorium lies over the city wall, both date back to Roman times.*

The paved ramp (Fig. 15) led up to the propylon FM. The entrance to the propylon measured 5.25 metres and possessed a door with two swinging flaps. This propylon (FM), built on the plan of a megaron, belonged to the Troy II c-g phases, i.e. the last period of the settlement. A little behind this rampart can be seen the remains of city walls, corresponding to the Troy II b phase in front, and to the Troy II a phase in the rear (i.e., the north). The northernmost ruins of a wall (shown in black on the plan Fig. 14), which lie more or less on the axis of the FM propylon, belong to Troy I. The gate FN in square E7 was the main entrance to Troy IIa. The large propylon (marked FO) was the main entrance to the city during the last phase of Troy II i.e. during its most splendid days (Fig. 15). This construction, like the FM propylon, was built on the plan of a megaron, open on the two narrow sides. The magnificent entrance led into an inner open square (Fig. 15) which was constructed in the period corresponding to the Troy II c-g phases (i.e. ca : 2200 - 2100 B. C.). This was made into a courtyard by levelling the top of the city walls of phases II a-b and putting down a pavement of pebbles. In order to enter the royal palace, it was necessary to pass through a small propylon, which was again constructed on a megaron plan. Judged by the width of the stone threshold block which lies on the ground, this propylon measured 1.82 metres across. A cobbled courtyard also lay between the II c phase propylon and the large megaron, and this had two walls 2.00 metres thick on its south and west sides; a stone base found *in situ* in the south corner discloses the fact that the structure was colonnaded (Fig. 15). People emerging from the megaron were therefore confronted by a fine piece of architectural decoration. On hot days when the sun blazed

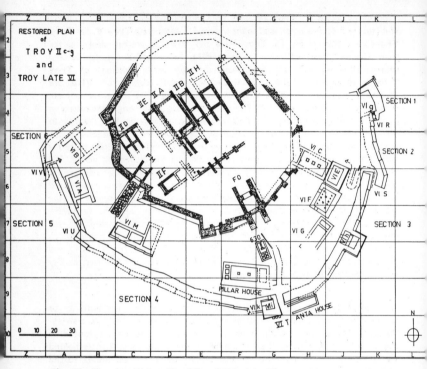

RESTORED PLAN
of
TROY II c-g
and
TROY LATE VI

Fig. 15 – Troy Late II (see Fig. 14) and Troy Late VI.

Troy Late VI. The city wall and the houses of VI f–h shown on the plan and representing the most brilliant period of this settlement (about 1425 to 1300 B. C.) are in a very good state of preservation. The most impressive remains of the city of Ilion are the fortifications of Troy VI f–h, which were built piecemeal during this golden age. **Section I** consists of a splendid watch-tower; in the centre of it is a cistern, enclosing a well, for use during time of siege. **Section 2** of the wall is largely hidden by a massive Roman wall; it overlaps the end of sections I and 3. In this way, an original type of city gate was formed at each end (VI R and VI S). The defenders were able to attack the enemy with cross-fire from the tops of the parallel walls forming the entrance. The walls (Pl. I) have sloping outer faces; they are vertically divided with offsets jutting out 10 to 15 cm. and occurring every ten metres. **Section 3** of the wall has the same character; Tower VI i, like Tower VI h, was constructed in the Troy VI h phase. The main gate to the acropolis was the entrance in the south marked VI T. The "**Anta House**", of which only a single stone is preserved at present, lay on the right-hand side as one entered the city gate; it was probably a sanctuary in which burnt sacrifices were frequently offered, perhaps in connection with ceremonial arrivals and departures. The four monoliths resembling menhirs and standing in a row at the foot of the south wall of Tower VI i may also indicate that worship *of some kind was practised in this area.* **Section 4,** *divided by thirteen vertical offsets, has the same beautiful masonry as the other parts of the city wall. The gateway VI U was blocked up in the later phases of Troy VI.* **Section 5** *belongs to an earlier phase of the sixth settlement; it shows an entirely different technique of masonry.* **Section 6,** *preserved only in parts, exhibits excellent workmanship; therefore, it also dates from the brilliant period of the sixth settlement (Troy VI f–h). The* **Pillar House,** *built during the VIf period, is the largest house on the acropolis. The two pillars, only one of which is in place, indicate that the house was two-storeyed.* **House No. 630** *dates back to the Troy VIb phase (ca. 1700 B. C.). The houses* **VI G, VI F, VI E** *and* **VI C** *are of the same type and date from the same period (Troy VI f–h).* **VI F** *and* **VI C** *were two-storeyed. The building* **VI M,** *constructed during the VIg phase, with its 27 metre-long south wall divided into five segments by four vertical offsets displays an attractive silhouette, like a miniature fortress. For further explanation see the text.*

down on the megaron, this provided a shady place in which to get cool. Mention has been made above of the orderly plan on which the acropolis of Troy II is based. All the buildings certainly conform to a well thought-out plan. In particular, the siting of the big megaron (IIA) on the summit of a hill, commanding the surrounding area, was highly effective. This house, with its 1.5 metre-thick walls, must have been a tall building, rising in the middle of the citadel as a mass attracting all attention. Although the greater part of the megaron was destroyed by Schliemann's north-south trench, it has been possible, by means of the present ruins, to establish approximately the plan of the construction. As will be seen from the plan (Fig. 15), only a part of this building has been discovered, and a portion of the east wall lies buried beneath the pinnacle of earth left after the German excavations. The width of the building, including the walls, is 13 metres; the length is not certain, but it must have been at least 35 to 40 metres. The interior measurements of the main room were 20 × 10.20 metres; in the middle of this room, Dörpfeld discovered the ruins of a platform which was 4 metres in diameter. From this it can be deduced that a hearth existed here in the centre of the room just as in all typical megaron structures. Places intended for seats and the marks of throne-like furniture have not been uncovered as such. Without doubt, various benches, tables and seats must have existed in this splendid building, which was used for a long time by the kings of the period comprising phases II c-g. The remains of two other megarons of the same type but comparatively smaller are evident on both sides of Megaron II A. The one (IIB) on the west was destroyed by Schliemann's north-south trench, but can be taken to be the twin of the well-preserved megaron on the eastern side (IIE). Both these megarons are thought to have been sitting or sleeping quarters for the royal family. Megarons II H, II R and II F, identified by Dörpfeld, must also have been reserved for the king and his family. The building II D (Fig. 15) was composed of a number of small rooms. Very probably this was a garrison or depot.

The level of culture in Troy II was high. This fact has been sufficiently elaborated in the first part of this book. Mention has also been made there of the treasure found by Schliemann. The American archaeologists have definitely established that the treasure which Schliemann unearthed belongs to Troy II g. Many other very valuable gold and silver works of art, like the aforementioned treasure, that have been brought to light as a result of excavation, reveal that Troy II g suddenly succumbed to attack. The layer of destruction which marks the end of Troy II g is on an average one metre thick and bears the marks of a raging fire. This was caused by an external enemy, very probably an arm of the hordes of Indo-European invaders. However, this enemy did not occupy Troy, since no evidence has been found of a change in culture during the subsequent settlements III, IV and V. We shall observe the arrival of a new people in Troy when we come to examine the VIth settlement in detail.

Troy III - V (2200 - 1800). In the first part of this book, mention was made of the connection that can be recognized between the disaster which destroyed Troy II at the end of the third millennium and the huge wave of Indo-European immigration. During this era (i.e., the period of Troy III, IV and V), which doubtless continued for a very long time, we notice the gradual fading of the former glory of Troy, and its decline in prosperity. We find the ruins of buildings dating from Troy III to the north-west of the ramp in C5. These were houses constructed of small, irregular stones. Excavations carried out by the Germans have proved that, during Troy IV, there was not even a fortifying wall. The remains of primitive buildings of this period have been discovered to the east of the house marked VIA (square B6). In the time of Troy V, the settlement is understood to have been encircled by an inferior kind of fortifying wall. The small wall in square 5A is of this period.

Troy VI (1800 - 1275). The VIth settlement is composed of eight strata and exhibits three main periods. The most splendid advances occurred during the Troy VI f-h periods. The houses and the city wall which were erected during this era, bear witness to a high standard of craftsmanship and good taste.

A close study of the city wall, which is still standing, reveals that it consisted of six sections, linked by five gateways (Fig. 15). The American archaeological team, benefiting also from Dörpfeld's earlier observations, has established the fact that, with the exception of Section 5 (Fig. 15), which was left in its former state and underwent no renovations, the city wall was rebuilt piecemeal during the VI f-g phases, from ca. 1425 to 1300 B. C., in place of a wall that previously existed. One of the best preserved and most impressive parts of the wall is Section I in square K 3-4 (Fig. 15). This section, which consists of a splendid tower, is 18 m. long and 8 m. wide. The height, according to calculations made by Dörpfeld, was 9 metres; the workmanship displayed in this bastion, referred to as VIg, is very fine. The interesting shape of this building, in particular the sharply angled corner, make it a very attractive structure. In the centre of the tower is a cistern which encloses a well, eight metres deep, carved out of the rock. This source of water was used during time of siege. On account of the great height of the bastion

VIg, it commanded the whole plain as well as the acropolis. Consequently, it is certain that it functioned as a look-out tower.

Section 2 of the wall (Fig. 15) was handsomely built and slopes in towards the top. It is 41.5 metres long, over 4.5 metres thick and today exceeds 4 metres in height. The wall is divided into five parts by four perpendicular offsets, with a slight angle between the divisions, for the offsets jut out from 10 to 15 centimetres. Unfortunately, this fine wall section is largely hidden by a massive Roman wall, which prevents it from being easily seen. It will be noticed that the north end of Section 2 is overlapped on its eastern side for about four metres by Section 1, whereas its southern end overlaps the northern end of Section 3 for five metres on the east. In this way, an original type of gateway was formed at each end (VI R and VI S on the plan in Fig. 15). From the point of view of defence, the gate marked VI S was especially practical. The defenders were able to ward off an attacking force from the two walls above this entrance, which was two metres wide and five metres long.

Section 3, which stretches for ninety metres, has been partially obliterated in the south by the erection over it of the Roman bouleuterion (Theatre B), and by Schliemann's north-east trench (Fig. 15). On the other hand, the eastern part is in a very good state of preservation (Pl. 1 a, b). Although the tower VI h, added during the very last phase of Troy VI, has been largely destroyed, it is still of impressive beauty (Pl. 1 a). This stretch of the wall is also divided into offsets. The main gateway, which was used during the final phase of Troy VI, lies in the gap between Sections 3 and 4. It has been noticed that the main gate to the acropolis has always been in the south, ever since the founding of Troy I (Fig. 14). Tower VIi, like Tower VI h, was built here in the Troy VIh phase, i.e. during the most glorious days of this settlement. In the earlier phases, the main gateway was defended by the tower VIk.

Section 4 of the wall is 121 metres long, and thirteen vertical offsets divide it into fourteen straight segments. The masonry of this section of the wall has, as in the other sections, been uniformly and excellently laid. The gateway VI U, formed by the ends of Sections 4 and 5, was later blocked up. It has already been stated that Section 5 was left in its original condition during the renovations of the phases VI f-h. This part of the wall is built of small stones and exhibits an entirely different building technique. Moreover, it is only half as thick as the other sections, and it was not founded on bed-rock, as were the others. Only the lower portions of Section 6 have been discovered; the upper parts were plundered for building stone during Hellenistic and Roman times. An examination of the present-day remains shows that the wall in this section was built in an especially beautiful and orderly fashion.

Without doubt, the wall surrounding Troy VI was small. Nevertheless, the original way it was planned, with offsets occurring every ten metres and with sloping outer faces, makes the city wall of Troy VI one of the finest and most interesting fortifications of its time in the whole ancient world.

The palaces and other important buildings of the Troy VI settlement evidently rose up on the summit of the hill, i.e. in the area occupying squares 4 - 7 B - K. However, the buildings of the acropolis of Troy VI at this spot were demolished when the temple of Athena was built, together with its stoas, in the Hellenistic age and when the ground was levelled during the enlargement of the temple and stoas during Roman times (Fig. 14). The parts which escaped these operations later fell victim to Schliemann's trenches. Nevertheless, the buildings which were identified by Dörpfeld and those which he excavated, together with those which have been brought to light by Blegen and his colleagues, are of exceptional value. Surprisingly enough, even in this state, the acropolis of Troy VI is among the best preserved of its contemporaries. In particular, the buildings on the lower terrace have survived to this day in quite good condition.

If, after entering the southern gate (VIT) of the acropolis, one follows the main road which goes slightly uphill, one comes to the largest building of this period a little further on to the left. This is known as the "Pillar House" (Fig. 15); it is slightly trapezoidal in shape and is 26 metres long and 12 metres wide. It had an entrance hall on the east, a large room in the centre and three small rooms at the back. One of the pillars, which shared the support of the roof with the walls and which may also have held up the second floor, is in good repair, but only one small remnant of the other has come to light. Since the south wall of the building was a retaining wall, it was thicker than the others. Food was cooked in an area at the west end of the house. The three rooms on that side were probably used as larders. The doorway of the house was in the north wall of the large room; if the plan conforms at all to that of a megaron, the fact that the entrance occurs in the long side and not in the narrow end indicates that it is not a typical one. The house was built during the Troy VI f phase. To the north-east of this dwelling is House No. 630, which has a very original plan (Fig. 15). The American expedition that unearthed this house has proved that it was erected in the Troy VI b phase, i.e. about 1700 B. C. This house certainly differs greatly from the other houses in that it possesses thin walls made of small stones, besides being built on a different plan. The southern part of House VI G, which is 20.90 metres long and 9.40 metres wide, has been destroyed by Schliemann's north-east trench; in spite of this, the plan is more or less definite. The American archaeological expedition discovered the original floor and, lying on it, a small stone base. A second block of about the same size, which can still be seen lying in Schliemann's trench, seems certainly to have belonged with the first. From this, we can deduce that the wide roof of the house was supported by two wooden pillars. The door was on the south side of the large room (Fig. 15). Steps must have led up to it from the outside and down from it on the inside, because the existing doorway is rather higher than street-level, whereas the floor of the room is even lower than the stone threshold. It is likely that, when the door was first constructed, it was on the narrow western side of this megaron-type dwelling; the alteration was probably made during the Troy VII period. Indeed, the large number of "pithoi" found in the house are of the Troy

VII era, as confirmed by the American archaeological expedition, which also judged the house to have been built during the VIg phase.

Just to the north of House VIG, we come upon House VIF (Fig. 15). The structure of the masonry differs from that of the other houses. The four walls are all of different thicknesses, the south face being fashioned of large stones in the Cyclopean style. It also is built on a trapezoidal plan, with the east wall 15.87 metres long and the west wall 14.70 metres long. The narrow faces measure 12.50 metres in length. Two vertical offsets divide the face of the eastern foundation wall into three sections; this Part of the house exhibits a most monumental structure. The house was proved to have been built in the VIe phase and renovated in the VIg phase. Twelve stone bases which were discovered within this one-roomed dwelling are still *in situ;* these are arranged in rows of five, the remaining two being in the centre of the room between the two side rows. Evidently, so many columns were not required to roof over a room only 8 metres in width; in any case, such a number of columns has never been found in any of the other constructions. Consequently, we can conclude that the roof of the first construction was supported by two columns which rested on the central stone bases, and that the side columns became necessary when an upper floor was added in the VIg phase. As has been confirmed by the American expedition, the doorway on the south side was blocked up during this period, and it can be assumed that the large stone block which lies close by was part of the wooden staircase leading to the upper storey. Following this alteration, entrance was gained to the house through the door in the west wall. A fire-place can be seen in the south-west corner; the lower part of an earthenware jar, which was partly buried in the stone floor here, probably served as a kind of grate.

Immediately adjoining the house described above on the north is House VIE. This slightly trapezoidal building has an east wall measuring 13.35 metres, whereas the west wall is 12.80 metres long. The walls on the narrow faces average 10.10 metres in length. The house is almost completely in ruins and, as a result, even the floor is missing. In sharp contrast to the general condition, the eastern retaining wall is well-preserved, and is a fine example of the style of masonry which was in fashion in Troy VI.

The plan of House VIC is fairly clear, although the central part of the house itself was destroyed by the intrusion of Schliemann's south-east trench. Its exterior measurements are 20.07 × 10.90 metres. The internal measurements of the main room are 15.50 × 8.40 metres. A stone base can be seen in the north-west corner of the room; basing their assumption on its discovery, first Dörpfeld and then Blegen came to the conclusion that the roof was supported by three columns situated along the longer axis of the room.

Of all the ruins of Troy VI which have been discovered up to the present, the building VIM is the one possessing the largest amount of visible remains (Sqs. 7 - 8 C - D). It was constructed during the VIg phase and the retaining walls on its western side are extremely well-preserved. The south wall, which stretches for 27 metres parallel to the city wall, is divided into

five segments by four vertical offsets. The building displays a very attractive silhouette, rising up in the form of a miniature fortress. This L - shaped
house consisted of a large room measuring 5 × 13 metres, and there used
to be six pithoi for storing grain along its western wall, but these have
been removed. A section in the north of the large room was used as a
kitchen and the two rooms on the west as larders.

House VIA is situated in squares 6A - B. Mycenaean pottery was first
found in quantity in this building. It measures 19.18 metres by 12.30
metres; the front porch is 4.25 metres deep. The interior of the main room
measures 11.55 × 9.01 metres. Since no trace of the floor remains, the former presence of stone bases is a matter for conjecture. However, it seems
certain that there must have been a central row of wooden pillars, which
would be needed to support the wide span of 9.11 metres. This is one of the
buildings of Troy VI, which is constructed on a typical megaron plan. Only
the porch of the adjoining house, VIB, has been preserved; the plan is
similar to that of House VIC, mentioned above.

Another of the Troy VI houses which is worthy of our attention is the
so-called "Anta House", situated near the south entrance (Fig. 15). The
stone from which the house got its name of "Anta" is still in its original
position. With the aid of a plan, it is possible to make out those portions
of the foundations which remain standing. The building has been largely destroyed by the overlying bouleuterion (Theatre B). A great number of animal
bones and burnt patches left by fires have been discovered inside the house
but no household effects have been found there. Consequently, it can
be assumed that this room was a sanctuary in which sacrifices were burnt
to a particular god or gods. One gets the impression that prayers were offered up in the building next to the main gate when people were about to
set out on journeys or go to battle, or when they returned to the city. As
a matter of fact, the monoliths resembling menhirs which lie at the foot of
the south wall of Tower VI, just at the entrance to the gateway, are doubtless stones connected with a religious cult, as has been stated by Dörpfeld
and Blegen. The fact that these menhirs were fixed in strong foundations
is an indication that they were formerly taller than they are at present and
that, in the course of time, they were reduced through demolition. A similar stone block has also been found at the entrance to House VIA. The fine
columns and pillars which we see in the sanctuaries attached to the Cretan
palaces also indicate that the Trojan blocks under discussion were connected
with a religious cult.

The majority of the houses on the acropolis which have been described
follow a trapezoidal plan. It will be noticed on closer investigation that
in all the houses of this type, i.e. VIM, the Pillar House, VIF, VIE and VIC,
the faces looking towards the city centre are narrower than those facing
the city wall, a point which is emphasized by Dörpfeld and Blegen. Thus the
trapezoidal houses conform to the overall plan of the acropolis, going from
north to south and radiating out in a fan-like manner. This means that
the hill was planned down to the last detail and that even the shape
which each house should take was determined by a master designer. Troy

VI exhibits another characteristic, namely that the terraces on which the buildings are situated, rise one above the other in concentric circles (Fig. 14, 15). A similarly planned sequence can be observed in the acropolis of the Hittite period at Boğazköy (Fig. 138). There also, one is struck by the arrangement of the isolated buildings in a concentric pattern. 1200 years later, one notices the same feature again in Asia Minor, this time on the acropolis at Pergamon, where a much more successful example of the fan-like city plan was realized (Fig. 24).

Troy VI, with its fine fortifications, its ingenious plan and its carefully constructed buildings, was one of the most beautiful and extraordinary cities of its day, not only in its immediate neighbourhood but in the whole ancient world. In the introduction to this book, we touched on the fact that the Trojans rose to a high cultural level during this period. It can be concluded from the statement of its architectural achievements that this brilliant period of Troy, which is reflected in the pomp of Homer's "Iliad", occurred during the VI f-h phases. This is the city told of in the "Iliad", the city which even after a siege lasting ten years still could not be overcome. Priam and his sons, Paris and Hector, or else the king and princes known to us by their names in myth, must have lived during the most glorious phase, VIh. The destruction of Ilion related in the "Odyssey", however, took place in the following architectural layer, VIIa. Blegen, with his acute perception, attributed the cause of the end of Troy VI to a catastrophic earthquake. The debris of the Troy VIh phase lying beneath Troy VIIa, as recorded by photographs taken during excavations, is clearly revealed as having been caused by an earthquake. It is still possible to observe the results of the earthquake in the area lying in squares G9 and J - K6.

Troy VII a (1275 - 1240 B. C.). Apparently, the earthquake did not strike without warning because no human skeletal remains have been discovered among the debris, and neither is there any evidence to prove that the houses were suddenly abandoned. The American archaeologists state categorically that there is no break in culture; indeed we see that the Grey Minyan ceramic ware found in the VIh stratum is of the same quality, and occurs in the same profusion, as in the VIIa stratum. In addition, they point out that the so-called Tan ceramic ware was fashioned as exquisitely as it had been in the previous habitation level. The American archaeologists have determined that the VIIa stratum lasted not much longer than one generation.

According to the American expedition, VIIa is Priam's city and the Ilion which we see mirrored in Homer's "Iliad" belongs to this period. However, our considerations of the architecture of the VIIa layer make it difficult to share this opinion. The inhabitants of VIIa repaired the city walls and the ruined houses but, from the point of view of workmanship, they built houses of low quality. A more important point is that the character of the city was completely changed as regards architectural planning and order. Not one work survived that was representative of the high artistic standards and intricately thought-out town planning which we so much admired in the Troy VIf-h strata. In place of the magnificent, free-standing buildings of Troy VI, there appeared houses of a character that displayed social class distinctions, houses which were huddled together and in complete contrast to the megaron-type dwellings. These houses are well-preserved; they can be seen between the gateways VIT and VIS, in the area behind the city wall. They simply cannot compare with Houses VIG, VIF, VIE and VIC, which flank them in a row to the west. What could have been the reason for this startling change in architecture and town planning in Troy? Could an earthquake have caused such a radical departure? One can perhaps suppose that this natural disaster brought about a change in the administration of the state, that the king and the royal family, accompanied by the nobles, were driven out of the city and that the lower classes who lived outside the acropolis moved in to take their place. It is inconceivable that the people who built the megarons and ramparts of the VIh stage would start building houses of this low standard and changed character solely as the result of a catastrophic earthquake. This change may be explained by the disappearance of the king and aristocracy. Possibly the common people, wearied in body and soul by more than five hundred long years of oppression by kings and nobles, were finally able to throw off their yoke, under the leadership of a rebel force which seized this opportunity to draw a parallel between the calamity and the people's lot; thus they rose up against the monarch and his wealthy entourage.

As we have attempted to state in this discourse, Priam's city of Ilion, found reflected in the glory of Homer's "Iliad", is actually Troy VIh. The archaeological situation fits in well with the epic. That is to say, it supports the account related in the "Odyssey" of the overthrow of Troy "VIIa" by the Achaeans after the stalemate struggle against Troy "VIh" as told in the "Iliad". Seen from this aspect, the stratagem of the wooden horse takes on a meaning. The Achaeans, unable to capture the city of Ilion after fighting for ten years, could only achieve their goal after the city had been destroyed in an earthquake and the rule of the acropolis had fallen into the hands of a usurper, leading the poor and inexperienced lower classes. Since the Achaeans well knew that they owed their victory to Poseidon, the Earth-Shaker, they offered up a wooden statue in the likeness of a horse as evidence of their gratitude to the god for his great help. Poetic fantasy then created the stratagem of the wooden horse in the 'Odyssey" from this event.

Troy VII bI (1240 - 1190 B. C.). The burnt layer in the VIIa level of habitation shows a thickness varying from 0.50 metres to 1.00 metre. In spite of this terrible disaster, the people of Troy returned to the city and repaired their dwellings and the city walls. With the continued production of Grey Minyan and Tan ceramic ware, the indigenous culture was uninterrupted. It is possible to see ruins of this period in squares E - F 8 - 9. The style of construction, first seen in VIIa, is continued.

Blegen is right in determining the date of the Troy VIIa catastrophe by means of the results obtained from research into the style of Mycenaean pottery. Moreover, as will be seen later, the year 1240 is in general agreement with other historical events.

Troy VII b2 (1190 - 1100 B. C.). A change in culture is encountered for the first time since the Troy VI settlement in Troy VII b2. In this stratum, the so-called Knobbed Ware and similar ceramics make their first appearance at Troy. This type of pottery, which heretofore was found only in the Balkan countries, is distinguished by its greyish hue, the decorative horn-like protuberances on its surface and the angular handles. There are changes also in wall-building technique. The lower courses of the walls are strengthened by the use of orthostats, i.e., by vertically placed blocks of stone. A house constructed in this style can be seen to the west of the gateway VI U in square A 7; in addition, there are the remains of an orthostat wall in J-K 5 and K7.

The people of Balkan origin who settled in Troy VII b2 probably gained entry with no great difficulty because no traces of fire or other disaster have been encountered between this layer and Troy VII b1. From this, we can conclude that, among the tribes that must have played a large role in the destruction of Hattusa about 1180 and fighting under the name of Muşki against the Assyrian king Tiglath-Pileser I around 1165 and which, after they had destroyed Arzawa and Kargamış, fought Rameses III (1198 - 1176), were nomads who had come from the Balkans and were living in Troy VII b2. It would appear that the first halt made by the "Aegean Immigration" was at Troy. Perhaps what actually happened was that the destruction of Troy VIIa by the Achaeans paved the way for the first wave of the "Aegean Immigration". The Trojan acropolis, which for hundreds of years had been acting as a fortress against the invasion of Asia Minor by European tribes, possibly lost its former strength and may have been instrumental in setting off mass movements of population in the world of that day.

Troy VIII. No traces of the Hellenic civilization found in Troy VIII can go back earlier than the 7th century B. C. This conclusion is in agreement with the discoveries of the earliest Hellenic finds in the north-west of Asia Minor. Cyzicus and Byzantium were also founded in the seventh century.

The remains of the first Hellenic building, called the "upper temenos" by the American expedition, are located beneath the sanctuary in squares A - B 7 - 8. The altar situated in the middle of the above-mentioned upper temenos was constructed in the Hellenistic era. The north-east facing wall of the temenos, lying immediately in front of and parallel to the city wall of Troy VI, is a fine example of the careful *rustica* stonework of Hellenistic times. However, another altar lying to the west of the centrally-placed altar, and also square in plan, dates from the Augustan age.

The sacred precinct south of the upper temenos in squares A 8 - 9, called the "lower temenos" by the American expedition, and containing two altars, was also erected in the Hellenistic period. To which gods the temenoi were dedicated has not been determined.

By far the most important building constructed in Hellenistic times is certainly the temple of Athena (Fig. 14). As was the case with many cities in western Asia Minor, a temple consecrated to Athena had long existed at Ilion. Herodotus writes (VII, 43) that here Xerxes sacrificed a thousand oxen to the goddess. Alexander the Great too, after his victory at Granikos, visited the temple and decorated it with beautiful gifts. In addition, he promised later, according to Strabo (13, 593), in a letter, that he would erect a splendid temple. To quote Strabo again, Lysimachos is said to have fulfilled Alexander's wish. Granted that this passage of Strabo's is controversial, it is a fact that the Helios head seen in a metope, and the acanthus leaves on fragments of the sima (gutter), are rendered in Hellenistic manner. Similarly, the temple of Athena at Pergamon is also of the Lysimachos period. The temple at Ilion, like the temple at Pergamon, was of the Doric order, which is an indication that it was built in the time of Lysimachos. Owing to the fact that the area containing the Athena temple has been completely dug up, the whole place is now a deep hole. Various parts of the temple lie at the bottom of this hollow and among the marble ruins of the Roman theatre. Some of them are kept in the local museum.

Troy IX. Since the Romans believed that the Trojan hero Aeneas, son of Aphrodite, was their ancestor (his son Ilus or Iulus having founded Alba Longa, the mother City of Rome), they attached great importance to Ilion (Troy). Julius Caesar, who traced his legendary origin back to Iulus and so to Ilion, offered sacrifices here, but it was Augustus who put concrete plans into effect. In this period, the temenos of the Athena temple was enlarged, and the construction of other buildings (Fig. 14) increased to cover the area. The temple was surrounded on all four sides by colonnades, each of which was 80 metres in length. While this huge square was under construction, the most important buildings of Troy VI and the houses of Troy VII were demolished. The Roman wall, which in part overlies the south-eastern section of the Troy VI wall and in part conceals the front of it, was erected in this period. The edifice in square G7 is the propylon to the temple of Athena, and it too was built in the Augustan age. A large number of Roman remains also exist in the open space lying between the south-eastern part of the Athena temple and the city wall. The bouleuterion (Theatre B), half of which was built over the city wall immediately to the east of the main entrance to Troy VI (VI T), and also the Theatre C (squares EF 9 - 10), the auditorium of which lies over the city wall, both date from the Roman period.

Alexandria Troas. This city was founded by Antigonos and Lysimachos at the command of Alexander the Great. Because of its artificial harbour, Alexandria Troas became a powerful and rich commercial centre. As the ruins lie on a sea route, their stones have been easily plundered. The theatre and the baths, constructed in the time of Hadrian by Herodes Atticus, have been reduced to rubble. The stones that formed the aqueduct erected by Herodes Atticus have also been completely pillaged.

NEANDRIA

This city was excavated by the German archaeologist Robert Koldewey in 1899. It lies about 13 km. inland from the coastal town of Alexandria Troas. It was founded on a granite crest of Mt. Çığrı at a height of 500 m. (Fig. 16). It covers an area 1,400 m. long and 450 m. wide. The city wall is 3 m.

thick and 3,200 m. long. This fortification was partially constructed in the
polygonal style and shows a very good state of preservation. In all probability it was erected in the 5th century B. C, since the houses in the town
were certainly inhabited for at least a period of one hundred years prior to
300 B. C. when, the coastal town of Alexandria Troas having been founded,
Neandria was completely abandoned. Quite long stretches of an earlier
city wall, laid in the polygonal style, are still standing (Fig. 16, No. 2).
This old wall encircled the highest part of the rocky acropolis in the north-

Fig. 16 – Plan of Neandria. 1) Archaic acropolis. 2) Ancient fortifications (probably 6th century B. C.). 3) Main entrance dating, together with the city wall,
from the late 5th century B. C. 4) Archaic temple, ca. 600 B. C.

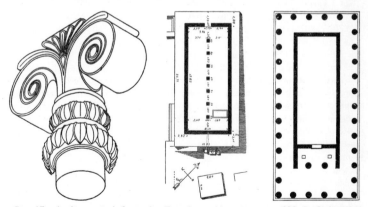

Fig. 17 – Aeolic capital from the Temple at Neandria, ca. 600 B. C. Istanbul.
Fig. 18 – Plan of the Temple at Neandria, ca. 600 B. C.
Fig. 19 – Temple of Athena at Assos. Peripteros of the Doric order with 6 × 13
columns and a frieze. Stylobate measuring 14.03 × 30.31 m., ca. 530 B. C.

west. The chief monument in Neandria is the temple that was built at the end of the 7th century or the beginning of the 6th (Fig. 16, No. 4). This temple consisted solely of a cella over a podium, with the exception of the west face (Fig. 18). The outer measurements are 12.87 × 25.71 metres, the inner measurements of the cella being 8.04 × 19.82 metres. A row of seven stone bases occupied the centre of the building. The wooden columns which rested on these shared the support of the roof with the thick walls of the cella. The upper parts of the columns were ornamented with fine Aeolic capitals (Fig. 17). These capitals are now kept in the Istanbul Museum.

ASSOS

The city of Assos, perched on a rocky hill which cuts off the Tuzla stream, the Satnioeis, from the sea, was founded by the inhabitants of Methymna, a town on the island of Lesbos. In the 6th century B. C. it came under the sovereignty of Lydia. At the end of the same century Assos, like the whole of the Troad, became part of the Persian province of Phrygia and the Hellespont. In the 5th century it joined the Athenian League. The governor Ariobarza-nes, who rebelled against the Persian King Artaxerxes, was defeated at Assos in 365 B. C. Later the town was governed by the banker Euboulos, who was succeeded as ruler by the eunuch Hermias, one of Plato's students. As a result of this connection, Hermias' friend Aristotle stayed with him at Assos for three years (348 - 345). Kleanthes, one of the heads of the Stoic school, came from Assos. From 241 - 133 B. C., Assos was under the domination of the Kingdom of Pergamon. Archaeological field research in the town of Assos was undertaken from 1881- 3 by an American expedition, directed by J. T. Clarke and F. H. Bacon. The acropolis, built on a hill command-ing approach by land and sea, is surrounded by magnificent walls more than 3 km. in length. These walls are the most complete fortifications in the Greek world (Fig. 20). They have been extremely skilfully constructed (Pl. 30). In particular, the gateways are exceptionally fine; they all differ from one another in kind and character and display a variety and originality of form (Pl. 30 a.). The large main gate (I) to the acropolis is on the west (Fig. 20). The eastern tower of the two guarding both sides of the gateway is intact up to the loopholes and the gutter; only the battlements are missing. The portion which is still standing reaches a height of more than 14 metres (Pl. 30b). The city wall was erected in the 4th century B. C. The polygonal wall seen near the gate on the west, the front of which is partly concealed by a 4th century wall, is older than the latter. Consequently, the other polygonal walls of Assos must be earlier than the 4th century. The temple of Athena, built on the highest platform of the acropolis about 530 B. C., stands out as the most important work in Assos (Fig. 20 No. 3). This temple, in andesite, was originally Doric in style, but the architrave below the row of triglyphs and metopes was decorated with a frieze, which is a feature of the Ionic order (Fig. 21). The naos is a "templum in antis" and the peri-stasis had 13 columns on the long sides and 6 on the ends (Fig. 19). Only the styiobate of the temple has been preserved and this measures 14.03 × 30.31 metres. Within the cella, a pebble mosaic dating from the Hellenistic period was preserved up to the time of the excavations. No trace of this mosaic is now visible. The altar is understood to have been completely destroyed by buildings erected in Byzantine times and the Middle Ages. The view, over the valley of the Satnioeis and the Bay of Edremit, that can be seen from the site of the temple 238 metres up, is magnificent. Reliefs from the Assos temple are housed in the museums of Paris, Boston and Istanbul. Well-preserved Doric capitals and various other fragments are scattered over the site.

Built upon terraces on the southern slopes of the acropolis, where the temple is situated, are also located the agora (4 - 9), the gymnasium (10) and the theatre (11). On the north side of the agora square there formerly stood a two-storeyed Doric stoa (4) measuring 111.52 metres in length and 12.42 metres in width. The columns were not fluted but, like those at Pergamon, they were prismatic in section and had 20 facets. On the lower floor, three metopes come between every two columns. The row of holes seen on the rear wall of the stoa held the timbers which formed the floor of the second storey.

The south stoa (5) possessed three storeys, but the top floor was built on a level with the first floor of the northern stoa (Fig. 22). The middle floor and the basement opened only to the south, whereas the top floor overlooked both the agora square and the sea (Fig. 20). When they wished, the people of Assos could either sit or stroll about in the large room on the upper floor of the north stoa and in the southern part of the third floor of the south stoa, enjoying the cool air and gazing at the splendid view of the Bay of Edremit. On the middle floor of the south stoa there were thirteen shops which formed a "covered bazaar". Windows existed in the south face of the middle floor. In the basement there were two cisterns, one measuring 41.60 × 2.75 metres, the other 14.85 × 2.37 metres. There were also 13 bathrooms. The middle floor of the stoa did not rest against the rock; there existed an intervening space of not more than 20 cms. As in the case of the so-called "peristasis" at Pergamon, this narrow air space ensured that the building was protected from moisture and that it was kept cool in summer and warm in winter. The building, which rises to the same height as the covered bazaar of the south stoa, is a prostyle (Fig. 22). We learn from an inscription that the inhabitants of Assos had this building erected in honour of Kallisthenes, the son of Hephaistogenes, for services he had rendered to the town. The building dates from Roman times.

Shops occupied an area opening on to a street lying to the southwest of the agora square (7), but only some parts of their foundations can be seen today (Fig. 22). Still other shops can be found outside the agora on the west of the north stoa (8). These give the impression of being small stores selling high class goods, but only some ruined portions of their foundations are now in existence.

Access to the agora was gained by a broad arched gateway on the west side. Immediately to the right of this is the site of the prostyle temple of the agora, of which only the foundations can be seen (Fig. 22). However, since this building was later converted into a church, not much is known about its original design. The ground plan of the temple and its situation

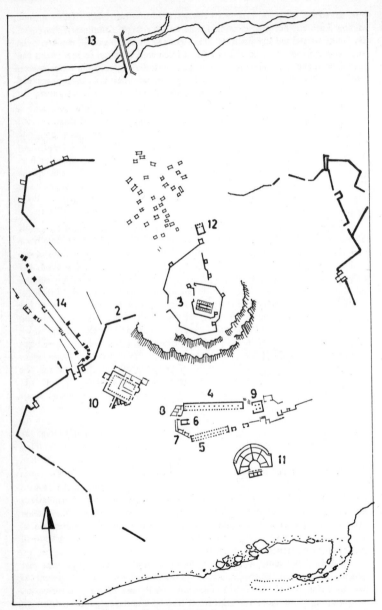

Fig. 20 – Plan of Assos.

Fig. 20 – Plan of Assos. 1) Main gateway (Pl. 30 b) together with city wall, dating from the 4th century B. C. 2) A smaller gate (Pl. 30 a), 4th century B. C. 3) Temple of Athena (see Figs. 19, 21), 530 B. C. 4) North stoa of the Agora, 3rd or 2nd century B. C. 5) South stoa of the Agora with a "covered bazaar", 3rd or 2nd century B. C. 6) The Agora temple, 2nd century B. C. 7-8) Shops built in Hellenistic times. 9) Bouleuterion, Hellenistic period. 10) Gymnasium, 2nd century B. C. 11) Theatre, built in the 3rd century B. C. and altered in Roman times. 12) Turkish Mosque, 14th century A. D. 13) Turkish bridge, 14th century A. D. 14) Necropolis of Hellenistic and Roman times.

Fig. 21 – Temple of Athena at Assos, of the Doric order with a frieze on the architrave. 530 B. C. (see also Fig. 19).

within the agora remind one of the temple in the upper agora at Pergamon (No. 22 in Fig. 24).

The official buildings of the agora are gathered together on its narrow eastern side (Fig. 22). Here are situated a bouleuterion (council chamber) and, just in front of it, a bema (the platform from which the orators delivered their speeches) and many other kinds of buildings, statues and small portable monuments with inscriptions. These andesite structures of the Doric order, surrounding the agora on four sides, in many ways recall Pergamon, an opinion which has also been expressed by Roland Martin. The fact that the rear of the temple is hidden by the west wall of the agora, like the temple in the agora at Pergamon, and that a narrow space has been left between the agora and the rock, again as was customary at Pergamon, has

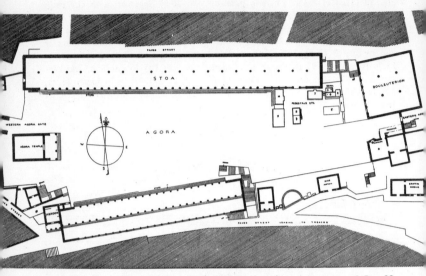

Fig. 22 – Assos. Plan of Agora. Hellenistic in date (see the caption of Fig. 20, Nos. 4-10).

been stated above. To these similarities can be added the characteristic of placing an Ionic profile above a Doric frieze. The agora temple and many other monuments at Pergamon are typical examples of this intermixture of Doric and Ionic styles. Therefore, it would not be wrong to date buildings in Assos according to the models at Pergamon. The rare occurrence of such features as the mixing of Doric and Ionic elements and the placing of only three metopes between every two columns indicates that the Assos architects were not yet familiar with the new trends of the Hermogenes period. Therefore, it would have been correct to date the stoas of the Assos agora to the 2nd half of the 3rd century B. C., had it not been for the longevity of the style; they could be as late as the 2nd century. Certainly the agora temple was built in the second half of the second century B. C. (see the similar temples at Pergamon in Fig. 33 a-e).

The ruins of a gymnasium (10) lie between the agora and the big west gate. Preserved here is a paved courtyard, measuring 32 × 40 metres, which had colonnades on its four sides. In the north-east sector of the courtyard can be seen a church which was erected in Byzantine times, and in the south-west corner, a cistern. The entrance was on the south. The three semicircular steps which were exposed during excavation can no longer be seen today. Fragments of the cornice and the epistyle of this gateway have been recovered. A few portions of the upper door of the gymnasium have been found. Entasis was absent in the columns of the gymnasium, which were made of andesite and had marble capitals of the Doric order. The echinus of the capitals is straight in profile. The building of the gymnasium at Assos was accomplished in the Hellenistic period. This multi-cornered colonnaded structure, forming a triangle and occupying the area to the right of the entrance to the gymnasium, also shows the influence of the architectural concepts of Pergamene kings and artists (see Fig. 35).

The theatre was situated immediately below the agora (Fig. 20). How sad it is that this building, which only a century ago was completely preserved, has been reduced to this miserable ruin. Nevertheless, with the aid of the remaining parts of the theatre, it has been possible to draw a plan of the building. The orchestra is horseshoe-shaped, as was customary in theatres of the Greek period. The theatre was originally built in the 3rd century B. C., and underwent renovation in the Roman era (Fig. 20, No. 11).

Both sides of the two roads, which began at the west and east gates of the acropolis, were flanked with sarcophagi and monuments (Fig. 20). The structure seen slightly to the north of the main west gate are the remains of the grave of Publius Varius. This road, passing out through the west gate, led to the River Satnioeis. The graceful bridge (13) with pointed arches that we see there is a Turkish work of the 14th century. To the north of the acropolis, the mosque, which stands in front of the tower dating from the Middle Ages, was also built by the Turks in the reign of Murat I (1359 - 1389).

PERGAMON

From a study of ceramic works that have been uncovered during the excavations, the place where Pergamon was founded is understood to have been a small settlement in the archaic period. Ancient records disclose the fact that Pergamon was ruled for a time by Gongylos of Eretria, who acted as viceroy to the King of Persia. During the so-called Expedition of the Ten Thousand, Xenophon occupied the town from 400 to 399. Since Lysimachos, the ruler of Anatolia from 301 on, gave 9000 talents for war expenses into the safe-keeping of Philetairos, the commander of Pergamon, one is entitled to suppose that the acropolis was well fortified with strong walls as far back as the 4th century B. C. On Lysimachos' death, Philetairos retained this money for himself and with it founded the Pergamon monarchy. For 150 years, Pergamon was one of the most brilliant cultural centres of the Hellenistic era (283-133 B. C.). Philetairos (283-263 B. C.) extended his kingdom as far as the shores of the Marmara; his nephew, Eumenes I (263-241 B. C.), managed to preserve these frontiers by paying tribute to the Galatians. Attalos I (241-197 B. C.), the son of Eumenes I, overcame the Galatians in battle and began to use the title of king. Attalos was deeply interested in art and culture. The first beautiful buildings to appear in the city were erected in his reign. Eumenes II (197-159 B. C.) raised the Kingdom of Pergamon to its rank of one of the strongest states of Hellenistic times, by means of the close ties he established with Rome. During this period, Pergamon held an important position among the cultural centres of the ancient world. The city possessed a library containing 200,000 volumes. The principal and most beautiful buildings to be found on the acropolis were erected by Eumenes II.

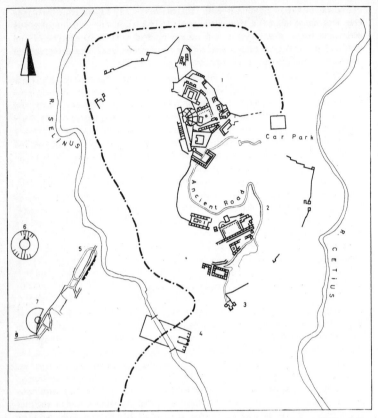

Fig. 23 – General plan of Pergamon. **1)** *Upper city (see the caption of Fig. 24).*
2) *Middle city (see the caption of Fig. 34).* **3)** *Gate of Eumenes (197–159 B. C.).*
4) *Serapis Temple, 2nd century A. D.* **5)** *Stadium, Roman Period.* **6)** *Amphitheatre,
Roman Period.* **7)** *Roman Theatre.* **8)** *Ancient road leading to the Asklepieion.*

With fine artistic feeling, Eumenes raised Pergamon to the level of the
most splendid cities of the Greek world of his time, by using the Athenian
acropolis as a model. Pergamon led the world of Hellenistic times in the
fields of architecture and sculpture. The example set by Eumenes II was
followed by his brother Attalos II (159-138 B. C.) and by the latter's son,
Attalos III (138-133 B. C.). The Kingdom of Pergamon died with Attalos III,
and he bequeathed it to the Roman Empire. Pergamon continued to be a
very important centre during the Roman period. Augustus re-erected the
monuments of the Kingdom Period commemorating victories. Hadrian
completed the Trajaneum (Fig. 24, No. 15), while Caracalla was responsible
for the restoration of the temple of Dionysus (Fig. 24, No. 17). Pergamon
became the centre of a diocese in the Christian era, and one of the seven

churches of the Apocalypse was located here. In Byzantine times, the city was encircled by a new wall, constructed from the remains of stone blocks, statues and reliefs dating from the Hellenistic and Roman eras. From A. D. 716 on, Pergamon was occupied by the Arabs for a period and, in 1330, it passed into Turkish hands.

The discovery by the German engineer Carl Humann of the high reliefs of the altar of Zeus, incorporated into that part of the Byzantine wall lying between the heroon (Fig. 24 No. 1) and the upper agora (Fig. 24, No. 21), led the way to the excavation of the ruins at Bergama. During the first campaigns (1878 - 1886), of which Carl Humann, Alexander Conze and R. Bohn were in charge, the upper city was unearthed (Fig. 24). During the second period of excavation (1900-1913), directed by W. Dörpfeld, H. Hepding and P. Schatzmann, the middle and lower districts of the city (Fig. 34) were uncovered. In the third period of excavation (1927-1936), the exploration undertaken by Theodor Wiegand resulted in the identification of the arsenals (Fig. 24, No. 14), the heroon (Fig. 24, No. 1), the Red Courtyard (Fig. 36) and the Asklepieion (Fig. 38). The fourth period of excavation (1957-1972) yielded under Erich Boehringer very important results. A new expedition headed by Wolfgang Radt is now in charge, and beginning with the Asklepieion, work is systematically extended to various parts of the city.

Pergamon was a place of flourishing social and cultural activity, in accordance with conditions prevailing in the world of Hellenistic times. In contrast to the Athenian acropolis, which was entirely religious and sacred in character, the hilltop of Pergamon was predominantly devoted to buildings and public squares constructed for purposes associated with the daily life of the people. Here, citizens could meet, walk, attend to personal or official affairs, or engage in sporting activities.

Although sacred buildings still seemed to be of importance, their outward appearance was their sole connection with religion. The altar of Zeus (Pls. 33 b, 34 b) was more a symbol of success in battle than a building dedicated to the worship of a god, and its significance arose from the fact that it was, in a sense, a monument to a victory won by the Kingdom. The Athena temple (Fig. 24, No. 7), dwarfed as it was by the three stoas lying along three of its sides, is another example showing that the religious function of buildings was only of secondary importance. The spacious stoas, which afforded ample shelter against heat and cold, together with the shady courtyard (Pls. 32-35) supplied a great need for public places where people could walk, sit, chat, observe and do business; therefore, they were given primary consideration. In the same way, the small buildings comprising the temples of Dionysus, Asklepios and Hera and those in the agora and the gymnasium were buildings of secondary importance, for performing the traditional religious ceremonies. Thus the principal buildings on the acropolis were apparently reserved for social and cultural functions. Not only classical drama and the new comedy, introduced in the Hellenistic period, were performed in the big theatre; it was also a place where philosophers and poets read their works aloud. The library, which overlooked the theatre from higher ground, was also instrumental in spreading knowledge. The

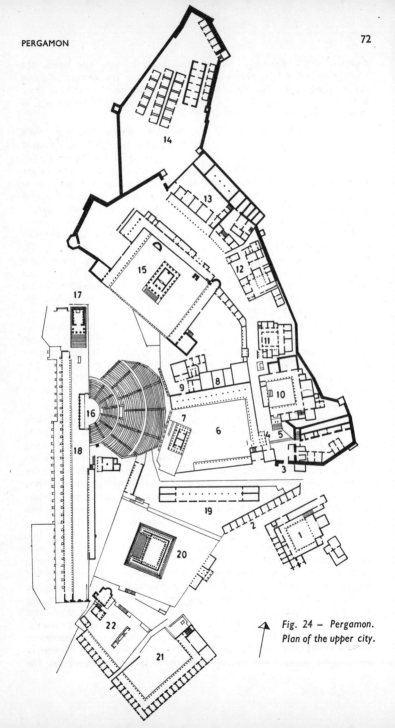

Fig. 24 – Pergamon.
Plan of the upper city.

Fig. 24 – Acropolis (upper city) of Pergamon. **1)** *Heroon, a peristyle building probably dedicated to the worship of the Pergamene kings Attalos I (241–197 B. C.) and Eumenes II (197–159). The andesite structure dates from the Hellenistic period; the Roman alterations were made of marble and are now lost.* **2)** *Shops built in the Hellenistic age.* **3)** *Main entrance of the Acropolis (the upper city). It dates, together with the city wall, from the time of Eumenes II. Parts of the fortifications on the right were repaired in Byzantine times.* **4)** *Outlines of the foundations of the Propylon, constructed by Eumenes II (see Fig. 27).* **5)** *Flight of steps leading up to the palaces.* **6)** *Sacred precinct (temenos) of Athena, surrounded by three stoas (colonnades) of the Doric order, built during the time of Eumenes II.* **7)** *Temple of Athena in the Doric order, constructed at the beginning of the third century.* **8)** *The renowned library which contained 200,000 volumes. It was erected by Eumenes II, but earlier than the north stoa of the temenos of Athena.* **9)** *A house - complex dating from Hellenistic times.* **10)** *Palace of Eumenes II in the form of a peristyle house.* **11)** *Palace of Attalos I, also of peristyle type.* **12)** *Remains of some Hellenistic houses, possibly belonging to officers.* **13)** *Barracks and command tower, built in the Hellenistic age. The view of the east side of the city wall behind the barracks, seen from the acropolis, is magnificent.* **14)** *Arsenals, erected in the 3rd century B. C. and altered in following periods. The andesite balls found in the Arsenals are now to be seen in the lower agora (Pl. 37 b).* **15)** *Trajaneum, a temple of the Corinthian order, erected to Trajan by his successor Hadrian (A. D. 117–138). In fact, both emperors were worshipped here, for colossal heads of two marble statues were found within the temple.* **16)** *Theatre, built during the third century B. C. and altered in Roman times.* **17)** *Temple of Dionysus (see also Figs. 29, 33 a), constructed in the second century B. C. and renovated by Caracalla (A. D. 211–217).* **18)** *Theatre terrace, second century B. C. There was, stretching for 250 m. along the west side of the narrow terrace, a Doric stoa with a splendid view overlooking the Kaikos valley. It was an ideal place for promenades (Pl. 32).* **19)** *Two-aisled stoa, late Hellenistic in date.* **20)** *Altar of Zeus, built by Eumenes II. It was adorned with reliefs (now in Berlin) representing the battle of Gods and Giants but symbolising, in fact, the victory of the Pergamene people over the Galatians.* **21)** *Agora, built in the Doric order, third century B. C. The altar of the agora was in the western part of the courtyard.* **22)** *Temple of the agora, built in the Doric order but intermixed with Ionic elements (see also Fig. 33 b). It was erected in the second century B. C. and probably dedicated to Zeus or Hermes. The building in the north-west corner of the agora, dating from the Hellenistic age, was converted into an apsidal structure during the Roman period.*

kings responsible for the arrangement of all these activities dwelt in the palace immediately behind the library. Here, as at Hattusa, (Fig. 138), the palaces occupied a position which could be most strongly defended, to the rear of all the other buildings on the hilltop.

Since the buildings of the acropolis had to conform to the topography of the site and to the road coming from the town (Fig. 23), they were arranged from south to north, but their main façades looked westwards, as they were required, and designed, to be seen from a distance. The agora, the altar of Zeus, the Athena temenos, the palaces, the theatre, and the building, doubtless of Hellenistic origin, which formerly occupied a site within the sanctuary of the Trajaneum, all overlooked the plain in the same direction. Since the altar of Zeus was originally intended to be seen from all sides, it was not surrounded by colonnades (Pl. 34 b), and the westward facing sides of the agora and the Athena temenos, which overlooked the plain, were likewise not enclosed (Fig. 24 Pls. 32-34).

The architectural plan of the Pergamene acropolis (Figs. 23, 24), calls to mind those of Büyükkale at Hattusa (Fig. 138) and of Troy VI (Fig. 14), which closely resemble it. In each case, the city is planned in terms of free-standing buildings which rise one above the other in concentric arcs on semi-circular terraces. The acropolis at Pergamon constitutes, from the points of view of form and conception, a splendid example of this type of city plan. Although the buildings were erected over a period of 150 years and are representative of different phases, the city exhibits a well-ordered plan and a highly successful tectonic composition. It can safely be said that work on the realization of the plan as a whole was first begun during the reign of Eumenes II, because the finest and most important works, i.e. the city wall, the altar of Zeus, the propylon of the Athena temple (Fig. 27) and the associated stoas, the library, the main palace (Fig. 24, No. 10), the theatre terrace (Pl. 32) and many other buildings, appeared in the reign of this king, and several earlier buildings were enlarged or completed. During this period of extensive development, the acropolis was set up according to a city plan which spread out fan-wise on three sides of the nucleus formed by the Athena temple and the theatre, which were built during an earlier period of the Kingdom.

It is perhaps no accident that the theatre, a building where all kinds of cultural activities took place, should form the centre of this structural composition. In this way, the city was presented to the eyes of the world as a magnificent architectural ensemble, and the inhabitants strove to express to mankind those achievements of the Hellenistic age that could be expressed in words through the medium of the theatre, which acted as a kind of mouth-piece for this tectonic organism.

The Acropolis of Pergamon (Fig. 24). The main entrance (3) to the acropolis of Pergamon was north of the heroon (1) and south of the palace of Eumenes (10). Today also, entrance to the ruins of the upper city is gained by following a ramp which ascends westwards from the car park through this same gateway (Fig. 23). The city wall was built by Eumenes II, and that part of it which adjoins the entrance is in a good state of preservation. Passing up the ramp, one can see, on the right, places in the Hellenistic wall which were repaired in Byzantine times.

The Heroon. The remains of a building (1), located below the main citadel gate, on the left of the ramp leading from the modern parking area to the acropolis, are known to be those of a heroon (Fig. 25). Here the Pergamene kings, especially Attalos I and Eumenes II, were worshipped as gods; the building can therefore also be designated by the name Attaleion or Eumeneion. The major sections of the structure can be enumerated as follows : a peristyle of approximately 18 × 21 metres, a 7-columned stoa to the east

of this, and a cult room adjoining the latter on the east. The main entrance
to the heroon was in the south-west corner, while another door was located at the north-west end of the north stoa beside the road. Moreover, those
descending from the acropolis could pass through two rooms in the south-
east section of the heroon. The plan offered here shows the building of
the Hellenistic period, which was probably erected during the time of
Attalos I (241 - 197 B. C.), but the changes made during the Roman period
are also indicated (Fig. 25).

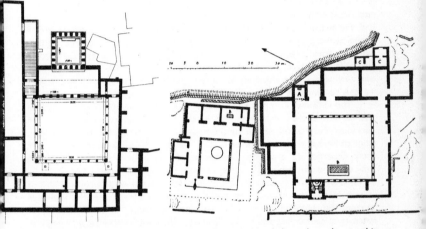

Fig. 25 – Heroon. Building of peristyle type probably, dedicated to the worship
of the Pergamene kings Attalos I (241-197 B. C.) and Eumenes II (197-159).
The andesite structure dates back to the Hellenistic age. Roman alterations were
made of marble and are now lost.

Fig. 26 – Palaces of Attalos I (left) and Eumenes II (right). Both are large houses
of peristyle type (buildings with central courtyards surrounded by rooms).
Eumenes' palace includes a cult room (A), a cistern (B), and another cistern
(in the centre of the courtyard).

No major alterations were carried out during the Roman era. In Hellenistic
times, the cult room proper measured approximately 6 × 12 metres
and had a rectangular niche in the north wall. During the Roman period, the
room was enlarged to a nearly square 12 × 13 metres and the inner walls
were faced with marble. A narrow podium was then erected in place of the
niche. In Roman times, a second storey surrounded by columns with Corinthian capitals was also added, and it is therefore possible that the heroon
resembled the Gümüşkesen tomb at Milas (Pl. 77). In the Hellenistic period,
only the columns of the stoa were of marble; the Doric columns of the peri-

style and the walls were of andesite. On the other hand, all the additions of the Roman period were constructed in marble. An earlier heroon, also erected by the Pergamene kings, lies under the Hellenistic heroon represented on the plan. This original building was composed of a simple courtyard with a cult room, in place of the later 7-columned stoa. Under the large building of the Hellenistic age, remains of houses, which are also Hellenistic in date, have been found. Discoveries include three houses under the peristyle and parts of a large house under the east edge of the cult room. Before excavation, a Byzantine city wall had covered the south-east corner of the heroon. The sacred building at Priene, probably dedicated to the worship of Alexander the Great, resembles the heroon at Pergamon.

The long building (2) north of the heroon (1) consists of a row of shops, and dates back to the Hellenistic era.

From the gate of the acropolis opening south, one passes into a fine stone-paved courtyard; on the right and left are quarters for the soldiers who guarded the gate. Directly opposite is a flight of steps (5) leading up to the palace of Eumenes II, while immediately to the left can be seen the outline of the foundations of the propylon (4) which formed the entrance to the temenos of Athena (Fig. 24, No. 6).

The Athena Temple and Stoas. The Athena temple, constructed on the terrace above the theatre, was of the Doric order, with 6 columns on the ends and 10 columns along the flanks (Pl. 33 a; Fig. 24, No. 7). Today, only some parts of the foundations of the temple remain, but the western flank is partly preserved up to a height of 1.20 m. It was built of andesite and stood on a two-stepped crepidoma; the stylobate measured 12.72 × 21.77 metres. The pronaos and opisthodomos were two intercolumniations in depth, and the distance from the naos to the pteron was the width of only one intercolumniation. The columns are slender and tall. The flutes were roughly worked and left unfinished. They are thus now prismatic in section. Three metopes occurred for every two columns. Fragments of the columns and the architrave are now in the Berlin Museum.

In western Anatolia, it seems that the most important temple of the city belonged traditionally to the goddess Athena, as observed, for example, in Izmir, Miletos, Erythrai, Phokaia and Assos. Despite this, however, it is apparent that the Athena temple at Pergamon is directly related to the Parthenon. The Pergamene temple, like the Parthenon, is of the Doric order and, unlike the Ionic temple with its many-stepped podium, rests on a crepidoma of a reduced number of steps in true Doric form. Indeed, like the Hephaisteion in Athens, the Pergamene temple has only two steps. Because of the great Doric influence, this monument must have been constructed at the beginning of the 3rd century, during the first days of the foundation of the Pergamene Kingdom, that is, in the art style, introduced by Lysimachos, which prevailed in those years. Thus Philetairos, using the acropolis of Athens as an example, constructed a temple of the Doric order and dedicated it to Athena, the chief goddess of the city. The three metopes for every two columns also indicate that the temple must be dated to the third century B. C.

Eumenes II, after his successful battles with the Seleucids, Galatians, and Macedonians, constructed two - storeyed stoas along the east and north sides of the Athena temple (Pl. 33a; Fig. 24, No. 6). These were built in the style of the Hellenistic age. The entrance, located on the east side (4), was a four-columned, two-storeyed propylon (Fig. 27). With the aid of the preserved fragments, this beautiful gateway has been restored in the Berlin Museum. As has already been mentioned, only traces of the foundations can now be seen on the original site. The lower storey was of the Doric order and the columns were only roughly worked, left to be fluted later, but never completed. The distance between the two central columns was wider than that between the remainder, as in old Ionic temples (Figs. 52, 83) and the propylaea on the acropolis at Athens. The preserved fragments of the inscription on the architrave have been restored as follows : "King Eumenes to the victory-bringing Athena". Five metopes occur over the two central columns, while four span the remaining intercolumniations (Fig. 27). The bases of the slender, tall columns are of the Attic-Ionic order. The narrow architrave has only two fasciae. The frieze is also very narrow and has a dentil moulding on its upper section. Two-thirds of the frieze, which is decorated with garlands, has been restored on the basis of the preserved fragments. The garlands are supported by alternating bulls' skulls and eagles. Between the garlands, phiales and the sacred owl of Athena are represented. On the balustrade of the second floor, the weapons taken as booty in the battles with the Galatians, Syrians and Macedonians are carved in relief. The round, decorated shields are those of the Macedonians, while the oval ones belong to the Galatians. The reliefs on the restored propylon are plaster casts which have been taken from the reliefs on the stoa balustrade. The tympanum was not decorated at all; however, both the horizontal and sloping geisons were embellished with dentils, as on the Zeus Sosipolis temple at Magnesia (Fig. 64, 66).

Akroteria are missing from the museum restoration and, owing to limited space, the reconstruction of the propylon is only half the actual depth. In the original, no walls existed in the upper and lower floors and there was free access between the columns. The space between the columns of the stoa was wide, and four metopes were accommodated over each inter-columniation. The top level was of the Ionic order and the lower section be-tween the columns was filled by a balustrade decorated with the weapon reliefs. The architrave had two fasciae and the five metopes and six triglyphs of each intercolumniation formed a Doric frieze. The columns, which divided the south stoa into two aisles, had capitals of the old Aeolic order, resembling those of the treasury house at Massalia, built in the 6th century B. C.

The Athena temenos was filled with a variety of offerings. According to Pliny (NH, XXXIV, 84), the artists Epigonos, Phyromachios, Stratonikos and Antigonos created statues representing the battles of Attalos I and Eu-menes II against the Galatians. Parts of stone blocks still found lying on the ground in this area were probably remains of a very large, high pedestal. It seems possible that bronze originals of some marble copies preserved

Fig. 27 – Pergamon. Propylon.

Fig. 27 – Propylon (entrance) to the sacred precinct of Athena in Pergamon. According to the inscription on the architrave, it was dedicated by "King Eumenes to the victory-bringing Athena". Reign of Eumenes II (197–159 B. C.). The propylon is restored in the Berlin Museum with the help of fragments found during excavations (Fig. 24, No. 4).

today may have been erected on this base. One of these marble copies is the group of the Galatian plunging a dagger into his chest after having killed his wife (Museo delle Terme, Rome) and another, the "Dying Gaul" (Museo Capitolino, Rome). It seems that both the weapon frieze on the stoa and the statues dedicated within the temenos expressed the victories of the Pergamene rulers. Thus a very sacred place in the Hellenistic period was enveloped in a political atmosphere. Moreover, the Attalids knew how to express these victories in the sensitive terms which had prevailed in Greek art since archaic and classical times. Looking at the statues representing the warrior committing suicide and the dying figure, we are not at first moved by the victory of the Attalids but respond rather to the heroic demise of the defeated Galatians.

The well, situated in front of the north stoa near the temple, dates back to the Hellenistic period. The round monument in the centre of the courtyard once supported, according to Otto Brendel and Harald Ingholt, the bronze original of the Prima Porta statue of Augustus, a marble copy of which is now kept in the Vatican.

The Library. Adjoining the east end of the north stoa was the library (8). According to Strabo (XIII 624), the Pergamene library was built during the time of Eumenes II. However, it must antedate the stoa, since the rooms of the library did not have doors opening on to the street or square. Those who wished to enter the library had to proceed from the upper storey of the north stoa (Fig. 28). The south wall of the library has disappeared, so the interior of the four rooms of the structure is now visible from the south, above the north stoa of the Athena temenos.

On the basis of the preserved architectural remains, it is clear that the floor of the second storey of the north stoa was at the same level as the

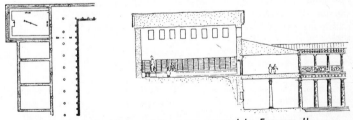

Fig. 28 a – Plan of the Library of Pergamon, erected by Eumenes II.
Fig. 28 b – The same library. Transverse section through the main room of the library and the north stoa of the Athena temenos. Entrance to the library was via the upper storey of this stoa.

first storey of the library. Thus, when the stoas were being erected, the second storey of the north stoa was constructed to give access to the library, one of the first works of the 38 - year reign of Eumenes II.

The reading room was a large hall measuring 13.53 × 15.95 metres, located in the eastern section of the library. The inner surfaces of the north and east walls are preserved to a height of 3.5 metres; at intervals of one metre, and at a height of 2.20 m., is a horizontal row of regular holes, each measuring 7.5 cm. in width, 4.5 cm. in height and 14 cm. in depth. The holes at the extreme ends of the line are 50 cm. from the corners of the walls. It would seem that these holes must have served to support book-shelves. If one examines the floor, a one metre-wide foundation can be seen at a distance of 50 cm. from the north and east walls (Fig. 28). Thus, the wooden shelves must have surrounded the hall on three sides, at a distance of 50 cm. from the walls, resting on this foundation and secured to the sides of the chamber by thick planks.

Since the shelves were not attached to the walls and a free space of 50 cm. was left, the books were protected from the damp. Similar precaution is evident in the library at Ephesus. According to preserved evidence, a podium measuring 1.05 × 2.74 metres and 90 cm. in height must have stood centrally in front of the north wall. The 3.50 metre-high Athena statue, discovered in front of the reading room, and now in the Berlin Museum, must have been erected on this platform. The statue, together with the podium, would have been 4.5 metres tall. Thus, the height of the hall must have been at least 6 metres. If we assume that the shelves were at least the height of the Athena statue, this room would have held many thousands of books. As stated above, manuscripts were primarily written on parchment, then rolled or folded and stacked on shelves in the way that we shelve books today. Nevertheless, even if we allow that the shelves were 4 to 5 metres in height, this room could not have held more than 15 - 20 thousand papyri or parchment books. Accordingly, the remainder of the 200,000 volumes known to have been housed in the Pergamene library must have been stored in the other three rooms and elsewhere.

This hall, which served as a reading room, had a wooden ceiling. The roof was pitched and light entered through the windows at the top of the side walls. Two of the remaining rooms could only have had windows at the top of the northern walls, and in the westernmost room the west wall alone could have held openings for light. There are no traces of shelves in any of these rooms.

During Caesar's campaign at Alexandria, the large library there was burned. Subsequently, Cleopatra ensured that books were brought from Pergamon to Egypt as the gift of Antony.

Remains of a large house (9) were found adjoining the most western room of the library (Fig. 24). This building is early Hellenistic in date. It has one large room preceded by an ante-room facing south and, in addition, three small rooms and another big room, also preceded by an ante-room, that opens to the west. The route to the acropolis used today passes through the centre of this house. The six steps overlooking the west are of modern construction.

The Palaces. The remains of the palaces (10, 11) of the Pergamene kings are located immediately to the east of both the stoa surrounding the Athena temple and the library (Pls 33a, Fig. 24). These were two large houses with central courtyards, that is, of peristyle form. It is accepted that the northern, smaller building (11) was constructed during the time of Attalos, while the larger palace (10) belonged to Eumenes. The columns of the smaller peristyle house were of wood and those of its larger counterpart of andesite.

The peristyle of the Eumenes palace was approximately 25 × 25 metres. A large hall was located in the north of the palace, an altar in the courtyard (B),a cistern in the south-west corner and a cult room (A) in the east, adjoining the large hall. The west wall of the Eumenes palace is at present entirely in ruins. The west wall of the aforementioned cistern, which was greatly altered in Roman times, is also no longer in existence. In the Hellenistic age, the entrance to this cistern was on the east, and it opened on to the courtyard. Mosaic fragments recovered within the palaces are now in the Berlin Museum. The kitchen and storage-rooms were in the south-east, just to the east of the acropolis entrance, at the foot of the city wall. A series of small rooms surrounded the courtyard of the Attalos construction. The altar was discovered in a room on the eastern side; water was supplied from a cistern in the peristyle. Large peristyle houses resembling the Pergamon palaces were found at Larisa and Priene (Figs. 39, 74). Barracks (13) were located to the north of the small palace, and immediately nearby are the poorly preserved remains of small houses (12). Those close to the king, officers must have resided here. The shops constructed of andesite, situated between the east corner of the library (8) and the north corner of the Trajaneum (15), go back to the Hellenistic period, but they underwent extensive restoration in Roman times.

The Arsenals. The arsenals (14) were located at the northern edge of the acropolis, at a level 10 metres below the palaces and the Trajaneum (15). These were five long buildings constructed parallel to one another. The westernmost measured 39 metres in length and the two to the east 48 metres each. Within were found 13 different sizes of andesite shot; the diameter of the smallest was 15 cm. and it weighed 2.8 kg., while the largest was 40.3 cm. in diameter and 75.2 kg. in weight. In Greek, these were called sphonduloi and were hurled by a weapon known as the palintonon. These andesite balls now occupy an area in the lower agora (Pl. 37 b).

The location of the arsenals at the edge of the north acropolis afforded a wide view of the surrounding plain; in turn, however, the arsenals themselves could only be sighted by the approaching enemy at close range. Thus, for the defence of the city, the placement was most appropriate. The arsenals were constructed during the reigns of both Attalos I and Eumenes II.

The barracks and command tower (13) were located on a terrace 5 metres above the arsenals, behind the Trajaneum (15) and adjoining the palaces (10 - 12). These military installations, built for the general protection of the city and especially of the palaces, were begun during the reign of Attalos I, and reached their final form during the time of Eumenes II. The part of the city wall which forms the east side of the barracks and overlooks the valley rises to a height of 32 courses and streches for 70 m. The view from this wall is strikingly beautiful.

At the north edge of the arsenals, re-used in a city wall of early Byzantine date, were found remains of a temple : architrave fragments, pieces of capitals and columns, as well as stones from cella walls. An architrave fragment, incorporated into the wall, was removed by plunderers some time before the start of excavations; however, the imprint of the inscription engraved on the architrave was clearly preserved in the mortar. On the basis of the impression, it would seem that this architrave belonged to the temple constructed for Faustina II, the wife of Marcus Aurelius. It is still not known, however, where on the acropolis this temple of Faustina was erected.

The Trajaneum. The buildings of the acropolis, apart from the temple of Trajan, were all built in the Hellenistic age. However, since these architectural works continued to be used in Roman times, some parts were restored or altered to suit the characteristic concepts of Roman art. In spite of additions to and completions of Kingdom period constructions on the Pergamon acropolis during the Roman era, we are struck at first glance by the essentially Hellenistic character of the buildings. The reason for this is that the buildings of the Kingdom Period were of andesite; marble was rarely used except for architectural ornamentation. Since the original plan of the buildings dating from Hellenistic times only underwent partial alteration, and since the marble additions were either removed to museums or stolen by plunderers of ruins, the majority of the remains seen *in situ* date from the Hellenistic age.

Trajan's temple (Pls. 32, 34a) rises up on a terrace measuring 68 × 58 metres. This level area was the highest point of the acropolis; a building of the Hellenistic age no doubt existed here prior to this. When the time came to build the Trajaneum, the area was levelled off by means of an arched and vaulted substructure, in the manner customary in Roman times, and the temple was built on this. The 23 m. high retaining wall of the terrace is decorated along the middle with a horizontal moulding, and also with a series of windows, which appear in the front faces of the vaulted arches in the upper part of the wall. From this point of view also, the Trajaneum has a different appearance from the Hellenistic buildings found at Pergamon. The temple is flanked on three sides by stoas. The rear stoa was built five metres higher than the side stoas because the rock face rises here. The temple lies exactly in the centre of the temenos, as was customary in Roman times. It is a peripteros of the Corinthian order, with 9 columns on the long sides and 6 on the short. With its podium and stairway on the front face, it strongly recalls the temple of Dionysus on the theatre terrace; but, in this case too, there is no doubt that the effect is due to Roman architectural concepts.

Although it seems that the temple was erected to Trajan by his successor Hadrian, both emperors, in fact, were worshipped here. In support of this theory are the heads of two colossal marble statues of Trajan and Hadrian, which were discovered within the temple. These works are now in the Pergamon Museum in Berlin (E. Rohde, Pergamon Fig. 16).

The Theatre. The Pergamon theatre (16), rising on a high and steep hillside and presenting a very impressive profile, is one of the most beautiful creations of the Hellenistic age. The architectural composition, in which all the other buildings of the acropolis are arranged fan-wise around the theatre, serves to increase the splendour and attractiveness of this fascinating structure (Fig. 24).

There remain only a few fragments of the retaining walls, in polygonal masonry, belonging to the original building, which was erected in the first years of the Kingdom on the same incline. Without doubt, the construction attained its most magnificent Hellenistic form during the reign of Eumenes II. The fact that the orchestra and the skene are set up on a terrace with a stoa fits in well with the architectural concepts which first became fashionable in the time of this king.

The auditorium consisted of 80 rows of seats the topmost row of which was 36 metres higher than the level of the orchestra. In order to facilitate exit and entry, the auditorium was divided horizontally into three sections by two wide landings (diazoma); in addition, the lower section was divided into seven and the middle and upper into six parts by wide steps, 0.74 cms. in breadth. The whole theatre could seat 10,000 people. Just above the centre of the lower landing was the king's box, which was made of marble. All the other rows of seats were of andesite. The stage was made of wood in Hellenistic times; it was erected only on the days of performance and was afterwards dismantled. Three rows of large square holes, in which were fixed the wooden supports holding up the proscenium and the skene, are still in evidence today. There were several reasons for this portable wooden installation at Pergamon. In the Hellenistic age, architectural structures blended harmoniously with the natural background. Theatregoers did not want the scene before them to be divorced from the outside panorama; it was important for them to be able to watch the city and the plain from where they were sitting (Pls. 31 a, 32). There was also a great need for this close link with nature when the festivals of Dionysus, the literature, poetry and music competitions, and other spectacles were held in the theatre at certain times of the year, since these would often go on from morning till nightfall and cover a period of many days. The place where the stage was actually set happened to be on the road leading to the temple of Dionysus (17). Those who wished to go to the temple would pass through a two-arched entrance on the south side of the theatre terrace (18) and then walk along a road roughly 250 metres in length (Pl. 32). The theatre terrace was one of the finest places on the acropolis for meetings and walks. Stretching for 246.50 metres along the west side of the road was a Doric stoa of andesite opening to the terrace and to the outside. On the east side of the road there was another stoa overlooking the terrace; this was also made of andesite, of the Doric order, but had a front only 75 metres long (Pl. 32; Fig. 24). Hence, the people of Pergamon could stroll and walk in the roofed stoas or along the road between, or else discuss their daily affairs, as the fancy took them. If they wanted to look at the view, however, they could sit down in one of the theatre rows or else gaze out from the side of the 246.50 metre-long

stoa that looked towards the plain of the river Kaikos. These were the reasons why the king and the people did not wish to shut off the centre of this
exceptionally beautiful promenade by building a construction of stone or
marble. If a permanent stage had been built, it would also have cut off the
front view of the temple of Dionysus.

The Temple of Dionysus. (Pl. 32; Figs. 29, 33a). Indeed, the kings
of Pergamon had the forethought to build this eyecatching temple
at the northern end of the nearly 250 metre-long theatre terrace, in such a
way that it would dominate the entire length of the promenade, People
walking from south to north along the theatre terrace had the opportunity
of gazing with pleasure and admiration, for the space of several minutes,
at this beautiful building (Pls. 31a, 32; Fig. 29). The temple of Dionysus is a

*Fig. 29 – Dionysus Temple of Pergamon (2nd century B. C.). The best example
of a Hellenistic temple set in a dominant position (Pl. 32). It represents, with
its rear and sides largely hidden from view (in constrast to the four-fronted character of archaic and classical Greek temples), a new architectural idea, later
developed in Roman times. The Dionysus Temple, originally built of andesite, was
largely renovated in marble by Caracalla (A. D. 211–217); this emperor was
then worshipped there as the "New Dionysus".*

prostyle of the Ionic order, rising on a richly profiled podium, and is in a very good state of preservation, as is its altar. The stylobate measures 11.80 by 20.22 metres. Since it had to conform to the topography of the site, the temple faced south. It was reached by a flight of 25 steps, which rose to a height of 4.5 metres (Fig. 33a). The temple of Dionysus, with its podium, the long flight of steps, its prominent position and with its rear and sides largely hidden from view, is a forerunner of the Roman temple. The building of this work at the point where a long road terminates, and in the form of a monument which is the focus of all eyes, was the first step towards Roman artistic feeling and the understanding of architectural town-planning, as conceived during the Baroque period in Europe. If one takes into account the close relationship between Pergamon and Rome, it might be said that the podium of this temple was inspired by Etruscan art forms. However, the Romans of this period were so much under the influence of Hellenistic artistic styles that the existence of such a counter-influence is open to doubt. Indeed this type of building, exhibiting an accentuated façade and pronounced axiality, is encountered not only at Pergamon but also in the mature stage of the Hellenistic period, i.e., from the second quarter of the 2nd century B. C. on, at Magnesia ad Maeandrum, Miletos, and Priene (Figs. 62, 63, 70, No. 6, 77, No. 20, 79, 80).

The side of the long stoa which faced the terrace was one-storeyed; the side which faced outwards possessed three storeys, and beneath these there was a supporting wall. The lower floors served as a depot and the dismantled sections of the portable stage were kept there.

Viewed from afar, the theatre, the stoas on the theatre terrace and the temple of Dionysus certainly formed an attractive architectural unit. The recurring vertical lines, created by the columns of the monuments and the buttresses of the terrace walls, made a pleasing contrast to the horizontal spread of the acropolis on the extensive hill.

The small building situated between the east stoa and the theatre also dates from the Hellenistic era. Although it is generally thought to be a meeting place for the artistic devotees of Dionysus, the exact function of this structure has not been determined. When Pergamon passed into Roman hands, the theatre underwent alterations. The orchestra, which had been horseshoe-shaped in the Hellenistic period, was now converted into a semi-circle, and a permanent stage construction was erected in marble. A magnificent multi-tiered façade was added to this same stage during the time of the Roman Empire. Not a trace of this Roman stage construction has survived to the present day. A gallery which encircled the top of the auditorium and decorated the lower side of the upper terraces was also built in the Roman Empire period. The ruins of the tower seen near the temenos of Athena, on the south-east side of the theatre, date from Byzantine times.

In Roman times, the temple of Dionysus also underwent changes. The pillars at the entrance to the naos and the life-size acroteria were added during the renovations that took place during the reign of Caracalla (211 - 217). In the course of the same structural restoration, the interior of the temple was also adorned with embellishments in marble. The dedicatory inscription which appeared above the architrave was written in gold-plated bronze lettering. Original fragments dating from the Hellenistic and Roman periods are now kept in the Berlin Museum. The ruler Caracalla was worshipped in this temple under the name of the "New Dionysus", in gratitude for the services he had rendered to the city of Pergamon.

The Altar of Zeus. The terrace of the Zeus altar was located to the south of the Athena temple, at a level 25 metres below. The altar (Pls. 33-35) rose precisely in the centre of this area, which measured approximately 69 × 77 metres. The propylon, shown on the general plan in the east section of the sanctuary, usually claimed as the entrance to the enclosure, is conjectural. However, access to the altar terrace must have been from this side, because the acropolis road skirted the area, and the terrace was built to correspond to the contours of this thoroughfare. Most probably, the altar proper was exposed on all sides to allow an unimpeded view of the monument; from the altar, the lower city of Pergamon, the Selinus and Ketios rivers and the entire plain could be scanned.

This monument, the most important and largest building on the acropolis dating from the Hellenistic period, must have been constructed in the golden age of the kingdom — that is, during the reign of Eumenes II.

The architectural fragments of the altar, as well as all of the high reliefs, were re-used in the section of the Byzantine city wall which extended from the heroon eastward to the upper agora. The discovery of these remains was made in the year 1871, by the German engineer Carl Humann. With the help of the preserved fragments, the altar has now been reconstructed in the Berlin Museum. Today, only the foundations of the altar can be seen on the acropolis (Pl. 35a). Below these foundations, houses of early Hellenistic date, as well as an apsidal building situated in the eastern part below the altar, have been unearthed.

The altar of Zeus consisted of a marble offering-table, set on a three-tiered podium, surrounded by a horseshoe-shaped stoa of the Ionic order (Pl. 34; Figs. 30-32). Twenty steps on the western side led up to the open rectangular area on which the marble altar was erected. Thus, the monument rose from bottom to top in four stages. The lowest was a 5-stepped crepidoma of nearly square form, measuring 36.44 × 34.20 metres. On top of this were the three horseshoe-shaped superimposed sections of the building proper. The lowest of these was a podium, the middle a relief frieze and the upper a columned portico in the form of an enclosing wall (Pl. 34 b).

Horseshoe-shaped altars closely resembling the Pergamon example were found at Magnesia on the Maeander and at Priene. As the earliest example of this building type, one can mention the altar of the archaic Hera temple at Samos. However, these three altars were associated with temples, unlike the Pergamon monument which, standing alone in its own temenos, was an independent cult building, dedicated to Zeus and Athena and possibly to all the gods. Originally, the Greeks worshipped only in front of an altar. The oldest altar dedicated to Hera at Samos, and the altar of Zeus at Olympia, built before the temple of Zeus, served as places of worship. At Sardis, prior to the erection of the Artemis temple, an altar was constructed which functioned for a century as a cult monument to the goddess (Fig. 44).

Fig. 30 – Zeus Altar of Pergamon, built during the reign of Eumenes II (197–159 B. C.). The largest and most impressive example of a Greek altar (see Pls. 33–35). The reliefs (now in Berlin) depicting the mythological battle between Gods and Giants symbolise the victory of the Pergamene kings over the Galatians. The Altar of Pergamon served as a model for the Ara Pacis of Augustus in Rome (see also Fig. 31).

The Pergamene altar was much larger in perimeter and height than the examples at Samos, Magnesia and Priene; it was the largest religious structure built in Hellenistic Pergamon. This altar must be older than those at Magnesia and Priene; it served as a model for the Ara Pacis of Augustus in Rome.

The Pergamene altar was a monument in which architecture and plastic art coalesced most successfully, since here the sculpture did not assume a secondary role but was equal in importance to the structural parts. The battle of the Giants and the Gods was represented in relief on the 120 metre-long and 2.30 metre-high frieze. The altar accordingly gains importance as a monument representing all of the Greek gods assembled; in this respect, it recalls the Hittite open-air sanctuary at Yazılıkaya (Fig. 118). The reliefs are on a par with those of Olympia and the Parthenon, being among the most important and beautiful of Greek sculptural works, as well as the most significant artistic achievement of the Hellenistic age.

The walls, which surround the marble altar on the podium on three sides, are decorated with reliefs representing the mythological life of Telephos, the son of Heracles, from the day of his birth to the time when he founded Pergamon. The Attalids, claiming Telephos as their forefather, linked their origin to Troy and a heroic demigod, much in the manner of the Romans.

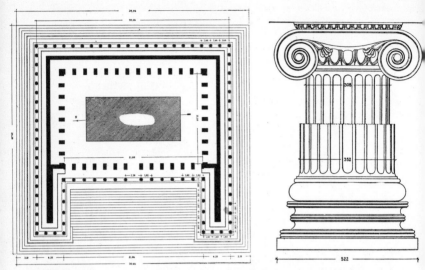

Fig. 31 – Plan of the Zeus Altar of Pergamon. This horseshoe-shaped monument, measuring 36.44 × 34.20 m., rose up in four stages (see also Fig. 30): 1) A 5-stepped crepidoma (still in place at Pergamon). 2) A podium. 3) A frieze. 4) A columned portico in the form of an enclosing wall. Twenty steps on the western side led up to the open rectangular area on which the altar proper was erected.
Fig. 32 – Column order of the Zeus Altar. The base and the capital are Hellenistic modifications of the classical models created by Pytheos (Fig. 69).

The Pergamene altar is not only a monument of great artistic and mythological importance but also a tribute to mankind, in the fine humanitarian manner employed to represent a victory over an enemy.

The Agora. Immediately below the altar of Zeus, at the southernmost end of the acropolis, was the site of the upper agora of Pergamon (Fig. 24, No. 21). The north-east and south-west sides of the agora square were each enclosed by an andesite stoa built in the Doric order. Topographical features dictated that the outward-facing sides of stoas built on a slope should be three-storeyed, and that the inward-facing sides should be only one-storeyed. In order to allow the road to pass from the lower and middle town areas, the south stoa was divided in two. As was customary at Pergamon, the front-facing one-storeyed side of the stoas was built in the form of a colonnade, while the three-storeyed stoas at the back and on the sides were erected as plain walls; at the rear and on the sides, there were doors to the ground floor and windows to the two upper storeys. There were rooms and storage places on the two lower floors.

After passing through the centre of the agora (Fig. 24 No. 21), the road follows the eastern side of the terrace, on which lies the altar of

Zeus (20); it then passes along the north-west side of the heroon (1) and from there turns west to reach the gate to the upper city, i.e. the entrance to the acropolis (Fig. 24, No. 3).

The altar of the agora was in the western part of the square. All that is now visible of a small temple that rose up on the west side of the agora and on the axis of the altar are the foundations, which are 12.30 × 6.70 m. in dimension (Fig. 33b). Judging by the marble fragments of architecture which have been found, this temple was a prostyle of the Doric order; however, the columnar flutes and the bases were in the Ionic style. In other words, the temple is a mixture of architectural styles. The podium was approximately 1 m. high. A many-stepped stairway was situated on the front

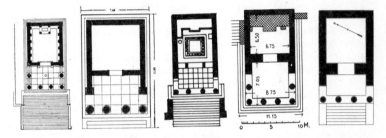

Fig. 33 – *Temples of the prostyle type at Pergamon:* **a)** *Temple of Dionysus (Fig. 24 No. 17), of the Ionic order (11.80 × 20.22 m.); second century B. C.* **b)** *Temple of the upper Agora (Fig. 24 No. 22), of the Doric order intermixed with Ionic elements (6.70 × 12.30 m.); second half of the second century B.C.* **c)** *Temple of Hera Basileia (Fig. 34 No. 1), of the Doric order (measurements: ca. 7.00 × 11.80 m.)* **d)** *Temple of Asklepios (Fig. 34 No. 8) of the Ionic order (9 × 16 m.); second half of the second century B. C.* **e)** *Temple in the Middle Gymnasium dedicated to the worship of Hermes and Heracles and to the cult of the Emperor (Fig. 34 No. 11), of the Corinthian order (7 × 12 m.); second half of the second century B. C.*

face of the temple. All that remains at present of the temple podium are six courses of stone on the long south-west face. The temple was believed to have been dedicated to Dionysus, because the gutter spouts were adorned with the heads of maenads and satyrs. However, since this was a temple for the agora, it is more likely to have been connected with Hermes or Zeus. The temple was erected at the beginning of the time when the Doric and Ionic styles were intermixed, i.e., in the 2nd century B. C., perhaps during the reign of Eumenes II. On the other hand, it can safely be stated that the agora was in existence since the beginning of the Kingdom period. The building to the north-west of the temple also dates from the Hellenistic period. This construction was converted into an apsidal building in the Roman era. The two buildings observed lying midway between the altar of Zeus, the temple of Athena and the heroon were erected at the end of the Kingdom period. The wider of these, lying south of and slightly below the temple of Athena, was a one-storeyed, two-aisled stoa (19). The narrower of the two, i. e. the one lying to the east of the former and slightly above the heroon (2), was composed of a row of shops, as has been stated above.

The Middle City (Fig. 34). As we go down from north to south, the buildings occupying the centre of ancient Pergamon were the sanctuaries of Hera and Demeter, the temple of Asklepios, the gymnasia and the city fountain (Fig. 34). The upper town was more especially the domain of the royal family, the nobility and the military commanders; consequently, it had an air of officialdom. The central district, on the other hand, contained the young people's sportsfields and the temples frequented by the less well-educated classes, i.e. those buildings which were not directly controlled by the city and the priesthood, and where the populace could come and go without hindrance.

The Temenos of Hera Basileia. To the north of the gymnasia, and about 20 metres above them, stood the temenos of Hera Basileia (Fig. 34, No. 1). The temenos dominated the gymnasia from its position on two terraces. The temple was built on the upper terrace, the altar on the lower. The temple of Hera, which faced south, was reached by a flight of eleven steps with a balustrade on both sides (Fig. 33c). The andesite wall lying between the two terraces is in a good state of preservation. The temple was a four-columned prostyle of the Doric order and was a monument intended to be conspicuous from a distance, just like the temple of Dionysus, which had a similar front stairway (Pl. 32; Fig. 29). Those parts of the buildings visible from the front, notably the pronaos, were built of marble; some parts were faced with marble, while those hidden from view were of andesite. The cella measured 5.80 × 6.80 metres. From the remains of an inscription, visible on some of the fragments of the architrave still lying in the pronaos, the temple is understood to have been built in the reign of Attalos II (159 - 138) and dedicated to Hera Basileia. To the east of the temple there is a stoa, to the west an exedra. Both of these are of andesite, but their function is unknown. In the north-east corner of the stoa can be seen a "kline" (couch) with three steps leading up to it. The front faces of the stoa and the exedra are in line with that of the temple. Five columns are thought to have stood along the front of the exedra and eight in front of the stoa.

The marble altar to the god Men, which now stands within the exedra, was placed there by the excavators. There is no connection between this altar and the temple of Hera, and it probably used to stand on the upper terrace. Not a fragment of the statue of Hera has come to light. A headless statue, however, has been discovered, and this is now kept in the Istanbul Museum. This fine marble statue resembles the god Zeus, but since the hair remaining on the nape of the neck is short, it is claimed to represent Attalos II, who commissioned the temple to be built, and not Zeus. Three metopes occurred in the intercolumnar span; the architectural ornamentation is carelessly executed, and the standard of workmanship is low, which indicates that the golden age of Pergamon was already on the decline. Excavation has only revealed the decorative border of the mosaics which adorned the centre of the cella. These comprised garlands and wave-like motifs shaped like volutes, both of which were popular in Hellenistic art. A wall enclosed the rear of the temple, the stoa and the exedra, at a distance of 60 cms. It functioned as a retaining wall, holding back the rising ground behind the buildings. The intervening space, which is termed a peristasis in Pergamon, protected the temple from the damp. The building (2) above the sanctuaries of Hera and Demeter is only partially excavated at present, and is thought to be the prytaneion (Fig. 34).

The Temenos of Demeter. The temenos of Demeter occupies an area of approximately 100×50 metres, on an extensive rectangular terrace (Pls. 9b, 37 a; Fig. 34, No. 3). People coming from the upper gymnasium passed through a gate and, having entered a square with a fountain (5) and a sacrificial pit (6), mounted a flight of five steps a little further on to reach the two-columned propylon (4) of the Demeter temenos (Pl. 37a). The fountain and the sacrificial pit were essential features of the Demeter cult and were instituted earlier in the Kingdom period. However, the present-day remains are of renovations and enlargements made in the Roman era.

The two columns of the propylon which constituted the entrance to the temenos of Demeter were re-erected during the excavations (Pls. 9b, 37 a). An inscription found on the frieze of the architrave over this small entrance states that the building of the colonnades and the oikoi in the sanctuary was commissioned by Apollonis, the wife of Attalos I (241 - 197). The andesite columns were of the Doric order (see Pl. 37a). Although a start was evidently made on the carving of 20 flutes on the lower portions of these, no opportunity arose to complete them, as in many other cases at Pergamon. The capitals, which were decorated with formal designs of palm leaves, were topped by thin abaci. This type of capital of the archaic period prevailed particularly in the Aeolian region. The reason that such capitals were used in the propylon must have been that Apollonis came from Cyzicus.

A flight of ten steps leads down from the propylon into the temenos (Fig. 34, No. 3). The temple is situated in the western half of the sanctuary, while the altar is more or less in the centre. Both of these are of andesite. Two identical inscriptions, one appearing on the temple architrave and the other on the eastern side of the orthostats forming the north-east corner of the altar, state that these two works were erected by Philetairos (283-263) and his young brother Eumenes, in memory of their mother Boa. The building was a "templum in antis" of the Ionic order, and measured 6.45 × 12.70 metres. A marble frieze adorned with garlands, interspersed with the skulls of bulls, appears on the architrave. The temple was converted into a prostyle during Roman times by marble additions in the Corinthian style to the front façade (Fig. 34, No. 3). The inscription on the architrave relates that the restoration was carried out by Claudius Silianus Aesimus, who belonged to the famous Siliani family of Pergamon and was a contemporary of Antoninus Pius, according to dates obtained from coins. The altar, which measured 2.30 × 7.00 metres, was rather large in relation to the size of the temple. This is an interesting work in that it bore marble volutes on two sides.

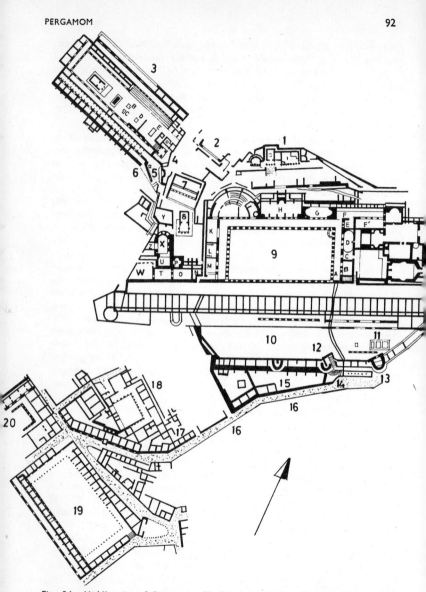

Fig. 34 – Middle city of Pergamon. **1)** Temenos of Hera Basileia. The sacred precinct, probably erected by Attalos II (159–138), contains the Temple of Hera Basileia (Fig. 33 c) of the Doric order, an exedra and a small stoa. **2)** Possibly the Prytaneion of Pergamon. **3)** Temenos of Demeter (Pls. 9 b, 37 a). This sacred precinct, founded in the early 3rd century B. C., was enlarged by Apollonis, the wife of Attalos I (241–197 B. C.) and altered in Roman times. **4)** Propylon (entrance) to the precinct with two columns surmounted by palm-leaf capitals (Pl. 37 a); commissioned, according to the inscription on the architrave, by Apollonis. The south stoa and the four oikoi (rooms) on the west side were also erected by Apollonis. The temple of Demeter and the altar were erected by Philetairos (283–263) and his younger brother Eumenes in memory of their mother Boa, according to the two identical inscriptions on the temple and altar. This first structure was a templum in antis of the Ionic order. In Roman times, the Pergamenes converted it, with marble additions, into a prostyle of the Corinthian order. In the precinct are to be seen four other altars (B, C, D, E), all dating from the Hellenistic age but showing alterations of the Roman period. A low stoa runs on the north side of the temenos, parallel with the temple and the big altar. The eastern half of the north side of the temenos contains a theatron, consisting of ten rows of seats sufficient for 800 people. The celebrants watched the ceremonies from these seats. **5)** A fountain in the shape of an exedra for ablutions. **6)** A pit, on the way to the temenos of Demeter, to receive the blood of sacrificed animals. **7)** Probably a meeting-house connected with the cult of Dionysus. **8)** Temple of Asklepios (see Fig. 33 d). Prostyle of the Ionic order; second half of the second century B. C. The rooms marked N–Z belong to the Roman baths of the upper gymnasium. **9)** The upper gymnasium was reserved for young men and ceremonies took place here. It consisted of a courtyard for athletic training, surrounded by colonnades erected in the Hellenistic age and much renovated in Roman times. In the north-west corner of the upper gymnasium lies the "auditorium maximum" for 1000 people, built during the Roman period. Major ceremonies took place here. The room with two apses marked G was reserved for the Emperor, according to an inscription on an entablature. The rooms to the east (shown in black on the plan) constitute Roman baths associated with the upper gymnasium. No remains of the south stoa of the upper gymnasium have been discovered. However, the basement stadium, lying beneath this stoa, is in a good state of preservation. Athletic races were held here during the summer and winter, while the spring and autumn games took place in the south stoa. **10)** Middle gymnasium. This served as the training place for adolescent boys. It was built in the Hellenistic period and underwent internal alterations in Roman times. **11)** The gymnasium temple, dedicated to Hermes and Heracles and to the cult of the Emperor, was a prostyle of the Corinthian order, constructed in the second half of the second century B. C. (Fig. 33 e). **12)** Stairway entrance, built in the time of Eumenes II. One of the oldest and most beautiful arch-and-vault constructions of the eastern Greek world. **13)** City fountain (Eumenes II's time). **14)** Propylon, entrance to the three gymnasia (Eumenes II's time). **15)** Lower gymnasium, also built during the reign of Eumenes II, reserved for children. The southern part has completely disappeared; the north side is well-preserved. **16)** Main street, built in the Hellenistic age and repaired in Roman times. **17)** Shops dating from the Hellenistic period. **18)** House of Attalos, erected in Hellenistic times. **19)** Lower agora (reign of Eumenes II), surrounded by stoas of the Doric order. The andesite balls exhibited in the courtyard were found in the arsenals. The modern building lying on the west side of the agora is the storage house of the German expedition. **20)** A peristyle house, built in the Hellenistic period and altered in Roman times. The modern structure occupying the courtyard of this dwelling is the house of the German archaeological expedition.

There were four other altars in the eastern section of the sanctuary. Two of these lay side by side (B. C), while the other two were one behind the other (D, E). Next to the altar B there was a sacrificial pit, but this is no longer visible. All four altars are attributed to the Kingdom period, and underwent various alterations during Roman times (Pl. 9b).

A stoa extended along the south side of the temenos for 91.50 metres. This colonnade had two aisles, formed by a row of columns on each side; one aisle faced in towards the temenos, the other to the south overlooked the plain. The capitals of the columns were decorated with conventional palm leaves, similar to those of the propylon. This stoa, which was built in Hellenistic times by order of Apollonis, was altered by the addition of marble structures, of possibly the Ionic or Corinthian orders, in the Roman era. The basement underlying the south-facing section of the colonnade is in a good state of preservation. Entrance was gained to the basement by gateways opening to the south. In the upper part of the south wall there are slit-like apertures, resembling the loopholes in towers through which arrows are shot. The basement was probably used as a depot for miscellaneous articles. The stoa was supported on the south by slanting buttresses, which rose to the level of the basement floor. Even today, the appearance of this buttressed wall is very impressive.

A low stoa runs parallel to the temple and the altar for a distance of 43 metres on the north face of the sanctuary. This must have been built during the initial construction of the temenos. Along the eastward continuation of the stoa for about the same distance, i.e. approximately 42 metres, ten rows of seats comprising the theatron have been unearthed. 800 people could be accommodated on these rows of stone seats. Behind the low stoa, and continuing westwards past the theatron, there was another stoa adjoining both of these structures. This was 80 metres in length and rose up en echelon, resembling a second storey. The rear wall of this stoa is preserved along its entire length. On the west side of the temenos, on the other hand, was built a four-roomed stoa. These four rooms were probably numbered among those oikoi mentioned in the inscriptions concerning Queen Apollonis.

It is possible to state that the chambers lying between the north stoa and the propylon also constituted some of the rooms referred to as "oikoi" in the inscription. If one judges from present appearances, these rooms seem to have been built in Roman times. However, the entrances are of the Hellenistic period, and bear witness to the fact that at least two large rooms existed here in Apollonis' time. Therefore, some of the rooms known as oikoi are understood to have been built between the north stoa and the propylon, i. e. along the east face of the temenos, during the time of Apollonis.

A close look at the temple and the altar reveals that the east-west axis of the temenos is slightly to the south of centre (Fig. 34). In all probability, the purpose of this asymmetric plan was to give the spectators assembled in the north stoa and on the steps a clear view of ceremonies taking place in front of the temple and altar.

According to the above-mentioned inscriptions, the first temple and altar, which were erected in early Hellenistic times, were devoted solely to the worship of Demeter, whereas, in Apollonis' time, Kore was worshipped as well as Demeter. The prostyle of the Corinthian order, which was built in the time of Antoninus Pius, was dedicated to Demeter Karpophoros and her daughter Kore. This cult, relating to the attractive promises made by the priests of Demeter and Kore concerning life after death, had been widespread among the unenlightened masses in Greece since the archaic period. In Asia Minor, such cults were associated with goddesses such as Cybele and Artemis. The spread of the Demeter cult in Asia Minor began in the Hellenistic era. At Priene too, there was a temple of Demeter contemporary with that at Pergamon. The cults of Serapis at Pergamon and Ephesus were similar in character, and they attracted huge crowds of people. Since the educated classes of Hellenistic times had lost their faith in religion, the illiterate masses, deprived of the positive beliefs postulated and developed by great writers and thinkers, were exploited by ignorant priests, and became the devotees of mystic religions.

The above-mentioned fountain (5) in the shape of an exedra, which lies in the outer court of the temenos and is in line with the south stoa, is connected with the cult of Demeter and Kore, as is also the sacrificial pit (6). The Greeks offered up burnt sacrifices to the gods of the heavens, but they slaughtered sacrificial animals to deities of the underworld, like Demeter and Kore, and allowed the blood to flow into a pit, in the manner customary in eastern religions.

The building (7) situated to the southeast of the Demeter sanctuary and north of the temple of Asklepios is considered to be a meeting-house, connected with the cult of Dionysus.

The Temple of Asklepios. The temple (8) which once rose up to the west of the upper gymnasium is now represented only by its andesite foundations. However, with the aid of fragments retrieved from the area, it has been possible to draw a ground plan (Fig. 33 d). The temple is a prostyle of the Ionic order and the stylobate measures 9×16 metres. Nevertheless, architectural remains which have come to light show that, when it was first constructed, the building was of the Doric order, and only later was it restored in the Ionic style. As a result, it can be stated that the first building came into being in the 3rd century or at the beginning of the 2nd century B. C., whereas the Ionic restoration was carried out in the time of the architect Hermogenes, when the Ionic style came into fashion, i.e. in the latter half of the 2nd century B. C. Within the cella, a platform runs the whole width of the temple in front of the south wall (Fig. 33d). The excavators have suggested that a group of three statues once stood on the proje tion in the centre of this platform. As the upper part of a statue representing Asklepios was discovered here, the temple is assumed to have been dedicated to this god.

The Gymnasia. Pergamon possessed a magnificent gymnasium built on three separate terraces, one above another (Fig. 34, Nos. 9, 10, 15). Mention is made of the Pais, Ephebos and Neos gymnasia in certain inscriptions which have been discovered. The places where these inscriptions were found indicate that the lower terrace was set aside for children, the middle for adolescent boys and the upper for young men. An alternative name for the upper gymnasium was the Ceremonial Gymnasium. Measuring from the south gate of the city (Fig. 23, No. 3), the height of the lower gymnasium was 50 metres, that of the middle gymnasium 74 metres, while the upper gymnasium was 88 metres in height. These three edifices were built with a special attention to form an importance that increased from the lower to the upper. When we consider how impressive even the present-day remains are, we can appreciate that the general appearance in Greek and Roman times must indeed have been unique in beauty and splendour. The propylon, which was situated alongside the large fountain on the main city thoroughfare, constituted the entrance to the three gymnasia. This was the sole entrance to both the lower and the middle gymnasia. However, the upper gymnasium could also be reached by a separate entrance in its eastern side. The three gymnasia date from the time of the Kingdom of Pergamon, and cannot have been built later than the second half of the 3rd century B. C. In Roman times, the greatest changes were made in the upper gymnasium, while the middle and lower gymnasia were more or less left in the same condition as they were in the Hellenistic period.

The Upper Gymnasium. The upper gymnasium (9) was erected on a terrace measuring approximately 200 × 45 metres. As has been stated above, the present-day ruins are largely those of restorations carried out during the Roman period. Since the parts dating from the Hellenistic period were constructed solely of andesite while in Roman times only marble was used, it is an easy task to distinguish the work of the two periods. In addition, the constructions of domes, apses and walls made with mortar point to the Roman period. In Roman times, the wall surfaces were covered with marble and marble mosaics.

The main building of the upper gymnasium consisted of stoas, which surrounded a courtyard on four sides. The most important rooms were in the northern stoa. The Asklepios temple, which has been described above, (Fig. 33 c) and the Roman baths, which were constructed during Roman times, belong to the upper gymnasium.

The courtyard, 74 metres in length and 36 metres in width, was made only of earth, since it was used as an athletic training ground. The stoas which surrounded it on four sides were of the Doric order during Hellenistic times, while in Roman times they were of the Corinthian order. Architectural fragments belonging to the styles of both periods have been discovered. As far as can be understood from the style of the architectural ornamentation of the Roman era, and from the inscriptions found on the fragmentary architrave remains, the ground floors of the stoas which surround the courtyard were built during the time of Hadrian (A.D. 117 - 138). On the other hand, the second storey, also of the Corinthian order, proves by its poor craftsmanship to belong to the late Roman period. In some places, fragments of an andesite stylobate of the Hellenistic period can be seen. The marble stylobate, which supported the columns of the Roman period, is preserved *in toto* on the west and north sides and partially on the east; but, on the south side, not a piece of either the stylobate or the columns has been found.

The beautifully paved semicircular area in the north-eastern corner of the courtyard was used as a wash-place.

Baths were an integral part of gymnasia of the Roman period. Therefore, they had an important position in the cities of Asia Minor. The buildings to the west of the gymnasium, indicated by the letters N-Z, are the wash-places erected in the Roman period (Fig. 34). The building marked Y next to the Asklepios temple (8) is nine metres higher than the big building marked X on the south. This shows that the construction was a water tank, built on high ground, and that it supplied water to the baths to the west. This tank was fed by a water-way, which was discovered over the gymnasium. The building U served as a furnace. During Byzantine times, all the western baths were used as cisterns. The buildings marked T, O, N and W are remains of the Hellenistic period (Fig. 34). The three andesite columns and capitals of the Doric order found in the building marked Z were brought from another locality and set up during the Roman period. Apparently, the baths of the Hellenistic period in the upper gymnasium were partially housed in this area. The room marked L, occupying the area behind the stoa is, in fact, the site of a bathroom in the Greek style. Here four marble bath-tubs were found at the foot of the north wall and three at the base of the south wall. As these were at a high level, it is more likely that they were wash-basins. On the other hand, they were also suitable for use as sitting baths, like hip-baths, as was customary among the Greeks. Immediately to the right of the entrance, there were two small andesite troughs at ground level for washing the feet. These now lie at the foot of the north wall. Very likely, the three big earthenware vessels (now in fragments) in this room are of the Byzantine period. It is not known what purpose the rooms K and M served in Hellenistic times, though in Roman times the room K was used as a salon attached to the auditorium, the building resembling a theatre. This theatre-like building on the west corner of the north stoa dates from the Roman period. A thousand people could be seated here. Apparently, the building was used mainly as a large auditorium for the gymnasium, since there is no orchestra.

The most important room in the gymnasium (marked H) is the middle room, i.e. the Ephebeion. All major ceremonies took place here. In the Hellenistic period, the façade of this room consisted of four Doric columns made of andesite. In the Roman period, the number of columns was increased; these were of marble and of the Corinthian order. The marble pillars seen in the rear wall of the room and the pillars of Greek origin taken from buildings and re-used during Roman times supported the vault which covered the enclosure. In the eastern corner can be seen part of a room belonging to the upper floor. According to an entablature inscription, the two-apsed room (G) was the room reserved in the gymnasium for the Emperor. The apses were roofed over with half-domes. It is not possible to say in what manner or with what material the central part of this room was roofed. During the Hellenistic period, this area consisted of two rooms. In Roman times, the dividing wall was removed. The front of this room opened on to the courtyard through columns with Corinthian capitals. The walls were faced with marble. Marble plaques were attached to the walls with iron nails, and the holes made by the nails can still be seen.

Only the foundations of the small room A in the east stoa remain. It is quite likely that a stairway led up from here to the next storey. The room marked B is in quite a good state of preservation. The east and north walls are fine examples of masonry in polygonal style dating from the Hellenistic age. Two marble columns with Ionic capitals, which stood on the west side, were of the Roman period. A base and a capital belonging to these have been found. The room marked C came into existence when Roman alterations divided it off from the room marked D. During the Roman period, this room (C) connected the eastern baths with the gymnasium. The rooms marked E and F were greatly altered in Roman times. The large room marked F' was built in the Roman period. The baths in the eastern section are quite well-preserved. Many of the rooms were faced with thin marble slabs. Some rooms with empty spaces underneath were equipped with a heating system. Remains of walls belonging to the Hellenistic period have been found in this area containing the eastern baths, thus proving that there were buildings here as far back as Hellenistic times. Although there was some relationship between these buildings and the gymnasia, it has not been possible to establish exactly what their function was.

The south stoa of the upper gymnasium was very probably of the Doric order of the Hellenistic period. However, not a single fragment of this stoa has been discovered. On the other hand, the basement stadium (measuring 210×6.80 metres) lying beneath this stoa is in a good state of preservation. Track races were held during the summer and winter in this basement stadium, while the spring and autumn races took place in the south stoa, which is assumed to have been of the same length. The basement stadium was illuminated by holes in the south wall. These windows resemble the apertures in towers used for shooting arrows in that they are narrow on the outside but widen inwards through the thickness of the wall. At the end of the Hellenistic period, sixty box-like rooms were constructed in front of the basement stadium in order to strengthen the upper gymnasium on the south side. There was no access to these rooms from the outside and they were completely filled in Hellenistic times with soil left over from construction. In this way, the danger that the terrace of the upper gymnasium would slip down and collapse was avoided. However, as the front of the basement stadium was sealed off, it thereafter ceased to be used as a running track and was employed only for storage purposes.

The Middle Gymnasium. This building (10) occupies an area of 150×36 metres on a narrow terrace (Fig. 34). The entire length of the terrace on the northern side was occupied by a large stoa built in the Hellenistic period, and this underwent internal alterations during the Roman period. A large area in the eastern half of this stoa is divided up into various rooms. Counting from the east, the sixth of these, called an "exedra" by the excavators, opens between two Doric columns on to the terrace. This room, according to an inscription found within, was dedicated to the worship of Hermes and Heracles, who were the gods of physical culture, and to the cult of the Emperor. The foundations of a temple (11) occupying an area of 12×7 metres have been discovered on the east part of the terrace. It was a prostyle of the Corinthian order with four columns (Fig. 33e). Remains of an altar have also been found on the west side of the temple. The names of the ephebes (the boys) written on the walls of the temple can be traced from the Roman period back to Hellenistic times. Consequently, it follows that the middle gymnasium belonged to the ephebes, and that the temple dates back to the time of the Kingdom of Pergamon. Indeed, the type of workmanship exhibited in the foundations, the shape of the metal clamps which fasten the stones together and the signatures of some of the masons all point to the Hellenistic period. Without doubt, this temple was of the same type as the agora temple, and that on the theatre terrace, both built in Hellenistic times. This is proved by the facts that the front of the prostyle was distinguished by a flight of steps, that the back and one side were in close proximity to other buildings, and, above all, that it was erected in a very conspicuous spot. These features determine that the building must have been constructed in the 2nd century B. C. According to the above-mentioned inscription found in the "exedra" lying opposite the altar, this temple was dedicated to the worship of Hermes and Heracles (the gods of exercise) and to the Emperor. The temple faced west because of its place in the terrain. The siting of the other Pergamon temples is also determined by the topography. The proximity of the entrance to the gymnasium no doubt also dictated the siting of this temple.

The Stairway Entrance. One of the most important constructions in the city of Pergamon is the vault-covered stairway (12) which forms the entrance to both the middle and upper gymnasia. This structure is in a good state of preservation and is very impressive, even in its present condition. The skill with which the walls and the vaulting have been fashioned and, especially, the craftsmanship manifest in the originality of the intersection of the arches at varying heights as they cover the winding stairway are highly impressive. This stairway entrance is one of the oldest and most beautiful arch-and-vault constructions of the eastern Greek world. The view over the plain of Kaikos at the point of exit beneath the vaulted arch is magnificent.

The Propylon. As we leave the bottom step of the vaulted stairway, we find the city fountain (13) on our left, and on our right a tower of Byzantine times and the remains of the lower gymnasium (15). The small open space lying in the form of a curve between the fountain, the lower gymnasium and the main road constituted the site of the entrance (14) to the three gymnasia. A study of the large plan (Fig. 34) and the small plan (Fig. 35a) in which the original lay-out is restored shows that the front wall of the fountain continued in a curve in the form of a quarter-circle to join the south wall of the lower gymnasium. There was a door exactly in the centre of this curved wall. It has been possible to reconstruct a plan of its former appearance through the discovery of the stone door-frame and the marks in the ground of two stone uprights. The rear wall of the propylon, which follows the same curve, can still be seen just to the west of the stair-

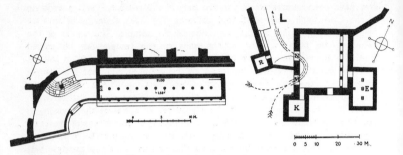

Fig. 35 a – Pergamon. The Propylon leading to the Middle Gymnasium and the City Fountain. Reign of Eumenes II.
Fig. 35 b – Pergamon. The South Gate of the city. Reign of Eumenes II.

way leading to the middle gymnasium. From an architectural point of view, this circular propylon, lying between the fountain and the lower gymnasium, constituted a very interesting corner of the city and of the main thoroughfare.

The City Fountain. This construction (13) was 21 metres long and 3.15 metres wide (Fig. 35a). The rear wall of the fountain has been discovered at its original level on the western corner. Two blocks belonging to the front wall have been set up in their correct places. People who stood in front of this low wall would dip their pots into the water and fill them. It is possible to see the marks made on the inside of this wall where the utensils have touched it and worn it away. Columns were built into the wall for half their height and then rose free as individual supports (Fig. 35a). These columns, together with a row of twelve others which divided the fountain in two, supported a stone roof about 3 metres in height. It has not been possible to establish to which architectural order this building belonged. However, it is more than likely that the propylon, the stairway construction and the fountain were built in the time of Eumenes II, when the city underwent such big changes.

The Lower Gymnasium. It has already been stated that the entrance to the lower gymnasium (15) for children was through the propylon on the main street. This gymnasium was 80 metres in length. The ground plan shows what it was originally like, but the southern part has disappeared completely. On the plan in the south-west corner we can distinguish five structures shaped like rooms. But these had no doors and were filled with earth, thus showing that they served only as supports. In spite of this, we can see that these roomlike supports, unable to withstand the pressure resulting from the weight of the terrace, collapsed. In contrast, the north side of the gymnasium is quite well-preserved. All along this side, supporting structures are built in the form of rooms, but they are again doorless and full of earth. In front of these, perpendicular buttresses were constructed to act as a second supporting wall. Lists containing the names of young winners of track events occupied some of the niches in the buttressed wall, while others housed statues of those winning greater distinctions. In the fourth niche to the west of the stairway entrance has been found a large stele, dating from the time of Attalos II, on which are inscribed the names of the ephebes of the year 147 B. C. The large towers constructed on the northern walls of the lower terrace, one of which is on the west side of the stairway entrance, were built in the Byzantine period.

The Main Street. After one leaves the gymnasium, the main street (Fig. 34, No. 16) of the city leads down to the lower agora and the entrance in the city walls. The road, which is 5 metres wide, is paved with massive blocks of andesite. On an average, these blocks are half a metre in width and sometimes one metre in length. In many places repair work done in ancient times and canals and drains installed at different periods are in evidence. The stones have been worn away by pedestrians, and chariot wheels have produced deep grooves.

The Shops. As we go down by way of the main street, the first buildings we come to on the right are 21 shops (17). In one of these was discovered a Roman copy of a herm, the original of which was the work of the sculptor Alkamenes. However, this had probably fallen down from the house of the Consul Attalos. The herm is now in the Istanbul Museum.

A Peristyle House. The house of Attalos (18) is built on the plan of a peristyle. A courtyard, measuring 20×13.5 metres, is surrounded on four sides by stoas containing rooms of various sizes (Fig. 34). The house was built in the Hellenistic period and underwent alterations in the Roman era. The mortarless walls of the Kingdom period, fashioned from regularly cut andesite stones, were built following the rectangular or polygonal method. In sharp contrast to this, the Roman walls are built of small, irregular stones, held together with mortar. The stoas surrounding the courtyard had two floors. The lower floor was made of andesite and was of the Doric order, and there were five metopes above every two columns. On the other hand, the upper floor, made of marble, was of the Ionic order. The largest room occupied an area of 10×10 metres on the west side of the courtyard. This was the sitting-room, facing southeast and receiving plenty of sunshine. In the Hellenistic period, the large sitting-rooms of houses were called "oikoi". This type of room can be seen in the houses at Priene (Fig. 74). In the oikos of the house of Attalos, there still exists, at the foot of the west wall, a small part of a triclinium which used to run along the base of three walls; these benches were used for sitting and sleeping. The floor was of marble mosaic. On the west wall at a height of 3 metres a delicate Corinthian niche was to be found. In a small room on the north side of the oikos a flight of stairs rose to the second floor. In the Roman period this was converted into a recess for worship. At the western end of the north wall of this niche stood a herm (i.e., a bust of a god or man surmounting a pillar with a representation of male sex), the bronze head of which was a portrait of the owner of the house. The bronze head has not been discovered, but the stone pillar of the herm still stands in its place. The inscription on the front of the herm states that the owner of the house was a certain Attalos, and that he was a consul. It is understood that the aforementioned herm of Alkamenes, found in one of the shops to the south of Attalos' house, stood formerly in the neighbourhood of the oikos or near the niche and that it tumbled down from there. In fact, the south-facing side of the house had slipped down and disappeared. The bathrooms of the house, built in the Roman era, were to be found in the basement-like ground floor of the south stoa. Excavations have proved the existence of a bathroom and a pool in the basement. The most westerly of the rooms in the north of Attalos' house was the bedroom. Here at the foot of the north wall is a wide stone bench where a bed could have been spread out. The second room from the west was a sitting - room attached to the bedroom. The middle room possesses a well-preserved Roman mosaic floor and partially preserved murals of the Roman era. To protect these rooms from moisture and to keep them cool in summer and warm in winter, a second wall was constructed along the entire length of the north side of the house, and between the two walls a "peristasis", that is, a narrow air-filled corridor was formed. In the centre of the courtyard is a semicircular cistern of fairly large dimensions. There is another small cistern of semicircular shape in front of the stoa lying on the eastern side of the courtyard. Both of these date from the Roman period; on the other hand, the 5 metre - wide and 13 metre - deep well which is situated between the two reservoirs and hollowed out in the shape of a beehive is of the Hellenistic era. It is now fitted with a modern cover. Throughout that period this well provided water for the lower agora by means of a channel.

The Lower Agora. The lower agora (19) must have come into being during the enlarging of the city in the reign of Eumenes II. Not only was the upper agora situated on high ground, but it was also reserved solely for affairs of state. These factors made it necessary to construct another agora near the plain. The new market-place must have been built during the first years of Eumenes II's reign, at the beginning of the 2nd century. The lower agora is a rectangle measuring 64 × 34 metres (Pl. 37b; Fig. 34) surrounded by stoas on its four sides. These colonnades, which possessed two aisles, were of two floors, both of which were of the Doric order. On both floors four metopes occurred above every two columns. Shops took up the area in the rear aisle. Following the custom prevalent at Pergamon, the part of the south stoa overlooking the public square was two - storeyed, whereas the back part situated on the sloping land beyond the terrace boasted three floors. In the year 1901, the excavators set up a museum on the west side of the agora. Professor Boehringer has now had the museum demolished and a fine storage place put up in its stead. Many archaeological finds are housed in this depot. Murals of the late Hellenistic period have been discovered in a room in the north-west corner. The splendid head of Alexander (Pl. 25), now in the museum in Istanbul, was found buried in the earth covering these rooms. The body to which this head belongs has nevertheless not come to light, but the complete statue with the head is believed to have stood in one of the houses higher up the slope. The andesite shot now exhibited in the lower agora was found in the arsenals, as mentioned above, and placed here. A well, situated in the centre of the agora, supplied all the water needed.

As has been stated previously, the water used to come from the big well in the house of Attalos. In Byzantine times, a small church occupied the courtyard of the agora. This church, with a nave, two aisles, an apse on the east side and a courtyard on the west side,was a basilica of the Asia Minor type and was built in the fourth century A. D. A peristyle house built in the Hellenistic era and altered in Roman times lies to the west of the agora on a higher terrace, but the southern part of this has slipped down and has been totally lost. On the other hand, the walls on the north side still stand 6 to 7 metres high. The German archaeological expedition is now housed in a building occupying the courtyard of this dwelling. During recent years, peristyle houses of the Hellenistic period have been excavated on the west side of the lower agora. These houses continued to be used in Roman times after undergoing alteration, and fine bronze statuettes have been found in them. The art objects mentioned are now kept in the Pergamon Museum.

The South Gate of the City. In the reign of Eumenes II, the city walls enclosed the upper, middle and lower districts of the city. Access to the city was gained through a big gate in the western city wall. The entrance to the city was a courtyard measuring 20 × 20 metres. It was fortified on three sides by the towers marked R, K and E (Fig. 35 b). Those desirous of entering the city went through the gate M into the courtyard and passed into the city via gate N. It is understood that this unusual method of entering the city arose from the fact that there was a bend in the main road at this point. The architect managed to make this complicated entrance interesting and attractive by building a portico in the eastern part of the courtyard. As people either passed into or out of the city via the south gate, a row of elegant columns appeared before them. Of these, the five in the middle of the row were complete columns, while one on each side of these was a half-column, all the columns being octagonal. The multi-cornered small square, created by means of the towers R and K, together with the gate M, was another attractive architectural feature of Pergamon.

The Temple of Serapis (Fig. 36). The largest building in ancient Pergamon was the temple dedicated to the Egyptian gods, which was constructed of red bricks and which is known popularly as the "Red Courtyard". Formerly the lower parts of the building were surrounded by colonnades, while in the case of the upper parts the old brick structure was not visible, since it was faced with marble of various colours. The marble bands in the upper part of the building are still in place today. The temple, together with the large courtyard lying in front of it, covers an area of 260 × 100 metres. The main structure of the temple consists of a building of the basilica type with one nave, two aisles and one apse (Fig. 36). Two identical and symmetrical buildings with courtyards on their western sides and big round towers on their eastern sides are situated one to the north of the basilica, one to the south. The temple and the two towered buildings open on to a courtyard measuring 200 × 100 metres. One of the rivers of Pergamon, the Selinus, ran beneath this big courtyard along two vaulted canals, then, as it does now. The large fragments of twice life-size statues of ·Egyptian

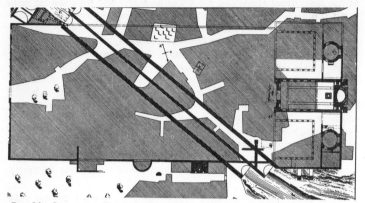

Fig. 36 – Pergamon. The Temple of Serapis. Reign of the Emperor Hadrian (A. D. 117–138).

type, which were found in the south round-towered building and which still stand there, prove that the temple was set apart for Egyptian religious practices, which were coming into fashion in the second century A. D. in the Roman world. The pools to be observed within the temple and in the two buildings with towers, and which were used for ritual bathing, i. e., for ablutions, and therefore not in accordance with Greek or Roman practices, are a further indication of the existence of a foreign religion. The statues are thought to have occupied positions as supports for the colonnades of the round-towered buildings. The statues are interesting, in that one side of each is carved as an atlant (a male figure) and the other as a caryatid (a female figure). The fact that the temple, with its array of Egyptian-type statues, faces towards the west leads one to think that it was dedicated to Serapis, the god of the underworld, and also to the associated goddess Isis and the god Harpocrates. The temple was erected in the reign of the Emperor Hadrian. During the Byzantine era, the main building was converted into a church and dedicated to St. John the Apostle.

The Roman City. The region lying between the River Selinus (the Bergama Çay) and the Asklepieion was settled in Roman times. Here on the Merak, a tributary of the Selinus, a theatre to hold 50,000 people was erected. Slightly to the south are the remains of a Roman theatre which had a seating capacity of 30,000. The imposing arch called the Viran (i. e. Ruined Gate) is the only part of this theatre still standing. Tumuli of both the Hellenistic and the Roman periods can be seen as one leaves the present-day town of Bergama. The largest of these reaches a height of 35 metres.

The Archaeological Museum. The first archaeological museum in Turkey devoted wholly to discoveries made during local excavations was set up at Bergama. A great number of the works of art found during excavation are housed here. In addition, other archaeological treasures found in the surrounding area are also exhibited in this museum. Among those worthy of mention are an archaic statue found at Pitane (present-day Çandarlı) and fine earthenware statuettes discovered at Myrina. All the works of art in the museum are well arranged and supplied with detailed labels of explanation. The town also possesses a rich Ethnographical Museum.

The Asklepieion (Asclepieum). The Asklepieion at Pergamon ranked equally in importance with the therapeutic centres of the same type at Epidauros and Kos in ancient times. According to Pausanias, the first temple of Asklepios was set up during the first half of the fourth century B. C. Excavations have also proved that the sacred precinct had existed since the fourth century, and developed during the Hellenistic period. However, the Asklepieion at Pergamon attained its most glorious heights in the second century A. D.

In Roman times, the Asklepieion was approached by a sacred way. This road was 820 metres in length. It began in the Roman city as a narrow road lined with columns, then passed by the Roman theatre and, continuing further on as a wide and magnificent road, finally reached the Asklepieion. In recent years, the whole of the second and more important sector of the sacred way has been exposed as a result of excavations under the direction of Erich Boehringer (Fig. 37). The latter sector, flanked by colonnades, is

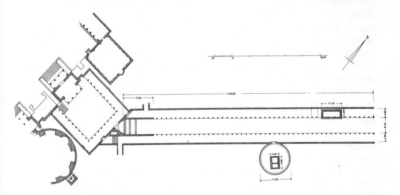

Fig. 37 – Pergamon. Via Tecta. Colonnaded street leading to the Asklepieion. Roman Imperial Age.

140 metres in length and 8.34 metres in width, or 18.14 metres in width if the areas with colonnades are also taken into account. Close to the mid-point of this colonnaded street and overlooking the south colonnade, a round building which is doubtless a sepulchral monument, has been discovered (Fig. 37). The craftsmanship exhibited in this work of art, which most probably was erected in the Augustan age, is very fine. Towards the end of this same sector of the road and situated in the north colonnade is a fountain which was built at a later date than the road. During the excavation of this

section, very beautiful statues and reliefs of the Hellenistic and Roman periods were unearthed. The most important of these is the splendid Hellenistic head (Pl. 38) mentioned above. The colonnaded road winds its way to the courtyard of the propylon (Fig. 38). The reason why the road twists in this fashion is that it has been in existence since the fourth century and, as was the case in Greek times, no attention was paid to building roads in straight lines. The courtyard, which is flanked on three sides by colonnades, is built in the Corinthian order. A propylon with four Corinthian columns stood in the west part of the entrance courtyard. The pediment which these columns supported and which now lies on the ground in the north-eastern corner of the courtyard bears an inscription to the effect that one Claudius Charax commissioned the building of the propylon. The front face of the propylon (Fig. 38) is built in the style of temple façades with a flight of steps which had persisted in Pergamon since the Hellenistic era (Pl. 32; Fig. 33). Today only two steps of the propylon are preserved.

The Asklepieion is an open space 110 × 130 metres in dimension, with stoas on three sides and various buildings on the east side (Pl. 39 a; Fig. 38). To the right of the foot of the stairs leading down from the inner gate of the propylon, was a small niche for worship which survives now only in its lower part (10). The square building next to this is the Emperor's room and was also used as a library (11). The statue of Hadrian which stood in the central niche in the east wall is now in the museum at Bergama. Hadrian was depicted naked as a deified emperor. The pedestal bears an inscription saying that the donor of this statue of the "god" Hadrian was Melitine. Formerly, there were shelves in the recesses seen in the north, east and south walls. They were used for storing manuscripts. The floor of the salon was paved with marble of various colours. The walls were decorated with coloured incrustations. There were windows above the niches. In those times, transparent marble or alabaster was used for window panes. The roof was made of wood.

The north colonnade (12) is very well-preserved (Pl. 30 a). It is built in the Ionic style. Ten of the columns nearest the library collapsed during the earthquake of A. D. 175 which caused so much damage in western Asia Minor. The new columns were of the Corinthian order. These were placed upon pedestals, since they were of insufficient height. The rear wall of the stoa was covered with a rich marble incrustation. In contrast to this, because it was necessary for the patients to be able to walk barefoot during certain rites, the floor of the stoa was made of earth just like that of the big courtyard.

The theatre in the Asklepieion (13) had seating accommodation for 3500 people (Pl. 39 b). The auditorium was semicircular in shape, as was the case in Roman theatres, and, also in accordance with Roman custom, the highest row of seats was crowned with a low gallery of the Ionic order. However, the auditorium was situated on a steep slope in the Greek manner. The first three rows below the middle row were reserved for persons of rank. The stage was three-tiered. The eastern stoa (14) was also of the Ionic order and the rear wall was covered with marble incrustations.

The central door of the stoa (15) opened on to buildings at a higher level on the west side of the courtyard. Here in 1967 the Germans uncovered a stoa in Doric style, which had two aisles and was 104 m. long and aligned from east to west. The function of the building (16) opening on to the colonnade close to the stairway is unknown. It is possible, that the fairly large room at the corner of the south and west stoas was used for conferences or meetings. The other two rooms (18, 19) at the same corner were lavatories; the smaller was reserved for women, the larger for men. In the middle of the larger room, four Corinthian columns supported the ceiling, which had apertures for ventilation and illumination. The floor was beautifully paved with marble. The men's lavatory was surrounded on all four sides by forty marble seats. The Corinthian capitals in this room are the finest of those found in the Asklepieion. In the women's lavatory, the number of seats was limited to seventeen and it was a simple room devoid of decoration.

The south stoa (20), unlike the other two stoas which were constructed on the earth itself or on rock, was built over a basement with columns. This stoa must have belonged to the Ionic order but no traces of it have been found. The basement possessed two aisles and, like other basement constructions of Hellenistic times, served as a support.

Let us now turn to those buildings in the Asklepieion which were concerned with religious worship and medical treatment. We learn of the methods of treatment at the Pergamene health centre from various inscriptions and more especially from the writings of the orator Aelius Aristeides, who stayed there for thirteen years around the middle of the second century A. D. During these years when the Pergamene Asklepieion was at the height of its glory, famous physicians such as Satyros and Galenos lived here and gave lessons. Generally speaking, various methods used in physiotherapy at the Asklepieion are still applicable today. The most important of these were water and mud baths, massage, the use of medicinal herbs and the application of ointments. In addition, the drinking of sacred water, courses of abstention from food and drink, colonic irrigation and running barefoot in cold weather were prescribed. Auto-suggestion and incubation played important roles in treatment. Judging by what we learn from the orator Aelius Aristeides, the type of treatment was determined by the patients' dreams. Probably these were induced by means of suggestion. For this purpose, specially constructed sleeping-rooms were provided (27, 28). Rites were held in the theatre described previously and the patients underwent treatment involving therapy accompanied by music.

There were three pools or fountains at the Asklepieion designed for bathing and drinking. The site of one of these (23) is at a spot opposite the theatre, close to the north stoa (Pl. 39a; Fig. 38). This marble structure is of the Roman period; the patients sat on the lower steps inside the bath and washed themselves. The water in this pool came from the sacred spring. Chemical analysis has shown this water to have radioactive properties. Very likely, the crack in the rock (24) was the site of the sacred spring. In ancient times, the water issuing from this spring was considered to have healing properties. The neighbouring round hollow is thought to be the

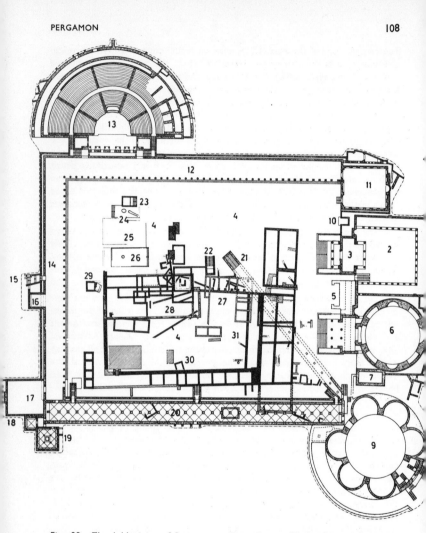

Fig. 38 – The Asklepieion of Pergamon. General view. **1)** *End of the colonnaded street (Fig. 37).* **2)** *Courtyard of the propylon.* **3)** *Propylon commissioned by Claudius Charax. Reign of the Emperor Antoninus Pius (A. D. 138–161).* **4)** *Place for religious festivities.* **5)** *Niche for worship.* **6)** *Temple of Asklepios, erected by the Consul L. Cuspius Pactumeius Rufinus, about A. D. 150. This cylindrical temple, preceded by a colonnaded entrance, was covered with a dome in the form of a half-globe measuring 23.85 m. in diameter. It was a small replica of the Pantheon, built in Rome twenty years earlier and supporting a dome 43.50 m. in diameter.* **7)** *Cistern.* **8)** *Peristyle building.* **9)** *This building, probably reserved for medical treatment, is a two-storeyed cylindrical structure 26.50 m. in diameter, with six*

apses inside and covered by a wooden roof overlaid with tiles. Second half of the second century A. D. **10)** *Niche for worship.* **11)** *The Emperor's room, which served also as a library. The naked statue of Hadrian kept in the museum at Bergama used to stand in the central niche in the east wall. Formerly there must have been shelves in the recesses seen in the north, east and south walls for storing manuscripts.* **12)** *The north colonnade, built about the middle of the second century A. D. in Ionic style. Ten of the columns nearest the library, standing on high pedestals and surmounted by Corinthian capitals, were built after the earthquake of A.D. 178.* **13)** *Roman theatre, built on a steep slope in the Greek manner, with accommodation for 3500 people.* **14)** *The eastern stoa (second century A. D.) was also in Ionic style.* **15)** *The central door of the stoa opened on to a Doric colonnade, discovered in 1967.* **16, 17)** *Rooms probably used for meetings.* **18, 19)** *Lavatories for ladies and gentlemen.* **20)** *South Stoa (second century A. D.), built over a colonnaded basement.* **21)** *Tunnel leading to the treatment building, Roman in date.* **22)** *Pool, built in Hellenistic times, with running water for drinking purposes. It was roofed like a house.* **23)** *Fountain, built in Roman times for bathing and drinking purposes. The patients sat on the lower steps inside the pool and washed themselves with radioactive water coming from the sacred spring.* **24)** *The crack seen in the rock today is very probably the site of the sacred spring.* **25, 26)** *Rectangular outlines in the rock probably show the traces of the temples of Apollo Kalliteknos, Asklepios Soter and of the goddess Hygieia, all three mentioned in written documents and built in the Hellenistic age.* **27, 28)** *Sleeping-rooms, specially constructed in Hellenistic times for incubation and auto-suggestion, which were two important methods of psychiatric treatment in Pergamon.* **29)** *Pool, probably used for mud-baths mentioned by the rhetorician Aristeides, who lived about A. D. 150 in Pergamon.* **30, 31)** *Remains of colonnades surrounding the temenos of Asklepios; Hellenistic age.*

hole dug to accommodate the roots of the sacred plane-tree mentioned by Aristeides.

The pool (22) lying to the west of the entrance to the tunnel, was a source of running water considered safe for drinking purposes. The occurrence of andesite as the building material and the excellent workmanship exhibited in the walls reveal that this structure originated in the Hellenistic era. The water coming from the sacred spring flowed into the pool through a spout fashioned in the shape of a lion's head. Water was taken from the pool in buckets. The walls of the pool rose vertically and the top was roofed over like a house, thus guaranteeing that the water remained pure. A small pool (29), referred to by the excavators as the rock-fountain, lay close to the exact centre of the west stoa (Pl. 39 a; Fig. 38). This was a pool carved out of rock. Marks seen in the rock on the four sides of the pool indicate that it also was formerly roofed over. The fact that the stone of the pool is considerably worn away shows that it was used a great deal. In the winter and spring months and the wet seasons, this and neighbouring areas were easily reduced to a muddy state. The mud-baths referred to by Aristeides are thought to have been taken in this pool.

The patients believed that the god Asklepios would restore them to good health. For this reason everything in this area was regarded as sacred. According to what can be gathered from the writings of Aristeides, the big courtyard was occupied by temples consecrated to Asklepios Soter, Apollo Kalliteknos, and the goddess Hygieia, and by a room dedicated to the cult of Telesphoros. In the rocky square to the south of the marble pool (23), rectangular outlines (24-26) big enough to have formed the foundation of each small temple are in evidence (Pl. 39a). It is reasonable to suppose that these three temples were built here in Hellenistic times and continued to be used throughout the Roman period (Fig. 38).

In all probability, the so-called incubation apartments were situated to the south of the area where these temples lay. The room indicated by the excavators on the plan by the number 27 is almost certainly of the Hellenistic period, while the front one of the group marked 28 seems to have been enlarged in late Hellenistic times for use as the "sleeping apartments". The whole area surrounded by walls and rooms was the site of the Hellenistic temenos of Asklepios. The walls marked 30 on the plan constituted part of the south stoa of the Hellenistic age; that marked 31 formed the east stoa, while the one across from the latter wall belonged to the west stoa.

The area containing the sacred pools and fountains, the temples and the sleeping - apartments was connected to the "treatment - building" by a tunnel (21). This tunnel, built in Roman times, was 80 metres long. The fact that the sleeping-apartments were connected to the house of treatment shows that they too played a part in the psychiatric cure. A tunnel such as this created a very suitable atmosphere for psychiatric treatment based on moral encouragement. Moreover, the patients were able to cool off inside the tunnel during the heat of summer.

The tunnel led to the ground floor of the house of treatment. This two-storeyed round building (9) was made rather later in the Roman period than the temple of Asklepios (6), which we shall examine later. It lay in a dip in the ground and its second floor was just above the ground level of the main courtyard. The lower floor is very well-preserved. The second and main floor of the building possessed two entrances : one on the side of the south stoa and the other directly opposite on the south-east side. The interior of the main building, which is cylindrical, is 26.5 metres in diameter. There are six apses situated round the periphery of this circular edifice. These apses are lower than the cylindrical body of the building, and the main part of the structure rises above the apses in the shape of a drum. This type of round building surrounded by apses became a model for the Byzantine age. The walls and the floor of the room with apses were covered with marble mosaics. The roof was not domed but constructed of wood overlaid with tiles.

The most important and most beautiful building to be found at the Asklepieion was the temple of Asklepios (6). L. Cuspius Pactumeius Rufinus, who was Consul in 142, had the building erected in 150 at his own expense. The west and main face of the building is modelled in the style customary at Pergamon since the Hellenistic period (Fig. 33). The fact that the part of the propylon (3) overlooking the courtyard was also decorated with a simi-lar temple façade gave the eastern side of the Asklepieion a beauty, in com-plete harmony with the Roman architectural concept. These two-staired en-trances, together with the intervening niche reserved for worship, formed, without doubt, an extremely attractive ensemble of architectural façades. The main part of the temple was cylindrical in shape and the top was covered with a dome in the form of a half-globe. There was a hole for illumination in the middle of the dome. The diameter of the dome was 23.85 metres. The walls were three metres in thickness. The interior walls of this circular building arouse a pleasant feeling of rhythmic movement, created by the device of alternating rounded and angular niches, seven in all. The floor and the walls were decorated with coloured marble mosaics.

In the centre, a statue of Asklepios occupied the niche directly opposite the entrance. The remaining recesses were also occupied, by statues of the gods of health and associated deities. The colonnaded entrance in front of the temple of Asklepios, with its cylindrical main body and half-globed dome, is a small replica of the Pantheon, built in Rome twenty years previ-ously. The dome of the Pantheon, being 43.5 metres in diameter, is twenty metres bigger than that of the temple of Asklepios. Nevertheless, the build-ing at Pergamon, displaying an extremely high quality of workmanship is an exceptional work of art. The painstaking labour manifest in the andesite blocks is proof that the art of masonry of Hellenistic times was still alive. The descendants of those Pergamene stonemasons who, three hundred years before, had fashioned the stairway entrance to the middle gymnasium with its vaults and arches still understood how to produce work of high quality in a truly artistic manner. The temple of Asklepios was Roman in form and style, but Greek and Pergamene in expression and spirit.

AEOLIS

The coastal region of western Anatolia lying between Izmir and the Bay of Edremit was known as Aeolis. Herodotus counts twelve Aeolian cities to correspond with those in Ionia. Nevertheless, the number of cities in this area must have greatly exceeded this. The most famous Aeolian cities are the following : Lesbos, Pitane, Elaea, Gryneion, Myrina, Aigai, Kyme, Neonteichos, Temnos, Larisa and Smyrna. Although the last city was founded as an Aeolian settlement, it was later inhabited by the people of Kolophon and absorbed into the Ionian League.

According to ancient sources, Aeolis was founded before Ionia by the descendants of Agamemnon. Lesbos appears to have been its most important centre. During the 7th century B. C. there was an immigration from Mytilene and especially from Methymna on this island to the opposite shores of Asia Minor. Since the inhabitants of the Aeolian cities were primarily engaged in agriculture, they did not play a large role in history. However, they were in the forefront in the fields of music and poetry. Sappho, Alkaios and Terpander, the inventor of the 7-tone scale, all came from Lesbos.

Going from north to south, the Aeolian cities which have yielded ruins and finds associated with archaeological excavation are Pitane, Myrina, Aigai, Kyme and Larisa (Buruncuk).

ÇANDARLI (PITANE)

At Pitane, vases and other small works of art from the archaic cemetery of the town, and of various dates between 625-500 B. C., have been discovered during excavations conducted by the present author. The finest and most plentiful specimens of Chian pottery yet found were unearthed on this site. Moreover, a large number of vases of orientalizing style, which were fashioned in the first half of the 6th century in western Asia Minor, have also been brought to light. The most important of these works are exhibited in the rooms devoted to vases on the top floor of the Istanbul Museum. Another fine if smaller collection is also displayed in the Izmir Museum. The works discovered during the initial exploratory excavation are now in the museum at Bergama; in addition, an archaic statue discovered before the excavations is housed in the same museum. One of the best preserved castles in Turkey is situated at Çandarlı, which is noteworthy for its beautiful bathing beaches. The castle was first built in the 13th or 14th century by Genoese knights and subsequently underwent renovations by the Turks, probably in the second half of the 15th century; this made it strong enough to withstand onslaught from weapons using gunpowder. The talus which encircles the base of the building was added at this time. The structure underwent further changes in 1814, and in 1955 it was restored according to its original style. Some fine blocks of stone taken from the city walls of the Greek period can be observed in the lower parts of some of the walls.

Myrina and Kyme. Hellenistic terracotta statuettes of great beauty, which were discovered at Myrina during excavations conducted by the Turks and the French within the last hundred years, can be seen in the Louvre and the Istanbul Museum, and a fine collection of similar works unearthed in the last few years is also on view in the museum at Bergama.

Since there are no visible remains in the ruined districts of Myrina and Kyme, only archaeologists would find it worthwhile to tour these two sites. On the other hand, the ruins at Aigai, especially those of the agora, are well - preserved. However, the climb up to Aigai is very difficult under present-day conditions.

LARISA

Field research at Larisa was begun by Swedish archaeologists in 1902 and continued as a German and Swedish joint dig from 1932 until its termination in 1934. The excavations carried out at Larisa are among the most fruitful field researches undertaken in western Anatolia. Architectural fragments of the archaic period discovered here have been sent to the Izmir Museum, while the terracotta revetments and pottery were conveyed to the Istanbul Museum.

It is very surprising that no Hellenic finds have been recovered at Larisa of a date earlier than the 7th century B. C. Especially now, when protogeometric pottery is being discovered in profusion at such places as Izmir and Foça, one is right to share the opinion of John Cook who believes that ancient Larisa must have been situated not here but elsewhere. In spite of this, the results of the discoveries pertaining to the archaic period are, as has been stated above, of great importance. The finds at Larisa are the most distinguished examples of the architecture of Aeolis in the 6th, 5th and 4th centuries, known at the present time. After the unparalleled beauty of the Bayraklı walls (i.e. those of ancient Izmir), which were built in the 7th and 6th centuries, we observe the continuation of the same tradition at Larisa.

Although grass covers the remains of buildings on the Larisa hill, those who climb it will have the opportunity of seeing some fine wall structures. The state of the Larisa acropolis as it was in 330 B. C. is shown on the accompanying plan (Fig. 39). Close examination reveals that the palace building in the north is a peristyle house with megarons on two sides. Similar peristyle dwellings exist at Priene (Fig. 74), but the pattern at Larisa is a continuation of the system that began in Troy II (Fig. 15) and survived at Tiryns and Gordion (Fig. 90), in which the megarons are arranged in rows, side by side. Here in a city where tyrannic rule prevailed, tradition had a stronger hold. On the plan, we can recognize a second peristyle house of smaller dimensions. Here again we observe a megaron complex. This second peristyle house, with two rooms in the rear like the megaron to the north, was constructed

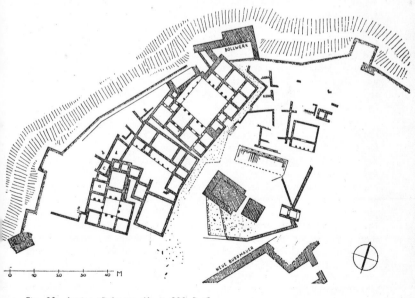

Fig. 39 – Larisa. Palaces. About 330 B. C.

in 500 B. C. Later, in about 450, three oikoi each with two columns, were added, one on each of the three sides, and thus a peristyle house came into existence. The same peristyle dwelling continued to be used as it was up to 330, except that, as can be seen from the plan, the oikos on the west side (marked "a" on the plan) was converted into a megaron, while the oikoi on the south and east sides were left in their original condition. It is interesting to observe that, in the palaces at Pergamon, megaron-type rooms (Fig. 26) have completely disappeared, and their place is taken by sunnier and better ventilated rooms, which are not so deep.

IONIA

The central part of the western Anatolian coastal region lying between the bays of Izmir and Bargylia, including the off-shore islands of Samos and Chios, forms the area known as Ionia. However, this term is usually employed to embrace a larger region of west Anatolia and the islands in the vicinity. The names of the twelve cities given by Herodotus are these : in the south, Miletos, Myus and Priene; in the central region, Ephesus, Kolophon, Teos and Lebedos; in the north, Erythrai, Klazomenai, Phokaia and the islands of Samos and Chios.

From the fact that the chief deity among the majority of the Ionian cities was Athena, we conclude that the various Hellenic centres on the coast of Asia Minor, arising from immigration to Ionia, were sponsored by Athens. Athena was revered as the chief goddess in the cities of Miletos, Priene, Phokaia and Klazomenai. We have recently discovered that Athena was also considered the most important deity in the cities of Erythrai and ancient Smyrna. It is now also clear, from the fact that the protogeometric and the geometric pottery of Bayraklı (ancient İzmir) resembles the type found in Athens, that there were close links between these cities. In this way, the recorded belief that the Ionian immigration was led by Neleus, the son of the legendary King Kodros of Athens, accompanied by some of his other children, has been confirmed.

Evidently the Ionian immigration was caused by the Dorian incursions which swept down the Greek peninsula. For this reason, the first Hellenic settlement in Asia Minor must have begun in the 10th century B. C. Indeed, the protogeometric pottery discovered during excavations at Bayraklı supports this date.

The twelve Ionian cities, including ancient İzmir, formed a federation called the Panionion, which doubtless had political objectives. Seeing that Smyrna joined the federation not later than the beginning of the 8th century B. C., the Panionion cannot have been founded later than the 9th century. The Panionion met in the sacred precinct associated with Poseidon Helikonios, in the locality of Güzel Çamlı, at the foot of Mt. Mykale. During his excavations in the district in 1957-8, G. Kleiner brought to light an edifice which must have been an altar. Kleiner proved that the altar he discovered dates from the end of the 6th century B. C. The structure, built in the form of a theatre with eleven steps and carved out of rock, is believed to have been the meeting house for the Ionian city delegates. From the very first day the Panionion was founded, a centralized organization was created which ensured the development of the Ionian cities. Owing to this federation, the Ionians not only created one of the most brilliant cultures in the history of the world but also, by ensuring their political unity, extended their area of settlement and their sphere of influence. The first step in the expansion of Ionia was the settlement of Smyrna by the people of Kolophon and Phokaia by the inhabitants of Teos and Klazomenai. This outward-spreading movement led to even greater expansion when, at the beginning of the 7th century, the Ionians founded such cities as Kyzikos, Lampsakos and Abydos in the Propontis (the area around the sea of Marmara). From the second half of the 7th century on, it took the form of large-scale colonial activity around the Black Sea and the Mediterranean.

As described in Part One, the most glorious period of the Ionian cities commenced in the second half of the 7th century, after the establishment of the colonies; but the golden age did not reach its peak until 600-545 B. C. In this period, the cultural leadership of the ancient world shifted from the Near East to the Ionian centres. The Ionia of this period led the world not only in the exact sciences and philosophy but also in the architectural and sculptural arts.

After the Achaemenid King Kyros defeated Kroisos, the king of Lydia, the Persian commander Harpagos seized many of the cities in western Asia Minor (545-540 B. C.). Following this, only one Ionian city-state remained independent in the real sense of the word; this was Samos, ruled by the tyrant Polycrates. In 522, Polycrates was killed, after being ambushed by the Persian governor Oroites at Magnesia ad Maeandrum. From then on, leadership passed from Samos into the hands of Miletos, a partly independent state. However, the Ionians were no longer able to bear a system of government founded on the harshness of the Persians and enforced by tyrants, and in 499, Miletos led them in a rebellion which resulted in the destruction of Sardis. Not long after, however, the Persians first retaliated by annihilating the Ionian navy, consisting of 353 ships, off the small island of Lade. At that time this was west of the city of Miletos, though now it is only a hummock surrounded by the clay soil brought down by the River Maeander. Then, in 494, they set fire to the city of Miletos and reduced it to ashes. The fact that Athens and Eretria had joined forces with the Ionians in their attack on Sardis caused the Persians to retaliate by destroying the Athenian acropolis in 480. Nevertheless, in the following year, 479, when they had gained their final victory at Plataea, the forces from the Greek homeland and the Ionians defeated the remaining Persian fleet at Mykale. Thus the Ionian cities regained their freedom. Thanks to the Delian League, which was formed in the same year, the whole of western Asia Minor, being allied to Athens, maintained its independence until 412. For the next century, until the time of Alexander the Great, the Ionian cities were mostly under Persian rule or control. At the beginning of the Hellenistic period, western Asia Minor became, for the second time, a world-leading cultural centre, and saw the emergence of densely populated wealthy cities as Ephesus, Pergamon and Smyrna, developed by the organized planning efforts of Antigonos and Lysimachos. In Roman times, Ionia belonged to the province Asia. Throughout this era too, the Ionian cities experienced glorious days and, with the other cultural centres of Asia Minor, were instrumental in preparing for the dawn of the Christian faith and the birth of Byzantine art.

FOÇA (PHOKAIA)

This city was the most northerly of the Ionian settlements and is situated in the Aeolian region. According to ancient writers, the Phokaians, directed from Athens, set up their first settlement on land given by the people of Cyme. The great quantity of grey pottery found during the excavations in Phokaia by the present author indicates that, like the Cymaeans, these first inhabitants were Aeolians. According to Pausanias (VII, 3, 8), Ionians later came to Phokaia from Teos and Erythrai and settled there. The protogeometric pottery discovered during excavations shows that the Ionians had probably lived at Phokaia at least since the end of the 9th century. From this we can deduce that the city of Phokaia was accepted into the Panionion after the Ionians settled in the area, at this early date.

The Phokaians were famed as navigators. Instead of big-hulled cargo boats, they employed 50-oared vessels capable of achieving great speed and carrying 500 passengers. Phokaian merchants took part in the flourishing of Ionian trade with Naukratis in Egypt and, in association with Miletos, they set up Lampsakos, at the northern entrance to the Dardanelles, and Amisos (Samsun) on the Black Sea. However, Phokaia actually established its major colonies in the western Mediterranean. The most important of these cities were Elea (Velia) on the western coast of Lucania in Southern Italy, Alalia in Corsica, Massalia (Marseilles) in France and Emporion (Ampurias) in Spain. Nice (Nicaea - Nizza) and Antibes (Antipolis) in the south of France were the "grandchildren" of Phokaia because they were set up by Marseilles. Thus Phokaia became the metropolis for some European cities. The city of Elea (Velia), founded by the Phokaians in southern Italy, produced a new wave of philosophy, with thinkers such as Parmenides and Zeno, and it became a cultural centre where these two important philosophers lectured.

As Herodotus relates, Phokaia possessed a very fine city wall, but this has completely disappeared. The building of the wall, which was erected to ward off the Persians, was financed by King Argonthonius of Tartessos in Andalusia, who was a great friend of the Phokaian traders. In 546 B. C., however, the Persians captured Sardis and, within a short time, devastated the majority of the cities in western Asia Minor, Phokaia among them. According to Herodotos (I 62) Harpagos, the Persian commander seized these cities by means of a mound of earth which he had piled up in front of the city wall. While the city was under siege, and after it had fallen to the Persians, many of the Phokaians emigrated to their Mediterranean colonies, but some of them are understood to have returned. In spite of this, there was no revival of the golden age experienced in Phokaia during the first half of the 6th century. In fact, the Phokaians were able to send only three ships to participate in the Battle of Lade in 494. Nevertheless, owing to their great skill in naval strategy, the command of the entire Hellenic fleet was given to Dionysius of Phokaia.

Phokaia was a member of the Delian League during the 5th century and paid tribute at the rate of two talents, but in 412 Phokaia rebelled and left the league. During the Hellenistic period, it was ruled first by the Seleucids and then by the Attalids. In 132 B. C., although it participated in Aristonikos' uprising against the Romans, Phokaia was saved from destruction with the help of Massalia, founded long before by the Phokaians. Pompey gave Phokaia its independence. In the early Christian era, the city became the centre of a diocese. In A. D. 1275, the Genoese, who were mining alum there, fortified the town with a castle and used it as a base for their operations. Akdes Nimet Kurat has stated that Foça (Phokaia) was one of the first coastal towns to fall into Turkish hands in western Anatolia, but the town did not definitely belong to the Turks until 1455.

The Phokaians were famous not only for their talent as mariners, traders and colonists, but also for their coinage made of electrum (an alloy of gold and silver), which was much in demand on the market. The town was also noted for its purple dye. Telephanes of Phokaia was a famous sculptor who worked at the command of the Persian Kings Darius and Xerxes in the 5th century. Theodoros of Phokaia wrote after Vitruvius (7 praef. 12) on Tholos at Delphoi and was for that reason probably the builder of it (Beginning of the fourth century B.C.).

Throughout history, Phokaia has been situated on a peninsula. However, the surrounding coastland has also been the scene of a settlement since the archaic period. The French archaeologist Felix Sartiaux carried out field research and initial excavations at Phokaia in 1913 and 1920. The present author also explored the archaic layer of the site during his excavations, carried out from 1951-55.

In ancient times there was a temple on the highest point of a rocky platform at the end of the peninsula at Foça, where the secondary school now stands. During the excavations, the half-finished framework of the secondary school building, in its abandoned state of construction, resembled, the ruins of an old temple. This impression was confirmed when the trenches which were opened up around the school during our investigations yielded an abundance of archaic architectural fragments. There is a strong possibility that the pieces of bases, columns, capitals and other upper structures found, were once part of the temple of Athena mentioned by Xenophon (Hellenica I 3,1) and Pausanias (II 31,6; VII 5, 4). This is indeed possible as the aforementioned site is in the most beautiful and prominent area of the peninsula, and as Athena was the principal deity worshipped at Phokaia, as was the case in many Hellenic settlements in western Asia Minor. Constructed of fine white porous stone, the building seems to have been erected in the second quarter of the 6th century B. C. and to have been restored approximately towards the end of the same century, after its destruction by the Persians. The architectural remains which have been recovered are housed in the Izmir Museum. Yet another large capital, adorned with palm leaves and probably once belonging to the temple, now stands in the garden of the school. Monochrome ware and protogeometric and geometric pottery, together with black-figured Greek vase fragments of the 6th century, were discovered in the exploratory trenches opened up on the peninsula, and these will shortly be on display in the Izmir Museum.

The rock monument rising to the north of the asphalt road, seven kilometres east of Foça, is worthy of special mention (Fig. 40). This work, which is 4.5 metres high, is connected with indigenous Anatolian tradition. The monument was not built as a separate edifice but was carved out of the rock, like the tombs found in Lycia, Lydia and Phrygia (Pls. 4, 5). The pattern found on the front entrance also appears on Lydian works in the immediate vicinity. On the other hand, the monument follows the Lycian custom of having two storeys, with the upper built in the form of a sarcophagus (Pl. 78 b). In contrast to the archaic Lycian custom, the burial chamber was on the ground floor. However, the architectural form of the building perpetuates ancient Lycian tradition. The presence of a stepped part between the two floors is indicative of Achaemenid influence. This building must have been erected in memory of a minor king. Consequently, such a princely monument can only have been built during a time when non-democratic Persian rulers dominated the region. Tyrants were living close by at Larisa during the 5th and 4th centuries. The Phokaian monument may have been that of a tyrant who ruled a small area in the neighbourhood in the 4th century B. C.

The tomb bearing the name of "Şeytan Hamamı" (the Devil's Baths), found in Foça itself, is carved out of rock like some of the Lydian tombs. The Greek sherds that the present author has found in this grave may be dated to the end of the 4th century, and confirm the date suggested for the tomb lying near Foça.

Fig. 40 – Rock-cut tomb near Foça (Phokaia), in Lycian and Lydian tradition, with Persian influence. Fourth century B. C.

SMYRNA

Ancient İzmir (Bayraklı). The investigation of East Greek civilization on a stratigraphical basis started with the excavations at Bayraklı. The first diggings between 1948 and 1951 were undertaken jointly by Ankara University and the British School of Archaeology at Athens, under the direction of John Cook and the author of this book. They were recommenced in 1966 by the latter under the auspices of the Turkish Historical Society and the General Directorate of Turkish Museums, as well as of the Universities of Ege and Ankara.

New information was gained concerning the history of the old city of İzmir, as a result of the joint expedition. The earliest settlement in İzmir was founded in the first half of the 3rd millennium B. C. at present-day Bayraklı, on the city mound where the vineyards managed by the Ministry of State Monopolies are situated. In antiquity the plain of Bornova was covered by the sea and the above-mentioned city mound seen there today was a small peninsula on the edge of the Bay of İzmir. The first comers, as was revealed by the excavations, built their houses on the rock; their settlement is contemporary with Troy I and II. Since the lowest layers of the hill have so far been little explored, nothing definite is known about the sequence of its periods. However, we do know that the 2nd millennium strata of Bayraklı were contemporary with the Troy VI and Hittite civilizations, and that a culture existed there which had close links with these. As a matter of fact, two important Hittite monuments, namely, the Tudhaliya relief at Kemal Paşa and the relief of a mother-goddess at Manisa, both testify to this relationship (Pl. 41 a, b).

The most important result of the Bayraklı excavations is the fact that a great quantity of protogeometric pottery has been found which shows that the first Hellenic settlement was founded in the 10th century B.C., as far as we know at present. The one-roomed building made of sun-dried brick (Pl. 41 c), which was brought to light at Bayraklı, is the oldest and best preserved house of its period. The houses found in the later strata of the 9th, 8th and 7th centuries B. C. are also the best preserved and most exactly dated dwellings of the Hellenic civilization in those centuries. The megaron, built in the 7th century and restored in the 6th, is a unique example of this type of house dating from the archaic period.

The temple dating from the end of the 7th century, which is being unearthed at Bayraklı, is the earliest and finest religious building of the eastern Greek world in Asia Minor (Pl. 42 b). According to the inscription on a bronze bar (probably a balance) found during recent excavations, the temple was dedicated to the goddess Athena. The capitals and column-bases are the oldest and most beautiful in the Hellenic world that are known to us at the present time (Pl. 42 a). In the new excavations, these capitals and bases were recovered in dozens of fragments (Fig. 41).

The symbol of the ancient city of İzmir was a lion's head. Today, in the British Museum, we can see a lion's head on a coin which was minted at the beginning of the 6th century B. C. (Pl. 43 a). Among the finds made during the field research of 1967 are fragments of four big lions' heads made of

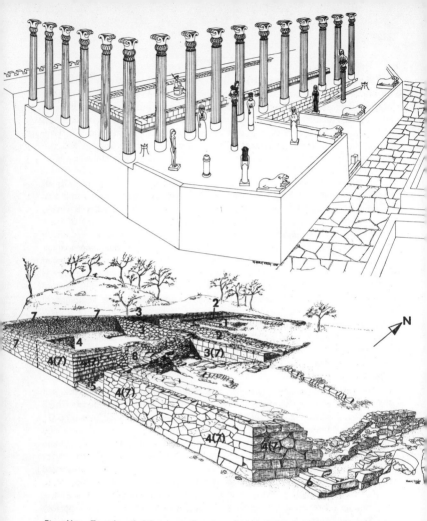

Fig. 41a – Temple of Athena at Smyrna. Archaic period (580 B. C.). Graphic reconstruction. The street and the structures along its southern side date back to the seventh century B. C. Judging from several stone blocks found in situ (now covered again) a few meters to the west of the main entrance, the street was paved.

Fig. 41b – Remains of the Temple of Athena at Smyrna after excavations. **1)** Cella wall of the temple in subgeometric period (ca. 650 B. C.). **2)** Podium wall of the Subgeometric Temple. **3)** Podium wall of the temple in the Orientalising period (625-600 B. C.). **4) (7)** Temenos walls in the Orientalising period. They were built soon after the construction of the podium walls **(3)** of the Orientalising structure. **5)** Main entrance. **6)** Side entrance. The Orientalising Temple and its temenos were destroyed by Alyattes (ca. 600 B. C.). After the Lydian *destruction, the Smyrnaians restored the temple and enlarged the temenos (ca. 580 B. C.). 7) The western wall and the western portion of the south-western wall of the temenos were added, while all the other walls of the temenos [4 (7)] as well as the main and side entrances (5, 6) were largely restored. The lower parts of these walls belong to the Orientalising structure. The half eastern portion of the southern podium wall of the Orientalising Temple [3 (7)] was completely restored in this archaic period. 8) The cross wall in the corridor was built in 545 B. C. against the Persians to block the entrance to the temple. However, the Persians completely destroyed the sanctuary. The temenos walls are restored with the help of the General Directorate of Antiquities and Museums in order to consolidate the ruins. The modern restoration work can easily be distinguished from the original constructions.*

stone, which may be assumed to have adorned the walls of temenos.

King Alyattes of Lydia captured ancient Izmir in 600 B. C. and utterly destroyed the temple and the houses. He drove the people of Izmir out of the city and they were forced to live in villages. Nevertheless, the next ten or twenty years witnessed a gradual return to the city; the devastated houses were repaired and new buildings were erected. In spite of this, however, Izmir was an insignificant city during the 5th and 4th centuries. Not long after, this site, which had been inhabited for three thousand years, was finally abandoned.

Izmir in Hellenistic and Roman Times. After Alexander the Great had conquered the East, the Greek world attained great prosperity. Cities began to grow larger. At this time, Alexandria, Rhodes, Pergamon and Ephesus achieved populations of over 100,000. Smyrna also had to develop. Only a few thousand people could be accommodated within the walls of ancient Izmir, which was situated on a small city mound. For this reason, a new, larger city was founded on the slopes of Mt. Pagos. This new settlement gained legendary fame. According to Pausanias, Alexander the Great went hunting one day on Mt. Pagos and afterwards fell asleep under a plane tree, which grew in front of the temple of the two Nemeses, situated near this spot. The goddesses appeared to him in a dream and told him to set up a new city there and have the inhabitants of the old city of Izmir move to it. Thereupon, the people of Smyrna consulted the oracle of Apollo at Klaros, as was customary when setting up a town, to inquire if the time was propitious. The answer they got was this : "Thrice and four times happy will those men be, who are going to inhabit Pagos beyond the sacred Meles". This legend was later depicted on coins of the time of Marcus Aurelius, Gordianus and Philippus Arabs. The coin shown in Plate 46 a dates from the time of the Roman Emperor Philippus Arabs (A. D. 244-249), and is in the von Aulock collection in Istanbul. The picture on the coin shows Alexander sleeping under the plane tree, and the two Nemeses.

Strabo the historian records that Smyrna was the finest Ionian city of his time, i.e., the turn of the 1st century B. C. At that time, a small part of the city was located on the city mound, but the greater part was centred around the harbour on flat land. The temple of the Mother Goddess and the gymnasium were also to be found on this level tract of land. The streets were straight and all perfectly paved with large stones. The orator Aelius Aristeides too, who came from Izmir, mentions the straightness and the well-paved state of the roads. He also states that the two main city thoroughfares, the Sacred Way and the Golden Road, ran east - west, and that the city was therefore cooled by the wind from the sea. When Eşref Paşa Road was being widened thirty years ago, an old road entering it at a slight angle was unearthed. It was recorded as being a well-paved road, 10 metres in width, with a roofed-over pavement for pedestrians along the side near the mountain. This road also ran east-west. The stretch of the old road was possibly a part of the Sacred Way. Strabo also mentions that a stoa called the Homereion (probably in the shape of a peristyle house) existed in Izmir. Within this house, as in a heroon, a statue of the deified Homer stood and a shrine was dedicated to his worship.

With the passing of time, the buildings of the Roman period that were constructed in Izmir disappeared from the scene. Nothing remains either of the theatre that formerly stood on the north-west slope of Mt. Pagos, or of the stadium on the west. The site of a silo, built by Hadrian, lay near the harbour. From this we can deduce that the commercial agora was situated close to the docks. However, it has not been possible to determine the exact site of this commercial market place. On the other hand, the state agora is very well-preserved (Pl. 46 b; Fig. 42). A large part of this fine con-

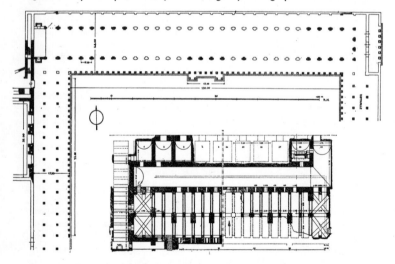

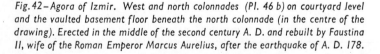

Fig. 42 – Agora of Izmir. West and north colonnades (Pl. 46 b) on courtyard level and the vaulted basement floor beneath the north colonnade (in the centre of the drawing). Erected in the middle of the second century A. D. and rebuilt by Faustina II, wife of the Roman Emperor Marcus Aurelius, after the earthquake of A. D. 178.

struction was excavated from 1932-1941 by Rudolf Naumann and Salahattin Kantar for the Turkish Historical Society and the General Directorate of Museums. The agora possesses a courtyard measuring 120 metres along one side and at least 80 metres along the other (Fig. 42). There was a stoa on the east side and another on the west; these were 17.5 metres in width and had two storeys, each of which was divided into three, longitudinally, by two rows of columns. On the north side there was a similar two-storeyed colonnade, consisting of a nave and two aisles, measuring 28 metres in width. The main stoa of the agora was called a "basilica". There is also a magnificent vaulted basement beneath the north colonnade, which is still in a splendid state of preservation to this day. The north aisle in the basement was composed of shops, which must have opened on to a street existing in Roman times. Court cases were heard in an exedra situated in the western part of the north colonnade. The west stoa was excavated for a length of 72 metres, and the east stoa for a length of 35 metres. The stoa on the south side, which has not so far been excavated, must also have consisted of two storeys with a nave and two aisles.

A severe earthquake occurred at Smyrna in A. D. 178 and the city is known to have been reconstructed with help from Marcus Aurelius. This information is confirmed by a portrait of Marcus Aurelius' wife, Faustina II, which still exists over an arch of the west colonnade. From this, we learn that the west colonnade was restored immediately after 178. Basing his conclusions on stylistic observations, Rudolf Naumann fixed the date of construction of the north stoa at the end of the 2nd century A. D.

The orator Aelius Aristeides of Smyrna relates that, in about the year 150 B. C., an altar to the god Zeus occupied a central position in the agora. High reliefs depicting a large group of gods have been recovered during the excavations; possibly they were connected with the altar. In these reliefs, Demeter is shown standing next to Poseidon (Pl. 49). The two high reliefs together constitute one of the best preserved and most beautiful specimens of Roman sculpture that has come to light in Anatolia (Pls. 16 b, 49-51). Demeter was the goddess of the harvest and the earth, while Poseidon held dominion over the sea. It is no accident that these two deities are found side by side among the other gods in the center of the agora. It may well be that the Smyrnaians of those days, by representing these two deities side by side wished to illustrate that their city dominated both the land and maritime commerce of their time

The Izmir Archaeological Museums. There are two well-stocked museums in Izmir : one near Basmahane and the other in the Fair. Until the outbreak of the Second World War, all the works of art found in western Anatolia were collected together in the first-mentioned museum, which was founded in 1927. In addition, many of the finds made during the excavations conducted over the last twenty years in western Anatolia are housed in this and in the newer museum at the Fair. Among these may be mentioned works of art from excavations carried out at Bayraklı, Foça, Çandarlı, Erythrai, Klaros, Labranda and Iasos.

One of the most important finds made in recent years is an archaic statue of a woman, recovered in Erythrai during excavations undertaken by the present author, together with H. Gültekin and C. Bayburtluoğlu. This statue, the head of which is missing, shows the influence of the Samian style of sculpture and was carved about 560 B.C. A ḥead found at Keramos dates from the archaic period, somewhere between 540 and 530 B. C. (Pl. 44). In the garden of the old museum at Basmahane stands a very attractive pair of statues, though the heads are missing. The grace inherent in the poses and movements, and the harmonious arrangement achieved in the composition of the garment folds exhibit an impressive Hellenistic interpretation (Pl. 45). A head of a young girl wearing a veil and showing a rather sorrowful expression on her idealized features, was discovered by chance in Izmir. This work (Pls. 47 and 48 b) is a very successful example of Roman sculpture produced in the 2nd century A. D. Plate 48a shows the head of a fine statue, representing a hunter, discovered in the Vedius gymnasium at Ephesus (p. 154). This statue, characterized by its bouffant "baroque" hairstyle, was carved in the second half of the 2nd century A. D. by an Ephesian sculptor. The head of another statue of a young woman (Pl. 48 c, d) is a 2nd century A. D. copy, of an original work, created in the 5th century B. C. and known as Aspasia.

Two portrait statues found at Ephesus may be considered among the most important works in the Izmir Museum. One of these represents a Sophist (Pl. 53); the other is a likeness of Flavius Damianus (Pl. 52). The former was found in the Vedius gymnasium at Ephesus (Fig. 55). It dates from the time of the Emperor Septimius Severus (A. D. 193-211). We recognize in this statue a typical intellectual of the time. The second statue represents Flavius Damianus, who was a man of means and commissioned the building of the palaestra, or wrestling school, in the east gymnasium. The ring which he wears on the index finger of his left hand signifies that he was a member of the equesterian order, and his diadem, adorned with sculptured busts tells us that he was an imperial priest as well. This statue belongs also to the period of Septimius Severus (see Inan-Rosenbaum, Roman and Early Byzantine Portrait Sculpture, pp. 127-128).

SARDIS

Sardis was the capital of the ancient Kingdom of Lydia. Gyges (680-652), the first man to make his mark in Lydian history, is mentioned in the annals of the Assyrian King Assurbanipal. The kingdom was subsequently ruled by Ardys (651-625), Sadyattes (625-610), Alyattes (609-560) and Kroisos (560-546). Sardis came under the sovereignty of Persia, following its capture by Cyrus in 546 B. C. The Persians transformed the city into the major stronghold of their western empire. The main Royal Road began at Susa and terminated at Sardis.

Within a century, Lydia had become the most powerful state in Asia Minor, and was to remain so for a long period. The Lydians won undying fame in the economic and commercial fields, through their invention of minted coinage at the end of the 7th century. After Alexander seized the city in 334 B. C., it became completely Greek in character, under the control of the Seleucids. During the period 180-133 B. C., Sardis first fell under the sway of the Kingdom of Pergamon and then under that of the Roman Empire. Sardis, which had been a very glorious Lydian centre in the 7th and 6th centuries B. C., also passed through an equally splendid period in the 3rd, 2nd and 1st centuries B. C. Like many other towns in Asia Minor during the Roman era, it became noted for its architecture and prosperity as it developed. In Byzantine times, Sardis became the centre of a diocese and in the 14th century, it was captured by the Turks.

From 1910-1914, fieldwork was carried out by an expedition formed mainly of members of Princeton University and, as a result, the temple of Artemis (13) and more than 1,000 Lydian tombs were excavated (Fig. 43). The works of art, dating from the 6th century B. C., that were brought to light at that time are now kept in the Metropolitan Museum in New York. Since 1958, excavations have been continued, under the direction of G. M. A. Hanfmann, on behalf of the American School of Oriental Research and Harvard and Cornell Universities. Some of the works now being recovered

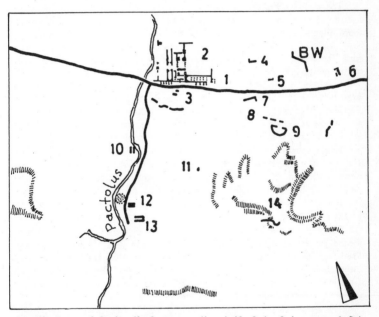

Fig. 43 – Ruins of Sardis. 1) Synagogue (1st. half of the 3rd century A. D.). 2) Gymnasium (beginning of the 3rd century A. D.). 3) House of Bronzes (ca. A. D. 550). 4) Roman Building. 5) Byzantine Church. 6) Roman and Byzantine Baths. 7) Roman Building. 8) Roman Stadium. 9) Theatre, built in Hellenistic times, altered in the Roman period. 10) Pactolus Cliff, with remains of Roman and Byzantine houses. 11) "Pyramid" tomb; remains dating from the Persian period 12) Excavation House. 13) Temple of Artemis. 14) Acropolis.

have been sent to the Manisa museum, while others remain in the depot on the excavation site at Sardis. The most important architectural works to be discovered were the synagogue (1) and the gymnasium (2), both of which lie just north of the Izmir-Ankara highway (Fig. 43). The synagogue, built in the 3rd century A. D., is a building of unequalled splendour, lying parallel to the east-west road. The gymnasium (2) is a huge construction, located next to the synagogue, immediately north of the asphalt road. The large area adjoining the synagogue on the north is the palaestra of the gymnasium. From what can be discerned of the remains of inscriptions that have been recovered, the ornate east-facing front of the gymnasium was constructed at the beginning of the 3rd century A. D., in the time of Geta and Caracalla. The members of the archaeological expedition are successfully carrying out one of the major restoration programmes in Turkey, in connection with the excavations at the gymnasium. Thanks to their efforts, two magnificent Anatolian buildings of antiquity are slowly rising once again in their former state.

The main road of the city passed along the south side of the gymnasium and the synagogue. It was paved with slabs of marble, and arcades with shops lined it on both sides. The colonnades on the south side of this marble road, built in the 4th century A. D., now lie beneath the modern asphalt road. The shops on the north side of the street and those along the south side of the gymnasium and the synagogue are of the Byzantine period.

South of the asphalt highway and opposite the gymnasium stands a large building (3) called the House of Bronzes by the American expedition (Fig. 43). Since many bronze works of a religious nature have been found within this as yet only partially-excavated house, built about A. D. 550, the excavators have concluded that it was inhabited by a high-ranking priest.

To the south-west, beyond the House of Bronzes is a large trench, which is known as the Lydian Trench, opened up by the American archaeologists. Here lie the remains of the Lydian market place, spanning perhaps the centuries from about 700 to 300 B. C. The walls are now reduced to mere rubble, but the area has yielded an abundance of ancient pottery. Small shops and a large building on the north-west corner of the house have been identified.

South of the highway and just below the acropolis on the north is a long arched structure which constitutes the northern side of the stadium (8). The southern flank was built on a natural slope, while the eastern end of the stadium lies at the foot of the ancient theatre (9). The latter, which had a seating capacity of 20,000, was erected in the 3rd century B. C. and later underwent restoration in Roman times.

The extensive substructures of a very long edifice, probably connected with the Roman civic centre, adjoin the highway on the south (7), and north of this road lie the remains of a Byzantine church (5), incorporating fragments dating from the Roman era. The ruins of a Roman building (4) can be observed north-west of the church. Further east, along the north side of the highway, we come to partly-excavated baths of Roman and Byzantine origin (6). Remnants of Byzantine walls (BW) occur north of the gymnasium and in areas north of 5 and 6, as indicated on the plan.

Other remains are encountered to the south, along the River Pactolus on the way to the temple of Artemis. On the right, i.e., on the west bank, rises the Pactolus cliff (10), on top of which appear walls of a Roman or Byzantine house dating from the 4th or 5th century A. D. Walls of Lydian structures, dating from the period between the 8th and 6th centuries B. C., lie at the bottom of a deep pit excavated by the river. After passing the village houses, the road dips to cross a ravine. To the left, half way up the southern side of the gorge, at a height of some 300 m., stand the remains of a stepped structure, the "Pyramid Tomb" (11). As pointed out by G.M.A. Hanfmann, these remains may belong to the funerary monument of Abradates, a noble of Susa, and his wife Pantheia. The ancient historian Xenophon relates that Abradates died fighting for the Persians and that his wife committed suicide over his body; thereupon King Cyrus had this sepulchre erected high up on a hill overlooking the Pactolus. The expedition camp (12), the temple of Artemis (13) and the acropolis (14) lie in an area at the end of the road.

The Temple of Artemis. One of the buildings at Sardis that have survived to the present day in a good state of preservation is the temple of Artemis. The ruins of this beautiful temple, set between the ridge of Mt. Tmolos and the acropolis of the capital of ancient Lydia, constitute some of the most attractive remains of antiquity (Pl. 54).

The Altar of Artemis. The original temple of Artemis at Sardis was built in 300 B. C., after Alexander the Great had converted the city to the Greek way of life (Fig. 44). As Gruben states, an altar to Artemis had existed in this area since the end of the 5th century. The remains of a red sandstone altar, measuring 21×11 m., referred to by the first American expedition as the Lydian Building, still stand on the original site, adjoining the temple on the west (Fig. 44-46). As will be understood from the alignment of the steps, the altar faced west. For this reason, when the first Artemis temple was constructed, it faced in the same direction, since it was attached to this sandstone altar. From the fact that the temples of Artemis at Ephesus and Magnesia ad Maeandrum also look towards the west, we may surmise that they were connected with an ancient Anatolian religious cult. Gruben suggests that the Artemis altar, in front of which Cyrus and Orontas became reconciled, according to Xenophon (Anabasis I, 6, 7), was actually this structure of red sandstone. This is plausible. Yet the fact that the reconciliation of two Persians took place before this altar makes it clear that not only was the Greek goddess Artemis worshipped here but also an indigenous goddess, doubtless Kybele. As a matter of fact, the altars sacred to Kybele in the so-called Midas-city and at Kalehisar near Alaca Höyük, like the Artemis altar at Sardis are also, approached by steps and associated with an open-air cult.

The First Phase. In the light of new discoveries made as a result of his close investigation of the building, G. Gruben recently proved in precise detail that the Artemis temple passed through three phases (Fig. 44-46). The first building, measuring 23.00×67.52 m., was (in my opinion) probably conceived as a dipteros, but the construction of the peristasis with two

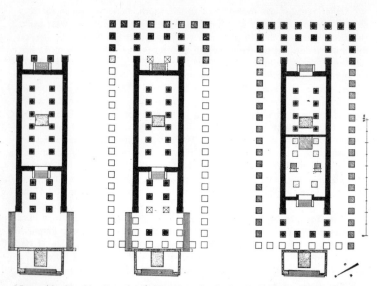

Figs. 44, 45, 46 – Temple of Artemis at Sardis (ground plans after G. Gruben).
Fig. 44 – First Building Phase (ca. 300 B. C.). West-facing Ionic temple, 23.00 ×
67.52 m. in area; traditional archaic elongated cella; square pronaos and narrow
opisthodomos, following the principles of the architect Pytheos. Originally intended
as a dipteros, a plan that was not realized. An Ionic capital from the first building
phase is now in the Metropolitan Museum in New York; two others are to be found
in the ruins (Pl. 56 a). West of the naos is the 21 × 11 m. altar of Artemis (the
so-called "Lydian Building"), made of red sandstone, with a flight of steps on the
west face. During the century preceding the erection of the temple, this altar
constituted the only place of worship dedicated to the goddess Artemis.

Fig. 45 – Second Building Phase (175–150 B. C.). In the second quarter of the
2nd century B. C., work was resumed for the completion of the temple as a pseudo-
dipteral amphiprostylos, though it was originally planned as a dipteros. As the plan
shows, however, only part of the project was realized. The completed portions
are indicated in black; those of which only the foundations were laid are dotted.
The capital surmounting the third column from the south in the front row, along
the east face of the peristasis, belongs to this period (Pl. 54 b, the capital on the
top of the left-hand column).

Fig. 46 – Third Building Phase (ca. A. D. 150): This period saw the completion
of those portions represented only by foundations in the previous phase. In addition,
the temple was divided in two so that the eastern half became a place of worship
dedicated to Faustina I, the wife of the Emperor Antoninus Pius. All the columns
of the peristasis, with the exception of the capital on the third column from the
south, in the front row on the east face (Pl. 54 b, left-hand capital), were carved
in this period.

rows of columns was postponed and only the naos was constructed to begin with (Fig. 44). Thus the main building (the naos) consisted of the pronaos, cella and opisthodomos; this structure, together with the interior columns, constituted the first phase. The fact that the naos was built on a long, narrow plan with the width one-third of the length (Fig. 44) and that it was quite an immense construction reveals the intention of the builders to create a dipteros of the Ephesian type. However, since the erection of the encircling columns was delayed, the idea of a dipteros was abandoned, following the artistic trend of the time, and in its place a plan for a pseudo-dipteros was put into effect (Fig. 45). The main point of difference between the Sardis temple and those at Ephesus and Didyma, which it took as models, was that the cella was not open to the sky in the form of a sekos. Since the building at Sardis was associated with an ancient cult and the altar of the temple was left out in the open, a sekos would have been redundant; therefore, the cella was roofed in the manner of a hall. Although the first temple was modelled on the archaic type, it also strongly showed the influence of Pytheos, the architect of the Athena temple at Priene. The square pronaos of the Artemision at Sardis, with its narrow opisthodomos just one inter-columniation wide, is an exact replica of that found in the Priene temple (Fig. 68). Indeed, two columns dating from the beginning of the 3rd century B. C., standing in the middle of the second row on the east side, have a smaller diameter of 1.56 m., which is exactly one-tenth of their original height (15.56 m.); this is a feature of the Priene model. Gruben points out that the 2.17 m.-high bases of the columns were intended to be carved with reliefs like those in the Artemision at Ephesus, but this was postponed so long that it went out of fashion and the bases remained in their unadorned state. However, as Gruben again states, these columns and bases, which were originally structures of some importance, very likely stood in the opisthodomos of the first temple and so were meant to be seen from the outside (Fig. 44).

The pseudo-dipteral plan of the temple must have been realized during the second phase. It is difficult to share the opinion that the temple was intended to be a pseudo-dipteros from its inception at the beginning of the 3rd century. If this had been so, the temple at Sardis would have been unique, because this architectural concept had not been thought of at the end of the 4th century or at the beginning of the 3rd. The most probable explanation is that which has been given above, namely, that the general plan tended more towards the idea of an archaic dipteros.

Gruben records that the platform between the altar and the naos was built in the first phase, and that steps led up to it on the south and north. This platform would have been necessary if the plan for a double peristasis and a portico on the western side had been realized. However, this plan was not put into effect during the first phase. Only the northern flight of steps belonging to this platform is in evidence today.

Three capitals, discovered during the excavations by the Americans and referred to by the letters G, D and C, have been identified as dating from the first phase. The capital known by the letter C is now in the Metropolitan Museum in New York, while the other two remain in the temple.

The capital D is illustrated in Plate 56 a. These capitals date back to 300 B. C., a fact which has also been confirmed by Gruben. The volutes of the capitals resemble archaic specimens in that they are large; each volute measures one-third of the width of the capital. In addition, the lower edge of the canalis of the volutes is distinctly bow-shaped. The egg - and - tongue on the echinus approximates to the classical type. On the other hand, the introduction of new features, as the acanthus leaves around the corner palmettes and on the canalis of the capital C is apparent. Thus, these columns are the work of crafstmen who, bound to classical and even archaic traditions, do not show traces of the mature Hellenistic style. Consequently, these columns must have been carved about 300 B. C. Since this is so, we can conclude that the pronaos, the cella and the opisthodomos of the temple, as well as the cult statue, were completed by the beginning of the 3rd century at the latest.

The Second Phase. As is clear in Gruben's plans, the second phase commenced with the building of the peristasis; the foundations of 13 columns were laid along the east front, but here the work was called to a halt (Fig. 45). Had it continued, the temple would have been a pseudo-dipteros with 8 columns along the short and 20 columns on the long sides. Instead of this, the two columns in the opisthodomos were brought forward and, by the addition of 4 more columns on this side, a portico in the form of a 6-columned prostyle was created. The erection of a corresponding portico on the west side had been planned, but in this case only the two westernmost columns of the pronaos were moved forward and no other renovations were made to the exterior. At the present day, the capital of the third column from the south in the front row on the east side (i.e., the more northerly of the two columns still standing in their entirety) is Hellenistic in style and actually belonged to one of the columns forming the prostyle (Pl. 54 b, the capital on the left-hand column). Gruben has proved that this capital is really too small for its present column, and that, in fact, it belongs to one of the columns 10 cm. smaller (i.e., with a lower diameter of 1.89 m) which were added to the east portico during the second phase. Thus the capital under discussion (Pl. 54 b, left) determines the date of the second phase. The straight line of the lower edge of the canalis on this capital marks it as being of the Hermogenes period, like the Didymaion capitals of the same type, i.e., it dates roughly from the second quarter of the 2nd century B. C. The plan shows that the arrangement of the foundations laid for the 8 columns of the front row during the second phase is also a feature of the Hermogenes era. The span of the intercolumniation between the two central columns in this row, which is much greater than that between the others in the same row, is equal to that between those that were moved forward in the same phase, i.e., the middle intercolumniation on the east side lies on the same axis as that on the west side (Fig. 45). As has been shown in the first part of this book, this tendency for precise strong axiality is especially noticeable in the Hermogenes temple of Artemis at Magnesia ad Maeandrum (Fig. 63). Therefore, the structures of the second phase were clearly erected in the second quarter of the 2nd century B. C.

The Third Phase. Gruben's plan of the third phase of the Artemis temple (Fig. 46) shows the work begun during the second phase in the east and west porticos in its completed form. While this building was in progress, the peristasis columns for which the foundations had been laid during the second phase were set up, with the exception of two; in addition, foundations were laid for all the columns on the two long sides and for just one column on the west side. The columns of the peristasis (Pl. 54) had a lower diameter of 2.00 m., while their height was 17.73 m., which gives a proportion of 1 : 9.9. Thus it is understood that the columns of the first phase were slim, those of the second phase had less slender proportions, while those of the third phase were relatively squat. Of the two columns standing intact on the east front of the peristasis, the southerly one (Pl. 54 b, right-hand column) supports the capital originally intended for it. The arrowhead-shaped tongues in the egg-and-tongue ornament carved on the echinus fixes this capital as a work of the second century A. D. If the plan of the naos is closely examined, other special features inherent in Roman structures of the third phase can be observed. It will be noticed that in this phase the division of the naos approximately across the centre resulted in the creation of two symmetrical temples of the prostyle type. A statue base for a new cult was placed within the cella of the westward-facing prostyle, while the east cella contained the old cult statue. Inscriptions of the Roman period, the oldest of which dates from A. D. 127, were originally situated in front of the stairway on the north-west, and Gruben has established the fact that these lay buried beneath building materials and debris of the third phase. From this, it is evident that the renovations in the naos were carried out after A. D. 127. Gruben is right in pointing out that the ornamentation on the eastern entrance also conforms to that typical of the 2nd century A. D. An inscription on the fourth column-base from the north in the front row on the eastern side was formerly considered to date from just after A. D. 17, but Franke has now dated it A. D. 150. Similarly, the capital of the seventh column from the north is shown to have been made in the middle of the 2nd century A. D. In addition to all this is the huge head representing Faustina I, wife of the Emperor Antoninus Pius, which was found in the cella of the eastern prostyle. Since Faustina I died in A. D. 141 and, as it is generally admitted that she was later deified, it is clear that this phase must be dated to the middle of the 2nd century A. D. After this date, the goddess Artemis was forced to share her 400-year old temple with Faustina.

The remains of a building lying beside the south-east corner of the Artemis temple belong to a church erected in the 4th century A. D., by which time paganism had been superseded by the Christian faith at Sardis.

The Acropolis. Although Greek and Lydian pottery dating from the 7th century B. C. has been found in the castle of the Lydian capital, the majority of the structural remains found *in situ* date from the Byzantine era. The marble tower of the Hellenistic age, which can be seen to the north of the central platform of the acropolis, was built by Antiochus III (223-187). This and the adjoining remnants of the tower wall, made of green sandstone and possibly dating from the Persian occupation, were excavated in 1960.

The Tumuli at Bin Tepe. The largest tumuli to be found in Anatolia are the burial mounds known as Bin Tepe (Thousand Hills), on the southern shore of the small Lake Marmara, north-west of Salihli. These barrows, containing the graves of Lydian kings and rich citizens, with their beautifully finished stone constructions, dromoi and krepidomata, carry on the tradition of the Mycenaean period like the other tumuli in Ionia and Caria. Phalloi were probably placed on the tops of the tumuli as on those at Izmir, Larisa and Hierapolis. Herodotus (I 93) records that five οὖροι stood on the summit of Alyattes' burial mound. The tumuli of the Lydian monarchs were certainly enormous and impressive works. These huge tombs were the "Pyramids" of Anatolia. The largest of all, referred to by Herodotus as Alyattes' Tomb, has a diameter of 355 m., a circumference of 1,115 m. and a height of 69 m. In all probability, this tomb was plundered far back in antiquity. The stonework seen in the constructions inside this tumulus dating from the end of the 7th century is of very high quality. The new American expedition is continuing its investigations of these burial mounds. The drive from Sardis to Bin Tepe takes two hours over rough roads.

MANİSA (MAGNESIA AD SIPYLUM)

Some important and interesting collections can be seen in the Manisa museum. Not only are discoveries made by the new American expedition housed here, but also many objects unearthed in the surrounding area. A fine statue portraying a young girl in the Manisa museum should be especially mentioned. The straight fringe covering the forehead is indicative of the hairstyle in vogue at the time of Trajan (A. D. 98-117). Moreover, the arrangement of the hair in an elongated bun at the back follows the style set by Plotina, the wife of the above-mentioned emperor. Consequently, this work must have been created at the beginning of the 2nd century A. D.

Visitors to the typically Ottoman town of Manisa are especially advised to see the exceptionally fine examples of Turkish architecture to be found there. The most beautiful among them is the "Muradiye Mosque" built in 1583-1586 by the Turkish Architect Ali Ağa.

The Kybele Rock Relief. On the north-east slopes of Mt. Manisa, about 6 km. from the centre of the town in the locality of Akpınar, a high relief depicting a woman sitting on a flat rock is to be found (Pl. 41 b). Carved out of the rock, this large figure measures eight to ten metres in height and, although it has been weathered away to a large extent, like so many other monuments, it is still possible to distinguish some of the details; the goddess clutches her breasts with both hands, and she wears a cylindrical head-dress. Faint traces of four Hittite hieroglyphs are barely visible in a square frame to the right of the head. Although it has not been possible to decipher these symbols, they are, nevertheless, quite definitely Hittite characters. Consequently, this high relief must date from the second half of the 13th century B.C., in common with the Tudhaliya relief (Pl. 41 a), which is to be found in the neighbourhood of Izmir. According to Pausanias (IV, 22, 4), this relief represents the goddess Kybele. This writer also states that it is the oldest portrayal of the mother goddess. Works of art of the Phrygian and Greek archaic periods depicting Kybele in a sitting position within a niche are strongly reminiscent of this work. The fact that in Phrygian and Hellenic art Kybele was so often depicted in a mountainous or rocky environment reveals that these works also must have been strongly influenced by this kind of Hittite rock-sculpture.

South-west of the Kybele relief near the place known as "Yarık Kaya" (Cleft Rock), are to be found houses and a throne, both of which were carved out of the rock. These works of the 7th and 6th centuries B. C. show Phrygian features, but they are in fact remains of Lydian culture. Two kilometres to the east of the Kybele relief is a rock tomb with two chambers one behind the other; this, like the other rock monuments in the area, is an example of a work of Lydian origin under the influence of Phrygian art.

The Niobe Rock. Mention can be made at this point of a rock eroded into the likeness of a weeping woman with bent head which, although not a work of art, was nevertheless once famous in history. This crag is to be found in the district of Çaybaşı about 1 km. east of Muradiye Square in Manisa, on the road to İzmir. Ancient writers relate that they saw at the foot of Mt. Sipylos a rocky crag which was really the form of Niobe, who was turned into stone when her twelve children were murdered in front of her very eyes by the arrows of Artemis and Apollo. Pausanias writes (1, 21, 3), "When I went up Mt. Sipylos I saw the rock known as Niobe. Viewed at close quarters, this crag neither resembles a woman nor a weeping figure, but when it is seen from a distance, one imagines it to be a woman weeping with a bowed head". The myth of the petrification of Niobe is very ancient; Sophocles was also acquainted with it (Antigone 806-816). Antigone likens her own tragic end to that of Niobe : "I once heard of the sad death of Niobe, the daughter of Tantalos of Phrygia, on Mt. Sipylos. They say that the rocks sprang out and entwined themselves around her like creeping plants, and now she is being worn away by the rain, and snow is everlastingly her companion. Tears streaming from her moisture-laden eyelashes constantly dampen her breast. Death haunts me in nightmares with the same fate."

KOLOPHON AND NOTION

One of the oldest and most important cities of Ionia was Kolophon. It is referred to in a poem as "lovely Kolophon" lying on "the charming coast of Asia" by the poet Mimnermos, who was either a native of this city or of İzmir, and who is known to have lived at the end of the 7th century B. C. or the beginning of the 6th. He also relates that it was founded by the emigrants of Pylos under the leadership of Neleus. Originally İzmir was an Aeolian city; but later, probably in the first half of the 8th century B. C., it became an Ionian settlement following the influx of Ionians from Kolophon.

The Kolophonians became very wealthy owing to the fertility of their land and their skill as mariners. The majority of the citizens were rich, but this easy life paved the way to an excess of luxury. At times, more than a thousand men entered the agora wearing purple clothing and perfumed with musk. In the opinion of ancient writers, luxury undermined the strength of Kolophon. However, the Kolophonians had formerly been renowned as fighters and especially as horsemen in the 8th and 7th centuries B. C.

Kolophon came successively under the dominion of Lydia and of Persia. First Gyges seized Kolophon some time in the first half of the 7th century. The city finally lost its importance when it came under Persian rule in the second half of the 6th century. The coastal settlement of Notion, that is the "city of the south", began to develop in its stead. For a time, while Kolophon was governed by the Persians, Notion was administered by Athens. Thucydides refers to Notion as belonging to the Kolophonians. When Alexander the Great came to free Asia Minor from Persian domination, the two cities regained their independence. However, Lysimachos forced the Kolophonians to live in the newly founded city of Ephesus and, since some of them also moved to Notion, Kolophon was reduced to a very feeble state. In spite of this, Kolophon was rebuilt in 281, after Lysimachos' death, and it continued to exist under the administration of the Seleucids and Attalids. During this period Kolophon was known as "archaic Kolophon", i.e., ancient Kolophon, and the fame it had lost gravitated to Notion in the south, about 15 km. away. Notion then became known as "New Kolophon" or else "Kolophon-on-Sea". Both settlements were in fact prevented from developing by the large new city of Ephesus. The only important remnant of Kolophon, which had known such a glorious past in the 7th and 6th centuries, was the famous temple at Klaros. In Roman times the city was independent and its real centre lay within the acropolis of Notion.

The ruins are not in a very good state of preservation (Fig. 86a). The city was set on three hills and the intervening valleys; the area enclosed by the triangular city wall is about 1 km. square. The city wall, which was fortified by a dozen semicircular towers, must have been built before the time of Lysimachos, at the end of the 4th century. The earliest settlement was founded on a hill overlooking the south-west plain, at a height of 200 m. Some of the ruins on the northern slopes still exist today. Excavations undertaken by the Americans on behalf of the Fogg Art Museum of Harvard University and the American School of Classical Studies in Athens have brought to light important architectural remains. Especially notable are the streets and associated houses, a stoa and a temple dedicated to Demeter Antaia. Shops and premises for official business were situated in the stoa, which was constructed in the first half of the 4th century. The houses, which were west of the stoa, were built in the 4th century and overlay remains of buildings dating from the archaic period. The pavement of one of the streets running between the houses was constructed with great care. Further west is a small street with steps and the ruins of Roman baths which are isolated from the houses. The building situated south of the western houses and constructed of porous stone was sacred to the mother goddess Antaia, who was much revered in the 4th century.

Notion occupied an area of 500 × 1,000 metres on two flat-topped hills which rose up on the coast and were separated from each other by a narrow neck of land (Fig. 47). The town was about 2 km. distant from the Klaros temple. A French archaeological expedition worked here under Charles Picard in 1921. The 4 km. - long city wall was erected in the Hellenistic age. It was built of regular square blocks and fortified with square towers; Roman mortar repair work can be observed on some of the faces. Two gates to the city are still visible : one on the west (1), the other on the north (2). Other gates must have existed, however. There was also an entrance with steps at the south-eastern end (3). The ruins themselves are poorly preserved, but there is a magnificent view from the top of the acropolis to Samos in the south, Kuşadası in the south-east and to Ephesus. A temple encircled with colonnades is to be found on the western hill (4). Only the foundation of this *templum in antis* of the Corinthian order is still standing; the measurements

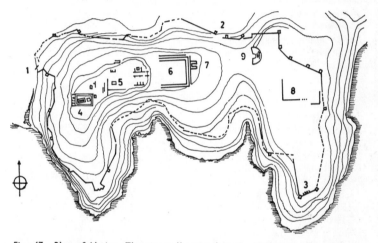

Fig. 47 – Plan of Notion. The city wall erected in the Hellenistic age possesses three surviving entrances: **1)** *West gate.* **2)** *North gate.* **3)** *South-east entrance with steps.* **4)** *Sanctuary of Athena, dating from the time of Hadrian (A. D. 117-138). Foundations of a templum in antis of the Corinthian order, with surrounding stoas of the Doric order.* **5)** *Remains of another temple.* **6)** *Central agora.* **7)** *Bouleuterion.* **8)** *East agora.* **9)** *Theatre, built in the Hellenistic age, altered in Roman times.*

of the temple were 7.50 × 16 m. The krepidoma (the platform) was three-stepped. The frieze was adorned with garlands made from sprays of bay leaves which supported the heads of bulls. The temple was consecrated to Athena Polias and dates from the time of Hadrian. To the east of the temple can be seen the remains of the foundations of an altar measuring 5.30 × 7.72 m. The temple and the altar were surrounded on all four sides by stoas of the Doric order. The exterior measurements of the temenos, including the stoas, were

17.10×38.15 m. Shops were arranged along the outer faces of the stoas on the east, west and south. The non-axial arrangement of the stoas, the temple and the temenos is reminiscent of the plan of the Athena temenos at Pergamon (Fig. 34, No. 7). This arrangement, which was contrary to that customary in Roman art, perhaps arose from the fact that the citizens of Notion in the Roman period wished to conform to the traditional style in which the aforementioned buildings of the Hellenistic period were constructed. The remains of a small temple (5) are to be found to the north-east of the sanctuary of Athena, but it is not known to which god the temple was dedicated. There were originally two agoras on the acropolis: one centrally placed (6), the other to the east (8); however, neither of these has yielded any well-preserved remains. Close by the east side of the agora, which lies in the middle of the acropolis, are the ruins of a bouleuterion (7). The city theatre (9) occupied an area in the north-east sector of the acropolis, to the north-west of the eastern agora. This small westward-facing theatre, which was erected in Hellenistic times, underwent extensive structural alterations in the Roman era. Although the horseshoe shape was retained, the theatron was rebuilt with an arched diazoma which conformed to the Roman constructional style.

KLAROS

The temple of Apollo at Klaros, famed in Hellenistic times, but more particularly in the Roman period, for its oracle, lies on a flat tract of land in a narrow valley within the boundaries of Kolophon, two kilometres from Notion. The most probable reason why the temple was not built on a hill but on level land was that there was a sacred spring and wood in that area. This holy place, according to the lays of Homer, had been the centre of an important cult as far back as the 7th and 6th centuries. Schuchhardt was the first to establish the fact that the temple was in the vicinity of Notion. Later, in 1907, Theodore Macridy discovered two columns from the propylon which stood at the beginning of the sacred way. At that time, these were thought to belong to the opisthodomos of the temple. Later still, in 1913, Charles Picard and Theodore Macridy opened up the area around these columns and proved that they actually belonged to the propylon. However, Louis Robert was the scholar who carried out systematic excavations of the temple from 1950 to 1960. The description given below is, to a large extent, based on the information given by Professor Louis Robert, the director of the excavation.

The propylon, erected in the 2nd century B. C. at the point where the sacred wood began, served as the entrance for those approaching by sea. It was approximately square in shape and built in the Doric style. The krepidoma was three-stepped. There were four columns on the south side facing the sea, two on the side turned towards the temple. The inner surfaces of the recovered columns are covered with inscriptions carved in the 2nd century A. D. These comprise lists of deputations from Asia Minor, Thrace, and Eastern Europe who had come to consult the oracle of Apollo. In addition, the names of the boys, girls and young people who sang hymns to the god Apollo are inscribed on the columns.

At a later date a colonnade set aside for business premises was built along the west side of the propylon, whereas on the east side there was a semi-circular exedra, measuring 8 m. across, which has been preserved *in toto*. On the north-east side can be seen remains of houses of the late Roman period.

Some bases and foundations of bases connected with the sacred way are in evidence north of the propylon. The west side of the road has been dug as far as the temple. In this area, several small monuments are arranged in rows. They contain bases, stelae and statues which were erected in honour of prominent men of the Roman period, particularly the governors of the Roman province of Asia. All of them were set up in the 1st century B. C. The most important memorial among these is the rectangular exedra which at one time accommodated three statues. Similar inscriptions to those which were written on the 2nd century propylon columns also cover this semicircular structure.

The sacred way came to an end exactly in front of the east face of the temple, which was 26 × 46 m. in size and of the Doric order. Built in the form of a peripteros with eleven columns on the long sides and six on the short, it rested on a five-stepped krepidoma. It is known that the temple collapsed as a result of an earthquake. Some of the columns lie on the ground, complete with the capitals and all the drums of the shafts. Seven capitals and 150 drums have been recovered. The column shafts were 1.60 m. in diameter. The temple must have been constructed, according to stylistic comparisons, in the late 4th century or at the beginning of the Hellenistic era. According to the inscription on the architrave, the peripteros was completed in the time of the Emperor Hadrian. It is thought that a temple to Apollo also existed here in earlier times, and this assumption is supported by remains which have been uncovered in the cella.

Sizeable portions of huge statues representing Apollo, Artemis, and Leto were discovered within the cella during the excavations and these remains are still *in situ*. With the help of Kolophonian coins, it should be possible to fit these pieces together. Apollo is depicted on the coins in a sitting position, with his left arm resting on a guitar. In his right hand he holds a spray of bay leaves. On his right stands his twin sister, Artemis, with her quiver on her shoulder, while his mother Leto stands on his left. We can assume that some of the pieces were part of the seated Apollo himself and that others belonged to the standing figures of the two goddesses. The existing remains reveal that the statue of Apollo was 7-8 m. high. The arm, for example, is 3.50 m. long.

The oracle was consulted beneath the cella of the temple. Greek and Roman authorities write that the divine revelations were not made through the medium of a woman, like the Pythia at Delphi, but through a male prophet. The seer would enter a cave or an underground chamber and, having drunk the mysteriously endowed holy water, would utter the prophesy in the form of scanned poetry. The oracle was always consulted at night.

The priests and the thespiodos, the composer of the poetry, were appointed for life, whereas the prophets were changed every year. In addition there were one or two scribes. No oracular inscriptions have been discovered at Klaros, but specimens of the Apollonian oracle were found, at Pergamon and Turgutlu, just as they came to light in Dalmatia, Algeria, Sardinia, Rome and even far-off Britain. The four steps on the east face of the temple are covered with inscriptions for their entire length. They consist of lists of delegations coming from distant towns and countries to seek the advice of the god Apollo. Besides the remote places already mentioned, inscriptions originating from the temple also were found at Olbia in southern Russia, and at Sivas, Amasya, Kayseri and Konya in Anatolia. We have already related above in the chapter on Izmir how, during the time of Alexander, the Smyrnaians, when leaving Bayraklı for Kadifekale (i.e. Pagos) sought the advice of the Klarian Apollo.

The remains obtained during the excavations have yielded a wealth of information as to how the functions of the oracle were performed. In the area around the entrance to the temple in the pronaos, there are two corridors of blue marble running parallel to each other, one in the north, the other in the south. These are 70 m. - wide and 1.80 m.- high. A little farther along, each corridor makes a right-angled bend and continues for some distance as a single passage-way. They later separate again and complete the symmetrical plan begun on the east. The two corridors both led to the adyton, i.e. the innermost shrine. The adyton consisted of two underground vaulted chambers and it lay beneath the cella, where the statue of the seated Apollo was situated. The first of these, i.e., the one on the east, which was at a depth of 6.43 m., was reached by two passageways, one on the right, the other on the left, as has been explained above. There were stone benches for seating purposes in this room, and also the sacred stone of Apollo, i.e., an omphalos (similar to that renowned at Delphi) fashioned from blue stone. This first chamber was a waiting room, and it was occupied by the above-mentioned prophet, the thespiodos and the scribe or scribes. The eastern chamber was separated from the western by a massive wall, 2.70 m. in thickness with a communicating door, 1.70 m. high in the exact centre. There was no other entrance to this second room, which was at a depth of only 4 m. It was entered solely by the diviner, and he entered it in complete darkness. A rectangular well, 0.96 m. × 1.41 m. in dimension, lies at the left of the entrance inside the room. This was the source of the holy water. As already stated, when the prophet had drunk this water, he would recite the metrical lines of poetry prepared by the thespiodos and answer the questions posed by those coming for advice.

27 m. east of the temple is a large altar measuring 9 m. × 18.45 m. The expedition in charge of the excavations records that there were two altar slabs here : one for offerings to Apollo, the other sacred to Dionysus.

South of the temple and parallel to it can be seen a small temple of the Ionic order and in front of that an altar. This temple must have been sacred to Artemis, because the statue of a goddess found near the altar was dedicated to Artemis of Klaros. Close to this small temple, six votive stones are to be found. These are all of the late period; one of them was set up to Poseidon Themeliouchos, another to the goddess Artemis Pythia of Miletos.

North of the altar attributed to the temple of Apollo, a well-preserved stone sundial can be seen, on which is an inscription to the effect that it was donated by the *agoranomos* in Hellenistic times. A stone with an inscription was set up to the south of the altar, in the name of Cicero's brother, Quintus Tullius Cicero, who was a governor of the province of Asia. Further south, a well-preserved exedra and a stone armchair can be observed. The armrests of the chair are shaped like winged serpents.

Some statues and reliefs of fine quality were brought to light during the excavations and these are now housed in the museum at Izmir. Mention can be made of a particularly beautiful fragment of a Hellenistic frieze and the statue of a man of the archaic period holding a sacrificial calf in both hands.

SIĞACIK (TEOS)

According to tradition, colonists from Minyas in Thessaly, with Athamas as their leader, were the first to settle in Teos, and they were followed by the Athenians, with some of the descendants of Kodros at their head. Teos, a member of the Panionion, developed rapidly and soon reached the stage where many of its inhabitants left for Phokaia and Ephesus. The main source of livelihood in Teos was trade by sea. About 600 B. C., Thales suggested that Teos be chosen as the main centre for the twelve Ionian cities, because of its position at the heart of Ionia. However, his suggestion was not accepted. When the Persians seized the cities of Ionia, some of the inhabitants of Teos founded the city of Abdera in Thrace, sometime between 545 and 540 B. C. Abdera was the home of Protagoras and Demokritos, two famous philosophers who lived in the 5th century. In spite of this emigration, the citizens of Teos were rich enough to take part in the Battle of Lade in 494 with seventeen of their ships, and to pay as tribute to the Delian League the high membership fee of six talents, in 476. Alexander the Great had the idea of linking Teos to the Bay of Izmir by canal.

The largest temple to Dionysus in the ancient world was built at Teos (Pl. 55, Fig. 49). Moreover the Ionian actors' guild was first established in Teos towards the end of the 3rd century B. C., and the players gave performances at various places, using Teos as their centre. It was important to Teos that the actors should live in their town because, as taking part in the celebrations during the festival of Dionysus was considered a sacred duty, the actors and the place where they resided had the right of asylum. However, towards the middle of the 2nd century B. C., the actors were forced to move to Ephesus on account of their intractability. But soon after that, Attalos II sent them on to Myonnesus because they caused trouble in Ephesus as well. Later, the Romans made the actors live in Lebedos and there they stayed, apart from a short time when Mark Antony had them brought to Priene to entertain Cleopatra. The most prominent personality produced by Teos was the famous lyric poet Anacreon, who lived in the 6th century B. C. Another native of Teos was the book-lover Apellikon, who kept Aristotle's library intact by buying it for an exorbitant sum in 100 B. C. Aristotle's books were later transported by Sulla to Rome, where they were published in revised manuscript form by a scholar called Tyrannion.

Teos was situated on the isthmus of a peninsula and possessed one large and one small harbour (Fig. 49). A portion of the city wall in polygonal masonry, dating from the archaic period, is still standing below the acropolis on the south-east side, while a well-preserved section of the Hellenistic city-wall can be seen just west of the enclosing wall of the Dionysus temple (Fig. 49). The theatre, built in the 2nd century B. C., lies at the south-west end of the acropolis (3). The auditorium is completely in ruins, whereas the stage, enlarged in Roman times, is in quite a good state of preservation. A very beautiful view over the city and out to sea can be enjoyed from above the theatre. The Teos theatre is a good example of the Greek type which blends harmoniously with the surrounding countryside. The odeion (a roofed theatre), lying south-east of the theatre and north-east of the sanctuary of Dionysus, is a well-preserved structure of the Roman period (5). The gymnasium (2), which was built just north-east of the acropolis, is still largely concealed by overlying earth. In the north part can be seen the ruins of a castle (7), built by the Turks in the late 15th century. Part of a Roman breakwater is visible south-west of this castle.

The temple of Dionysus (4), the principal building in Teos, is in fine condition. Field research and excavations were carried out in this area in the 18th century by an expedition of the Society of Dilettanti founded by the British, in 1824 by French archaeologists and in 1964-1965 by the Turkish archaeologists Y. Boysal and B. Öğün. A provisonal anastylosis has been

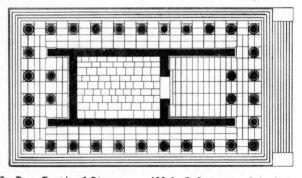

Fig. 48 – Teos. Temple of Dionysus ca. 130 B. C. Peripteros of the Ionic order, with 6 by 11 columns and stylobate measuring approximately 18.5 × 35.00 m. Built by Hermogenes, according to Vitruvius. The intercolumniation is $2\,^{1}/_{4}$ times the lower columnar diameter, which fully conforms to the eustyle principle attributed to Hermogenes by Vitruvius. The Attic column base and sculptured frieze are also "Hermogenic" features of this structure. Since the temple of Dionysus does not exhibit a pseudodipteral arrangement but follows the Priene ground plan (p. 21 ff. and Fig. 68), one may assume that it was one of Hermogenes' earlier creations.

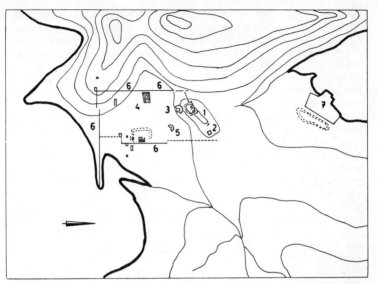

Fig. 49 – Map of Teos. **1)** Archaic city wall in polygonal masonry, part of which still stands below the acropolis on the south-east side. **2)** Gymnasium, built in the Hellenistic age, altered in Roman times. Still largely concealed by overlying earth. **3)** Theatre. 2nd century B. C. Although the auditorium is in ruins, the stage, enlarged in Roman times, is well-preserved. A fine example of the typical Greek theatre, which blends harmoniously with the surrounding countryside. **4)** Temple of Dionysus (see Fig. 48). **5)** Odeion. Well-preserved structure, built in Roman times. **6)** City wall of Hellenistic age, a section of which can be seen just west of the Dionysus temple. **7)** Turkish castle, from the end of the 15th century A. D. Part of a Roman breakwater is visible south-west of the castle.

carried out by re-erecting the bases, capitals and other upper structures which have survived up to the present. Some of the various architectural remains seen strewn about the site are Hellenistic in origin, while others date from the Roman period. The fragments of an acroterion, now in the Izmir Museum, exhibit Hellenistic workmanship, but the majority of th. Ionic capitals show Roman technique. It seems that the temple was erected in the Hellenistic era and underwent extensive restoration in the time of Hadrian (see also pp. 21-25).

The temple of Dionysus (Fig. 48) is of the Ionic order with six columns on the shorter sides and eleven on the longer. The building strongly resembles Pytheos' temple of Athena at Priene in that it has a deep two-columned pronaos and a narrow two-columned opisthodomos (Fig. 68). The main difference in the plan is that the cella in the temple at Priene was exactly twice the size of the pronaos, whereas in the temple at Teos, the cella is only slightly larger than the pronaos. Vitruvius, the famous architect of the Au-

gustan age, records that the temple was built by Hermogenes, and adds that it
was planned on Hermogenes' eustyle principle, i.e., with the intercolumniation
$2\,^1/_4$ times the lower diameter of the columns. It has been positively confirmed that the temple at Teos follows this eustyle plan. In the case of the
Dionysus temple, the cross walls of the pronaos and the opisthodomos
lie on the same axis as the columns opposite them in the peristasis;
this, as has already been mentioned (pp. 22-29), is a feature of the Hermogenes temple of Artemis at Magnesia. Study of the frieze with reliefs,
formerly decorating the temple but now in the Izmir Museum, and examination of the column-bases, which conform to the Attic style, reveal
other features of Hermogenes in the temple. The opinion has already been
stated in the first part of this book that this building, which is not a pseudo-
dipteros and which faithfully follows the design of Pytheos, is an early work
completed by Hermogenes. If the other considerations mentioned there
are also correct, the temple must have been erected in the second quarter
of the 2nd century B. C. On the other hand, the present author does not
consider that the inscription relating to Antiochus III, i.e. Antiochus the
Great (223-187 B. C.), discovered here during recent Turkish excavations
and so well commented by Peter Herrmann, will solve the problem of
dating the temple of Dionysus. In any case, Herrmann himself writes very
reservedly on this subject and suggests various possibilities. Probably it
seems that the construction of the temple was delayed and that the stones
bearing the inscription were never used to build the "parastas of the temple".
Indeed, the four blocks bearing the inscription were found during the
excavations, in the temenos wall, twenty metres away from the south-west
corner of the temple.

EPHESUS

According to tradition, the founder of Ephesus was Androklos, one of the
sons of the legendary King Kodros, though Lelegians and Carians inhabited
the area earlier. Like the other Ionian settlements, the city must have
been colonized by the 10th century B. C. at the latest. On reaching this spot,
the Greeks found that the mother goddess, Kybele, held sway as chief deity,
as in almost every part of Anatolia. In order to placate the indigenous peoples,
they adopted a policy of syncretism and introduced the worship of Artemis and Kybele in the same deity. The original settlement is thought to
have been established 1,200 m. west of the Artemision, at the port of Koressos
(Fig. 50). In the beginning, Ephesus was ruled by kings, then by an oligarchy
of aristocrats and later by tyrants. During the first half of the 7th century
B. C., the Cimmerians seized Ephesus, and it only began to develop about
the middle of the same century. Towards the middle of the 6th century, it
came under the sovereignty of Lydia. Judging by the columnae caelatae Kroisos
presented to the temple, cordial relations existed between Lydia and Ephesus.
However, the Ephesians had to leave their strongly fortified city in the port
of Koressos and settle in the neighbourhood of the Artemision. As this
second settlement lies below water level today, it has not been possible to

excavate any remains except those of the temple of Artemis (Figs. 52-54). After the death of Alexander, Ephesus, together with the whole of Ionia, fell into the hands of Lysimachos, who had the foresight to re-establish the city (Fig. 50) on the northern slopes of Mt. Koressos (Bülbüldağ) and on the southern and western slopes of Mt. Pion (Panayırdağ), within a large area, enclosed by a city wall with a height of 10 m. and a perimeter of 9 km. The stretch of wall exhibiting fine stone craftsmanship seen today on the side of Bülbüldağ, i. e., Mt. Koressos, is part of this original city wall (Fig. 50, No. 29). Lysimachos ensured the growth of population in Ephesus by forcing the people of Kolophon and Lebedos to reside there. Indeed, in a short space of time, Ephesus became the most densely populated city in Anatolia. In Hellenistic times, Ephesus was administered by the Seleucids and, after 190 B. C. was governed by the Pergamene kings. Ephesus came under the joint rule of the Kingdom of Pergamon and the Romans until 133 B. C. and, like the other cities in Asia Minor, was heavily taxed during the time of Julius Caesar; but in Augustus' reign there began a period lasting two hundred years, during which Ephesus passed through its most glorious and happy period. According to Aristeides, who lived about A. D. 150., Ephesus was the most prosperous commercial centre of that time and controlled the banking affairs of the whole of western Anatolia. The city of Ephesus was referred to as the metropolis of Asia, i.e., of Ionia. After a period famous in ancient history for strife and upheaval, lasting throughout the 3rd century A. D. and subsequently to the middle of the 4th century, Ephesus entered into a third golden age which continued until the Justinian era (A. D. 527-565). With the rapid expansion of Christianity in the area, many important and beautiful buildings came into being. The castle at Ayasoluk and the church of St. John within it, were erected during this period. Ephesus enjoyed a further period of prosperity in the Seljuk era, during the 14th century. In this time, the city occupied the area where the Ayasoluk Castle and the present day town of Selçuk now stand. During the time of the Ottomans, the city declined but now it is again developing well.

The British archaeologist J. T. Wood undertook the first excavation of Ephesus in 1869, when the Artemision was discovered. He was succeeded from 1895-1913 by Austrian scholars, who found remains of the city dating from Hellenistic and Roman times in their extensive investigations on the slopes of Mt. Koressos (Bülbüldağ) and Mt. Pion (Panayırdağ). The Austrians continued to uncover this richest and best preserved of the ancient cities of Turkey after the First World War, with Josef Keil in charge of the project, and also following the Second World War, when Franz Miltner and then Fritz Eichler directed operations. Excavations are still progressing favourably with Hermann Vetters as director of a distinguished team of scholars.

Ayasoluk Hill (Fig. 50, Nos. 1-3). This hill was defended throughout the early Christian, Byzantine and Seljuk periods by a well-fortified castle. The fine ramparts, which still exist, were constructed in the early Christian era and underwent extensive restoration during Seljuk times. The main gateway in the castle wall (1) was built in the 6th century A. D. from stones rifled from Roman constructions, in particular the stadium (6).

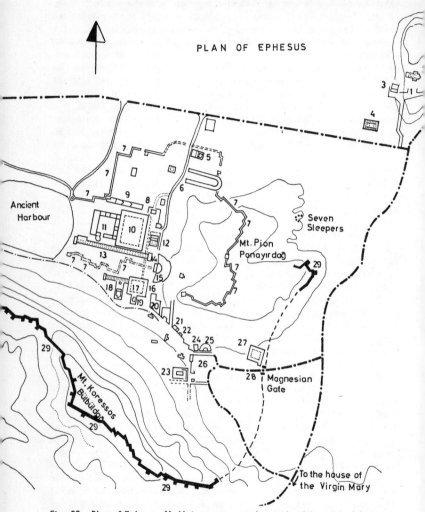

PLAN OF EPHESUS

Fig. 50 – Plan of Ephesus. **1)** *Main gateway to the castle of Ayasoluk, 6th century A. D.* **2)** *St. John's Church (see Fig. 51).* **3)** *İsa Bey Mosque, A. D. 1375; a magnificent example of the transitional style of Turkish art, between the Seljuk and Ottoman periods.* **4)** *Temple of Artemis (see Figs. 52-54).* **5)** *Vedius Gymnasium (see Fig. 55).* **6)** *Stadium. Reign of Nero (A. D. 54-68).* **7)** *City wall of the Byzantine period.* **8)** *Byzantine baths, 6th century A. D.* **9)** *Church of the Virgin Mary, beginning of the 4th century A. D. Converted from a Roman building, used for* *banking and commercial purposes. Second century A. D.* **10, 11)** *Harbour gymnasium and baths. Huge baths complex combined with two large palaestrae for athletic training, begun in the reign of Domitian (A. D. 81-96), completed and decorated by Verulanus in Hadrian's time.* **12)** *Theatre gymnasium. Second century A.D. The palaestra has been completely excavated, but the baths only partially so. The steps along the entire length of the palaestra on the north side functioned as seating accommodation, most probably during prize-giving ceremonies.* **13)** *Arkadiane. No doubt, this colonnaded street leading to the harbour was erected in Hellenistic times. However, according to an inscription, it was rebuilt and decorated by Arcadius (A. D. 395-408) and named after him (see p. 157).* **14)** *Hellenistic fountain.* **15)** *Theatre (see Fig. 56).* **16)** *Marble road. A section of the sacred road of Ephesus. The marble pavement seen today was laid by Eutropios, who probably lived in the 5th century A.D.* **17)** *Commercial agora. Market place, built in Hellenistic times, enlarged by additions erected in the reigns of Augustus, Nero and Caracalla.* **18)** *Temple of Serapis (see Fig. 57, No. 3).* **19)** *Celsus Library (see Figs. 57 and 58, No. 4).* **20)** *Scholastikia Baths (see Fig. 58, No. 9).* **21-26)** *For descriptions of these buildings, see Figs. 58 and 59).* **27)** *East gymnasium. The same type of structure as the Vedius Gymnasium; probably built by Flavius Damianus (Pl. 52) and his wife Vedia Phaedrina.* **28)** *Magnesian Gate. According to fragments of an inscription, probably built in the time of the Emperor Vespasian (A. D. 69-79).* **29)** *City wall, built by Lysimachos, the founder of Hellenistic Ephesus.*

St. John's Church (Fig. 50, No. 2; Fig. 51). According to a Christian legend going back to the 2nd century A. D., St. John lived on this hilltop and, on his death, was buried there. At first, the grave was marked by a memorial, which was enclosed in the 4th century A. D. by a church with a wooden roof; a century later, Justinian (A. D. 527-565) erected over the spot a domed basilica remains of which are still standing (Fig. 51). Entry to this cross-shaped building was gained on the west through a courtyard called the atrium, leading into the narthex to the east and so into the nave

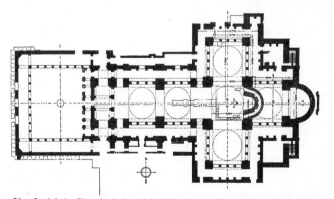

Fig. 51 – St. John's Church. A domed basilica erected by Justinian (A. D. 527-565).

of the church proper. Six domes formed the roof of the nave and the transept, while galleries stretched in an unbroken line over the aisles from the narthex as far as the apse. St. John's grave was situated under the most central of the domed sections. Sacred dust rising from the grave through a hole was believed to have healing properties. Throughout the Middle Ages, St. John's grave was one of the most important shrines in the Christian world to which pilgrimages were made. East of the central chamber and separated from the place where the presbyters sat is a synthronon of semi-elliptical shape.

Excavations have recently been carried out to the east of St. John's church, under the auspices of the museum authorities, backed financially by George B. Quatman; these have led to the discovery of a centrally domed building, the baptisterium, in the middle of which lies a baptismal pool. Frescoes depicting saints seen in the accompanying chapel probably date from the 10th century A. D.

The İsa Bey Mosque (Fig. 50, No. 3). One of the major works representative of Turkish Seljuk art is the mosque on the hill at Ayasoluk, which was built by İsa Bey, a member of the ruling family in the Aydın district. This building, which is in a fair state of preservation, was completed in A. D. 1375, according to an inscription. As has been established by Katharina Otto-Dorn, this building constitutes the oldest known example of a Turkish mosque with a courtyard. It is, moreover, the earliest representative of an Anatolian columned mosque with a transept. The details of the ornamentation in the İsa Bey mosque, especially the arabesque and the network, the shape of the stalactites, the faience mosaics in the south dome, the monumental height of the main west portal and the lavish decoration are features that typify the Seljuk style. Like the İlyas Bey mosque in Miletos, this mosque is a very impressive work of the Turkish style, transitional between the Seljuk and the Ottoman periods, both from the point of view of the exquisite quality of the details and of the beauty of the marble carving it exhibits.

The Archaeological Museum. One of the finest local museums in Turkey is situated in Seljuk. Here are housed the works of art brought to light among the ruins of Ephesus and its environs. The majority of the finds made before the First World War were conveyed to the museum in Vienna, while all of the statues discovered after that war have been taken to the İzmir Museum. However, all the removable discoveries made after the Second World War are housed in the local museum. The most important works displayed there are the following: the Mycenaean vases found on the hill at Ayasoluk, fragments from the Artemision, the sarcophagus and Corinthian columns of the Belevi Mausoleum (in the garden), the altar of the temple of Domitian (in the garden), two statues of Artemis Ephesia (Pl. 58), a fresco depicting Socrates, various statues taken from different monuments, notably from fountains, a Theodosian relief from the temple of Hadrian and extremely valuable full-length portraits and busts of the early Christian period.

The Temple of Artemis at Ephesus (Fig. 52-54). The Artemision, considered one of the seven wonders of the world, was indeed a building unparalleled in splendour. This is because it was the largest edifice in the Hellenic world and also the first architectural work of monumental proportions ever to be constructed entirely of marble. Today nothing but a part of the foundations remains of the Artemision; nevertheless, it has been possible to draw a reconstruction of this extremely important work, with the help of fragments recovered during excavation (Fig. 54).

Before the coming of the Greeks, the site of the temple of Artemis was occupied by an area sacred to the Anatolian mother goddess Kybele, who was worshipped by the local inhabitants. This is borne out by the fact that, although there were no topographical features to dictate the siting of the Artemision, it faced west like the temples of Artemis at Sardis and Magnesia (Figs. 44-46, 63). Excavations undertaken by British archaeologists have proved the existence of three building phases beneath the archaic Artemision. The first building (phase A) consisted of an altar, while the second and third constructions (phases B and C) each comprised a naiskos. As the oldest of the beautiful ivory and gold works of art found under the temple (and now housed in the Istanbul Museum) date from the beginning of the 7th century B. C., the first Hellenic edifice, i.e., the altar corresponding to phase A, must have been constructed about 700 B. C. The naiskos which immediately preceded the archaic Artemision, i. e., the cult building representing phase C, lay within an area measuring 14.63 × 28.20 m.; it was surrounded by a temenos wall. According to Wilhelm Alzinger, this sanctuary must have been built in the time of the tyrant Pythagoras, i. e., at the beginning of the 6th century B. C. The two ivory works of art, pictures of which appear in this book (Pl. 7), can be attributed to phase C. The ivory figurine bearing a phiale (libation bowl) and a small oinochoe (wine-jug) is also one of the works presented to the goddess in this naiskos.

The Archaic Artemision (Fig. 52-54). The golden age of the Ionian world reached its peak in the second quarter of the 6th century B. C. Consequently, a temple of the modest proportions stated above would not have sufficed for a wealthy city-state the size of Ephesus. Moreover, in 570 B. C. or slightly earlier, work was begun on a temple on Samos with a stylobate measuring 52.5 × 105 m. Two architects called Rhoikos and Theodoros were in charge of the construction, which was intended to replace the outdated small Heraion. The Ephesians would not allow a rival city to get ahead of them, and they lost no time in sending to Crete for Chersiphron of Knossos and his son Metagenes to come and construct a huge and magnificent temple. In addition, they got the architect Theodoros to come from Samos, since they were compelled to set the foundations of the Ephesian Artemision in swampy ground, just as those of the Heraion on Samos had been. However, it is apparent that the services of the guest architect were not required only for the laying of the foundations, since, in many respects, the Artemision resembles the Heraion. Nevertheless, a work of art was created which was in every way more beautiful and more mature. It may well be that the Cretan architects had an intimate knowledge of Egyptian, Assyrian and Hittite architecture and sculpture, which inspired them. It is also possible that they had produced other large-scale buildings before this. Whatever the case, they certainly created an exceptional work of colossal proportions. The stylobate of the Artemision measured 55.10 × 115.14 m. in area and, as has been stated above, it was the largest building in the Greek world. The most

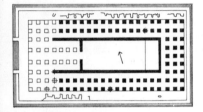
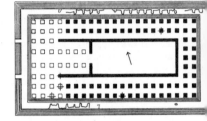

Fig. 52 – Archaic Artemision (560-550 B. C.). This Ionic temple, a dipteros measuring 55.10 × 115 m., was the first monumental structure ever to be made of marble, as well as being the largest building in the Greek world. According to Pliny, the total number of columns was 127, of which 36 in the front, i.e., the western part, were carved with reliefs (Fig. 54). The cella was long and narrow, the pronaos deep. The statue of Artemis stood in a naiskos or a baldachin inside the unroofed cella over the remains of the altar, erected at the beginning of the 7th century B. C. The column bases and capitals were realized in canonical style (Fig. 54). The columns were 19 m. in height, which was twelve times the lower diameter. The shafts were carved variously with 40, 44 or 48 shallow flutes which formed sharp edges (arrises). The entablature consisted of an architrave with three fasciae, a row of dentils decorated above and below with cymations, and over this the sima, bearing reliefs depicting chariots. The architects were Chersiphron of Knossos, his son Metagenes, and Theodoros of Samos.

Fig. 53 – Later Artemision (334-250 B. C.). One of the seven wonders of the world in Hellenistic times. Since the later Artemision was erected on the foundations of its predecessor, the dimensions were the same. In order to protect the new temple from the underlying swampy ground, it stood on a 13-stepped crepidoma, 2.68 m. in height. This high base was probably the only difference between the two temples. The cult statue stood in the cella in the same position as the earlier one. The new statue was probably of the Roman type known to us as the Artemis Ephesia (Pl. 58). Column bases with reliefs are also in evidence. In accordance with Pytheos' models, the height of the columns (18 m.) was ten times the lower diameter. Another resemblance to Pytheos' models was that there were 24 flutes with sharp edges (arrises). Although the proportions of the capitals are different, they follow the old style. The entablature was composed of an architrave with three fasciae, a row of dentils with a cymation above and below, and a sima or cornice with anthemion reliefs and lion-headed gargoyles. The altar of the later Artemision was discovered by Austrian excavators, who have confirmed that it was a horseshoe-shaped building standing on a marble-paved square.

important point is that it was the first monumental construction in the world to be built entirely of marble, as has also been mentioned above. The architects followed the dipteral plan, which originated on Samos. Thus the temple, surrounded on four sides by a double instead of a single row of columns, was saved, by the gain in width, from appearing too elongated. Besides this, it is also possible that the Ionian architects drew their inspiration from the temples in Egypt and Urartu, in which it was fashionable to have many columns. This forest of columns formed a very beautiful setting and a most suitable sanctuary for the goddess Artemis, the ruler of Nature. Pliny (NH 36,96 b) states that the temple was 220 × 425 ft. in area and contained 127 columns. Using this information, many theories have been propounded on the reconstruction of the temple. The first successful one was that of H. Drerup; then G. Gruben and W. Alzinger each made new suggestions based on the same plan with slight alterations. Drerup maintains that there was one row of columns at the rear and two in front. Gruben states that there were three in the front and two in the rear, while Alzinger suggests the existence of three rows on each side. Each theory is possible. However, since the Hellenistic structure had, as Pliny says, strictly the same plan, proposals including an opisthodomos cannot be considered, because such a structure did not exist in Ionian art before the time of the architect Pytheos. Drerup's theory is acceptable because it confirms the 127 columns recorded by Pliny. However, Pliny states that 36 columns carved with reliefs were to be found in the front part of the temple. This is not in accordance with Drerup's plan. Moreover, the elongated archaic character of the naos is lost if a fourth row of columns is added to it following this same plan. In contrast to this, Alzinger assumes (Fig. 52) that over the statue of Artemis there existed a baldachin supported by four columns, and thus his plan not only agrees with the figure of 127 columns, but also leaves room for the 36 sculptured columns in the front area. (The empty squares in Figs. 52-53 indicate the columns with reliefs).

Pliny, of course, saw the later temple. However, since the Hellenistic structure was erected on the foundations of the archaic temple, his observations are valid for this earlier building as well. The only differences between the two temples are that the later structure stood on a 13-stepped podium and probably had a flight of steps at the front, i.e., the west side, while the archaic building was erected on a low-stepped crepidoma. These considerations are strictly based on Pliny's information. If we suppose that the number of columns given by Pliny is not exact, we may admit that the new Artemision showed some alterations and, for instance, possessed an opisthodomos which was absent in the archaic structure (see p. 152).

When the archaic Artemision was under construction, the above-mentioned naiskos and the temenos enclosing it remained within the unroofed cella of the new building, and so the statue of Artemis was set up over the former cult area. This cult statue stood either under a baldachin or within a naiskos, and was different from the type known to us through Roman copies (Pl. 58). The rear of the cella (known also as the adyton or sekos) was closed, i.e., there was no opisthodomos, a feature also lacking in Heraions

Fig. 54 – Ephesus. The Artemis Temple. 560-550 B. C. See also Figs. 52, 53.

III and IV. The pronaos also resembled the two Samian models and the archaic Didymaion in that it took the form of a long hall.

Although the plan of the Artemision shows the marked influence of the Samian prototype, it exhibits many new features, improvements and developments. Mention can be made of the column bases, which began at the bottom with a plinth, followed by a spira, consisting of three tori and two trochili, and ended with a large torus (Fig. 54). The Ephesian base exhibited a less intricate and delicate profile. As it was much more tectonic and practical compared with the models in Heraion III or even Heraion IV, it became a standard architectural element in Ionian art and continued in use for two hundred years. It is generally accepted that the height of the columns was 12 lower diameters, i. e., 19 m. The number of flutes varied : shafts with 40, 44, and 48 arrises have been encountered. Some columns exhibit alternating narrow and wide flutes. According to Pliny, 36 "columnae caelatae", i.e., columns carved with reliefs, existed in the temple. Fragments of some have been recovered. One such piece, inscribed "presented by King Kroisos", attests to the truth of Herodotus' writings on this subject. This "columna caelata" has been restored and is now in the British Museum. There is no doubt that the columns bearing carved reliefs were created under the influence of eastern models. Probably, Ionian craftsmen who saw the reliefs on the orthostats in the city walls, palaces and temples of Assyrian and Hittite centres, or their pictorial designs fashioned in gold, bronze and ivory, adopted this idea by inventing the "columna caelata". In the case of Greek temples, only columns could be seen from the outside; the cella walls were hidden from view. Therefore, column bases carved with reliefs took the place of orthostats and created an original element in Ionian architecture.

The volutes on the capitals in the archaic Artemision also took a canonical form (Fig. 54). Since no capital from Heraion III is in existence today, we have no idea what form the Samian prototype had. When a comparison is made with the column capital of the Sphinx of Naxos, which must have been about 570 B. C., one is struck by the far greater elegance and organic appearance achieved in the Ephesian specimens. It is generally accepted that the entablature of the archaic Ephesian temple consisted of an architrave comprising three fasciae, with a row of dentils on the upper and lower edges decorated with an Ionic cymation, surmounted by a cornice and finally a sima. The space between the two central columns on the front end was 8.74 m. and calculations prove that the single block forming the architrave which they supported must have weighed 24 tons. Lifting such a weight to a height of 20 m. with the primitive equipment of those days and placing it on the columns was an astonishing feat. Indeed, the legend arose among the people that one night the goddess Artemis placed the marble block in position herself. No precise information has come to light concerning the dentils, but the existence of an Ionic kymation, 28 cm. in height, has been confirmed. Recovered fragments of the sima, also 28 cm. high, are decorated with lion-headed gargoyles as well as scenes depicting chariots and warriors. We learn from coins stamped with a representation of the second Artemision that it had a pitched roof, i. e., that there was a pediment. However, no pieces of the archaic Artemision have been found which could throw light on how it was roofed. The material of the roof, ceilings and the inner architrave was of wood.

The temple can be dated by the ivory works of art discovered in the foundations and by the columnae caelatae presented by Kroisos. The afore-mentioned ivory statuette of a priestess bearing a Phrygian phiale in one hand and a small oinochoe in the other has the most recent date of the objects recovered in the foundations. The simplicity of the bunched folds of the skirt between the legs, ending with a slight zigzag edge just above the feet, dates the statuette to about 570 B. C. The columnae caelatae commissioned by Kroisos must have been set up during his reign. Since these columns cannot have been erected after the devastation of the Persians in 546, it may be con-cluded that the greater part of the temple was finished by 550. However, the late archaic style of the sima reliefs reveals that some parts were comp-leted or restored in the last quarter of the 6th century and yet others in the 5th century.

The Later Artemision (Fig. 53). The magnificence and beauty of the archaic Artemision was a source of admiration for a period of one hundred years. However, in 356, the year of Alexander the Great's birth, a man called Herostratos, idiotically in search of fame, had the idea of rendering his name immortal by setting the temple on fire. The ceiling and inner architrave, being made of wood, were completely destroyed in the blaze. Before marching against Persia in 334, Alexander offered up sacrifices amid the ruins of the Artemision and expressed the desire to undertake its reconstruction. Accord-ing to Strabo (XIV, 641), the Ephesians acknowledged his proposal with this superb but flattering refusal : "It is not fitting for a god to build a temple to a god". Thereupon, the city of Ephesus decided to rebuild the Artemision to its original plan. Consequently, new columns and walls rose up on the exact sites of the originals. The main difference was the placing of the new temple on a 2.68 m. high podium with 13 steps (Fig. 53). The presence of un-derlying marshy ground necessitated the construction of a high platform. The foundations of the archaic Artemision are understood to have been waterlogged even in those days. In fact, the channels recently discovered around the later Artemision altar, which Austrian archaeologists have been engaged in uncovering since 1965, were obviously constructed to carry off the water rising from below. At the same time, however, a podium of such a height becomes an architectural form, and must have been built for aesthetic reasons as well. Just as the Ionic column had been given a specific structural appearance, like that of a human figure with feet, a trunk and head, so the Ionian architects may now have felt the need to give a similar organic form to the temple as a whole. Without doubt, the Ionic temple gained a far more attractive silhouette, owing to this high base. When the temple was viewed from its narrow ends, the diagonal lines formed by the two sides of the steps, together with those formed by the sides of the trian-gular pediment, presented a particularly pleasing harmony. The Hellenistic Didymaion, constructed after the later Artemision but not built on marshy ground, also rests on a similar podium with 7 steps, which is in fact higher than that of the temple of Artemis, reaching a height of 3.15 m. On this point the architect was probably influenced by Pytheos' Mausoleum. If we admit an opisthodomos in the new Artemision, this element would also indicate the influence of Pytheos. As was stated in the chapter on Priene, prior to this time the opisthodomos did not exist as a feature of Ionic architecture, but after its introduction by Pytheos, it became a characteristic of practically every temple. The second Artemision was affected by Pytheos' style in yet other ways. The measurements and proportions of the columns also conform to those of the columns of the Athena temple at Priene. Pliny records that the columns in the later Artemision rose to a height of 60 ft. (17.65 m.), which was 9.6 times the lower diameter of the shafts. This means that they appeared shorter and thicker than those in the archaic Artemision. The height of the columns of the Athena temple at Priene was ten times the measurement of their lower diameters. Like the specimens found at Priene, the column shafts in the second Artemision were carved with 24 flutes joined by narrow strips. Although the column bases were replicas of the archaic examples, the style of the reliefs on the new columnae caelatae followed the latest trends in classical art. A large part of one of these has been preserved to the present day and is now in the British Museum. This column, bearing reliefs depicting Hermes, Thanatos and possibly either Eurydice or Alcestis, was produced by an Ionian sculptor under Attic influence and is one of the finest examples of stone carving dating from the 4th century B. C. The entablature of the new Artemision was similar to that of the archaic building, except that the reliefs with figures found between the lion-headed gargoyles on the sima, were replaced by conventional anthemion designs.

As stated above, representations of the new Artemision on coins indicate that its narrow faces were surmounted by pediments and the building was covered with a pitched roof. The same coins show a large door in the pediment with a big window on each side. The purpose of these openings was doubtless to relieve the weight of this huge pediment, which measured 50 m. along the lower edge.

The temple was completed in the first half of the 3rd century B. C. Its magnificent rows of columns must have appeared like an imposing phalanx. Those who approached the temple were no doubt impressed by the quality of the stonework as well as by the beauty and perfection of the reliefs and ornamentation. It is on account of this that the Hellenistic Artemision, as we learn from the epigram of Antipatros of Sidon, was considered the most impressive of the seven wonders of the world.

The excavations undertaken by the Austrian expedition of 1965 led to the discovery of the altar belonging to the later Artemision. This was a horseshoe-shaped edifice, faced with marble, 15 cm. thick, and erected on a site 32 × 22 m. in area. Since the ruins lie beneath water level, the archaeologists had to resort to the use of pumps. A number of channels were discovered around the altar; these show that the water rose to this level even in the 4th century. Among the finds, those worthy of mention are column drums belonging to the archaic Artemision, and various decorated portions of the altar, dating from the classical period. Of special importance is the 33 cm.-high piece of cornice that has been retrieved. In 1901, an Amazon relief of the Berlin-Lansdown-Sciarra type was discovered among the marble paving stones in the road running by the Ephesian theatre, and is now preserved in the museum in Vienna. A comparison with the remnant of cornice mentioned above led to its identification as an original part of the Artemision altar, as was earlier surmised by Hans Schrader. A. Bammer, a member of the expedition, has proved that the marble plates decorated with the Greek fret used in the theatre and the İsa Bey mosque were also originally parts of the altar. Other discoveries made during the excavation of the altar include the body and part of the legs of a statue representing a horse, as well as many other fragments of statues. For the new excavations and observations made by Anton Bammer see the annex at the end of this book.

The Vedius Gymnasium (Fig. 50, No. 5; Fig. 55). This gymnasium, one of the best preserved buildings to be found in Ephesus, was erected in A. D. 150 by Publius Vedius Antoninus, one of the prominent wealthy Ephesians of the time. He dedicated it to the goddess Artemis and the Emperor Antoninus Pius, who was his friend and protector. This building emerges as a combined gymnasium and baths, as was customary in Roman architecture. East of this building complex lay the palaestra, with a propylon on its south side. This entrance was formerly decorated with statues. The elongated room to the west of the propylon was a lavatory, with access from the west, i.e., from the street, and the south.

In the western section of the west colonnade in the palaestra is a large room, open on the front, which must have been the hall found in all Roman gymnasia, and used for ceremonial purposes or reserved for the

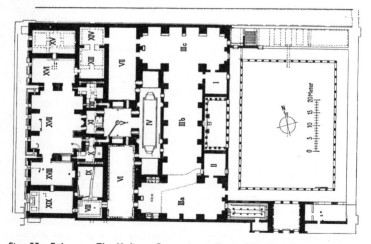

Fig. 55 – Ephesus. The Vedius Gymnasium. Erected by P. Vedius Antoninus about the middle of the 2nd century A. D. This is the best preserved and most completely excavated gymnasium at Ephesus (see p. 154).

Emperor. The base of a now lost statue in a central niche in the west wall of the hall is still in its original position. Since Vedius dedicated this building to Antoninus Pius (A. D. 138-161), the statue that occupied the niche was most probably a likeness of this emperor. The portrait statue of a sophist (Pl. 53), dating from about A. D. 200, has been found here. On ceremonial days, teachers and scholars offered up sacrifices on the altar which stood in front of the niche. The large hall (No. III on the plan), stretching the entire width of the building, was a place devoted to sports and gymnastics. Two doors gave access to Room VI, which was the apodyterium or dressing-room; another door at the south-east corner opened to the street; however, the latter cannot be seen on the accompanying illustration (Fig. 55, No. VI). The holes over the bench running around the base of the four walls of this room were made to contain boxes, in which valuables could safely be kept. The hall in the centre (marked V) housed the frigidarium or cold baths. Two bathtubs supplied with cold water were to be found there, one along the south side of this room and the other along the north, while a small pool, with water issuing from a central jet, occupied the middle of the room. The area marked IV, lying east of Room V, contained the natatio or swimming-pool. Room XI was supplied with hot water running through earthenware pipes, but since there was no form of underground heating, this must have been the tepidarium or warm baths. It was possible to reach Rooms X and XI by passing underground. These basements were occupied by small domed ovens or furnaces, in which fires burned day and night, ensuring the constant stream of hot air that flowed through channels beneath the floor and into the hollow bricks of the walls in the caldarium, or hot baths, indicated by the numbers XV-XIX. In addition, the furnaces heated the water sent to the hot-water tubs in the caldarium.

Throughout the Roman period, there also existed at Ephesus other buildings devoted to bathing and sports. These are known as the Harbour Baths (Fig. 50, No. 11), the Theatre Gymnasium (Fig. 50, No. 12), the Varius Baths (Fig. 59, No. 22) and the East Gymnasium (Fig. 50, No. 27). In the early Christian era, the Scholastikia Baths (Fig. 58, No. 9) and the Byzantine Baths (Fig. 50, No. 8) were added.

The Stadium (Fig. 50, No. 6). The stadium, lying south of the Vedius gymnasium, was the scene of all kinds of ceremonies, athletic contests, chariot races and gladiatorial fights. Seats for the spectators on the south side were constructed on the slopes of Mt. Pion, i.e., present-day Panayırdağ, while those on the north were built over a vaulted substructure. Since the stone seats were used to build the city wall around Ayasoluk in the early Christian era, the stadium was reduced to ruins. Only the west side of the stadium has so far been excavated. Judging by the pillar bases lying on the ground, entry to the stadium was gained through an arcade. Recovered inscriptions reveal that the stadium was erected in the reign of the Emperor Nero (A. D. 54-68). Among the pillar bases near the entrance were found poorly-fashioned marble vases representing sports trophies, and plaques decorated with designs incorporating olive branches and rabbits; all these date from a period when alterations were carried out, in the 3rd or 4th century A. D.

Gladiatorial fights and the baiting of animals for amusement took place at the eastern end of the stadium.

The Byzantine Baths (Fig. 50. No. 8). The lavish use of apses in the building situated west of the processional road that passes in front of the Vedius gymnasium and the stadium, reveals that these baths were probably constructed during the Christian period in the 6th century A. D.

The Church of the Virgin Mary (Fig. 50, No. 9). This church, the most important of the Christian edifices at Ephesus, is situated within a Roman building, constructed during the first half of the 2nd century A. D. It is 30 m. in width, 260 m. in length, and divided by two rows of columns into a nave and two aisles; at each of the narrow ends is an apse-shaped exedra. It can be classified as a basilica (Fig. 42), a type of building found in Roman agorae. The aisles were divided into a series of small sections, very probably at a later date, but still in the first half of the 2nd century. When one remembers that the rhetorician Aristeides, who lived about the middle of this century, mentions Ephesus as being the bank for the whole Province of "Asia" (western Anatolia), and the main commercial centre of the period, one may assume that this large building might have been the corn and money exchange. Perhaps customers gathered to examine the produce on display in the nave of this 260 m. - long building, while bankers and brokers occupied the small rooms in the aisles. In all probability, business connected with the courts was attended to in the two exedrae in the apses at the ends of the building, as was the customary practice in the basilica within an agora. The opinion that this was a building for business and exchange is further strengthened by the fact that it was situated at the city centre and very near the harbour.

Perhaps the extremely difficult and critical times during the 3rd century A. D. put an end to the activity of the exchange building. Meanwhile, the local Christians built their first church, entered by a large, square atrium and a mosaic-paved narthex, in the western part of this then-abandoned large Roman building, at the beginning of the 4th century A. D. At a later period, they converted rather more than the western half of the Roman basilica by the addition of two more churches, placed one behind the other. The remaining eastern section of this building, however, was reserved as the place where the bishop and other religious officials sat. The baptisterium, built on the north side of the atrium, dates from the 4th century. This cylindrically-shaped building is in a fine state of preservation. In accordance with the first Christian rites, those who wanted to be baptised immersed themselves three times in the pool in the centre of the building, and after this, they were anointed with fragrant oils. The surface of the walls between the niches and entrances were adorned with large signs of the Cross, and, judging by the holes present, with rosette motifs worked in metal.

The third meeting of the Ecumenical Council was held in this church in A. D. 431, and after a stormy discussion, the members agreed to accept as dogma the statement that Jesus, the son of the Virgin Mary, was also born the Son of God. Perhaps the Virgin really did live in Ephesus during the second quarter of the 1st century A. D., and that is why the first church dedicated to her was erected in Ephesus and the above-mentioned council reached its decision in this same church. It is well known that Jesus gave his mother into the care of St. John at the crucifixion ". . . and from that hour the disciple took her to his own home" (Gospel according to St. John, Ch. 19, v. 25). When we consider that St. John spent part of his life in Ephesus, it is quite conceivable that St. Mary also lived in the city, and on her death was buried there. Indeed the Christian world favours this belief, to which Pope Paul VI gave his blessing in a religious ceremony held in this church in 1967, attended by many thousands of visitors.

The Harbour Gymnasium and Baths (Fig. 50, Nos. 10, 11). Although only a very small part of these buildings constituting the largest architectural complex in Ephesus has as yet been excavated, those remains still standing are extremely impressive. There were formerly two palaestrae or athletic training grounds (Fig. 50, Nos. 10, 11), one of which was 90 sq. m. in area and the other 200 × 240 m. The entire construction attained a length of 360 m. The building of this huge gymnasium commenced and must have neared completion in the reign of the Emperor Domitian (A. D. 81-96). In Hadrian's time (A. D. 117-138), Claudius Verulanus, the chief priest of Asia, i.e., of western Anatolia, had the whole of the larger palaestra faced with marble plaques. The use of 13 different kinds of coloured marble has been confirmed. The plaques themselves have long since disappeared, but holes in the walls for holding them in position are still in evidence. The hall in the northern section of the smaller palaestra (11) must have been devoted to the cult of the Emperor, while lectures and meetings no doubt took place in the one to the south, where a fine Roman copy of a Greek bronze statue of an athlete was found. This copy is now in the Vienna museum; the original dates from the 4th century B. C. The remains of the baths section of the building complex still stand as ruins of immense proportions, and those able to spare the time would be well advised to take at least a short walk within them.

The Theatre Gymnasium (Fig. 50, No. 12). This structure was built in the period of the Roman Empire, most probably in the 2nd century A. D. So far, only the palaestra has been completely uncovered, while the rest of the building has only been partially excavated. Nevertheless, it has been possible to produce quite a good reconstructed plan. In place of a stoa, rows of steps, used for seating, run the entire length of the north side of the palaestra, which measures 30 × 70 m. Thus the athletic training ground in this gymnasium functioned also as a small "stadium".

Arkadiane (Fig. 50, No. 13). This colonnaded street, attributed to the Emperor Arcadius and known by his name, according to the evidence of an inscription, is in present-day opinion definitely considered to have existed since the Hellenistic era. In point of fact, the recovered fragments and foundations of the harbour gateway or propylon, lying on exactly the same axis as the western end of the Arkadiane, are Hellenistic in date. The Arkadiane is a fairly well-preserved colonnaded street, 11 m. in width and 600 m. in length.

The two pedestrian walks in the colonnades were 5 m. wide and paved with mosaics. A series of shops stretched along the inner sides of the colonnades. Thus shoppers or those wishing to take a stroll walked on the pavements protected from the rain and sun, and in summer got the benefit of the cool breezes blowing from the nearby sea. From the inscription which states that Arcadius erected the colonnades, it is also learnt that street-lighting existed.

About half-way down the Arkadiane is to be seen a monument composed of four columns with Corinthian capitals. In all probability, these columns supported statues of the four apostles. The niches in the round column bases and other details are features betraying the style of the Christian period. Therefore, this four-columned monument was evidently erected in the reign of Justinian (A. D. 527-565), a time when Ephesus was at the zenith of its final glorious period.

A Hellenistic Fountain (Fig. 50, No. 14). Sunk into the north-west corner formed by the theatre terrace wall is a fountain opening westwards between two columns of the Ionic order, on to the courtyard in front of the theatre. Both the elegant proportions of this fountain and the skill manifest in the fine stonework are features revealing the style of the Hellenistic era. Judged by the beautiful way in which the Ionic capitals and the flutes on the columns shafts are carved, this is definitely a creation of the 3rd or, at the latest, the 2nd century B. C.

The Theatre (Pl. 57 b; Fig. 50, No. 15; Fig. 56). The largest and most impressive of the buildings in Ephesus that are well-preserved is the theatre.

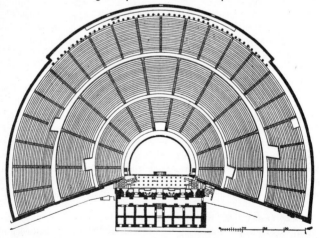

Fig. 56 – Ephesus. The Theatre. The most impressive building at Ephesus. The auditorium had a seating capacity of 24,000 and reached a height of 30 m. Originally constructed in the Hellenistic age, it was altered and enlarged in the reigns of Claudius (A. D. 41-54), Nero (A. D. 54-68) and Trajan (A. D. 98-117). St. Paul preached here (see p. 158).

In Roman times, the appearance of this marble construction, measuring 145 m. in width and possessing an auditorium 30 m. in height, must have had a profound effect on the beholder. Even today, as one approaches the ruins of Ephesus from Kuşadası, the remains of the theatre present an attractive and majestic appearance.

Work on the construction of the theatre commenced in Hellenistic times. Later, in the reign of the Emperor Claudius (A. D. 41 - 54), the diameter was enlarged, but the building was not completed until Trajan's time (A. D. 98-117). The first two storeys of the skene were erected in the Emperor Nero's reign (A. D. 54-68), while the third storey was probably added in the middle of the 2nd century A. D. The auditorium had a seating capacity of 24,000. The stage measured 25×40 m. and the auditorium rose to a height of 30 m. above the level of the orchestra. Portions of the skene belonging to the Hellenistic theatre have been found in the stage of Roman times and thus have yielded important information concerning the style and shape of the earlier building. In the Hellenistic era the performers acted in the orchestra, but in Roman times the 7 m. wide proscenium was used for this purpose.

St. Paul preached in the theatre at Ephesus, but a jeweller named Demetrius, fearing a drop in the sale of Artemis statues, started a demonstration against the Apostle by stirring up the multitude to shout "Great is Diana of the Ephesians", for the space of several hours. Only the calming words of the "grammateus" (the head of the municipality) prevented the episode from reaching more alarming proportions.

The Marble Road (Fig. 50, No. 16). A sacred road starting at the Artemision in Ephesus passed west of the Vedius gymnasium, the stadium and the theatre and then continued east of the agora until it turned east in front of the library and came to the State Agora (Fig. 59, No. 20). After reaching the Magnesian gate, it took a northerly direction and so regained the temple of Artemis. As will be noted, this was also the main thoroughfare of the city. At various times, this road underwent repairs and alterations in many sections of the city; the stretch beginning south of the theatre and running the length of the commercial agora was paved with marble slabs by a man named Eutropios, thought to have lived in the 5th century A. D. This marble street, which even now has a very pleasing aspect, was reserved for vehicles. Today, abundant remains of a late Roman colonnade lie along the eastern side of the street, while on the western side stretches a 1.70 m. - high socle in the *rustica* style belonging to the Doric stoa of the agora. This socle was erected in Nero's time (A.D. 54-68). There was a flight of stone steps at the northern end of the Doric colonnade and another at the southern. Pedestrians could go up these steps and walk through the colonnade.

The Celsus Library (Pl. 57 a; Fig. 50, No. 19 and Figs. 57, 58, No. 4). At present, there is no doubt that one of the principal buildings at Ephesus is the extremely well-preserved Celsus library. Its façade was two-tiered; the interior consisted of a single large, lofty hall, measuring 10.92×16.72 m., comprising the Celsus library itself, which rose up on a platform built over a vaulted substructure and was reached by a nine-stepped stairway,

21 m. in width. A wall surrounded the building on the outside, thus insulating it on each side and ensuring protection against the effects of dampness. When looking closely at the ruins still standing today (Pl. 57 a), one notices an upper and lower row of square niches on the inner faces of the rear and side walls. Originally there existed a third row of niches, so that the interior of the library was three-storeyed. Manuscripts in the form of scrolls or volumes were kept in cupboards or on shelves in these niches. Access to the second and third rows of niches was gained by a two-tiered gallery of horse-shoe shape, running around three sides of the main hall, much in the manner employed in some modern libraries. A librarian would give the books to the readers. The central niche consisted of a large arch, rising to the height of the third row of niches and very probably, was occupied by a statue of Athena, the patroness of wisdom and learning.

The library possessed a very elaborate architectural façade. It has been possible to make a graphic reconstruction of the entire façade with the help of fragments found during the excavations. Judging by columns bases still in place along the front of the façade, it was supported by four pairs of columns. The remains of the façade wall, which stood just behind the aforementioned bases, show that there were evidently three entrances to the building. In addition, three windows were to be found over the entrances, set into the second tier. In this way, the reading room received light through these windows and doors.

According to inscriptions in Latin and Greek on the wings of the front steps, the Celsus Library was erected in A. D. 110 by the Consul

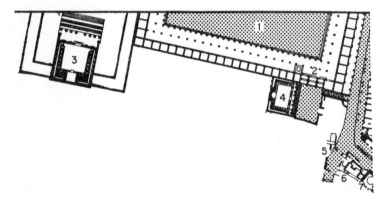

Fig. 57 – Ephesus. 3) The Temple of Serapis (Fig. 50, No. 18), one of the most impressive buildings at Ephesus. It was erected in the Antonine period (A. D. 138-192) by Egyptian colonists. 4) The Celsus Library (see also Fig. 50, No. 19) was erected in A. D. 110 by the Consul G. J. Aquila for his father, G. J. Celsus Polemaeanus. The library was completed in A. D. 135 by his heirs. The sarco-phagus containing the remains of Celsus lies in the vaulted substructure under the main niche of the library.

Gaius Julius Aquila as a heroon for his father, Gaius Julius Celsus Polemaeanus.
Aquila left 25.000 denarii for the purchase of books and the upkeep of the
library, which was completed in A. D. 135 by his heirs. The skeletal remains
of Celsus still lie buried in a lead casket kept in a marble sarcophagus, installed under the large niche in the vaulted substructure.

The reading room was destroyed in a fire of unknown date, but the
façade did not suffer damage. For a time, the library was left filled with the
resulting debris. About A. D. 400, the area in front of the building was converted into a pool. The façade, still in existence, served a decorative purpose,
with its beautiful silhouette mirrored in the water. Huge reliefs belonging
to a monument erected to commemorate a victory over the Parthians won
by Marcus Aurelius and Lucius Verus were found within the pool, in front
of the steps, during the excavations. These reliefs are now kept in the museum
in Vienna.

Very probably, the auditorium mentioned in an inscription occupied the
space lying between the street and the pool in front of the library. Professors,
rhetoricians and poets held lectures in this hall, and its proximity to the
library must have been very convenient. No trace of this auditorium has
survived; on the other hand, a portion of the platform of a circular building
of Hellenistic origin, destroyed when the auditorium was under construction,
is still in evidence.

Some important remains lie immediately south-east of the library. Those
that can be seen near the beginning of Curetes Street, a little way up on the
south side, are the ruins of a monumental gateway (Fig. 58, No. 5), which
resembled Hadrian's Gate in Athens. Just south of the road lie the remains
of a building, shaped like a pool. These are the ruins of a heroon of the Augustan age which was later converted into a fountain (Fig. 58, No. 6). The
remains of a building, situated south-east of the fountain are of an octagonal
tomb dating from the 1st century A. D. (Fig. 58, No. 7). The inscriptions
it bears were carved at a later date, in the 4th century.

The Commercial Agora (Fig. 50, No. 17 and Fig. 57, No. 1). The
commercial market-place in Ephesus was set up in Hellenistic times.
In fact, the Ionic architectural fragments of the west gate that have been
discovered bear characteristic signs of the Hellenistic period. Nevertheless, this agora, measuring 110 m.sq. and enclosed on all four sides by stoas,
was altered by additions erected in the reigns of Augustus and Nero. It
is further understood to have been extensively restored in the time of
Caracalla (A. D. 211-217). The two-storeyed double colonnade of the Doric
order forming the eastern side of the agora was built when Nero was
emperor (A. D. 54-68). The south-east gate to the market-place, however,
was erected in the year either 4 or 3 B.C. Two inscriptions written in Latin
and Greek appear on the attic of this triple gateway. They record that
two slaves emancipated by Agrippa, Mazaeus and Mithridates, built the
gateway in honour of Augustus and his wife Livia, and Agrippa, who
was Augustus' deceased son-in-law, and Augustus' daughter Julia. The
inscriptions on the 2.52 m.-high attic lie in large fragments at the foot
of the inner wall of the agora near the gate. They were written in

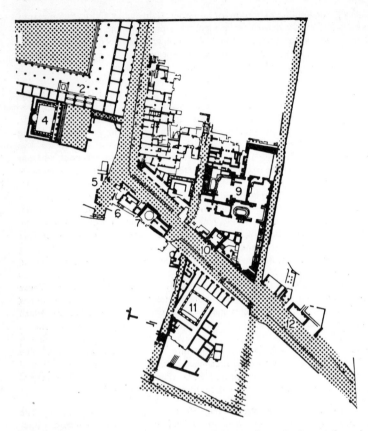

Fig. 58 – Ephesus. Buildings on both sides of Curetes Street leading up from the Celsus Library (4) to the State Agora (Fig. 59). 5) Ruins of a monumental gateway resembling Hadrian's Gate in Athens. 6) Remains of a pool-shaped structure. These constitute the ruins of a heroon of the Augustan Age, later converted into a fountain. 7) Ruins of an octaganal tomb, first century A. D., with inscriptions on the socle dating from the 4th century A. D. 8) Round building on Panayırdağ, several fragments of which have been found in the vicinity, although only the quadrangular base of the monument survived on the spot (not shown on the plan). Middle of the 1st century B. C. 9) Scholastikia Baths. Originally constructed ca. A. D. 100 and enlarged at the end of the 4th century A. D. by a Christian lady named Scholastikia. A large lavatory and a section identified through an inscription as a brothel both belong to the first building phase. The entrance to these two sections is on the marble sacred street. 10) Temple of the Corinthian order dedicated to Hadrian (A. D. 117-138). The second sanctuary especially built for the cult of an emperor, the first being the temple dedicated to Domitian (Fig. 59,

No. 17). **11)** *House on the slope. Constructed in the 1st century A. D. but inhabited for centuries, it rises up on 5 successive terraces each supporting a storey of the same house. A fresco representing Socrates found here has been removed to the museum in Selçuk.* **12)** *Trajan's Fountain (A. D. 98-117). A colossal statue of the emperor formerly stood in the middle of the façade. The surviving base with the two feet of the statue and a globe (the earth symbol) has been restored to its original position. The water cascaded from beneath the statue into a large basin and then flowed into the pool, from which it was drawn by the citizens.*

gold-plated bronze letters, only the sockets of which remain today. The word "Imperator" (Emperor) on the eastern part of the attic appears as "Imberator". It is probable, however, that this textual eror was corrected in the metal form. The inscription, written in Greek for the benefit of the Ephesians, whose language it was, states that the gateway was previously dedicated to the Ephesian "demos", that is, the autonomous populace. It is interesting to note that it did not seem necessary to use this formula in the Latin rendering. Nevertheless, it is certain that Ephesus was self-governing from the time of Augustus onwards.

A horologion, or combined water-clock and sundial, stood in the middle of the agora, and there were hundreds of statues on all sides. Although only the bases exist at the present time, the inscriptions appearing on them disclose important information concerning the social life of Ephesus. The statues represented rhetoricians, philosophers, athletes and various state officials.

The Temple of Serapis (Fig. 57, No. 3). One of the most interesting buildings to be found at Ephesus is that which must have been erected by Egyptian colonists. An addition in the form of a stoa (Fig. 50), measuring 24 m. in width and 160 m. in length, was built on the axis of the west gate of the commercial agora. This led to the temple of Serapis, which today is reached by the flight of steps at the south-west corner of the agora.

The temple was a conspicuous edifice, built partly on the rear wall inside a square enclosed on three sides by colonnades. It consisted of a cella roofed with stone vaulting and a porch containing eight Corinthian columns The walls were exceptionally thick to enable them to support the weight of the vault over the 29 m. wide cella. The monoliths, i.e., the columns formed of single blocks of stone, had a lower diameter of 1.5 m., a height of 14 m. and a total weight of 57 tons. A two-leaved doorway was also very wide, being 6 m. across. Fragments of the entablature lying on the ground bear deeply carved architectural ornamentation, a feature of the baroque style of the Antonine period (A. D. 138-192). This building of such conspicuously large proportions must have been a temple set up to the god Serapis, for the following reasons: firstly, fragments of a statue made of Egyptian granite have been discovered among the ruins; secondly, a recovered inscription records the rites of an Egyptian cult; and finally, according to another inscription, it was dedicated to the adherents of Serapis-worship. Indeed, a similar temple of huge proportions also existed in the same period at Pergamon (Fig. 36). In antiquity, Egypt was mainly a wheat-producing country.

Consequently all the other countries of those times established firm commercial relationships with her.

In the Christian era, the Serapis temple was converted into a church. Ruins of a baptisterium are to be seen at the east corner of the temple.

The Scholastikia Baths (Fig. 58, No. 9). The large baths, situated at a bend in the main road stretching along the south-west slopes of Mt. Panayır, were erected in the second half of the 1st century A. D. or at the beginning of the 2nd century. In A. D. 400 the baths were extensively renovated by a Christian lady named Scholastikia. A large lavatory and a section identified through a recovered inscription as a brothel both belong to the first building phase, i.e., the 1st century A. D. Compared in size with the small brothels of Pompeii, the one in the Scholastikia baths draws much more attention. Franz Miltner was of the opinion that the rooms on the top floor were reserved for the girls and the hall on the ground floor for visitors. The main hall of the brothel contained a dining-room (tablinum) covered with mosaics. On the floor in each of the four corners of the room was a personification of one of the seasons. Winter (with the head covered) and Autumn (wearing a garland of flowers) are in a good state of preservation. The Austrian archaeologists record that the large-scale alterations carried out in the Roman building by Scholastikia took place about A. D. 400. They also state that a great number of Roman buildings, especially the Prytaneion (Fig. 59, No. 19), yielded the materials used in its construction. The headless statue of Scholastikia, together with the base bearing an inscription, have been restored to their original position.

The Temple of Hadrian (Pl. 56 b; Fig. 58, No. 10). Although small in size, the temple of Hadrian is one of the most attractive edifices in Ephesus. Built in the Corinthian style, it consists of a cella and a porch; the former was originally roofed with stone vaulting. There are two columns in the middle of the porch façade, with a pillar at each end. The straight architrave and overlying frieze found at the sides curve in an arch over the two columns. The arch, adorned with the bust of a tyche (city goddess), is framed by a pediment, now represented by fragments at the two corners. The figure of a girl is depicted rising from an interlaced acanthus decoration on the arch-shaped tympanum over the entrance to the cella. The inscription over the architrave states that the temple was dedicated to the Emperor Hadrian (A. D. 117-138) by a man named P. Quintilius. As was customary in many Anatolian cities wishing to secure the friendship and support of Rome, a temple especially dedicated to the worship of the emperor was built in autonomous Ephesus; this temple was the second of its kind in Ephesus, the first sacred building consecrated to an emperor being the temple of Domitian (Fig. 59, No. 17). When these cities listed their titles, that of "Temple-Wardenship" was especially mentioned.

Before it was partially demolished in A.D. 400, the temple of Hadrian underwent restorations, in the course of which four decorative reliefs were added to the upper part of the inner walls of the porch. The original reliefs, now in the safe-keeping of the museum, have been replaced by plaster casts. Three of the reliefs date from the 3rd century A. D. and were taken from other buildings in Ephesus. The fourth one, however, was made during the restorations and is of considerable importance in relation to Christian history in that the Christian King Theodosius, a strong opponent of paganism, accompanied by his wife and son, stands side by side with a figure of Artemis Ephesia. The above-mentioned relief appears on the block, at each end of which appears a portrayal of Athena with her round shield and helmet. The fourth figure from the right represents Artemis Ephesia. To the right stands Theodosius, and next to him comes a portrayal of his father in the form of a half-naked dead figure. Immediately left of Artemis appears Theodosius' wife and then his elder son Arcadius.

The House on the Slope (Fig. 58, No. 11). This is the largest house in Ephesus excavated to date. Constructed in the 1st century A. D. but inhabited for centuries, it rises up on a series of terraces with a frontage on the south side of Curetes Street. The excavators have uncovered, up to the present, 5 successive terraces, each supporting a storey of the same house. A mural portrait of Socrates shown seated, which dates from the 1st century A. D., was found in this house and has now been conveyed to the museum in Selçuk. For the detailed plans of this house and of a second house on the slope, see the annex at the end of this book.

The Fountain of Trajan (Fig. 58, No. 12). Curetes Street continues as a column-lined road climbing in a south-easterly direction. The fountain occupies an area of 5.20×11.9 m., at a point 40 m. east of the side street bordering the end of the Scholastikia Baths which lie on the north side of Curetes Street. It takes the form of a pool, flanked on three sides by a two-storeyed building. The columns used on the ground floor are composite in style, whereas those on the upper floor are of the Corinthian order. A colossal statue of the Emperor Trajan, rising to the height of the two-storeyed edifice, stood in the middle section of the building where water flowed into the pool. The surviving base, with the two feet of the statue accompanied by a globe, has been restored to its original position. Water cascaded from beneath the statue into a large basin and then flowed into a 1.90 m.-wide elongated pool, from which it was drawn by the populace. The many statues formerly decorating the fountain of Trajan have been removed to the Ephesus Museum. The excavators hesitated to carry out a complete anastylosis, as the height of the original columns is not known.

A short way past Trajan's fountain can be seen the remains of reliefs, depicting Hercules and decorated bases, all of which were incorporated in a gateway erected in the 4th or 5th century A. D. Further on, one comes to a junction where the road, referred to by the excavators as Domitian Street, leads off to the south. Various monuments stand at the junction; north of Curetes Street, a base formed of stone blocks in *rustica* style can be seen. According to the fragments of a recovered inscription, the monument that rose on this base was erected in the late Hellenistic period to Memmius, one of the grandsons of the dictator Sulla (Fig. 59, No. 14). The building adjoining the Memmius monument on the north-west is described in an inscription as a hydreion or fountain (Fig. 59, No. 13). The round Roman altar situated exactly in the centre of the junction comes from another place and was set up here temporarily.

At the junction of Curetes Street and Domitian Street, on the south-east corner, there stands an edifice showing walls with stone blocks in *rustica* style, referred to by the excavators as the "Socle Structure" since its function is not known (Fig. 59, 15). The monument (Fig. 59, No. 16), situated a short way along Domitian Street, was erected in honour of C. Sextilius Pollio, the builder of the Marnas aqueduct. An inscription records that this structure was built in the reign of Augustus by C. Ofillius Proculus and was embellished in A. D. 93 by the addition of an apsidal fountain construction and various statues, some of which have been discovered and are now kept in the Ephesus Museum. The monument (Fig. 59, No. 18) at the end of Domitian Street is a fountain set up in A. D. 80 by C. Laecanius Bassus.

The Temple of Domitian (Fig. 50, No. 23; Fig. 59, No. 17). The first sacred building in Ephesus to be dedicated to a Roman emperor was the temple of Domitian. The Ephesians built this temple, which from many points of view was of great importance, to the monstrous tyrant Domitian (A. D. 81-96), who referred to himself as "ruler and god". At great expense, they erected the temple on the best and most central site in the town, opposite the state agora on the slopes of Mt. Bülbül, on a terrace supported by a substructure measuring 50×100 m. in area. The view south from the road junction reveals this terrace in all its grandeur.

The building, like all Roman temples, was essentially a small prostyle, having four columns in front, a peristasis of eight columns on the short and thirteen columns on the long sides. The cella measured only 9×17 m., and the stylobate, 24×34 m. in size, rose up on an 8-stepped krepidoma. In contrast to the small dimensions of the temple, the cult statue of Domitian, of which only the head and an arm have come to light, was of colossal proportions. In a sitting position, it would have been 5 m. in height, and standing it would have measured 7 m. The well-preserved head and the forearm, itself as big as a man, are now on display in the Izmir Museum; the altar is deco-rated with reliefs showing weapons, and it has now been re-erected in the garden of the Ephesus Museum at Selçuk. Nothing much remains on the site. Following the construction of this temple, the city of Ephesus, known as "the first and largest city of Asia", was granted the privilege of adding to its titles that of "Temple Warden" of the Roman Emperor.

After the Domitian Street junction, Curetes Street continued as far as the entrance to the state agora, where it came to an end. Of the gateway that at one time stood here, only two pillars decorated with reliefs have survived. One relief depicts Hermes with a ram, another a youth with a goat, and yet another, a tripod with an omphalos. The figure of Hermes no doubt indicated the proximity of the state agora.

The State Agora (Fig. 50, No. 26; Fig. 59). Excavations have been going on for several years in the state agora, and the north and east stoas have been brought to light. The north stoa is referred to as a basilica, on a piece of an architrave that has been found. This stoa was divided into two aisles and a central nave by two rows of columns. The aisles were two-thirds the height of the nave. A series of columns rose along the side of the south aisle overlooking the agora. The basilica, Ionic in style, was erected in the late Augustan age, and bulls' heads decorated the Ionic capitals on two sides. In late Roman Imperial times, columns with Corinthian capitals were placed between those adorned with bulls' heads, in order to give extra support to the nave. Excavations have confirmed the existence of a single-aisled Hellenistic stoa, 1.30 m. beneath the basilica. Very probably, certain municipal activities, such as meetings of the law courts, took place here in the basilica of the agora. Indeed, the fact that the prytaneion, where state affairs were attended to, was situated immediately behind the basilica is no mere coincidence.

The Prytaneion (Fig. 59, No. 19). This was the town hall of the autonomous city of Ephesus, with the accompanying temple of Hestia Boulaia, where burned the perpetual fire that was never permitted to go out. Besides being the place where political business was conducted, the prytaneion was also the scene of other important ceremonies, banquets and receptions. The excavators have placed various architectural fragments of the Doric courtyard in front of the assembly hall. This prytaneion was built in the Augustan age, but a prytaneion must have existed here since the time of Lysimachos, for it would not have been practical to move the altar containing the everlasting flame from one site to another. The courtyard of the prytaneion was adorned with a mosaic, composed of Amazon shields and whirls. The style of the columns with composite capitals indicates that the building underwent alterations in the 3rd century A. D. As has been stated above, a Christian woman named Scholastikia demolished several buildings, in particular the prytaneion, in order to acquire stone and marble for building material in the construction of the baths named after her (Fig. 58, No. 9). Nevertheless, she did not touch the two beautiful statues of Artemis Ephesia which stood here in pagan times, and these have survived to the present day. One of these, already mentioned, is kept in the Ephesus Museum. It is twice life-size, and was carved in the reign of Domitian (A. D. 81-96). It had stood in the middle of the courtyard, in front of the main hall of the prytaneion. The other is a life-size statue with a very beautiful countenance (Pl. 58). Judged by the hairstyle and rendering of the eyes, it is a work of the Hadrianic period (A. D. 117-138). Franz Miltner found the statue buried with great care under the soil in one of the side rooms of the Hestia Boulaia temple. Perhaps some of the workers employed by Scholastikia did not dare to use this beautiful piece of sculpture as building material and, for this reason, concealed it so carefully in the earth. It is now in the Selçuk Museum.

The Odeion (Bouleuterion). The building resembling a theatre is known as the odeion. (Fig. 59, No. 21). However, considering that the prytaneion is situated close by and the state agora is just in front of it, we may be right to assume that it functioned as a bouleuterion, or else did duty as a bouleuterion as well as an odeion. There are channels hollowed-out in the orchestra which could have drained off rain water, and it is very likely that the building was at one time roofed over; therefore this auditorium, with a seating capacity of 1,400, was suitable for a bouleuterion.

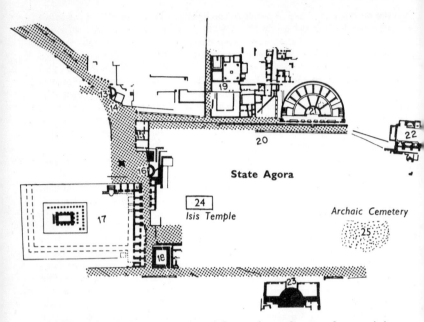

Fig. 59 – Ephesus. The upper section of Curetes Street, Domitian Street and the buildings surrounding the State Agora.

A short way past Trajan's Fountain can be seen the remains of reliefs, depicting Hercules, and decorated bases, all of which were incorporated in a gateway erected in the 4th or 5th century A. D. Further along, at the Domitian Street junction, three buildings are to be seen: **13)** Semicircular monument described in an inscription as a hydreion, i.e., a fountain. **14)** Monument erected in the late Hellenistic period to Memmius, one of the grandsons of the dictator Sulla. **15)** Edifice situated on the north-west corner of Domitian Street, called by the excavators the "Socle Structure". Function unknown. The round Roman altar at the centre of the junction comes from a different locality and is only set up here temporarily. Then follow buildings along Domitian Street: **16)** Monument erected in honour of C. Sextilius Pollio, the builder of the Marnas Aqueduct. An inscription records that this structure was built in the reign of Augustus and embellished in A. D. 93 by the addition of an apsidal fountain and various statues, some of which have been discovered and removed to the Selçuk Museum. **17)** Temple, built on a terrace supported by huge vaulted substructures. Erected for the cult of Domitian (A. D. 81-96), self-styled "ruler and god". Nothing much remains on the site. **18)** Fountain, set up in A. D. 80 by C. Laecanius Bassus.

At the end of Curetes Street beyond the Domitian Street junction, lie the remains of a gateway which formed the entrance to the State Agora. Only two portions of pillars decorated with reliefs have survived from this gateway. One relief depicts Hermes with a ram, another a youth with a goat, and yet another, a tripod with an omphalos. The figure of Hermes no doubt indicated the proximity of the State Agora. **19)** The Prytaneion, the town hall of the autonomous city of Ephesus, with the adjoining temple of Hestia Boulaia, where burned the perpetual fire. **20)** The north stoa of the agora, referred to in an inscription as a "basilica". It constituted a tripartite colonnade of the Ionic order, erected in the late Augustan Age and altered in late Roman Imperial times, when the columns with Corinthian capitals were added. **21)** Odeion. A formerly roofed-over edifice, which was probably not an odeion at all but a bouleuterion (senate house) because it adjoined the Prytaneion (see p. 167). **22)** Private baths, probably built by Flavius Damianus (Pl. 52). **23)** Monumental fountain, built in the 2nd century A. D. and restored in the 4th century A. D. **24)** Isis Temple (?). **25)** Archaic Cemetery.

In any case, as regards the seating-area, there was no difference between a bouleuterion (council chamber) of Roman times and a theatre (Pl. 59 b). Finally, the podium of the "odeion" is not a typical proscenium, and in this respect also it is similar to a Roman bouleuterion. Consequently, it is reasonable to assume that this building, erected, according to the fragments of an inscription, by Publius Vedius Antoninus just after A. D. 150, was in fact a bouleuterion.

The Private Baths (Fig. ,59, No. 22). The excavators consider that the well-preserved remains of a building lying east of the odeion are the ruins of baths. In accordance with information disclosed by an inscription, this structure is thought to be the one-roomed Varius Bath, erected by the famous Ephesian sophist, Flavius Damianus (Pl. 52).

The Large Fountain (Fig. 59, No. 23). The water that supplied the monumental fountain situated on the south side of the state agora and opposite the odeion came from the River Marnas (the present day River Dervent), flowing 6 km. east of the ruins of Ephesus. The two-tiered aqueduct seen crossing a narrow valley 5 km. east of Ephesus along the Aydın road carried water from the Marnas. This water channel, built by Caius Sextilius Pollio sometime between A. D. 4 and 14, was partly swept away by a flood about 5 or 6 years ago. The aqueduct, until then the best preserved and oldest in Turkey, will soon be repaired.

The East Gymnasium (Fig. 50, No. 27). Situated on the edge of the town, this gymnasium is a fine work in quite good condition. Basing their assumption on the finding of portrait statues of the sophist Flavius Damianus (Pl. 52) and his wife Vedia Phaedrina in the Emperor's salon, the excavators are of the opinion that this couple was responsible for the construction of the palaestra.

The Magnesian Gateway (Fig. 50, No. 28). This sadly ruined building, erected by the Emperor Vespasian (A. D. 69-79), is the only Ephesian city gate to survive to the present day. An inscription unearthed during the excavations records that the Processional Road began at the Artemision, continued to the theatre via the Magnesian Gateway, and then, having passed through the Koressos Gateway at the eastern corner of the stadium, finally regained the Artemision. Beyond the processional road a colonnaded street, built by the sophist Damianus about the third quarter of the 2nd century A. D., stretched between the Magnesian Gateway and the Artemision.

The City Walls (Fig. 50, No. 29). The fine wall constructed by Lysi-machos at the beginning of the 3rd century B. C. can still be seen stretching along the ridge of Mt. Koressos (Bülbüldağ) and a portion of this same wall is also in evidence on Mt. Pion (Panayırdağ).

The wall built in the early Christian era follows a winding course on Panayırdağ, thus enclosing the stadium and the Vedius gymnasium before descending as far as the harbour (Fig. 50, No. 7).

The House of the Virgin Mary. It has been stated above, in the discussion of Mary's Church, that the Virgin most probably lived and died at Ephesus, and this belief was further strengthened all over the Christian world by the visit of Pope Paul VI in 1967. Indeed, the celebration of High Mass, organized every year on the anniversary of Pope Paul's visit to Ephesus, is attended by a vast gathering of visitors. A wonderful view can be seen from the heights where the house, believed to have been the abode of the Virgin, is situated.

The Belevi Mausoleum. The monument standing at the spot known as Belevi, to the east of the road junction II km. from Ephesus, ranks as the largest and highest tomb in ancient Anatolia after the Mausoleum at Halicar-nassus, one of the seven wonders of the ancient world.

Judging by the surviving fragments of the Belevi Mausoleum, the podium, proved to have been 11.37 m. high, was composed of local rock, faced on four sides with beautifully cut blocks of stone. It was based on a square plan, measuring 29.65 sq. m. The rock core was hewn into shape at the sides and top to render it suitable to receive the stone facing. The mass of rock was hollowed out on the south side to form a burial chamber in which was originally placed the sarcophagus now in the Ephesus Museum. As can still be seen on the site, the lowest part of the podium has a three-stepped krepidoma, on which stands the podium wall with a moulded base-course (teichobate), and a Doric entablature at its top edge.

On the podium stood a peristasis of the Doric order, with 8 columns on each of the four sides. Statues of lion-griffins the size of a lion stood on the edges of the roof, but these are now kept in the museums at Ephesus and İzmir.

The twenty-four ceiling coffers were decorated with reliefs depicting the funeral games organized for the deceased, and a centauromachy. Accord-ing to existing fragments, the height of the peristasis, from the top of the podium to the level of the cornice, was 11.32 m. The total height of the monument, the roof not included, was about 23 m. No remains have been uncovered that could throw light on the manner in which the roof was finished.

The craftsmanship displayed in the architectural ornamentation, the mouldings and the Corinthian capitals (Pl. 73) is of a high standard. Basing his calculations on the reliefs appearing in the ceiling coffers and the charac-teristic features shown in the Corinthian capitals, G. Kleiner is of the opinion that the Mausoleum dates from the middle of the 3rd century B.C. W. Alzinger supports this date because of the shape of the Lesbian cymation and the shape of the astragals. In addition, G. Kleiner has identified the occupant of the tomb as one of the Macedonian *Epigones* of Alexander because, in the manner of a Macedonian king, he lies on a couch and wears a diadem in the form of a headband. Kleiner declares that, most probably, he was the Seleucid King Antiochos II, Theos, who died at Ephesus in 246 B. C. Thus the suggestion, previously put forward by J. Keil, but subsequently retracted, has now been definitely confirmed. Kleiner is right in saying that the Persian motifs on the monument accord well with the idea of a Seleucid monarch. In fact, if the lion-griffins on the Belevi Mausoleum are compared with those in the temple at Didyma, the former will be seen to be much more under the influence of Achaemenid art. The stylized pattern of a full moon and a crescent appearing on the haunches of the Belevi lion-griffins was copied from those on similar lion-griffins at Susa, and this Achaemenid stereotyped carving of the muscles does not appear on any other Greek representation of a lion. The presence of such marked Achaemenid influences no doubt indicates that the grave was that of a Seleucid King.

The tumulus observed next to the Belevi Mausoleum, but at a slightly higher level exhibits fine worksmanship in its krepis, and from this point of view must also have been built in the 3rd century B. C.

APHRODISIAS

One of the most attractive ruins of Turkey is located at Aphrodisias, now being successfully excavated by Kenan T. Erim under the auspices of New York University. The following description is based almost entirely on information given by Professor Kenan Erim.

In ancient geographical context, Aphrodisias lay in the north-eastern confines of Caria, in the vicinity of the Maeander valley. The impressive remains of this once-splendid city are situated on a high plateau, ca. 600 m. above sea-level, at the foot of the Baba Dağ range. The site is about 230 kms. south-east of İzmir by road, and lies near the hamlet of Geyre, in the *Vilâyet* of Aydın and the *Kaza* of Karacasu (Pls. 14 a, 60-63; Fig. 60).

Ancient sources furnish little information about Aphrodisias. According to a late writer, Stephanus of Byzantium, the city was also known as Ninoe (after Ninos, a semi-legendary Babylonian ruler) and under several other names. It is more probable that Ninoe was connected with the Akkadian Nino, Nin or Nina, names for the goddess Astarte or Ishtar. The strong eastern overtones of the cult of Aphrodite and the affinities between Ishtar and Aphrodite are generally well-recognised. Therefore, Aphrodisias may well be a Greek version of Ninoe, which began to be used in the Hellenistic period. Whatever its precise origins, the antiquity of the cult of the goddess of Aphrodisias cannot be underestimated. The similarities of this Aphrodite to Kybele, Artemis of Ephesus and other Anatolian mother-goddesses are especially evident in her late Hellenistic cult-image. At that time, she took the form of an ancient idol-like figure, a nature goddess sovereign on earth, in heaven, the seas and the underworld, in short, a symbol of life and fertility in all its aspects. The first clear allusion to the Carian divinity (and by implication to Aphrodisias) is found in Appian (second century A. D.), where the Roman dictator Sulla is reported to have sent Aphrodite a golden crown and a double-axe in 82 B. C. in response to a Delphic oracle. The name of Aphrodisias also appears on several silver and bronze coins in conjunction with Plarasa, a neighbouring town, in the late second and early first centuries B. C. In the latter part of the first century B. C., Mark Antony, following a decree of Julius Caesar, recognised the autonomy of both Aphrodisias and Plarasa, as well as the inviolability of the sanctuary of Aphrodite. These privileges were reaffirmed by the Emperor Tiberius in A. D. 22 and maintained throughout the Empire. It was during these centuries that Aphrodisias reached its heights of fame and prosperity, flourishing not only as a significant religious site, but also as an important centre for the arts, literature and other intellectual endeavours. Despite the advent of Christianity and the establishment of a bishop in the city, paganism lingered for a long while at Aphrodisias, most probably because of the great popularity of the cult of Aphrodite. Perhaps in order to eradicate any such remnants, the city was suitably renamed Stavropolis ("City of the Cross") or simply referred to as Caria, since it was the chief city of the Carian province. The appearance of Seljuk and Turcoman raiders between the eleventh and thirteenth centuries contributed much to the decline of several cities along the Maeander valley. Aphrodisias-Caria was captured several times by raiders during this time, until it was gradually depopulated and abandoned. Eventually a Turkish village, Geyre, whose name surely derives from Caria, grew up among the ruins (Pls. 60-63; Fig. 60).

The site of Aphrodisias attracted the attention of several early travellers to Asia Minor, among whom were Laborde, Texier and the Society of Dilettanti, who reported on the impressive ruins and the abundant epigraphical documents. In 1904 - 5, a French mission headed by Paul Gaudin conducted two short but fruitful campaigns of excavation on the site. Work was briefly resumed by A. Boulanger in 1913. The Italian scholar Giulio Jacopi directed successful excavations for several weeks in 1937. Finally, since 1961, a new and more thorough series of yearly campaigns has been initiated by Kenan T. Erim under the auspices of New York University and has produced brilliant results. In addition to well-preserved monuments and much historical information, each of these investigations has brought to light an unprecedented quantity of sculpture and statuary of the highest quality. It appears now more than ever, since Maria F. Squarciapino conceived the notion of a school of sculpture flourishing at Aphrodisias during the Roman Empire, that the art of sculpture indeed found a congenial environment in the Carian city. This activity was much encouraged by the presence of excellent white and blue - grey marble quarries 2 kms. east of the city along the lower slopes of Baba Dağ. The stone also appears to have been exported to other parts of Asia Minor and the Mediterranean in blocks or roughly finished form. Many signatures of Aphrodisian artists have been found on fragments, bases, full statues and reliefs in Rome, Italy, Greece and elsewhere, and testify to the great appreciation of the work of the Carian sculptors. The school of Aphrodisias, however, was not merely a school of copyists of earlier models, as believed by some ancient art historians, but represented a group of sculptors who, though often inspired by

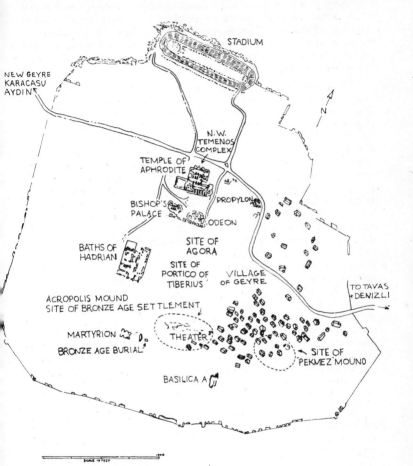

Fig. 60 – Plan of Aphrodisias.

earlier masterpieces, managed to inject a great deal of spirit and originality into their work. Aphrodisias' contributions, on the other hand, were not limited to the field of art alone. Xenocrates, a medical writer, was a native of the city in the days of Nero and the Flavians. Chariton, an ancient novelist, lived at Aphrodisias in the second century A. D. Another native son was Alexander, who expounded Aristotelian philosophy in Athens in the third-century A. D.

The site of Aphrodisias is enclosed in its essential part by a circuit of fortifications over 3.5 kms. in length, encompassing an area of approximately 520 hectares. These walls, built in late Roman times and much restored subsequently with a variety of re-used material including architectural blocks and inscriptions, possibly dislodged by earthquakes, were interrupted by several gates. The old, half-abandoned village of Geyre survives in the south-eastern sector of the site. A new village, built by government decree following a serious earthquake in 1956, is located 1 km. to the west of the West or Antioch Gate.

The ground is mostly flat, except for a small conical hill, ca. 15 m. in height, in the south, the so-called "acropolis". During recent excavations, this hill was proved to be a prehistoric mound, formed by the accumulations of several settlements dating at least as far back as the Early Bronze Age (ca. 2800 - 2200 B. C.). Another slight rise in the ground to the south-east, named "Pekmez" and partly investigated in 1967, also revealed traces of early prehistoric occupation. On the eastern slope of the "acropolis" an imposing theatre with a capacity of several thousand spectators is now being slowly brought to light under the abandoned houses of Geyre. The chief sanctuary of the city, the temple of Aphrodite, has fourteen columns of its peristasis still standing. The building was transformed into a Christian basilica in the fifth century and later, by the removal of its cella, the shifting of columns along the sides to form a nave and two aisles and the addition of an apse to the east end. The original structure, apparently an octostyle with thirteen columns on the sides, according to recently uncovered evidence, was erected in late Hellenistic times. An elaborate precinct or temenos was thrown around the temple in the reign of the Emperor Hadrian (A.D.117 - 138). Indications of earlier buildings, presumably shrines going back at least to the seventh century B. C., have been uncovered here in recent campaigns. To the east of the temple, eight columns of an imposing propylon, or monumental entrance-way, have been newly excavated and re-erected. This attractive gateway was probably built in the second century and consisted of four rows of columns, the two easternmost ones forming a handsome façade arrangement, including spirally fluted columns and beautifully carved pedimental relief decoration.

South of the temenos of Aphrodite, a very well-preserved odeion, or concert-hall, was discovered in 1962. Its sunken orchestra and stage were elaborately decorated with mosaics and statuary (at present in the temporary depot at Geyre). The odeion had more rows of seats than are now visible. The upper tiers collapsed in antiquity. A backstage corridor opened on to a porticoed area, decorated with handsome portrait-statues of prominent Aphrodisians and connected with the agora or market-place. This agora, as yet unexplored, lay immediately to the south-east and comprised a vast area (ca. 205 × 120 m.) enclosed by Ionic porticoes on at least three sides. A magnificent series of these columns is preserved in the south-eastern corner among the graceful poplar groves planted by the farmers. Another impressive porticoed area, the Portico of Tiberius, so called after the emperor in whose reign its construction began, was partly excavated by the Italian mission of 1937, immediately south of the agora. Its southern side skirted part of the "acropolis", while to the west it led to the imposing Baths of Hadrian. This thermal establishment consisted of at least five large galleries, now being excavated, and a colonnaded courtyard or palaestra, cleared by the French in 1904 - 5. It was built under Hadrian (A.D.117 - 138) and was decorated with magnificent reliefs and statuary. Recent operations here have revealed a number of heated rooms and halls intended for the various stages of Roman bathing practices (*caldarium, tepidarium, sudatorium,* etc.). Another most impressive public building and certainly one of the best preserved of its kind anywhere is the stadium, located in the north-west quarter of the city. It is 262 m. long and 59 m. wide and could accommodate about 30,000 spectators (Pls. 14, 62 b).

West of the odeion, an elaborate complex of halls and rooms, including a triconch and a peristyle, is thought to have been a residence for the bishop of Aphrodisias. Seven blue marble columns of its peristyle were re-erected in 1964. Part of another luxurious residence, probably of official character and from the Byzantine period, was uncovered north of the temenos of Aphrodite along the road leading into Geyre. Also pertaining to the Byzantine period are two churches, partly excavated during recent investigations. One, to the south-east of the "acropolis", was a basilica, originally of Roman date but converted into a church; the other, at the south-west base of the hill, is a trefoil structure, probably dedicated to a martyr (a martyrion), surrounded by a large Byzantine cemetery.

PAMUKKALE (HIERAPOLIS)

The fairy-like panorama and the richness of Roman and early Christian architectural remains make Hierapolis one of the most famed of the ruins surviving from antiquity. Pamukkale means "Cotton Fortress". The magnificent cotton-white plateau formed by the travertine deposits of the calcium oxide-bearing waters of a stream rising on the southern slope of the Çaldağ is certainly of fascinating beauty. The well-preserved and extensive necropolis of the city is one of the most impressive cemeteries of the past.

The city (Fig. 61) is thought to have been founded by the Pergamene King Eumenes II and named after Hiera, the wife of Telephos, the legendary founder of Pergamon. In 133 B. C. the city was bequeathed, along with the entire Kingdom of Pergamon, to the Romans, in accordance with the testament of Attalos III. During the reign of Tiberius in A. D. 17, Hierapolis was destroyed by a terrible earthquake. The city was rebuilt and experienced the height of its prosperity during the 2nd and 3rd centuries A. D. Hierapolis contained a large Jewish element which might have favoured the rapid expansion of Christianity. Nevertheless, it was here that the Apostle Philip was martyred in A. D. 80. In the Byzantine period, Hierapolis became the seat of a diocese and possessed a large church erected to St. Philip.

Towards the end of the last century, a German archaeological expedition made preliminary excavations at Pamukkale, and the results were published in book form: "Altertümer von Hierapolis" by Humann, Cichorius, Judeich, and Winter, Berlin 1898. Since 1957, Italian archaeologists directed by Paolo Verzone have been engaged in fruitful excavations and highly skilled restoration.

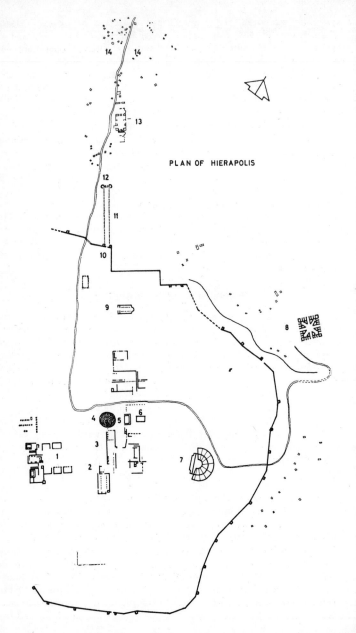

PLAN OF HIERAPOLIS

Fig. 61 – Plan of Hierapolis.

1) *City Baths.* This is the first structure reached on gaining the plateau, and is in quite a good state of preservation. In the eastern part of this complex is a palaestra, measuring 36.13 × 52.25 m. It is flanked by two large rooms, one in the south, and one in the north, reserved for the Emperor and for ceremonial use. Along the entire west side of the courtyard, i.e., the palaestra, stretched a large hall, doubtless used for athletics and gymnastic exercises. This led into the frigidarium and then into the barrel-vaulted rooms comprising the caldarium. The small barrel-vaulted room adjoining the large hall now functions as a museum. Here are stored magnificent sculptures, which have been unearthed by the Italian excavators, generally showing the influence of the school of Aphrodisias. It is assumed that the baths were constructed in the 2nd century A. D.

2) *Christian basilica,* consisting of a nave and two aisles. It dates from the 6th century A. D. and was probably built just after Hierapolis became the seat of a bishopric. **3)** *Colonnaded Street;* the section in the city centre. This was the main road of Hierapolis, leading from the southern gateway in the city wall to the Arch of Domitian (No. 12). **4)** *Modern swimming-pool and casino.* **5)** *Monumental fountain,* 4th century A. D. **6)** *Temple of Apollo,* the principal deity of Hierapolis. According to G. Carettoni, the foundations go back to the late Hellenistic period, though the present remains of the upper structure date no earlier than the 3rd century A. D. **7)** *Theatre.* 2nd century A. D. The structure is well - preserved and has been successfully restored by the Italian expedition. The reliefs of the pulpitum (podium), depicting a Dionysiac cortege, are now in the local museum in the City Baths (1). **8)** *Martyrium of St. Philip.* An imposing octagonal building erected on a square measuring 20 × 20 m., and dating from the beginning of the 5th century A. D. **9)** *Building in the form of a basilica,* composed of a nave, apsed at the eastern end, and two aisles. **10)** *Byzantine gateway.* **11)** *Colonnaded Street;* the section built in the reign of Domitian (A. D. 81-96). **12)** *Arch of Domitian.* A monumental gateway erected by Julius Frontinus, Proconsul of Asia (western Anatolia) from A. D. 82-83. **13)** *Building erected as baths,* dating from the end of the 2nd century or the beginning of the 3rd century A. D. (Pl. 59 a). It was converted into a church during the Early Christian period (probably in the 5th century A. D.). **14)** *Necropolis,* containing tumuli, sarcophagi and house-shaped tombs, lying on both sides of the road, and stretching 2 km. to the north. Spanning the centuries from the late Hellenistic age to early Christian times, it represents one of the best preserved of the ancient cemeteries in Turkey and is pervaded by a fairyland atmosphere.

MAGNESIA ON THE MAEANDER

Although the town of Magnesia on the Maeander (Figs. 61 a - 66) is situated in the central region of Ionia, it was founded by Aeolians coming originally from Magnesia in Northern Greece. The first settlement started at the junction of the Lethaeus and the Maeander. Magnesia was ruled for a time by the Lydian King Gyges (680-652 B. C.) and devastated by the Cimmerians about 650. The Milesians rebuilt Magnesia, but it was captured by the Persians in approximately 530. Herodotus records (III, 39) that in 522 B. C. Oroites, Satrap of Sardis, crucified Polykrates, the famous tyrant of Samos, not far from the city of Magnesia. After Themistocles, the Athenian statesman and victorious commander at the Battle of Salamis, had been ostracized, he made friends with the Persian King Artaxerxes and settled in Magnesia. The inhabitants held him in high esteem. He later erected a temple to the Phrygian mother goddess and installed his daughter as a priestess there. Upon his death, he was given a magnificent funeral, and a memorial to him was set up in the agora.

The Spartans controlled Magnesia from 400 to 398, and the commander Thibron moved the city to its present site in the district called Leukophrys (White Eyebrowed) where the Leukophryene temple to Artemis was situated. Thus the city was saved from the inundations of the Maeander and, in addition, gained importance and power by virtue of its status as a religious centre. Magnesia first began to develop and enjoy the rank of an important city in the time of the Seleucids and later under the Attalids (189-133). In 87 B. C., the city closed its gates to the Pontic King Mithradates Archelaos, who had started particularly bloody operations against the Romans and, as a result, it continued as an independent city befriended by Rome from the time of Sulla onwards. In the Byzantine era, Magnesia was the seat of a bishopric. The city was excavated from 1891-1893 by Carl Humann, and the results were published in 1904 by J. Kohte and C. Watzinger.

Of the buildings brought to light during the excavations of Magnesia on the Maeander, only the remains of the Artemis temple can be seen today (Figs. 63-65). The agora, the temple of Zeus Sosipolis and many other buildings (Fig. 61 a) have vanished beneath the silt brought down by the River Lethaeus. The orchestra of the theatre has likewise disappeared under muddy deposits and only the tops of the columns are visible. Part of the auditorium is still in existence. The whole of the stadium is overgrown with grass and trees. Nevertheless, in many parts of the stadium, the presence of marble seats with armrests can be verified by parting the grass.

The wall enclosing the Artemision on the north and east and traversed by the highway dates from Byzantine times. The remains of a large building lying east of the main road are probably, according to R. A. Staccioli, the ruins of Roman baths.

The Artemis Temple. Judging by the remains uncovered during excavations, this was built on the site of an older temple, probably dedicated to the mother goddess. The ancient Artemision was constructed of rough limestone, and its column bases were of the Ephesian type. The column shafts were carved with 32 flutes with a semi-elliptical cross-section. It is assumed that this earlier temple was of smaller dimensions and had six columns across the front.

Although many architectural fragments have been removed to the Berlin Museum and portions of frieze reliefs to the Paris and Istanbul Museums, it would be possible to carry out a partial anastylosis(i.e., a re-erection), using the many remains which lie on the ground at the present time.

According to Vitruvius, the temple of Artemis was the work of the architect Hermogenes. It measured 41 × 67 m. and took the form of a pseudodipteros of the Ionic order with 8×15 columns rising up on a nine-stepped platform. This building faced westwards like other temples perpetuating the tradition of the Phrygian mother goddess, such as the Artemis

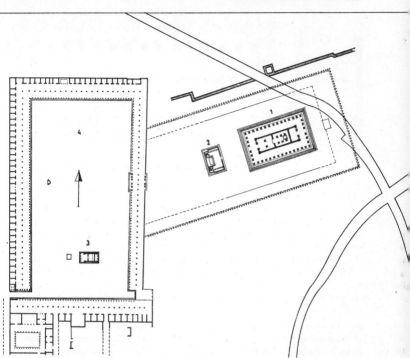

Fig. 61 a – Plan of Magnesia on the Maeander. 1) The Temple of Artemis (Fig. 63).
2) The Altar of the Artemis Temple. 3) The Temple of Zeus Sosipolis (see Fig. 62).
4) The Agora. The Agora, the Temple of Zeus Sosipolis and many other buildings
are now covered by the silt brought down by the River Lethaeus after the excavations. The wall enclosing the Artemision on the north and east and traversed by
the highway, dates from Byzantine times. The remains of a large building lying
east of the main road are, according to R. A. Staccioli, very probably the ruins
of Roman baths.

temples at Sardis and Ephesus (Figs. 44-46, 52, 53) and the temples at Ankara
(Fig. 118) and Pessinus. The pronaos was as big as the cella, following the example of the Athena temple at Priene, created by Pytheos. The opisthodomos
was enlarged to conform to the middle Hellenistic concept of spaciousness.
The statue of Artemis stood in the cella upon a base, the foundations of which
are still in existence. The intercolumniation measured 3.94 m; only the
central columns on the short sides had an interaxial span of 5.25 m. The
wide spacing of the central columns was a traditional Ionic feature in Anatolia and also conformed to the architectural concept of the Hellenistic
period. The accentuation of the central columns also served to emphasize
the pronounced tendency towards axiality, typical of the Hellenistic era. It
should be noted that the columns within the pronaos, cella, and opisthodomos

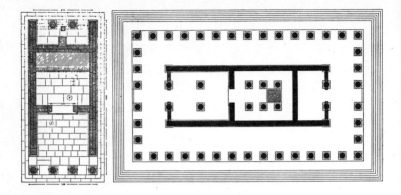

Fig. 62 – Magnesia on the Maeander. The Temple of Zeus Sosipolis is now lying under the silt brought down by the River Lethaeus following excavations. It was probably an early work of the architect Hermogenes (p. 183).

Fig. 63 – Magnesia on the Maeander. Temple of Artemis. ca. 130 B. C. A pseudo-dipteros of the Ionic order, with 8 by 15 columns and stylobate measurements of 41 × 67 m. According to Vitruvius, it was a work of the architect Hermogenes, and one of the most important architectural creations of Greek art (p. 178).

lie on the same axis as the middle columns found on the east and west sides of the peristasis (Fig. 63). In the same way, the two doors appearing respectively in the middle of the east and west pediments create a second axis (Fig. 64) parallel to that shown in the plan (Fig. 63). The tendency towards axiality is also apparent in a north-south direction. A look at the plan reveals that all the columns in the pronaos, cella, and opisthodomos are exactly in line with the ones opposite them along the long sides. This alignment had not been so exactly carried out in any previous Greek temple.

Since the lower diameter of the columns was 1.40 m. and the space between them 3.94 m., their proportion was 2.80, i.e., $2\,^4/_5$; consequently, the temple is an example coming somewhere between the eustyle and the diastyle of the five Hermogenian types of intercolumniation (see p. 23). That is to say, Hermogenes placed the columns slightly farther apart, in this instance, than in the temple at Teos, where the ratio is $2\,^1/_4$ (eustyle). The columns in the Artemision reach a height $9\,^1/_2$ times the lower diameter; thus Vitruvius was right in attributing this feature to Hermogenes.

The order of the architectural elements in the Artemision (Figs. 64, 65) is as follows: 1- Nine-stepped krepidoma. 2- Plinth (a square block) surmounted by a base consisting of torus, trochilus and torus. 3- Column shaft with 24 flutes (semicircular in cross-section). 4- Ionic capital with a straight lower edge of the canalis and an abacus with a Lesbian kymation. 5- Architrave with 3 fasciae. 6- Frieze bordered above and below with an Ionic kymation. 7- Row of dentils. 8- Pediment with a central door, flanked on each side by a window. 9- Sima. 10- Acroteria.

The new features to be observed in the Artemision may be enumerated as follows :

1. The pseudo-dipteral plan, i.e., a modification of the dipteral scheme (Figs. 52, 53, 83, 84) with the innermost row of columns omitted so as to form wide colonnades around the temple suitable for walking; shady and cool in summer, sheltered in winter. The first step towards the architectural concept of spaciousness (Raum), and large scale, roofed buildings.

2. The pleasing contrast between the mass of the temple, shining in the sun, and the deep shadow caused by the wide colonnades.

3. The further development of the concept of "Raum" by the attainment of width and depth in the pronaos and opisthodomos.

4. The initiation and development of the tendency to produce contrasting ornamental features meant to be seen from afar, in place of detailed calligraphic designs observable only at close quarters. Thus, slender, delicate base profiles (Figs. 4 b, 54, 66, 69) were superseded by more practical forms (Fig. 65); the calligraphically expressed curves of the lower canalis (Figs. 32, 54, 68) were replaced by a straight line (Fig. 65), and all kinds of deeply incised ornamentation produced sharp contrasts in light and shadow. This idea can also be noted in the frieze reliefs of the Artemision and in those of the temple of Dionysus at Teos, in which detail is neglected in favour of sweeping lines and animated compositions utilizing the play of light and shadow to produce an impressive effect at a distance.

5. The increased number of Attic art forms in Ionic buildings in Anatolia. For example, the occurrence of the Attic profile, i.e., torus, trochilus, torus, at the base of the walls, as in some earlier Anatolian buildings; and finally, yet another Attic feature: the incorporation of a frieze with reliefs in the entablature of the temples.

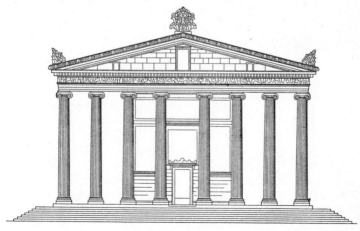

Fig. 64 – Magnesia on the Maeander. The Temple of Artemis. Graphic reconstruction (see p. 178 and Figs. 63, 65).

6. The necessity for producing a lighter entablature, as a result of the wider intercolumniation. This, in fact, is why the frieze reliefs of the middle Hellenistic period were discontinued in late Hellenistic times, why the three fasciae of the architrave were reduced to two, and the metopes and triglyphs were decreased in height and consequently increased in number. The first

Fig. 65 – Magnesia on the Maeander. The Temple of Artemis. Elevation (see p. 178 and Figs. 63, 64).

step towards the lightening of the upper structure was taken in the later Ephesian Artemision. With this purpose in mind, a door and two windows were opened in the pediment, which not only animated the blank surface with light and shadow, but also relieved the columns of an excessive load. At the same time, it is also reasonable to suppose that the doors in the pediment were opened on ceremonial days so that a portable statue of the goddess Artemis could be shown to the multitude as an act of epiphaneia. However, the actual reason for making these doors and windows was to solve structural and aesthetic problems.

7. The tendency towards pronounced axiality, present in the Artemision and already mentioned, is also apparent in the gymnasium (Fig. 79 a) and the bouleuterion (Fig. 80) at Miletos, both buildings contemporary with the Artemision. This architectural concept was later to be developed in Roman art and Baroque city-planning in Europe.

The innovations in the Artemision related above explain why it is one of the most important works in the history of art. Its monumental dimensions and the magnificent 200 m.-long sculptured frieze also place it among the major buildings of antiquity.

As has been established by A. von Gerkan, the altar (Fig. 61 a) lying west of the temple derives from the Pergamene prototype, and its construction definitely shows the influence of the Zeus altar of Pergamon.

The Temple of Zeus Sosipolis (Figs. 62, 66). This temple, situated in the courtyard of the agora (Fig. 61 a), is a small marble prostyle of the Ionic order, the stylobate of which measured 7.38×15.81 m. Most Hellenistic temples of small proportions were of the prostyle type. The earliest examples of this style of building in Anatolia are the naiskos in the Didymaion (Fig. 84) and the temple of Zeus in the agora at Priene (Fig. 70), while the Pergamene representatives (Fig. 33) were erected in the 2nd century B. C. The prostyle at Magnesia can be dated somewhere between these earlier and later specimens. In fact, the Magnesian prostyle exhibits a different form, in that it possesses an opisthodomos. G. Gruben is rightly of the opinion that this temple of Zeus Sosipolis (Figs. 62, 66) is one of the earliest works to be attributed to Hermogenes. The reasons produced by Gruben are very convincing: 1. The eustyle principle ascribed to Hermogenes has nowhere else been applied in the exact ratio of $2\,^1/_4$. 2- Another characteristic of Hermogenes' work to be seen in this temple is the feature in which the height of the columns is $9\,^1/_2$ times the measurement of the lower diameter. 3- The presence of a deep and therefore shady pronaos. 4- The Attic profile of the base of the cella wall, consisting of torus, trochilus, torus. 5- The introduction of the frieze and the production of a composite style comprising Ionic and Attic elements.

In our opinion, these views are right. It will be noticed that the Zeus Sosipolis temple is closely related to Hermogenes' Artemision as regards plan. In contrast to all the previous Hellenistic prostyles (Figs. 84, 75 a, 33), the temple of Zeus Sosipolis, like the Artemision, possesses a tripartite composition; it also resembles the Artemision in that the pronaos is approximately as big as the cella. We are therefore convinced that, from the point of view of its plan too, the Magnesian prostyle reveals features characteristic of Hermogenes.

Fig. 66 – Magnesia on the Maeander. The Temple of Zeus Sosipolis. Elevation (see p. 183 and Fig. 62).

PRIENE

Since the Panionion, the centre of politics and religion, was situated on Prienian soil, this city was one of the earliest Ionian settlements. Nevertheless, it has not so far been possible to ascertain the exact site where it was founded. The first city was probably a peninsula with two harbours. It participated in the Battle of Lade in 495 with twelve ships. According to tradition, Bias, who was considered one of seven world-famous philosophers and wise men, lived in Priene at the beginning of the 6th century B. C. The only one work of art which has survived from this first settlement is a coin made of electrum, minted in 500 B. C. and bearing the head of Athena on the obverse side.

In 350 B. C., the new city of Priene was founded on its present site, with the help extended by Athens and the interest she showed. In those days Priene was much nearer the sea than it is now, and possessed a port called Naulochos. Priene never played a very important role in politics; at first it was subject to the influence and rule of Athens; it then passed first to the Kingdom of Pergamon and finally to Rome, which began to govern it about the middle of the 2nd century B. C. In spite of this state of affairs, the works of art of the 4th century and the Hellenistic era which have been recovered here can be counted among the foremost creations of Greek art in value and importance. The clay deposits brought down by the River Menderes gradually increased the distance between Priene and the sea, and finally, at the end of the Roman period, it sank into insignificance. However, it was the centre of an important diocese in Byzantine times. Archaeological diggings at Priene were first begun in 1895 by Carl Humann, and were then continued under the direction of Th. Wiegand until 1898. The results of research carried out prior to the excavations, under the auspices of the British Society of Dilettanti were published in The Antiquities of Ionia, Vol. IV. in 1881.

Immediately after the establishment of Priene in 350 B. C., it was enclosed by a fine, strong city wall. Even today, the eye is drawn to the outstanding workmanship of the *rustica* masonry work displayed in some sections of this city wall, built entirely of local marble and preserved in an excellent state of repair. The wall shows the same type of serrated plan as the Trojan ramparts (Pl. I) in that there are numerous offsets separated by short gaps (Fig. 67). If an attempt were made to undermine the city wall, the citizens of Priene would have been able to attack any enemy force on the flank by standing, well protected, behind these projections and fighting it off with arrows and spears. The principal entrance to the city was the north-eastern gateway (16). In addition there were two other entrances: one at the western end of the main road (19) and the other at the eastern end of the street passing through the south stoa of the agora (17).

Priene was built on the Hippodamian system, i.e., according to a city plan in which streets intersect at right angles, and is the oldest and finest example of this type to be found among Hellenic cities (Fig.67). The atmosphere of the town as it was in antiquity still pervades the well-preserved main roads and streets lined with buildings. The city as a whole faces south; the

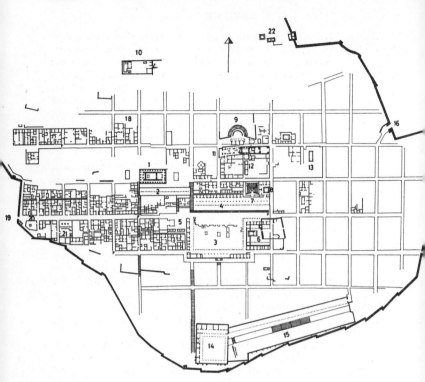

Fig. 67 – Plan of Priene (Pls. 8, 66). The best example of a Greek city with streets intersecting at right angles. The plan of the city was already laid out in the 4th century B. C. The city wall, the Athena temple (1), the theatre (9), the sanctuary of Demeter (10) and the upper gymnasium (12) were also erected in the 4th century B. C. The agora (3) and the temple of Zeus Olympios go back to the 3rd century B. C., while the sacred stoa (4), the bouleuterion (7), the lower gymnasium (14) and the stadium (15) date from the 2nd century B. C. In spite of alterations carried out in Roman times, the essentially Greek character of the city was largely preserved. **1)** *Temple of Athena (see Figs. 68, 69).* **2)** *Stoa south of the Athena Temple (see Fig. 68).* **3)** *Agora (see Fig. 70).* **4)** *The Sacred Stoa (see Fig. 70).* **5)** *Market place for foodstuffs.* **6)** *Temenos of Zeus Olympios (see Fig. 70).* **7)** *Bouleuterion (Figs. 71 a, b).* **8)** *The Prytaneion.* **9)** *Theatre (see Figs. 72, 73).* **10)** *Sanctuary of Demeter. One of the oldest places of worship in Priene. The visitor must be prepared to make a short climb (see p. 202).* **11)** *Archbishop's Church. A Byzantine basilica with a nave flanked by two aisles. The entrance vestibule or narthex had two doors. The pulpit still stands in the nave, but only the foundations of the altar have survived. Only part of the apse has been excavated.* **12)** *Upper Gymnasium. Built in the second half of the 4th century as a peristyle consisting of rooms surrounding a courtyard. The earliest school and*

athletic training centre were situated in this gymnasium. In Roman times, baths were added to the north part of the gymnasium but this area has so far only been partly excavated. In the west part of the courtyard stand the remains of a small Roman temple devoted to the cult of the emperor. To the east of this is a pool dating from Byzantine times. **13)** Temenos of the Egyptian Gods. This is merely an altar, 7.31 × 14.60 m. in area and 1.73 m. in height (see p. 196). Before visiting the lower gymnasium (14) and the adjacent stadium (15), it would be as well to take a look at the houses in Priene (see below, No. 18 and p. 203). Nos. 19 and 20, also described below, could be included in the same walk. **14)** Lower Gymnasium. This is in a fair state of preservation and vividly recreates the atmosphere of a Greek school and athletic centre (p. 201). **15)** Stadium. A fine example of the Greek type (see p. 201). **16)** North-East Gateway. **17)** East Gateway **18)** Largest House in Priene (see. p. 203). **19)** West Gateway. **20)** Temenos of Kybele (p. 205). **21)** House of Alexander the Great (see p. 205).

main roads follow an east-west direction and the side-streets, rising in steps, run north-south, intersecting the former at right angles. The theatre (9), the stadium (15), the principal colonnades , i.e., the sacred stoa (4), the south stoa of the temple of Athena (2) and the oikoi (sitting rooms) of many of the private houses faced south (Fig. 74). Thus the sitting rooms and meeting places received sunshine throughout the winter, whereas in summer the sun gave less heat, passing over the tops of the buildings. Blocks of houses measured 47.20 × 35.40 m. In general, there were four houses to a block, whereas the official and religious buildings were so planned that they fitted into one block, or else occupied exactly two or three blocks. The side-streets were usually 3.50 m. and the main roads 4.44 m. wide; the main road which passed in front of the sacred stoa, however, was 7.36 m. across. Ancient Greek writers attribute the invention of this type of city-planning to Hippodamos of Miletos and also state that Miletos and Piraeus were built on the same plan in the second quarter of the 5th century B. C. (see the chapter on Miletos).

Priene was supplied with water from the mountains via an aqueduct which passed into the city through the city wall on the north-east. After the water had been allowed to stand in three pools (22), it was distributed all over the city through earthenware pipes. The mortared walls of the pools are of the Byzantine period (22). However, the fine *rustica* stonework of the encircling wall bears witness to the fact that these settling pools had been in existence since Hellenistic times. Water flowed from fountains at many points in the city. One of these stood at the south-east corner of the theatre skene; another was to be found on the same road at the south - east corner of the second block from the west , i.e., just around the corner of the side street (F). There was another fountain at the east end of the sacred stoa on the main road and yet another on the south side of the temple of Athena (I) on the east wall of a side street around the corner where the road with steps reaches the main road (F). Still another fountain was located in the western part of the road passing through the south stoa of the agora; it stood in front of the house occupying the eastern corner of the second street past the agora (F).

The Temple of Athena. The oldest and most important building in Priene and the one built on the highest spot in the city, at a height of 96.76 m. above sea-level, was the temple of Athena (Fig. 67, No. 1, Fig. 68). As has already been stated, according to the evidence of an electrum stater found in a treasure unearthed at Klazomenai, Athena was also worshipped in ancient Priene. Indeed, the excavations at Erythrai and İzmir have revealed that Athena occupied the first place among the deities in western Asia Minor in the 7th century B. C. Thus, it is possible to accept that Athena enjoyed the esteem of the population at an even earlier date than the 7th century in Ionian cities.

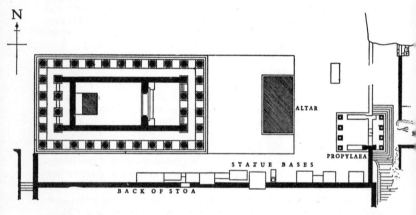

Fig. 68 – Temple of Athena, the classic model for Ionic architecture, built by Pytheos, the architect of the Mausoleum at Halicarnassus, in the third quarter of the 4th century B. C. A peripteros with 6 by 11 columns and a stylobate measuring 19.55 × 37.20 m. In the cella adjoining the west wall is still preserved the base on which once stood the cult statue of Athena, made after the model at Pergamon, now in Berlin. It was presented to the temple by Prince Orophernes of Cappadocia, in the second half of the 2nd century B. C. The Doric stoa which extended along the entire southern side of the temple and faced the town was also constructed during this period. According to inscriptions on the architraves of the temple and the altar, in the Augustan Age, the emperor was worshipped in the temple beside the goddess Athena. In this period, a propylon was set up on the east side of the sacred area. The front steps and a section of the south wall of this structure (Pls. 8 a, 66 a) are still standing.

The temple of Athena at Priene was built by Pytheos, the architect responsible for the Mausoleum at Halicarnassus, considered to be one of the seven wonders of the ancient world. The Athena temple became the classic model for Ionic architecture and, according to Vitruvius, Pytheos published a book dealing with his principles of architectural design. This building was a peripteros with 6 columns on the short sides and 11 on the long ones, and it was of the Ionic order. The stylobate measurements were 37.20 × 19.55 m.

The whole naos was 100 Attic feet, or 29.5 m. in length. The cella measured 50 ft. in length and the pronaos 30 ft. The opisthodomos was very small,
being only 12 ft. or 3.53 m. long. The sides of the temple were 50 ft. high,
which was the length of the cella; the columns   rose to 43 ft. of this
height, the remaining 7 ft. being taken up by the entablature. The building
material was local Mykale marble. The ornamented sections were painted,
the dominant colours being red and blue.

The columns of the north side of the peristasis, which were re-erected
a few years ago, produce an impressive scene. It is only regrettable that
in the restoration of the column bases, one part, the torus, has been overlooked (compare the restorations with Fig. 69).

The order of the temple of Athena (Fig. 69) can be described, going
from the bottom to the top, as follows :

1) The platform (the three-stepped krepidoma, or krepis).

2) The column-base. This shows the Ephesian form of the old Anatolian type
   and consists of a plinth, a spira and a torus. The spira, resting on the
   plinth (a square block), is composed of three sets of double astragals
   (roundels) and two concave mouldings called scotiae or trochili. The
   torus, overlying the spira, is a large convex moulding fluted horizontally.
   The Pythean type, however, is fluted only in its lower half (Fig. 69).

3) The column. The lower diameter of the column was one-tenth the height
   of the shaft, which has twenty-four flutes, each separated from the next
   by a narrow strip. The top of the shaft just below the capital is profiled
   with a roundel, which makes the transition from the column to the capital.

4) The capital. This is composed of an "echinus" carved with the egg-and-
   tongue, two volutes, a canalis (channel between the two spirals) edged
   by small mouldings, and an abacus on the top, in the *cyma reversa* profile,
   decorated with the Lesbian leaf-pattern.

5) The entablature. This begins with an architrave composed of three fasciae
   (bands). Over the top fascia runs the egg-and-tongue overlying an astragal
   carved with the bead-and-reel. Above this lie the dentils representing
   wooden beam-ends. An egg-and-tongue also runs above the dentils over
   an astragal carved with the bead-and-reel. Finally come the cornice (corona
   or geison) and the sima (rain gutter).

The pronaos was large in comparison with earlier designs. This characteristic persisted into the next period, and in the middle Hellenistic period
most pronaoi were of large proportions to give an effect of spaciousness,
as was the case in the Zeus Sosipolis and Artemis temples at Magnesia ad
Maeandrum (Figs. 62, 63).

There was no opisthodomos in the older Ionic temples. Pytheos adopted this feature from the Doric order and included a narrow opisthodomos
in his own type of plan; in later periods an opisthodomos was almost
never omitted from temples of Ionic design (Figs. 44-46, 62, 88). Another
Pythean feature maintained by succeeding architects was the rule of 24 flutes
on the column shafts. Be that as it may, the temple as a whole did not
arouse much admiration because it slavishly followed the scheme laid down

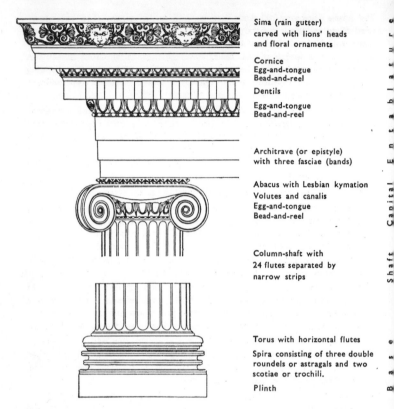

Sima (rain gutter)
carved with lions' heads
and floral ornaments

Cornice
Egg-and-tongue
Bead-and-reel

Dentils

Egg-and-tongue
Bead-and-reel

Architrave (or epistyle)
with three fasciae (bands)

Abacus with Lesbian kymation
Volutes and canalis
Egg-and-tongue
Bead-and-reel

Column-shaft with
24 flutes separated by
narrow strips

Torus with horizontal flutes

Spira consisting of three double
roundels or astragals and two
scotiae or trochili.

Plinth

Fig. 69 – Priene. The Ionic Order of the Temple of Athena. Third quarter of the 4th century B. C.

for the Doric style of temple, and was at cross-purposes with Ionic architectural concepts. Pytheos' plan, with slight modifications, was put into practice only in the temple of Dionysus at Teos (Fig. 48).

The construction of the eastern part of the temple was begun in the middle of the 4th century B. C., and was completed by Alexander the Great. The topmost block of the south anta in the naos, now in the British Museum, bears an inscription which reads : "King Alexander presented the temple to Athena Polias". The western half of the temple, which exhibits an entirely different and later style of ornamentation, is understood not to have been completed until the middle or the second half of the 2nd century B. C., when the cult statue and the altar were renovated. Prince Orophernes of Cappadocia, who possibly spent his childhood at Priene, gave the state treasury of 400 talents into the safe-keeping of the town of Priene when, in 158

B. C., he seized his brother Ariarathes' kingdom. The Prienians later returned this money to him, and maybe this is the reason why he helped to beautify the city. Indeed there is no doubt that the cult statue was presented by him. This fact is proved by the finding of some silver coins (the only ones minted, as far as we know, in Orophernes' reign and now kept in the Berlin Museum) in a hollow, specially carved to hold them, in the base of the statue. Consequently, it would not be wrong to suppose that other works were completed with his financial aid. Pictures of the Athena statue which Orophernes presented to Priene are found on Priene coinage of the Roman Empire era. On these coins, Athena is depicted standing, wearing her helmet and goatskin, bearing her shield and spear, and grasping a small Nike in her extended right hand. This portrayal strongly resembles the Parthenon Athena. During their excavations in the temple, which were undertaken prior to those of the Germans, the British discovered fragments of the left foot, the left hand and left arm belonging to a marble cult statue and also the gold-plated bronze wings of a Nike statue. Judged by these remains, the statue must have been $6^1/_2$ m. tall or half the height of the Athena in the Parthenon on the Athenian acropolis.

The only part of the temple altar still standing is the foundation. Nevertheless, we can conclude, from a study of the recovered pieces, that the design of the altar resembled that of Zeus at Pergamon (Pl. 34 b) and that its reliefs must have been influenced by the style of Pergamene sculpture.   One part of the base of the Priene altar, which was decorated with high reliefs of gods and giants, has been discovered, and this is now in the Istanbul Museum. The style of sculpture exhibited in this work also indicates that the altar was erected in the middle or in the latter half of the 2nd century B. C. It has been confirmed that the portrayals of fighting giants, unlike those of the Pergamene model, did not occur on the frieze but were framed in the form of metopes. The paving of the open space in front of the temple with regular stones was undertaken at the same time that the altar was being built.

During the construction that took place in the second half of the 2nd century, a stoa was erected, in keeping with the style in vogue and with Pergamene models (Fig. 24, No. 6). This stoa, with one row of Doric columns, was 78.40 m. long and obstructed the entire side of the temple that faced the town (2). This neglect of a religious edifice in favour of an architectural work playing an important role in everyday life was characteristic of the Hellenistic concept of architecture.

The rear of the stoa was turned towards the temple, but the whole façade looked over the valley of the Menderes. The stoa, with its 32 columns and the fine 7 m. high terrace wall below, doubtless presented a very attractive appearance. The citizens used to go about their daily business within the colonnade; they would stroll to and fro and gaze at the sea, which was clearly visible from there in those days. According to inscriptions carved on the architraves of the temple and the altar, in the Augustan age, the Emperor was worshipped here beside the goddess Athena. In this period, a propylon was set up on the east side of the area sacred to Athena (Fig. 68). The front steps and a portion of the south wall (Pls. 8 a, 66 a) of this structure are still standing.

The Agora. The agora (3), built in the 3rd century B. C. and covering almost two blocks (75.63 × 35.40 m. square), formed the centre of the city (Fig. 70). Stoas were built along three of its sides; the main thoroughfare of the city passed along the northern side. The stoas were Doric in style. On the west side of the agora was built a row of shops. As the land in the southern part of the agora sloped down, there was a basement under the south stoa. Shops were found only in the east and west sections of this stoa, while in the centre between these two sections there was a room divided into two by eight columns (Fig. 70). In order to protect this hall from the cold north winds of winter, the inter-columnar spaces in the front row were enclosed by a wall to a height half that of the columns themselves. The holes into which this protecting wall fitted can be seen in some of the columns which lie on the ground.

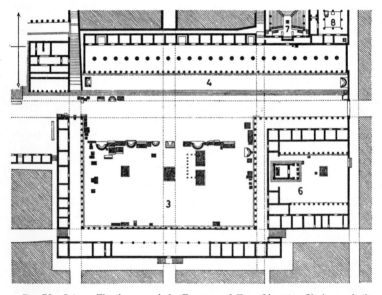

Fig. 70 – Priene. The Agora and the Temenos of Zeus Olympios. **3)** Agora, built in the third century B.C.; it was enclosed on three sides by stoas and formed the centre of the city. The main city thoroughfare passed in front of it (see p. 192). **4)** The Sacred Stoa was added in the second half of the 2nd century B. C., (see p. 193). **6)** The temple of Zeus Olympios, erected in the 3rd century B. C., was second in importance only to that of Athena in Priene (see p. 193; Pl. 8 b; Figs. 75 a, b). **7)** Bouleuterion. **8)** Prytaneion.

The Priene agora, like all market-places in Greek cities, was an open space where public meetings were held, festivals celebrated and business conducted. An altar dedicated to the god Hermes occupied a central position in the square (Fig. 70). Immediately east of the altar can be seen two stone-paved platforms, which were specially set apart so that they could be covered over by a baldachin. It is assumed that persons of rank could take their places here on ceremonial occasions. Wooden pillars to support the awning were erected on twelve stone bases (Fig. 70) in front of the two rectangular paved areas on the days when these functions were held.

The agora square and the area in front of the stoas were filled with memorial statues in antiquity (Fig. 70). Bronze figures next to marble statues painted in bright colours, and the surrounding buildings in vivid blues and reds created an atmosphere which would appear very exotic to our present-day tastes. All that now remains of this open-air exhibition of statues are the pedestals and their foundations. Since the pedestals were usually in the form of benches or exedrae, they also served as seats; the statues stood on the backs of these.

There was a separate market-place for foodstuffs. Adjoining the agora on the western side and marked 5 on the plan (Fig. 67) was the place where vegetables, fruit, meat, cereals and clothing were sold.

In the second period of prosperity in Priene, i.e., in the latter half of the 2nd century B. C., the agora was surrounded by new buildings of impressive size. Of these, the main one was the large colonnade which was known as the Sacred Stoa (4) in inscriptions. It is 116 m. in length and, since a piece of an architrave discovered here bears the first three letters of the name of King Ariarathes VI of Cappadocia, it is understood to have been erected by him. Therefore, the Sacred Stoa must have been built in 130 B. C. Six steps led up to the Sacred Stoa along its entire length. The citizens also used to sit upon these steps and watch the activity in the main road and the agora. After ascending the steps, one reached a 6.47 m.-wide promenade, paved with marble and open to the sky. At various times of the day and especially towards evening, this also formed an ideal place for a stroll, where promenade-loving Greeks could take the air (Fig. 70). The Sacred Stoa itself was 12 m. broad. There was a series of 49 Doric columns along the façade; the 24 Ionic columns that divided the inner hall longitudinally in two also carried the roof. The lower parts of the latter columns were not fluted, in accordance with the peculiarities of Hellenistic architecture. The roof was made of wood. Various inscriptions were carved on the side walls of the stoa. On the west wall alone there were 1400 lines of writing; these and other inscriptions related the main facts concerning the city of Priene and life there. In the rear of the Sacred Stoa there were 15 rooms opening on to the main hall. In Roman times, the ninth of these, counting from the west, was probably dedicated to the worship of the goddess Roma and later to Augustus. There were important inscriptions on the walls of this same chamber. One of these relates how the province of Asia (western Anatolia) began to use the Julian calendar in 9 B. C.

The Temenos of Zeus Olympios was situated next to the east stoa in the agora. This sacred area, built by modifying the construction of the eastern part of the agora, must have been established as far back as the 3rd century B. C. The temple, only the foundations of which exist today, was a prostyle of the Ionic order with a stylobate of 8.50 × 13.50 m. (Pl.

8 b; Fig. 75 a, b). The altar also is now only represented by its foundations. Nevertheless, it has been possible to draw a plan of the temple in a restored condition from a study of remains situated in the vicinity and others which have been sent to the Berlin Museum. The influence of Pytheos' style can definitely be discerned in all the architectural features and embellishments. The column bases (Fig. 75 b) are of the same type as those in the Athena temple (Fig. 69). From the standpoint of form and composition, the sima repeats the model found in the temple of Athena. In spite of all this, there are some stylistic differences. In keeping with the Hellenistic style, the spaces between the columns are wider, for example. The temple must have been erected in the 3rd century B. C. Because of the width of the base in the cella (Fig. 75 a), it is generally agreed that statues of two deities must have occupied it at the same time, and that very probably Zeus and Hera were worshipped here.

During the construction of the temple of Zeus in the 3rd century, the shops in the east stoa of the agora were abandoned. The entrance was on the east (Fig. 70) and no gate existed between the temenos and the agora. The colonnade on the north side of the temenos came into being at the same date as the Sacred Stoa. Thus, the colonnade with its shops on the main road, the sanctuary of Zeus and the Sacred Stoa all formed a highly attractive architectural unit.

The ruins in the eastern corner of the temenos of Zeus are the remains of a Byzantine castle. The rear part of this same fortress, together with its small chapel, is on the eastern block lying along the street passing east of the temenos (Fig. 67).

The Bouleuterion (7) is one of the best preserved buildings in Priene (Pl. 66 b). The bouleuterion and the adjacent prytaneion (8) together cover one whole block. The building is roughly square in shape and is approximately 20×21 m. in area (Fig. 71 a, b). The bouleuterion was a hall with an altar in the middle and with steps, used as seats, rising parallel to the walls on three sides. On the north side there were 16 tiers, while the east and west sides possessed only ten each. The south side differed in that it had no steps, but in their stead there were two entrances to the building. The hall could seat 640 people; the seats were reached by narrow stairways in the east and west corners, and also through doors opening to the upper rows from the side street and from the road passing in front of the temple of Athena (Fig. 71 b). Between the two doors on the south side, there was a rectangular niche, like a theatre box, which was used as a rostrum by orators. The altar was fashioned out of one single block of marble. Busts of gods in the form of "imagines clipeatae" and boukranions (bulls' skulls) holding up laurel garlands were portrayed on the four sides of the altar. The hall was roofed with a wooden structure. During the initial construction, this roof was supported by the walls and by stone pillars which stood on the top seats. The area to be covered was originally 14.50 m. but, when it was realized that this was too wide a span, the rows of pillars that were opposite each other were moved inwards two metres each; thus, the span was reduced to 10.50 m. Moreover, as will be seen on the site, the pillars were strengthened

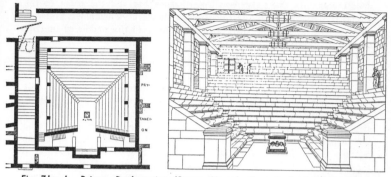

Fig. 71 a, b – Priene. Bouleuterion (Senate House). One of the best preserved buildings in the city (Figs. 67, 70, No. 7). Possibly constructed about 150 B. C. This once roofed hall with a central altar could seat 640 people (Pl. 66 b). Immediately next to the bouleuterion lies the prytaneion, possibly also dating from about 150 B. C. The officials forming the executive committee for the "boule", elected by the senators, carried out their daily duties in this building. This was also the place of the perpetual fire (see p. 195).

by additions, each one-third the width of the bases, made on two sides of each base. It is certain that there were windows in the bouleuterion and that these occurred in the upper parts of the walls, although, no proof has been found to support this theory (see the senate house of Termessos, pl. 95 a). It is also probable that the part of the hall which was beyond the place for sitting, i.e., that between the south wall and the steps, was open to the sky, and that the building received light by this means.

The fact that only 640 people could be seated in this hall supports G. Kleiner's opinion that this was a meeting place for the senate, i.e., a bouleuterion, and not an ekklesiasterion, which was a place of assembly for the people's parliament, consisting of all the people with the right to vote. In fact, this hall would have been too small for an ekklesiasterion. For meetings of the people's parliament, the theatre, which could seat 5,000, was probably used. The bouleuterion at Miletos (Fig. 80), which could accommodate 1,200 people, was used as a senate house and not as an assembly hall for the people's parliament. The Priene bouleuterion was obviously built before the Sacred Stoa, because the latter conforms to the architectural setting of the former (Fig. 70). However, the bouleuterion cannot have been very old; possibly it was built after the Milesian bouleuterion, in 150 B. C. As a matter of fact, the ornamentation of the altar supports such a date. **The Prytaneion** was immediately next to the bouleuterion (Fig. 70, No. 8). The officials who formed the executive committee for the "boule", created by the senators, carried out their daily duties in this building. The prytaneion was also the building where the municipal or state council representatives met. It was a great honour to be chosen by the people's parliament to partake of daily meals here. The middle room on the south was the entrance hall and the room to the east of this, containing the sacrificial hearth of the prytaneion, was evidently built at the same time as the bouleuterion, in the middle of the 2nd century B. C.

The Temenos of the Egyptian Gods (13) occupied a site in the east of the city (Fig. 67). In the south Part of this 47×31 m. area there is a retaining terrace wall exhibiting very attractive stonework. There is only one altar for religious worship; this consists of a platform, 14.60×7.31 m. in area and 1.73 m. high, on which there are no traces of any architectural structures. A close examination of a marble block which has been recovered shows that, at one time, seven marble steps, each 5 m. wide, rose up to the platform on the south wall of the altar. The entrance to the temenos was in the form of a square propylon on the north-west corner. A small altar-stone, 0.68 m. in height, found within the temenos was sacred to Isis, Serapis and Anubis, according to the inscriptions it bears. Other incriptions appear on the anta of the propylon. They give detailed instructions concerning the worship of these deities and, in addition, state that rites must only be performed with a suitable Egyptian presiding, and that those other than initiates should not officiate at the sacrifical ceremonies of Isis. The fine for violation of these rules was 1,000 drachmae; trialwas by court. Thus the inscriptions lead one to believe that the Egyptian gods were foreign to the people of Priene. However, trade considerations may have led to the establishment of a temple to please Egyptian businessmen. The profile of the various architectural elements and the skill manifest in the fine lettering of the inscriptions disclose the fact that the temenos and the altar were built in the Hellenistic age.

The Theatre. The theatre (9), which is situated in the north-east of the town, was one of the principal works not only of the Hellenistic period in Priene, but also throughout antiquity. In spite of the changes and additions made in Roman times, the building still retains most of its Hellenistic features (Pl. 67; Figs. 72, 73). The theatre was the place where dramatic works were performed and where various cultural activities occured. Moreover, it was also used as a meeting-place for the "ekklesia", i.e., the people's parliament. This fact is indicated by the presence of a water-clock, which will be mentioned again below, and which stood at the point where the west side-wall came to an end, by the orchestra. In keeping with designs of the classical and Hellenistic ages, the theatre was horseshoe-shaped and the walls of the parodoi were diagonal. Only the lower rows of seats have been preserved, but it is estimated that the spectators' stands were composed of 50 rows which could seat 5,000 people. To make it easy for people to find their seats, there were six narrow stairways placed at regular intervals (Fig. 72). In the middle of the fifth row, there were some seats added at a later date which were called the prohedria, i.e., special seats with back-rests reserved for important people. This feature will be discussed again below. The square holes which are visible in the seats were used to hold the uprights of canopies, put up to keep off the sun and the rain. It will be noticed that the holes outline a rectangular area (Fig. 72). The two ends of the wall on the south side of the theatre show some very fine *rustica* stonework. This wall must have been erected in the 4th century B. C. or, at the latest, in the Hellenistic age, at the beginning of the 3rd century. The sections of the side-walls descending towards the orchestra finally end in two squat stone pillars, on each of which there stood a statue (Fig. 73). A close scrutiny of the hollowed out places which held the feet shows that the limbs must have been set apart, which is an indication that the statues portrayed figures in agitated motion. For this reason, one concludes that these statues were made of bronze. As will be understood from the inscriptions on them, the sculptor Kleandros won the title of "stephanephoros" and they were dedicated by him to the god Zeus Olympios and to the people of Priene.

The orchestra was floored with beaten earth. No traces of a central altar have been discovered. On the other hand, there was an altar in the middle of the prohedria, which was in the horseshoe-shaped curve of comfortable seats reserved for people of rank (Pl. 67 a). Like every theatre altar of antiquity, this was sacred to the god Dionysus. Performances used to start

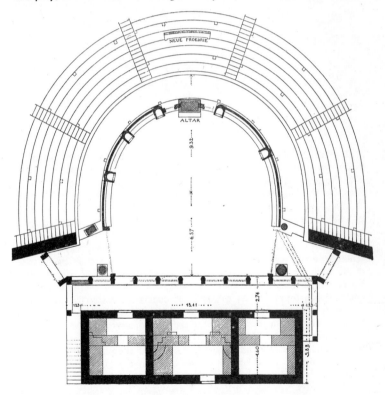

Fig. 72 – Priene. Theatre. Ground Plan (see Fig. 73).

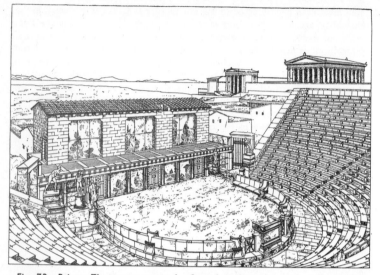

Fig. 73 – Priene. Theatre, as restored. One of the best preserved of the earliest Greek theatres (Pl. 67). Built in the second half of the 4th century B. C., it exhibits two phases going back to the Hellenistic age and a final renovation dating from the 2nd century A. D. (see the description on p. 196).

with sacrificial rites. This particular altar, according to the inscription it bears, was presented by Pythotimos. A study of the type of lettering shows that this altar dates from about the beginning of the 2nd century B. C. Since this is so, there must have been another altar in the theatre at an earlier date.

The prohedria encircled the horseshoe-shaped orchestra in the form of a bench with a back rest. This contained five armchairs, separated from each other at varying intervals by gaps of different sizes (Pl. 67 a; Fig. 73). Inscriptions occurring on the fronts of these seats state that they were presented by a man named Nysios. It will be observed, from a close examination of the foundations, that the altar and the armchairs were built later than the bench. Although the style of the lettering found in the inscriptions on the chairs differs from that on the altar, it does not necessarily follow that they were of different periods. This dissimilarity of the inscriptions could also be explained by the possibility that they were carved by two different men. Consequently, the armchair-type seats might also have been built at the beginning of the 2nd century, together with the altar. A space, 1.85 m. wide, paved with irregular stones, lies between the prohedria bench and the auditorium. This gave room to the spectators when they were going to their seats, and also drained off rainwater to the outside. At the south-east end of this way stands a statue pedestal and at the south-west extremity, the base of the aforementioned water-clock. The hollows on top of the latter pedestal were made to allow water to flow in and out of the water-clock. When a second prohedria was erected in the auditorium, two small entrances, fenced with railings, were built to allow the passage of the high priest to and from the altar (Fig. 73).

The proskenion is very well-preserved. It consists of a colonnade, 21 m. in length and 2.74 m. in width, and twelve supports in the form of Doric half-columns, still *in situ*, decorate the front face of the building (Pl. 67 b; Figs. 72, 73). The architrave and the triglyphs are also in very fine condition. As was the custom with colonnades of the Hellenistic era, four metopes occurred between every two columns. The extreme eastern and western intercolumniations on the front and those on the side faces were closed off with iron bars, as can be seen on the reconstructed plan (Fig. 73). However, the performers used to make their entrances and exits through the 3rd intercolumniation from the east, the 6th (the middle one) and the 9th. The remaining two intercolumnar spaces on each side of the central intercolumniation were used for setting up the wooden scenery or "pinakes". There were holes in these pillars for the purpose of holding up this wooden structure. Two statue pedestals are to be found in front of the proskenion: one in front of the second intercolumniation from the west, the other in front of the second from the east. Inscriptions relate that the former held a statue of Apollodoros and the latter of Thrasyboulos. The Apollodoros statue was erected by the city state of Priene, and that of Thrasyboulos by his wife Megiste. Both these men were famous personalities of Priene, and we know that there were other statues of them in the agora, and that they lived about 130 B. C. Since this is so, the proskenion must have been built no later than 130 B. C., which agrees with the date claimed by von Gerkan.

The skene was a two-tiered structure measuring 18.41 × 5.82 m. Only the lower storey is partly standing today (Pl. 67 b). On each floor, there were three rooms, those on the lower floor opening on to the proskenion through separate doors (Fig. 72). One end of the stone joists which covered the ceiling of the proskenion rested on the north wall of the skene (Pl. 67 b). Only one piece of a stone block has been discovered to show that there was an upper floor : this is part of the door and the wall of the western narrow face of the skene. There is a narrow shaft rising like a chimney inside the north wall of the skene behind the fifth pillar from the western end of the proskenion. It continues up past the next floor and emerges on the roof (Fig. 73); in all probability this was used for a kind of "deus ex machina" operation during scenes of "epiphaneia" in tragedies.

The skene underwent extensive alterations in the Roman period, probably in the 2nd century A. D. In Roman times when the actors performed their roles entirely on the proskenion, the structure measuring only 2.74 m. from front to back, which had been built at the end of the Hellenistic period, was found insufficient for this purpose. Therefore, the second floor of the stage was demolished and a new second floor constructed with the front wall 2 m. further south and with supporting arches underneath. In this way, the stage on which the actors performed was extended in depth to 4.74 m. by an addition of 2 m. The façade of the new stage presented three doors facing the audience. It is an easy matter to distinguish the Roman construction of mortar-bonded tiles from the Hellenistic walls made of beautifully cut stones. Two lateral gangways called parodoi passed between the auditorium and the skene and proskenion buildings: one on the west, the other on the east (Pl. 67 b; Figs. 72, 73). These gangways were at first open to allow free passage of the spectators into the theatre. Later they were closed off by gates made of iron railing (Fig. 73). Many of the uprights of these gates remain in the ground on both sides (Pl. 67 b).

Let us now summarize the four building phases which the Priene theatre went through in various periods.

1) Shortly after the foundation of the city in the second half of the 4th century, the theatron, orchestra and the first prohedria were erected. In addition, there probably existed a skene which functioned as a backdrop. In this period, dramas and other shows were performed in the orchestra.

2) At the beginning of the 2nd century B. C., the present-day proskenion and the skene were built, and armchair-like seats and an altar were added to the first prohedria. During this phase, performances continued to be given in the orchestra; some productions or scenes must have been presented on the roof of the proskenion (Pl. 67 b); otherwise, there would have been no point in building such a podium in front of the skene.

3) In this phase, from the middle of the 2nd century B. C. onwards, all performances were held on the flat roof of a proskenion, measuring 18.4 × 2.74 m. For this reason, the prohedria in the orchestra no longer had the best seats, and a new prohedria was built at the fifth row up from the front of the auditorium, in such a way that the flat roof of the proskenion would be at the spectators' eye-level (Fig. 73). In this period, the high priest sat in the second prohedria, and two small entrances with iron railings were built, one on each side of the altar, to give him access to the sacrificial rites performed there (Fig. 73). The iron railings of the parodoi must also have been constructed in this phase.

The Priene theatre, which was built in 130 B. C. and a large part of which is in evidence at the present day, remained thus, without undergoing any changes to speak of, until the 2nd century A. D. (Pl. 67 b; Fig. 73).

4) When, in the 2nd century A. D., there was another blossoming of Ionian culture, the 2.74 m. - deep platform of the proskenion, on which the players acted, was considered to be too small and was renovated, as explained above.

After visiting the theatre, those who enjoy a climb can wander around the temple of Demeter (Fig. 67, No. 10), perched in its lofty position 130 m. above sea level. This temple will be described later. Before visiting the lower gymnasium (Fig. 67, No. 14) and the adjacent stadium (Fig. 67, No. 15), it would be well to take a look at those houses in Priene which are particularly notable (to be discussed later). In the north - east corner of the theatre stands a sepulchral monument of the Augustan age. Mortar has been used in the construction and it presents a fine marble façade to the street. South of the theatre lies the archbishop's church (Fig. 67, No. 11), which has a central nave flanked by two aisles; the entrance vestibule or narthex has two doors. The pulpit was found in the nave, but only the foundations of the altar have survived. Part of the apse has been excavated.

The Gymnasia. Priene possessed two gymnasia: one to the north of the bouleuterion (Fig. 67, No. 12), the other in the south of the city (Fig. 67, No. 14). The upper gymnasium underwent extensive alterations in Roman times. The Hellenistic construction is understood to have been a peristyle consisting of rooms surrounding a courtyard, judging by the present-day remains. In Roman times, baths were added to the north side of the gymnasium, but they have, so far, only been partially excavated by the German archaeological team. In the west part of the courtyard, there stood a small temple which must have been devoted to the cult of the emperor; to the east of this, a pool of Byzantine origin may be observed. As we shall see below, the earliest school and athletic training centre was in the upper gymnasium. Consequently, the first building must date from the 4th century B. C. The lower gymnasium (Fig. 67, No. 14) is in a fair state of preservation and creates the atmosphere of a Hellenistic school and athletic centre. Like the upper gymnasium, it too was a peristyle structure. The courtyard functioned as a palaestra, i.e., a place where athletes practised their various exercises, and it was encircled by four stoas of the Doric order. An entrance in the form of a propylon having two columns at the front and the rear was situated on the west face of the gymnasium. It was also Doric in design and opened on to the stepped street leading down from the south-west corner of the agora. Various reading and training rooms lay behind the north and west stoas. On the northern side was a hall that opened to the outside between two Ionic columns; according to information given by Vitruvius about Greek gymnasia, it must have been an ephebeion. Here students were given lessons. It is still possible to make out the names of students, written in their own hand, on the rear wall. Each inscription began with an expression of place, ὁ τόπος, which was followed sometimes by the student's own name, and sometimes the father's name too, both in the genitive case. An English translation of two typical inscriptions reads "This is Theophilos' place" and "This is the place of Epikouros, son of Pausanias". In another room, a punch-ball must have been hung for boxing practice; in yet another, the athletes were oiled. To the south of the entrance that was on the west side are found well-preserved washrooms. The stone basins that are arranged around the walls at half the height of a man were used like present-day wash basins; slightly above these is a stone guttering or sima, hollowed out of the stone. Water ran perpetually from spouts fashioned like lions' heads, while low troughs for washing feet are still visible on the floor.

A gateway in the north-east corner of the palaestra led into the **Stadium.** One first steps on to an unroofed promenade, measuring 6 m. wide and 190 m. long (Fig. 67, No. 15). This is 74 m. longer than the similar promenade in the Sacred Stoa in the northern part of the agora (Fig. 67, No. 4). A stoa of Doric design stretched for the same length behind the promenade area.

Here, athletic trainers used to exercise during temperate weather. On hot or cold days they would exercise in the stoa or attend to their lessons. Races were run on the 190 m. -long track below. Guests sat on the stone steps beneath the promenade area and watched the races. The places reserved for spectators, the exercising ground and the stoa were all reached by the stairway on the west. The stone finishing- post for the runners should appear to the east of the stadium track, but has not been discovered. On the other hand, the starting point at the western end is well- preserved. In the front row, there are eight stones with holes through the centre. These were the starting posts for races in Hellenistic times, while the ten similar stones behind them (i.e. to the west) served the same purpose in Roman times. The holes in the stones erected in Hellenistic times are bigger than those in the others. Very possibly, the umpire stood here. Columns of the Corinthian order, which supported an architrave, stood on the Roman markers. If the bases are examined closely, hollows will be found in the sides. Similar grooves exist on the fragments of the architrave. It appears that barriers, formed of sheets of some kind of material, were placed in front of the runners, who waited for the start between the columns, and that these were raised simultaneously by the umpire or his assistant. According to inscriptions that have been found, a decision was made in the middle of the second century B. C. to build a new gymnasium at Priene. This date is more or less confirmed by architectural fragments that have been recovered. The lower gymnasium was very likely constructed in 130 B. C., as were many of the buildings in Priene. In any case, the upper gymnasium was now too small for the rapidly expanding town at that date, and one imagines that a new athletic ground and school were built during that period. When the new gymnasium and its adjoining stadium had been completed, they were reserved for the neoi, i.e., the young men, while the upper gymnasium was left to the ephebes (the youths) and the paides (the children). In the Roman period, the upper gymnasium was equipped with up-to-date conveniences, that is, the halls had hot-air heating installations. In contrast to this, the young people in the lower gymnasium still carried on the old Greek custom of washing in cold water.

The Sanctuary of Demeter (Fig. 67, No. 10), one of the oldest places of worship in the city, was dedicated to Demeter and Kore, the deities of plenty. Their emblem, a wheat sheaf, appears on the earliest Priene coinage. The entrance to this temenos measuring 45.05 × 17.75 m. was on the east, and just outside it the pedestal of a bronze statue portraying the priestess Timonassa is to be found. Another pedestal stands immediately next to the entrance. On this stood a marble statue of the priestess Nikeso, but this has been removed to the Berlin Museum by the excavators. Just south of the entrance lie the ruins of simply constructed houses that were inhabited by the priestesses. The temple occupies a site at the western end of the temenos, whereas the altar lies a short distance to the right of the main gateway. There was a two-columned vestibule in the square entrance area in front of the temple; the shrine, which was also a square construction, was reached through this. A podium can be seen running the whole length of the west

wall and half-way along the side walls. Three of the stone slabs paving the
north-west corner of the podium have hollows carved in them; these were
used to hold stelae which had been presented to the goddesses. In front
of the podium, was placed a votive slab for sacrifices, and parts of this
still lie there at the present time. Outside the temple, to the south, a small
chamber with a saddle roof lies buried in the earth. This was the sacrificial
pit. When the Greeks offered sacrifices to the gods of the heavens, they
burned animal flesh on the stone altar, but when they made offerings to
deities of the underworld, such as Demeter and Kore, they made an ablu-
tion of the blood of the slaughtered animal. This pit was surrounded by wierd
figurines in a grotesque style.

The houses of Priene rank with those of Delos and Pompeii as regards
size, beauty and state of preservation. Many of them exhibit early Hellenistic
features. Although the majority are overgrown with grass at the present
time, some of these houses still create an atmosphere of bygone days. In
general, house walls were made of small stones; the upper parts of some of
the side walls were made of sun-dried brick. In contrast to this type of
construction, the walls of some very attractive houses overlooking the
street are excellently built of well-cut stone and exhibit careful
workmanship. The rooms reached a height of 5.5 to 6 m., which is
customary in Mediterranean lands. Although no buildings with upper storeys
have been discovered, the beginnings of stairs have been found in one or
two places, and from this we may assume that many of the houses had two
floors. In most cases the flooring is made of clay soil. The walls of some of
the houses are plastered with stucco so that the lower parts look like marble.
Some of the houses are thought to have possessed windows. Slabs of baked
clay, measuring 79×52 cm. and pieced by six arch-shaped holes, have been
found inside the dwelling, and these are thought to have been shutters.
The windows were unglazed and were set into the upper walls at a height to
prohibit passers-by from gazing in. Fresh air and sunlight also entered through
the doorways facing the courtyard. The roofs were tiled. Among the many
household effects that been discovered are bronze bedsteads, earthenware grills and oil-lamps, and stone and terracotta statuettes. In addition, a
bathroom, 1.82×1.06 m., in area, was unearthed in a house in the north part
of the fourth block, west of the main road. Inside it was found an earthenware
tub measuring 1.08×0.51 m. in which a person could bathe in a sitting
position.

The finest, largest and best preserved of the houses is by the road
on which the theatre is situated, and which occupied a whole block between
the fourth and fifth streets west of the theatre (Fig. 67, No. 18; Fig. 74 b).
The façade is practically as wide as the temple of Athena including the
peristasis, since its breadth of 35 m. falls just two metres short of the latter's.
The fine *rustica* work of the front wall, the size of the house, which contained 26 rooms, and the valuable objects discovered within suggest that
this building belonged to a man of means. An altar dedicated to Zeus
Olympios stands in the house, and this indicates that the former
owner was a stephanephoros. To win this title was a great honour; the person

who was the "wearer of the wreath", i.e., who wore a circlet around his head, was put in charge of all sacrificial processions in the name of the state for one year, and he would defray the expenses of all the festivals out of his own pocket. The year when he was in office would bear his name. Consequently, the man who lived in the above-mentioned house in Priene must have been one of its wealthiest citizens. The entrance to the house was in the centre of the front and opened on to the theatre street (Fig. 74 b). One entered a small square courtyard and then stepped into another open space through a gate. The first door on the right led to the porter's room, the second on the same side was the door to the men's apartments, and the one opposite went to the women's quarters. There was a central rectangular courtyard in the men's section, which took the form of a peristyle house with rooms of various sizes on the four sides. The women's section was also

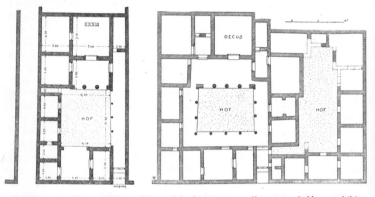

Fig. 74 a, b – Priene. Houses. Some of the houses are well-preserved. Many exhibit early Hellenistic features and deserve at least a short visit (see description on p.203).

a peristyle house, with rooms of different sizes surrounding a courtyard. If the plan and the remains are examined carefully, it will be seen that in fact the men's and women's quarters were contained in two separate buildings with a street between, and that later these were joined into one (Fig. 74 a, 74b). The women's apartments, i.e., the building on the west marked XXXIII, have been effectively revealed in their earlier condition as a result of the excavations (Fig. 74 a). When the building was first constructed, there was a large megaron north of House XXXIII; this constituted the men's hall, while the other rooms served as the women's apartments (Fig. 74 a). When the two houses were joined together, the old-fashioned dark and stuffy megaron was turned into a sunny, airy room by knocking down the west wall of the front room and adding a third column to the two existing Doric columns and a pillar in both corners, so that a beautiful colonnade was created opening south to the courtyard. As a result, the main room of the megaron received light and air and, in addition, the women and children were able to pass the time in a well-aired abode, which was cool or temperate according to the season of the year. This alteration must have been made in the 2nd century B. C., the period in which colonnades became so popular. When the two houses were turned into one, three rooms on the east were joined on to those on the west; thus two houses were formed, one consisting of 16 rooms for the women, the other of only 10 rooms for the men. Careful scrutiny shows that the door of the women's house was added later. In this way, the two apartments were completely cut off from each other. Strangers calling at the house would go straight into the section reserved for the men without passing through that set apart for the women.

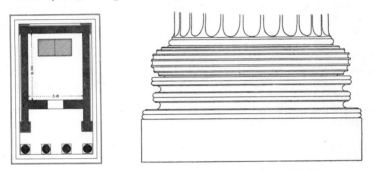

Fig. 75 a, b – Priene. Temple of Zeus Olympios. a) Ground plan. b) Column base. 3rd century B. C. (see description on p. 193).

An irregular five-sided courtyard can be observed at the western end, and on the south side of the main road running between the agora and the Sacred Stoa (Fig. 67, No. 20). This construction, the temenos of the goddess **Kybele** (Cybele), was built parallel to the city wall and is closed on that side. Inside it there is nothing but a sacrifical pit. Kybele was worshipped by the poor; although land was reserved for this purpose inside the city, the institution received no financial support from the state. This is the reason why it consists of a humble five-walled structure. The headless stone statuette of Kybele found here is now in the museum in Istanbul.

The House of Alexander the Great. The house occupying the western half of the second block east of the temenos of Kybele was also a place of worship (Fig. 67, No. 21). An inscription now kept in the museum in Berlin states that only people wearing white would be admitted to the sacred precinct. The house contained a large courtyard, a sizeable room with three columns and many other rooms. In order to reach the large room, one had to pass through the said three-columned room, which had a podium in the form of a sort of bench half-way along the north and east walls. In addition, the legs of a marble table made of two stone slabs have been found in front of the podium on the east wall. It has been established that there was a sacrificial pit in front of this marble table, which was actually an altar. Several marble and terracotta figurines were found standing on the podium. The small room to the south-east of this large one also possessed a sacrificial table.

Especially worth noting is a marble statuette representing Alexander the Great, which was among the works of art found in this house of worship and which is now in the Berlin museum. The lower parts of the body are missing, but since the head and bust are quite well-preserved, much importance is attached to it. The head shows stylistic peculiarities of the Hellenistic period, with the features of Alexander the Great. This rather triangular-shaped head resembles another head of Alexander depicted in the large mosaic representing the Battle of Issus and kept in the Naples museum. In addition, another smaller portion of the statuette has been recovered and from this we can see that Alexander carried a dagger in his left hand. We have seen that the statue of Alexander the Great found at Magnesia (Pl. 25) also grasped a dagger in the left hand. The finding of the statuette of Alexander in this sacred building is an indication that the place was dedicated to his worship. Since Alexander the Great was responsible for the completion of the Athena temple, it is not difficult to imagine that such a hieron should be consecrated to him. As a matter of fact, an inscription that has been found states that there was a sacred place dedicated to Alexander in Priene and that, in 130 B. C., the sum of 1,000 drachmas was contributed by wealthy citizens for its repair. Very possibly, Alexander the Great stayed in this house during his siege of Miletos in 334 B. C., and therefore the city later converted it into a house of worship as a memorial to him.

MILETOS

Miletos, one of the oldest and most important settlements in Ionia, was a coastal city with four harbours (Fig. 76). One of these was on the eastern bay and the other three were inlets on the west. Owing to the silting of the area by the River Menderes, the present-day town lies in the middle of a plain. The famous island of Lade, which in antiquity was off the coast to the west of Miletos, is now left high and dry for the same reason and is actually the hill four miles west of the theatre. As has already been stated, the Persian armada set fire to the Ionian fleet near this island in 494 B. C. and burnt it entirely.

An important Mycenaean colony existed in Miletos from the middle of the 2nd millennium on. The city wall, some houses and an abundance of pottery, all dating from the Mycenaean period, were brought to light during excavations recently carried out by the Germans. The people who settled here came mainly from Caria and, to a lesser extent, from Crete. In the "Iliad", Homer relates that the Milesian princes fought side by side with the Trojans. Tradition also has it that Miletos was founded by the Ionians, led by Neleus, son of the Athenian King Kodros. The story goes that the Greeks slew the male inhabitants and then married the widows. It is possible that the Greeks settled in the area as far back as the 10th or even the 11th century. Miletos passed through a very prosperous period in the 7th and 6th centuries. From about 650 B. C. onwards in particular it grew very wealthy, owing to the establishment of colonies on the Black Sea and the Mediterranean, and became the metropolis of the Ionian world. According to ancient sources, the Milesians founded ninety colonies, of which the principal ones were Naukratis in Egypt, Kyzikos on the south coast of the Sea of Marmara, and Sinope, Amisos and Olbia in the Black Sea region. The famous tyrant, Thrasyboulos, who lived at the end of the 7th century B. C. and the beginning of the 6th, successfully warded off attacks by Sadyattes and Alyattes, Kings of Lydia. The first steps towards the establishment of western culture, especially in the field of exact science, were taken mainly by the city of Miletos. The natural philosophers, Thales, Anaximander and Anaximenes, the famous historian and geographer, Hekataios, the town-planning architect, Hippodamos, and Isidoros, one of the designers of St. Sophia in Istanbul, were all native Milesians. Aspasia, the mistress of Pericles, came from Miletos. Towards the end of the 5th century B. C., the Milesian alphabet was officially adopted by Athens and so became the standard writing system of the Greeks. In 546 B. C., the city of Miletos, together with the Lydian centre of Sardis, passed into Persian hands. Miletos, the instigator of the Ionian rebellion, assisted by the other Ionian cities, destroyed the lower city of Sardis by fire in 499 B.C. Eighty Milesian ships took part in the Battle of Lade. However, the result was that the Milesians were deprived of their fleet by the victorious Persians, who then seized and demolished the city in 494 B. C. Some of the citizens were taken captive and forced to settle in Ampe, at the mouth of the Tigris. After this, Miletos lost its position as leader of the Ionian cities and never regained its former strength. Although Miletos had dwindled in importance in classical times, in the Hellenistic period it is known to have been one of the main centres of commerce and art in Ionia. Miletos, an independent city in the Roman era, was one of the principal metropolises of Asia, i.e., western Anatolia.

Excavations at Miletos were first begun in 1899 by Th. Wiegand. Carl Weickert took over when work was resumed in 1938, after a period of inactivity enforced by the First World War, and he also continued the investigations following the Second World War. In recent years Professor G. Kleiner has been in charge of the excavations. (See G. Kleiner, Die Ruinen von Milet, Berlin 1968, published by Walter de Gruyter).

One of the most important and beautiful works in Miletos is the huge **Theatre** (Fig. 76, No. 1). The front face of the theatre is 140 m. in width and the present-day auditorium reaches a height of 30 m. When the missing upper galleries were standing, in the Roman period, the height was 40 m. Without doubt, the colossal bulk of the theatre standing on the seashore in ancient times must have been extremely impressive (Pl. 13). The first construction was erected in the fourth century and later enlarged in the Hellenistic era; in Roman times the theatre attained its present-day proportions. More than 15,000 people could be seated in the theatre. The emperor used to sit in the lowest row. During performances, a baldachin was stretched over four columns, two of which are still *in situ* (Pl. 13 b). It is an easy matter to distinguish the parts of the skene built in classical and Hellenistic times from those added in the Roman period. G. Kleiner has proved that some parts of the theatre façade date from the Hellenistic era and others from the Roman period. The same scholar has identified those portions of Hellenistic origin in the north-west corner of the auditorium. The oblique position of the

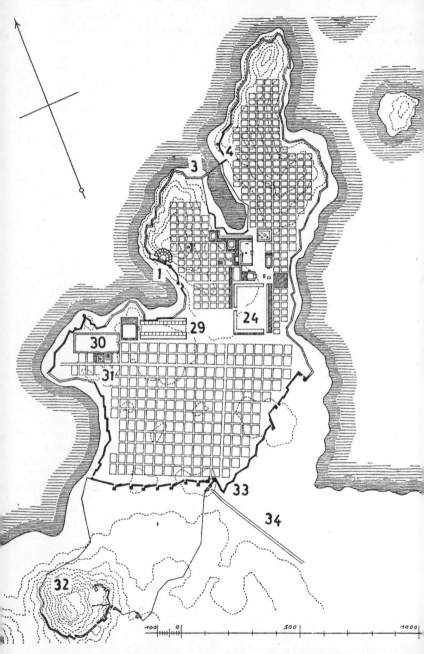

Fig. 76 – Miletos. General Plan. **1)** *Theatre (Pl. 13). The huge theatre at Miletos is one of the most impressive buildings of antiquity in Turkey. According to G. Kleiner, the initial construction was erected in the 4th century, which was earlier than that at Priene. The same scholar distinguishes three phases of construction, one of Hellenistic date and two of Roman date. Over 15,000 people could be seated in the theatre of the final phase, which is well-preserved (see p. 207).* **3, 4)** *Two lion statues dating from the Hellenistic era still stand in their original antithetic position on either side of the harbour entrance, guarding it in an apotropaic sense, with their heads turned towards the harbour.* **24)** *South Agora (see Figs. 77, 78).* **29)** *Stadium. Erected ca. 150 B. C. and altered in Roman times (see p. 217).* **30)** *West Agora, the most recent of the city market places in Miletos, probably erected in late Hellenistic times.* **31)** *Temple of Athena, dating from the first part of the 5th century B. C. (see p. 221).* **32)** *Kalabak Tepe. One of the sites where German archaeologists have uncovered remains going back to the archaic period (see p. 221).* **33)** *Sacred Gate.* **34)** *Sacred Way, connecting the city of Miletos with the temple at Didyma.*

parodoi clearly shows a perpetuation of the Hellenistic design. Remains of city walls going back to Hellenistic times and the archaic period lie beneath the theatre façade. An archaic tower can easily be identified below, close to the eastern end of the façade and in line with the proskenion. The German excavators have removed the Byzantine city wall that passed over the stage. Further sections of this same wall still stand on a slope just above the theatre (Pl. 13 b). An inn dating from the Seljuk period and erected at the beginning of the 15th century occupies the level area immediately opposite the theatre. Stables took up the ground floor, while the upper floor consisted of rooms for travellers.

A building of the Hellenistic period is in evidence below and to the east of the aforementioned Byzantine castle (Fig. 78, No. 2). This was reserved for the worship of some deified person. On the east and west sides of the building are to be found rooms, and in the middle, a courtyard with a circular tomb. The bay known in archaeological literature as the Bay of Lions constituted the greatest strategical means of defence for the city in antiquity (Fig. 78). The extremely narrow entrance could be closed off by a chain and thus a well-protected naval base was formed. Two stone lions (Fig. 76, Nos. 3, 4) stood one on each side of the entrance and guarded the harbour in symbolic fashion. These lion figures, carved in the Hellenistic period, still occupy their original sites today.

Miletos in Classical Times (Fig. 77). Since the Bay of Lions was so favourably equipped for the protection and shelter of ships, the idea springs to mind that at least a portion of the initial settlement must have been set up around this port. However, although this district of the town was the scene of active development from the first half of the 5th century B. C., no trace has been found of the original settlement, apart from a few remains going back to the archaic period. On the other hand, it has been established that many of the buildings around the harbour which were used in the Hellenistic era (Fig. 77) were actually erected in the classical period, i. e., in the 5th and 4th centuries. These comprise the harbour stoa (9), the small market place (12), the prytaneion in the south-west of the northern agora (13), as well as the western half of the Delphinion (10). The strictly east-west orientation of the temple of Athena (Fig. 76, No. 31), built in the first half of the 5th century B. C., shows its alignment with the buildings in the Lions' Bay district. From this it clearly follows that the city plan of the Hellenistic period, characterized by its straight streets, was actually that drawn by Hippodamos of Miletos as far back as the first half of the 5th century, as is related by ancient writers. According to the ancient Greeks, the originator of the right-angled city plan was Hippodamos. He not only re-planned his birthplace but also reconstructed Piraeus on these same principles in 445 B. C. and, in the following year, the city of Thourioi in the bay of present-day Taranto. The destruction of Miletos at the hands of the Persians in 494 gave Hippodamos the opportunity to realize a completely new plan. As a matter of fact, both Piraeus and Thourioi were entirely reconstructed settlements. However, Hippodamos was definitely inventor of this type of city plan, since there already existed cities in the Near East, such as Nineveh and Babylon, that had straight streets. Furthermore, as has been stated above, in ancient İzmir the houses were arranged in north-south or east-west directions as far back as the 7th century. Nevertheless, Hippodamos was obviously a great architect and town-planner since he systematized this type of city design, using a strictly right-angled geometric pattern.

Miletos in Hellenistic Times (Figs. 77 and 81). Miletos, founded on a peninsula $2^1/_2$ km. in length (Fig. 76), had the distinction of being one of the most beautiful and important cities of the ancient world for over a thousand years. In particular, those structures in the city centre that came into being throughout the Hellenistic and Roman periods are creations that rank highly in the history of architecture. On the south side was situated a 160 m.-long stoa of the Doric order, constructed in the Hellenistic era (Fig. 77, No. 9). 64 columns stood along the front of the stoa and, inside, there were 30 shops.

The chief religious centre in the town was the **Delphinion** (10), lying to the east of the stoa. Here Apollo Delphinios was worshipped. As the delphis (dolphin) was an intelligent and music-loving fish, it was believed in the Hellenic religion to be an animal sacred to Apollo. This god, apart from his many other qualities, was known particularly as the protector of sailors and ships. The original temenos was established in the archaic period; however, the present-day remains are of a building erected in Hellenistic times and enclosed on three sides by stoas (Fig. 77, No. 10), which later underwent alterations in the Roman period (Fig. 78, No. 10). In the Hellenistic era, entrance to the 50 × 60 m. temenos was gained through three gates on the west, whereas in Roman times a propylon, also on the west side, served this purpose. The stoas in Hellenistic times were of the Doric order, but were modified in the Corinthian style in the Roman era. An altar, a round structure and the remains of foundations belonging to three exedrae, together with four portable altars, have been discovered within the courtyard. On entering the courtyard from the west, one is immediately confronted by the remains of a rectangular foundation in a central position, which belongs to the temenos altar (Fig. 77, No. 10). The extremely beautiful corner acroteria and some portions of a cornice attributed to this building were discovered during excavations, and they reveal that the altar was erected in the second half of the 6th century B. C. The round portable altars are also archaic and date from the same period. One of these is older than the others; this is the one which rests against the eastern foundations of the altar. It is understood from an inscription that this altar was dedicated to the goddess Hekate. The two exedrae (i. e., semicircular platforms on which statues were set up and which could also be used as seats) seen facing each other east of the altar foundations, (Fig. 81) are Hellenistic in date. The columned edifice on a high cylindrical base with a large circular foundation lying east of the two exedrae was, in all probability, part of a heroon. Just below the circular foundation was found another exedra, similar to those previously mentioned. For this reason, the round monument to which we attribute the function of a heroon was either late Hellenistic or Roman in date.

Lying between the aforementioned Apollo Delphinios sanctuary and the harbour stoa was the 16-columned harbour gateway (11), constructed at the beginning of the Roman Empire (Fig. 78). This district, lying just south of the harbour, formed the city centre from the 2nd century B. C. onwards, and the north agora (13), the gymnasium (17), the bouleuterion (20) and the south agora (24) were located here. At that time, the east stoa of the north agora did not exist, and this side was enclosed by a wall; entrance to the courtyard was gained through a propylon (Fig. 77, No. 13). The agora temple was situated in the middle of the west stoa. This temple took the form of a prostyle with four Ionic columns on the front face. The Zeus Olympios temenos at Priene also exhibits the same concept of a temple set in a stoa (Fig. 70). The agora temple at Pergamon too is built more or less in the same manner and is situated at the foot of the agora wall (Fig. 24, No. 22). This seems to have been typical of the Hellenistic period. The four-columned façade of this temple in the north agora in Miletos is also in fact a Hellenistic feature, and the same characteristic is met with in the previously-mentioned temple at Priene (Fig. 70), in many temples at Pergamon (Fig. 33), and in the temple of Zeus Sosipolis at Magnesia (Fig. 61 a). Milesian architects preferred to incorporate this attractive type of façade into their buildings. The same four-columned prostyle can be observed in the gymnasium and the bouleuterion (Fig. 77, Nos. 17, 20). The 27 × 27 m. square courtyard with a colonnade, which lies in the western part of the north agora (12), was obviously a market place with shops on its four sides. The **gymnasium** (17) consisted of a propylon and a palaestra with five rooms for study (Fig. 79 a). Although it is difficult to decipher the ground plan with any certainty, owing to the fact that the remains brought to light by the expedition were later covered with earth, the main lines of the building are still observable on the ground. The individual shape of each study and the way these rooms are arranged calls to mind the lower gymnasium at Priene. Here, just as in the latter case, the ephebeion was in the centre and opened to the outside between two columns of the Ionic order. Moreover, the Milesian

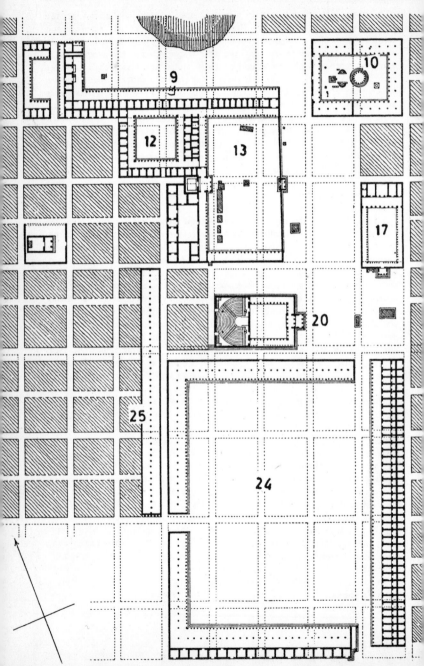

Fig. 77 – Miletos in Classical and Hellenistic times. The city plan of geometric design was already laid out by the first half of the 5th century B. C. (see p. 209). For description see p. 210 and the caption to Fig. 78, also Fig. 82 a.

structure also resembles that at Priene in that the columns standing in front of the studies were noticeably more widely spaced than those in the colonnade on the other side. In this way, the studies received comparatively more light. The propylon leading to the gymnasium consisted of a four-columned Ionic prostyle such as we have already encountered in Pergamon and Priene. The great similarity between this imposing entrance and the propylon erected by Eumenes II in the Athena temenos at Pergamon should also be pointed out here (Fig. 27). It has been stated in the first part of this book that the Milesian gymnasium conformed to a system characterized by pronounced axiality. Indeed, the two columns of the ephebeion were not only in line with the outer and inner columns of the propylon but also with the two central columns of the north stoa (Fig. 79 a). It has been recorded in relevant passages above that such a feeling for axiality was a feature of the Hellenistic period in the time of the architect Hermogenes and was particularly prominent in his own works (P. 24 ff.). Inscriptions have given no indication of the date when the gymnasium was constructed. Nevertheless, when the propylon is compared, from the standpoint of axiality, with buildings at Pergamon and Magnesia, and when we contrast its plan with the lower gymnasium at Priene, the date of construction emerges as the 2nd century B. C. This date is also in accordance with the style of the palmettes and acanthus leaves carved on sima fragments lying in the vicinity.

The Bouleuterion (Pl. II b; Fig. 77, No. 20 and Fig. 80). This building comprised a propylon, a colonnaded courtyard, and an auditorium (Fig. 80). The columns of the propylon are Corinthian in style. A photograph is given of one of the fine Corinthian capitals (Pl. 72). The propylon frieze, composed of reliefs depicting the implements of war, is a small replica of the reliefs made by order of Eumenes II in the propylon and the stoas of the Athena temenos in Pergamon (Fig. 27). The propylon had three separate entrances. Stoas of the Doric order stretched along three sides of the courtyard. The centrally-placed tomb dates from the Roman period (Fig. 78, No. 20). A meeting hall was situated in the west part of the courtyard from which it was entered by four doors. Two other doors also led into the assembly room on the west side; people entering by these reached the upper rows of seats by means of two stairways. The wooden roof was supported by the walls and four Ionic columns (Fig. 80). The auditorium had a seating capacity of 1,500. It is generally agreed that there were windows in the west wall of the hall. Half-columns built along the upper half of the exterior walls counterbalanced the horizontal aspect by means of vertical lines, and, with their perpendicular movement gave a liveliness to the massive body of the structure. The lower half of the exterior walls exhibits the fine technique employed by the masons of the Hellenistic period. An inscription found on the bouleuterion architrave overlooking the courtyard states that the building was constructed at the command of Antiochos Epiphanes, King of Syria. If this

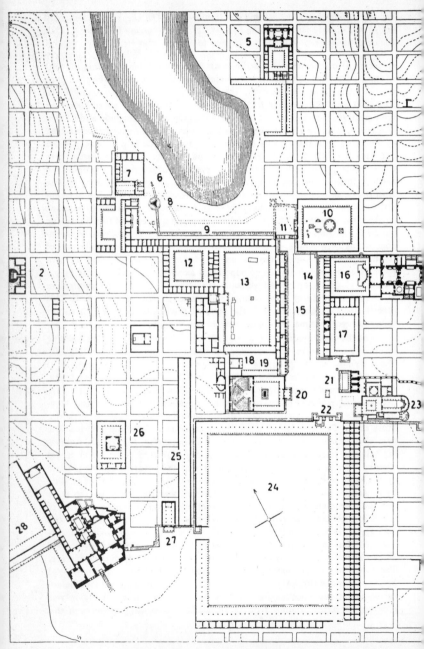

Fig. 78 – Miletos. The present-day ruins in the city centre. **I)** *Theatre. (described in the caption to Fig. 76).* **2)** *Heroon. A building consisting of a courtyard with a circular tomb and rooms on the east and west sides. Built in the Hellenistic age, it was devoted to the cult of a deified person.* **3, 4)** *Two Hellenistic lion statues still to be seen in situ on either side of the harbour entrance (see description in the caption to Fig. 76.)* **5)** *Roman Baths. Well-preserved building with a palaestra, dating from the end of the first century A. D., and representative of the type of baths developed from a combination of the Greek house and gymnasium plans.* **6)** *Small Harbour Monument. This structure, a portion of the base of which still lies on the ground, was a concave, three-sided monument, probably built in the second half of the first century A. D., during the Flavian dynasty and modelled on the larger harbour monument (see Fig. 82 b).* **7)** *Synagogue. This basilica-type building (a nave flanked by two aisles) is Roman in date. Little remains of the marble lavatory, built in Roman times to accommodate 40 people, that is situated at the south-west corner of the harbour stoa (not shown on the plan).* **8)** *Large Harbour Monument. The three-stepped round base of the structure is still in exist-ence. The whole of the monument has been convincingly restored with the help of recovered fragments (see Fig. 82 b). According to its inscription, it was set up in honour of an emperor, very probably Augustus, on the occasion of his victory near Actium in 31 B. C. Some sculptured reliefs of tritons (minor sea-gods, half-man, half-fish) are still to be seen on the site.* **9)** *Harbour Stoa. A marble-paved quay, constructed in Roman times, curved around three sides of the harbour, and on the south side stretched 160 m. - long harbour stoa in Doric style, built in Hellen-istic times. Sixty-four columns stood along the front of the stoa, and inside there were thirty shops.* **10)** *Delphinion. The chief religious centre, where Apollo was worshipped from archaic times onwards (p. 210). The present-day foundations are of a building erected in the Hellenistic age and altered in Roman times; the remains found inside the courtyard, however, date from various periods (see p. 210).* **II)** *Harbour Gateway. A 16-columned entrance giving access to the city centre, built at the beginning of the Roman Empire period.* **12)** *Small market-place sur-rounded by shops. Erected in classical times and enlarged in the Hellenistic and Roman periods.* **13)** *North Agora. Built in classical times; enlarged in Hellenistic and Roman times (p. 211).* **14)** *Ionic stoa with shops opening on to the main street. Erected in the reign of Claudius (A. D. 41-54). A specimen of the Ionic order of this stoa, consisting of base, column, capital and entablature, can be seen at the south-east end of the processional road.* **15)** *Processional Road. This attained a length of 100 m. and was 28 m. across. In addition, there were 5.75 m.-wide pave-ments for pedestrians on either side.* **16)** *Capito Baths, erected by Cn. Vergilius Capito, Procurator of Asia Minor in the reign of Claudius. The small baths built partly on the northern end of the stoa and partly along the road are Seljuk in date (not shown on the plan).* **17)** *Gymnasium (see also Fig. 79 a). Second century B. C. This consisted of a propylon and a palaestra with five rooms for study, and resembled the lower gymnasium in Priene in plan and in the arrangement of the rooms (Fig. 67, No. 14).* **18)** *Asklepios Temple (?).* **19)** *Sanctuary for the Imperial cult (?).* **20)** *Bouleuterion (senate house). Eercted sometime between 175 and 164 B. C., this building comprised a propylon, a colonnaded courtyard and a roofed auditorium to seat up to 1500 (p. 213).* **21)** *Nymphaion (Fountain). Second century A. D. A monumental three-storeyed city fountain with very rich architectural* ornamentation. The ground floor is still intact but deprived of its decorative embellishment in marble, parts of which are lying on the ground. **22) North Gate.** The monumental entrance (see Pl. 74 b) leading to the south agora. Second half of the 2nd century A. D. These two Roman buildings, with their markedly projecting and recessed façades, no doubt made a pleasing contrast with the harmonious fronts of the Hellenistic bouleuterion and gymnasium. The shady colonnade with the fountain lavishly providing water must have been very refreshing and soothing on hot Ionian days. The whole square, together with the processional road, doubtless formed one of the most impressive architectural ensembles of antiquity. **23) Diocesan Church at Miletos.** An apsidal basilica with a nave flanked by two aisles and preceded by a square atrium. The round building adjoining the apse of the basilica is a martyrion, and the square building to the north of the atrium must be a baptisterium. The church is earlier than the city wall of Justinian's time that encloses it and was probably built in the 5th century A. D. The propylon with four columns serving as the entrance to the church belongs to a Roman architectural complex and dates from the 3rd century, A. D. **24) South Agora.** An enormous courtyard 164 × 196 m. in area, erected in the Hellenistic age and altered in Roman times (p. 216). **25) Storage Building** (163.40 m. long by 13.40 m. wide). A Hellenistic structure, probably dating from the 2nd century B. C. **26) Heroon** from Roman times. **27) Serapis Temple.** A building of basilical type dedicated to the Egyptian gods, with a nave flanked by two aisles and preceded by a four-columned portico. Third century A. D. A section of the city wall dating from the period of Justinian lies between this temple and the Faustina Baths. **28) Faustina Baths.** Eerected by Faustina II, the wife of Marcus Aurelius (161-180 A. D.). A well-preserved structure meriting close examination (see the description on p. 220).

is so, it must have been erected sometime between 175 and 164 B. C., the years when this king was reigning. The fact that the aforementioned reliefs depicting military weapons on the propylon frieze were copies of originals made in the time of Eumenes II (197-159) also bears out this date (Fig. 27). The ruins that may be seen today in the centre of the bouleuterion courtyard (Pl. II b) are the remains of a heroon constructed in Roman times (Fig. 78, No. 20). The tendency towards axiality so noticeable in the gymnasium is also apparent here. The central columns of the propylon are in line with the middle entrance and, in order to conform to this arrangement, the middle columns of the east stoa are more widely spaced than the others so that they too lie on the same axis. A look at the "orchestra" of the assembly hall shows that it also conforms to this symmetrical arrangement (Fig. 80).

The South Agora (Figs. 77, 78, No. 24) This market-place was set up in Hellenistic times as an enormous colonnaded courtyard of 164 × 196 m. Although the whole area is only partly excavated, the plan has been disclosed in every detail. As will be clear from the plan, stoas had surrounded the agora on all four sides since Hellenistic times. Although the colonnades are built in three free-standing separate blocks, they all belonged to the same construction project. All three are of the Doric order. The east stoa was composed of 39 pairs of shops arranged back-to-back in such a way that half the shops were entered from the east and the remainder opened to the west, i. e.,

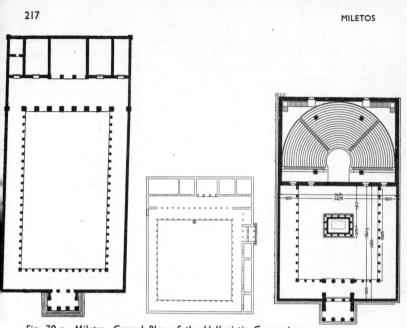

Fig. 79 a – Miletos. Ground Plan of the Hellenistic Gymnasium.
Fig. 79 b – Ground Plan of the Hellenistic Gymnasium at Priene.
Fig. 80 – Miletos. Ground Plan of the Hellenistic Bouleuterion.

towards the agora courtyard (Fig. 78). Those shops opening to the agora
also possessed storage rooms at the back. 19 shops stood along the south
side of the south-western stoa; these were arranged so that some faced
outwards and some inwards, but no particular order was followed. The three
stoas of the south agora each follow the same general plan as that observed
in the bouleuterion and the gymnasium; it is obvious from the plan, in which
the siting of the stoas conforms to that of the bouleuterion and gymnasium,
that they were constructed during the same period, i. e., about the middle
of the 2nd century B. C. It is also clear from its position on the plan that the
storage building (Figs. 77, 78, No. 25), stretching along the entire length
of the west side of the south agora and the bouleuterion, was also constructed in the Hellenistic era.

   The Stadium (Fig. 76, No. 29). This structure was also erected
during the realization of the city plan under discussion, i. e., in the middle
of the 2nd century B. C. The alignment of this structure is parallel to that
of the bouleuterion and at right angles to the south and north agoras (Fig.
76). Moreover, in contrast to stadia of the Roman period, the ends ware
not rounded but terminated in two opposing wings, calling to mind the
blocks already seen in the south agora, which are distinctly separated from
each other. Indeed, a portion of the wall unearthed at the east end of the
stadium definitely shows the excellent wall-building technique thought

to be of the Hellenistic period by reason of the beautifully cut stones and the precise way in which they are laid. Besides this, the gateway overlooking the stadium is typically Hellenistic, both in design and ornamentation. On the other hand, the east gate of the stadium dates from the Roman period. The stadium was 191 × 29.5 m. in area and could seat 15,000 people.

The City Centre in Roman Times (Figs. 78, 82). Miletos was the scene of renewed and vigorous development from the very beginning of the Roman Empire. The basilica-type building and adjacent courtyard situated to the north of the stoa wing evidently comprised a synagogue (Fig. 78, No. 7) dating from Roman times. A lavatory for 40 people, which occupies the south-west corner of the stoa, was of the Roman period; but this construction does not appear on the plan in this book. A harbour monument occupied a position in the north part of the west wing of the stoa (Fig. 78, No. 8; Fig. 82). An inscription records that this monument, of which the round base and some other portions have been preserved, was set up by the Milesians in honour of an emperor, very probably Augustus. As far as can be deduced from fragments, some of which have been conveyed to the Berlin Museum and others still lie on the site, a second base, smoothly concave and triangular in shape, rested on the round base. On this was a ship. The whole was crowned by a tripod. Recovered portions of the monument also reveal that it was decorated with reliefs depicting tritons or minor sea-gods (see Fig. 82 b). The three-sided edifice (Fig. 78, No. 6), fifteen metres north of the harbour monument, was set up, according to an accompanying inscription, in the name of one Grattius, a Roman. This small structure resembled the harbour monument, except that the round base was lacking; it rose immediately as a concave three-sided monument (Fig. 82 b).

One of the earliest building of Roman times was the 16-columned harbour gateway, set up between the Delphinion and the stoa in the first half of the 1st century A. D. The entrance in the centre was 3.84 m. wide and there were two other entrances on each side of it, both composed of four pairs of columns. Passing through the gateway towards the south, one came to a splendid processional road measuring 28 m. in width (15). There were 5.75 m.–wide sidewalks on either side. The baths (16) were built by Cn. Vergilius Capito, Procurator of Asia Minor under Claudius. The stoa (14) of the Ionic order was erected by Tiberius Claudius Sophanes. It lies opposite the north agora, and east of that baths (16). The stoa stretched for 100 m. as far as the southern end of the gymnasium (17). Shops opening on to the street were located in the arcade (Fig. 78). Parts of the upper structure of the stoa, consisting of column bases, shafts and capitals, can be seen placed one upon the other on the site. The palaestra attached to the Capito baths was surrounded by two-storeyed stoas and occupied a site between the gymnasium and the Delphinion, whereas the actual baths extended eastwards. The small baths sharing the road frontage with the palaestra and the stoa of Ionic style (14) were built in the Seljuk period at the beginning of the 15th century. This extremely well-preserved bath-house does not appear on the accompanying plan. As has been stated above, the palaestra of the Capito baths was surrounded by two-storeyed colonnades.

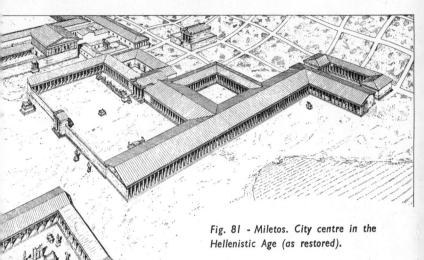

Fig. 81 - Miletos. City centre in the Hellenistic Age (as restored).

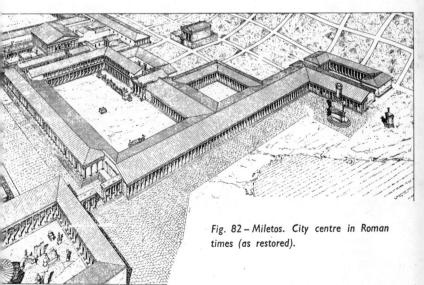

Fig. 82 – Miletos. City centre in Roman times (as restored).

The main building was reached through the central front room. This was the tepidarium, i. e., the cool room; the rooms on the right and left comprised the apoditerium, or dressing-rooms. Two rooms formed the caldarium, or hot rooms. These were the rooms east of the entrance, i. e., the one in the centre of the building, and the largest room of all, which lay east of the first room. The north agora underwent changes in the 2nd century A. D. The propylon on the east was demolished and the shops that stretched back-to-back in two rows along the entire length of the east side of the agora were constructed at this time; the remains of mortar walls still observable *in situ* today belong to these stores. A three-stepped krepidoma ran the whole length of the stoa in front of the shops facing the street, while a row of columns stood before those opening on to the agora courtyard.

The nymphaion or fountain (21) and the north gateway (22) to the south agora, two important buildings of the Roman period situated in front of the bouleuterion, were both constructed in the 2nd century A. D. (Fig. 78). The essential part of the fountain is still in position (P. II b) and important parts of the decorated façade lie on the ground nearby. The north gateway (22) of the south agora also presented a very richly ornamented architectural façade. Members of the German archaeological expedition have removed architectural pieces of this edifice to the Berlin Museum, where they have been restored to their original condition (Pl. 74 b). All that remains on the site of the ruins today are the foundations (Pl. II b). These two Roman buildings, with the marked projections and recesses of their façades, made a pleasing contrast with the harmonious fronts of the bouleuterion and the gymnasium. The shady promenade in the colonnades with the fountain spouting great jets of water, must have been very refreshing and soothing on hot Ionian days. The remaining buildings in the city centre dating from Roman and Byzantine times, are as follows. The basilica type building (23) east of the south agora gate was a Byzantine church. The small elongated building adjoining the bouleuterion courtyard on the north was probably used as a sanctuary for the Imperial cult. The megaron-like edifice lying just north of the auditorium of the bouleuterion is thought to have been an Asklepieion. The building lying 60 m. west of the west end of the south agora was a heroon (26). Yet again, the three-aisled structure preceded by a portico lying parallel to the end of the elongated storage building in the west of the south agora was the temple of Serapis (27). The baths of Faustina (28) are situated in the western sector of the south agora. A long stretch of the city wall dating from the period of Justinian lies between the temple of Serapis and the Faustina baths.

The Faustina Baths (Fig. 78, No. 28). This structure, which is in a very good state of preservation, does not conform to Hippodamos' city plan. The palaestra approximated a square, measuring 77.5×79.41 m. The colonnades encircling the courtyard were of the Corinthian order. The apodyterium or dressing-room, was a long hall leading off the palaestra. The statues of the Muses that occupied the niches at the northern end of the apodyterium are now housed in the Istanbul Museum. From the apodyterium, one passed into a three-roomed frigidarium, the cold section of the baths. In the central rooms of the frigidarium was a large pool. The statue of a river god and another of a lion, both of which served as fountains, can still be seen in their original positions. The frigidarium opened into the hot section, or caldarium, which consisted of two large rooms with apses, situated in the south-east part of the baths. Both these rooms were heated from below by hot air flowing from the furnaces in the south into spaces beneath the floor. In addition, the rooms were also warmed by hot air passing through earthenware pipes concealed in the walls. The bathers then passed westwards via the larger hall in the caldarium to the tepidarium, or lukewarm room, and so returned to the apoditerium where they had deposited their clothing on entering the baths. Inscriptions found during the excavations disclose the fact that these baths were erected by Faustina II, wife of Marcus Aurelius (A. D. 161-180).

The Mosque of İlyas Bey. Those visiting Miletos would be well advised to see one of its chief monuments, the İlyas Bey Mosque situated south of the south agora (24). It would be hard to find another edifice to equal this excellent building as regards the exceptional beauty of its architectural decoration and the precision and skill displayed in its marble carving. In particular, the skilful selection of ornamental details and the way in which they are employed to make the transition from one tectonic element to another compel admiration. The stalactite capitals, the marble window-lattices and the lustre of the coloured marble surfaces are all extremely effective. The sacred niche is a masterpiece in itself. The mosque, completed in 1404, is a domed construction based on a square plan, measuring 18.30 × 18.30 m. The transition from the square to the dome is accomplished by the use of a type of pendentive squinches.

Ancient Miletos (Fig. 76). Mention has been made above of the archaic tower seen beneath the foundations of the theatre, and of archaic remains in the Delphinion. Quite a number of archaic finds have been made in the vicinity of the temple of Athena (31) in the south part of the peninsula and also at Kalabak Tepe (Fig. 76, No. 32). Thus the city is understood to have covered an extensive area in archaic times. It is obvious that Miletos, the most powerful and prosperous centre in ancient Ionia, could not be contained within narrow boundaries. The greater part of G. Kleiner's research concentrates on the archaic period. Without doubt, we shall soon be in possession of some important results.

Only the foundations of the cella belonging to a temple situated at Kalabak Tepe have come to light (32). Judging by the fragments of baked earthenware sima found in the vicinity, the building was erected in the second half of the 6th century B. C. In the south of the west agora (30) lies a temple measuring about 18 × 30 m., and dedicated to Athena (31). This must have been constructed in the first half of the 5th century B. C. It definitely conforms to the city plan of Hippodamos. All that remains of this building at the present time are the rough stones forming the podium. Those pieces which have been uncovered reveal that the structure was of the Ionic order. The naos was a *templum in antis* and the peristasis had 6 columns on the short sides and 10 on the long. However, it is possible that, as von Gerkan suggests, there were 6 columns on the front side of the peristasis, i. e., on the south, but 7 on the north. There were usually fewer columns along the front face of Ionic temples than along the rear. As a result, the spaces between the front columns were wider and facilitated entry to and exit from the temple.

During his excavations undertaken in 1938 and 1955-57 in the immediate neighbourhood of the Athena temple, Carl Weickert unearthed the remains of a city wall and some houses dating from the Mycenaean period. Beneath the Mycenaean stratum, moreover, he found remains of a habitation level containing Minoan pottery. The excavations in this area finally yielded traces of the earliest Hellenic settlement of Miletos, characterized by protogeometric and geometric pottery, dating from between 900 and 700 B. C.

The Temple at Didyma (Pls. 68-72; Figs. 83-85). Beginning at the sacred gate of Miletos (Fig. 76, No. 33), the sacred road (Fig. 76, No. 34) winds its way south along the coast to the port of Panormos at Didyma. It then continues southwards and comes to an end north-east of the Didyma temple, in front of the terrace associated with votive offerings (Fig. 83). The final stretch of the sacred road going to Didyma was lined on the left and right with statues representing seated priests and priestesses as well as recumbent lions. These statues are now in the British Museum.

The Didymaion became very famous for a hundred years during the archaic period, i. e., the 6th century when it was in the charge of a family of priests who were known as the Branchids. Gifts were presented to the Didymaion in 600 B.C. by the Egyptian King Necho (see Herodotus II, 159) and later by King Kroisos. Herodotus also relates (1,92) that the presents sent by Kroisos were comparable to those he dispatched to Delphi, since they were made of gold and were of the same weight and design.

Pausanias relates (VII, 2, 6) that the sacred area dedicated to Apollo at Didyma was older than the first Ionian settlement. Thus, it follows that, as in so many other places in Anatolia, the Greeks replaced an indigenous cult with their own. The cult statue in the Didyma temple dated from 500 B. C. and depicted Apollo Philesios seizing a deer. The iconographic type of this statue is, in fact, closely related to the Hittite-Anatolian tradition, as has been established by Erwin Bielefeld.

The earliest signs of building at the Didymaion were discovered by German archaeologists as a result of their investigations in and around the temple in 1962. Heinrich Drerup unearthed, for a stretch of 5 m. in each case, the remains of the north and south foundations of the wall enclosing the initial sanctuary, which must have been built in the 8th or 7th century B. C. (Fig. 83). Judged by the traces of the exposed foundations, the original sanctuary must have measured 10.20 m. in width and at least 24 m. in length; it narrowed slightly towards the east. Within the sacred courtyard of the temenos were situated an altar, a well connected with the oracle, and various cult symbols such as Apollo's laurel tree. Again, in the year 1962, R. Naumann and Klaus Tuchelt excavated a colonnade measuring approximately 3.60×15.50 m. at the south-western end of the Hellenistic structure of the Didymaion. The colonnade was erected at the end of the 7th century B. C., and, since it overlooked the ancient sekos (sanctuary), we can conclude that the first Didymaion was enlarged in the 7th century by means of this addition (Fig. 83 No. 3).

The Archaic Didymaion (Fig. 83). As has been seen, the first temenos, which was probably built at the end of the 8th century, and the colonnade, which was added to it about a hundred years later, were actually unpretentious constructions of no great size. On the other hand, the temple at Didyma gained particular recognition in the most glorious period of the entire Ionian world during the first half of the 6th century B. C. Miletos is regarded as a place of special importance among the Ionian cities; when we consider that at İzmir there existed a temple with a magnificent peristasis consisting of bases, columns and capitals made of tufa even as far back as the end of the 7th century or the beginning of the 6th century (Pl. 42; Fig. 41), we come to the conclusion that a great part of the archaic Didymaion was completed by 560-550 B. C. at the latest. It is also beyond doubt that King Kroisos would only have sent his valuable gifts of gold to a temple of great size. The principal parts of the archaic Didyma temple show the influence of the temples of Samos and Ephesus which must have been built about the year 560 B. C. Although the archaic Didymaion lies beneath the Hellenistic construction, it has been possible to reconstruct it graphically. The accompanying plan is that produced by G. Gruben (Fig. 83). This building was a dipteros measuring 85.15 × 38.39 m., that is to say, the naos was encircled by a double row of columns. Just as in the case of the Ephesian temple, the outer peristasis (i. e., the outer ring of columns) consisted of 21 columns on the two long sides; the east face had 8, while the west face contained 9 (Fig. 83). If the columns in the inner circle are added to these, the naos was surrounded by 104 columns, and if those in the naos itself are included, the total for the entire temple is 112 columns.

When the new building was constructed, the original courtyard was altered. Actually, it merely became an enlarged version of the former sekos in the archaic Didymaion (Fig. 83, No. 1). The laurel tree and the well, connected with the oracle, were again in evidence. On the other hand, a naiskos, that is, a small temple, must have been erected to house the cult statue of Apollo. This naiskos seen within the first sanctuary (Fig. 83, No. 2) was a *templum in antis* and, as we shall see below, it was built during the restorations undertaken in the Didymaion at the end of the 6th century. The archaic Didymaion, which was built about 560-550, must also have had a naiskos; however, no traces of this have been unearthed. The naiskos constructed at the end of the 6th century stood in the open air within the new sekos, which was 50.25 × 17.45 m. in size (Fig. 83, No. 2). However, since the sacred courtyard was surrounded by walls approximately 17.5 m. in height, the archaic Didymaion gave the impression of being roofed, when viewed from the outside; but, as the distance between opposite pilasters along the sekos walls was 13.5 m., it is obvious that the area could not have possessed a roof. On the other hand, the presence of two rows of columns in the pronaos shows that this part was covered. The interior faces of the sekos walls, like those in the second hekatompedos on Samos, were reinforced with pilasters in the form of half-columns (Fig. 83). The effect of

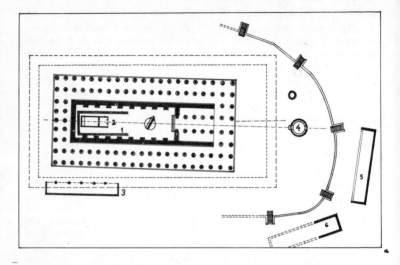

Fig. 83 – Archaic Didymaion (560-550 B. C.). Dipteros of the Ionic order, measuring
38.39 × 85.15 m. The plan shows the archaic Didymaion drawn inside the Hellenistic Didymaion. The unroofed cella (also known as either the sekos or the adyton)
is elongated; the covered pronaos is deep. Within the cella can be seen 1) the
temenos of the first Didymaion (end of the 8th century or beginning of the 7th
century B. C.) 2) the naiskos inside the initial temenos (520 B. C.). The statue
of Apollo, the work of the sculptor Kanachos of Sikyon, stood in this naiskos. The
inner surfaces of the cella walls are decorated with pilasters to form a kind of
architectural façade. 3) The recently uncovered 3.60 × 15.50 m. stoa is preserved
in the south-west corner of the dipteros, it was built in the 7th century B. C. The
outer peristasis of the dipteros contained 9 columns across the west face, 8 across
the east face and 21 along each side. Some of the columns at the east end were
decorated with reliefs in the manner of those in the Ephesian temple (Fig. 54).
The bases and capitals also resembled Ephesian models; the column shafts
were carved with 36 flutes. By the use of one column less on the eastern side, the
central intercolumniation was made wider, thus forming a kind of entrance, as
in other Ionic temples. In this way the front was accentuated. 4) A circular altar
stands on the axis passing through the middle of the central intercolumniation. The
sacred way from Miletos (Fig. 76, No. 34) led up to the north-east corner of the
Didymaion. The east face of the temple was enclosed by a 3.50 m- high wall,
portions of which are still standing. It was built about 550 B. C., as indicated by
the form of the kymation on its upper cornice. The wall supported the front of a
platform where offerings were placed. Five flights of steps led up to this at various
points. 5, 6) Two stoas, as well as diverse statues and portable altars, stood on this
platform.

these pillars was to relieve the horizontal line formed by the long walls and also to animate the otherwise uninteresting surfaces. The columns, column bases and capitals were of the type found in the Artemis temple at Ephesus (Fig. 54); the shafts were carved with 36 flutes. The principal building material of the temple was tufa. However, those parts visible from the outside, the whole of the upper structure and also the capitals and the columns in the pronaos were made of marble. The lower parts of the pronaos columns were decorated with reliefs, like the columns on the front of the Ephesian temple (Fig. 54). Two splendid female heads that have been recovered from these reliefs are now in the Berlin Museum. These highly successful specimens of Ionian art were created, at the latest, about 550 B. C., i. e., they date from the first building phase of the archaic Didymaion. On the other hand, the two winged gorgons forming the acroteria at each corner of the pediment, one of which is kept in the Istanbul Museum and the other in the Berlin Museum, have been proved to be late archaic works which were made during restorations carried out in the temple at the end of the 6th century. The bronze cult statue known as Apollo Philesios, mentioned above, also dated from the end of the 6th century, according to Pausanias, who states that it was the work of Kanachos of Sikyon, a sculptor living about 500 B. C. The naiskos which housed the statue is therefore understood to have been rebuilt during these alterations.

Standing in the eastern part of the archaic Didymaion is the altar, which is circular in design and aligned on the axis passing between the two columns of the naiskos (Fig. 83, No. 4). The well to the west of the altar must also have had a religious function. A semicircular wall, 3.5 m. in height, surrounds the whole of the eastern section of the temple. As will be understood from the Ionic kyma decoration appearing along its upper edge, this wall was built either during the first building phase of the Didymaion or shortly afterwards. Two stoas on the east and south sides of this same wall can similarly be said to date from the 6th century (Fig. 83, Nos. 5,6). Votive statues and other monuments erected in the name of the god stood on this platform. Five steps, each 2.5 m. wide, led up to this terrace.

After the Ionian rebellion, the Persians, having won the Battle of Lade, devastated Miletos and the Didymaion. Meanwhile, the conquerors banished the Branchids, i. e., the priests of the temple, to Baktria, on account of their treachery, and took Kanachos of Sikyon's bronze cult statue to Ekbatana.

The Hellenistic Didymaion (Pls. II a, 68-72; Fig. 84). Towards the end of the 4th century, after Alexander the Great had regained independence for the Ionian cities, he set about rebuilding the Didymaion. While this was going on, Seleukos I, King of Syria, had the cult statue of Apollo brought back from Ekbatana about 300 B. C. and also helped with the construction of the new temple, designed by the architects Paionios and Daphnis. The former, who came from Ephesus, was one of the architects responsible for the Artemision. The new temple took the form of a dipteros, though it was bigger than the first Didymaion. On G. Gruben's plan, which is reproduced here, the Hellenistic Didymaion is drawn over that of archaic times (Fig. 83). The outer measurements of the peristasis in the first building have

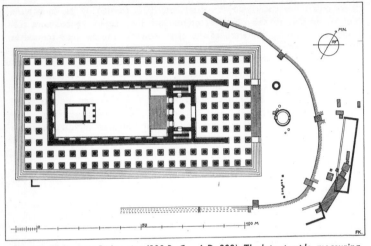

Fig. 84 – Hellenistic Didymaion (300 B. C. – A.D. 200). The later temple, measuring 51.13 × 109.34 m., was the third largest structure of the Hellenic world, being exceeded in size only by those at Ephesus and Samos. Although the Hellenistic Didymaion was of greater dimensions than the archaic temple, it was merely an adaptation of the original plan. It rose, like the Artemision (Fig. 53), on a high krepidoma (3.5 m. in height, with 7 steps). In addition, there was a flight of 14 steps in the middle of the east front. The naiskos within the cella (sekos or adyton) took the form of a prostyle and was erected at the beginning of the 3rd century B. C. The two-columned chresmographeion (the oracle room), its two flanking labyrinths (roofed corridors with ramps), and the pronaos were also built in the first half of the 3rd century and belong to the first building phase. The anta capitals of the pronaos, however, date between 150-100 B. C., while the griffin friezes decorating the upper parts of the adyton or cella walls as well as the inner row of the peristasis with three columns still standing (Pls. 11 a, 68, 69, 71) were made in the first half of the 2nd century B. C. The columns forming the outer row of the peristasis were completed in the 2nd century A. D. The busts of gods, the capitals decorated with griffins and bulls' heads, together with the friezes adorned with Medusa heads (Pl. 74 a) surmounting the architrave, were also the work of this period. The 7-stepped structure (late Hellenistic period) lying 13 m. south of the temple is the remnant of a stadium where ceremonies associated with the Didymaion were held.

been given above. The stylobate of the initial construction measured roughly 87.65 × 40.89 m. whereas that erected in the Hellenistic era measured 109.34 × 51.13 m. and the naos 87.41 × 29.16 m. Thus, this temple was nearly as big as the Artemision (Fig. 52) and the Heraion on Samos and was third in size of all the religious buildings in the Hellenic world. The outer perimeter of the peristasis was bounded by 21 columns on each of the longer sides and 10 on the shorter. Those along the front face were not widely

spaced; this was a departure from the old Ionic style. The total number of columns in the double peristasis was 108; in all there were 120
Ionic columns including those in the pronaos. At the entrance to the
chresmographeion, i. e., the room where the oracle was written and delivered, stood two half-columns; inside this room there were two more columns with Corinthian capitals, which makes a total of 124 columns in all.
Another original feature of the second Didymaion was that it stood upon
a 3.5 m.-high platform with seven steps leading up; there was also a separate
flight of 14 steps in the centre of the east front (Pl. 68 a). Both these
special features were also evident in the Artemision of classical times
(Fig. 53).

The major part of the temple still stands at the present day and, even in
its ruined state, it is a very impressive building (Pl. 68-71). It will one day
be possible to restore a great part of the Didymaion by re-erecting the
fragments lying on the site.

Such a large building could not have been completed in a short time.
Indeed, the construction continued throughout the 3rd and 2nd centuries
B. C., and one section was finished only in Roman times, while it is understood
that the outer columns on the south-west and north were never completed.
Remains which have come to light reveal that the first part to be built comprised the naiskos, lying within the unroofed cella (which we referred to as the
sekos or adyton), the two-columned hall and the pronaos. Although many
pieces of the naiskos have been discovered, only the foundations can be seen
at the site (Pl. 68 b). The plan of this small building, measuring 14.23 × 8.24 m.,
shows a prostyle with four Ionic columns in front of the antae, an architectural form much favoured in Hellenistic art (Fig. 33). One of the earliest examples of this small type of temple was that dedicated to Zeus Olympios at Priene
(Fig. 62). Nevertheless, if the cella of the Didymaion naiskos is compared with
other Hellenistic models of the same design, it is found to be rather longer
and to be the forerunner of this type. The architectural ornamentation of the
naiskos certainly closely resembles classical examples and exhibits very
fine workmanship. Moreover, the fact that the column bases are of the Ephesian type and that the lower edge of the canalis on the capitals is bow-shaped
are further indications that this is an early Hellenistic building. There is no
doubt that the bronze statue of Apollo, which was brought back from Ekbatana by Seleukos in 300 B.C., was not kept long in the open but that the naiskos was built and the ancient statue of the god placed within it. It is particularly notable that the naiskos at Didyma was the first Anatolian building of the Hellenistic period to show the influence of the Attic style.
The base of the walls, the profile of which consists of torus, trochilus, torus,
and the placing over the architrave of a narrow anthemion frieze, composed
of floral motifs, both betray the influence of the Attic art of classical times.
Moulding of the Attic order along the base of walls is also encountered in
the Zeus Olympios temple at Priene. On the other hand, as regards the plan
of the naiskos of the Didymaion and the high quality of its architectural
decoration, we may state that the building already shows an early Hellenistic
character.

The sekos of the Hellenistic Didymaion was naturally also enlarged. This sacred courtyard, known in inscriptions as the adyton, 53.63 × 21.71 m. in area, was unroofed and the surrounding walls had a height of more than 25 m. However, the huge encircling walls no doubt had produced the impression of a covered cella. The temenos was actually transformed into an architectural interior by means of the elaborate architectural and ornamental additions that were made to the walls by skilled craftsmen (Pl. 68 b; Fig. 85). The profile of the walls began with a high base; the middle section comprised pilasters topped with capitals and a frieze depicting heraldically disposed griffins, and above this was the cornice.

Several fragments of the pilaster capitals and the griffin frieze still lie on the ground nearby. These pieces bear characteristic features of Hellenistic art forms. From the point of view of style, we may date them between the aforementioned naiskos and the works of Hermogenes; consequently, the walls of the adyton must have been built at the beginning or in the first half of the 2nd century B. C.

On the eastern side of the adyton we see a stairway 15.20 m. in width and comprising 24 steps (Pl. 68 b). This flight of steps led up to the chresmographeion, that is, the hall where the oracle was written and delivered. The two half-columns standing in the three-doored entrance were surmounted by Corinthian capitals. The chamber measured 14.04 × 8.74 m. and was 20 m. high with a marble roof. East of the room, a doorway 5.63 m. wide and 14 m. high, led to the pronaos. The supporting pillar on the south side of the doorway is still intact and weighs 70 tons; it is known to be the largest

Fig. 85 – Temple at Didyma (Hellenistic structure). The sekos enclosing the naiskos. The small temple was built at the beginning of the 3rd century B. C. while the enclosing wall was completed in the first half of the 2nd century B. C.

monolith of antiquity. The threshold stone of this opening to the oracle room was 1.46 m. higher than the floor of the pronaos; hence, we can understand that there was no entry from the pronaos to the chresmographeion. The priests delivered the oracle of Apollo here, and those interested in the pronouncement would listen from the pronaos. It was possible to reach the roof via stairways gained by two doorways, one of which was located in the north wall of the chresmographeion and the other in the south wall. These stairways are referred to in inscriptions as "labyrinths" because of the decorations on the ceiling showing the Greek fret. The "labyrinths" must have played a great role in cult ceremonies. There were two doors measuring 2.25 m. in height and 1.2 m. in width, one on either side of the pronaos; both opened on to a narrow vaulted corridor which led down to the adyton, that is, the unroofed cella. At the lower end of each corridor there is a room resembling a propylon with a ceiling decorated in squares and a door ornamented with Doric mouldings. The profile of the upper door frames was characterized by the presence of taenia (the fillet lying between the frieze and the architrave) and regula (the strip with guttae on the underside), elements which strongly recall the profile of the Propylaea, the entrance to the acropolis in Athens. The use of such Doric features in an Ionic temple heralds the mixed Ionic and Doric style which first came into fashion in the 2nd century B. C. in the Hellenistic period.

From the standpoints of type and style, the Corinthian capitals at the entrance to and within the oracle room were closely related to the classic model of Epidauros. The Didymaion capitals exhibit a striking resemblance to the prototype of Epidauros, because of the arrangement and proportions of the upper and lower rows of acanthus leaves, and the impression that the outer volutes have a quasi-structural and supporting role. The capitals of the Laodike building at Miletos, those of the Belevi monument (Pl. 73) and of the Olba temple (Pl. 102) conform to the same type. Since the Laodike building was in all probability erected by the wife of Antiochus II (251-246), the Didymaion example together with those mentioned above are understood to have been built during the first half of the 3rd century B. C. When one takes into consideration that the Didymaion capitals are superior in workmanship and quality to the specimens of the Laodike building, it is possible to conclude that the former, i. e., those of the Didymaion, appeared earlier and were used as models for the others. Indeed, from the standpoint of the quality of execution and measured proportions, in the classical sense, which are manifest in the arrangement of its leaves and volutes, the Didymaion capital is the closest of all the Anatolian specimens to the Epidauros model. Thus it can be said that the chresmographeion and the pronaos, like the naiskos, were completed by the beginning of the 3rd century. As the essential feature of the Didyma temple of Apollo was really the oracle, the chresmographeion and the pronaos, with which it formed a unit, was naturally the section first commenced and the first to be completed. On the other hand, the antae, together with the winged busts of women and the acanthus leaves forming the lower parts of their bodies, which together decorated the pillars in the north-west and south corners of the antae, must, as stated by H. Knackfuss, have been created sometime between 150 and 100 B. C.

Very probably the inner peristasis, that is, the inner row of columns, was completed in the first half or the middle of the 2nd century B. C., because the carving of the acanthus leaves at the inner corners of the volutes on some of the capitals belonging to this peristasis calls to mind the acanthus leaves on the pilasters in the adyton. Some capitals, three of which are still standing on their columns (pls. 11a, 69, 71), exhibit a classical and academic style; however, since the bow-shaped feature formerly found on the lower edge of the canalis has been superseded by a straight line, these capitals cannot have been made earlier than the 2nd century. Furthermore, as the rows of egg motifs and the volutes of these same capitals have been carved in rather shallow relief (Pl. II), they differ from the Hermogenean type of capital which appeared in the middle of the 2nd century and which was characterized by deep carving to produce a play of light and shadow. Thus it is possible to date the inner row of columns to the years between 200-150 B. C.

In contrast, the outer row of columns shows an entirely different style. The eight column bases in the middle of the outer peristasis on the east side are of the Roman era. The base which is given as an example in the photograph produced here (Pl. 70) exhibits characteristic Roman workmanship as regards

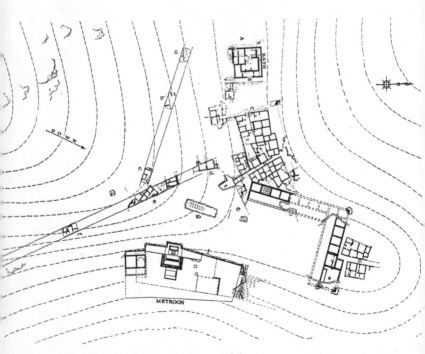

Fig. 86 a – Plan of Kolophon (see p. 134).

the decorative motifs and sculptured bas-reliefs. Perhaps the bases were constructed in the time of Caligula (A. D. 37-41), who tried to take the place of the Apollo of Didyma. The busts of deities (Zeus, Apollo, Artemis and Leto) on the two corners of the outer row of columns and the associated capitals decorated with the heads of griffins and bulls are works of art of attractive baroque style, conforming to the fashion of the 2nd century A. D. In the same way, the Medusa heads forming the frieze over the archi-trave of the outer row of columns (Pl. 74 a) were completed in the 2nd cen-tury A. D. and are most likely to have been carved along with the figured capitals by craftsmen from Aphrodisias.

Fifteen metres to the south of the temple was a seven-stepped stadium. On some of the rows of seats were carved names belonging to the late Hellen-istic period. It is understood that this stadium was used for the sacred races which took place in connection with the religious ceremonies held at Didyma.

ILDIRI (ERYTHRAI)

The ancient site of Erythrai is today partly occupied by the small village of Ildıri, located 20 km. to the north-east of the famous beach of Çeşme. The four islands which lie in the gulf opposite the city were called Hippoi, i. e., horses in ancient Greek times (Strabo XIV 644). Inscriptions mention a river, Aleon, which is noted by Pliny. However, the coins of Erythrai repre-sent a river-god named Axus. Yet, actually, there is only one stream in Erythrai, which flows into the gulf of the city.

According to Pausanias (VII 3,7), Erythrai was founded by Cretan settlers under the leadership of Erythros, "The Red", son of Rhadamanthys and, at the same time, inhabited by Lycians, Carians and Pamphylians. However, the city of Erythrai, as Pausanias notes, was later reinforced by Ionian colonists under Kleopos, or Knopos (Strabo XIV 633), a descendant of the legendary Athenian King Kodros. Erythrai belonged to the Panionion, which consti-tuted the mighty political league of the Ionian cities, and which was already founded in the 9th century B. C. After it was founded, the city was governed for a time by members of the aforementioned Athenian royal house. Aristotle mentions an oligarchy of Basilidae at Erythrai in ancient times (Pol. 1305 b). Together with Teos, Erythrai sent noblemen of Ionian descent to reinforce the Ionic settlement (p. 116) at Phokaia (Pausanias VII 3,8). The local historian, Hippias, which probably lived in the Hellenistic period, reports that King Knopos was dethroned by the tyrants Ortyges, Iros and Echaros, who were friends of the tyrants Amphiklos and Polyteknos of Chios.

According to Hippias, these tyrants, who ruled as terrible despots, were expelled by the brother of Knopos and died during their flight. This king, whom Hippias probably confuses with the legendary Knopos, must have lived in the 7th century B. C., i. e., at a time in which most of the Ionian cities were governed by tyrants. From ca. 560 B. C., Erythrai was under Lydian domination and after 545 B. C. was subject to the Persians.

It joined the Battle of Lade (494 B. C.) with eight ships. In the Delian Confederacy, the Erythraean tribute was the considerable sum of seven talents. Erythrai possibly left the Delian league ca. 453 B. C. Together with Chios, it revolted against the Athenian hegemony in 412 B. C. and served as a base for the Peloponnesians. Afterwards, it was allied alternately with Athens and Persia. About the middle of the 4th century, it developed a friendly relationship with Maussollos. In an inscription honouring this monarch, that was found on the site, he is called a benefactor of Erythrai. In approximately the same period, Erythrai signed a treaty with Hermias, Tyrant of Assos and Atarneus (p. 64), based on reciprocal aid in the event of war (Syll.[3] 229). In 334 B. C. the city regained its freedom through Alexander the Great, who, according to Pliny (N. H. V, 116) and Pausanias (II, 1,5), planned to cut a canal through the peninsula of Erythrai to connect Teos Bay with the Gulf of Smyrna. Erythrai was associated with Pergamon and with Rome. After the death of Attalos III in 133 B. C., when the Pergamene Kingdom had been bequeathed to the Romans, Erythrai flourished as a free city attached to the Roman province of Asia.

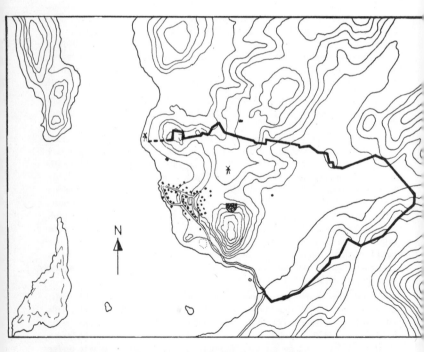

Fig. 86 b – Plan of Erythrai (after Cevdet Bayburtluoğlu).

The fortification wall which protected the city of Erythrai on the landward side is still in a very good state of preservation, and exhibits fine ashlar masonry. It is from 4 to 5 m. thick, and included several gateways. From three different inscriptions found on the site (Magie, *Roman Rule in Asia Minor*, 79), it can be surmised that the city wall was built either at the end of the 4th or at the beginning of the 3rd century B. C. Near the coffee-house in the village, there is a part of a pebble mosaic, still *in situ*, representing griffins, and dating from the Hellenistic period. The theatre, which is cut into the north slope of the acropolis hill, is extremely damaged and plundered. The aqueduct that stands to the south of the acropolis hill and shows a south - north course crossing the Aleon (?) river, dates from Byzantine times. Opposite the coffee - house and close to the school there is a small depot containing a few works of art discovered in Erythrai. The andesite pilaster capitals kept in the garden of the Izmir Museum date from the 5th century B. C.

The site of the sanctuary of the Tyrian Herakles, the Herakleion, is not known. A cult statue of Egyptian type is described by Pausanias (VII 5,4) and depicted on the coins of the city. The prophetic sibyl of Erythrai, named Herophile, enjoyed a great reputation in the ancient world. She was the most famous sibyl after that of Kyme in Italy. The seat of Herophile is said to have been discovered at Ildırı. In 1891, a structure was found that resembled a nymphaion and provided a number of inscriptions, among them one relating the Erythraean origin of the sibyl Herophile. However, this building has not yet been identified.

The excavations that the present author has been conducting at Erythrai since 1964, in collaboration with Hakkı Gültekin and Cevdet Bayburtluoğlu, have brought to light important finds which are now exhibited in the Archaeological Museum in Izmir. The trenches dug on top of the acropolis hill yielded a large amount of pottery and small offerings in bronze and ivory, dating from ca. 670 to 545. It appears that Erythrai was destroyed by the Persians shortly after the middle of the 6th century B. C. The pronounced Cretan and Rhodian style of the ivory statuettes confirms the statement of Pausanias (VII 3, 7) that Erythrai was originally founded by Cretans and inhabited by Lykians, Karians and Pamphylians.

According to a graffito on a bowl dating from the beginning of the 6th century B. C., the offerings belonged to the temple of Athena Polias, mentioned by Pausanias (VII 5,8). The small lion figurines in bronze, dating from the first half of the 6th century B. C., very much resemble the lion statue from Bayındır, now in the Izmir Museum (Pl. 43 b, c). They are the earliest Ionian examples of a lion type which served as a model for Etruscan artists. In the same trench, dug on top of the acropolis hill, a monumental archaic statue of a woman, now also kept in the Archaeological Museum in Izmir, was uncovered. The well-preserved statue, the head of which is missing, exhibits folds on its chiton (tunic) which recall such Samian sculptures as the Hera of Cheramyes in the Louvre and the statues made by Geneleos. The Erythraean statue is the work of an Anatolian artist of ca. 560 - 550 B. C.

SULTANHİSAR (NYSA)

The city of Nysa is situated in a romantic setting on both sides of a precipitous gorge. The engineering skill evident in the vaulted substructures supporting buildings, streets and squares, is very impressive. The city was probably founded by Antiochos I, Soter, son of Seleukos, in the first half of the 3rd century B. C. Its name may, therefore, have been taken from some unknown member of the Seleucid family (Magie,RR in AM,128). Strabo, the Greek geographer, who was born ca. 63 B. C. in Amasia and who died after A. D. 21, studied in this city. He reports (XIV, 650) that he was, in his youth, a pupil of Aristodemos in Nysa. Strabo gives a short but clear description of the city (XIV, 649). He says that Nysa was "a double city, so to speak", divided by a torrential stream that forms a gorge. He first speaks about three structures which were built over or in the gorge: a bridge that joined the two cities, an amphitheatre and a hidden underground passage for the torrential waters; he then mentions the theatre and, below it, the gymnasium of youths on one side and the agora and gerontikon on the other side. All these structures have survived; however, most of them were greatly enlarged or altered during Roman Imperial times.

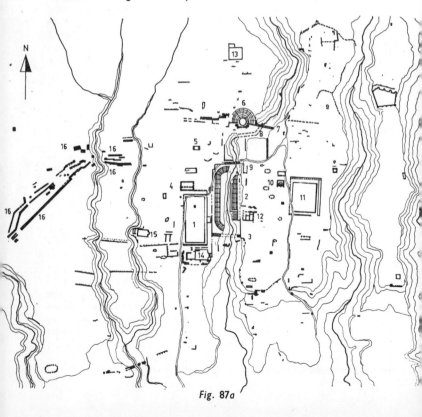

Fig. 87a

Fig. 87 a – Plan of Nysa. **1)** *Gymnasium.* The structure mentioned by Strabo
(see above) was certainly not as large as this one. The present day ruins belong
to a building with a palaestra, 70 by 165 m. in area, erected in late Roman times.
Its north side has been destroyed by the modern road passing through the ruins.
2) *Stadium.* This structure is 44 m. wide and 192 m. long. It may be the amphitheatre quoted by Strabo (see above). Strabo, in using the word "amphitheatre"
doubtless meant a στάδιον 'αμφιθέατρον which was curved at both ends. The seats
have been completely destroyed by torrential waters. **3)** *Remains of a Roman
bridge* connecting the two opposite parts of the city. **4)** *Byzantine building.*
5) *Library.* Roman in date. It stands 150 m. to the north of the gymnasium. This
two - storeyed structure is the best preserved ancient library of Turkey, next
to the Celsus library at Ephesus (Fig. 87 b, c). The reading hall measured 13.40
by 14.80 m. in area. Manuscripts in the form of scrolls or volumes were kept
on shelves installed in niches. **6)** *Theatre.* This well-preserved and conspicious
structure was built in Roman Imperial times. The diameter of the orchestra measures 27 m. Below the portable scene of the theatre, there is a large basin which
was filled with water and used in spectacles representing sea-fights. In front
of the theatre was a wide square of ceremonial character, supported by imposing
substructures. It is a splendid example of city planning and engineering work.
7) *Roman bridge.* **8)** *Tunnel.* This high, barrel - vaulted and 150 m. - long tunnel
is doubtless the hidden underground passage mentioned by Strabo (see above).
It served as a canal for the torrential waters coming from Mt. Mesogis and, at
the same time, supported the large square in front of the theatre. **9)** *Roman bridge,*
joining the two opposite parts of the city. **10)** *Bouleuterion.* This very well-preserved,
attractive building (Pl. 59 b) dates from the latter half of the 2nd century A. D.,
according to the style of the architectural ornaments; it is probably the Roman
phase of the gerontikon mentioned by Strabo (see above). **11)** *The Agora* consisted of a market place measuring 89 by 105 m. in area, with colonnades surrounding it on all four sides. On the east and perhaps the south sides were double
colonnades of the Ionic order while on the south and west sides stood single
colonnades of the Doric order. From the differences in architectural order and in
the style of the ornaments, we learn that the agora, also mentioned by Strabo,
was greatly altered and, perhaps, enlarged during Roman Imperial times.

*Fig. 87 b, c – The Library of Nysa
(see Nysa ad Maeandrum, Berlin
1913, Pl. 8, 10).*

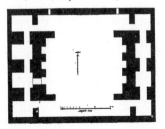

12) *Roman baths.* 13) *Basin.* 14,15) *Byzantine churches, probably built on the sites of ancient temples.* 16) *Necropolis. The graves of Nysa consisted of two-tiered, barrel-vaulted structures which were built side by side joining each other Thus they often formed a continuous front, composed of two - storeyed arcades. The dead were deposited in the vaulted rooms, some of which contained sarcophagi.*

AYDIN (Tralleis). Tralleis was an important city of Karia, both in the Greek and Roman periods. Excavations, which were carried out by archaeologists from the Istanbul Museum in 1902 - 1903, yielded important results. The remarkable finds are exhibited in a special hall in the same museum. They include the fine statue of a young athlete (Pls. 26 - 28). On the site where the ruins of a stadium, a theatre, an agora and a third century A. D. gymnasium stood in the last century, only the still impressive remains of the latter structure have survived.

LAODICEIA AD LYCUM

The ruins are situated on the south bank of the river Lykos. The city was founded by a king of the Seleucid family, very probably Antiochos II, Theos, who named it after Laodike, his wife, between 261 and 253 B. C. After the assassination of Seleukos III, his lieutenant Achaios rebelled against Antiochos III, and in 220 B. C. assumed the crown in Laodikeia, proclaiming himself King of Asia Minor. For part of the second century, at least, Laodikeia seems to have belonged to the Pergamene Kingdom (Magie 127). Laodikeia witnessed the most prosperous period in its history during the second century A. D. The city called itself the "metropolis of Asia". It received Hadrian as a visitor in A. D. 29. Laodikeia also enjoyed a brillant period in early Christian times, where an important council was held in the 4th century A. D. (Laodicée du Lycos p. 11).

According to Strabo (XII, 578), Laodikeia produced sheep that were known for the softness of their raven-black wool. He says that these animals provided the Laodikeians with a splendid revenue. The city also developed a reknowned textile industry. Certain cloth called "Laodikeian" is listed in the edict of Diocletian (Magie, p. 813). The tunics known as trimita, also manufactured in Laodikeia, were so famous that the city was named "Trimitaria" (Gagniers, Laodicée du Lycos, p. 7).

Excavations on the site were carried out in 1961 - 1963 by an expedition on behalf of Laval University of Quebec, Canada, under the direction of Professor Jean des Gagniers, during which a very interesting fountain was completely uncovered. The publication of this successful field research has now appeared, containing excellent studies on the fountain (Laodicée du

Lycos, Le Nymphée, Paris 1969, see Bibliography at the back of this book).
The following description is based mainly on the information given in the
first volume of the publication.

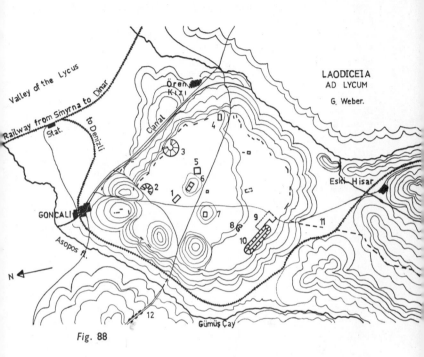

Fig. 88

Fig. 88 – Plan of Laodiceia ad Lycum. **1)** *Unidentified temple of the Ionic order.*
2) *Small theatre. Roman in date.* **3)** *Large theatre of the Greek type.* **4-6)** *Un-identified buildings.* **7)** *Nymphaion. This monumental fountain, situated on the southeastern corner of two streets intersecting each other at right angles, consisted of a basin occupying the corner, that was flanked by two niches, one facing northwards and one facing westwards. According to Professor René Ginouvès (Laodicée du Lycos pp. 13 - 1835), it was erected in the time of Caracalla (A. D. 211 – 217) and witnessed four successive periods of restoration, the last dating from the first part of the 5th century A. D. The parapet of the basin was adorned with mythological reliefs depicting Theseus, the Minotauros and the abduction of Ganymedes.* **8)** *Odeion.* **9)** *The Gymnasium. This was dedicated to Hadrian and Sabina under the proconsulate of Gargilius Antiquus.* **10)** *Stadium. According to an inscription, this structure was erected in A. D. 79. It took the form of a Roman stadium with both of its ends curved. A similar plan was employed in the stadium at Nysa which, probably for this reason, was called an "amphi-theatre" by Strabo.* **11)** *Aqueduct.* **12)** *Sarcophagi.*

MYUS

Myus, which was, in ancient times, a promontory on the sea-shore, today lies 15 km. north-east of Miletos and 100 m. south of the Maeander river. The site is now called Avşar Kalesi. The scanty ruins would be of interest only to archaeologists.

According to Strabo (XIV, 633), Myus was founded by Kydrelos, a son of the legendary King Kodros of Athens. It was one of the cities of the Panionion (Strabo XIV, 636), but never played any significant role in history, and fell, at an early date, under the domination of Miletos. The Persian fleet, composed of 200 warships, under Megabates, anchored at Myus in 499 (Herodotus V, 32 and 36). At the Battle of Lade in 494, Myus contributed only three ships. In the Delian Confederacy, Myus was assessed at the normal tribute of one talent. Together with Magnesia on the Maeander and Lampsakos, Myus was given to Themistokles, hero of Salamis, in 480, by Artaxerxes, (Thukydides I, 138,5; Plutarch, Themist. 29,7), who welcomed him when he fell into disgrace and made his way as a refugee to Asia Minor (about 465 B. C.). When Philip V, of Macedon, captured Myus in 201 B. C., he gave it to Magnesia on the Maeander, in exchange for food for his army (Strabo, XIV 636). Soon afterwards, however, the city came into the possession of Miletos (Magie, RR in A.M. 883). In the time of Strabo (XIV 636), the city was thirty stades from the sea, and could be reached only by small boats. Pausanias (VII 2,11) reports that, from the Gulf of Myus, which was blocked with silt brought down by the Maeander, arose such dense swarms of mosquitoes that the inhabitants were forced to abandon their city. Pausanias relates

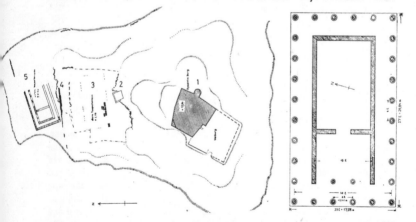

Fig. 89 a – Plan of Myus (after Hans Weber, Istanbuler Mitteilungen 15, 1965, p. 44 Fig. 1). 1) Byzantine castle (ca. A. D. 1200-1250). 2) Niche, cut into the rock, dating from the archaic period. 3) Scanty remains of an Ionic temple, built in the late archaic period. 4) Archaic wall supporting the upper terrace and flanking the lower terrace. 5) Remains of a peripteral Ionic temple (see Fig. 89 b). Fig. 89 b – Restored plan of the archaic temple at Myus (H. Weber).

that the citizens moved to Miletos, taking with them all portable property including cult statues. He says that, in his time, there was nothing else in Myus but a temple of Dionysus, in white marble. However, in the 3rd century A. D., Myus was almost entirely deprived of its monuments. During the German excavations in Miletos under Th. Wiegand, several fragments of architecture in very fine archaic style were found reused in the theatre, the Athena temple and the stadium. Some of these bore inscriptions, referring to Myus and its temple of Apollo Termintheus. These inscriptions, which have now been published by Peter Herrmann (*Ist. Mitt.* 15, 1965, 90 ff.), support the identification of Myus with the Avşar Kalesi.

The site of Myus is marked by a small hill, sloping from south to north, on which stood its sacred monuments. On top of the temple hill stands a conspicuous Byzantine castle. The lower slope of this hill consists of two rock-terraces, arranged one above the other. On each of these, in ancient times, stood a temple, whose scanty remains were still partly visible on the surface and have now become clearer since the German excavations conducted by Hans Weber in 1964 and 1966 (Fig. 89 a, b). The city proper, with remains of houses and cisterns cut into the rock, lies to the south-east of the temple hill.

Myus was first excavated in 1908 by Theodor Wiegand, who sent all the architectural fragments remaining on the site to Berlin, together with the archaic reliefs representing chariot-races, which he found reused in a later wall. According to Wiegand, the temple of Apollo Termintheus stood on the higher terrace and the structure on the lower terrace was the temple of Dionysus, reported by Pausanias. Hans Weber uncovered foundations and fragments of architecture on the lower terrace. These helped him to restore, graphically, the ground plan (Fig. 89 b) and to obtain important conclusions concerning the upper structure of the building. It was a westward-facing peripteral temple of the Ionic order, with 6 by 10 columns and stylobate measurements of 17.275 × 29.84 m. A trench dug on the east side of the temple gave no evidence of an altar there. The column-bases were of the Ephesian type and the column-shafts had 32 shallow flutes. The reliefs of chariot-races, now in Berlin, belonged to the frieze, which probably decorated the exterior wall of the naos, or cella. According to the style of these reliefs and to that of the egg-and-dart-fragments, also kept in Berlin, Weber correctly dates the temple to about the middle of the 6th century. Weber points out that there is no particular evidence for attributing the temple to Dionysus. He proposes that Apollo Termintheus and Poseidon could also have been divinities of the temple. As the temple faces west, although there is enough room to build an altar on the east side of the sanctuary, the present author would like to suggest a Greek goddess, like Artemis, who could easily have been combined with one of the autochthonous Anatolian deities, whose sanctuaries are always oriented to the west. The field work done by Hans Weber in 1964 on the higher terrace shows that, sometime in the late archaic period, a temple of the Ionic order was begun on this site; it was larger than that on the lower terrace, but its construction was interrupted before the columns could be erected.

HERAKLEIA UNDER LATMOS

Herakleia (Fig. 90), with its splendid city wall and its fascinating land-scape, is one of the most impressive Anatolian ruins dating partly from Hellenistic times (Pl. 75 b). The site is easily accessible both from Lake Bafa and by land. A motorboat can be hired from the southern shore of Lake Bafa and a rough jeep-road leads from the village of Bafa to the ruins.

In the Greek period Herakleia was connected with the sea. From Strabo we learn that, in his time (ca. the last quarter of the first century B. C.), it still had an anchorage. Strabo (XIV, 636) reports also that it was first called Latmos, i.e., by the same name as the mountain which lies above it. It paid a tribute of one talent as a member of the Delian Confederacy in the 5th century B. C. Around the middle of the 4th century B. C., it was dominated temporarily by Maussollos and Artemisia II. Both in the Hellenistic and Roman periods, the city flourished and its prosperity must have come from sea-trade. Herakleia also blossomed during Early Christian and Byzantine times, The small romantic islands situated in Lakc Bafa bear well- pre-servad churches and monasteries dating from the Erly Christian and Byzantine periods.

Fig. 90 – Plan of Herakleia under Latmos.

1) *The city wall was probably built by Lysimachos about 287 B. C. in a large circuit of 6.5 km. with 65 towers; later, however it was reduced by an intermediary wall and then measured only 4.5 km. (Pl. 75 b).* 2) *City plan. Herakleia at Latmos was one of the cities planned after the Hippodamian system. The streets were arranged in a strictly axial and symmetrical plan, oriented either from south to north or from west to east.* 3) *The Athena Temple, standing on a hill and dominating the entire site, is the most attractive building of Herakleia. This Hellenistic structure is identified as the temple of Athena from an inscription still lying on the spot. It was a templum in antis, consisting of a cella and a pronaos of approximately equal size.* 4) *The Agora, which was built in the Hellenistic period, still exhibits a very well-preserved south wall of exquisite beauty.* 5) *The remains of the bouleuterion (council chamber) are scanty at present. According to fragments found during the excavations, the upper half of the walls of the building were adorned with half-columns of the Doric order. Fragments of an architrave, a triglyph-frieze, a row of dentils and a pediment, have also been found. It seems that the council chamber of Herakleia followed the example of the bouleuterion at Miletos, where the walls were also adorned with half-columns in their upper half (p. 213). The seats of the bouleuterion at Herakleia, built of stone, are arranged in a U shape parallel to the walls. The structure probably dates from the 2nd century B. C.* 6) *Roman baths.* 7) *Theatre, Roman in date.* 8) *Scanty vestiges of a nymphaion (fountain).* 9) *Insignificant remains of an unidentified temple.* 10) *Sanctuary of Endymion. A prostyle temple, consisting of a pronaos and an apsidal cella. According to Greek legend, Selene (the moon goddess) visited a beautiful young shepherd each night as he slept an eternal sleep in a cave on Mt. Latmos.* 11) *Unidentified temple.* 12) *Byzantine*

castle. Beyond this castle, going to the headland, there is a cemetery that is worth a visit. The graves, mostly arranged side by side, are cut into the rock and covered with a separate lid. Some of them lie in the lake, close to the shore.

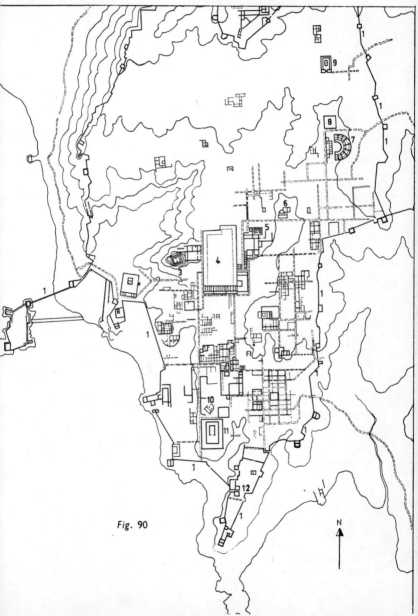

Fig. 90

N

KARIA

The mountainous region of the south western coast of Anatolia, encircled by Ionia, Phrygia and Lykia, was called Karia. We have already dealt briefly with the earlier history of Karia, in the first part of this book (p. 16). During the 7th century and the first half of the 6th century B. C., Karia seems to have been absorbed into the Kingdom of Lydia. When, in 546 B. C., Lydia was conquered by Kyros, Karia, too, passed under Persian rule. However, autochthonous princes managed to establish themselves and to extend their domination even to the Greek cities. They were especially powerful in the 4th century B. C. According to Strabo (XIV, 657), Hekatomnos was king of the Karians (died ca. 377 B. C.). He had three sons, Maussollos, Idrieus and Pixodaros, and two daughters. Maussollos, the oldest of the brothers, married Artemisia, his elder sister. Idrieus, the second son, married Ada, the other sister. Maussollos was a satrap (377 B. C.), but he became the virtual ruler of Karia. He took part in the revolt against Artaxerxes II, Mnemon, and conquered considerable parts of Lydia and Ionia, as well as some Greek islands. He helped the Rhodians in their war with Athens and removed the Karian capital from Mylasa to Halikarnassos. He was an admirer of Greek culture and invited famous Greek architects and sculptors to embellish his capital and the other Karian cities with excellent works of art (see Halikarnassos and Labranda). The Maussoleion, named after Maussollos, was the most monumental tomb of the Greek world and was prized as one of the seven wonders of ancient times. It achieved such fame that the word "Mausoleum" was used in Roman times to designate its most distinguished tombs, such as those of Augustus and Hadrian. The term is still employed for the monumental tombs of the modern world.

When Maussollos died childless (353 B. C.), he left the kingdom to his wife, Artemisia. After her death, Idrieus became ruler (351-344 B. C.). He died of disease and was succeeded by Ada, but she was expelled from Halikarnassos by Pixodaros, the remaining son of Hekatomnos. The latter, being pro- Persian, asked for a satrap to share the ruling power with him; when he, too, departed from life, the Persian Satrap Othontopates took possession of Halikarnassos. His wife was Ada, who was the daughter of Pixodaros by Aphenis, a Cappadocian woman (Strabo, XIV, 657).

Ada, the daughter of Hekatomnos, after being banished from Halikarnassos, became Queen of Alinda. When Alexander came to Karia, in the summer of 334 B. C., he wrecked Halikarnassos and handed it over to her. Following the death of Alexander, Karia was included, first in the empire of the Seleucids, then in the Pergamene Kingdom (ca. 180 B. C.), and finally in the Roman Province of Asia (133 B. C.).

ARAPHİSAR (ALABANDA)

The attractive ruins of the ancient Karian city of Alabanda are situated 4 km. west of the Marsyas (Çine Çay), a river that flows into the Maiandros. In the 3rd century B. C., it was a member of the Karian League. Alabanda developed good relations with Rome and was a free city almost throughout the Roman era. It was a prosperous city. Strabo (XIV, 661) reports that the people of Alabanda lived in luxury and debauchery and had many girls who played the harp.

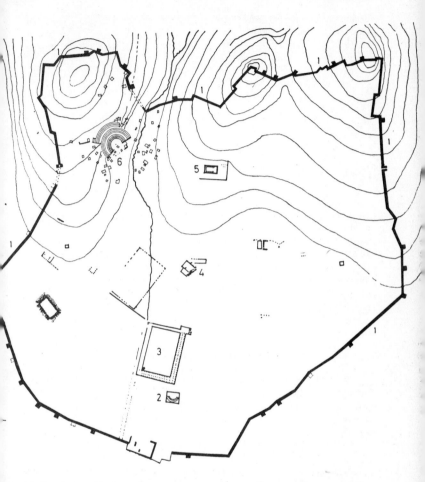

Fig. 92 – Plan of Alabanda. **1)** *The city wall, built in fine rustica ashlar masonry, dates from the Hellenistic period.* **2)** *Bouleuterion (Council Chamber). This rectangular building, measuring 26 × 36 m. in area, was approached by four doorways on its south side and by two other entrances on its west and east sides. The seats formed a semi-circle. The upper part of the northern exterior wall was adorned with pilasters (Pl. 75 a) in the manner seen in the Bouleuterion at Termessos (Pl. 95 a). The structure dates from the Hellenistic period.* **3)** *The large rectangular structure, measuring 72 m. wide and 114 m. long, may be the agora of Alabanda, because it is close to the bouleuterion.* **4)** *Roman baths.* **5)** *The Temple of Apollo (Stylobate measuring 21.66 × 34.53 m.). According to Vitruvius (III, 2,6) there was a pseudodipteral temple of Apollo, designed by the architect*

Menesthes. Edhem – Bey, who carried out excavations at Alabanda (CRAI, 1906), uncovered the temple marked 5 on our map. However, his plan shows a peripteros with 8 by 11 columns (loc. cit. Fig. 5). Moreover, Edhem-Bey points out that the columns have no bases and that the temple, for this reason, was of the Doric order (see p. 31 in this book). On the other hand, Arnold Schober restores it, rightly I believe, as a pseudo-dipteros with 8 by 13 columns (see Fig. 4, p. 30 in this book). According to him, the columns stood on bases (Lagina, Ist. Mitt. 2, 1933, p. 17). The large frieze fragment found in Alabanda (CRAI, 1906, Pl. 5) and depicting an Amazon combat, with an Ionic ovolo on the top border, must have belonged to this temple. Thus, the structure can be identified as the temple mentioned by Vitruvius and was a pseudo-dipteros of the Ionic order, built very probably in the latter half of the 2nd century B. C. 6) The theatre, built in the Hellenistic period, was altered in Roman times.

Alinda. The well - preserved, impressive ruins of Alinda are situated on a rocky acropolis, close to the village of Karpuzlu. Ada, the daughter of Hekatomnos, who was expelled from Halikarnassos by his brother Pixodaros, made this city into her capital (ca. 344 B. C.). When Alexander the Great came to Karia, she welcomed him; in return, Alexander granted her the satrapy of Karia, with the exception of the Greek cities which were declared free. The magnificent city wall must have been erected in the time of Ada. The theatre has fine masonry. It was built in the Hellenistic age and was altered in Roman times. (Pl. 65 a). The agora, with its imposing terrace walls, dates from the Hellenistic period.

LABRANDA (LABRAUNDA)

One of the best preserved ancient sites of Turkey is situated in the mountains, 14 km. north of Milas. It can only be reached by jeep, as the path is difficult. It was a sacred precinct, connected with Mylasa in ancient times by a paved "Sacred Way". The site was successfully excavated by a Swedish expedition between 1948 and 1953, and the important results are published in the form of excellent monographs. The following description is based mainly on the book of Alfred Westholm, *Labraunda*, Lund 1963.

The excavations have revealed that a sanctuary existed on the site already in the 5th century B. C. The Zeus Temple was a prostylos with antae. Indeed, Herodotus (V, 119) mentions a temple of Zeus Stratios at Labranda. However, the initiator of the planning of the hieron, i.e., the sacred place, was Maussollos (377 - 353 B. C.); many of the structures were completely built or started in his time. Others were accomplished by his brother, Idrieus (351 - 344 B. C.). The following structures were completed in the reign of Maussollos : the north stoa; Andron B, with its annexes and terrace; the large terrace wall, south of the temple; the structure west of Andron B; the large flight of steps in the east; the large structures called palaces (?). The structures started or completed in the time of Idrieus are : Temple II, a peripteros of the Ionic order (Pl. 64 b); Terrace House II; Oikoi; Andron A with a terrace to the south; the Well-House Stoa; the East Propylaia; the Doric House; the South Propylaia with adjoining buildings.

Androns A and B were doubtless megaron-type palaces reserved for the royal family, like the megara at Troy II and VI (Fig. 14, 15), and at Gordion (Fig. 117 a). The structure named "oikoi" was a house, composed of two single rooms which never had an antechamber, in contrast to megarons. We have seen similar houses with oikoi at Larisa (Fig. 39), Pergamon (Fig. 26) and Prlene (Fig. 74 b). The house "oikoi" at Labranda were probably, like Terrace Houses I and II, reserved for the priests. Andron A (Pl. 10 b, 65 c) is the best preserved structure with windows, clearly revealing that windows were used in Greek architecture. Other structures showing the use of windows are the council chambers of Termessos (Pl. 95 a) and Alabanda (Pl. 75 a).

The remaining structures of Alabanda are Roman in date : Andron C, the Well - House with a terrace, the East Baths and the restored parts of the Doric house, the West Stoa and adjoining terraces, the South Baths. The East Church and some additions in " oikoi " and Andron B date from the Byzantine period.

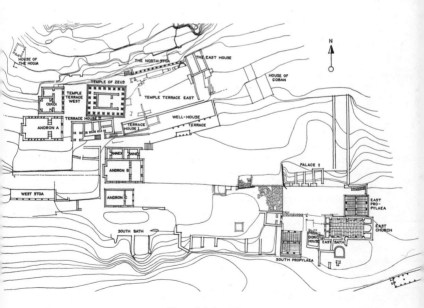

Plan of Labranda

EUROMOS

Euromos is mentioned in inscriptions and by ancient writers from the 2nd century B. C. on. In two decrees, Mylasa and Euromos are quoted as combined cities (Magie 908 No. 130). The ruins of the Zeus Temple at Euromos are in a very good state of preservation (Pl. 78 a). The structure is a peripteros of the Corinthian order with 6 by 11 columns (Fig. 93). The excavations carried out by Ümit Serdaroğlu revealed that the stylobate measured 14.40 × 26.80 m. Judged by the fine quality of workmanship of the Corinthian capitals and the mouldings (Pl. 78 a), as well as the neo-classical character it discloses, the temple must have been built not later than the time of Hadrian (A. D. 117 - 138).

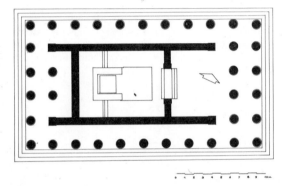

Fig. 93 – Plan of the Zeus Temple at Euromos (after Ümit Serdaroğlu). Peripteros of the Corinthian order with 6 by 11 columns. Time of Hadrian (A. D. 117-138).

Stratonikeia. Only a few vestiges remain of this city, which was an important religious centre in Hellenistic and Roman times. Strabo reports (XIV, 660) that there were two temples in the country of the Stratonikeians, the most famous of which was the Hekateion at Lagina (Fig. 3, p. 30). The other was the temple of Zeus Chrysaoreus, the common sanctuary of all Karians. Among the ruins can be recognized a theatre, the foundations of an unidentified temple and a still attractive portion of a gateway, all dating from the Roman period.

IASOS

An Italian expedition, under Professor Doro Levi, has conducted excavations on the ancient site of Iasos, which is one of the most successful field operations carried out on the western coast of Anatolia. The interesting and important finds are kept in the Izmir Museum. According to tradition,

Iasos was founded by colonists from Argos but was later occupied by emigrants from Miletos. The chief deities of the city seem to have been Apollo and Artemis. However, the cult of Dionysus was also of great importance; the theatre was dedicated to him, and his festival made Iasos a musical and dramatic centre.

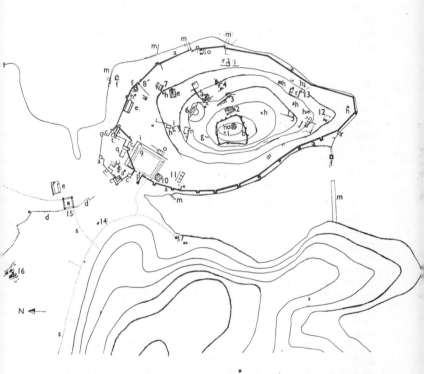

Fig. 94 – Plan of Iasos (see Annuario 1968). 1) Temple on the acropolis. 2) Early Christian basilica. 3) Wall of the acropolis. 4) Excavated area east of the acropolis. 5) Theatre quarter. 6) Theatre. 7) Basilica. 8) City-gate. 9) Roman Agora. 10) Roman Bouleuterion. 11) Stoa, dedicated to Artemis and the Emperor Commodus (A. D. 180-192). 12) Sanctuary of Demeter and Kore. 13) House with mosaic. 14) Tomb on the isthmus. 15) Mausoleum, excellently restored by the Italian expedition. 16) Necropolis. 17) Excavation House. a) Remains of Greek periods. b) Medieval castle. c) Byzantine castle. d) Aqueduct. e) Early Christian church. f) Byzantine structure. g) Wall of the acropolis. h) Cistern. i) Fountain. l) Greek temple. m) Quay or mole. n) Roman temple. o) Roman structure. p) Dipylon. q) Gymnasium r) Roman House. s) Modern road. t) Roman baths.

MİLAS (MYLASA)

Mylasa was originally a Karian city. Its ancient temple of a native god, renamed Zeus by the Greeks, became the common sanctuary of "all the Karians". Labranda formed a part of Mylasa and was connected to it by a paved "Sacred Way". The temple of the Karian Zeus seems to have been greatly altered in the late Hellenistic period. In Mylasa, in the quarter called "Hisarbaşı", there are remains of a temple with its temenos wall in fine ashlar masonry. The temple stood on a podium, 3.50 m. in height. An elegant slim column, surmounted by a beautiful Corinthian capital, is still standing. The style of the masonry of the temenos wall and the shape of the acanthus leaves of the Corinthian capital reveal that this phase of the temple dates from the first century B. C. The doorway called "Baltalı Kapı", because of the representation of a labrys or a double axe on the key-stone of the arch, is the only vestige that remains from the city wall; it probably dates from the 2 nd century A. D. The most important ancient structure of Mylasa is the well-preserved tomb called Gümüşkesen (Pl. 77), which seems to be a smaller copy of the famous Mausoleum. It probably dates from the 2nd century A. D. This monument will be discussed when we deal with the Maussolleion of Halikarnassos at Bodrum.

BODRUM (HALIKARNASSOS)

According to Herodotus, a native of Halikarnassos, the city was founded by Dorian colonists. It was one of the six members of the Dorian Confederacy, the other five being Knidos, Kos, Lindos, Kamiros and Ialysos. Representatives from the six cities met in the Temple of Apollo at Knidos. The original inhabitants of the area were Lelegians and Karians. From the middle of the 6th century on, Halikarnassos was under Persian domination. In the first half of the 4th century B. C., the whole of Karia including Halikarnassos, was ruled by Hekatomnos and his son Maussollos (Mausolus), who, on becoming king, chose Halikarnassos as the capital of his kingdom. He was succeeded in 353 B. C. by his sister, also his wife, Artemisia, who reigned two years. On her death, the remaining children of Hekatomnos ruled in turn : first Idrieus, second Ada, and then Pixodaros, with whose daughter, Ada, the satrapy passed to the Persian Othontopates. The principal buildings in Karia which have survived to the present day date from the time of this dynasty (Pls. 64, 65).

No remains of buildings of an earlier date than the Middle Ages can be found standing in the city proper of Halikarnassos today (Fig. 95 a). However, a Danish archaeological expedition, under the direction of Kristian Jeppesen, has recently met with success and has unearthed several sections of the peribolos (i.e., the enclosing wall) of the Mausoleum (Fig. 95 a, No. 4). Professor Jeppesen summarizes his results on this point as follows: "The precinct of the Mausoleum was surrounded by a peribolos wall of white marble, ca. 242 m. long on the north side and ca. 105.5 m. on the east side. The length of the south and west sides cannot be determined with certainty for the present, but it may be said with some confidence that the precinct is likely to have had a perfectly rectangular plan." (See Fig. 95 a, No. 4).

According to Pliny (NH, XXXVI, 30-31), the Mausoleum, reckoned to be one of the seven wonders of the world in antiquity, was built for Mausolus by his wife Artemisia about 350 B. C. Pliny also states that the Mausoleum consisted of a high base, a pteron (peristasis) of 36 columns, a pyramid of 24 steps, and finally a crowning quadriga (a four-horsed chariot), the total height of the edifice being 140 ft., i.e., about 42 m. The accompanying reconstruction is the work of K. Jeppesen (Fig. 95 b). Pliny's information proves to be correct because the Gümüşkesen sepulchral monument, which is probably a copy of the Halicarnassus Mausoleum, also consists of a high base, a peristasis and a stepped pyramid (Pl. 77). The small dimensions of the Gümüşkesen monument must have precluded the placing of a quadriga on the pyramid.

Vitruvius records (VII, Praef. 12-13) that the architect responsible for the Mausoleum was Pytheos, the designer of the Athena temple at Priene (Fig. 68, 69) and that the reliefs with which the memorial was embellished were the work of the greatest sculptors of the time, such as Leochares Bryaxis, Skopas and Timotheos. The reliefs uncovered during excavations undertaken by Lord Stratford in 1846 and Newton in 1857, together with the statues of Maussollos and his wife Artemisia, are now in the British Museum. The newly found sculptured slab from the frieze of the Mausoleum is kept in the Museum at Bodrum (Pl. 76).

The unique Turkish marine museum devoted to works of antiquity, is situated at Bodrum. In this well-arranged and attractive museum are exhibited finds discovered by chance on the sea bed and also those resulting from underwater excavations being carried out by George F. Bass of the Pennsylvania University Museum. In the section of the Bodrum museum reserved for discoveries made on terra firma can be seen vases of the Mycenaean period, brought to light by Yusuf Boysal at Musgebi in the neighbourhood of Bodrum. Also on display in this section of the museum are vases dating from the 9th and 8th centuries B. C. and a terra-cotta sarcophagus of the 9th century B. C., all belonging to the earliest Dorian colonization known at present in Anatolia, uncovered by the present author at Dirmil near Bodrum.

The Castle of St. Peter (Fig. 95 c). Work on this extremely well-preserved, magnificent architectural building complex was begun immediately after the capture of Bodrum in 1402 by the Knights of Rhodes. In 1409, a papal bull offered absolution to all who participated in this work. The German architect Heinrich Schlegelholt (1415-1437), constructed the first walls; however, the castle was altered several times to keep pace with the development of ballistic weapons. Blocks of stone, statues and reliefs, originally part of the Mausoleum, which was apparently destroyed in an earthquake, were used as building material in the castle. The Italian tower was constructed in 1436 by Angelo Muscettola. The fosse was begun in 1476. The English tower (soon to be restored by the Turkish Department of Antiquities) was built by John Candall in A. D. 1486. The most recent alterations in the castle were carried out under the Grand Master Pierre d'Aubusson (1476-1503). The castle passed permanently into Turkish hands in 1523.

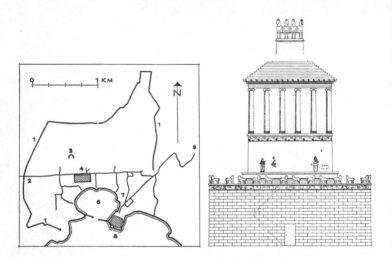

Fig. 95 a – Plan of Bodrum, after Kristian Jeppesen. **1)** Ancient city wall. **2)** Myndos gateway. **3)** Ancient theatre. **4)** Precinct of the Mausoleum. **5)** Modern road to Mylasa. **6)** Inner harbour. **7)** Centre of the modern city of Bodrum. **8)** Castle of St. Peter.

Fig. 95 b – Reconstruction of the Maussolleion after Kristian Jeppesen (east front).

Fig. 95 c – Bodrum. Castle of St. Peter (after A Maiuri and W. Müller-Wiener). It was built on the site of a Turkish fortress in the 14th century by the Knights of Rhodes, utilizing blocks and sculptures acquired from the Mausoleum that probably was destroyed by earthquake.

In the west fösse, on the west wall built by the Turks and enlarged in its upper part by French knights, can be seen three coats of arms surmounted by a cardinal's hat; they are the arms of the order, the arms of the Grand Master d'Aubussons (1476-1503) and those of the commandant of the castle in 1492. Above the 6th gate are three coats of arms, including that of Guy de Blanchefort (1512-1513). Various coats of arms appear over the 5th gateway; among those facing the outside can be discerned the arms of the Grand Master Emery d'Amboise (1503-1512), and among those overlooking the interior of the castle, those of Jacques de Mily (1454-1461). On the west wall of the English Tower rising up at the south-east corner of the castle is to be observed an archaic marble lion surmounted by the arms of Edward Plantagenet. For a detailed description of the coats of arms, see Maiuri in Annuario IV-V, 1921 - 1922, pp. 290 - 343.

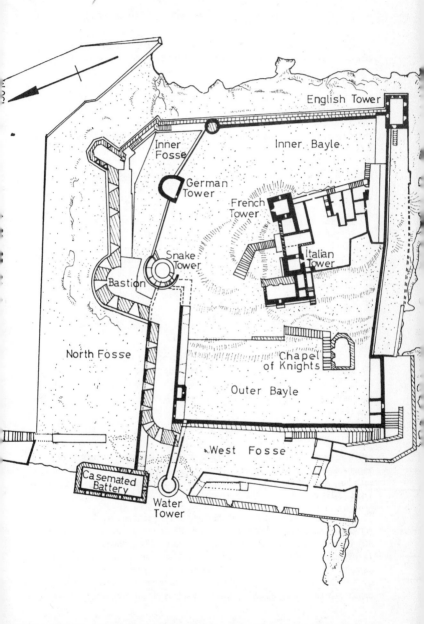

English Tower

Inner Bayle

Inner
Fosse

German
Tower

French
Tower

Italian
Tower

Snake
Tower

Bastion

North Fosse

Chapel
of Knights

Outer Bayle

West Fosse

Casemated
Battery

Water
Tower

KNIDOS

Knidos was one of the most important cities on the west Anatolian coast. It belonged to the Dorian Hexapolis, consisting of Lindos, Ialysos and Kamiros in Rhodes, the island of Kos, and Knidos and Halikarnassos on the west Anatolian coast. The temple of Apollo, which was the common sanctuary of the Hexapolis, stood at Knidos. Strabo (XIV, 656) reports that the city of Knidos was built on terraces, rising like a theatre from the coast to the acropolis. The projecting headland, called triopium, was connected with the city by moles. Thus Knidos possessed a double harbour. Strabo says that one of the harbours was a naval station which could be closed and had a capacity for berthing twenty triremes. The moles have now silted up, creating an isthmus, but traces of walls show that there had been a channel about 10 m. wide connecting the two harbours (Love, TAD, 1968, 134).

Knidos developed excellent commerce and exported a famous wine. From the 6th century B. C. on, the city already played an important role in the Greek world. The Knidians, like other rich cities, erected a Structure at Delphi, ca. 540 B. C., called thesauros or treasury which contained works of art dedicated to Apollo. The Lesche (pavilion) of Knidos at Athens was noted for its mural painting by Polygnotos (ca. 450 B. C.). The city was the birth-place of Eudoxos, one of the most important astronomers and mathematicians in history (ca. 400 B. C.). The architect, Sostratos, designer of the lighthouse of Alexandria (p. 28), one of the seven wonders of the world, was also a native of Knidos.

In the temple of Aphrodite stood the greatly prized statue of the goddess by Praxiteles (see the head of a Roman copy of this work Pl. 97). In 1857 C. T. Newton carried out excavations with important results. His finds, including the magnificent seated statue of Demeter, are now in the British

Fig. 96 – Plan of Knidos (After I. C. Love, Türk Arkeoloji Dergisi 1968, 130, Fig. 2). Knidos was one of the Anatolian cities built on a Hippodamian geometric townplan. Its splendidly preserved city walls may date from the beginning of the Hellenistic era.

1) *Roman Tomb.* **2)** *Terrace Building.* **3)** *Lighthouse.* **4)** *Tower.* **5)** *Agora.* **6)** *Doric remains.* **7)** *Building Podium.* **8)** *Roman complex.* **9)** *Foundations.* **10)** *Cistern.* **11)** *Foundations.* **12)** *Roman complex.* **13)** *Sunken court.* **14)** *Corinthian Temple. According to Professor I. C. Love, the temple stood on a high podium and was approached on the east by a flight of seven steps. The plan made by the Dilettanti society shows a pseudo-peripteros (with engaged half-columns on the exterior walls), which has a tetrastyle prostyle pronaos and an opisthodomos*

Museum. Knidos is now being excavated again. In 1967, under the auspices of Long Island University, Professor Iris Cornelia Love began new field work, which has already brought to light notable remains. The following description is based mainly on information taken from the reports that Professor Love has published in TAD 1968, 1969 and AJA 1968 - 1970.

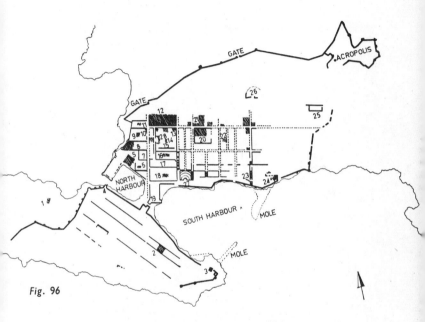

Fig. 96

with two columns in antis. The style of carving of the well-preserved capitals and moulding suggests a date in the period of Hadrian (Love, TAD 1969, p. 124). **15)** Doric stoa, dating from the Hellenistic period. **16-18)** Terraces. **19)** Bridge abutment. **20)** Terrace. **21)** House complex. **22)** Temple of Muses. **23)** Steps. **24)** Bouleuterion, Roman in date. **25)** Temenos of Demeter. The beautiful seated statue of Demeter, ca. 330. B. C., that is now in the British Museum, was found in this sacred precinct. **26)** Theatre. **27)** The lower theatre. Its capacity is estimated at about 4,500 people. The calculations of the American expedition reveal that the plan of the theatre conforms to the Vitruvian canon for a Hellenistic theatre.

In 1969 the American expedition discovered a circular building on the highest, most western terrace of the city. Since, according to Pliny, the famous statue of Aphrodite stood "in a shrine which allowed the image of the goddess to be viewed from every side", Professor Love is inclined to identify this structure with the temple of the Praxitelian Aphrodite. However, the temple, as Miss Love has already pointed out, is certainly later than the 4th century B. C.

KAUNOS

According to Herodotos (I. 172), the Kaunians were natives of Karia; he says, however, that the Kaunians considered themselves to be of Cretan origin. Strabo (XIV, 651) reports that the city of Kaunos had dockyards, and a harbour that could be closed (Fig. 97). Professor Baki Öğün and Associate Professor Ümit Serdaroğlu have been conducting field work on the site since 1967. The following description is based on information given by Dr. Serdaroğlu.

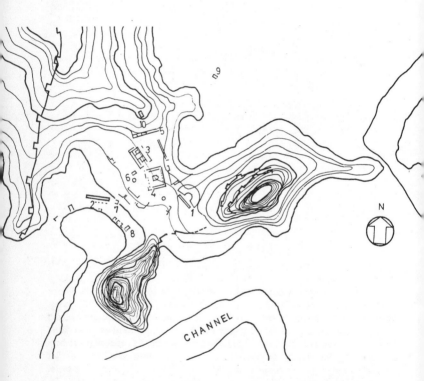

Fig. 97 – Plan of Kaunos (after Ümit Serdaroğlu). 1) Roman Theatre. 2) Stoa, Hellenistic in date (?) 3) Roman baths. 4) Palaestra, probably Roman in date. 5) Water reservoir. 6) Templum in antis and tholos (monopteros). 7) Nymphaion, built in Roman times. 8) Temple, prostylos tetrastylos, of the Corinthian order (Roman period). 9) Templum in antis, of the Ionic order. 10) Temple. Peripteros with 6 by 9 columns (Roman Period).

LYKIA

The ruins situated in Lykia, the coastal district between Karia and Pamphylia, are among the most attractive antiquities on Anatolian soil. Here, monuments dating from the 5th and 4th centuries B. C. stand side by side with buildings, tombs and sanctuaries of Hellenistic and Roman times (Pls. 5, 6, 78 b). The archaeological sites are often in picturesque settings of great natural beauty. Especially fascinating are rock-cut tombs of various types, dating from the 5th century B. C. to the Roman period (Figs. 104 - 106).

A people called *Luku* or *Luqqa* is mentioned both in Egyptian and Hittite records, dating from the latter part of the 2nd millennium B. C. According to Herodotos (I, 173), the Lykians came originally from Crete, under the leadership of Sarpedon, brother of Minos. In the Iliad, the Lykians are allies of the Trojans, fighting under their leaders Sarpedon and Glaukos. Lykian is an Indo-European language containing some early Anatolian pre-Hittite elements; its script (Fig. 103) derives from the Greek alphabet.

The oldest known archaeological remains in Lykia do not date earlier than the 6th century B. C. The strata contemporaneous with the Hittite Empire period and those from the first half of the 1st millennium have not yet been discovered. The first steps in such an investigation have been made by Professor M. J. Mellink, who has been conducting systematic excavations in Karataş Semahöyük - Bozüyük since 1963, under the auspices of Bryn Mawr University. Her results, should be of great importance for the pre-historic periods of the Lykian district. The centre of the excavated site at Karataş is a rectangular house with an oval courtyard and outer enclosures. A village with houses of the megaron type grew around this complex. The site existed in the Early Bronze Age II and IIIa periods (ca. 2600 - 2200 B. C.) and some habitation continued in the 2nd millennium B. C. We hope that Lykian habitation levels of the latter part of the 2nd millennium will soon be discovered at this or other sites.

The Lykians were the only people in Asia Minor that maintained their independence from the Lydian Kingdom. However, after 545 B. C., they came under Persian domination. In spite of some Achaemenid influences, they developed their own architecture, which was of outstanding originality (Pls. 5, 6, 78 b; Figs. 104 - 106). Their sculptural art was Greek in style, but Lykian in spirit and expression.

Each Lykian city has a different and special charm. Some of them display a fairyland atmosphere. In the following pages we shall describe Fethiye Pinara, Xanthos and Patara, because they are easily accessible (Fig. 98 - 100). In addition, we shall mention very briefly the ruins of Kaş, Demre, Limyra, Olympos and Phaselis. We must also note that the following cities also display ruins that are in a splendid state of preservation : Tlos, Kadyanda, Oinoanda, Hoiran, Kekowa and Rhodiapolis (Fig. 97a).

FETHIYE (Telmessos). Some beautiful Lykian tombs of the Greek type, i.e., in the form of *a templum in antis*, are preserved at Telmessos. The most remarkable among them is the splendid tomb of the Ionic order which bears the name of Amyntas. According to the shape of the Ionic ovolo which adorns the lintel, the monument dates from the 4th century B. C. (Above the lintel, to the left, Charles Texier, the famous French traveller, has inscribed his name). A well-preserved Lykian tomb of the sarcophagus type with a handsome pointed arch, that is situated in the modern town, is particularly worth seeing.

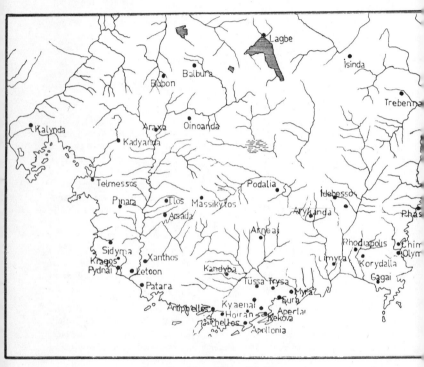

Fig. 97 a – Map of Lykia.

PINARA

Pinara lay on the main road of Lykia. It was one of the six largest cities in the powerful Lykian league; each of them possessed three votes. The other five were Xanthos, Tlos, Patara, Myra and Olympos (Strabo XIV, 665).

Fig. 98 – Plan of Pinara. The ruins are fairly well-preserved; however, the whole site is greatly overgrown. The city was situated between the large **(1)** and small **(2)** hills. **3)** The well-preserved odeion was built in Roman times. The agora must have been close to it. **4)** Remains of a sanctuary or a funerary temple. Probably a peripteros with 6 × 8 columns (Serdaroğlu). **5)** Scanty remains of a templum in antis, enclosed in a temenos wall (funerary temple ?). No remains from the upper structure of the temple (Serdaroğlu). **6)** Theatre, in a good state of preservation, is of the Greek type.

Pinara is rich in tombs. On the east slope of the large hill *(1)* are rock-cut tombs of the Roman period. The Lykian type tombs are mostly in the southern part of the city (Fig. 105. Nos. 7, 9, 12). Notable are one with reliefs representing a Lykian city (Fig. 105, No. 9) and another one with a pointed arch, crowned by a pair of ox-horns and ears in high relief (Fig. 105, No. 7).

XANTHOS

The ruins of Xanthos are among the most attractive ancient remains of Turkey and deserve a special visit. Xanthos was the principal city of Lykia. Its name, which it shares with the River Xanthos (today Eşen Çayı), means "yellow" in Greek. The city was independent until the Persian conquest. Herodotos (I, 176) reports the heroic fight of the Xanthians against the Persian general Harpagos, who invaded Lykia in 545 B. C. The Xanthians enclosed their women, children, servants and property on the acropolis and set it on fire. All the men of Xanthos sallied forth against the besiegers and died fighting. Only 80 families, who were absent from the valley of Xanthos at that time, survived. The Xanthians had to fight against the Athenians during the Peloponnesian war in order to defend their independence. Like many other cities of Lykia, Xanthos enjoyed prosperous times during all periods of history. After the arrival of Alexander the Great, it became greatly Hellenized.

The ruins were first investigated in 1838 by Charles Fellows, who transported all reliefs and a great part of the architectural fragments to London. They are all now exhibited in the new Lykian room of the British Museum. Since 1950, a French expedition has been excavating the site, first under Pierre Demargne and then under Henri Metzger. Most of the important results obtained during the excavations are published in excellent volumes (see Bibliography at the end of this book).

Fig. 99 – Plan of Xanthos. **1)** *The city gate, built in the Hellenistic age.* **2)** *The gateway of the Emperor Vespasian (A. D. 69 - 79).* **3)** *The site of the Nereid Monument, which was a monumental heroon, consisting of a high podium surmounted by a funerary structure in the form of an Ionic Greek temple. Today only a part of the foundations have survived. The monument was erected ca. 400 B. C. Its reliefs are now in the British Museum. For the result of new research work, see Demargne, Le Monument des Nereides, Paris 1969 (Fouilles de Xanthos III).* **4)** *Hellenistic wall.* **5)** *Polygonal wall, dating from the 4th century B. C.* **6)** *Byzantine Church.* **7)** *Remains of a Lykian pillar-tomb. The present height is 4.35 m. The funerary chamber which surmounted this pillar has not survived. The tomb was probably erected in the 4th century B. C., somewhere on the Lykian acropolis. It was then transferred to its present site when the theatre was constructed.* **8)** *The theatre is well-preserved and dates from the Roman period (Pl. 78 b).* **9)** *Remains of a Roman pillar-tomb, probably dating from the 1st century A. D.* **10)** *Lykian pillar-tomb, supporting a sarcophagus with a pointed arch (Pl. 78 b). The height of the pillar, which, unlike other examples in this category, is not monolithic but built with large blocks, is 3.37 high. The height of the sarcophagus is 3.56 m. and the whole monument is 8.59 m. high. This handsome tomb dates from the 4th century B. C. An archaic relief found in the interior of the pillar dating ca. 540 - 530 B. C. and representing wrestlers, is now in the Istanbul Museum (see Akurgal, Kunst Anatoliens Fig. 86).* **11)** *The Harpy Tomb (Pl. 78 b). The whole monument measures 8.87 m. in height. The pillar is a monolith, 5.43 m. in height. The chest which was the funerary chamber of the monu-*

ment is adorned with reliefs representing a dynast and his wife receiving hommage from their children and the other members of their family. The original slabs, which were removed to the British Museum, were replaced by plaster casts ten years ago. Also depicted are sirens, erroneously called harpies, who carry diminutive female figures representing the souls of the dead. According to the style of the reliefs, the monument may be dated ca. 480 - 470 B. C. **12)** The Agora dates from the 2nd or 3rd century A. D. **13)** The Inscribed Pillar. This monument consisted of a pillar mounted on a two – stepped krepis, a funerary chamber,

Fig. 99

a projecting horizontal roof and a crowning statue of a dynast sitting on a lion-base. Except for the statue, all other parts of the monument are completely or partly preserved. The height of the tomb reached ca 11. m. The slabs constituting the funerary chamber, built on top of the pillar below the projecting horizontal roof, were adorned with reliefs representing the victories of the dynast. They were uncovered by Pierre Demargne and are now in the Istanbul Museum (Fouilles de Xanthos I). The essential part of the monolithic pillar has survived. It is inscribed in Lykian on all four faces. The inscription, evidently of historical character, has not yet been deciphered. However, from the proper names mentioned in it and from the Greek epigram in twelve verses on the north face, and finally from the reliefs, we may surmise that the dynast who erected this pillar-tomb recorded on it his fights for independence against the Athenians during the Peloponnesian war. 14) The lion tomb. The pillar of this earliest Lykian tomb found up to the present is now lying on the ground. The slabs which constituted the funerary chamber and which bear reliefs dating ca. 550-540 B. C., are now in the British Museum. 15) The site of the Payava tomb (4th century B. C.). This entire monument has been transported to the British Museum. 16) The pillar-tomb standing on the Roman acropolis dates from the 4th century B. C. This splendidly preserved monument (Pl. 5 a) consists of a three - stepped rock-cut base, a monolithic pillar, a funerary chamber built of marble, and a roof with three projecting horizontal members. The height of the whole tomb is 6.39 m.

The rock-cut tomb with an Ionic façade which is in the neighbourhood of the pillar-tomb described above, also dates from the 4th century B. C. The tombs on the necropolis date from different periods. A sarcophagus with a relief representing lions devouring a bull, dates from the middle of the 5th century B. C.

Letoon. On the west bank of the River Xanthos was situated Letoon, the Lykian federative sanctuary. A French expedition, under Henri Metzger, has conducted excavations on this site since 1950 and has achieved important results.

The following description has been given by Professor Metzger :

"The sanctuary comprises three temples. The one in the middle, the smallest, is of the Ionic order without a peristasis. It was no doubt consecrated to Artemis and dates from the 4th century B. C. To the west of this small temple there is an Ionic temple with a peristasis. It is excellently preserved and dates to the 2nd century B. C. We do not know to which divinity it belonged. To the east of this two temples and parallel to them lies a third temple which is of the Doric order and may also date back to the 2nd century B. C. It was greatly damaged during the destructions of the Byzantines.

To the south-west of the terrace with three temples is situated a sumptuous fountain (nymphaion) in the form of a semicircular portico with a basin 27 m. in diameter. An inscription found in situ reveals that the structure was built in the time of Hadrian (A. D. 117 - 138). Below this Roman structure there are remains of Hellenistic installations which are not yet excavated.

A small church dating from the 4th century A. D. with a beautiful mosaic is located in the south-eastern angle of the excavated area.

A theatre not yet excavated lies on the slope of the hill about a hundred meters from the temples.

In the small local museum are kept architectural fragments belonging to the temples and the nymphaion, some pieces of sculpture from Roman times and a great number of Greek and Lycian inscriptions.

PATARA

The city of Patara possessed one of the principal harbours of Lykia, flanked by a hill, on which probably stood a lighthouse. The port is now a marsh (Fig. 100). During the Roman Empire, Patara was the judicial seat of the Roman governor. The city was visited by Hadrian and his wife Sabina. It was, moreover, famous because of its ancient oracle of Apollo, which functioned only in winter.

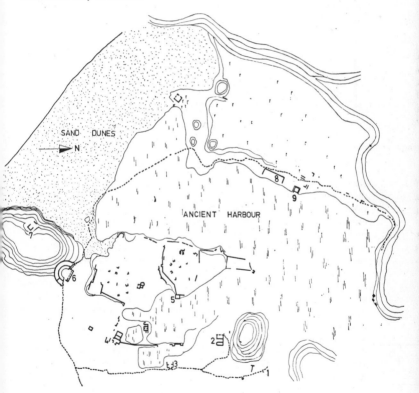

Fig. 100 - Plan of Patara. **1)** *Gateway. This handsome and well-preserved monument was erected about A. D. 100. According to its inscriptions, the six consoles on both sides of the gateway supported busts of members of the family of Mettius Modestus, who was the Roman Governor of Lykia. Near the gateway are many sarcophagi of Roman date.* **2)** *Roman Baths.* **3)** *Christian Basilica.* **4)** *The Baths*

of Vespasian (A. D. 69-79). **5).** A very well-preserved temple of the Corinthian order. This structure has recently been investigated by Ümit Serdaroğlu, who proposes that it was a templum in antis without a row of columns surrounding it (apteros). It stood on a platform measuring 13 by 16 m. in area. The maximum preserved height of the structure is 10.30 m; the cella door is 6.10 m. high. The pronaos is 8 m. wide and 2.10 m. deep, while the naos has a width of 7.50 m. and a depth of 2.75 m. **6)** The theatre is fairly well-preserved but it is partly buried in the sand. The stage building was built in the middle of the 2nd century A. D., according to an inscription on its outer wall. **7)** Scanty remains of an unidentified temple. The view to the sea from the top of this hill is splendid. **8)** Granary of Hadrian. This well-preserved structure (Fig. 101) is identified by its Latin inscription. **9)** An excellently preserved pseudoperipteral structure, probably a funerary temple (?).

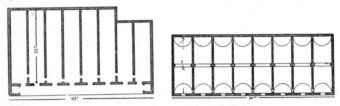

Fig. 101 – Granary at Patara. Reign of Hadrian.
Fig. 102 – Granary at Andriake. Reign of Hadrian.

Kaş (Antiphellos). A portion of the city wall close to the shore displays fine masonry of the Hellenistic period. The small theatre dominating the landscape is of the Greek type. It has neither a stage - building nor vaulted substructures. This splendidly preserved structure, with its beautiful ashlar masonry, must also have been erected in the Hellenistic age. Nearby are the remains of an unidentified temple. On the slope of the hill west of the modern town stands a rock-cut tomb in an excellent state of preservation. The façade representing the front of an anta house with pediment is Greek in its architectural order; however, the tower shape of the structure and the cubic mass surmounting it, reveal some Achaemenid influences. The interior is adorned with a frieze depicting 24 female figures. It probably dates from the 4th century B. C. A well-preserved characteristic Lykian tomb of elegant, slim proportions stands in the town, northeast of the harbour. It consists of a two - tiered podium and a sarcophagus with pointed arch and lion-heads on the lid. It most certainly dates from the 4th century B. C. The rock-cut tomb in Antiphellos with a pointed arch, seen in Pl. 6, is also a Lykian work. It too dates from the 4th century B. C.

↑ Β Ж Ξ Ν Ѡ : Γ Ρ Ξ Ν Ꝺ Ϝ Ѵ Μ Ѡ Τ Ε Γ Ρ Ξ Ν Ꝺ Ϝ Ꝺ Τ Ѡ
Τ Ρ Ε Ι Ꝺ Τ Ρ Β Β Ꝺ + Ε Γ Ξ Ν Ο Τ Ρ + Ε Ο + Ρ + Ε + Ρ Γ Γ Ε

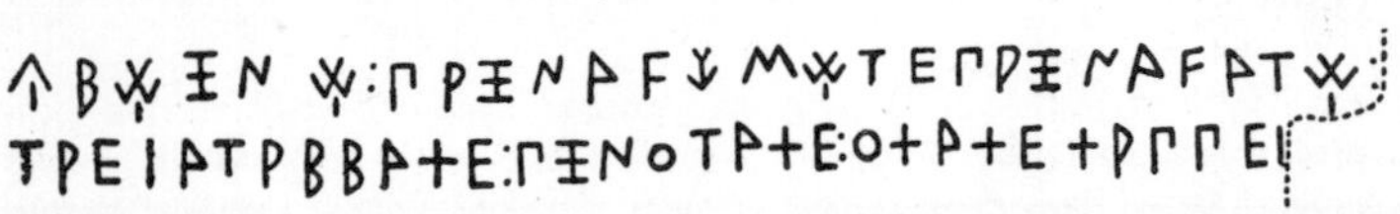

Fig. 103 – Lykian inscription from the Tomb of Merehi (see British Museum, The Nereid Monument, London 1900 p. 5), dating from the 4th century B. C.

Demre (Myra). The village of Demre contains the famous Church of St. Nicholas. It consists of a Byzantine structure with three apses and a basilica restored in the 11th century A. D. The basilica is preceded by an atrium and a double narthex. A sarcophagus, believed to be the tomb of St. Nicholas, is early Christian in date. The lid, dating from the Roman period, which bears two recumbant figures, does not belong to this sarcophagus. The cupola which covers the eastern part of the nave of the basilica was adorned with frescoes; figures of the apostles are still visible. Some other murals which adorn the walls of the church are also in a poor state of preservation. This Saint is perhaps now better known as Santa Claus, the bearer of gifts to children at Christmas time.

Myra was one of the earliest Lykian cities. The ruins and necropolis are a few km. to the north of Demre. The rock-cut Lykian tombs of Myra are among the most fascinating historical remains of Turkey (Fig. 104). Tombs of different Lykian types are cut into the face of the rock, creating a picturesque composition (see Akurgal, Kunst Anatolians Pl. VI). There are also tombs with reliefs representing the dead and their families or friends, all similarly cut out of the rock. The general effect is splendid. These tombs and sarcophagi, together with accompanying high reliefs, date from the 4th century B. C. The Roman theatre, built to the right of the rock tombs,

Fig. 104 – Rock-cut tombs at Myra! (Drawn by Charles Fellows, Discoveries in Lycia, London 1841, Pl. 23).

is in a very good state of preservation. Some km. sw. of Demre is the granary of Hadrian (Fig. 102). It measures 36 by 45 m. On the walls of the monument are many inscriptions and reliefs. Over the middle door are depicted the busts of Hadrian and Faustina.

Limyra. The ruins of Limyra are situated to the north of Finike. The well-preserved tombs are spread out in groups along the road for several km. Some of them are adorned with reliefs that reveal strong Greek influences and date from the 4th century B. C. (see Akurgal, Kunst Anatolians Pl. IV b). One monumental tomb at Limyra, of the sarcophagus type with a pointed arch, is a splendid example of Lykian art. It is adorned with reliefs which may be dated to the 4th century B. C. The little theatre is in a good state of preservation and dates from Roman Imperial times.

Dr. Jürgen Borchhardt of the German Archaeological Institute in Istanbul discovered and excavated, high on the south slope of the acropolis of Limyra, a fine heroon which is closely related to the Nereid Monument. A rock-cut terrace of 19 × 18 m. was the setting of the heroon. The foundations of the tomb (10.40 × 6.80 m.) stood on this terrace. The hyposorion, 3.40 m. high, enclosed a tomb chamber which was accessible from the south. The long east and west sides had a frieze with scenes of an ekphora, moving south. The superstructure (ca. 5.30 m. high) had the shape of an amphiprostyle temple with karyatids instead of columns, 4 each on the north and south sides. In ancient Ionic tradition, the karyatids stood on round bases;

Fig. 105 – Rock-cut tombs in Lykia (Drawn by Charles Fellows, Discoveries in Lycia, London 1841 Pl. IX).

1 and 6 at Massikytos. 2, 3 and 4 at Telmessos. 5 and 8 at Tlos. 7, 9 and 12 at Pinara. 10 between Limyra and Arykanda. 11 at Limyra.

they carried an architrave with rosettes and dentils. The sima was adorned with lion-head spouts. The acroteria are preserved on the north side. At the corners were female figures in running poses (ca. 1.25 m. high) in the style of the Nereid Monument; the central acroterion was probably a descending Nike, supported by two female protomes. Statues must have stood in the intercolumniations, but remnants of a horseman and a warrior suggest that they were set up in late classical times (Borchhardt, AJA 1970 p. 169).

Fig. 106 – Varieties of built tombs in Lykia. (Drawn by Charles Fellows, Discoveries in Lycia, London 1841, Pl. X).

1 and 8 at Telmessos. 2 and 5 at Kadyanda. 3 Xanthos. 4 and 6 at Sidyma. 7 at Kalynda. 9 at Massikytos.

Olympos. The much overgrown picturesque ruins of the ancient city of Olympos are situated at the mouth and on both banks of a torrential stream, which flows from east to west into the sea. In the city in ancient times, the river bed was constructed of regular stones to form a channel. It was crossed by a bridge, one abutment of which has survived. Along the south bank, a well-preserved portion of the quay may still be seen, built in the fine coursed polygonal technique and dating from the Hellenistic age. However, the quay betrays repair work of the Roman and Byzantine periods.

The small, steep acropolis lying close to the river-mouth bears remains of late and insignificant buildings. However, the panoramic view seen from the top of the hill is splendid. A small, much overgrown Roman theatre, also erected on the south bank of the stream, is in a poor state of preservation, with the exception of one side of the entrance.

The most attractive structure at Olympos is the cella-door of a temple, still in place, which has recently been investigated by Ümit Serdaroğlu. It lies ca. 150 m. west of the mouth of the river. The inside measurements of the door are 2.90 by 7.85 m. According to Serdaroğlu, it was a *templum in antis* of the Ionic order. The cella measured 10.70 × 12.53 m. From the inscription of a statue-base lying at the foot of the door, we learn that a statue of Marcus

Aurelius stood somewhere in the temple. The sanctuary, therefore, may have been erected in the reign of this Emperor (A.D. 161-180).

Chimaira. A few km. to the north-west of Olympos, in mountains some 300 or 400 m. in height, a flame issues permanently from the ground. This miraculous natural phenomenon is very impressive at night. Since the chimaera was thought to be a fire breathing monster living in Lykia, (Homer, Iliad VI, 168-182; Hesiod, Theogony 324), the place called Chimaira seems to have been identified in ancient times with the home of this hybrid figure that came into Greek mythology from a Hittite source (Akurgal, The Birth of Greek Art 187, 188). It must be noted, however, that, according to Strabo (XIV, 666), the scene of the myth of the chimaira was the neighbourhood of Mt. Kragos, in the western part of the Lykian land.

Phaselis. The ruins of Phaselis, largely covered by rich vegetation, may be considered among the most picturesque ancient remains of Turkey. The city was founded by colonists from Rhodes at the beginning of the 6th century B. C. It had three harbours : one on the north, one on the north-east, and one on the southwest side of the peninsula. The buildings still visible on the site are concentrated on the neck of the peninsula, between the north-eastern and south-western harbours. A fine paved street connected both of these harbours. It began near the south-western harbour, and there stands the gateway which was erected in honour of Hadrian's visit. The theatre, much overgrown, lies on the west side of the paved street; near the north-eastern end is located the agora of the city. South of Hadrian's gate, a cistern, remains of an unidentified temple, as well as a portion of the city wall can be distinguished. To the northeast of the paved street there is a church, and north of this an aqueduct begins. Stone built and sarcophaguslike tombs are located north of the city and east of the aqueduct.

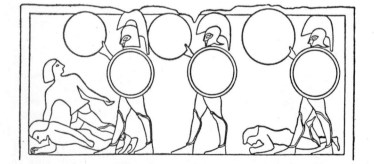

Fig. 106 a - Lycian warriors depicted on the Isinda Tomb in the Istanbul Museum, ca. 530 B. C. After Ekrem Akurgal, Lykische Reliefs, Berlin, 1942. P. 57. Fig. 8.

ÇAVDARHİSAR (AIZANOI)

One of the best preserved archaeological sites in Turkey is located at Aizanoi, 54 km. south-west of Kütahya. From the evidence of terra-cotta figurines discovered here, Aizanoi dates back to the 1st century B. C. The goddess Meter Steunene was worshipped in the city and the surrounding area. The magnificent remains, which are still standing, bear witness that the town passed through a very glorious period in the 2nd century A. D. Aizanoi was the seat of a bishopric in the Christian era, when the temple of Zeus was converted into a church. Rudolf Naumann has now published an excellent study on the subject of Meter Steunene of Aizanoi. (İstanbuler Mitteilungen 17, 1967, 218-247). The results of the excavations carried out at Aizanoi from 1926-28 by Schede and Krencker under the auspices of the German Archaeological Institute, together with studies made on the temple by Rudolf Naumann, are about to be published.

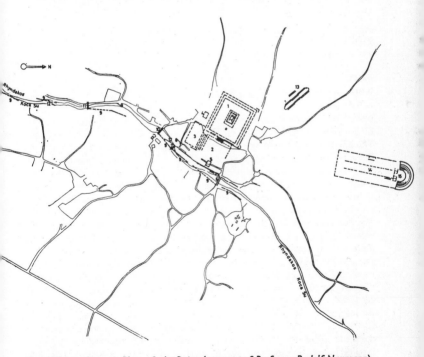

Fig. 107 a — Aizanoi, Plan of the Ruins (courtesy of Professor Rudolf Naumann). **1)** *The Temple of Zeus.* **2)** *The large Agora.* **3)** *Doric Agora.* **4)** *Foundations of an ancient building.* **5)** *Remains of a Roman structure.* **6)** *Roman bridge.* **7)** *Roman bridge.* **8)** *Remains of a Roman structure.* **9)** *Quay.* **10)** *Roman bridge.* **11)** *Roman bridge.* **12)** *Dam.* **13)** *Roman baths.* **14)** *The Stadium.* **15)** *The Theatre.*

The Temple of Zeus (Pls. 12, 79, 80). The temple at Aizanoi is the best preserved of all the sacred buildings of antiquity in Turkey, standing almost in its original form. Built of marble, it is surrounded by a peristasis in a pseudodipteral arrangement with 8 Ionic columns on the short sides and 15 on the long sides. (Pl. 79). It stands on a many-stepped podium measuring 32.962 × 36.920 m. (Pl. 79; Figs. 108 a,b). The naos itself is a prostyle

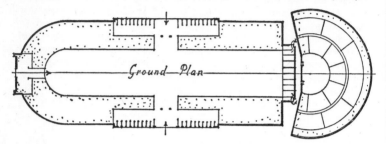

Fig. 107 b – Aizanoi (Çavdarhisar). Theatre and Stadium (after Fyfe, Hellenistic Architecture, p. 158, Fig. 48). Reign of Hadrian (117-138 A. D.) See also Pls. 12, 79, 80.

with four columns surmounted by composite capitals and has an opisthodomos with two columns in antis, also crowned by capitals of the composite order (Pl. 80). Although the temple was built in the Roman period, it discloses many features of a temple of the Greco-Anatolian type (Fig. 108). The peristasis, surrounding the naos at a distance of two intercolumniations, has a typical pseudo-dipteral arrangement, as laid down by Hermogenes in his rules for Hellenistic architecture (Fig. 63). The naos resembles the Zeus Sosipolis temple at Magnesia ad Maeandrum (Fig. 62) in that the pronaos is preceded by four columns and the opisthodomos is narrow (p. 183). It was an old Ionic principle that the span between the central columns on the short front side of the peristasis be wider than that between the remaining columns. However, it was Hellenistic tradition for the central intercolumniation in front of the pronaos to be equal to that between the two columns of the opisthodomos and for all central columnar spans to lie on the same axis (Fig. 63). The many-stepped podium may also be identified as a feature of Hellenistic architecture. In contrast, the placing of the cella over a barrel-vault is a characteristic of Roman architectural art, as we see in the temple of Trajan at Pergamon (Pl. 34a) and the temple of Hadrian at Cyzicus (Pl. 29). One is struck by the neo-classical character of the art forms of the Hadrianic period, as manifest in the rendering of the architectural ornamentation, the egg-and-dart, the composite capitals (Pls. 80), and especially the acanthus leaves on the middle akroterion (Pl. 12). As a matter of fact, inscriptions carved on the walls of the temple indicate that the building was constructed in the days of Hadrian; they also reveal that it was erected in honour of Zeus. A statue of the god once stood in the cella, but not a fragment of it was recovered. Nevertheless, a statuette of an eagle, the bird sacred to Zeus, has been found within the temple. Coins found in Aizanoi give some idea of the appearance of the statue of Zeus; on these the god is depicted standing, an eagle perched on his right hand and a spear grasped in his left.

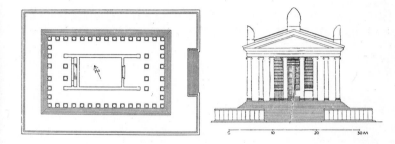

Fig. 108 a – The Temple of Zeus at Aizanoi. Built in the reign of Hadrian (A. D. 117-138). The naos (the temple proper) is a well-preserved prostyle preceded by a porch with four columns of the composite order and a narrow opisthodomos with two columns in antis, also of the composite order. The peristasis of pseudodipteral arrangement, with 8 Ionic columns along the short sides and 15 on the long, is in great part still extant. The many-stepped podium measured 32.962 × 36.912 m. (after Martin Schede, Der Tempel in Ankara, p. 30, Fig. 38).

Fig. 108 b – Temple of Zeus at Aizanoi. Reconstruction after Martin Schede, Der Tempel in Ankara, p. 31, Fig. 39.

    Rudolf Naumann has rightly suggested that the barrel-vaulted substructure of the temple served for the worship of the Goddess Kybele, i.e., the Meter Steunene. He gives the following arguments. 1) In the vaulted substructure were found terracotta figurines representing Kybele. 2) In an inscription Zeus and Kybele are mentioned together, apparently, as the chief deities at Aizanoi. 3) Entrance to the vaulted substructure was gained from the opisthodomos by means of wooden steps.' 4) The central acroterion of the pediment above the opisthodomos which constituted the entrance to the cella with its statue of Zeus was a male bust, while that above the opisthodomos was a female bust (Pl. 12). The fact that this front of the temple (Fig. 108 a) looks to the west, is, I believe, additional corroboration of Rudolf Naumann's statements. Indeed, all Greek and Roman temples in Anatolia connected with the ancient cult of Kybele were oriented to the west (Figs. 44-46, 52, 53, 63, 116, 118).

The earthquake in 1970 caused damage to the temple; however the toppled columns were later re-erected by a Turco-German team.

There were at Aizanoi a large agora with remains of a heroon in the center, and a second one of the Doric order with a round fountain in the middle, the exterior wall of which bears a copy of the famous edict of Diocletianus indicating maximal wages and ceiling prices of agricultural and industrial products.

Two very well-preserved bridges over the River Rhyndokos, still in use today, together with the quay protecting the river against flooding, were built in Roman times (Fig. 107 a).

PHRYGIA

Phrygian art and culture occupy an outstanding position in Anatolian history. We have already dealt with the most important problems of this remarkable civilization in the first part of the present book (pp. 14-15). In the following pages, we shall describe some of the well-preserved rock-cut monuments situated in the districts of Eskişehir and Afyon Karahisar (see the map of Phrygia).

The Phrygian rock-cut monuments situated at Midas City near Eskişehir (Figs. 109-114) have been thoroughly investigated and excellently documented by Albert Gabriel, *Phrygie* II, IV, Paris 1952, 1965. For the other group of Phrygian monuments (Pls. 81,82, Figs. 115 a,b) located in the neighbourhood of the railway station of the Mineral Water Source of Afyon Karahisar (see the map of Phrygia), consult Ekrem Akurgal, *Kunst Anatoliens*, Berlin 1961, p. 88-89, Fig. 52-53, p. 116 Fig. 73. The rock-cut Phrygian tomb at Arslantaş has been mistakenly described, in Pl. 81, as near Eskişehir. The tomb is located near Afyon Karahisar (see the map of Phrygia. Fig. 109a No. 1).

Fig. 108 c - Lion and Ibex depicted on a terracotta revetment from Pazarlı. After Ekrem Akurgal, The Birth of Greek Art. London, 1968, P. 198, Fig. 135, 136.

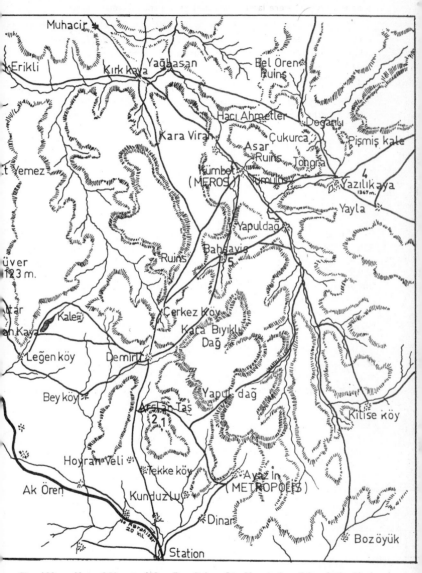

Fig. 109 a – Map of Phrygia (after F. v. Reber, Die Phrygischen Felsendenkmäler 1898 p. 544, Fig. 1).

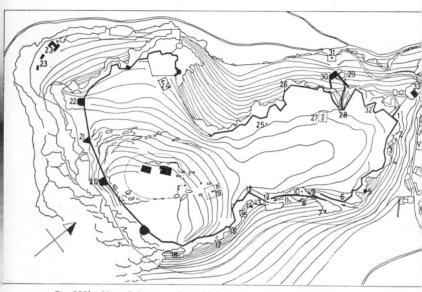

Fig. 109b – Plan of the acropolis at Midas City near Eskişehir (after Albert Gabriel, Phrygie II and IV). See the map of Phrygia, Fig. 109a, No. 4

The Phrygian ruins all date from the 6th century B. C. **1)** *Midas Monument or Yazılıkaya (see the caption to Fig. 111).* **2-5)** *Rock-cut Phrygian tombs.* **6)** *Altar.* **7-8)** *Phrygian rock-cut tombs.* **9)** *Steps.* **10)** *Altar.* **11)** *Arcosolium.* **12)** *Steps leading to the plateau of the acropolis. On the right hand side of the rock is carved a row of figures dating from the Neo-Hittite period (see the caption to Fig. 110).* **13)** *Large Phrygian Inscription.* **14)** *Large Phrygian altar with Phrygian inscription.* **15)** *Monumental Phrygian niche.* **16)** *Rock-cut tomb.* **17)** *Rock-cut tomb and rock-reliefs.* **18)** *Phrygian inscription, carved into the rock.* **19)** *Rock-cut throne (see the caption to Fig. 112).* **20-22)** *Insignificant cuttings in the rock face.* **23)** *A group of underground steps.* **24-25)** *Altars.* **26)** *Küçük Yazılıkaya (see the caption to Fig. 113).* **27)** *Cuttings in the rock.* **28)** *Steps leading down to a well.* **29)** *Underground grotto.* **30)** *Fortification wall.* **31)** *Fountain.* **32)** *Altar with Phrygian inscription.* **33)** *Sepulchral chamber.* **34)** *Sepulchral Chamber with Latin inscription.*

The Phrygian cult monument of Arezastis (Pl. 4 a) is very near Midas City and receives sunlight for only one hour after sunrise. (see Akurgal, Kunst Anatoliens 113 Fig. 70).

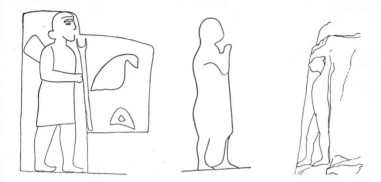

Fig. 110 a, b – Neo Hittite Reliefs at Midas City, cut into the rock face above
the steps leading to the plateau of the acropolis (Fig. 109b, No. 12). After Ekrem
Akurgal, Anatolia 1958, pp. 151-154, Figs. 1-5, Pls. 23-25. 8th or beginning of
the 7th century B. C.

Fig. 110 c, e – Neo-Hittite Reliefs at Midas City, cut into the rock-face above
the steps leading to the plateau of the acropolis (Fig. 109b, No. 12). After Ekrem
Akurgal, Anatolia 1958, pp. 151-154, Figs. 1-5, Pls. 23-25. 8th or beginning of
the 7th century B. C.

Fig. 111 – The Midas Monument or Yazılıkaya (after Albert Gabriel, Phrygie IV, p. 55 Fig. 30). Rock-cut Phrygian cult monument. 6th century B. C. The modern name, "Midas Monument", derives from the word MIDAI, mentioned in the inscription on the upper left-hand side of the façade. A portable statue of Kybele was installed in the niche during religious ceremonies. 6th century B. C. (see Ekrem Akurgal, Kunst Anatoliens 106 Figs. 67, 68). See the map of Phrygia, Fig. 109a, No. 4.

Fig. 111 a – Phrygian inscription engraved on the right edge of the Midas Monument (Fig. 111). After Ekrem Akurgal, Kunst Anatoliens, Berlin 1961, P. 108, Fig 68.

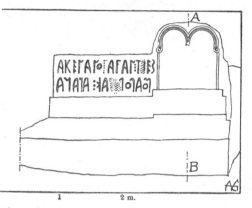

Fig. 112 – Rock-cut throne with Phrygian inscription, on the acropolis at Midas
City (see Figs. 109b, No. 19). After Albert Gabriel, Phrygie IV. p. 45 Fig. 26. During
religious ceremonies, a seated statue of Kybele was placed on this throne. 6th
century B. C. (see Ekrem Akurgal, Kunst Anatoliens p. 116, Fig. 74).

Fig. 113 – Rock-cut Phrygian cult monument called Küçük Yazılıkaya. Unfinished
(see Fig. 109b, No. 26). After Albert Gabriel, Phrygie IV, p. 75, Fig. 37. 6th century
B. C. (E. Akurgal, Kunst Anatoliens p. 110, Fig. 69).

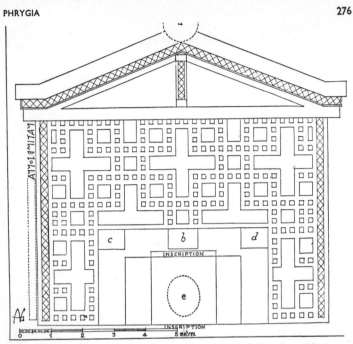

Fig. 114 – Rock-cut Phrygian cult monument called Maltaş (see the map of Phrygia, Fig. 109a, No. 2). After Albert Gabriel, Phrygie IV, p. 87, Fig. 41. 6th century B. C.

Fig. 115 a, b – Reliefs from a Phrygian rock-cut tomb called Kırık Arslantaş (see Akurgal, Kunst Anatoliens P. 95, 306). a) Relief depicting a warrior killing Gorgon; another warrior, on the left side, also killing Gorgon, is lost. The relief was sculptured on the front face of the tomb, which has collapsed. It is at present hidden from view, as the stone fragment on which it was carved has fallen face down on the ground. A cast of this relief is now exhibited in the Archaeological Institute of the University of Ankara. According to the folds on the shoulder of the warrior, the monument dates from ca. 540-530 B. C. b) On the same stone is depicted a relief of a lion which can be seen on the spot. This lion head is part of two antithetically arranged lions which adorned a lateral surface of the tomb.

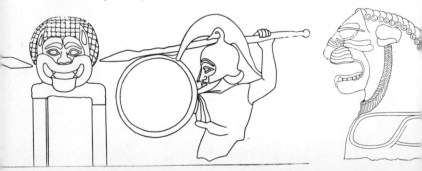

PESSINUS

The ruins lie in Ballıhisar, near Sivrihisar, on the Ankara - Eskişehir highway (136 km. from Ankara). The distance from the junction on the highway to the ruins is 16 km. It was an ancient Phrygian city in the form of a temple-state, with the famous sanctuary of the Great Mother of the gods, Kybele, also called Meter Dindymene, Agdistis or Magna Mater. The cult statue of the Great Goddess was an unshaped stone (Baitylos), supposed to have fallen down from heaven. The city was under Pergamene domination but its priests seem to have enjoyed a limited independence in spite of the Galatian invasion. A chief priest ruled, together with five Phrygian and five Galatian priests. According to Strabo (XII, 567), the priests profited very much from their religious influence. Pessinus reached its highest fame in 204 B. C., when the Roman Senate, in consequence of a Sibylline prophecy, sent envoys to Pessinus (or to Attalos I) and transported the cult statue of Kybele to Rome, where it was set up in a temple erected on the Palatine for this occasion. Pessinus passed to the Romans in 25 B. C. when Augustus constituted the province Galatia.

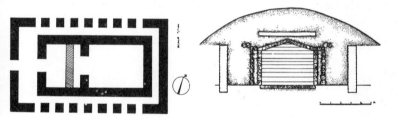

Fig. 116 – Temple at Pessinus (after Pierre Lambrechts, De Burg XII p. 282).

Fig. 116 b) Gordion. Midas Tomb. Section through the tomb, looking north (after R. S. Young. AJA, 62, 1958 Pl. 25 No. 12).

The site has been successfully excavated since 1967 by the Belgian scholar Professor Pierre Lambrechts, on behalf of the University of Ghent. In this book we have already dealt, on several occasions, with the temple which Professor Pierre Lambrechts has now completely uncovered. The building has a very curious ground plan (Fig. 116) which, despite its provincial features, seems to be a modification of a Greek temple, with a peristasis of 6 columns on the short sides and 11 on the long sides. Among the pottery and small finds that the excavations on this spot yielded, there is, as yet, not a single fragment which could be dated earlier than the Hellenistic period. The ground plan, together with the wall - building technique, reveals that the temple also dates back to sometime in the Hellenistic period at the earliest. Seven pillars in the middle of each long side indicate that the structure follows the form of a Greek peripteral temple. The ends of the long sides and the short sides are built in the form of walls for solidity. Yet, the whole plan seems to correspond to a peripteral scheme with 6 by 11 columns. It may represent a provincial Hellenistic expression of the Athena temple at Priene, built by Pytheos (p. 188, Fig. 68). For this monument, in the first edition of this book I had suggested a date in Roman times while in the second edition in the Hellenistic age, thinking that if the building stood on the ground level it must date back to early Hellenistic period, for such a provincial structure could not have been built in the Augustan age in a city in which, according to Strabo (XII, 567), the sacred precinct was embellished by "the Attalid kings with a temple and with stoai in marble". However, the building seems to be the substructions of a temple the upper parts of which must have been disappeared completely. In this case it is equally possible to date it either in the Hellenistic or Roman period. Nevertheless, it seems more likely that the building was erected in the Roman period. Indeed it shows the form of a hypogeum and was probably devoted to ceremonies, which were held in buildings below ground level, as in the vaulted substructure of the temple at Aizanoi (Fig. 108). We may finally point out that this structure, as Pierre Lambrechts has already indicated, faces westwards, in accordance with Greek temples related to the ancient cults of Anatolia, such as the sanctuaries of Artemis at Ephesus, Sardis, Magnesia ad Maeandrum and the temple of Kybele and Men at Ankara (Figs. 44-66, 52, 53, 61 a, 118).

Professor Lambrechts has also carried out excavations on the necropolis of Pessinus, which yielded some fine examples of late Roman tombs with door façades. Their gravestones, which date from the 3rd to the 4th centuries A. D., according to Mrs. İnci Bayburtluoğlu, who studied the pottery of the necropolis, are now kept in the local depot at Ballıhisar. The most important among them is a stele surmounted by a lion statue. According to its inscription, the stele was the tomb of a priest called Asklepios, who had the title, "gallos", when this grave was executed, but later became archigallos, great priest of Kybele. According to Pierre Lambrechts who published and commented on the inscription, the word "archi", which was added afterwards, indicates that a "gallos" could become "archigallos". He says, "this means that the theory after which the archigallos was a Roman citizen and could not have belonged to the category of castrated priest, is no longer valid".

During its 1969 campaign the Belgian expedition uncovered a broad and probably long canal, constructed in the shallow valley of Pessinus. It was many-stepped along both sides. The steps gave the citizens easy access to the water when its level dropped in summer. The Belgians have found, moreover, on the northern end of the canal, a dam system which regulated the water of a stream that seems to have existed in Roman times. The discovery of this fine canal, reveals that the field work in Pessinus is highly promising, and that the plan of the ruins drawn by Texier was not pure fantasy.

GORDION

The ruins of famous Gordion, the capital of the Kingdom of Phrygia, lie near the Ankara-Eskişehir highway, close by the confluence of the River Sakarya and the Porsuk, 29 km. north-west of Polatlı (94 km. from Ankara).

Gustav and Alfred Koerte started the excavation of five tumuli at Gordion and also of the city mound in 1901, and they brought to light very fine works of art which are now housed in the Istanbul Museum. Excavations carried out from 1949 onwards, under the direction of Rodney S. Young of the Pennsylvania University Museum, have led to extremely important discoveries which have considerably increased our knowledge of Phrygian art and culture. The majority of the finds unearthed as a result of the American digs are kept in the Ankara Archaeological Museum, while a small number are exhibited in the local museum. Rodney S. Young's excellent guide book to the excavations and the museum can be obtained both in Ankara and at Gordion.

The discoveries made during the German and American excavations indicate, as has been pointed out in various publications by the present author, that the Phrygian capital does not date earlier than the middle of the 8th century B. C. Gordion passed through its most glorious times during the period between 725 and 675 B. C. In this city lived Midas, referred to as "Mita of Muşki" in the annals of the Assyrian King Sargon covering the years 717-709. Although Gordion was destroyed at the beginning of the 7th century B. C. as a result of the Cimmerian invasion, many of the finds made on the city mound and in some of the tumuli reveal that the city was the scene of prosperous occupation until the very end of the 6th century B. C. Nevertheless, Gordion was ruled by Persia from the middle of the 6th century until Alexander the Great restored its independence. During the time of the Persian occupation, the older Phrygian cities declined as the centre of importance gravitated westwards, and major Phrygian settlements began to flourish in the region between Eskişehir and Afyon.

It happened that, while he was wintering at Gordion in 333 B. C., Alexander the Great cut through the famous knot tied by King Gordios. However, no traces have as yet been found of the temple in which stood the legendary chariot of King Gordios with its problematical knot.

The City Mound (Fig. 117 a). The Phrygian town, now a low flat mound measuring about 350 × 500 m., is located just east of the River Sangarios. The American expedition uncovered a monumental gateway and a great number of royal houses, as well as an imposing ensemble of fortifications and dwellings (Fig. 117 a) dating from the most prosperous period of the Phrygian Kingdom (ca. 725-667 B. C.).

The City Gateway (Fig. 117 a). Constructed of soft limestone and even now attaining a height of 9 m., the Phrygian Gateway, erected at the end of the 8th century B. C., must have been a monumental entrance of great attractiveness. The actual entrance to the city was approached by an unroofed corridor, 9 m. wide and 23 m. long (Fig. 117 a). This kind of city gateway, incorporating a long, narrow passage, is strongly reminiscent of the type used in Troy. The propylons FL, FM and FN observed in Troy II (Fig. 14),

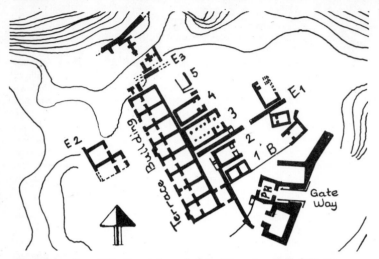

Fig. 117 a – Plan of Gordion at the end of the 8th century B. C. **1-3)** *Megarons.*
4) *Temple (?).* **B)** *Wall of sun-dried brick separating the royal courtyard
from the city gateway.* **E 1-3)** *Inner fortification wall surrounding the royal palaces.
During the excavations in the northern part of the city centre in 1969, new houses
of the megaron-type, with flights of steps, and other portions of the northern
section of the city wall have been uncovered. However, these are not indicated
on our plan.*

and the VIR and VIS gateways in Troy VI (Fig. 15) all exhibit the same ground
plan. Thus, in Gordion as in Troy, these long corridors served to trap an
attacking force, which would come under the cross-fire directed from three
sides by the defenders ranged along the tops of the walls. Both towers
flanking the gateway possess a courtyard opening to the city. The north
courtyard, which has been completely excavated, was utilized for storage
purposes. The south courtyard, on the other hand, has been left undug
by the excavators in order to preserve the massive south wall of the Persian
gateway. It is more than likely that both courts functioned as barracks and
that the wooden galleries installed in each were the quarters of the
king's bodyguard. The building constructed of stones of various colours
and therefore termed the Polychrome House by the American expedition
(PH) was the gateway in an earlier city wall, probably dating from the first
phase of the Phrygian settlement (750-725 B. C.).

     The City Centre (Fig. 117 a). The central part of the city mound was
occupied by the palace area. A light dividing wall made of sun-dried brick (B)
separated the first royal courtyard containing four buildings from the city
gateway. A stronger wall (marked E1, E2, E3) enclosed the inner royal courtyard on the north, west and south, and probably continued, as Young
assumes, along the east side of the royal buildings as well, thus completely
isolating them. This system of barring or enclosing walls is also to be observed

in Troy II (Fig. 15), in Hattusa (Fig. 137) and is a marked feature of the Mycenaean acropolis at Tiryns. In all probability, the cross-wall (B) was built to cut off the view of the palace area from the barracks located in the city gateway, whereas the function of the stronger wall was to protect the royal residence as a kind of inner fortification.

The Palaces (Figs. 1-5). Two of the buildings in the first court (Fig. 117 a, Nos. 1, 2) are megarons, i.e., structures composed of an anteroom and an inner room with a central round hearth. In the last decade of the 8th century, at a later date than the initial construction, Megaron 2 was paved with a mosaic of deep red, white and dark blue natural pebbles arranged in geometrical designs. This constitutes the earliest known example of a pebble mosaic to be discovered in its entirety. A part of this mosaic is exhibited in the local museum at Gordion.

Basing his conclusions on the evidence provided by his digs, Rodney Young rightly points out that Megaron 2 had a pitched roof with a crowning akroterion on the front gable and two lions' heads of limestone (now in the Ankara Museum), one on each side of the front. The walls of the house were of sun-dried brick, strengthened by a framework of timber resting on a stone socle. The roof was of reeds, covered by an outer layer of clay.

Megaron 3 (Fig. 117 a, No. 3). This megaron seems to be the most important building unearthed so far at Gordion. Measuring 18.30 × 30.40 m., it is the largest structure on the Phrygian acropolis and lies in the strongly fortified inner court of the city mound. It was divided into a nave and two aisles by two rows of wooden posts, bedded on timbers set below floor level (not visible today). In the opinion of the excavators, the nave was a one-storey-high hall, while the aisles consisted of two-tiered wooden galleries. Among the debris of the floor were found fragments of elaborate furniture worthy of a royal residence. Megaron 3 was obviously one of the oldest buildings, constructed in the second half of the 8th century B. C. Another large megaron called M4 by the American expedition lies to the north of Megaron 3 at a higher level. Professor Young's deductions lead him to conclude that this was a temple. He states, "The Phrygians evidently liked to site their temples on high places. M4 was the only building at terrace-level facing directly on to the square, and was approached by a processional ramp."

The Terrace Building (Fig. 90). In the western part of the terrace, west of megarons 1-5, lie 8 megarons, placed side by side each measuring about 11 × 14 m. Each had a central hearth, while a wooden gallery supported by posts ran along the sides. The abundant finds made by Rodney Young have enabled him to identify these buildings as the centre of the great domestic activity connected with the royal residence. A flight of steps was built alongside the large Megaron 3 to give access to the newly erected terrace.

This system of placing megarons in long rows reminds one of the town-planning methods employed in Troy II (Fig. 15). and at Tiryns. The same principle applied at Gordion is also noticeable in connection with the treasuries at Olympia. The large megarons in the palace area are also arranged side by side (Fig. 117 a, Nos. 1-5). A house at Bayraklı (ancient İzmir) shows a similar plan, in which two megarons lie side by side, and the megarons, as well as the oikoi incorporated in the peristyle houses of Larisa (Fig. 39) and Priene (Fig. 74), are likewise arranged side by side. The marked similarity between the town-planning of Gordion and that of other centres of culture in the western world of that day provides further striking evidence of the East European descent of the Phrygian people.

The Great Tumulus (Fig. 116 b). The whole area around Gordion is covered with tumuli of various sizes, dating from a period beginning in the last quarter of the 8th century and extending to the mid-6th century B. C. The largest of these, possessing a magnificent silhouette, is nearly 300 m. in diameter and at present attains a height of 53 m., though this must be lower than was the case before its erosion by wind and rain. It is the second highest tumulus in Anatolia and the ancient world, being exceeded in this respect only by the Lydian tumulus referred to by Herodotus as Alyattes' Tomb (p. 132).

The Phrygians customarily buried their dead in a wooden chamber accommodated in an oblong pit dug in the ground, the whole being subsequently covered with large masses of stones and earth or clay. After the interment of the deceased together with burial offerings in a wooden cabin, first a heap of stones and then a mound of earth or clay was piled over the chamber. Unlike Lydian and Greek tumuli, those of the Phrygians possessed neither a krepidoma nor a dromos. Phrygian tombs also differed from the Lydian and Greek type in that the chamber was built of wood instead of stone blocks. The excavation of the Great Tumulus at Gordion is one of the most important achievements of modern archaeology. The wooden construction within the huge mound is in an excellent state of preservation (Fig. 116 b).

The tomb chamber is a departure from the usual Phrygian type, since it was not installed in a pit dug in the earth but was built at ground level. It is surrounded by a 80 cm. - thick wall built of rough limestone blocks; the space between it and the chamber is filled with small stones. The interior measurements of the chamber are 5.15 × 6.20 m. and it is aligned north to south. The walls reach a uniform height of 3.25 m. from floor to roof, though the number of beams varies from ten to eleven. These beams, of juniper or cedar, are very precisely fitted together, presenting an excellent finish on the interior face. The double-pitched roof rests at both ends and in the centre on triangular gables. Stones were piled over the edifice to a height of nearly 4 m., and then came large masses of clay forming the mound (Fig. 116 b).

The skeleton that lay on a large bed in the burial chamber was that of a male over sixty years of age and of small stature, his height in life estimated at 1.59 m. The chamber was full of grave offerings. Of these, nine tables, two inlaid screens, three large bronze cauldrons, 166 fragments of smaller bronze vessels and 154 fibulae have been discovered. Most of these are in the Ankara Archaeological Museum; only a small number are on display in the local museum at Gordion.

Professor Young is of the opinion that an undertaking on such a scale could not have been carried out immediately after the Cimmerian catastrophe when King Midas possibly committed suicide; he believes the tomb to have been the resting place of King Gordios and therefore dates it sometime between 725 and 720 B. C. However, this date hardly agrees with the age of the Assyrian and Urartian objects found among the grave offerings in the great tumulus. The Urartian cauldrons and a bronze situla ending in a lion's head definitely betray stylistic features peculiar to the Sargonid period, i.e., 721-705 B. C. Thus it is improbable that they could have been made before 721 B. C. It is important to draw attention to a fact already observed by Young, namely, that all the ring-handles of one of the Urartian cauldrons are missing, as well as the lower ends of two of the bird tails. This shows, without doubt, that this particular vessel had seen considerable use before being placed in the tomb. This deduction and other stylistic considerations lead one to conclude that the great tumulus must be that of King Midas, who probably died in 696 B. C. The destruction of the city by the Cimmerians and the resulting suicide of Midas need not have prevented the Phrygians from honouring their great sovereign with the colossal tumulus he no doubt deserved. Moreover, the Cimmerian invasion, which was only a temporary wave of devastation, did not put an end to the Phrygian Kingdom. Although the glorious period linked with the name of Midas was definitely over, Phrygian culture continued to exist at Gordion.

ANKARA

Several settlements dating from prehistoric times have been identified within and just beyond the city limits of present-day Ankara. Although it is certain that the city and adjacent areas were the scene of small-scale settlements in the Hittite era also, no sites with habitation levels belonging to that age have so far been identified. The first settlements of any importance appear to have been founded in Phrygian times. Tumuli, scattered over a wide area around the Atatürk Mausoleum within the confines of Ankara, date from the Phrygian period. The finds made in these piles of earth are now housed in the Ankara Museum. Three further tumuli of the same Phrygian area have been recently excavated under the auspices of the Middle East Technical University in Ankara by the present author in collaboration with Cevat Erder and Sevim Buluç. The material discovered in these three tumuli is exhibited in the newly founded Museum of the Middle East Technical University. The great number of tumuli (there were at least twenty) seem to indicate the existence of an important Phrygian settlement in Ankara between 750 and 500 B. C., but the city to which this large necropolis belonged has as yet not been discovered.

After the Phrygians, the Galatians occupied Ankara from the second quarter of the 3rd century B. C. onwards. The city was the capital of the Galatian tribe called the Tektosages. During this period the deities, Men and Kybele were worshipped on the citadel. The corbel-vaulted burial chamber of Deiotaros, Tetrarch of Galatia, who died ca. 40 B. C., was discovered, together with an inscription at a place callèd Karalar near Ankara. In 25 B. C., Augustus annexed Galatia for Rome. In 1147 Ankara passed into the hands of the Seljuk Turks and since 1923 it has been the capital of the Turkish Republic.

Those places in Ankara worth seeing, apart from the Archaeological Museum, are the temple of Augustus and Roma, the Roman baths, the citadel, and, especially, the Ethnographical Museum with its rich collection. In addition, a visit to the Atatürk Mausoleum, a magnificent monument erected to the founder of modern Turkey, is recommended.

The Ankara Temple (Pl. 83; Fig. 118). Sixteen months before his death, Augustus placed four documents in the hands of the vestal virgins : his private will and testament, orders for his funeral, a statement about the financial and military situation of the Empire and, finally, a systematic account of the deeds he accomplished during his life-time. Only the last of these, the "index rerum gestarum" has been preserved through the bilingual inscription in Latin and Greek carved on the walls of the temple in Ankara. The original Latin text, which was engraved on plaques of metal and placed in front of the Emperor's Mausoleum in Rome, has entirely disappeared.

Strangely enough, the remnants of the two other copies of the "Res Gestae Divi Augusti" (The Deeds of the deified Augustus) known at present were also discovered in Anatolia. Excavations carried out at Antiochia in Pisidia (present-day Yalvaç) have brought to light some fragments of the Latin text, which are now displayed in the Ankara Museum, and which have filled in some of the gaps in the copy of the Latin text belonging to the Ankara temple. On the other hand, the Greek version discovered at Apollonia in Phrygia (present-day Uluborlu) has contributed nothing to a further understanding of the original text.

The Latin text relating the deeds of Augustus appears on the inner faces of two walls in the pronaos, while the Greek version is carved on the exterior of the south-west side of the naos (Pl. 83 a).

Four columns stand in front of the entrance to the temple, i.e., the pronaos. Access to the cella, the inner shrine, was gained after passing through a well-proportioned doorway of imposing height, which constituted the sole source of daylight for the windowless cella (Pl. 84; Fig. 118).

At the other end of the temple was the opisthodomos, containing two columns in antis. In Roman Imperial times, the temple was consecrated to the deified Augustus and the goddess Roma. Before the Roman conquest, the deities, Men and Kybele, were probably worshipped here.

In the 2nd century A.D. (about A.D. 150), the temple was encircled by a peristasis of the Ionic order, with 8 columns on the short sides and 15 on the long sides (Fig. 118). The space between the peristasis and the wall was twice the intercolumnar span; thus the temple took the form of a pseudodipteros. The building stood on a podium measuring 36×54.82 m., which was reached by several steps. The naos itself was 12.8×28.21 m. in area.

The roof, the architrave and the colonnade have not survived. When the temple was converted into a church, the dividing wall between the cella and the opisthodomos was demolished, and the two columns in antis were removed to make room for the construction of the choir and the crypt. The three windows in the south-east wall also date from this period (Pl. 83 a).

When Ankara was taken by the Turks at the beginning of the 15th century, the Hacı Bayram Mosque was erected adjoining the north-west corner of the temple. Although part of the north-west wall of the cella was destroyed in 1834, the temple is in quite a good state of preservation at the present time. The workmanship is of such a high standard that some specialists have been inclined to recognize in this temple a work of the Hellenistic era. Without doubt, the inscription concerning the text of August-us' deeds was carved at a later date, i.e., after the temple was built, for the presence of joints indicates that the blocks were not intended to hold an inscription. However, the high quality of workmanship seen in the marble blocks and the ornaments as well as the fact that the inscription was engraved after the construction of the sanctuary, do not help us to date

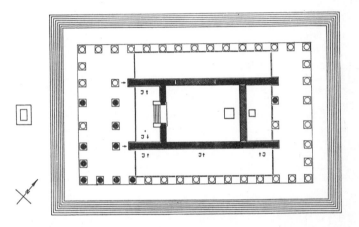

Fig. 118 – Ankara. Temple of Augustus and Roma. Probably built between 25-20 B. C. after the annexation of the province of Galatia for the Roman Empire by the Emperor Augustus, on the site of a sanctuary of Men and Kybele. The Ankara Temple, which seems to have served as a model for that at Aizanoi (Fig. 108), stood on a many-stepped podium about 2 m. high, measuring 36 × 54.82 m. The naos itself measured 12.8 × 28.21 m. and was a prostyle preceded by a porch with four columns of the Corinthian order and had an opisthodomos with two columns in antis, probably also Corinthian in style. The inscriptions in Latin and Greek report-ing the deeds of Augustus (30 B. C. – A. D. 14) were engraved after his death. In the latter half of the 2nd century A.D., the naos was probably surrounded by a peristasis in pseudodipteral arrangement with 8 Ionic columns on the short sides and 15 on the long. The temple faces west in the manner of all Greek temples based on local Anatolian tradition, such as the temple at Pessinus recently discovered by Pierre Lambrechts, and the sanctuaries of Artemis at Ephesus, Sardis and Magnesia ad Maeandrum (Figs. 44-46, 52-53, 61 a).

The Christians who converted the temple into a church opened the three windows in the south wall of the cella and built a crypt in the rear of the naos, having demolished the wall between the cella and the opisthodomos. The Turkish mosque of Hacı Bayram, which adjoins the north wall of the naos at an angle, was built at the beginning of the 15th century A. D.

the temple to the 2nd century B. C., as Martin Schede suggested thirty years ago. On the contrary, the temple seems to have been erected just after 25 B. C. to celebrate the occasion when Augustus annexed the province of Galatia to Rome. Indeed, the decoration on the oldest parts of the temple, for instance, the palmettes and especially the acanthus leaves along the foot of the opisthodomos wall, does not appear to be earlier than the early Augustan age (see Pl. 83 c). When compared with middle Hellenistic specimens dating from the latter half of the 2nd century, they are less fine in execution. On the other hand, the ornamentation on the upper part of the cella wall may date from a later time, judging by the broad form of the beads (Pl. 83 b). Indeed, Ümit Serdaroğlu and Sevim Üner have observed that the blocks in the upper parts of the naos walls do not show anathyrosis (marginal bands surrounding the blocks) and, consequently, are additions subsequent to the first period of construction.

Since Hamit Koşay unearthed only three Corinthian capitals in the excavations which he carried out thirty years ago, it is not possible to state with certainty whether they belonged to the pronaos, the opisthodomos, or the peristasis. However, the Corinthian order of the pilaster-capitals in the pronaos seems to imply that the capitals discovered may belong to the columns standing in front of the pronaos. The arrangement of the acanthus leaves and their compact form disclose, as pointed out by Y. Boysal, that they are of early Augustan date. Likewise, the "eyes" on the edges of the acanthus leaves on the capitals resemble those seen at the base of the wall in the opisthodomos (Pl. 83 c), which we have already dated to the early Augustan age. These comparisons enable us to conclude that the capitals found during excavations surmounted the columns standing across the front of the porch (the pronaos). The missing capitals of the peristasis may have been of the Ionic order, like the temple at Aizanoi and as the coins of Ankara seem to illustrate. This suggestion has already been put forward by Martin Schede, who observed that the temple of Zeus at Aizanoi closely resembles the Ankara temple in many ways, notably in the type of ground-plan and the arrangement of the ornamental bands on the cella wall.

From an inscription on the north-west anta of the porch we know that the temple was dedicated to Augustus and Roma. Basing his judgement on the evidence of coins, Martin Schede concluded that the temple was originally erected to Men and Kybele. We are now in a position to confirm his suggestion. During the successful excavations which Pierre Lambrechts has been carrying out over the last three years at Pessinus, he has unearthed a temple with a very curious ground-plan which, despite the provincial features it exhibits, is a modification of a Greek temple with a peristasis having 6 columns on the short sides and 11 on the longer sides. Among the pottery and small finds that the excavations on this spot have yielded, there is not a single piece or fragment which could be dated earlier than the Hellenistic period. The plan together with the wall-building technique also disclose that the temple at Pessinus actually dates from the Hellenistic age. We may also point out that this temple, as Pierre Lambrechts has already indicated, faces west in accordance with Greek temples related to the ancient cults of Anatolia, such as the sanctuaries of Artemis in Ephesus, Sardis and at Magnesia ad Maeandrum (Figs. 44-46; 52, 53, 61 a). The fact that the temple of Augustus and Roma in Ankara also faces towards the west (Fig. 118) reveals, beyond doubt, that it was one of the Greek temples based on local Anatolian tradition and used for the worship of Men and Kybele before becoming the sanctuary of Augustus and Roma.

Roman Baths (Fig. 119). At the foot of the Ankara citadel, crowned by the temple of Augustus, are located the well-preserved Roman baths, dating from the days of Caracalla (A. D. 211-217). These baths lie 400 m. from the square of Ulus on the left-hand side of the main street leading to the north. The huge construction contains a palaestra and centrally-heated rooms. The small round bricks piled in columns 1.30 m. high supported the floors of the baths and retained the heat provided by furnaces (Plan after M. Akok).

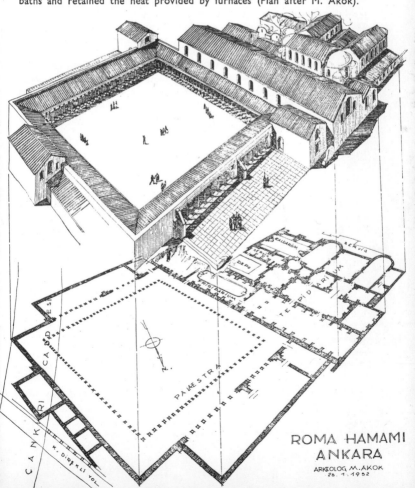

ROMA HAMAMI
ANKARA
ARKEOLOG M. AKOK
26. 1. 1952

GÂVURKALESİ

Gâvurkalesi (Figs. 120 a, b), "the castle of infidels", is about 60 km. southwest of Ankara, near Haymana. The ruins consist of a Hittite cult relief depicting three deities (Fig. 120 a, No. 1), and a subterranean chamber (Fig. 120 a, No. 2) which was a monumental tomb, dating from the Hittite Imperial period. The site probably formed an important centre of worship.

Gâvurkalesi is a rocky elevation rising 60 m. in a deep valley. During the Hittite era, the site was smoothed to form a raised level surface, measuring 35 by 37 m., and was fortified by Cyclopean walls. On the rock front facing the valley are carved two standing gods (Fig. 120 b) before a seated goddess, who is only slightly visible to the left of the rock-cleft. The cap of the foremost male figure is adorned, both in front and in back, with three horns, while the cap of the other god bears only three horns in front. The male figures very probably represent the weather god, followed by his son. The goddess also wears a pointed cap. The two gods, together with the goddess, constitute a triad, consisting of father, mother and son, such as we see in the main scene of Yazılıkaya at Boğazköy (Fig. 151, Nos. 42-44). West of the seated goddess, the face of the cliff has been smoothed over for an area of 6.00 × 4.20, below which appears another offset, about 2 m. above the original surface. The cult scene seems to be related to a subterranean chamber which lies directly opposite it, at the north side of the platform

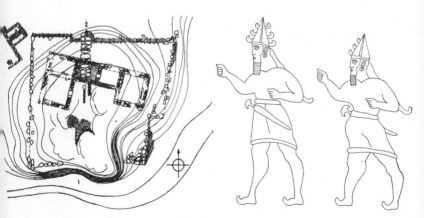

Fig. 120 a, b – Gâvurkale. Hittite place of worship and underground tomb. 13th century B. C. a) Plan of the fortified plateau. 1) Rock-cut reliefs representing two gods and a seated goddess. 2) Funerary chamber of the Isopata type. b) The figures of two gods, probably the Weather God and his son.

(Fig. 120a,No.2). The underground chamber, built in the Hittite Cyclopean wall technique, measures 3 by 4 m. and is covered by false vaulting. It reminds one very much of the tomb of Tantalos and the subterranean graves at Ras Shamra of the Isopata type. Tombs with burial chambers constructed in stone and covered by false vaulting were in vogue in the second millennium B. C. in the Creto-Mycenaean world. It is only natural to expect that they had some influence on Hittite funerary architecture. Indeed, Hittite texts describing detailed burial rites relate that, after cremation, the bones of the dead were placed in a "stone house". Since there is mention of a couch and bedroom, the burial places quoted in the Hittite texts must have consisted of a chamber like this one at Gâvurkalesi (Akurgal, Belleten 1943, 7 n. 36).

Thus, Gâvurkalesi was, like the sanctuary of Yazılıkaya (Fig. 143), a holy place, which consisted of a cult relief, representing the most important Hittite deities, and a burial chamber, reserved for royal worship. On the fortified platform in the Hittite period, probably stood a structure of religious character and some houses built for the priests. The portion of the fortifications still standing to the east of the reliefs, like the subterranean chamber on the north side, exhibits the characteristic building technique of the Hittites. Hans H. v.d. Osten, who carried out excavations at Gâvurkalesi in 1930, uncovered, on the fortified platform, some remains of walls, constructed in whitish limestone (Fig. 120 a). However, they date from a later period. The Hittite structures seem to have been completely destroyed. The foundations and sherds found by v.d Osten reveal that the slopes around the platform were inhabited in the Phrygian period.

The Ankara Museum. One of the world's most important and interesting museums is in Ankara. This museum is housed in the covered bazaar, built in the second half of the 15th century by Mahmut Pasha, one of the Great Viziers of Mehmet II, the Conqueror of Constantinopolis, and contains the magnificent finds made in Turkey belonging to the prehistoric, Hattian, Hittite, Phrygian and Urartian civilizations.

Statues and reliefs of the Hittite Empire period and the Neo-Hittite age (Figs. 123 ff.) are on display in the central hall of the covered bazaar, which is roofed with ten domes. Works representative of the prehistoric, Hattian, Hittite, Phrygian, Urartian, Persian, Greek and Roman civilizations, on the other hand, are exhibited in the surrounding halls. An informative illustrated catalogue of the museum, written by Raci Temizer in English, French and German, is available. The most important digs which provided the finds displayed in the museum are those of Çatalhöyük, Hacılar, Can Hasan, Alişar, Alacahüyük, Beyce Sultan, Kültepe, Eskiyapar, nİandık, Acemhöyük, Boğazköy, Malatya, Kargamış, Sakçegözü, Altıntepe, Toprakkale, Patnos, Gordion, Ankara, Pazarlı and Ikiztepe. The present book contains photographs (Pls. 84-92) and drawings (Figs. 121-136) of some of the specimens on display in the museum representative of the civilizations referred to above. It is possible to get an idea of the various civilizations that have existed in Anatolia by means of the detailed captions accompanying these illustrations.

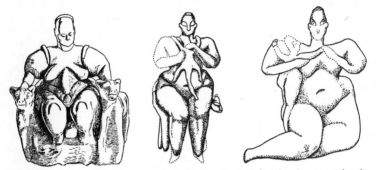

Fig. 121 a, b, c – Clay statuettes of the Mother Goddess found in houses at Level VI at Hacılar (ca. 5500 B. C.). Archaeological Museum, Ankara.

Fig. 122 a, b – A Hittite warrior god that once protected the east city gate of Hattusa, now kept in the Archaeological Museum, Ankara (see Fig. 137, No. 6). This relief, dating from the beginning of the 14th century, is the best preserved and most outstanding example of Hittite sculpture. It gives the impression of free-standing sculpture as it is carved in pronounced high relief. Three-quarters of the head emerges from the background, and the body displays plastic modelling similar to that of the lions and sphinxes from the same city. The horn on the helmet identifies the warrior as a god. Probably the naked breast and bare feet are further indications that he is a god. The pointed helmet has cheek and neck flaps, and a plume. The short skirt is fastened with a belt, from which a long sash extends diagonally to the right knee. Stuck into the belt on the left side is a sword with a crescent-shaped pommel and a scabbard ending in a hooked curve. The right hand grips a long-handled axe with a tassel dangling at the end. The workmanship manifest in the carving of the relief is extremely fine; the ornamentation is very precisely chiselled. The minute execution of the details goes so far as to represent the hair on the chest and the cuticles of the nails. The modelling of the face and body and the rendering of the collar-bones and muscles is masterful. The sculptor must have been one of the greatest artists of his time. By producing a front view of the right leg, while the left is in profile, he has given his work an animated aspect, creating the effect of a marching figure. A concrete cast of the relief now replaces the original on the site.

Fig. 123 – King Sulumeli offering a libation to the Storm God. Orthostat block from Malatya, now in the Archaeological Museum in Ankara. Early Neo-Hittite style 1050-850 B. C. In this relief two scenes are depicted in succession. In the one on the left, the Weather God is seen riding in his chariot, drawn by the sacred bulls Serri and Hurri. The scene on the right shows him after alighting, receiving the libation from King Sulumeli. The god holds a boomerang in his right hand and a thunderbolt in his left. Two hieroglyphs carved between the two images of the god confirm his identity. The upper hieroglyph means "god" and the lower W-shaped thunderbolt signifies "the Weather God".

The hieroglyphs on the king's cartouche are easy to read. The conical signs in antithetic position mean "king" and the three superimposed symbols in the centre can be deciphered as "Sulumeli". The two lower signs "li" and "mi" (or "ma") are known from the names Mursili and Suppiluliuma, which have been identified from bilingual comparisons. The meaning of the upper sign can be deduced from the name Sulumeli in the Assyrian annals, mentioned as being a king of Malatya. The bull being led by a man is to be sacrificed to the Weather God.

Fig. 124 – Lion of a statue base from Carchemish. Early to middle Neo-Hittite style (traditional school). Reign of Pisiris (Katuwas). Second half of the 8th century B. C. Archaeological Museum, Ankara (see also Pl. 89 b).

Fig. 125 – Lion of a column base from Carchemish. Early to middle Neo-Hittite style (traditional school). Second half of the 8th century B. C. Archaeological Museum, Ankara. The type of lion portrayal in these two reliefs from Carchemish served as a model for Greek sculptors at the beginning of the 7th century B . C.

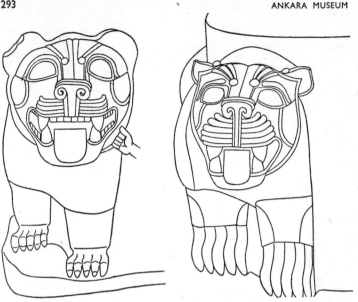

Fig. 126– Chimaera, from Carchemish. Early to middle Neo-Hittite style (traditional school). Reign of Pisiris (Katuwas). Second half of the 8th century B. C. Archaeological Museum, Ankara. This hybrid figure, typical of Hittite art, first made its oppearance in Greece in literature (Homer and Hesiod) and in Corinthian vase painting about the beginning of the 7th century B. C.

Fig. 127– Griffin demon. Carchemish. Early to middle Neo-Hittite style (traditional school). Reign of Pisiris (Katuwas). Second half of the 8th century B. C. Archaeological Museum, Ankara.

Fig. 128a– Warrior. Carchemish. Early to middle Neo-Hittite style (traditional school). Reign of Pisiris (Katuwas). Second half of the 8th century B. C. Archaeological Museum, Ankara.

Fig. 128 b– Ibex bearer. Carchemish. Early to middle Neo-Hittite style (traditional school). Reign of Pisiris (Katuwas). Second half of the 8th century B. C. Archaeological Museum, Ankara.

Fig. 128 c – King Katuwas (Pisiris) of Carchemish. Middle Neo-Hittite style (modern school). Second half of the 8th century B. C. Archaeological Museum, Ankara.

Fig. 129, 130 – Portal lion from Sakçegözü. Aramaean style, composed of Assyrian and Hittite elements, ca. 730-700 B. C. Archaeological Museum, Ankara. This type of lion portrayal served as a model for Greek and Etruscan artists in the first half of the 7th century B. C.

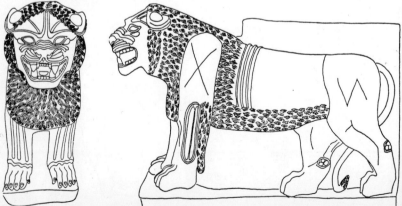

Fig. 131 – Head of a griffin demon
on an orthostat relief from Sakçegözü. Aramaean style, composed
of Assyrian and Hittite elements,
730-700 B. C. Archaeological
Museum, Ankara.

Fig. 132 – Griffin head from an
orthostat relief found in Ankara.
Aramaean style composed of Assyrian and Hittite elements, ca. 700
B.C. Archaeological Museum, Ankara. This type of griffin portrayal
served as a model for Greek and
Etruscan artists in the first half of
the 7th century B. C. (Akurgal, The
Birth of Greek Art, London 1968).

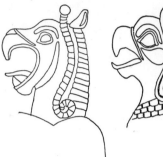

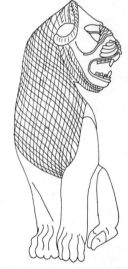

Fig. 134 – Ivory lion, found in the Urartian
city at Altıntepe. North Syrian style, with
marked Assyrian influence. 7th century
B. C. The lion from Altıntepe is the earliest
example illustrating the sitting posture,
with the head turned to the side; later
repeated in Greek archaic art, as in the
statue of a lion from Perachora, now in
the Boston Museum (Akurgal, The Birth of
Greek Art, London 1968).

Fig. 133 – King Araras with his son Kamanas.
Carchemish. Late Neo-Hittite style. 717-691 B.C.
Archaeological Museum, Ankara.

Fig. 135 – Ivory plaque showing a griffin demon, found in the Urartian city at Altıntepe. North Syrian style with marked Assyrian influence. 7th century B. C.Archaeological Museum, Ankara.

Fig. 136 – Ivory lion, found in the Urartian city at Kayalıdere. Middle Urartian style (685-645 B. C.). Archaeological Museum, Ankara.

BOĞAZKÖY (HATTUSA)

The ruins of Hattusa, the capital of the Hittite state, are situated overlying a terrace and a huge crag rising above the present-day village known either as Boğazköy or Boğazkale (Fig. 137). Hattusa is derived from Hattus, the original name given to it by the Hattic people. On capturing the city, the Hittites (p. 7 ff.) continued to use the name, except that by adding the suffix "a" or sometimes "as", they turned it into the Hittite adaptation "Hattusa" or "Hattusas". The oldest Hittite document discovered at Boğazköy reveals that Hattusa was devastated at the beginning of the 18th century B. C. by Anitta of Kussara (p. 7), who is understood to have been the greatest Hittite king during the time of the city states. The document also states that he put a curse on the city in the following words : "Whoever shall be king after me, if he re-settles Hattusa, he shall be struck by the Storm God". However, the fact remains that the Hittites re-inhabited Hattus shortly after Anitta's death, as is proved by a letter of the Hammurabi period, discovered at Mari, in Syria, during the excavations of the French archaeologist, André Parrot, in which

Hattus is referred to by its Hittite name, "Hattusa." This evidence reveals that the city had become Hittite by 1700 B. C. at the latest.

North of the Great Temple (Fig. 137, No. 1), the German expedition, now carrying out excavations at Hattusa, recently unearthed the remains of buildings and small works of art belonging to the Karum Hattus settlement, which occurred in the final phase of the Hattic era of the city. One of the Assyrian colonies called "Karum" in ancient written sources existed at Hattusa in this phase covering the 19th and 18th centuries B. C. (see p. 7).

Throughout Hittite history, both during the Old Kingdom period (1750-1450) and that of the Empire (1450-1180), Hattusa was the capital city. The first city wall around Hattusa is thought to have been built by King Hantili I about the beginning of the 16th century. In spite of this fortification, the Kaska people destroyed and sacked the city about a century later in the reign of Tudhaliya III. Nevertheless, it is understood that, within a short time, the city and its defences were rebuilt. The old city occupies the area between the Great Temple and the Great Citadel, and was the scene of settlement in the Hattic age (pp. 5, 7), the City State period (2000-1750), and the time of the Old Kingdom (1750-1450). On the other hand, the upper city, rising up south of the sally ports (see Fig. 137), came into being in the Empire period (1450 - 1180 B. C.). The city wall, which is very well-preserved in some places, stretches for a total of 6 km. (Fig. 137). The Hittite state came to an end with the devastation of Hattusa by Thracian tribes in 1180 B. C. (p. 12).

The excavation of Hattusa first began in 1906, under the direction of Hugo Winckler and Theodor Makridi. These two archaeologists were joined in the following year by Otto Puchstein, and their work continued until 1912. A great sensation was caused by the discovery during these excavations of tablets bearing cuneiform writing in the Great Temple (Fig. 140). The tablets could be read, since cuneiform writing was already known, but the deciphering of the Hittite language took a long time. After some unsuccessful attempts by various scholars, the riddle of the Hittite tongue was finally solved by the Czech linguist, F. Hrozny, in 1915. The excavations were recommenced after the First World War in 1931 with Kurt Bittel in charge and, disregarding the interruption caused by the Second World War, have continued successfully up to the present day.

Those important places worth visitting are listed here in the order in which they should be seen : Yazılıkaya (Figs. 143-157), the Great Temple (Figs. 140-141), the Great Citadel (Fig. 138), the King's Gate (Fig. 137, No. 6), the Sphinx Gate (Fig. 137, No. 11), the Tunnel (Fig. 139), the city wall in the vicinity of the Sphinx Gate (Fig. 139), temples 2-4 north of the Sphinx Gate (Fig. 142), the Lion Gate (Fig. 137, No. 12), and the local museum. Those who intend spending just one day at Hattusa are advised to visit Yazılıkaya before proceeding to the city, because the reliefs at Yazılıkaya only receive direct sunlight between 11 a. m., and 1 p. m.; after this time they are not distinctly visible.

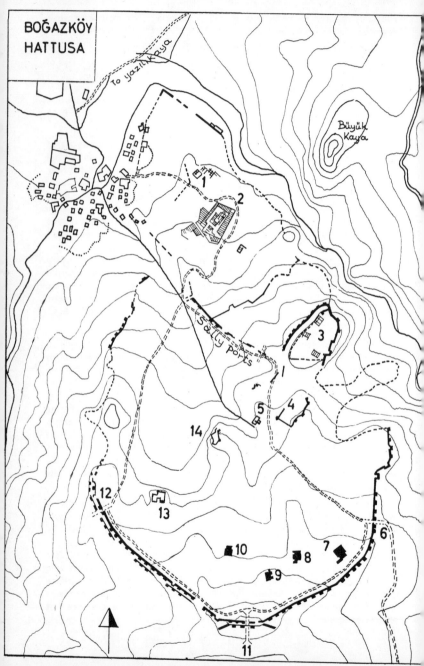

BOĞAZKÖY
HATTUSA

To Yazılıkaya

Büyük
Kaya

1

2

Sally Ports

3

4

5

14

12

13

10

7

8

6

9

11

Fig. 137 – Plan of Boğazköy (Hattusa). **1)** *Settlement dating from the Karum Hattus period (19th-18th centuries B. C.).* **2)** *The Temple of the Weather God of Hatti and the Sun Goddess of Arinna (Fig. 140).* **3)** *Büyükkale (the Great Citadel), the acropolis of Hattusa (see Fig. 138).* **4)** *The Southern Citadel, probably one of the most important fortresses of the 13th century B. C., not yet excavated.* **5)** *Nişantepe (Target Hill), with remains of a once imposing Hittite castle dating from the 13th century B. C. On the west side of the modern road can be seen an 8.50 m.-long hieroglyphic inscription carved in the rock. This is badly weathered, but, starting in the top right-hand corner, reference is made to "the Great King Suppiluliuma, son of the Great King Tudhaliya and grandson of the Great King Hattusili". Since the two Hittite kings called Suppiluliuma happen to have had the same genealogy, we are not in a position to determine which is meant here* **6)** *King's Gate (beginning of the 14th century B. C.). The high relief originally adorning the west face of the north door jamb of the entrance overlooking the interior of the city is now kept in the Ankara Archaeological Museum (Fig. 122 a, b). On the site, the original work is now replaced by a concrete cast. The attractive outer face of the King's Gate is relatively well-preserved. The door jambs were made up largely of tall andesite monoliths forming the pointed arch characteristic of Hittite architecture. The city wall is built in Cyclopean masonry with huge, roughly worked stone blocks. The height of the stone wall was about 6 m., and this was overlaid with sun-dried brick.* **7-10)** *Temples dating from the 13th century B. C., constructed according to the classic type of Hittite sanctuary (see Figs. 140, 141) with a central courtyard and an adyton containing the cult statue.* **11)** *Yer Kapı, the Sphinx Gate (see Fig. 139).* **12)** *Lion Gate (beginning of the 14th century). Constructed like the King's Gate in the form of a pointed arch, the upper part of which is now lost. The outer (western) fronts of the door jambs are each adorned with the head and fore-quarters of a lion. The animal on the right-hand side, almost intact, is a valuable example of large-scale Hittite sculpture. Like the apotropaic dogs mentioned in Hittite texts, these lions, with their threatening open mouths, were intended to ward off evil spirits.* **13)** *Yenice Kale (the New Castle), showing well-preserved Hittite walls, dating from about the 13th century B. C.* **14)** *Sarı Kale (the Yellow Castle). Beautifully laid Hittite walls going back to the 13th century B. C. are also in evidence here. The other walls in the same castle are built of small stones, showing the remains of repair-work carried out in Phrygian times.*

Fig. 137 a, b – Impressions of Hittite royal seals with bilingual inscriptions in cuneiform and picture writing (hieroglyphs).

a) Impression from a seal of king Muwatalli (1306-1282 B. C.)

b) Impression from a seal of king Urhi Teşup, i. e., Mursili III (1282-1275 B. C.). After H. G. Güterbock, Siegel aus Boğazköy I, No. 38A and No. 13 B, C.

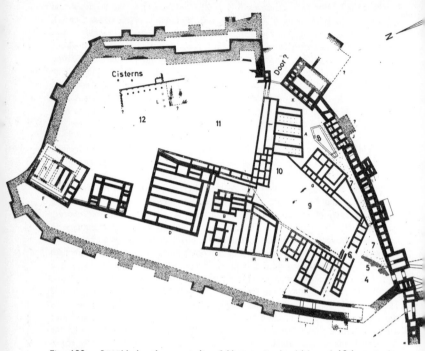

Fig. 138 – Büyükkale, the acropolis of Hattusa in the 14th and 13th centuries
B. C. 1) City Gate, built in the early Empire period (beginning of the 14th century).
2) Acropolis Gate (13th century B. C.). 3) Postern, 34 m. long, built on the corbelling
principle, with large Cyclopean stone blocks (beginning of the 14th century).
4) Lower courtyard of the Acropolis. 5) Road paved with red marble slabs,
stretching from the Acropolis Gate to the South-West Hall (13th century B. C.).
6) South-West Hall, portico giving access to the acropolis (13th century B. C.).
The walls beneath the portico date from the early Empire period (beginning of
the 14th century B. C.). 7) Broad, well-paved road running parallel to the south
fortifications on the inside (13th century B. C.). This has been uncovered for a
length of 40 m. 8) Basin, in which votive offerings were found; probably used for
ritual purposes (13th century B. C.). 9) Middle Courtyard (13th century) surrounded
by Buildings M, N, H, B, 10, A, G, 6. The courtyard seems to have played the
role of an important square for public and official meetings, and may be regarded
as a kind of "State Agora". A) Archives of the Hittite Empire (13th century).
The oldest building in history known to have been built as a library. The main
structure is 32 m. long and consists of store-rooms on the ground floor. In the
four southern rooms, double rows of rectangular limestone pillar bases have been
uncovered, but some of these have since disappeared. The pillars and the walls
of the rooms shared the support of the first floor. A staircase leading to this was

probably installed in the easternmost and narrowest room, in which no pillar bases have been found. Most of the 3,350 clay tablets inscribed with cuneiform writing, which have been preserved either whole or in fragments, were found in the three southern rooms. The tablets stood on end, like modern books, on wooden shelves fitted along the walls. Labels were discovered, also in clay, indicating the contents of the tablets, for instance, "Tablets concerning the deeds of Mursili" or "Thirty-two tablets concerning the Purulli festival of the city of Nerik". **G)** *This structure, as the remains show, was embellished with limestone and granite orthostats, as well as with mural paintings; therefore it can be considered one of the most important buildings of the acropolis. (13th century B. C.).* **M)** *Built in the 13th century B. C. and preceded by a pillared hall, this building was probably reserved for administrative and official purposes.* **N)** *From its tripartite ground plan, this building can be identified as a monumental gateway of the 13th century. It is comparable with the gate-houses of the temple of the Storm God at Hattusa (Fig. 140) and of the temple at Yazılıkaya (Figs. 143, 150), which follow similar schemes. It seems that the "processional way" reached the courtyard of the public and official buildings (9) through Gatehouse N. Actually the front of the Citadel Gate is not oriented in the same direction as the entrance to the South-West Hall (6) but rather overlooks the road skirting Buildings M, N, H, C, D, E and F.* **B, H)** *The function of these two buildings dating from the 13th century is unknown.* **C)** *This 13th century structure may be taken to have been a small shrine, since jugs, plates, beakers, and shells, probably all votive offerings, were found in its central room.* **D)** *The largest structure on the acropolis so far unearthed. It dates from the 13th century and measures 39 × 48 m. The ground floor was occupied by narrow, rectangular rooms. As Rudolf Naumann suggests, the first floor probably comprised a spacious audience hall with a wide view of the surrounding landscape, including the temple of the Weather God of Hatti.* **E)** *Building E, erected in the 13th century, was very probably a small reception hall. With its almost symmetrical ground plan, this edifice is entirely different from the other buildings at Hattusa and recalls the Bit Hilani type of building first encountered in the plan of Niqmepa's palace (15th or 14th century) at Tell Açana near Antakya.* **F)** *Building F, constructed in the 13th century in the north-west corner of the citadel, may be regarded as one of the private houses used by the royal family. Its dominating and strategic position above the highway leading to the capital and the magnificent view it commands in three directions must have made it a very suitable residence for the Great Kings.* **10)** *The Palace Gate, built in the 13th century B. C. displays the same triple ground plan, with three rooms along each side, as observed in Building N. It gave access to the upper courtyard in the palace area.* **11)** *The palace buildings proper were situated in the highest part of the acropolis.* **12)** *The summit has been levelled off over a wide area. Holes in the rock marking the positions of pillars are still visible.*

The foundations and remains of walls belonging to structures built of roughly cut small stones situated on the south and south-west slopes of the acropolis go back to the Phrygian period. They date from the 7th and 6th centuries B. C. The narrow paved road leading up for a stretch of 45 m., winding its way from a well at the foot of the acropolis as far as the gate to the citadel in the south-west, is also a Phrygian construction dating from the 7th century B. C.

Fig. 139 – Boğazköy. Yer Kapı, i.e., the central portion of the southern fortifications, with the Sphinx Gate and the big postern (beginning of the 14th century B. C.). On the east and west, the city was naturally defended by steep slopes which are absent in the centre of the south side. Therefore, the Hittite architects constructed a strong bulwark for offensive sorties in this weak section. The 70 m. - long postern beneath the Sphinx Gate served as a sally port against the enemy. The outer door of this subterranean tunnel, built on the corbel system and employing huge Cyclopean stone blocks, is visible in the centre of the picture. When this section of the defence works was in danger, Hittite warriors used this tunnel and descended the two steep stairways on both sides of the gateway in order to attack the enemy from the rear. One of the towers stood on the axis of the postern, flanked by sphinxes on the inner side. Three of these sphinxes were found during the excavations. Of the two sphinxes formerly adorning the gateway on the city side, one is now in Berlin, the other in Istanbul. Parts of the third sphinx are still observable in situ.

Fig. 140 – The Temple of Weather God of Hatti and the Sun Goddess of Arinna. 13th. century B. C. Drawing, based on the plan of P. Neve (MDOG 1969 p. 5 Fig. 1). The entire complex, including the storerooms surrounding the temple proper, measures 160 × 135 m. in area. This large precinct seems to be encircled by a temenos wall, a part of which has been uncovered in the northern area of the sanctuary. The main entrance to the precinct of the temple lies on the southeast side of the complex; both the doorway built of huge blocks and the two sentry rooms flanking it, are preserved only in parts. During religious festivals, processions passed through this propylon and entered the courtyard surrounding the sanctuary proper. The temple was approached by the monumental gate building which lies to its south (opposite room 65 on the plan). The temple had three additional entrances : one on the south front (between room 64 and 71 a), one on the west (40) and one on the east (17) sides. They were most certainly reserved for the personnel attached to the sanctuary. The narrow rooms surrounding the temple served several purposes and, especially, provided storage space for provisions and for the sanctuary treasure. Many storage jars, resembling those in Cretan and Mycenaean palaces, were found in situ, arranged in two rows (Pl. 93 b). Some of these jars bear incised signs indicating their capacity. Others have real impressions with hieroglyphs. In the south-east storerooms and also in rooms 10 to 12 there were found, in 1907, thousands of cuneiform tablets. The extremely narrow form of the storerooms suggest that they supported upper structures.

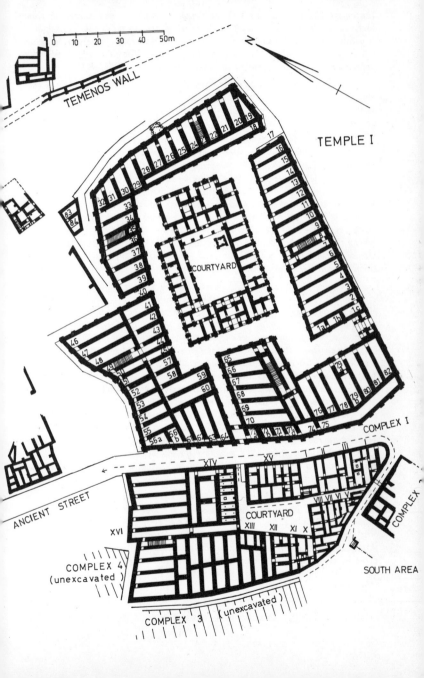

0 10 20 30 40 50m

N

TEMENOS WALL

TEMPLE I

COURTYARD

COMPLEX I

COMPLEX 2

ANCIENT STREET

XIV

XV

COURTYARD

XVI

XIII XII XI X

VIII VII VI V

III

COMPLEX 4
(unexcavated)

SOUTH AREA

COMPLEX 3 (unexcavated)

The topography of the area where the temple is erected slopes downwards from south to north. This must have made it necessary to build the surrounding structures in several stories. It seems that the west, south and east sides were two-tiered while the north side had three floors. The stairs which led to the upper stories can still be traced in several rooms (8, 23, 35, 49).

The temple itself consists of an entrance on the south front, a series of rectangular rooms surrounding a courtyard, and an annex of twelve ritual chambers on the north-east. The main building is of limestone, while the sacred annex is of granite (Fig. 141).

The gate building (opposite room 65) is an architectural unit in itself, exhibiting a tri-partite ground plan, with rooms arranged in threes for the length and breadth of the building. After crossing a monolithic threshold, one entered a small vestibule connecting two rooms, one on the left and one on the right, both of which opened onto the courtyard attached to the encircling store - houses. Then came the central room of the entrance, flanked by two sentry rooms. Beyond the middle room was a second vestibule, again with a room on either side, which had access to the temple courtyard. In sharp contrast to the markedly symmetrical ground plan of the entrance is the assymmetrical arrangement of the rectangular rooms surrounding the temple courtyard. The rooms in the western aisle differ from those in the eastern aisle, both in shape and in number.

In the north east corner of the paved courtyard of the temple lie the remains of a "wash house", mentioned in tablets dealing with the ceremonies held in Hittite temples. According to these texts, the king passed through a "hilammar" (gateway), crossed a "hilas" (courtyard) and washed his hands before entering the holy of holies, where he conducted the ritual ceremonies. A portico, opening onto the courtyard through three pillars, gave access to the sacred complex of the temple. In the large north-eastern room of this annex stands a stone base which probably supported the statue of the Sun Goddess of Arinna. The large north-western room which has recently been uncovered must have contained the cult statue of the Weather God of Hatti. As the excavators have rightly pointed out, the equal size and the symmetrical position of the two large rooms reveal that the temple was consecrated to the Weather God of Hatti and the Sun Goddess of Arinna. These deities are, indeed, represented side by side on the north wall of the sanctuary of Yazılıkaya (Fig. 151), depicting the alliance between the autochthonous Hattian Goddess Wurusemu (Sun Goddess of Arinna), and the Indo - European god of the Hittites (Akurgal, The Birth of Greek Art. 208; Späthethitische Bildkunst, p. 111 - 118).

Each temple room possessed at least one window, set into the exterior wall. These windows almost reached floor level (Fig. ~~114~~). The room with the stone base projects in such a way that the cult statue would have received sunlight on three sides. The other cult room, which possessed four windows, also received constant sunlight. This love of light suggests that, originally, Hittite religious ceremonies were held in the open air, as was the case in the sanctuary at Yazılıkaya (Fig. 144).

The temple was constructed of stone only in its lower part, and this is entirely preserved (Fig. 141). The upper part consisted of sun-dried bricks. The rows of round holes seen on the upper surface of the top stone blocks, served to mortise the horizontally placed beams of the wooden frame, strengthening the mud-brick construction. The temple was covered with a flat roof, also composed of mud-brick.

In 1967 and 1968, the German expedition carried out excavations in the southern area of the temple, which yielded important results. They uncovered a street, eight metres wide, paved with large slabs of hard limestone and extending along the south-west front of the temple precinct. They also found several complexes of storerooms and other buildings surrounding a courtyard. Although the complexes show an irrational plan, as in the Cretan palaces, several groups of rooms can be discerned. Group XIV comp.'ises two large rooms and seven rooms in a row, the central one being larger than the six other rooms. This larger room has a monolithic base in its northern section and a pilaster on its south wall, while the six rooms each have two sandstone bases on their middle axes. The excavators believe that this group of rooms served some purpose connected with the religious and administrative activities of the whole sanctuary. In this complex, a half-preserved cuneiform tablet was found bearing one column with a list. According to Professor Bittel it reads: "Altogether two hundred and eight persons of the É GIS KIN-TI, eighteen of whom are priests, twenty-nine musicians, nineteen scribes of clay tablets, thirty-three scribes of wooden tablets, thirty-five priests of divination, ten singers in Hurrian". This list totals one hundred and forty-four persons.

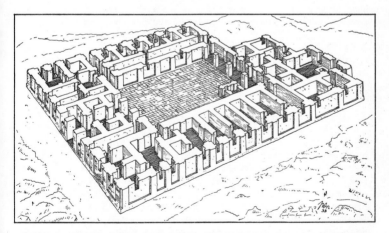

Fig. 141 – Temple of the Weather God of Hatti at Boğazköy (erected in the 14th century B. C.). As seen in this picture, the lower part of the temple was built of stone blocks, while the upper part was of mud brick. Round holes arranged in rows on the upper surfaces of the stone blocks held the horizontally-placed beams of the wooden frame that strengthened the mud-brick construction.

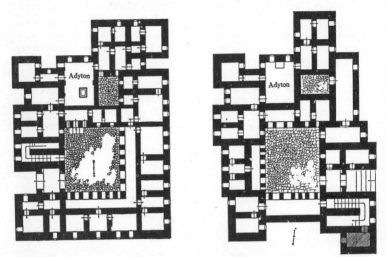

Fig. 142 – Ground plans of Temples II and III at Boğazköy. The four 13th century-temples located in the southern part of the city (Fig. 137, Nos. 7-10) have ground plans similar to that of Temple I (Fig. 140). The rooms marked "adyton" each contain a stone base which once supported a statue of the Weather God.

YAZILIKAYA

The national sanctuary of the Hittite Empire, today called Yazılıkaya, lies 2 km. north-east of Hattusa (Boğazköy). It was a natural rock shrine, open to the sky. The temple buildings later erected in front of this cult area display remains of three different periods. The accompanying ground plan (Fig. 143), howe-ver, shows only the second phase of the temple. Nevertheless, an examina-tion of the ruins on the spot reveals that at the lowest level was a simple en-closing wall, which separated the rock shrine from the outside world in the first period. In the second phase a temple was built in the canonical type of Hittite sanctuaries ((Fig. 143) developed in Hattusa (Figs. 140 - 142). A gate-house (Fig. 143 c) was constructed at this time, similar to the gateway in the Great Temple at Hattusa (Fig. 140), which served as a monumental entrance to the sanctuary. During the same phase, a gateway was erected in front of the small gallery (Fig. 143 E). In the third period, the east wing of the main building (Fig. 154) was altered to accommodate the construction of a more appropriate entrance in front of the small gallery. The temple of

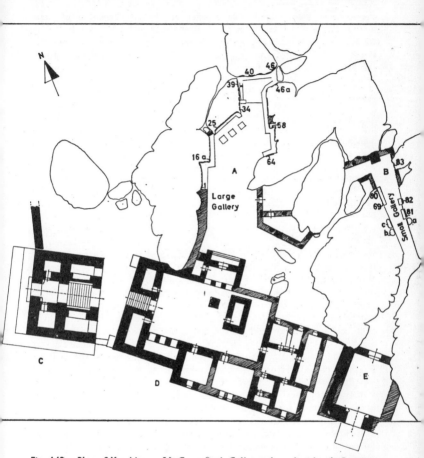

Fig. 143 – Plan of Yazılıkaya. **A)** *Great Rock-Gallery adorned with reliefs representing 63 Hittite divinities. Probably erected by Hattusili III (1275-1250 B. C.).*
B) *Small Rock-Gallery, a mortuary temple reserved for the royal cult. Probably
erected by Tudhaliya IV (1250-1220 B. C.).* **C)** *Monumental Gateway leading to
the temple (D), erected by Hattusili III.* **D)** *Main building of the temple. Probably
erected by Hattusili III (see p. 262).* **E)** *Entrance giving access to the small gallery.
Possibly it was erected by Tudhaliya IV.*

A third open-air chamber, connected with the Small Gallery and marked
C (not shown on our plan), was excavated last year. The function of this
room, which has no reliefs, is not known yet.

the second phase, like the sanctuaries at Hattusa, consisted of rooms surrounding a courtyard with a lustral chamber and a pillared hall giving access to the cult room (Fig. 143). However, religious ceremonies, which in the temple of Hattusa took place in closed rooms before the statue of the Storm God, were performed in the rock gallery in the open air, below reliefs representing almost the entire Hittite pantheon.

The west wall in the large gallery is adorned with reliefs of gods (Fig. 146, Nos. 1-39), while those on the east wall are devoted to goddesses (Fig. 146, Nos. 43-63). Both rows meet at the junction of these walls with the north wall (Fig. 146, Nos. 40-46 and Fig. 151). The division into male and female deities is not absolute; three goddesses can be discerned among the gods (Fig. 146, Nos. 36-38; Figs. 148, 149), and one god is noticeable in the row of females (No. 44). The central scene on the north wall depicts the chief divinities, which are described in the caption to Fig. 151.

A place of particular significance has been allotted to the relief of King Tudhaliya IV (1250-1220 B. C.). It is the largest relief in the gallery (Fig. 143, No. 64; Fig. 152), being 2.95 m. in height, one third more than that of the main scene, which is only 2.18 m. high. We may assume that Tudhaliya had his picture carved on the east wall overlooking the main scene because he was personally interested in the completion of the sanctuary. This was originally erected by his father Hattusili III (1275-1250 B. C.), in collaboration with Puduhepa, his ambitious mother. No doubt Puduhepa, who was a powerful queen and afterwards reigned with her son Tudhaliya IV, played an important part in the construction of this sanctuary. As Emmanuel Laroche has recognized, this contained, a magnificent representation of the Hittite pantheon, arranged according to the ceremonial order of the Hurrian religion. She was a princess of Kummanni in Kizzuwatna, one of the chief cult centres of the goddess Hepatu, who is depicted in the main scene at the sanctuary (Fig. 151, No. 43). Her very name betrays that she was a devotee of Hepatu. The Egyptian version of the treaty between Hattusili III and Rameses II describes the royal seal appearing on the Hittite silver tablet as showing the queen in the embrace of the Sun Goddess of Arinna, the Hittite counterpart of the Hurrian Hepatu. On the whole, however, the divinities were represented in their Anatolian Hittite character. Although the composition of the reliefs follows the ceremonial order observed in the Hurrian religion, the deities themselves are depicted entirely according to Hittite iconographic principles. A beholder from Hattusa would only see representations of Hittite deities before him. The artistic style of the reliefs is also wholly Hittite in character.

The small gallery, which was approached by a separate entrance (Fig. 143), also contains a number of relief sculptures in a good state of preservation (Figs. 154-157). Kurt Bittel and his colleagues, the excavators of Yazılıkaya, are of the opinion that this small gallery was dedicated to the cult of a dead king, either Tudhaliya II or III. Although this clever interpretation is in complete agreement with written sources and with the non-oriental character of the Hittite culture and religion, it would seem that this gallery was nevertheless reserved for the apotheosis of King Tudhaliya IV in his lifetime; for there are two portrayals of the monarch in the small gallery as well as the large relief in the main one. Apart from the magnificient relief sculpture in the small gallery showing the king in the embrace of the god Sharruma (Fig. 153), there was also a statue of him which is now lost, though its statue-base and cartouche on the wall still exist (Fig. 143, No. 83). It is significant that not only is the entrance directly opposite the statue-base, but, in addition, all the figures in the gallery are turned towards it (Figs. 153, 155, 156). Bearing in mind that the king was represented three times and that his reliefs and statue occupied the most important position in both galleries and, further, that he was depicted to the exclusion of all other rulers, one is inclined to assert that these images were made during his lifetime. On the other hand, none of these portrayals can have represented Tudhaliya III, who reigned from 1400 to 1380 B. C., Reliefs which reflect such a marked Hurrian influence and display such iconographical uniformity could only have been realised in the time of Puduhepa, the daughter of the high priest from the Hurrian country of Kizzuwatna. She had clay tablets from Kizzuwatna copied for the Hisuwa festivals. Consequently, Tudhaliya IV was introduced to the Hurrian religion in his mother's house. Thus he reorganised the Hittite state cult according to Hurrian rites. The stylistic differences between the three cartouches may have no chronological importance as they were probably carved by different sculptors or at different periods during the monarch's life. We, therefore, believe that the temple of the second phase, together with the reliefs of divinities in the large gallery, was built in the reign of Hattusili III (1275-1250 B. C.), and the relief of Tudhaliya (Fig. 152), the small gallery and the third phase of the temple were achievements of Tudhaliya IV (1250-1220 B. C.). The possibility that his son Arnuwanda IV (1220-1190 B. C.) could have erected the sanctuary is out of the question, for his reign fell in so troubled a period that he could hardly have been in a position to make artistic and religious undertakings of such magnitude.

The three rectangular niches in the small gallery may have contained the burial urns of the Hittite royal family, beginning with Hattusili III and his wife Puduhepa.

Fig. 144 – Rock sanctuary at Yazılıkaya. General view of the great gallery. The reliefs, which consist of 64 figures and represent 63 deities of the Hittite pantheon, were carved in the reign of Hattusili III (1275-1250 B. C.).

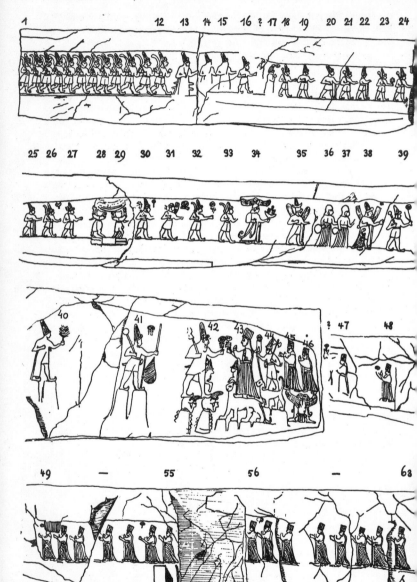

Fig. 146 – Rock sanctuary at Yazılıkaya. Sixty-three deities representing a reduced version of the "thousand gods" of the Hittite Empire.

The gods (**1-42**) are depicted on the west and the goddesses (**43-63**) on the east side of the gallery. The chief divinities are portrayed in the main scene on the north wall (**40-46**). As they appear in profile, they are generally described as being in a procession. However, it must be understood that, with the exception of the monument of Eflatunpınar, it was not customary in Hittite art to carve front views of figures. Therefore, we do not consider these deities to be marching in a procession nor advancing to meet one another. Rather, we believe that the artist meant his figures to be standing ceremonially in front of the beholder. The division into groups of male and female deities is not rigid. Three goddesses stand among the gods (**36-38**), and one god (**44**) is observed in the row of goddesses. The 42 gods represented start on the left of the entrance to the gallery with a relief consisting of 12 figures. **13-27**) These gods are not clearly identified. **28** and **29** show two bull men standing on the hieroglyphic symbol for the earth and supporting the sky. **34**) Representation of a deified king with the hieroglyphic signs of the Sun God of Heaven (see also Fig. 147). **35**) Moon God. **36, 37**) Ninatta and Kulitta, handmaids to Ishtar. **38**) Shaushga, the Hurrian Ishtar. **39**) Ea, Mesopotamian God of Water and an important deity in the Hurrian religion. **40**) God of Grain, holding an ear of corn. **41**) Weather God of Hattusa. **42**) Weather God of Heaven (Weather God of Hatti). **43**) Hepatu. **44**) Sharruma. **47**) Hutena. **48**) Hutellura. **49**) Nabarbi. **56**) A sculptured block representing Ishtar-Shaushga, found in Yekbaz, a neighbouring village, now leaning against the wall below the row of goddesses. Very probably originally from the gap between 55 and 56.

Fig. 147 – Personification of the divine kingship. This relief at Yazılıkaya represents the figure of a king with hieroglyphic symbols of the Sun God of Heaven (Fig. 146, No. 34). Kingship is indicated by the winged sun-disc and the kalmush, the long staff curved at the end. Both of these, according to the texts, were signs of sovereignty. The round skull-cap and the cloak further identify this figure as a monarch. (See also the portrayals of Tudhaliya, Figs. 152, 153). On the other hand, the hieroglyphic symbols designate him as the Sun God of Heaven. Owing to the absence of ideograms for an individual name, this figure seems to be the image of a deified ruler in a general sense. Consequently, it symbolically represented the monarch in power in each period.

Figs. 148, 149 – Ishtar, accompanied by her attendants (Fig. 146; Nos. 38, 37, 36). The great Babylonian goddess Ishtar was worshipped in Anatolia under the Hurrian name of Shaushga. She was the sister of Teshup and held sway as the Goddess of Law and War. She appears here with her attendants, the goddesses Ninatta and Kulitta, as the Hurrian Goddess of War. In her place among the male deities at Yazılıkaya, she wears, like them, a pointed cap with one horn and bears an axe (this is absent in the illustration given here). She was represented unarmed in the row of female deities at Yazılıkaya, in her capacity as the Goddess of Law. The latter relief now rests on the ground below the figures of the female divinities. The hieroglyphic ideograms accompanying the two portrayals of the goddess are identical.

Fig. 150 – Yazılıkaya. Monumental gateway as restored (see Fig. 143, C).

Fig. 151 – The main scene in the shrine at Yazılıkaya (see Fig. 146, Nos. 40-46 and Fig. 144). **41)** Weather God of Hattusa, standing on two mountain peaks. **42)** Weather God of Heaven, astride the deified mountains, Nanni and Hazzi. He possessed two sacred bulls called Serri and Hurri, one of which accompanies him here, while the other is shown with his consort Hepat (43). In the Hurrian language, Serri and Hurri mean, respectively, day and night. Hazzi is the Mons Cassius near Antakya, which was in Hurrian country. In view of these religious elements and the Hurrian name of his spouse (43), one may be sure the god was intended to be known by his Hurrian appellation, that is, "Teshub", although his name appears here in the usual Hittite ideograms, which mean the "Weather God of Heaven". As the highest ranking god in the hierarchy, his cap is adorned with five superimposed god-ideograms (half ellipses) and six horns at the front and back, while the Weather God of Hattusa (41) and the god Sharruma (44) are permitted to wear pointed caps with only six frontal horns in the chief god's presence. **43)** The leading female deity of the Hittite Empire, the Sun Goddess of Arinna, wife of the Weather God of Heaven, bears the Hurrian name of Hepatu, at Yazılıkaya clearly written in the hieroglyphic script as it should be pronounced. Like the other female deities, she wears a high polos, ending in the form of a Greek city crown; but hers is much higher than those of the other goddesses. She is shown standing on a panther. **44)** The God Sharruma. He usually appears with his mother Hepatu. The Hurrian texts record that he is the son of Teshub. Like his mother, he also stands on a panther. He carries a long-handled axe, resting on his shoulder. **45, 46)** The two goddesses standing on a double-headed eagle have not been identified as yet. The three divinities Nos. 42-44 form a triad, composed of father, mother, and son. When participating in the erection of this sanctuary, the ambitious Puduhepa probably identified her husband Hattusili III with Teshub, herself with Hepatu and her son Tudhaliya IV with Sharruma.

Fig. 152 – A place of particular significance in the great gallery is occupied by the relief (No. 64) of King Tudhaliya IV (1250-1220 B. C.). It is the largest relief in the gallery. He is represented armed, wearing a skull-cap and holding in his left hand a kalmush, the sign of sovereignty. The two antithetic hieroglyphs in the form of an Ionic capital mean "Great King". The name of this king, which was originally that of a sacred mountain, is expressed by the figure in the middle and the sign below it. Since other holy mountains existed, such as Arnuwanda and Ammuna, and all were represented by the same figure as this appearing here, the sculptore has added the signe below it, which corresponds phonetically with the syllable "tu". Thus the beholder understood that this picture represented King Tudhaliya. Standing on two mountain peaks, Tudhaliya is depicted here as a deified king. According to Hittite texts, a king became a god after death. However, the impression of a seal, found in Ras Shamra, in which he is shown wearing a pointed cap adorned with horns, clearly reveals that Tudhaliya allowed himself to be represented as a god. Therefore, this picture of Tudhaliya at Yazılıkaya was quite possibly carved in his lifetime.

Fig. 153 – The scene in which the god Sharruma holds King Tudhaliya in his embrace is one of the most beautiful reliefs in the sanctuary at Yazılıkaya (Fig. 143, small gallery, No. 81). As understood from the testament of Hattusili I, the embrace was a gesture signifying honour and protection. Sharruma's pointed cap is adorned with god-ideograms, unlike the plainer one he is shown wearing in his portrayal in the main scene in the great gallery (Fig. 151, No. 44). This is possibly because he is not in the presence of the Weather God of Heaven and, therefore, can allow himself to wear headgear showing marks of a higher rank. However, his cap is not adorned at the back, and so still possesses fewer horns than that of the Weather God of Heaven. Thus the hierarchy is respected. The hieroglyphs of Sharruma, indicating his name, consist of a god-ideogram and a headless body.

Güterbock interpreted them as Sharruma not only because this figure, following
Hepatu (Fig. 151, No. 44), is, according to the texts, most probably Sharruma, but
also because the two parallel strokes on either side of his shoulders are to be read
as "ma". The same sign occurs as the last syllable of the hieroglyphic signs of
the name "Suppiluliuma", which was deciphered with the assistance of bilingual
inscriptions on royal seals found in the excavations at Hattusa.

This relief is an exquisite example of Hittite art. We may admire the mastery
of the calligraphic outlines, which were the strong point of the Hittite sculptors.
The pyramidal composition is most successful. The figures rest on a rhythmic
horizontal line, achieved by the alignment of up-turned shoes. The vertical edges
of the garments and the ruler's staff merge into the rounded forms of the bodies
of the king and the god. The pointed cap of the god, with its superimposed horns
and god-ideograms, counterbalances the horizontal rhythm of up-turned shoes
with a vertical movement and with its harmonious proportions provides a graceful
finale to the entire composition.

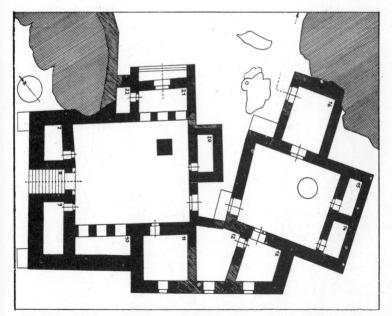

Fig. 154 – Temple of Yazılıkaya. Third phase. Probably erected by Tudhaliya
IV (see Fig. 143).

Fig. 155 – The relief of twelve gods in the small gallery (Fig. 143, Nos. 69-80) is in a very good state of preservation. It is covered with a brownish yellow patina, like the figures of Ninatta and Kulitta (Fig. 148) and that of the deified Tudhaliya (Fig. 156). The Hittite sculptor has achieved the effect of figures marching side by side in parade by the device of overlapping the limbs.

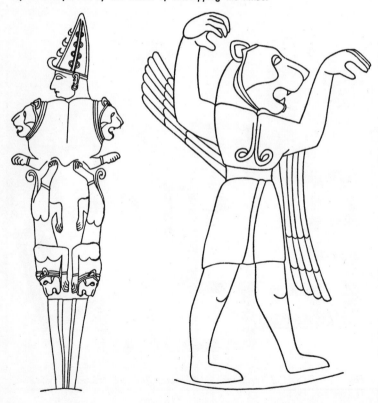

Fig. 156 – Up to the present there has been no satisfactory answer concerning the religious significance of the Sword God (Fig. 143, No. 82).

Fig. 157 – Two hybrid figures, depicted on either side of the entrance (Fig. 143, Nos. 67-68 not shown, however, on our plan) giving access to the smaller gallery, were supposed to protect, in an apotropaic sense, the mortuary chamber reserved for royal cult.

ALACAHÖYÜK

During the summer, when the evenings are long, visitors to Boğazköy can easily stop to see Alacahöyük on the return journey. Alacahöyük, with its still extant sphinx gate, its interesting architectural remains and its local museum, is certainly an archaeological site that is well worth seeing. We mention here that, in the caption to plate 93 a, the Sphinx Gate, wrongly said to be at Yazılıkaya, should read Alacahöyük.

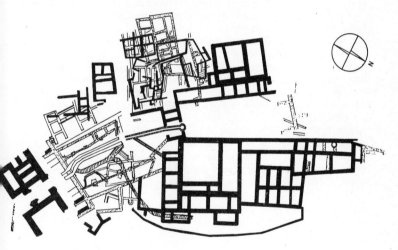

Fig. 158 – General plan of Alacahöyük

Alacahöyük was an important centre as far back as the Chalcolithic Age, that is, from the 4th millennium on. Artifacts dating from this period and brought to light by Hamit Koşay are in the Ankara Museum.

The settlement reached the peak of its importance in the Early Bronze Age. During Turkish excavations initiated thirty-five years ago by Atatürk, archaeologists Remzi Oğuz Arık and Hamit Koşay unearthed one of the most valuable artistic treasures of ancient times. These fascinating works of gold, silver and bronze, including mysterious standards, now form an unrivalled collection in the Ankara Museum (Pls. 84 b, 85, 87).

The Hittite era, too, witnessed glorious times in Alacahöyük. The remains which are still standing at the present day (Fig. 158) belong to the Hittite Empire period (1450-1180 B. C.). The sphinxes (Pl. 93 a) guarding the city gate can be seen on the spot, while the orthostats decorating the city wall have been removed to the museum in Ankara. However, they are now replaced by concrete casts. On the left side of the entrance facing east, we see from right to left on the orthostats: 1 - King and Queen, worshipping a bull. 2 - Animals for the sacrifice. 3 - Priests. 4 - Jugglers (sword - swallower and a man climbing a ladder that stands up in the air. 5 - Musicians. 6 - Unfinished relief, representing a bull and a chariot (?).

On the right side of the entrance is depicted, in sitting position, the Sun Goddess of Arinna (?), the main female deity, worshipped by a number of adorants. The six male figures depicted on the southward-facing wall inside the entrance, may also represent adorants, venerating the Sun Goddess of Arinna, who is seen on the aforementioned orthostat of the east front. The meaning of the scene with four persons, depicted on the northward-facing wall inside the entrance, is unknown. The inward-looking sides of the sphinx - blocks were also adorned with reliefs. However, the relief of the southern sphinx-block is entirely broken away; that of the northern sphinx-block is partly preserved; it represented a female divinity supported by a double - headed eagle, gripping two hares in its talons. From the standpoint of stylistic peculiarities, these reliefs belong to an artistic school differing widely from that found at Boğazköy. Adjoining the east wall of the city is a large building resembling a temple rather than a palace, with a courtyard, measuring 18-20 m. in width and 80 m. in length. The examples uncovered at Hattusa clearly indicate that in Hittite cities the large structures served religious purposes, while the palaces were comparatively small. An excellent model showing the superimposed cultural levels of Alacahöyük is exhibited in the middle hall of the Ankara Archaeological Museum.

KÜLTEPE (KANESH)

One of the most important ancient settlements in Turkey is situated at Kültepe, which has been successfully excavated by Professor Tahsin Özgüç since 1948. The numerous finds of exquisite beauty and considerable historical value which were brought to light in Kültepe, are among the finest works of art exhibited in the Ankara Museum. The following description has been prepared by Professor Özgüç.

Kültepe is situated 20 kms. north-east of ancient Mazaka, called Kayseri in modern times. Here was established the capital city of Cappadocia on the main route that formerly connected the east and the west. Situated in the centre of the fertile Kayseri plain, Kültepe, one of the largest ruins of ancient Anatolia, is composed of two main sections. The mound of Kültepe which is 20 m. higher than the level plain and which has a diameter of 500 m., forms the first part; the second part is an area, 1500 m. long and 1000 m. wide, which covers the trading centre built on the north-eastern, eastern and south-eastern rims of the mound (Fig. 159).

The primary importance of Kültepe, in relation to history, is its being the site of the earliest Anatolian written documents. The first appearance of Anatolia into the light of history was in this era and through these documents. The clay tablets were written in an ancient Assyrian dialect, using the cuneiform script.

At the beginning of the 2nd millennium B. C., Anatolia enjoyed one of the most prosperous periods in its history. The Assyrians who inhabited Northern Mesopotamia, established great trading outposts in Anatolia which they called Karums. Among these, the Karum of Kanesh was the controlling centre to which all the other Karums were subordinate; in its turn, it was directly connected to Assur. Using routes through Assūr - Diyarbakır - Malatya - Kayseri, or Assur - Urfa - Adana - the pass of Külek, Assyrian merchants imported tin, garments, and cloth by means of caravans of 200-250 donkeys, and sold their goods to the native people, in exchange for gold and silver. The Assyrians did not exercise power or influence of a political or administrative nature in Anatolia. To the local princes who ruled Anatolia at that period, the merchants were obliged to pay taxes, in return for a guarantee of safety. The majority of the written documents are commercial, economic and legal in nature; in addition, there are some historical and literary texts. The envelopes in which these letters, contracts or deeds were placed, bore cylindrical seal impressions, belonging to such people involved in these business transactions as the lender, the borrower and the witnesses. In this manner, the habit of using cylindrical seals, widely practised in Mesopotamia, where they constituted the basis of art, was introduced to Anatolia, along with writing. This stimulated the native craftsmen to create very evolved examples of this branch of art, and to develop a native style.

The natives and the princes of Kanesh inhabited the mound, while the foreign traders lived at the Karum, which was somewhat in the nature of a lower city. However, the Assyrian merchants mixed with the natives, and intermarriages took place.

Karum, the settlement of the Assyrian merchants. The Karum occupies four building levels, the last of which occurs in two phases. In Level IV, which is the earliest and which is built on virgin soil, and in the subsequent Level III, writing is unknown. The most advanced phase, called the "Assyrian Trading Colonies Age" in Anatolian history, is represented by Level II, and dates approximately from 1950 to 1850 B. C. At this level, quarters were formed by a close arrangement of regular buildings around squares and streets. The houses have stone foundations and mud-brick walls; wood was also used extensively as a building material. The houses are spacious in their accommodation. The majority have 3-4 or 5-6 rooms and a wide hall.

The archive-rooms are separated from the living rooms, which, in their turn, are distinct from the bedrooms, the kitchens and the store-rooms. By means of the archives, it is possible for us to learn the owners' identities, and to establish their Assyrian or native origins. The great fire which destroyed the city barely allowed the inhabitants to escape with their lives, and to save what they had on their persons; all kinds of household utensils, marvellously evolved pottery, animal-shaped drinking cups and statuettes were abandoned, waiting for future discovery. The houses of this level, which had one or two storeys, were uncovered in good condition; this has considerably simplified the task of reconstructing the site. So far, 15,000 tablets and envelopes have been discovered at this level, which represents the most brilliant phase of the Assyrian Trading Colonies. As the dead were buried in their own houses, burial gifts were discovered as well. Rich with gifts, stone cist-graves are found in all quarters of the city.

The reason for the burning of the city and the identity of its destroyers are not known. The place remained deserted for 40-50 years after the destruction of Level II, when finally, in approximately 1800 B. C., people of the same origin built city Ib upon the debris. The new city is contemporary with Hammurabi the Great, King of Babylon. In Level Ib, the houses were built very close together. The plans are more spacious and the number of rooms has been increased. The number of houses with wide rooms and with large store-rooms is considerable. In spite of the fact that there are few written documents, this level enjoyed at least as much prosperity as Level II. It was likewise destroyed in a great fire. However, as the use of wood as a building material was less common here than stone, the destructive force of the fire was diminished. On both levels, the Karum was surrounded by a city wall, with a diameter of no less than 2000-2500 m. After its second destruction, the importance of the Karum of Kanesh entirely waned; it was abandoned as an area of inhabitation and was left in ruins. With the end of this settlement, the Assyrian language and cuneiform script ceased to be used in Anatolia.

The houses of Levels II and Ib can be observed together at Excavation area No. I, situated at the centre of the Karum; in Excavation area No. 2, Levels Ib, II, III, and IV are all represented together, while area No. 3 covers the houses, roads and squares of Level II exclusively (Fig. 159).

During the Age of the Assyrian Trading Colonies, the Anatolian people not only mastered the foremost invention of human history, namely writing, but also established connections with the Mesopotamian civilization, which constitutes the basis of all ancient civilizations. In this manner the indigenous people of Anatolia found a means to develop their way of thinking, their philosophy of life and their art. Through contact with and assimilation of ancient Mesopotamian art, a new Anatolian style came into being, which is called "Hittite Art" by archaeologists (see p. 7). After the Karum area fell into decay for obscure historical reasons, habitation of the mound continued.

The settlement of the autochthonous people. The mound of Kültepe was inhabited from the 4th millennium B. C. on, that is, from the Chalcolithic Age, to the end of the Roman period. With its spacious buildings, its large alabaster idols, fashioned into a single body and many heads, its statuettes, either clothed or naked, and its painted pottery, Kültepe was one of the most important sites of Anatolia in the Early Bronze Age, especially in the late phase (2500-2000 B. C.). At Kanesh, which was the capital of the Kingdom of Kanesh during the Age of the Assyrian Trading Colonies, princes lived on the mound, within the city walls in great palaces which have been unearthed during excavations. Still intact, the palaces form a great complex, possessing wide courts faced with stone, large halls, long corridors and suites used by the princes, and for the administrative functions of the kingdom (Fig. 159).

Fig. 159 – Plan of Kültepe (courtesy of Professor Tahsin Özgüç).
The houses of Levels Ib and II can be observed together in area 1. In excavation area 2, Levels Ib, II, III and IV are all represented together, while area 3 covers the houses, roads and squares of level II exclusively.

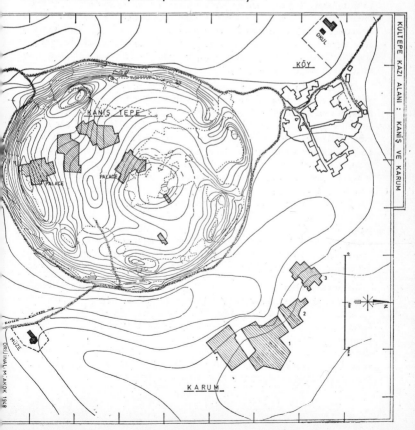

After the Assyrian Trading Colonies Age, Kültepe lost much of its political and economic importance and was unable to re-achieve the status of a great centre during the Old Hittite or Hittite Imperial periods.

During the Neo-Hittite Age, from 1000 B. C., Kültepe was one of the foremost cities of the country called the Kingdom of Tabal by the Assyrians. However, the city was considerably destroyed during the Hellenistic and Roman ages; consequently it has not been possible to find traces of the palaces, decorated with sculptured slabs, the existence of which we know. In spite of this, sculpture, painted pottery and seals have been discovered in sufficient abundance to indicate the importance of Kültepe during this era. During the Hellenistic and Roman periods, Kültepe was one of the most important cities of Cappadocia despite its closeness to Kayseri.

The first excavation of the Kültepe mound was started by the French explorer, Ernst Chantre, in the years 1893-1894. He was succeeded in 1906 by H. Winckler, the discoverer of the Boğazköy archives. B. Hrozny, who made a great contribution to archaeological knowledge by deciphering Hittite cuneiform script, performed the first excavations at Karum in 1925. Unfortunately, the excavations were not carried out systematically, as their sole objective was to discover tablets, and thus caused a great deal of destruction. The first systematic excavations of the mound and of the Karum area were begun under the auspices of the Turkish Historical Association and the General Directorate of Antiquities and Museums in 1948, and have since been regularly continued.

Sultan Han. In the vicinity of Kültepe, there are two Seljuk buildings which have an unforgettable effect on visitors. The first is situated on the Kayseri-Sivas road, 47 km. from Kayseri. It was built by the great Seljuk Sultan, Alâeddin Keykubad I., during the years 1232-1236, and is one of the most splendid examples of Seljuk civic architecture. Karavanserais were built along important trade routes for the caravans to rest overnight. A mosque stands at the centre of the karavanserai's great courtyard, which is surrounded on three sides by chambers that serve as bedrooms for travellers, store-rooms, administrative rooms and a baths complex. The left side of the entrance contains arcades, open to the courtyard; rooms were also built beyond the arcades, on the right-hand side. Winter quarters were sited within the portal and were covered with barrel-vaults, supported by thick stone pillars. The Karavanserai was built with regular stone blocks, and reinforced by towers. The entire surface of the portal, the mosque and its mihrab are adorned with beautiful ornaments of Seljuk art.

Karatay Han. This Karavanserai is situated 50 kms. east of Kayseri and is on the Kayseri-Malatya highway. It was built by the great Seljuk vizier, Celâlettin Karatay, in the year 1240-1241. The walls of the building are entirely faced with regular stone blocks. The plan is identical to that of the Sultan Han, except for the position of the mosque, which is not in the centre of the courtyard, but at the front, to the right of the entrance. This Karavanserai is an exceptionally handsome building owing its beauty to its perfect architectural design and to the high quality of its ornamentation.

Acemhöyük : One of the important ancient sites of Anatolia ending with a rich Early Hittite level (2000-1750 B. C.), is Acemhöyük. The site is now being excavated with excellent results by Professor Nimet Özgüç. Mrs. Özgüç has kindly contributed the following note.

"The settlement is situated 225 km. to the south of Ankara, and is 18 kms. to the north-west of Aksaray (the ancient Garsaura, Archaleia). It is on the southern bank of Tuz Gölü (Salt Lake) and is in the town of Yeşilova. It is west of the Ankara-Adana highway and is 10 kms. to the north of the main east-west highway which connects Kayseri to Konya.

Acemhöyük had been a settlement area since the Chalcolithic and Early Bronze Ages, but its most brilliant phase occurred during the age of the Assyrian trading colonies. Apart from private houses, the discoveries of the period include a monumental palace which was destroyed by a great fire. The foundations were made of stone, while the walls were constructed of mudbrick and reinforced with wooden beams. So far, only 40 of the palace's rooms have been uncovered. The ruins are still intact and indicate it to be the largest Anatolian palace of this age. The discoveries in the rooms include ivory works of art that belonged to furniture, crystal and obsidian vases, bronze objects and also large quantities of stamp seal impressions on clay bullae. Some rooms were full of large pithoi used for storage purposes. After the first quarter of the second millenium B. C., Acemhöyük lost its importance and was not inhabited for a long time. The south-western part of the mound reappeared as a settlement during the Hellenistic and Roman ages. The objects from Acemhöyük are being preserved and exhibited in the Ankara Archaeological Museum. A very fine collection of ivories, obtained from illegal diggings, is in the Metropolitan Museum of Art in New York."

❋

THE SOUTHERN MEDITERRANEAN COAST
(Districts between Antalya and Adana)

Those wishing to visit the ruins along the southern coast of Anatolia are advised to go by way of Konya and see the impressive monuments in this centre of Seljuk culture. The Konya Museum is also of importance as it houses works representative of indigenous Anatolian civilizations. A photograph of a fine sculptural work in the Konya Museum, namely, a columnar sarcophagus (Pl. 15 b, 94) is included in this book. Two ancient monuments well worth seeing are the Hittite sanctuary of Eflatunpınar (13th century B. C.) at Beyşehir and the Ivriz relief at Ereğli (Pl. 2).

Proceeding from west to east along the Mediterranean coast, the ancient settlements most worth seeing are Termessos, Attaleia (Antalya), Perge, Silyon, Aspendos, Side, Alanya, Anamur, Silifke, Uzuncaburç (Diocaesarea= Olba), Korasion, Korykos, Mersin, Tarsus, Adana, Karatepe and Antakya. This book deals with the most important of these, and those that are comparatively easy to visit.

Antalya (Attaleia). This city, founded by Attalos II, King of Pergamon (159-138 B. C.), is particularly worth seeing because of the Archaeological Museum and Hadrian's Gate (Fig. 160). In addition, it is a charming, characteristically Turkish city with picturesque streets and houses, and attractive minarets and mosques.

The archaeological Museum of Antalya is one of the most important local museums of Turkey. The numerous and splendid sculptural works of the Roman period, excavated by Arif Müfit Mansel in Perge, are kept in this museum. The broken heads of the "headless statues" in the garden are kept in the central hall of the museum. The beautiful head of a statue of Aphrodite found at Perge and depicted in this book (Pl. 97), is also in the Antalya museum. The caption to this head I owe to Professor Jale Inan.

Fig. 160 – City gate of Attaleia (after G. Niemann). Time of Hadrian (A. D. 117-138).

TERMESSOS

Termessos is one of the best preserved and most attractive archaeological sites in Turkey. Since the construction of the new road, it is much more accessible than formerly. It is situated 1050 m. above sea level, some 30 km. to the north-west of Antalya, on a natural platform between two mountains. The one to the east is Mount Güllük (Güllük Dağ), known in ancient times as Mount Solymos. The Termessians referred to themselves in inscriptions as Solymians, a native people of Pamphylia. Their language seems to have been a dialect of Pisidian. Although mentioned in the "Iliad", in connection with the story of Bellerophon, Termessos does not make its first appearance in history until 334 B. C., when Alexander the Great passed through the region. According to Arrian, the conqueror left these brave people unmolested in their stronghold and continued on his way into Central Anatolia. Termessos enjoyed its first period of prosperity in the Hellenistic age, and its second in Roman times. The inhabitants were acknowledged by the Roman senate as "friends and allies" of the Roman people, and were granted the right to "formulate their own laws". Nothing is known about the Christian period in Termessos.

Fig. 161 – Plan of Termessos. The ruins of Termessos owe much of their charm to their picturesque setting in dense woodland, but the trees also make it very difficult to find many of the remains, including the attractive tombs, without the help of a guide. The accompanying plan shows practically all the surviving buildings, and is followed by short explanatory notes. Those who have time and would like to see the beauties of the site for themselves will greatly enjoy their adventurous walk. The buildings in the city centre are, for the most part, well-preserved and quite accessible.

1) *Agora. The market-place was enclosed on the west, north and possibly the east by stoas which are now in a very ruined state, consisting merely of piles of stone blocks.* 2) *Stoa of Attalos. According to fragments of its dedicatory inscription found on the ground, this was erected by Attalos II, King of Pergamon (159-138 B. C.) as a two-storeyed structure of the Doric order with the basement floor only opening onto the sloping side of the site, in the manner customary at Pergamon.* 3) *This edifice, presented to the city by Osbaras, was erected, according to a fragmentary inscription, during the Roman period, in imitation of Hellenistic models. On the south-west side of the agora are the remains of a tomb, consisting of a semicircular bench preceded by a broad flight of steps.* 4) *Theatre (Pl. 95 b). The most attractive building in Temessos is the well-preserved theatre, with a seating capacity of 4,200. It is of the Greek type and dates from the Hellenistic era with its beautiful ashlar masonry, its auditorium exceeding the half-circle and the absence of vaulted substructures. Moreover, the stage building is separated from the auditorium by open parodoi (passages); this was definitely a Greek feature. The south parodos was later covered by vaults (Pl. 95 b), while the one on the north remained in its original open form. During the same*

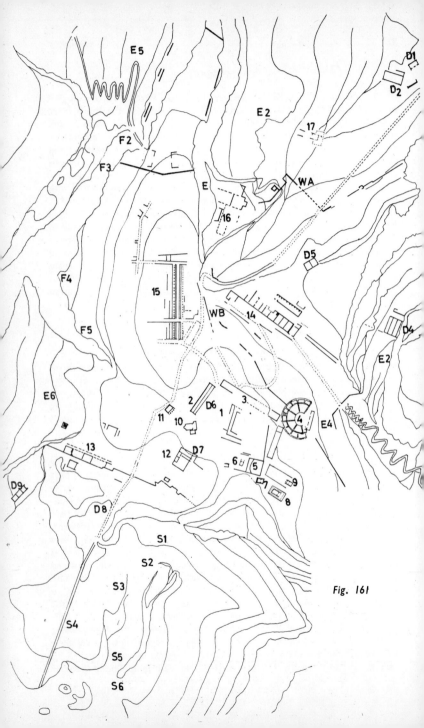

Fig. 161

phase of construction, the section of the auditorium above the north parodos was made to accommodate some 60 extra seats (Pl. 95 b). The stage building underwent considerable alteration in Roman times. It consisted of the scaenae frons (stage) with a long, narrow room behind it, and the proscenium (podium on which the players acted). The stage had five doors, the largest being in the middle. Judging by the architectural ornaments lying on the ground, the stage building must have been erected in the late second century A. D. **5)** Bouleuterion (Pl. 95 a). This attractive building with handsome ashlar masonry is the best preserved structure at Termessos. The walls still stand over 10 m. high, but the whole is densely overgrown and the interior is largely filled with debris. It dates, no doubt, from Hellenistic times, like the theatre; however, the wall-building technique employed is different. The upper part of the outer face is decorated in the mixed architectural style typical of Pergamon, with Doric pilasters standing on Attic-Ionic column bases. The arrangement of the pilasters along the outer face (Pl. 95 a) recalls the bouleuterion at Miletos, in which the upper half of the exterior wall surface was adorned with half-columns. The members of the Austrian expedition, having examined the odeion without removing the rubble, state that they discerned portions of slightly curved rows of seats. The windows to be seen in the east and west walls suggest that the whole building must have been roofed. However, the question of how the width of 25 m. was spanned will perhaps be answered when the debris in the interior has been completely cleared away. Pieces of green, yellow, violet and white marble, found on the ground, seem to indicate that the roughly dressed interior faces of the walls were covered with polychrome marble mosaics. In the rear wall is a wide entrance for the senators. All kinds of meetings, no doubt, took place in this building; it probably served as a bouleuterion and a theatre when the weather turned cold. **6)** Temple of Zeus Solymeus (?). This beautifully constructed temple, comprising only a cella measuring 6.10 × 7.36 m. in area, still reaches a height of 4 m. The Austrian expedition considers this structure to have been one of the temples devoted to the worship of the Solymian Zeus. **7)** Artemis Temple. This small, well-preserved prostylos, with a cella measuring 5.50 × 5.50 m., dates from the Roman period. The inscription on the lintel of the practically intact door reports that one Aurelia Armasta erected the temple at her own expense, and the cult statue with the help of her husband. Pedestals still in situ on either side of the door supported statues (not preserved) of her paternal uncles. **8)** Main Temple of Termessos. This temple is now represented only by its foundations, but judging by the architectural fragments strewn about, it was built in the reign of the Antonines (138-192 A. D.) as a peripteros of the Doric order, with 6 by 11 columns. A dedicatory inscription to Artemis, and reliefs depicting the goddess in the sacrificial scene from "Iphigenia", were found among the ruins; consequently it can be concluded that the main temple at Termessos was dedicated to Artemis. The proximity of the small Artemis temple to it is a further indication that the large religious building was connected with the worship of the same deity. **9)** Templum in antis.

This small shrine, with a cella measuring 5.78 × 6.90 m., was probably of the Corinthian order and stood on a high podium (base). Architectural fragments observed in the vicinity indicate that it dates from the late Roman period. It is not known to which deity this shrine was devoted. 10) Corinthian Temple. A prostylos of the Corinthian order, with a cella measuring 9.50 × 10.85 m. in area. 11) Small Corinthian Temple. Another prostylos of the Corinthian order, with a cella measuring 6.70 × 7.20 m. in area and preceded by a flight of steps. Late Roman period. 12) Founder's House. This well-preserved structure was a Roman house of the type having an unroofed atrium (courtyard), in the middle of which was sunk an impluvium (square basin for catching rain water). The front door was of the Doric order and is still standing to a height of 6 m. on the west side of the house. Windows also were set into the walls. The inscription on the left jamb of the door refers to the owner of the house as "founder of the city", a title no doubt indicating that he helped defray the cost of erecting important public buildings in the city. 13) Remains of houses. 14) Gymnasium. This huge structure, standing at a lower level to the north-east, is composed of handsome blocks but is completely overgrown. 15) Colonnaded street. Promenade bordered on either side by colonnades and shops. 16) Remains of houses. 17) Propylon of Hadrian, leading to a ruined Ionic peripteros with a cella ca. 8 m. in width. **D** 1-9) Cisterns. Termessos possessed many reservoirs and cisterns which can still be observed in several places.

An important and impressive feature of Termessos is the attractive necropolis lying south, west and north of the city. Most interesting are the tombs cut in the rock and the grave monuments built in the form of temples and containing sarcophagi : **E** 1-6) Small tombs. **F** 1-5) Rock-cut grave monuments. The majority of these tombs are of the Lycian type resembling houses. The most important tomb in this category is the grave of Alketas (F 4). Within the tomb can be seen a relief depicting a man fighting on horseback. He has been convincingly identified by Niemann as Alketas, a general of Alexander the Great, and brother of Perdikkas. According to the historian Diodorus (18, 47), he fought against Antigonos and came to a very tragic end. Defeated by Antigonos, Alketas took refuge in Termessos. When Antigonos demanded his surrender, the elders of the city decided to give him up. The young Termessian warriors, however, would not countenance such an act of betrayal. The elders, therefore, came to a secret agreement with Antigonos and sent out their young men to fight against him. While the young men were engaged in combat at some distance from the city, the elders prepared to surrender Alketas to Antigonos. Rather than submit to this, Alketas committed suicide. The elders delivered his corpse to Antigonos, who caused it to be shamefully mutilated and left unburied. The young Termessians finally retrieved his body and gave it a splendid burial. This grave contained a sarcophagus carved out of the rock; within this lay the bones or ashes of the Macedonian commander. Treasure seekers have destroyed all but the lower parts of the sarcophagus. Lower down, to the right of the Alketas relief, can be seen the partially smashed representations of his armour, consisting of a helmet, a pair of greaves and a round shield with a sword set behind and diagonally across it. **S** 1-9) Tombs of a larger scale. The majority of the larger tombs lie buried among the trees to the south-west of the city. Dating from the 2nd and 3rd centuries B. C., they mostly *consisted of sarcophagi mounted on podia (bases). Some are extremely well-preserved, attractive monuments of temple form, containing one or more sarcophagi.* **WA)** *Lower fortification wall.* **WB)** *Upper fortification wall.*

❄

PERGE

Statue bases recovered in the older gateway of the city (7), and inscribed with the names Kalchas and Mopsos, bear evidence that the Pergaians believed their city was founded by Greek heroes after the Trojan War. Nevertheless, Perge does not appear in history until Alexander the Great's arrival there in 333 B. C. The city must have been fortified before it came under Seleucid domination, in the 3rd century B. C. Its first period of prosperity coincides with that of Side, in the 2nd century B. C. In fact, it was in this period that Pergaian coins, depicting the cult statue of Artemis Pergaia standing in an Ionic temple, became abundant. The image took the form of a baitylos consisting of a roughly rectangular block, surmounted by a human bust. Like other Anatolian cities, Perge reached the peak of its fame in Roman Imperial times, during the first three centuries A. D.

The first settlement was probably established on the acropolis situated on the east side of the city (Fig. 162, No. 16). However, the present-day ruins in this area date from Byzantine times. Professor Arif Müfit Mansel of the University of Istanbul conducted successful excavations in Perge on behalf of the Turkish Historical Society in 1946 and from 1953 to 1957. Professor Mansel resumed field-work here in 1967 and this has already led to important new results. The following description is based mainly on information given by Professor Mansel, director of the excavation.

Fig. 162–Plan of Perge. **I)** *Theatre (Pls. 96 a,). This theatre is of the Greco-Roman type. The auditorium built against the hillside and exceeding a semicircle in extent, as well as the unroofed parodoi (passages) separating the auditorium from the stage-building, all perpetuate the Greek tradition, while the diazoma (the horizontal passage around the auditorium) supported by vaulted substructures, the colonnaded gallery running around the top of the auditorium, and the high stage building are architectural features characteristic of the Roman period. The theatre could accommodate 15,000 spectators, who gained access from the hillside and from ground level by means of passages on either side of the diazoma and also via the parodoi. The stage-building, erected in the second half of the 2nd century A. D., still stands to a considerable height. Judging by the architectural ornaments found, it was two-tiered and richly decorated. It stood on a narrow*

*podium, decorated with reliefs representing mythological scenes. We observe the
representation of the local river god, Kestros, and the narration of the life of Dionysus, god of wine and spectacle: Dionysus, who was born prematurely and sewn
into the thigh of Zeus, is seen here, emerging from his father's body; he is taken*

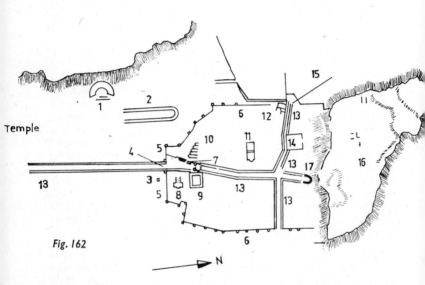

Temple

Fig. 162

N

*by Hermes and delivered to the nymphs of Mt. Nysa; the nymphs give the child
Dionysus a bath; Dionysus is brought up by the nymphs and finally sits as a god
in a chariot, led by panthers and accompanied by satyrs and maenads. The five
niches adorning a long wall backing against the outer face of the stage building
disclose that at a later date the theatre was probably combined with a nymphaion.
In the late Roman period, when the custom of gladiatorial shows and fights
with wild beasts was introduced in Greek cities, a perforated parapet surrounding
the orchestra was built on the lower seats of the auditorium, in order to protect
the spectators.* **2)** *Stadium. One of the best preserved stadiums of antiquity, being
second only to that at Aphrodisias. Probably erected in the 2nd century A. D. The
well-preserved rows of seats supported by barrel-vaulted construction had a seating
capacity of 12,000. The entrance of the 34 × 234 m. arena lay at the southern end,
but the monumental gateway, only a few fragments of which have been discovered,
is no longer in existence. Below the seats on the east side, thirty chambers are to be
found, opening to the outside and possessing communicating doors. The spectators
passed through every third chamber, which led to the arena. The remaining twenty
rooms served as shops. On the walls are inscribed the shopkeepers' names or their
trades.* **3)** *Tomb of Plancia Magna. Scanty ruins of a monument erected, according
to the recovered fragments of an inscription, in honour of a rich lady called Plancia
Magna. Her name occurs in over a dozen inscriptions found in the city. It is interesting to note that in the inscriptions on two statue bases in the older city gate (7)*

mention is made of M. Plancius Varus and C. Plancius Varus, in a reference to the distaff side of the family, as being the father and brother of Plancia Magna. **4)** Later city gate, (Pl. 98a) dating from the 4th century A. D. **5)** Later southern city wall, built in the 4th century A.D. The archway lying behind the southern city gate has now been restored by Turkish archaeologists under the direction of Professor A. M. Mansel. **6)** City wall, erected in the Hellenistic age. It is well-preserved; some of the towers on the east side are particularly so, since they attain practically their original height. **7)** The city gate complex (see Fig. 163). **8)** Church with an eastern apse. **9)** Agora. A large square 65 × 65 m. in area, surrounded by colonnades lined with shops and rooms on the outer sides. It was built when the city was enlarged in the 4th century A. D. A round structure in the middle of the market-place recalls a similar building in the centre of the agora at Side (Fig. 165, No. 10). In 1968, Professor Mansel unearthed, near the agora, a colonnade measuring 4.30 × 96 m. **10)** Roman baths. They consist of structures arranged side by side, with large windows facing southwards. The baths were approached by a propylon located inside the large courtyard of the city gate (Fig. 163, No. 5). **11)** The Bishopric basilica of Perge comprising an apsidal nave flanked by two aisles. **12)** Baths. **13)** Colonnaded streets. The city was divided into four quarters by two colonnaded streets (Pl. 96 b). A water channel ran along the middle of each street. **14)** Palaestra. This well-preserved building, measuring ca. 76 × 76 m. in area with windows overlooking the street, was dedicated to the Emperor Claudius (A. D. 41-54) by a certain C. Julius Cornutus and his wife and children. **15)** Streets lined with tombs uncovered by Professor Mansel in 1946 under the auspices of the Turkish Historical Society. **16)** Acropolis. The flat hill to the east of the city is probably the site of the original colonial settlement. However, the ruins to be observed there today date from the Byzantine period. **17)** Nymphaion i. e. fountain (Period of Hadrian).

Fig. 163 – Plan of the city gate complex at Perge (courtesy of Professor A. Müfit Mansel). **1)** *The older city gate, flanked by two round towers, dates from the Hellenistic age (Pl. 98 b). This well-preserved structure, consisting of a horseshoe-shaped courtyard like that at Side, is the most impressive ruin in Perge. The handsome ashlar masonry exhibited in the lofty towers is very attractive. The interior of the horseshoe-shaped courtyard was transformed in to a magnificent courtyard in the years A. D. 120-122 by Plancia Magna, daughter of Plancius Varus, governor of Bithynia. The walls of the Hellenistic structure (Pl. 98 b) were faced entirely with marble, the number of niches was increased and a two - tiered columnar marble façade of the Corinthian order was built in front of them. In the niches of the upper storey once stood statues, only the bases of which have survived. According to the inscriptions engraved on these bases, the statues represented the city founders of Perge; among them are mentioned legendary heroes such as Mopsos and Kalchas. Two of the bases bear the names of M. Plancius Varus and his son C. Plancius Varus, who were apparently also considered founders of the city. The niches on the ground floor contained statues of deities such as Hermes, Aphrodite, Pan and the Dioskouroi, etc.* **2)** *Plancia Magna also commissioned a two-tiered gateway with three doorways, which was erected on the north side of the horse-*

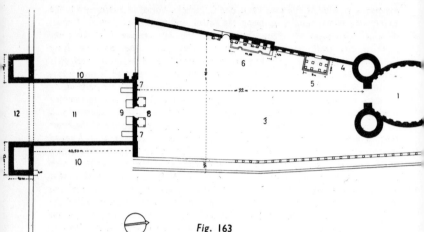

Fig. 163

shoe-shaped courtyard. It is a structure which reminds one very much of the gateway of Hadrian at Antalya (Fig. 160). The niches contained statues of Roman emperors and empresses, as well as members of the Imperial house, from the reign of Nerva until the period of Hadrian. Most of the statues which stood on bases with inscriptions were discovered by Professor Mansel during his excavations in 1943-1956 and they are now kept in the Antalya Museum. **3)** The large courtyard, 92 m. long, which lies between the horseshoe-shaped entrance on the north side (1) and the complex of gateways on the south side (7-9), is a monumental ensemble of architectural structures built in the 2nd century A. D. Some of the monuments and statues which embellished this large ceremonial courtyard in Roman times were discovered by Professor Mansel in his recent campaigns. **4)** In the three niches in the west wall of the large courtyard, to the south of the northern Hellenistic tower, Professor Mansel discovered three statues, two of which are likenesses of Plancia Magna, according to the inscriptions on their bases. One of these portraits, found in an excellent state of preservation, is a magnificent work of exquisite beauty. It has now been transported to the Antalya Museum. **5)** Propylon. The large baths of Perge (Fig. 162, No. 10) were approached through this propylon, which was uncovered by Professor Mansel during his 1968-1969 campaigns. The soffits (the lower surface of the architrave) of the propylon, large fragments of which lie on the spot, were decorated with reliefs depicting deities such as Helios, Selene, Dionysus, Pan, Eros etc. This beautiful gateway was erected in the reign of Septimius Severus (A. D. 193-211), according to its inscription and stylistic peculiarities. **6)** Nymphaion (fountain). This structure consisted of a wide basin and a richly decorated architectural façade. From its inscription we learn that it was dedicated to Artemis Pergaia as well as to Septimius Severus, his wife and their sons. The statues of the Emperor and Empress and the members of the Impe- rial House, which have survived in a very good state of preservation, are now in the Antalya Museum. **7)** South wall of the large courtyard, adorned with niches, *probably dates from the 2nd century A. D. 8) The gateway in front of the south wall was erected in the time of Septimius Severus (A. D. 193-211). 9) Large bases, which once supported a columnar façade that was built with marble blocks taken from earlier structures. The façade dates perhaps from the 4th century A. D. 10) City wall, built in the 4th century A. D. 11) Rectangular courtyard, probably of the 4th century A. D. 12) Outer gate. The arcades that we observe in this structure (Pl. 98 a) were probably built in the time of Hadrian. From the large marble blocks lying on the spot, we learn that a gateway, dating approximately to the reign of Septimius Severus, was erected in front of the arcades. When, sometime in the 4th century A. D., a new city wall was built, this city gate was incorporated in it. The central arch was left open and it continued to be used as the entrance to the city. On both sides of this city gate, the excavators found a great number of statues representing the principal gods and goddesses of Perge. They are now in the Antalya Museum.*

Silyon. In the middle of the plain, left of the road going from Perge to Aspendos, a conspicuous hill rises to a height of 200 m. This is the site of the town of Silyon, the ruins of which are in a fine state of preservation. They form an architectural ensemble which is well worth seeing and which also contains Hellenistic buildings showing the influence of Pergamon.

ASPENDOS

According to Greek tradition, Aspendos was founded by colonists from Argos, under the leadership of Mopsos. The name of the city on coins of the fifth and fourth centuries B. C. is Estwediya. This is possibly derived from a certain King called Asitawadia or Asitawada, mentioned in the Hittite hieroglyphic inscriptions found near Adana at Karatepe, dating from the end of the 8th century B. C. (Pl. 106).

Aspendos was the only city besides Side which was minting silver coins by the early 5th century B. C. For a time, the city was a member of the Athenian Maritime League, also known as the Delian Confederacy. In his Anabasis (1, 2, 12), Xenophon speaks of mercenaries from Aspendos among the troops of Kyros the Younger. As recorded by Scylax and Strabo, the River Eurymedon, which flows 500-1000 m. east of Aspendos, was then navigable as far as that city, so that the Persian fleet was able to anchor there in 468 B. C. before the Battle of the Eurymedon. In 330 B. C., Alexander the Great occupied the lower city. Like Side, Aspendos was a prosperous settlement in Hellenistic times. After the Battle of Magnesia ad Sipylum in 190 B. C., Aspendos entered into a good relationship with Rome. On the death of Attalos III, it was incorporated into the Roman province of Asia, and continued to prosper under Roman rule. The present-day ruins date from this period. No traces have been found so far of pre-Roman Aspendos.

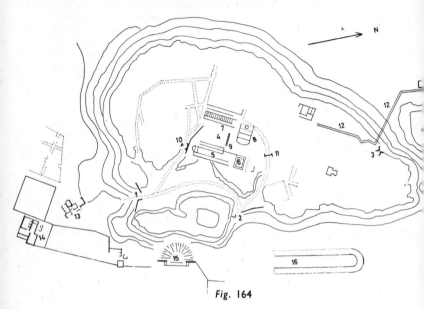

Fig. 164

Fig. 164 – Plan of Aspendos at the time of the Roman Empire. 1-3) City gates. The southern gateway is well-preserved but at the present time is almost completely buried. 4) Agora, surrounded by public city buildings. 5) Basilica. Commercial business was transacted in the 105 m. - long building which was divided into a central hall and two aisles. Only the foundations are in evidence today. 6) Section of the basilica devoted to civic affairs. Tribunals and affairs of state were probably conducted in this excellently preserved structure. 7) Market hall. This 70 m. - long hall consists of a row of shops with a stoa in front. 8) Bouleuterion. This building, taking the form of a roofed auditorium, was situated close to the basilica (5) and served as a council chamber. 9) Nymphaion (fountain). The only surviving part of this building is the well-preserved façade, which very much resembles the nymphaion at Side (Fig. 165, No. 3). Parts of the richly decorated entablature can still be observed over the niches. 10) Exedra. This curvilinear open recess, overlooking the road leading from the main gateway (1) to the agora once contained statues and seats for the public. 11) Arch spanning the road leading from the eastern gate to the agora at a point half-way between the two. 12) Aqueduct. One of the best preserved and most impressive Roman aqueducts to be found in Turkey. 13, 14) Vaulted structures which probably served as baths and gymnasia. 15) Theatre (Pls. 100, 101). This magnificent structure is the best preserved theatre of antiquity. It represents the culmination of an architectural development that started at the end of the classical age. The architects of Hellenistic times made important advances in theatre design, as witnessed in the examples at Priene (p. 198). However, it was the Roman architects who achieved the perfect unity of the auditorium with the stage buildings, as exemplified at Aspendos. The Greek theatre was a harmonious blending of architectural forms with the surrounding countryside. At Pergamon, for instance, the spectators sat in the heart of the city but faced a landscape visible from every seat in the auditorium. The Aspendos theatre, on the contrary, is cut off from the outside world and forms a self-contained, architecturally-framed space (Willy Zschietzschmann).

Although almost entirely built over barrel-vaulted substructures, the theatre at Aspendos rests in part against a hillside, thus indicating the architect's desire to conform to the age-old Greek custom of erecting a theatre on the slope of a hill. The horseshoe-shaped auditorium was also a Greek feature which was probably dictated by architectural considerations. As a matter of fact, an exactly semicircular auditorium would probably render the exterior view of the building less pleasing. In other respects, the Aspendos theatre is built to conform with the principles of Roman architecture. The parodoi (side entrances), which in Greek theatres are always unroofed and set diagonally, are here parallel with the auditorium and, what is more significant, are roofed. The auditorium is divided by a horizontal gangway (diazoma) and surmounted by a colonnaded arcade. Some of the half-columns in this gallery show brick repair work dating from the Seljuk period. The well-preserved stage building consists of a scaenae frons (façade) and a proscenium (platform on which the play was performed). The scaenae frons had five doors giving entry to the proscenium. The large one in the middle was called the porta regia, the smaller ones, portae hospitales. The entire wall was adorned with a two-tiered architectural façade which still reaches its original height.

The outer wall of the stage is an exact replica of the interior arrangement. A row of arches on the outer rear wall corresponds to the arcade crowning the auditorium, and the two-tiered articulation of the stage building facing the interior is reproduced on the outer façade. A buttress and the tower-like portal were added in the Seljuk period. A simple moulding marks the division between the two tiers. A row of seventeen upper windows is set on a level with the arcade surmounting the auditorium. The architect designed the rear wall of the stage building in a severely tectonic form.

We learn from an inscription that the Aspendos theatre was designed by the architect Zeno, son of Theodorus during the reign of Marcus Aurelius (A. D. 161-180). Greek and Latin inscriptions carved over the entrances on either side of the stage building further disclose that two brothers, namely Curtius Crispinus and Curtius Auspicatus dedicated it "to the gods of the country and to the Imperial house". **16)** Stadium. This structure is in fairly good condition and merits a visit.

❊

SIDE

According to Strabo (XIV 667), Side was founded by the inhabitants of Kyme, an Aeolian city located north of Smyrna. The settlement dates back to the second half of the 7th century B. C., as proved by the Greek pottery found in the lower strata of the city. The colony was set up during the period of large-scale emigration from the cities of western Asia Minor. Its geographical siting on a peninsula is a further indication that the colonists came from the western seaboard of Anatolia, where almost all cities were located on offshore islands or on narrow necks of land. In Hesychius' dictionary, the meaning of Side is given as "pomegranate". This fruit is depicted on the city coinage from about 500 B. C. down to Roman Imperial times.

Arrianos (Anabasis 1, 26,4) reports that, soon after their arrival, the colonists from Kyme began to speak a barbaric dialect which was probably the original Anatolian tongue of Pamphylia. This Sidetan form of the language has long been known from the legends on the city coinage. In recent years three texts in this dialect, dating from about the 3rd century B. C., have been found, two of them accompanied by a Greek version. Greek became the official language in Side after its conquest by Alexander the Great, as is proved by inscriptions on stone dating from the beginning of the 3rd century B. C. Although Side was first under Ptolemaic and then under Seleucid domination during the 3rd century (301-218 B. C.), it profited from the rivalry existing between the Hellenistic rulers. Attalos II (159-138 B. C.) founded Attaleia (Antalya) to gain control of the southern coast of Anatolia. Nevertheless, Side at no time came under the sway of Pergamon. On the contrary, in the 2nd and 1st century B. C. Side enjoyed its first period of prosperity, owing to its friendship with Rome. The attractive wall, marking the greatest extent of the city to the east (Fig. 165, No. 1), must have been erected sometime during this period, as pointed out by Professor Mansel. Side reached the height of its glory in the 2nd century and the first half of the 3rd century A. D. The most magnificent of the city buildings were erected during this phase of the Roman era.

The general decline of the Roman Empire resulted in the impoverishment of the Anatolian cities. In the middle of the 4th century, an inner city wall was constructed across the narrowest part of the promontory (29), thus reducing the city to half its former size, and the north-eastern part of the peninsula was abandoned. The 5th and 6th centuries saw a revival of the city after it had become the centre of a diocese, and, during this period, the settlement extended beyond its original limits. A short survey was made by the Austrian expedition, directed by Niemann and Petersen, and later published under the title "Lanckoronski, Städte Pamphyliens und Pisidiens, Wien 1890". During the twenty years from 1947 to 1966, systematic excavations were carried out by Professor Arif Müfit Mansel on behalf of the Turkish Historical Society and the University of Istanbul. The results are now available in the form of an excellent, comprehensive guide-book : A. M. Mansel, *Die Ruinen von Side*. Berlin 1963.

Fig. 165 – Plan of Side (after Mansel, Die Ruinen von Side). **1)** *City Wall. Built of regular breccia blocks, this attractive fortress wall was erected in the 2nd century B. C., when the city was passing through its first period of prosperity. The best preserved sections of the wall can be seen in the neighbourhood of the main gate (2), where it is reinforced by towers at irregular intervals and decorated by a cornice-moulding on the outer face. Two rampart walks divide the inner side of the wall into three tiers; the middle of the latter was relatively broad and con-tained casemates (small vaulted rooms with loopholes), whereas the uppermost tier was composed of only a narrow rampart walk and a parapet with embrasures (loopholes). Thus there were two rows of loopholes through which missiles could be hurled at an attacking force. The section of the wall on the three seaward sides of the peninsula has undergone considerable modification and some parts were completely renovated during Roman and Byzantine times. The section running across the neck of the peninsula (29) was constructed in the 4th century A. D.* **2)** *Main Gate. A fine defence-work resembling that at Perge. The four small doors, two at each end of the semi-circular wall around the courtyard, allowed the defenders to attack the enemy in the rear should he manage to force an entry through the gate. Towards the end of the 2nd century A. D., which was a time of peace, the inward-facing walls of the courtyard were enriched with architectural decorations, now in the safe keeping of the museum (12).* **3)** *City Fountain. The nymphaion opposite the main gate is similar to that at Aspendos. In the opinion of Professor Mansel, it was constructed during the same period as the aqueduct (4), i.e., in the Antonine period (A. D. 138-192). A magnificent three-tiered façade rose behind the large basin. The lowest of the tiers is still in situ and contains three large niches, once fitted with several spouts. The statues and reliefs found during the excavations are in the museum (12). Some fragments are still lying on the ground.* **4)** *Aqueduct. This structure was probably built in the last years of the 2nd century A. D. It supplied water from the source of Melas river (Manavgat Çayı). Ten sec-tions of the aqueduct between the source and the city still standing, at different distances from each other, are in a good state of preservation. The aqueduct was greatly restored in the first quarter of the 3rd century A. D. by Lollianos Bryonianos, a wealthy citizen, and his wife Quirinia Patra. Slightly west of the fourth tower from the main gate(2)can be seen a small section of the aqueduct and a hole in the city wall. Water passed through this gap in a main pipe and was then transported by means of the aqueduct to the baths and fountains in the city centre.* **5, 6)** *Colon-naded Streets. In the 2nd century A. D., two streets lined with columns in the Corinthian order led into the city from the main gate. These once splendid roads are now moderately well preserved. The one running south (5) is now overgrown; the other (6) leading to the agora is still in use today.* **7)** *Building with a sacred fountain. Fifth or sixth century A. D.* **8, 9)** *Two houses of peristyle type, i.e., consisting of a courtyard surrounded by rooms. Erected in the 2nd or 1st century B. C., they continued to be used in Roman times. After a temporary abandonment in the 4th century A. D., they were restored and reinhabited in the 5th and 6th centuries. The three rooms between the house marked 8 and the colonnaded street are shops, no doubt belonging to the owner of the same house.* **10)** *Agora. Second century A. D. This huge structure, measuring 90.80 × 94.00 m. and originally consisting of a courtyard surrounded by colonnades containing shops, is now represented only by the foundations. A monumental gateway opening onto the main street gave* access to this market-place, which was the centre of all kinds of commercial and cultural activities. In addition, it was the place where captives seized by pirates were auctioned off into slavery. Indeed, according to Strabo (XIV, 664), Side was a flourishing slave market. The ruins lying near the centre of the agora belong to a round structure, convincingly identified by Professor Arif Müfit Mansel, the director of the excavations, as the Temple of Tyche or Fortuna depicted on Side coins. It dates, like the agora itself, from the 2nd century A. D. The lavatory situated in the north-west corner of the agora is in a good state of preservation. This building had a semicircular corridor with seats for 24 people and was roofed with a barrel-vault. The walls were faced with marble. **11)** Theatre. With the sea in the background, this structure is the most impressive and conspicuous of the ruins at Side. It dates back, in its present form to the middle of the 2nd century A. D. and belongs to the Roman type of theatre, built on barrel-vaulted substructures. However, the native Anatolian architect has paid tribute to the earlier Greek style by building the auditorium in a curve greatly exceeding a semicircle. The outer-facing side of the theatre was two-tiered, with superimposed arcades the lower one of which is still well-preserved (Pl. 99 b). The stage, composed of a proscenium and a skene, was three-tiered, forming a richly decorated façade with columns, niches, statues and reliefs. The plays were performed on the proscenium, which was 6 m. broad and 3 m. above the level of the orchestra. The foot of the scene behind the proscenium was adorned with reliefs depicting mythological events, but these are in poor condition (cf. the similar frieze at Perge which is in a relatively good state of preservation). When, in late Roman times, the gladiatorial shows and fights with wild beasts also became the fashion in Greek cities, a thick wall, 1.50 m. in height, was built on the 1.80 m. - high bench surrounding the orchestra of the Side theatre in order to protect spectators on these occasions. According to two large inscriptions, the theatre was converted into an open - air church in the 5th or the 6th century A. D. Additional evidence for this are two small chapels containing poorly preserved paintings at either end of the auditorium and inscriptions on the seats of the auditorium indicating the places reserved for the priests. **12)** Baths near the agora (now the local museum at Side). This structure belongs to the ring type of baths building complex and dates from the 5th century A. D., as stated by Arif Müfit Mansel. It is now restored, thanks to financial aid given by Ragıp Devres and Mrs. Devres, and contains a great number of excellent sculptural works and sarcophagi dating back to various periods in Roman times. The richly decorated façades of the square, formed in the late Roman era by the western front of the agora, a monumental gate (13) and three fountains, no doubt produced the impressive atmosphere of an architectural ensemble. The fountain situated on the western corner of the street by the baths (now the museum) is preserved in its lower part. It was a structure 17.50 m. in length built of marble about the second half of the 3rd century A. D. with three water-basins between four podiums (bases), each supporting an aedicula containing a statue.

Between this fountain and the eastern inner wall of the monumental gate (13) lie the remains of a semicircular building covered by a half dome; a marble spout in the middle of the niche indicates that this structure also served as a fountain. The structure to the north-west of the above-mentioned fountains is a cistern dating probably to the 2nd or 3rd century A. D. Further to the north-west is an open cistern dating from Byzantine times. The small elegant building next to the western inner face of the monumental gate (13) and backing onto the 4th century city wall, was erected, according to the architrave inscription, as a monument in honour of the Emperor Vespasian (69-79). This edifice, which originally stood elsewhere in the city, was later brought here and converted into a fountain. **13) Monumental Gate.** Arched entrance giving access to the inner city in Roman times. The present height of the whole doorway measures 13.45 m., but, formerly, it must have reached a much greater height with the overlying entablature and an attica probably surmounted by a quadriga. In the 4th century, the arch was blocked up with a wall containing a smaller gate. The central part of the blocking wall was recently removed by the villagers to gain a much wider entrance. It is regret-

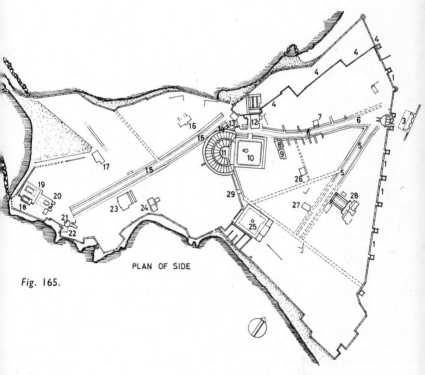

PLAN OF SIDE

Fig. 165.

table that this, the most striking monument at Side, is threatened with collapse because of this alteration **14)** Dionysus Temple. A podium (base), measuring 7.23 m. × 17.55 m. in area and 0.65 m. in height, lies between the theatre and the colonnaded street. According to recovered fragments, it was a pseudoperipteral temple (with half columns set against the outer face of the cella) erected in the Early Roman Empire period. Professor Mansel has assigned this temple to Dionysus because of its proximity to the theatre. **15)** Colonnaded street leading from the city centre almost as far as the shore. It is continuation of the colonnaded street marked 6. Since this stretch lies under the modern village, it has not been excavated. **16)** Christian Basilica, only partly preserved. **17)** Harbour Baths. This attractive ruin of monumental character has been identified by Professor Mansel as baths constructed in the 2nd century A. D. **18)** Temple of Apollo. Peripteros of the Corinthian order with 6 by 11 columns and a stylobate measuring 16.37 × 29.50. Second half of the 2nd century A. D. **19)** Temple of Athena. Peripteros of the Corinthian order with 6 by 13 columns. The stylobate measures 17.65 × 35.00 m. Second half of the 2nd century A. D. **20)** Christian Basilica, erected in the 5th century A. D. A church consisting of a nave, two aisles and an atrium (courtyard), built on the foundations of the temples of Athena and Apollo. This huge structure seems to have been abandoned for some reason at an unknown date. The small church installed in the nave of the ruined basilica dates from the 8th or 9th century A. D. and is in a very good state of preservation. **21)** Temple of Men (the Anatolian Moon God). The temple took the form of a semicircular cella (cult room) with a platform in front supporting a colonnaded vestibule approached by a flight of steps. The 2.20 m. - high podium (base) supporting the cella and the vestibule still survives. Basing his opinion on the style of the architectural decoration, A. M. Mansel dates the temple to the beginning of the 3rd century A.D. **22)** A Byzantine fountain. **23)** The most imposing baths of Side. Not yet excavated. **24)** Byzantine house. This dwelling consisting of several rooms built in brick and covered by vaults is preceded by a courtyard measuring 14.50 × 17.50 m. Next to this house can be seen a cistern 10.5 × 14 m. in area. **25)** Building M. This was probably the State Agora of the city. It consisted of a courtyard surrounded by 7 m. - broad colonnades, with a monumental structure on the east side composed of three large rooms. The whole complex measured 69.20 × 88.50 m. in area. A recovered fragment indicates that the colonnades surrounding the courtyard were of the Ionic order. The inner surfaces of the walls in the middle room of the monumental structure on the east side were richly decorated and divided into two tiers, a fact deduced from the surviving niches and aediculae, and from architectural fragments lying on the ground. It seems likely that the courtyard was the market place, and that the above-mentioned large, ornate room was reserved for the emperor's use on ceremonial occasions. The walls of the rooms on both sides of the central hall contain large niches; perhaps they served as a library and archives. The magnificent sculptural works found by the excavators in the niches and aediculae within the ceremonial hall are in the local *museum (12).* **26)** *Byzantine building. The function of this well-preserved two-storeyed structure is unknown.* **27)** *Small Byzantine church, probably dating from the 8th or 9th century A. D.* **28)** *Byzantine basilica, built with architectural pieces taken from Roman buildings. This, together with a trikonchos and a baptisterium, constitutes a huge complex, probably dating from the 5th or 6th century A. D.* **29)** *Inner city wall, limiting the inhabited area to half its former size. About the middle of the 4th century A. D. The north-eastern part of the city was left deserted. The arch of the inner city gate (13) was filled in during this period; thereafter, only a small doorway in this blocking wall gave access to the city.*

✻

Alanya. Known in antiquity as Korakesion, Alanya is one of the most attractive towns on the southern Anatolian coast. The magnificent fortifications and the handsome arsenal, both constructed by the Great Seljuk ruler Alaeddin Keykubad, the covered bazaar and mosques, and the natural beauty of the setting all contribute to make this a characteristically Turkish town, unrivalled in charm and splendour.

Anamur. Formerly known as Anemurium. The ruins of Anamur are worth seeing. The theatre, the odeion and the mediaeval fortress near the shore are well-preserved. Thanks to the recent excavations undertaken by the archaeologist Elisabeth Rosenbaum (Mrs. Alföldi), the whole ancient city has now been unearthed.

Silifke (Seleukia on the Kalykadnos). The city was founded by Seleukos I at the beginning of the 3rd century B. C. on the south bank of the River Kalykadnos. The bridge passing over the river today is modern. According to an inscription found in the district in 1870, a bridge was erected in precisely the same spot in A. D. 77 or 78 by Governor L. Octavius Memor, in honour of the Emperor Vespasian and his two sons Titus and Domitian. Frederick Barbarossa was drowned in the same river (the present-day Göksu) in A. D. 1290, during the Third Crusade. No traces of the pre-Roman settlement have yet been found. On the other hand, remains of Roman date include a theatre, a temple and quite a large necropolis. The temple lay 200-300 m. south of the river and about 100 m. from the Cumhuriyet school. Some of the columns, including one fluted column surmounted by a Corinthian capital, are still *in situ*. The edifice was a peripteros with 8 by 14 columns of the Corinthian order and was erected in the 2nd century A. D. The remains of a mediaeval castle top a hill rising to a height of 184 m. west of the city. About 1 km. south of Silifke lies the Christian site called Meryemlik, with the Church of St. Thekla dating from the 5th century A. D.

Uzuncaburç (Olba, Diocaesarea). 30 km. north of Silifke are some of the most important and best preserved ruins in Turkey. These are identified as Olba in archaeological literature. Among the ruins here are preserved the Zeus Temple and some other architectural remains (Fig. 166).

Judging by the writings of Strabo, by the many inscriptions unearthed here and, above all, by the presence of the Temple of Zeus Olbius, we can safely conclude that this district bore the name of Olba in the Hellenistic period. On the other hand, the evidence found in an inscription and on Roman coins proves that the same place was known by the name of Diocaesarea from the time of the Emperor Vespasian onwards.

Ruins of Roman date line the Silifke-Mersin highway on the northern side. The buildings that most often catch the eye are tombs resembling small temples. This road, flanked on one side by the ruins of ancient cities and on the other by a chain of small bays, passing in addition through pine woods and orange plantations, is one of the most beautiful and attractive coastal highways in the world. The chief examples of these ruins are described below.

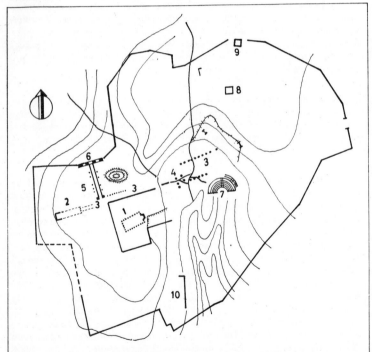

Fig. 166 – Plan of Uzuncaburç (Olba-Diocaesarea). **1)** *Temple of Zeus Olbios (Pl. 102). A peripteros with 6 by 12 columns of the Corinthian order, which is in a fairly good state of preservation. The Corinthian capitals are of the earliest type,*

*(see p. 229) and therefore no doubt date from the 3rd century B. C. It seems likely that the temple was erected in the reign of Seleukos I at the beginning of the 3rd century B. C. The same king founded Seleukeia, which was named after him. The sanctuary at Olba is the earliest temple of the Corinthian order known at present. In the early Christian period, it was converted into a church, with an apse at the eastern end which was later removed. **2)** The Tychaion (Tychaeum). According to an inscription on the architrave (Pl. 103 a), this structure was a temple dedicated to the goddess of good Fortune. Judging by the style of the Corinthian capitals, it probably dates from the latter half of the 1st century A. D. **3)** Colonnaded street. Main road of the city leading in an east-west direction from the vicinity of the theatre to the Tychaion. **4)** Monumental arch spanning the colonnaded street (Pls. 103 b, 104). Consoles projecting from a point half-way up the column shafts and carved in one piece with the column drums used to carry statues or busts. The arch dates from the Roman period. **5)** Colonnaded street leading from the north-western city gateway to the main road. **6)** City gateway. **7)** Theatre. Inscriptions on a fragment of the architrave state that the theatre dates from the co-reign of Marcus Aurelius (161-180) and Lucius Verus (161-169). **8)** Tomb. Late Hellenistic in date. **9)** Tower. It is from this 22.50 m. – high Hellenistic structure that the Turkish name of Uzuncaburç (i.e., high tower) is derived. **10)** Gymnasium (?). Roman in date.*

Korasion (Çok Ören). The first ruins encountered after leaving Silifke are those of a town founded, according to an inscription, by Flavius Uranius (A. D. 367-375), Governor of Isauria. The existing remains date from the period between A. D. 400 and 700. The little town is enclosed by a wall with graveyards to the north and south. Within the area encircled by the wall can be discerned a baths-complex, a large storage hall, a structure with a central courtyard and a church. Another church is also in evidence on the southern necropolis.

Korykos. Known by the local inhabitants as Cennet and Cehennem (Heaven and Hell), this city lies 50 km. south-west of Mersin and the main road passes through the ruins, cutting through the east section of the city wall. The castle standing on the beach south of the highway was built at the beginning of the 12th century A. D. by the Armenian kings of the Rubenian Dynasty. Another castle built on an islet about 200 m. off shore opposite Korykos is contemporary with the one on the beach. Both castles were once connected by a sea wall.

The attractive city founded on the hill slopes north of the road is especially interesting because of the two natural chasms which reminded the neighbouring people of Heaven and Hell. The larger one, called Heaven, is 200 m. long and 70 m. deep. On the north-east edge of this huge grotto is situated a sanctuary consisting of a peribolos, within which stands a church.

The precinct wall is constructed of fine polygonal blocks and probably dates from Hellenistic times. The north wall of the church also resembles the splendid ashlar masonry of the mature Hellenistic style. The other walls of the church were built later. It seems that the sanctuary was erected some time in the 3rd or 2nd century B. C. and converted into a church in the 5th century A. D. Recently, Otto Feld and Hans Weber, two German scholars, declared that the Hellenistic wall of the sanctuary had been transported from some nearby temple and re-erected here as part of the church (Istanbuler Mitteilungen 1967). Two fragments of Corinthian capitals from the apse, which are now lying on the ground, indicate that the church was built in the 5th century A. D. In all probability, this sanctuary was originally dedicated to Zeus Korykios. Similarly it can be assumed that the abode of the monster Typhon, according to myths and legends recorded by ancient writers, must be sought somewhere in Korykos. Josef Keil, who investigated the ruins of Korykos forty years ago, reported that he and Miltner had discovered a grotto conforming to the description of the cave of Typhon as given by Mela, the Latin geographer. Keil writes of visiting this cave (MAMA, III, 215), the site of which is not known at the present day. Nevertheless, the gigantic chasm at Korykos may be a part of the Korykian cave associated with the myth of Typhon.

Today the only extant ruin inside the larger chasm is that of a church erected to the Virgin Mary, located right at the bottom of the southernmost part, at a depth of 70 m. and dating from the 5th century A. D. It is a chapel with an apse flanked by two formerly domed sacristies. The apse and the walls bear traces of paintings, probably of Christ, accompanied, on either side, by saints. Judging by the windows, which take the form of small arcades, the nave was perhaps covered by a wooden pitched roof. The presence of the Virgin's church inside Typhon's cave was a symbolic guarantee for the Christians that the demons had been put to flight. The second chasm is about 200 m. to the north of the larger. Since the walls are very steep, the depths can be reached only by the use of special equipment. Perhaps the people called it Hell because whoever fell into the chasm had no hope of getting out again.

The rock-cut reliefs to be seen in the vicinity of Korykos, depicting standing warriors or figures reclining on couches, are all tombs dating from Roman times.

Left of the road going to Mersin are the ruins of several other ancient towns. The ruins of the ancient town of **Elaiussa-Sebaste**, in the neighbourhood of Ayas, cover a wide area stretching from 3-5 km. north-east of Korykos, as far east as the district known as Kanlıdivane. The road passes through the ancient site, which possesses an abundance of the temple-like grave monuments and sarcophagi noted elsewhere. A pile of stones surmounting a promontory jutting out towards the road is the remains of a temple. This was a peripteros with 6 by 12 columns in the Corinthian order, measuring 17.6 × 32.9 m. and dating from Roman times. In the early Christian period, a chapel was installed within the temple. There is also a theatre, from which most of the tiers of stone seats have been removed by pillagers. Two aqueducts are also visible, one to the east and the other to the west of the city. On the south side of the road, on a small hill which was formerly an island, stands a ruined basilica with an apsidal nave and two aisles.

The ruins of the ancient city of **Kanytelis** are to be found in the locality of Kanlıdivane. The temple-like tombs and sarcophagi, all dating from the Roman era, are very fascinating.

Pompeiopolis. The ruins lying 11 km. west of Mersin, near the modern town of Viranşehir, date from Roman times. The ancient town of Soloi was built in the same district by colonists from Rhodes about 700 B. C. Pompey, the famous Roman general and statesman, subdued the local pirates and settled them in Soloi towards the middle of the 1st century B. C. and changed the name of the city to Pompeiopolis. The surviving ruins are insignificant. Only a few Corinthian columns are left, representing the colonnaded street dating from Roman times.

Mersin. This beautiful city has a very long history. Excavations carried out by the British archaeologist John Garstang 3 km. west of the city at Yumuk Tepe resulted in the discovery of one of the most important centres of prehistoric Anatolian civilization. Yumuk Tepe was also a town of importance in Hittite times. Finds made as a result of the excavations are housed in the Adana Museum.

Tarsus. Today no spectacular remains exist to give evidence of the former importance of the very ancient town of Tarsus. On the other hand, works of the Hittite period unearthed at Gözlükule by Professor Hetty Goldman and now kept in the Adana Museum can be counted among the major historical discoveries of Anatolia.

Both the prehistoric and Hittite finds now housed in the Adana Museum are particularly well worth seeing. The well-preserved sarcophagus from Tarsus of the so-called Greek type, depicting Achilles with Priam, Hector and Patroclus, is a magnificent work made at the beginning of the 3rd century A. D. The ancient bridge in Adana known as Taşköprü, was, according to an inscription kept in the museum, probably built by an Auxentius (CIG 4440); he was perhaps identical with the "comes et mechanicus" Auxentius, who lived and worked around A. D. 384 in Rome, as a constructor of bridges. Originally it was composed of 21 arches only 14 of which have survived. A relief of the Hittite King, Muwatalli (1306-1282 B. C.), carved on a rock on the banks of the River Ceyhan at Sirkeli near Adana, constitutes the oldest large-scale sculptured work of Hittite times known at the present-day.

Karatepe. This Neo-Hittite site, situated 130 km. south-east of Adana not far from Kadirli, has been turned into an exceptionally fine open-air museum by Professor Halet Çambel. Excavations undertaken in this district twenty years ago by Bossert, Alkım and Çambel led to the discovery of the longest Hittite hieroglyphic inscription known so far. It is accompanied by a Phoenician version and dates from about 700 B C.

The finely-placed citadel of Karatepe, the "Black Mountain", overlooking the Ceyhan valley, was the summer residence of King Asitawada, whose name is mentioned in the bilingual inscriptions on the orthostats. We see the king at a daily meal in the main scene. With his right hand he reaches for one of the flat loaves in a large bowl, while he holds a meat patty in his left hand. Three more meat patties lie in the bowl. Two servants wave fans to drive away annoying insects and provide fresh air. The next slab to the left shows cooks and servants bringing more dishes for their lord : roast hare, meat, fruit and drink. On the lower portion of the main scene, servants lead in an ox and a lamb for the feast. We may think of the musicians as playing monotonous though perhaps highly rhythmic melodies. The shape of the lyre closely resembles that of the earliest lyres known in Greek art. Terpander of Lesbos, who was active at the beginning of the 7th century, may have had his seven-string lyre, which signifies the invention of the heptaton system, made after the model of these Near Eastern instruments.

Some markedly expressionistic scenes of the Karatepe reliefs are animated by a gayer approach that seems almost comical. The monkey under the king's dining-table, the scene with the birds of prey pecking at a hare, the dancing bears, the warriors displaying their weapons, as well as the Bes with two monkeys on his shoulder, are merry scenes of burlesque that reveal the strength and special charm of this provincial but attractive sculpture. These carvings, imbued with a Mediterranean spirit of gaiety, should not be regarded as formal reliefs of a palace but as those of a summer residence. The mother nursing her child (Pl. 105) is a masterpiece of its kind, not because of its beauty of execution or the naturalism of its volumes, but because of the unique expressiveness of its naive method of narration. Domuztepe, on the east bank of the River Ceyhan opposite Karatepe, is another Neo-Hittite site of major importance which has been excavated by Bahadır Alkım.

Antakya. One of Turkey's finest and most important museums is that at Antakya. The exhibits comprise finds made in the plain of Amik, works of art unearthed at Tel Açana, Tel Tainat (Pl. 107) and Al Mina, as well as the rich collection of mosaics brought to light in Antiocheia, during the excavations of the Princeton University (Pl. 108).

ARSAMEIA AND NEMRUD DAĞ
IN KOMMAGENE

The most remarkable ancient site in Turkey is situated on Mt. Nemrud (2150 m. above sea-level) near the village of Eski Kâhta, close to Adıyaman, in the south-east part of the country. The climb up and down again by foot and on horseback makes a long journey, but the fascinating beauty of the monumental sculptures as well as the splendour of the scenery are unrivalled. The district between the Taurus Mountains and the Euphrates was called Kommagene in Greek and Roman times, and it includes the cities of Samosata, Perre, Doliche and Germanikeia Kaisareia as well as Nemrud Dağ. This region, occupied today by the modern cities of Adıyaman, Maraş and

Gaziantep, has been identified with Kumuhu, the territory comprising the Neo-Hittite kingdom mentioned in Assyrian annals.

Kommagene was set up as an independent kingdom at the beginning of the first century B. C. by Mithradates I Kallinikos during the civil wars that ended the Seleucid Dynasty. The kingdom flourished in the reign of Antiochos I Epiphanes (ca. 62-32 B. C.), who was the son of Mithradates Kallinikos. Antiochos I was succeeded by Mithradates II. The Kommagenian Dynasty lasted until A. D. 72, when the region was incorporated in the Roman province of Syria by Vespasian.

Arsameia on the Nymphaios. This city was discovered by Professor Friedrich Karl Dörner of Münster University during his systematic investigations in connection with the Kommagene project. In 1951 he found a monumental inscription cut in the rock on the south flank of Eski Kale (Ancient Castle) near Eski Kâhta (in Adıyaman) on the River Nymphaios (the present-day Kâhta Çay). The inscription : "*the Great King Antiochos, God, the Righteous, Epiphanes, the Romanophile and Hellenophile, son of King Mithradates Kallinikos and Queen Laodike, daughter of Antiochos Epiphanes*", states that this site was chosen by his father as his "Hierotheseion", or sacred last resting-place. The king Antiochos Epiphanes, father of Laodike mentioned in the inscription, is Antiochos VIII Philometor (Grypos), one of the later kings of the Seleucid Dynasty, who was assassinated in 96 B.C. The inscription also discloses that Arsameia on the Nymphaios was founded by Arsames, an ancestor of Antiochos and further that the city had a fortifying wall and contained palaces and other buildings. Antiochos records that, here, a common cult of father and son should be established, both in his own honour and in memory of his ancestors.

The excavations supervised by Professor Dörner have yielded some very important finds, among which was a 3.43 m. - high relief, now re-erected in its original place above the aforementioned monumental inscription. This well-preserved relief, half in Parthian and half in Greek iconography but entirely Greek in style (Pls. 109-111), has been thoroughly studied by John Howard Young. It shows King Mithradates Kallinikos shaking hands with Herakles, who in Kommagene also represented Ares and the Persian god Artagnes. The relief must have been carved in the reign of Antiochos I, about 50 B. C.

Two or three kilometres south-west of Arsameia, the handsome bridge spanning the Cendere Çay, a branch of the Kâhta Çay, (the Nymphaios, was erected, according to a Latin inscription on columns, by four Kommagenian cities in honour of Septimius Severus, his wife Julia Domna and his sons Caracalla and Geta. The four columns originally stood in two pairs on either side of the bridge, but the one set up in honour of Geta is missing. Probably it was removed after Geta was murdered by his brother Caracalla.

About 10 km. south-west of Arsameia on the Nymphaios is a tumulus where the royal womenfolk were buried. The three Doric columns on its southern side are each surmounted by a statue of an animal : one by a lion, another by a bull and the third by an eagle. Since they overlook the Kâhta

Çay and form part of the view of the tumulus from the top of Nemrud Dağ, they also must date from the reign of Antiochos I (62-32 B. C.).

Nemrud Dağ. As a result of successful research and digs directed since 1953 by Theresa Goell on behalf of the American School of Oriental Research, New Haven, Connecticut, the most striking archaeological site in Turkey has now been systematically examined. The tumulus and the hierotheseion of Antiochos I Epiphanes are situated on the summit of Nemrud Dağ, a partly isolated mountain, 2150 m. above sea-level, lying among the Ankar Mountains immediately north-east of Kâhta. The tumulus, piled with fist-sized stones, is 50 m. high and 150 m. in diameter. It is bounded on the east, west and north by three terraced courts, hewn from the living rock. The east court forms the most important ensemble of architectural and sculptural monuments. It is surrounded on the west by colossal statues, on the east by a pyramidal fire altar, and on the north and south by low walls composed of orthostats (upright stone slabs) standing on a long, narrow base. The orthostats overlooking the court on the north were adorned with reliefs depicting the Persian ancestors of Antiochos, while those on the south bore reliefs portraying his Macedonian antecedents. In front of each relief there still stands a rectangular incense altar. The names of the persons depicted in the reliefs on the fronts of the orthostats were engraved on the outer faces. The greatly damaged orthostats now lie in small fragments on the ground. Professor Dörner, who assembled and studied these pieces, has established the genealogical trees of Antiochos of Kommagene, both on the paternal (Persian) side and on the maternal (Seleucid-Macedonian) side. According to his genealogy, Antiochos I of Kommagene claimed descent through his father, Mithradates, from Dareios I (522-486 B. C.) and through his mother, Laodike, from Alexander the Great (336-323 B. C.). The steps of the pyramidal altar bordering the east side of the eastern court are still partially preserved (see Figs. 167, 168).

The colossal statues of seated figures overlooking the court on the east terrace are fairly well-preserved and reach a height of 8-10 m. These block-like statues recall the very similar portrayals of seated deities to be found at Yesemek, some 50 km. south-west of Gaziantep, on the borders of ancient Kommagene. The latter date from the Hittite period and have been systematically investigated by Professor Bahadır Alkım. Each god of Kommagene incorporates several deities, following the principle of syncretism. In this way, the Macedonians, from the time of Alexander onwards, tried to unite the Greeks, Persians and other peoples of the Near East by identifying their various deities with one common type. Inscriptions state that the colossal statues on the east terrace, proceeding from left to right, are as follows : 1)Apollo-Mithra-Helios-Hermes.2) Fortuna, or the fertility goddess of Kommagene. 3) Zeus-Oromasdes (Ahuramazda). 4) Antiochos. 5) Herakles-Artagnes-Ares. An eagle and a lion statue stood, one on each side of the divinities. The heads of all the statues, except that of the goddess of fertility, have toppled down and can now be observed lying in the same sequence on the ground. They are exceedingly fine examples of the idealized late Hellenistic style, bearing handsome faces with noble features. The gods wear the Persian tiara and diadem. Zeus and Antiochos have lost the tops of their headdresses. The necks of Antiochos and the other gods are protected from the sun by lappets in the Persian fashion. A crown of fruits adorns the head of Fortuna, who bears a veil as a symbol of womanhood. The sides of the pedestals overlooking the court and the tumulus are engraved with inscriptions giving

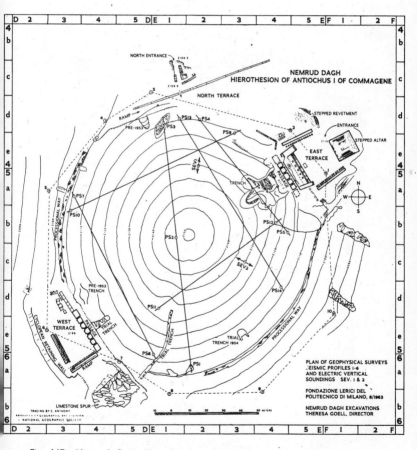

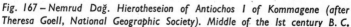

Fig. 167 – Nemrud Dağ. Hierotheseion of Antiochos I of Kommagene (after Theresa Goell, National Geographic Society). Middle of the 1st century B.C.

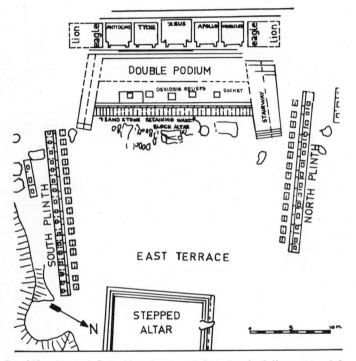

Fig. 168 – Nemrud Dağ. Hierotheseion of Antiochos I of Kommagene (after Theresa Goell, National Geographic Society). Middle of the 1st century B. C.

details of cult procedure, the birthday of the ruler, as well as the prescriptions and laws of his country.

The row of statues on the west terrace (Fig. 167) follows the same sequence. Though the heads of these statues also lie on the ground, they are in a better state of preservation. The face of Fortuna on the other terrace is badly eroded but the one on this terrace is in quite good condition. The heads of Herakles, Zeus and Apollo are also much better preserved than those on the eastern side of the tumulus. Owing to different topographical features, the orthostats bearing reliefs and inscriptions of ancestors on the west terrace are not arranged in the same way as on the east side. The slabs of the Macedonian ancestors of the king are, in this case, placed opposite the monumental statues, while those bearing reliefs of the Persian ancestors are set up on the southern border of the west terrace. In the same way, the reliefs in the west court depicting Antiochos shaking hands with several deities are excellently preserved, while the slabs with the same figures on the east terrace are represented by only a few fragments. On the west side can be seen the following hand-shaking scenes : Antiochos and Apollo-Mithra-Helios-Hermes; Antiochos and Zeus-Oromasdes; Antiochos and Herakles-Ares-Artagnes.

The lion relief in the west court deserves special attention. According to Professor Otto Neugebauer of Brown University, this relief bears astronomical symbols. Nineteen stars seen in the background of the relief and on the lion's body, a crescent moon on its breast and the conjunction of three planets corresponding to the Greek words for Jupiter, Mercury and Mars can be interpreted as the date July 7, 62, or 61 B. C. This happens to be the date when Antiochos was set on the throne by the Roman general Pompey.

The north terrace took the form of a processional way linking the east and west terraces. Slabs lying on the ground were originally part of a wall, 3 m. in height and 80 m. in length. There was an entrance in the middle of the wall giving access to a ramp leading from the valley to the mountain top. This entrance was guarded by the colossal statue of an eagle. Trenches dug into the tumulus indicate that it was piled up on a rocky hill. It is therefore very probable, as Theresa Goell states, that the bones or ashes of Antiochos I of Kommagene were preserved in a chamber cut in the living rock and covered by the tumulus.

GLOSSARY

ABACUS. The uppermost member of a capital (Fig. 69).

ACROTERIUM. The figures or ornaments crowning the apex or the lower angles of a pediment (Figs. 21, 27, 29).

ADYTON. The most holy room of a temple.

AGORA. Market-place.

AKROTERION. (See Acroterium).

ANTA. Pilasters of slight projection terminating the lateral walls of a cella in a Greek temple.

ANTEFIX. The decorative termination of the covering tiles.

APSE. A semicircular recess in a wall.

ARCHITRAVE (epistyle). A lintel resting on the columns. The lowest member of the entablature (Fig. 69).

ARRIS. The sharp edge formed by the flutes of a Doric column or of an old Ionic column.

ASHLAR MASONRY. Masonry composed of rectangular blocks.

ASIATIC BASE. Ionic base consisting of one plinth, two large scotiae with separating roundels and an upper torus (Figs. 54, 69).

ASTRAGAL. A moulding of rounded section, usually adorned with a carved or painted bead-and-reel and often combined with an egg-and-tongue (Fig. 69).

ATRIUM. 1) The court of a Roman house roofed at the sides, but open to the sky in the centre. 2) The entrance court of a Byzantine church (Fig. 51).

ATTIC BASE. The Ionic base consisting of an upper and lower torus and a scotia (or trochilus) between (Fig. 65).

BARREL VAULT. Covering of a room semicircular in cross-section.

BASILICA. 1) A Roman building consisting of a central hall with aisles which are lower in height than the central hall. 2) A Byzantine church composed of a nave and two or four aisles, which are lower in height than the nave.

BEAD-AND-REEL. The carved or painted ornament adorning an astragal (Fig. 69).

BOULEUTERION. Greek Senate House (Fig. 80).

CANALIS (channel). The space between the two volutes of an Ionic capital.

CAPITAL. The topmost member of a column.

CARYATID. Figure of a maiden replacing a column.

CAVEA. The auditorium of a theatre.

CELLA. The main chamber of a Greek temple containing the cult statue.

COFFER. A sunken pannel in a ceiling.

COLONNADE (also stoa or portico). A long covered hall with columns in front.

COLUMNAE CAELATAE. Sculptured columns (Fig. 54).

COMPOSITE CAPITAL. Corinthian capital combined with Ionic ovolo and volutes (Pl. 80).

CORNICE. The upper member of the entablature (Fig. 69).

CREPIDOMA, Crepis (Krepidoma). The stepped platform of a Greek temple.

CYCLOPEAN MASONRY. Walls composed of large blocks of irregular shape.

DENTIL. Rectangular blocks originally representing the ends of joints which carried a roof (Fig. 69).

DIAZOMA. The horizontal passage separating the rows of seats in a theatre.

DIPTEROS. A temple surrounded by two rows of columns (Figs. 52, 53, 83, 84).

DROMOS. A long narrow passage.

DRUM. One of the cylindrical sections of a column shaft.

EGG-AND-TONGUE or Egg-and-dart. This is the Ionic ovolo profile, originally consisting of a row of leaves (Fig. 69).

EKKLESIASTERION. Hall for the meeting of the sovereign assembly of a Greek city.

ENTABLATURE. The superstructure of a temple carried by columns (Fig. 69).

EPISTYLE. The Greek term for architrave.

EUSTYLE. Well-spaced columns (p. 23).

EXEDRA. A rectangular or semicircular open recess containing statue-bases which served also as seat places.

FASCIA. Slightly projecting bands of architrave of the Ionic and Corinthian orders (Fig. 69).

FLUTES. The vertical channels of columns separated one from the other by an arris (in the Doric order) or by a fillet (in the Ionic order).

FORUM. Market place in Roman times.

FRIEZE. The middle member of the entablature in the Ionic order (Fig. 65).

GEISON. The Greek term for the cornice.

HEART-AND-DART or leaf-and-dart. See Lesbian kymation and Kyma reversa.

HEROON (Heroum). Shrine dedicated to a deified or semideified dead person.

HIERON. Temple or sacred enclosure.

INTERAXIAL. The measurement of two adjacent columns from centre to centre.

INTERCOLUMNAR DISTANCE. The distance between two columns from surface to surface.

IONIC KYMATION. Another name for Egg-and-dart or Ionic ovolo (Fig. 69).

KREPIDOMA, KREPIS. See Crepidoma.

KYMA REVERSA (Lesbian Kymation). A wave moulding of which the upper convex part is protuding. It is usually adorned with heart-shaped leaf-and-dart.

LEAF-AND-DART. Another name for heart-and-dart. An ornament decorating the Lesbian kymation i.e. kyma reversa.

LESBIAN KYMATION. Another name for kyma reversa.

MEGARON. A long, narrow, isolated house consisting of one front-room as entrance and a hall with a hearth in the middle (Fig. 14, No. 102).

NAOS. The Greek term for temple. It is also used as equivalent to cella.

ODEION (Odeum). A roofed building in which rehearsals and musical contests were held.

OPISTHODOMOS. The porch at the rear of a Greek temple.

ORCHESTRA. Originally the dancing place of the Dionysiac ceremonies and hence the place of action for the chorus and the actors in Greek theatres of Classical and Hellenistic times.

ORTHOSTATS. Upright slabs forming the base of walls.

OVOLO. A quarter-round moulding decorated with egg-and-tongue. See Ionic Kymation.

PALÃESTRA. Literally "wrestling school"; but often used to mean training school for all kinds of physical exercises.

PARODOS. One of the lateral entrances left between the auditorium and the stage (Fig. 72).

PEDIMENT. The triangular termination of a pitched roof (Figs. 21, 27, 64).

PERIBOLOS. An enclosure wall.

PERIPTEROS. A temple surrounded by a row of columns (Fig. 68).

PERISTASIS. A row of columns surrounding a temple (Fig. 68).

PERISTYLE. A courtyard surrounded by colonnades (Fig. 26).

PLINTH. A square block forming the bottom of an Ionic base (Fig. 69).

PODIUM. A continuous and raised base carrying columns, sarcophagi, statues or temples.

PORCH. Vestibule.

PORTICO. Colonnade or stoa.

PRONAOS. The porch in front of a cella in a Greek temple.

PROPYLEIA, Propylaeum, Propylon. The entrance gate-building of a precinct or a sacred enclosure (Fig. 27).

PROSKENION. A raised platform in front of the stage-building on which the actors played in the Roman period (Fig. 73).

PROSTYLOS (Prostyle). A temple preceded by a porch with columns in front (Fig. 33).

PRYTANEION (Prytanaeum). The administrative building of a Greek city, containing the perpetual fire (Fig. 59, No. 19; Fig. 70, No. 8).

PSEUDO-DIPTEROS. A dipteral temple of which the inner row of columns are omitted (Fig. 63).

PTERON. The Greek word for wing. A row of columns surrounding a Greek temple.

SCOTIA. A concave moulding used in the Ionian column base (Fig. 69).

SKENE. The Greek word for tent. The stage building of a Roman theatre (Pl. 101 a).

SHAFT. The body of a column between the base and the capital.

SIMA. The gutter of a building.

SOCLE. The projecting foot of a wall or pedestal.

SOFFITE. The lower surface of an architrave as well as of an arch and a lintel.

STOA (Colonnade or Portico). A long covered hall with columns in front.

STYLOBATE. The upper step of a temple forming platform for the columns.

TEMENOS. A sacred enclosure containing one or more temples.

TYMPANON (tympanum). The triangular wall of the pediment.

TORUS. A large convex moulding of semicircular profile (Fig. 69).

TROCHILUS. The Greek term for Scotia.

BIBLIOGRAPHY

GENERAL WORKS

Prehistoric Period

AKURGAL - MANGO - ETTINGHAUSEN, Treasures of Turkey, Skira, Geneva 1966. Also in French, German, Italian and Spanish.

ALKIM, Bahadır, Tilmen Höyük, Belleten, 1958-1960, 1962 ; — Excavations at Gedikli, Belleten 1966 . — Anatolie I, Nagel-Génève 1968.

BITTEL, K. Grundzüge, Tübingen 1958; — Einige Idolen aus Kleinasien, Prähistor. Zeitschrift 34/35, 1949-1950, 135-144 .

BLEGEN, BOUTLER, CASKEY, RAWSON, SPERLING, Troy I-IV, Princeton 1950, 1951, 1953, 1958; BLEGEN, Troy and the Trojans. London 1963.

BORDAZ, J., The Suberde excavations, southwestern Turkey, TAD, 17, 1968, 43-713 .

BOSTANCI, E., Belbaşı, Belleten 36, 1962 ; — Beldibi, Anatolia 4, 1959 .

BRAIDWOOD, Reflexions on the origin of the village-farming community, Studies presented to Hetty Goldman , New York 1963.

FRENCH, D. H., Can Hasan, Anat. Studies 12, 1962; 13, 1963-1968·.

GARSTANG J., Prehistoric Mersin, Oxford 1952.

ESIN-BENEDICT, Recent developments, Current Anthropology 44, 1963 .

GOLDMAN, Hetty, Excavations at Tarsus I-III, Princeton, 1950, 1956.

KANSU Ş. A., Eti Yokuşu, Ankara 1937.

KÖKTEN, K., Karain, Anatolia 7, 1936, 59-88.

KOŞAY - AKOK, Büyük Güllücek, Ankara 1957.

LAMB, W., Kusura, Archaeologia 86, 1936; 87, 1937 .

LLOYD, Seton, Early Anatolia, Penguin Books, London 1956; Seton Lloyd and Mellaart, Beyce Sultan I, II, London 1962, 1964; Seton Lloyd, Early Highland peoples of Anatolia, Thames and Hudson, London 1967.

MATZ, Friedrich, Kreta und frühes Griechenland, Baden-Baden 1962.

MELLINK, M., Anatolian Chronology (Ehrich, Chronologies in old world Archaeology, Chicago 1954, 101-131); — Excavations at Karataş - Semayük, AJA 68, 1964, 269-278; 69, 1965, 251-241.

MELLAART, J., Earliest Civilisations, London 1965.

NAGEL W., Vordynastisches Keramikum, BjV 1-2, 1961-1964 .

ORTHMANN, W., Keramik der frühen Bronzezeit, Berlin 1963.

SCHACHERMEYR, F., Neufunde zur ägäischen Frühzeit, AA 1962, 106 ff. .

STRONAH, D. B., Metalltypes in early Anatolia, Anat. Studies 7, 89-125 .

TEZCAN, Burhan, New finds from Horoztepe, Anatolia 5 1960 .

WEINBERG, Saul S., The Stone Age in the Aegean, CAH I, 1965 ; — Relative Chronology in the Aegean (Ehrich, Relative Chronologies in old world Archaeology).

Hattian and Hittite Periods

AKURGAL, Ekrem, Die Kunst der Hethiter, München 1961; — The Art of the Hittites, London-New York 1962; — Arte degli Ittiti, Firenze 1962; — Kunst der Hethiter, Historia, Einzelschriften, Heft 7, 74-118 .

ALBRIGHT, W. F., The Anatolian Goddess Kupaba, AfO, 5, 1929 ; — New light on the history, BASOR 77/78, 1940 .

ALKIM, B., Excavations at Domuztepe, Belleten XVI, 1952, 238-250 .

ALP, Sedat, Nam-Ra-Leute, JKFI ; — Personennamen, Ankara 1950; — Kanis = Anisa = Nisa, Belleten 1963, 377-386 ; — Eine hethitische Bronzestatuette, Anatolia 6, 1961/62 ; — Libationsgefässe, Belleten 31, 1967, 513-549 ; — Zylinder - und Stempelsiegel aus Karahöyük bei Konya, Türk Tarih Kurumu, Ankara 1968.

ARIK, R. O. Alaca Höyük, Ankara 1935.

BALKAN, Kemal, Chronological Problems of the Karum Kanis, Ankara 1955; — Letter of King Anum Hirbi, Ankara 1957.

BILGIÇ, Emin, Ortsnamen der kappadokischen Urkunden AfO 15, 1-37 ; — die einheimischen Appellativa, Ankara, 1954.

BERAN, Thomas, Hethitische Siegel, Bogazköy III, Bittel , Berlin 1957, 42-57; — Ausgewählte Siegel, MDOG, 89, 1957, 39-48 ; — Die Siegel der hethitischen Grosskönige, Istanbuler Mitteilungen, 17, 1967, 72-77 ; — Die hethitische Glyptik von Bogazköy, Berlin 1967.

BITTEL, Kurt, Boğazköy, Kleinfunde, Leipzig 1937; — Nur hethitische oder auch hurritische Kunst, ZA, 49, 1950 ; — Hethiter und Protohattier, Historia I, 1950, 267-286 ; — Yazılıkaya Deutsche Orientgesellschaft, 61, Leipzig 1941 .

BOSSERT, H. Th., Altanatolien, Berlin 1942.

BOZKURT - ÇIĞ - GÜTERBOCK, Boğazköy Tabletleri I-II, İstanbul 1947/1948.

CAVAIGNAC, E., Subbiluliuma et son temps, Paris 1932.

BRANDENSTEIN, C. G. v., Götter nach Bildbeschreib. Leipzig 1943 MVAeG, 46, 2.

DANMANVILLE, J., Un roi hittite honore Ishtar de Samuha, RHA 59, 1956; — La libation en Mésopotamie, RA, 49, 1955; — Istar-Sausga RA, 56, 1962.

DARGA, Muhibbe, Huwası (Belleten 33, 1969, 493 - 504).

DEMİRCİOĞLU, Halil, Der Gott auf dem Stier, Berlin 1939.

DOLUNAY, Necati, Hasanoğlan Heykelciği IV. T. T. Kongresi.

FISCHER, Franz, Die hethitische Keramik von Boğazköy, Berlin 1963.

FRIEDRICH, J., Aus dem hethitischen Schriftum AO, 24, 3; 25, 2.

FURLANI, G., Sugli sulla Civilta degli Hittiti, Udine 1939.

GARELLI, P., Les assyriens en Cappadoce, Paris 1963.

GELB, I. J., Hittite Hieroglyphic Monuments, Chicago 1939, OIP 45.

GOETZE, A., Kleinasien, München 1957; — The Cultures of early Anatolia, Proc. of Am. Phil. Soc. 2, 1953; — Annalen des Mursili, Kl. Forsch. I 161-251, 1929.

GURNEY, O. R., The Hittites, Penguin Books 1968; — "Mita of Pahhuwa", LAAA, 28, 1948.

GÜTERBOCK, H. G., Siegel aus Boğazköy I, II, AfO, Beihefte 5, 7, 1940, 1944 ; — The deeds of Suppiluliuma, JCS, 10, 1956 ; — Kumarbi, Zürich-New York 1946; — Götterdarstellungen, Belleten, 7, 1943, 295 ff; — Kanes and Nesa, Eret - Israel, 5, 1958.

HANCAR, F., Der Kult der grossen Mutter, AfO 13, 1939-41 ; — Wiener Beiträge zur Kunst -und Kulturgeschichte Asiens XII, Wien 1959.

KAMMENHUBER, A., Vom Mond, der vom Himmel gefallen ist, ZA, 17, 1955; — Hattische Studien I, RHA, 20, 196 a, 1-29; — Die sprachen des vorhellenistischen Kleinasien, Münchener Studien zur Sprachwissenschaft 24, 55-123, München 1968; — Die Arier im Vorderen Orient, Heidelberg 1968; — Die sprachstufen des Hethitischen, Zeitschrift für Vergleichende Sprachforschung 83, 1969, 256-289.

KINAL, F., Géographie et l'histoire des pays d'Arzawa, Ankara 1953.

KOROSEC, V., Hethitische Staatsverträge, Leipzig 1931.

KOŞAY, H., Alaca Höyük, Ankara 1938, 1951; — M. Akok, Alaca Höyük, AJA 51, 1947; Koşay - Akok, Alacahöyük, Ankara 1966.

LANDSBERGER, B., Assyrische Handelskolonien in Kleinasien, AO, 1925 ; — Assyrische Königsliste und "dunkles" Zeitalter, JCS, 8, 1954, 31-133.

LAROCHE, E., *Recueil d'onomastique hittite*, Paris 1952; — Le panthéon de Yazilikaya, JCS, 6, 115-123; — Etudes "Protohittites", RA 41, 1947; — Hattic deities and their epithets, JCS, 1947; une conjuration bilingue Hatti-Hittite, JKF, I, 1950; — Les Hiéroglyphes Hittites, Paris 1960; — documents en langue hittite et hourrite, Ugaritica V 447-544, 769-784 Paris 1968; — Les noms des Hittites, Paris 1966.

MELLINK, M., The Royal Tombs at Alaca Höyük, Studies presented to Hetty Goldman; — A Hittite cemetery at Gordion, Philadelphia 1956.

MERIGGI, P., Die längsten Bauinschriften in "hethitischen Hieroglyphen, MVAeG 29, I, 1934; — Listes des hiéroglyphes hittites, RHA, 4, 1937. 69-114; — La ricostruzione di Kargamis, Rivista degli Studi Orientali 29, 1954, 1-16.

MOORTGAT, A., Die bildende Kunst des alten Orients und die Bergvölker, Berlin 1933; - Nur hethitische oder auch churrische Kunst, ZA, 48, 1944, 152-160; — Vorderasien bis zum Hellenismus in Ägypten und Vorderasien (Scharff und Moortgat), München 1950.

NASTER, P., L'Asie Mineure et l'Assyrie, Louvain, 1938.

NAUMANN, R., Die Hethiter, Berlin 1948; — Architektur Kleinasiens, Tübingen 1955.

NEVE, Peter, Hoftürme in den hethitischen Tempeln Hattusas, Ist. Mitt. 17, 1967.

OTTEN H., Die hethitische "Königlisten" und die altorientalische Chronologie, MDOG, 83, 1951, 47-71; — Zu den Anfängen der hethitischen Geschichte, ibid. 33-45; — Hethitische Totenrituale, Berlin 1958; — Keilschrifttexte, MDOG, 91, 1958, 73-84, — Die hethitischen historischen Quellen und die altorientalische Chronologie, Wiesbaden 1968; — Sprachliche Stellung und Datierung des Maduwatta - Textes, Wiesbaden 1969.

ÖZGÜÇ, N., The Anatolian Group of cylinder Seal impressions from Kültepe, Ankara 1965.

ÖZGÜÇ, T., Excavations at Kültepe 1948, 1949, Ankara, 1950, 1953; — Kültepe-Kaniş, Ankara 1959; — Horoztepe, Ankara 1958.

PRITCHARD, J. B., Ancient Near Eastern Texts, Princeton, 1950.

SCHAEFFER, Claude, Ugaritica III, Paris 1956.

STEINER, G., Die Ahhijawa-Frage heute, Saeculum 15, 1964, 365-392.

STEINHERR, Franz, Die Hieroglyphenhethitische Inschrift des Reliefs A am Karabel, Istanbuler Mitteilungen 15, 1965, 17-23.

SCHULER, E. von, Hethitische Dienstanweisungen für höhere Hof und-Staatsbeamte, AfO, Beiheft 10, 1950 ; — Staatsverträge, Historia, Einzelschriften, Heft 7, 30-53.

TEMIZER, R., Un bas-relief de Cybèle, Anatolia IV, 1959, 183-187; — Archaeological Museum, Ankara 1969.

TOSUN, M., Styles in Kültepe seal-engraving as expressions of various cultural influences, Festschrift für Landsberger, JCS, 183-188, 1968.

VIEYRA, M., Hittite Art, London 1955.

Neo - Hittite Period

AKURGAL, Ekrem, Remarques stylistiques sur les reliefs de Malatya, Istanbul 1946; — Späthethitische Bildkunst, Ankara 1949; — Orient und Okzident, Baden-Baden, Holle Verlag, 1966; The English, American and French Editions of the same book: — The Birth of Greek Art, Methuen - London 1966; — The Art of Greece : The Origins, New York 1968.; — Orient et Occident, Albin Michel, Paris 1969.

ALBRIGHT, W. F., dark ages, Studies presented to Hetty Goldman 144-164.

ALKIM, Bahadır, Les résultats archéologiques des fouilles de Karatepe, RHA, 9, 1948-1949, 1-29; — Excavations at Domuztepe, Belleten 116, 1952, 238-250.

BARNETT, The key to the Hittite Hieroglyphes, Anatolian Studies 3, 1953, 53-95.

BOSSERT, H. Th., ALKIM, ÇAMBEL, ONGUNSU - SÜZEN, Die Ausgrabungen auf dem Karatepe, Ankara 1950.

ÇAMBEL, H., Some Observations on the Karatepe Sculptures, Belleten 12, 1949, 35 ff.; — Oriens I, 1948, 147 ff.

KALAÇ, Die Wettergott - Stele mit Hieroglyphen (Athenaeum 47, 1963, p. 160 - 167).

LANDSBERGER, B., Samal, Ankara 1948.

MATTHIAE, P., Studi sui relievi di Karatepe, Roma 1963.

MELLINK, M., Bibliotheca Orientalis 7, 1950.

PECORELLA, P. E., Una Stele neoetea da Malatya (Athenaeum 47, 1969, 226 - 235).

PUGLISI - MERIGGI, Malatya I, Roma 1961.

TEZCAN, Burhan, Göllüdağ Kazısı, TAD, 17, 1968, 211-235.

Urartian Art And Culture

AKURGAL, Ekrem, Die Kunst Anatoliens, Berlin 1961, 23-69; — Urartäische und Altiranische Kunstzentren, Türk Tarih Kurumu, Ankara 1968.

AMANDRY, P., Grèce et Orient, Etudes d'archéologie Classique I, 1955-1956, 3-20; — Chaudrons à Protome de taureau, Studies presented to Hetty Goldman 239-261 .

BALKAN, K., Ein urartäischer Tempel auf Anzavurtepe bei Patnos, Anatolia 5, 1960, 99-131 .

BARNETT, R. D., Excavations of the British Museum at Toprakkale near Van, Iraq, 12, 1950, 1-43; — Iraq, 16, 1954, 3-22.

BİLGİÇ, Emin - **ÖĞÜN**, Baki, Excavations at Kef Kalesi of Adilcevaz, Anatolia 8, 1964, 93-124 .

BURNEY, C. A., Urartian Fortresses and towns in the Van region, Anatolian Studies 7, 1957, 37-53 ; Burney und G. R. I. Lawson, Anatolian Studies 10, 1960, 177-196 ; Burney, Excavations at Kayalıdere, Anat. Studies 16, 1966, 55-111.

ERZEN, Afif, Untersuchungen in der urartäischen Stadt Toprakkale bei Van in den Jahren 1959 - 1961, AA, 1962, 382-414 .

GHIRSHMAN, R., Perse, 259-301, Paris 1963.

HANFMANN, George M. A., Urartian Bull's heads, Anatolian Studies 6, 1956, 205-213 .

LOON, Van, Urartian Art, Istanbul 1966.

MAXWELL-HYSLOP, K. R., Urartian Bronzes in Etruscan Tombs, Iraq 18, 1956, 150-167 .

NAUMANN, Rudolf, Bemerkungen zu urartäischen Tempeln, Ist. Mitt. 18, 1968, 48 - 57.
OGANESYAN, K. L., Arin Berd, Erivan 1961.
ÖĞÜN, Baki, Ausgrabungen von Kef Kalesi, A.A. 1967, 481-503 .
ÖZGÜÇ, T., Excavations at Altıntepe, Belleten 98, 1961, 253-290 ; — The Urartian architecture on the summit of Altıntepe, Anatolia 8, 1963, 43-57 ; — Altıntepe, Ankara 1966.
PALLOTTINO, M., Urartu, Greece and Etruria, in "East and West" 9, 1958 Roma 29-52 .
PIOTROVSKI, B. B., Vanskoie Tsarstvo, Moskva 1959; — Iskusstvo Urartu, Leningrad 1962.
; — Urartu, Nagel, Paris 1969.
SALVINI, M., Nairi e Ur(u)atri, Edizioni dell' Ateneo, Roma 1967;— Studi sul Verbo Urarteo
Studi Micenei ed Egeo-Anatolia 5, 1968, 97-127; — Inscrizioni Urartee... Studi Mic. ed
Egeo-Anatolici 9, 1969, 7-24; — Urartäisch-hurritische Wortgleichungen, Orientalia 39, 1970,
409-411 .
SÜMER, Osman, Urartu Keramik eserleri, Anatolia 5, 1961-1962, 245-248.

Phrygian Art And Culture

AKURGAL, Ekrem, Phrygische Kunst, Ankara, 1945; — Die Kunst Anatoliens, Berlin 1961.
70-121; — Huitième Congrès International d'Arch. Classique, Paris 1963, 467-474.
BARNETT, R. D., Phrygia and the peoples of Anatolia in the Iron Age, The Cambridge Ancient History II Chapter XXX, 3-32.
BERAN, Thomas, Eine Kultstatuette phrygischer Zeit in Boğazköy, MDOG, 94, 1964, 44-52.
BITTEL, Kurt, Kleinasiatische Studien, Istanbul 1942, 66-127.
BOSSERT, E. M., Funde nachhethitischer Zeit, MDOG, 89, 1957, 58-67; 94, 1963, 53-71.
GABRIEL, Albert, Phrygie II, La cité de Midas, Topographie, le site et les Fouilles, Paris 1952. — Phrygien IV, Architecture, Paris 1965.
HASPELS, C. H. Emilie, Phrygie III, La Cité de Midas, Céramique, Paris 1951.
LEJEUNE, Michel, À propos de la titulature de Midas, Athenaeum 47, 1969, 179-192 ; — Discussion sur l'Alphabet phrygien, Studi Micenei ed Egeo-Anatolici 1969, 19-47;— Notes Paléo – Phrygiennes, Rev. des Etudes Anciennes. 71, 1969, 287 — 300; — Les inscriptions de Gordion et l'Alphabet phrygien, Kadmos, 9, 1970, 51 — 74.
MELLINK, Machteld, AJA 61, 1957, 292—295.
MERIGGI, P., Una prima attestazione epicorica dei Moschi, Athenaeum 42, 1964, 52-59 .
MUSCARELLA, Oscar white, Phrygian Fibulae from Gordion, London 1967.
YOUNG, Robert, S., see Gordion .

Greek And Roman Periods

AKARCA, A., Les Monnaies grecques de Mylasa, Paris 1959; — Milas, Istanbul 1954.
AKURGAL, Ekrem, Die Kunst Anatoliens, Berlin 1961. Akurgal-Mango-Ettinghausen, Treasures of Turkey, Skira, Geneva 1966, also in French, German, Italian and Spanish . Akurgal, The Birth of Greek Art. London 1968 (The Art of Greece : The Origins. New York 1968: Orient und Okzident, Holle, Baden-Baden 1966: Orient et Occident, Albin Michel, Paris 1969).
BAYBURTLUOĞLU, Cevdet, Arkaik Kuros başı, Belleten, 31, 1967, 331-334 .
BEAN, G. E. Aegean Turkey, London 1966; — Turkey's southern shore, London 1968.
BIEBER, M., Sculpture of the Hellenistic age. New York 1961.
BILABEL, F., Die Ionische Kolonisation, Leipzig 1920.
CAHN, Herbert, A., Frühhellenistische Münzkunst, Basel.
CARRUBA, O., Ahhijawa e altri nomi di popoli e di paesi dell' Anatolia occidentale, Athenaeum 42, 1964, 269-298 .
CASSOLA, E., La Ionia nel Mondo Miceneo, Napoli 1957.
COOK, John, Ionia and the East, London 1962.
DENTZER, J. M., Reliefs au Banquet dans l'Asie Mineure du Ve siècle, Rev. Arch. 2, 1969, 195 - 224.
DEVAMBEZ, P., Grandes bronzes du Musée de Stamboul, Paris 1937.
DINSMOOR, W. B. The Architecture of Ancient Greece, London-New York 1950.
DOLUNAY Necati, Daskyleion, Ist. Ark. Müzeleri Yıllığı 1966, 1 ff.
DRERUP, H., Pytheos and Satyros J d I, 69, 1954, 1-31; — Zum Artemistempel von Magnesia, Marburger Winckelmann-Programm 1964, 13-22; — Prostashaus und Pastashaus, Marburger Winckelmann-Programm 1967, 6-17; — Griechische Architektur zur Zeit Homers, AA, 1964, 180-219; — Bericht über die Ausgrabungen in Didyma 1962 A.A. 1964, 333-368; — Griechische Baukunst in geometrischer Zeit, Göttingen 1969.

DUNBABIN, T. J., The Greeks and their eastern neighbours, London 1957.

DUYURAN, Rüstem, Batı Anadolu, Istanbul 1948 — Priene Kılavuzu, Istanbul 1948.

ERDER, Cevat, Hellenistik devir Anadolu mimarisinde Kyma Rekta, Kyma Reversa, Middle East Technical University, Ankara 1967.

FIRATLI, Nezih, Les stèles funéraires de Byzance greco-romaine. Paris 1964.

GEHRIG-GREIFENHAGEN-KUNISCH, Führer, Antikenabteilung in Berlin, Berlin 1968.

GERKAN, Armin von, Griechische Städteanlagen, Berlin 1924.

GÖTZE, Bernt, Antike Bibliotheken Jdl, 52, 1937, 225-247.

GRUBEN, G. Zum Artemis-Tempel von Sardis AM, 76, 1961, 155-196; — Das archaische Didymaion, Jdl, 78, 1963, 78-182; — Die Tempel der Griechen, Hirmer, München 1966.

GÜLTEKİN, Hakkı, Izmir Agorası, Izmir 1951 — Izmir tarihi, Izmir 1952. — Miletos, Izmir 1961. — A guide to Ephesus, Izmir 1965. — A guide to the Museum, Izmir 1965.

HAMPE, Roland, Kretische Löwenschale des siebenten Jahrhunderts v. Chr., S. B. Heidelberger Akademie 1969, 9 - 42.

HANFMANN, G. M. A., Ionia, Leader or Follower, Harvard Studies in Classical Philology 41, 1953, 1-37; — Hellenistic Art, Dumbarton Oaks Papers 17, 79-94 1963.

HOEPFNER, Wolfram, Herakleia Pontike — Ereğli, Wien 1966.

HUMANN-PUCHSTEIN, Reisen in Nordsyrien und Kleinasien, Berlin 1890.

INAN, Jale, Römische Porträts aus Antalya, Ankara 1965. J. INAN and E. ROSENBAUM, Roman and Early Byzantine Portrait Sculpture, Oxford 1966.

KASPER, Sandor, Eine Nekrople nordwestlich von Soma, AA 1970, 71 — 85.

KESKIL, Süheyla, Hatay Müzesi, Ankara 1964.

KLEEMANN, I., Der Satrapen-Sarkophag, Berlin 1958.

KRISCHEN, Fritz, Weltwunder der Baukunst in Babylonien und Ionien, Tübingen 1966.

KÜNZL, Ernst, Frühhellenistische Gruppen, Köln 1968.

LAWRENCE, A. W., Greek Architecture, Penguin Books 1957.

LULLIES, Greek Sculpture, London 1960.

MAGIE, David, Roman Rule in Asia Minor, Princeton University Press 1950.

MANSEL, Arif Müfit, Stockwerkbau der Griechen und Römer, Berlin 1932; — Die Kuppelgräber von Kırklareli in Thrakien, Türk Tarih Kurumu, Ankara, 1943; — Excavations at Perge, Ankara 1949; — Ausgrabungen in Side, Ankara 1951; — Die Ruinen von Side, Berlin 1963. AA 1956, 34-119. — Osttor und Waffenfries von Side AA, 1968, 239-279.

MARTIN, Roland, Recherches sur l'Agora Grecque. Paris 1951. — L'Urbanisme dans la Grèce Antique, Paris 1956; — L'Agora (Etudes Thasiennes VI) Paris 1959; — Manuel d'Architecture Grecque I. Paris 1965; — Living Architecture, Greek, Oldbourne-London 1967.

MELLINK, Machteld, J., Anatolia : Old and new perspectives, Proceedings of the American Philosophical Society 110, 1966, 111-129.

MENDEL, G., Catalogue I-III, Constantinople, 1912-1914.

METZGER, H., Catalogue des monuments votifs du Musée d'Adalia, Paris.

OĞUZ, Erol, Observations on Anatolian Coastline, Changes during the Holocene, Coğrafya Araştırmaları Dergisi 2, 1969, Ankara University 95-102.

OLCAY, Nekriman et SEYRIG, Henri, Le trésor de Mektepini en Phrygie, Paris 1965.

POLACCO, Luigi, Topaklı (Studi Micenei ed Egeo - Anatolici 10, 1969, 54 - 68).

RIDGWAY, Brunilde Sismondo, The Bronze Lady from the sea (Expedition 10, 1967, 3-8).

RIEMANN, H., Pytheos (Pauly-Wissowa, XXIV).

ROBERT, L., — Villes d'Asie Mineure, Paris 1935; — Etudes Anatoliennes, Paris 1937; La Carie, Paris 1954; — Les Fouilles de Claros, Conférence donnée à l'Université d'Ankara, 29 pages, Paris 1954; — Noms indigènes dans l'Asie Mineure Greco-Romaine, Paris 1963; — Nouvelles inscriptions de Sardes, Paris 1964; — Inscriptions d'Aphrodisias (L'Antiquité Classique 35, 1966, 377-432).

ROBERTSON, D. S., Greek and Roman Architecture. Cambridge 1945.

ROEBUCK, C., Ionian Trade and Colonisation, Newyork 1959.

ROHDE, E., Griechische und Römische Kunst in den Staatlichen Museen zu Berlin, Berlin 1968.

ROSENBAUM, E., Huber, G. Onurkan, Somay, A survey of coastal cities in western Cilicia. Türk Tarih Kurumu Ankara 1967.

SAKELLARIOU, M. B., Migration Grecque en Ionie. Athènes 1958.

SCHOBER, Arnold, Der Fries des Hekateions von Lagina (Istanbuler Forschungen 2), Wien 1933.

STARK, Freya, Ionia, London 1954; — The Lycian Shore. London 1956; — Alexander's path from Caria to Cilicia, London 1958.

WALTER - KARYDI, Elena, Äolische Kunst (Antike Kunst 1970, 3 - 17).
WEBER, H. Zum Apollon Smintheus - Tempel in der Troas (Istanbuler Mitteilungen 16, 1966, 100 - 114).
YURDKORU, Suad, Büyük İskender'in Anadolu Savaşları, İzmir 1961.
ZSCHIETZSCHMANN, Willy, Die hellenistische, und römische Kunst (Die Antike Kunst II Potsdam 1939).

SPECIAL WORKS

ACEMHÖYÜK : Nimet ÖZGÜÇ, Excavations at Acemhöyük (Anadolu X, 1966). Kutlu EMRE, The pottery from Acemhöyük (Anadolu X 1966). Nezahat BAYDUR, N. Kültepe ve Kayseri tarihi, İstanbul 1970.

ADANA : Seyyide ÇELİKKOL, Adana Taşköprüsü, Adana 1946. M. Hadi ALTAY, Çukurova, Adana 1946. H. I. MUSSCHE, Aphrodite in het Museum te Adana (Gentse Bijdragen tot de kunstgeschiedenis en de Oudheidbunde, Gent 1959, 27 - 30).

AIZANOI : Charles TEXIER, Description de l'Asie Mineure I, 97, pl. 23. Charles FELLOWS, Asia 137. LE BAS - REINACH 142. Körte (Festschrift für Otto BENNDORF, Wien 1898, 209). SCHEDE - KRENCKER, der Temple in Ankara, Berlin 1936, 30 - 31. T. FYFE, Hellenistic Architecture 1936, 35 - 38. V. F. NOACK, Baukunst des Altertums 47 - 58. W. B. DINSMOOR, Architecture 274. A. W. LAWRENCE 216 - 218. WEIGAND, Gnomon 1937, 414 - 422. ROBERTSON, Handbook, 218 - 220, 342, 358, 94. R. NAUMANN, Das Heiligtum der Meter Steunene, Istanbuler Mitteilungen, 17, 1967, 218 - 247. P. LAMBRECHTS, ANAMNHCIC (Gedenbock Leemans), Brugge 1970, 235 - 253.

ALABANDA : EDHEM - BEY, Fouilles d'Alabanda (CRAI, 1905, 1 - 16). SCHOBER, Der Fries des Hekateions von Lagina, Wien 1933, 16 - 19). H. WEBER, zum Apollon Smintheus - Tempel in der Troas (Istanb. Mitt. 16, 1966, 114 n. 12).

ALACA HÖYÜK : R. O. ARIK, Alaca Höyük, Ankara 1935. Hamit KOŞAY, Alaca Höyük, Ankara 1951; KOŞAY and AKOK, M. Alaca Höyük (AJA 51, 1957); — Alaca Höyük, Ankara 1966. MELLINK, M. The Royal Tombs at Alaca Höyük (Studies Presented to Hetty Goldman).

ANKARA : KRENCKER - SCHEDE, Der tempel in Ankara, Berlin 1936, it includes previous bibliography) (rev. by E. WEIGAND, Gnomon 1937, 414 - 422). H. KOŞAY Augustustempel in Ankara (Anatolia 2, 1957, 133 - 138). Afif ERZEN, İlkçağda Ankara. T.T.K. Ankara 1946. E. BOSCH, Quellen zur Geschichte der Stadt Ankara im Altertum. T.T.K. Ankara, 1967. Mahmut AKOK, Ankara Roma Hamamı (Türk Ark. Derg. 17, 1968, 5 - 37). Can GÜLEKLI, the guide of Ankara, Ankara 1961.

APHRODISIAS : Kenan T. ERIM, Ancient Aphrodisias and its Marble Treasures (National Geographic 132, 2, August 1967 pp. 280 - 294); — Two new early byzantine statues from Aphrodisias (Dumbarton Oaks papers 21, 285 - 286); — Portraits, Aphrodisias (Belleten 32, 1968 pp. 4 - 18). L. ROBERT, Inscriptions d'Aphrodisias (L'Antiquité Classique 35, 1966, 377 - 432). M. SQUARCIAPINO, La scuola di Afrodisia, Rome 1943.

ARSAMEIA : DÖRNER - NAUMANN, Forschungen in Kommagene (Istanb. Forschungen 10) Berlin 1939. DÖRNER, Arsameia in Kommagene (Neue Deutsche Ausgr.), Berlin 1959. DÖRNER - GOELL, Arsameia am Nymphaios (Istanbuler Forschungen 23), Berlin 1963. DÖRNER, Zur Rekonstruktion der Ahnengalerie des Königs Antiochos I. von Kommagene (Ist. Mitt. 17, 1967, 195 - 210). John H. YOUNG, Skulpturen aus Arsameia (Dörner - Goell, 197 - 226); — Commagenian Tiaras : Royal and Divine (AJA 68, 1964, 29 - 34).

ASPENDOS : LANCKORONSKI I (Pamphylien), Wien 1890, 83 - 124.

ASSOS : CLARKE - BACON - KOLDEWEY, Investigations at Assos, Cambridge Mass. 1902 - 1921. W. B. DINSMOOR, The basis of Greek Temple Design (Atti del VII Congresso Internaz. d'Arch. Classica, Roma 1961, I, 355 - 368). A von GERKAN, Betrachtungen zum Ionischen Gebälk (Jdl 61 - 62, 1946 - 47, p. 28). Arif Müfid MANSEL (AA, 1956, 71 - 72 and note 43). Fred E. WINTER, Hellenistic Fortifications (Amer. Philos. Soc. Yearbook, 1958, 388 - 393). R. MARTIN, L'Agora Grecque 427.

BOĞAZKÖY : Kurt BITTEL, Die Ruinen von Boğazköy, Berlin 1937. Kurt BITTEL, NAUMANN and others, Yazılıkaya Leipzig 1941 (Deutsche Orient - Gesellschaft, 61). E. LAROCHE, Le panthéon de Yazılıkaya JCS, 6, 115 - 123. Franz FISCHER, Boğazköy und die Chronologie der altassyrischen Handelsniederlassungen in Kappadokien (Ist. Mitt. 15, 1965, 1 - 16). BITTEL, Bericht 1968 (MDOG, 101, 1969, 5 - 13). Kurt BITTEL, Hattusa, The Capital of the Hittites, New York, Oxford University Press 1970.

BELEVI : Josef KEIL, Öst. Jhft. Beiblatt 28, 1933, 28 ff; 29, 1935, 103 ff; 30, 1936, 173 ff. Camilo PRASCHNIKER, Die Datierung des Mausoleums von Belevi, Öst. Akademie, Anzeiger 1948, 271 - 298. G. KLEINER, Diadochengräber, Wiesbaden 1963, 83 ff. W. ALZINGER, Anzeiger für die Altertumswissenschaft 17, 1964, 106. Sandor KASPER, Grabtumulus von Belevi, Österreichisches Archäologisches Institut, Grabungen 1966, 12 - 16. Ekrem AKURGAL, Griech. Reliefs aus Lykien, Berlin 1942, P. 102.

DIDYMA : Th. WIEGAND (H. KNACKFUSS), Didyma, Baubeschreibung, Berlin 1941. A. V. GERKAN, Das säulenproblem des Naiskos von Didyma (Ist. Mitt. 13/14, 1963/64, 63 - 72). G. GRUBEN, Das archaische Didymaion (Jdl, 78, 1963, 78 - 182). H. DRERUP, Bericht über die Ausgrabungen in Didyma 1962 (AA, 1964. 333 - 368). W. HAHLAND, Didyma im 5. Jh. (Jdl, 79, 1964, 142 - 244). NAUMANN - TUCHELT, Ausgrabung im Südwesten des Tempels von Didyma (Ist. Mitt. 13/14, 1963/64, 15 - 62).

EPHESOS : Franz MILTNER, Ephesos, Wien, 1958. K. OTTO DORN, Die Isa Bey Moschee in Ephesos (Istanbuler Forschungen 17, 115 - 131). Josef KEIL, Führer durch Ephesos, Wien, 1964. Fritz EICHLER, Heroon von Gjölbaschi; — Trysa, Wien 1950; — Die Österreichischen Ausgrabungen in Ephesos 1960 - 1968. Wilhelm ALZINGER, Ionische Kapitelle aus Ephesos I (ÖJH 46, 1961-63, 105 - 136); — Ritzzeichnungen in den Marmorbrüchen von Ephesos (ÖJH. 48, 1966 - 67, 61 - 72); — Alt-Ephesos (Das Altertum B, 1967, 20 - 44); — Koressos (ÖJH 12, 1967, 1 - 9). Anton BAMMER, Der altar des Jüngeren Artemision von Ephesos (AA, 1968), 400 - 423); — Zur Topographie und städtebaulichen Entwicklung von Ephesos (Öst. Jh. Beiblatt 46, 1961 - 63, 136 - 157); — Zum jüngeren Artemision von Ephesos (Öst. Jh. 47, 1964 - 65, 126 - 145); — Die gebrannten Mauerziegel von Ephesos (Öst. Jh. Beiblatt 47, 1964 - 65, 290 - 299); — Tempel und Altar der Artemis von Ephesos (Öst. Jh. Beiblatt 48, 1966 - 67, 22 - 43); — Doppelmäander in Ephesos (Festschrift für Fritz Eichler, Wien 1967, 10 - 22). Hakkı GÜLTEKIN, A guide to Ephesos, Izmir. 1965. ATALAY – TÜRKOĞLU, Guide du Musée d'Ephèses Ankara, 1969. Beat BRENK, Datierung der Reliefs am Hadrianstempel in Ephesos (Ist. Mitt. 18, 1968, 238 - 258). H. WIEGARTZ, Zu den columnae caelatae des jüngeren Artemision (Marburger Winckelmann - Programm 1968, 41 - 73).

ERYTHRAI : H. GAEBLER, Erythrae, Berlin 1892. G. WEBER, AM 26, 1901, 103, ff. MAGIE, RR in AM 68, 79, 889, 897. C. J. CADOUX, Ancient Smyrna 62, 65, 113. Hakkı GÜLTEKIN, TAD 17, 1968, 103 - 116.

GÂVURKALESİ : H. H. v. d. OSTEN, Oriental Institute Communications 14, Chicago 1933, 56 - 90. Ekrem AKURGAL, Belleten 1943, 77 n. 36; — Späthethitische Bildkunst 5, n. 31;— The Art of the Hittites 105 - 106. NAUMANN, Architektur Kleinasiens, Tübingen 1955, 407.

GORDION : G. and A. KÖRTE, Gordion (Jdl, Ergänzungsheft V, Berlin 1904). Ekrem AKURGAL, Phrygische Kunst, Ankara 1955; — Die Kunst Anatoliens, Berlin 1961 (includes previous bibliography). M. MELLINK, Hittite Cemetery at Gordion, Philadelphia 1956. Robert S. YOUNG (AJA. 59, 1955, 1 - 18; 60, 1956, 249 - 266; 61; 1957, 319 - 331; 62, 1958, 139 - 154; 63, 1959, 263 - 268; 64, 1960, 227 - 243; 66, 1962, 153 - 168; 68, 1964, 179 - 292; 70, 1966, 267 - 278; 72, 1968, 231 - 241; — Gordion, A Guide to the Excavations and Museum, Ankara 1968.

HALIKARNASSOS : C. T. NEWTON, and R. P. PULLAN, A History of Discoveries at Halicarnassus, Cnidus and Branchidae, London 1862. A. H. SMITH, Catalogue of Sculpture in the British Museum II. 1900, 65. F. ADLER, Das Mausoleum zu Halikarnassos, Berlin 1900. W. R. LETHABY, Greek Buildings represented by Fragments in the British Museum, 1908, 37. J. BÜHLMANN, Z. G. A. II, 1908 - 9, I. E. KRÜGER, Bonner Jahrbücher, CXXVII, 1922, 84. F. Krischen, ibid. CXXVIII, 1923, I. Kristian JEPPESEN, Paradeigmata, Aarhus University Press 1958. — Excavations at the site of the Mausoleum, Copenhagen 1968. Wolfgang RADT, Siedlungen und Bauten auf der Halbinsel von Halikarnassos (Ist. Mitt., Beiheft 3, 1970). R. MARTIN, Chapiteau ionique d'Halicarnasse (REA 61, 1959, 65 - 76). W. MÜLLER - WIENER, Burgen der Kreuzritter, mit Plan und Photos, Deutscher Kunstverlag 1966. G. KARO, Die Burg von Halikarnassos (Arch. Anz. 34, 1919, 59 - 76). A. MAIURI, I castelli dei Cavalieri di Rodi a Cos e a Budrum, (Annuario della Scuola di Atene 4/5, 1921/22, 290 ff.).

HERAKLEIA : Fritz KRISCHEN, Die Befestigungen von Herakleia am Latmos (Milet III 2, 1922). A. Von GERKAN, Griechische städteanlagen 14 - 17, 96 - 110. W. B. DINSMOOR 244 - 273. R. MARTIN, l'Agora 515;—L'Urbanisme 194. MAGIE, RR in AM, 882 - 3, 909, 917 - 18. John M. COOK, Ionia 150.

HIERAPOLIS : HUMANN - CICHORIUS - JUDEICH - WINTER, Altertümer von Hierapolis (Jdl Ergänzungsheft 4), Berlin 1898. Gianfilippo CARETTONI, Scavo del Tempio di Apollo a Hierapolis (Annuario della Scuola Archaelogica di Atene 41 - 42, 1963-64, 411 - 433).

IASOS : Doro LEVI, Annuario 1961 - 1969; — TAD, 7, 1968, 117 - 121.

İZMIR : CADOUX, Ancient Symrna, Oxford 1938. NAUMANN - KANTAR, Agora von Symrna (Istanbuler Forschungen 17). Ekrem AKURGAL, Symrne à l'époque archaïque, (Belleten X, 1946, 55 - 80). AKURGAL, Bayraklı 1950. John M. COOK and others, BSA 53 - 54, 1958-59. J. M. COOK, Greek settlement in Asia Minor (CAH, 1961, 3 - 33). John M. COOK, The Geeks in Ionia, London 1962. AKURGAL, Kunst Anatoliens, Berlin 1961, 8 - 21, 182 - 190. AKURGAL, The Early period and the Golden Age of Ionia (AJA 66, -1962, 369 - 379). Hakkı GÜLTEKİN, İzmir Agorası, İzmir 1951; — İzmir Tarihi, İzmir 1952; — A guide to the Museum İzmir 1965. Muhsin YENİM, The İzmir's Museums, İzmir 1969.

KARIA (see also the bibliography of the cities described in this book pp. 242 - 250) : Louis ROBERT, La Carie, Paris 1954. Olivier MASSON, Textes Cariennes d'Egypte (RHA 55, 1953, 32 - 37). L. DEROY, Les inscriptions Cariennes de Carie (L'Antiquité Classique 24, 1955 305 - 345). Franz STEINHERR, Der Karische Apollon (Die Welt des Orients, 1955, 184 - 192). P. MERIGGI, Karisch (Kadmos II, 1963). V. SEVOROSKIN, on Karian (RHA, 12, 1964, 1 - 55); — Aegyptisch - Karische Inschrift am Sockel einer Isisstatue (RHA 12, 1964, 57 - 64). G. M. A. HANFMANN — Olivier Masson, Carian inscriptions from Sardis and Stratonikeia (Kadmos 157). HANFMANN - WALDBAUM, Two Sub Mycenaean vases and a tablet from Stratonikeia in Caria (AJA 72, 1968, 51 - 56). See also the bibliography in Ekrem AKURGAL, Kunst Anatoliens 320, note 2. – J. M. COOK, W.H. PLOMMER, The sanctuary of Hemithea at Kastabos, Cambridge at the University Press 1966.

KAUNOS : Baki ÖĞÜN, (Türk Ark. Derg. 16, 1967 121 - 132); — Excavations at Caunos, Belleten 32, 1968, 15 - 160. Paavo ROOS, Research at Caunos, Opuscula Atheniensia 8, 149 - 166. Lund 1968 (includes previous bibliography); — Topographical and other notes on southeastern Caria, 59 - 93). Ümit SERDAROĞLU, Theatre at Caunos, Türk Ark. Derg. 16, 1967, 133 - 136.

KNIDOS : DILETTANTI, Antiquities of Ionia III ff. V ff. Ch. TEXIER, Description de l'Asie Mineure (Paris 1849) III, 171 - 176, Pls. 159 - 164. Sir Ch. NEWTON, A History of Discoveries at Halicarnassus, Cnidus and Branchidae II, London 1865. Bernard ASHMOLE, Demeter of Cnidus (JHS 71, 13 - 28). G. E. BEAN and J. M. COOK "The Cnidia" BSA 47, 1952, 171 - 212; — The Carian Coast III, BSA 52, 1957, 85 - 87. J. M. COOK, The Greeks in Ionia and the East, London 1962, New York 1963, 142 - 147. Iris Cornelia LOVE, AJA 72, 1968, 137 - 139, Pls. 56, 58 - 59; 73, 1969, 216 - 219, Pls. 61 - 62; 74, 1970, 149 - 155; — Türk Ark. Derg. 16, 1967, 133-159; 17, 1968, 123 - 143. Herbert A. CAHN; Knidos, Die Münzen des 6. und 5. Jhs, Berlin 1970.

KOMMAGENE : See Arsameia and Nemrud Dağ.

KORYKOS : KEIL - WILHELM, Monumenta Asiae Minoris Antiqua, Otto FELD, Bericht über eine Reise durch Kilikien (Istanbuler Mitteilungen 13/14. 1963/64, 88 - 107). FELD - WEBER, Tempel und Kirche über der Korykischen Grotte (Cennet Cehennem) in Kilikien (Istanbuler Mitteilungen 17, 1967, 254 - 278). Alois MACHATSCHEK, Die Nekropolen und Grabmäler von Elaiussa Sebaste und Korykos, Wien 1967.

KÜLTEPE : Nimet ÖZGÜÇ, The Anatolian Group of Cylinder Seal Impressions from Kültepe, Ankara 1965; — Seals and Seal Impressions of Level Ib, T. T. K., Ankara 1968. Tahsin ÖZGÜÇ, Excavations at Kültepe, Ankara 1950, 1953.; — Kültepe — Kaniş, Ankara 1959; — Kültepe in the Iron Age, Türk Tarih Kurumu, Ankara 1971. Sedat ALP, Kanis= Anisa = Nisa (Belleten 1963, p. 377 - 386). Franz FISCHER, Boğazköy und Chronologie der Altassyrischen Handelsniederlassungen in Kappadokien, Istanbuler Mitteilungen 1965 p. 1 - 16. Nezahat BAYDUR, Kültepe ve Kayseri Tarihi, Istanbul 1970.

KYME : Ekrem AKURGAL, Les sondages de Kyme (Anatolia I. 1956, 3 - 4. Schäfer — Schlager, Zur Seeseite von Kyme in der Aiolis (AA 1962, 42 - 56).

KYZICUS : F. W. HASLUCK, Cyzicus, 1910, 187. Bernard ASHMOLE, Cyriac of Ancona and the temple of Hadrian at Cyzicus (Journal of the Warbourg and Courtauld Institutes 19, 1956, 179 - 191). Ekrem AKURGAL, Recherches à Cyzique (Anatolia I, 1956, 15 - 24). H. P. LAUBSCHER, zum Fries des Hadrianstempels (Istanbuler Mitteilungen 17, 1967, 211 - 217).

LABRANDA : Kristian JEPPESEN, Labraunda I, I, The propylaea, Lund 1955. A. WESTHOLM. Labraunda I, 2, The architecture of the Hieron, Lund 1963. HELLSTROM, Labraunda II, I, Pottery, Lund 1965.

LARISA : L. KJELLBERG, Uppsala Universitets Arsskrift, 1903, 30 AA. XXI, 1906, 265. H. KOCH, R. M. XXX, 1915, I. SCHEFOLD, BOEHLAU, GERKAN and others, Larisa am Hermos I (Bauten), Berlin 1940. KJELLBERG - AKERSTRÖM and others, Larisa II, Die Architektonischen Terrakotten), Stockholm 1940. SCHEFOLD and others, Larisa III (Keramik), Berlin 1942.

LYDIA (see also Sardes) : Hans KALETSCH, Zur Lydischen Chronologie (Historia VII, 1958, 1 - 47). Alfred HEUBECK, Lydiaca (Erlanger Forschungen A. g. 1959, 1 - 88). P. MERIGGI, der indogermanische Charakter des Lydischen (Festschrift H. Hirt 2, 1936, 283 - 290). Onofrio CARRUBA, Lydisch und Lyder (Mitteilungen des Instituts für Orientforschung VIII, 1963, 383 - 408). O. MASSON, Un nom pseudo-lydien à Sardes (Athenaeum 47, 1969, 193 - 197). G. NEUMANN, Lydisch - hethitische Verknüpfungen (Athenaeum 47, 1963), 217 - 225); — Der lydische Name der Athena (Kadmos 6, 1967, 80 - 87); — Lydisch - hethitische Verknüpfungen (Athenaeum 47, 1969, 217 - 226). See also the bibliography in E. AKURGAL, Kunst Anatoliens 319 - 320.

LYKIA : Charles FELLOWS, A journal written during an excursion in Asia Minor, London 1839; — An account of Discoveries in Lycia, London 1841. O. BENNDORF- G. NIEMANN, Reisen im südwestlichen Kleinasien I, Reisen in Lykien und Karien, Wien 1884. E. PETERSEN - F. v. LUSCHAN, Reisen im südwestlichen Kleinasien II, Reisen in Lykien, Milyas und Kibyratis, Wien, 1889. E. KALINKA, Tituli Asiae Minoris I, 1901, II, Baden, 1930. G. RODENWALDT, Griechische Reliefs in Lykien (S. B. Berlin 1933). Ekrem AKURGAL, Griechische Reliefs des VI. Jhs. aus Lykien, Berlin 1942. Fritz EICHLER, Ostwand des Heroons von Trysa (Öster. Akademie d. Wiss. 1947, 55 - 72);–Heroon von Gjölbaschi-Trysa. Wien 1950. F. J. TRITSCH, "Lycian, Luwian and Hittite, Archiv Orientalni 18, 1 - 2, 1950. M. MELLINK, Lycian Wooden Huts and Sign 24 on the Phaistos Disk (Kadmos III 1969, 1 - 7). P. DEMARGNE, Fouilles de Xanthos I, Paris 1958. Henri METZGER, Fouilles de Xanthos II, L'Acropole Lycienne, Paris 1963. P. Coupel - P. DEMARGNE, Fouilles de Xanthos III, Le Monument des Nereides, Paris 1969. O. AKŞİT, Likya Tarihi, Istanbul 1967. Jürgen BORCHHARDT, Limyra, Sitz des Lykischen Dynasten Perikles (Ist. Mitt. 17, 1967). Jürgen BORCHHARDT, GÜNTHER, NEUMANN, Dynastische Grabanlagen von Kadyanda (AA 1968, 134 - 238). H. METZGER, Letoon, TAD 1966, 103 - 106; 1967, 113 - 120). Ümit SERDAROĞLU, Karia ve Lykia'da Roma devri tapınakları (in preparation). Hans L. STOLTENBERG, die termilische Sprache Lykiens, Leverkusen 1955 (Rev. by Olivier MASSON, Kratylos, 1, 1956, 49 - 52). See also the bibliography in : Ekrem AKURGAL, Kunst Anatoliens 318 - 319. COUPEL - METZGER, Reliefs inédits de l'Acropole de Xanthos (Rev. Arch. 2, 1969, 225 - 232).

MAGNESIA ON THE MAEANDER : C. HUMANN, Magnesia am Maeander, Berlin, 1904. H. DRERUP, Zum Artemistempel von Magnesia (Marburger Winckelmann - Programm 1964, 13 - 22). Armin von GERKAN, Der Altar des Artemis Tempels in Magnesia am Maeander, Berlin 1929. R. A. STACCIOLI, Sulla cosidetta "caserma" di Magnesia al Meandro (Rivista Archeologia Classica 9, 1957, 250 - 256). G. GRUBEN, Tempel der Griechen 364 - 372.

MIDAS CITY : See Phrygia.

MILETOS : Carl WEICKERT, Die Ausgrabung am Athena - Tempel in Milet 1955 (Ist. Mitt. 7, 1956, 102 - 132). KLEINER, Alt-Milet, Wiesbaden 1966; — Die Ruinen von Milet, De Gruyter, Berlin 1968 (includes previous bibliography 155 - 160). Alfred MALWITZ, Athena - Tempel (Istanbuler Mitteilungen 18, 1968, 89 - 143). Wolfgang SCHIERING, Athena - Tempel (Istanbuler Mitteilungen 18, 1968, 144 - 160). Peter HOMMEL, Archaischer Jünglingskopf aus Milet (Ist. Mitt. 17, 1967, 115 - 127). Musa BARAN, Guide to Miletos, Ankara 1965. Hakkı GÜLTEKİN, Miletos, Izmir 1961.

MYLASA : A. AKARCA, Les Monnaies grecques de Mylasa, Paris 1959; — Milas, Istanbul 1954. P. DEVAMBEZ - C.H.E. HASPELS, Le sanctuaire de Labraunda près de Mylasa, Paris. 1959.

MYRINA : POTTIER - REINACH, La Nécropole de Myrina, Paris 1887. MOLLARD - BESQUES, Louvre, Terrecuite, catalogue II, Myrina, Paris 1963.

MYUS: Wiegand, AA 1904, 8 ff. A. von GERKAN (Milet I. 8, 69 ff.). A. von GERKAN (Milet II, I, 32, pls. 6, 7). D. MAGIE, Roman Rule in A. M. 74, 883 - 4. Peter HERRMANN, Urkunden zur Geschichte von Milet (Ist. Mitt. 15, 1965, 90 - 117). H. WEBER, Ausgrabungen in Myus (Ist. Mitt. 15, 1965, 43 - 63 and 17, 1967, 128 - 143).

NEANDRIA : R. KOLDEWEY, Neandria (55. Winckelmannsprogramm, 1891 3 - 49), Berlin 1891.

NEMRUD DAĞ : Theresa GOELL, Nimrud Dagh (Archaeology 5, 1952, 136 - 144); — Throne above the Euphrates (National Geographic 119, 1961, 390 - 405); — Das Grabmal Antiochos I in Kommagene (Mitteilungen der Deutsch - Türkischen Gesellschaft 30, Bonn, 1959, 1 - 15); — Geophysical survey of the Hierotheseion and Tomb of Antiochus I of Commagene 1963.

OLBA : HEBERDEY - WILHELM, 84. Bent, T. J. H. S. XII, 1892, 220. E. HERZFELD and S. GUYER, AA, 1909, 434. J. KEIL and A. WILHELM, Öst. Jh. XVIII, 1915, Beibl. 7., E. WEICKERT, Gnom. III, 1927, 88. KEIL - WILHELM, Monumenta Asiae Minoris Antiqua III, Manchester University Press 1931, 44 - 79. Y. BOYSAL, Korinthische Kapitelle (Anatolia II, 1957, 123 - 130). — Uzuncaburç ve Ura, Istanbul 1963.

PATARA : E. KALINKA, (Tituli Asiae Minoris, Baden 1930, 141 - 180). F. J. TRITSCH - Ahmet DÖNMEZ, Discoveries in Lycia (ILN - March 21, 1953). Ümit SERDAROĞLU, Karia ve Lykia'da Roma devri tapınakları (in preparation).

PERGAMON : A. CONZE and Others, Altertümer von Pergamon, 8 vols. E. PONTREMOLI and M. COLLIGNON, Pergame, Paris 1900. E. BOEHRINGER, Pergamon (Neue deutsche Ausgrabungsarbeiten zu Pergamon im Jahr 1965 (AA 1966. 415 - 483). Otfried DEUBNER, Das Asklepieion von Pergamon Berlin, 1938; — Pergamon und Rom. (Marburger Jahrbuch für Kunstwissenschaft XV 1949 - 50. 95 - 114). H. KÄHLER, Der Grosse Fries von Pergamon, Berlin 1948. G. KLEINER, Nachleben des Pergamenischen Gigantenkampfes (105. Winckelmannsprogramm, Berlin, 1949). H. LUSCHEY, Funde zu dem grossen Fries von Pergamon (116/117. Winckelmannsprogramm) Berlin, 1962. E. SCHMIDT, Der grosse Altar zu Pergamon, Leipzig 1961. E. ROHDE, Pergamon, Burgberg und Altar, Berlin 1966. PINKWART Pergamon, TAD 1966, 107 - 111, 1967, 113 - 115. G. KLEINER, Die Istanbuler Platte vom pergamenischen Gigantenfries (Ist. Mitt. 17, 1967, 168 - 172). Jörg SCHÄFER, Hellenistische Keramik aus Pergamon, Berlin 1968. Oskar ZIEGENAUS - Giola de LUCA, Das Asklepieion I, Berlin 1968. Harald INGHOLT, The Prima Porta Statue of Augustus (Archaeology 22 1969, 176 - 187, 304 - 318). Otto BRENDEL, Gnomon 36, 1964, 501 (Augustusstatue of Prima Porta).

PERGE : LANCKORONSKI I, Pamphylien, 33 - 63. Arif Müfit MANSEL, Excavations at Perge, Ankara 1949; — Perge (TAD 1967, 101 - 106).

PESSINUS : LAMBRECHTS, Pierre, "De Brug" 1967 (p. 247 - 267), 1968 (p. 280 - 291), 1969 (p. 267 - 280); — Türk. Ark. Derg. 1967, 113 - 131; 1968, p. 83 - 91, Les Fouilles de Pessinonte : La Necropole, L'Antiquité Classique 38, 1969, 121 - 146; — Asclepios, Archigalle pessinontien de Cybèle (Hommages à Marcel Renand, II collection Latomus vol. 102, Gent 1969, 404 - 414); — La Famille de Lollii à Pessinonte (Etudes Classiques vol 37, 1969, 302 - 307); Inscriptions inédites de Pessinonte (l'Antiquité Classique 1968, 540 - 550). Kurt BITTEL, Beobachtungen in Pessinus, AA 1967, 142 - 150 (includes the plan of Pessinus by Texier and Bogaert).

PINARA : E. KALINKA (Tituli Asiae Minoris, Baden 1930, 183 - 200). Ümit SERDAROĞLU, Karia ve Lykia'da Roma devri tapınakları (in preparation).

PRIENE : Th. WIEGAND and H. SCHRADER, Priene, Berlin, 1904. W. WILBERG, A. M. XXXIX, 1914, 72. A. von GERKAN A. M. XLIII, 1918, 165; — Das Theater von Priene, München 1921, W. DÖRPFELD, A. M. XLIX, 1924, 50. GERKAN, Zum Skenengebäude des Theaters von Priene (Istanbuler Mitteilungen 9/10 1959 - 60, 97 - 108). G. KLEINER, Priene (RE, Pauly-Wissowa); — Diadochengräber, Wiesbaden 1963. SCHEDE, Die Ruinen von Priene, Berlin 1965. Rüstem DUYURAN, Priene Kılavuzu, Istanbul 1948. Otto BAUER, Bericht über die Neubearbeitung des Athena - Tempels zu Priene (Ist. Mitt. 18, 1968, 212 - 220).

SARDIS : H. C. BUTLER, Sardis. Vol II. Part, 1. Leyden, 1925. R. VALLOIS, R. E. G. XXXIX, 1926, 367. G. GRUBEN, Zum Artemis - Tempel von Sardis (AM, 76 1961, 155 - 196). G.M.A. HANFMANN, Excavations at Sardis (BASOR, 154, 1959, 5 - 35); – The ninth campaign at Sardis (BASOR, 86, 1967, 17 - 52); – The tenth campaign at Sardis (BASOR, 191, 1968, 2 - 41); – Sardis und Lydien (Akademie der Wissenschaften, Mainz 1960 No: 6, 500 - 536); — Guide to Sardis (BASOR, 154, 1959, 5 - 35). G. M. A. HANFMANN - Olivier MASSON, Carian Inscriptions from Sardis (Kadmos VI 2, 1967, 123 - 134). Ann K. KNUDSEN, From a Sardis Tomb, A Lydian Pottery Imitation of a Metal Bowl (Berytus 15, 1964, 59 - 69). L. ROBERT, Nouvelles inscriptions de Sardes, Paris 1964. PEDLEY, John GRIFFITHS, Sardis in the Age of Croesus, Oklahama Press 1968.

SIDE : LANCKORONSKI I : Pamphylien 125 - 152. Arif Müfid MANSEL, Ausgrabungen in Side, Ankara 1951; — Die Ruinen von Side, Berlin 1963, AA, 1965, 34 - 119 (includes previous bibliography); — Osttor und Waffenfries von Side (AA, 1968. 239 - 279). Sabahat ATLAN, Untersuchungen über die sidetischen Münzen, Türk Tarih Kurumu, Ankara 1967. Muhibbe DARGA, Side dili ve yazısı (Belleten 31, 1967, 49 - 66). Claude BRIXHE, L'Alphabet épichorique de Sidé (Kadmos VIII, 1969, 54 - 84).

SOUTHERN SHORE (Districts between Antalya and Adana) : Karl Grafen LANCKORONSKI, Städte Pamphyliens und Pisidiens, I Pamphylien, Wien 1890; II, Pisidien, Wien 1892. KEIL - WILHELM, Monumenta Asiae Minoris Antiqua III, Manchester, University Press 1931 (includes bibliography on south Anatolian cities described in this book, see pp. 287 - 290). A. M. MANSEL, Studien zur Geschichte Pamphyliens T. T. K., Ankara 1957. G. HUBER, Städteplanung in den Küstenorten des westlichen Kilikiens (TAD, 1964, 140 - 147). Jürgen BORCHARDT, Epichorische, gräco-persisch beeinflusste Reliefs in Kilikien (Ist. Mitt. 18, 1968, 161 - 211). Otto FELD, Bericht über eine Reise durch Kilikien (Istanbuler Mitteilungen 13/14. 1963/64, 88 - 107). FELD - WEBER, Tempel und Kirche über der Korykischen Grotte (Cennet - Cehennem) in Kilikien (Istanbuler Mitteilungen 17, 1967, 254 - 278). Alois Machatschek, Die Nekropolen und Grabmäler im Gebiet von Elaiussa Sebaste und Korykos, Wien 1970 (Österr. Akademie der Wissenschaften).

TARSUS : Hetty GOLDMAN, Tarsus I (The Hellenistic and Roman periods, Princeton); Tarsus II (From the Neolithic through the Bronze Age, Princeton 1956); Tarsus III (The Iron Age, Princeton 1963).

TEOS : DILETTANTI, Antiquities of Ionia IV, 35, V, 10, 13, 28. A. LAUMONIER and T. BEQUIGNON, B. C. H. XLIX, 1925, 281. P. DEVAMBEZ, Bas relief de Teos, Paris 1962 (Institut Français d'Archéologie d'Istanbul XIV). W. HAHLAND, Der Fries des Dionysostempels in Teos (Öst. Jh. 38, 66 - 190). Peter HERMANN, Antiochos der Grosse und Teos (Anatolia IX, 1965, 29 - 159).

TERMESSOS : LANCKORONSKI II, Pisidien 43, 99.

TRALLEIS : Gustave MENDEL, Istanbul Museum, catalogue II 257 - 271. H. P. LAUBSCHER, ein ostionischer Frauenkopf (Istanb. Mitt. 16, 1966, 95 - 99). H. SICHTERMANN, Knabe von Tralles (Antike Plastik IV Berlin 1965).

TROY : BLEGEN, BOUTLER, CASKEY, RAWSON, SPERLING, Troy I - IV. Princeton 1950, 51, 53, 58 (includes previous bibliography). BLEGEN, Troy and Trojans, London 1963. Dorothy Bates THOMPSON, Troy, The Terracotta Figurines, Princeton 1963. GOETHERT - SCHLEIF, Der Athenatempel von Ilion, Berlin 1962. Beatrice Mills HOLDEN, The metops of the Tempel of Athena at Ilion, Northampton, Mass. 1964. Roland HAMPE, Heinrich Schliemann (Gymnasium 69, 1962, 530 - 549).

UZUNCABURÇ : See Olba.

XANTHOS : See Lykia.

ACKNOWLEDGEMENTS

The plans and the line-drawings were executed by the architect Murat Erdim in accordance with sketches and directions given by the author. The following line-drawings were made by the artist Refik Epikman (Figs. 5, 8, 93, 103, 117, 120-126, 128). See also the foreword.

The photographs were taken by: E. Akurgal, Ankara 1 a, b, 4 b, 5, 6, 8, 9 b, 11 b, 13, 29, 41 b, 66, Efe Berna, Ankara, 12, 15 b; Y. Boysal 102 a, b; Eva Maria Czako 19; M. Ali Düğenci, 2, 7, 10 b, 11 a, 14, 15 a, 16 b, 20, 24, 25-28, 35, 42 a, 43-48, 54, 56 b, 58, 64, 65 b, c, 75, 78, 81, 83 b, c, 86, 97, 101, 105; Halit Gökberk; 30, 31, 36, 37, 39, 41 a, 42 c, 42 b, 49-53, 55, 60-63, 68, 69; Bürhan Görgüç, 3, 88-89; Ara Güler, 84 a; Max Hirmer 21-23; Ministry of Tourism, 17, 18, 40, 56, 57, 59, 67, 74 a, 77, 83 a, 84 b, 85, 90 a, 91, 95 a, b, 98-100, 103, 104, 106, 108; Selahattin Öztartan, 82, 87, 92, 94; Dr. Georg Röhrig, 4 a; Ozan Sağdıç 16 a, 112; Ümit Serdaroğlu 79-80; Nicole Thirerry 10 a. See also the foreword. The following photographs were kindly supplied by: Professor E. Boehringer 38, and Professor F. K. Dörner 109-111.

LIST OF FIGURES

INDEX

(Sites mentioned in the Table of Contents are not included in the index)

Philippus Arabs, 121.
Piotrovski, 14.
Pisiris, 292-294.
Pixodaros, 242, 244, 248.
Plancia Magna, 330–332.
Polykrates, 115, 177.
Pompey, 117, 345, 351.
Priam, 47, 59, 60, 345.
Propontis, 18, 47, 115.
Prytaneion at : Ephesus, 164, 167, 169, –
Pergamon, 91, 92, – Priene, 186, 194-196.
Puduhepa, 308, 309, 313.
Pylos, 133.
Pytheos, 19-22, 31, 88, 128, 129, 141, 142,
148, 149, 153, 179, 188-190, 194, 249, 278.

Ramesses II, 308 III, 13, 61.
Ras Shamra, 289, 314.
Robert, Louis, 19, 136.
Rosenbaum, Elisabeth, 341.

Sabina, 237, 261.
Sadyattes, 124, 207.
Sakçegözü, 14, 289, 294, 295.
Samos, 18, 41, 114, 115, 135, 149, 177 Altar
of Hera, 86, 87   Hekatompedos II, 21, 223
Temple of Hera, 21, 86, 147, 149, 151, 226.
Samosata, 346.
Sangarios, 279.
Sappho, 41, 111.
Sarpedon, 255.
Satrap Sarcophagus, 41, 42.
Schede, Martin, 267, 269, 286.
Schefold, Karl, 18.
Schliemann, H, 6, 47, 50, 53-57.
Schober, Arnold, 30, 244.
Schrader, Hans, 154.
Schuchhardt, 136.
Scylax, 333.
Sea peoples, 13.
Selene, 240, 332.
Seleukos I, 225, 341, 343.
Seleukos III, 236.
Septimius Severus, 34, 332, 333, 347.
Serapis, temple at : Ephesus, 95, 145, 160,
163, 164, – Miletos, 216, 220, – Pergamon, 70,
95, 103-104, 163.
Serdaroğlu, Ümit, 246, 254, 262, 265, 286.
Shaushattar, 11.
Sidon, 19, 41 - 43.
Sidyma, 265.
Simon, Erika, 32.
Sinope, 207.
Sirkeli, 345.
Socrates, 146, 163.
Solymos, 325.
Sophocles, 133.
Sostratos, 28, 252.
Squarciapino, Maria, 172.
Stadium at : Aizanoi, 268, – Aphrodisias,
175, 330, – Aspendos, 335, – Didyma, 231, –
Ephesus, 143, 144, 155-157, 159, 170, – Lao-

diceia ad Lycum, 237,– Magnesia on the Maeander, 178,– Miletos, 209, 217, 218,– Nysa, 235,
237,– Pergamon, 70, 93 98,– Perge, 330,– Priene, 29, 186, 187, 201, 202,–Sardis, 125, 126,
– Smyrna, 122, – Tralleis, 236.
Stoa at : Aphrodisias, 173, 174, – Aspendos,
334, – Assos, 65, 67, 68, – Athens, 27 Delphi,
27, – Didyma, 224, 225, – Ephesos, 159, 161,
163, 166, 169, – Iasos, 247, – Kolophon, 134, –
Labranda, 244, – Miletos, 210, 211, 215-218, –
Notion, 135, – Pergamon, 71-74, 77, 79-83,
85, 88, 92-94, 96-98, 101, 102, 106, 107, 109,
110, – Priene, 185-188, 191-195, 201, 205, –
Smyrna, 122, 123, – Termessos, 325
Stratford, Lord, 249.
Straton I, 43.
Stratonikos, 77.
Sulla, 26, 140, 165, 168, 172, 178.
Sulumeli, 13, 292.
Susa, 124, 127.
Synagogue at: Miletos, 215 – Sardis: 125, 126.
Tantalos of Phrygia, 133.
Tektosages, 283.
Tel Açana, 301, 346.
Telephanes, 117.
Telephos, 32, 87, 175.
Telesphoros, 110.
Tel Tainat, 346.
Temizer, Raci, 14, 289.
Temnos, 111.
Temples : (see under the names of divi-
nities). Unidentified temples : Aeolic temple
at Neandria, 63, 64. Corinthian temples at :
Diocaesarea, 343, – Elaiussa Sebaste, 344, –
Kaunos, 254, – Knidos, 252, 253, – Patara,
261, – Pergamon, 89, 93, 99, – Seleukia on the
Kalykadnos, 341, – Three temples at Termes-
sos, 327, 328. Doric temples Pergamon, 73,
89 Ionic temples: Kaunos, 254, – Labranda,
244,– Laodiceia ad Lycum, 237,– Miletos, 211,
– Two temples at Myus, 238, 239, – Olympos,
265, 266. See also temples at: Antiphellos,
262, – Assos, 65, 67, – Gordion, 280, 281.
Temples at Hattusas, 297, 299, 302 - 306,– He-
rakleia under Latmos (three temples) 240, –
Iasos (three temples), 247, – Kaunos (two
temples) 254, – Knidos, 253, – Miletos, 215, –
Notion, 136, – Patara (two temples), 262,
– Phaselis, 266, – Pınara (two temples), 257,
– Priene, 187, – Stratonikeia, 246, – Yazılı-
kaya, 306-317.
Terpander, 111, 346.
Teshup, 312, 313.
Thales, 139, 207.
Theatre at : Alabanda, 244, – Alinda, 244, –
Antiphellos, 262, – Aphrodisias, 173, 174,
– Aspendos, 33-35, 334-335, – Assos, 65, 67,
69, – Athena (Dionysos) 27, – Diocaesarea,
343, – Elaiussa Sebaste, 344, – Ephesus, 33,
34 145, 154, 158, 159, – Erythrai, 233, – He-

SUPPLEMENT

SUPPLEMENT TO EPHESUS

In the last few years, the excavations at Ephesus have yielded some very important discoveries. In the following pages we shall report on buildings uncovered and observations made by the excavators.

House Blocks on The Slopes of Bülbüldağ (Mt. Koressos)

Two insulae with private houses have now been almost completely uncovered (Figs. 169-170). Found in an extremely good state of preservation, they are situated on the Curetes street opposite the temple of Hadrian on the northern slopes of Bülbüldağ (see p. 162 Fig. 58 No. 11).

Fig. 169 – The eastern insula, covering an area of 50.10 × 54.6 × 46.5 74.70 = 2540 m², is comprised of private houses built on three successive terraces. There is a splendid domus which belonged to a wealthy man and several houses of middle class citizens. The front, overlooking the Curetes street, was in the form of a colonnade. The initial construction goes back to the beginning of the first century A. D. However, the houses were inhabited until the time of Arcadius (A. D. 611-641) and were restored or altered several times during this period. All of the houses had their own entrances opening directly onto the street and each was provided with running water.

A) *Colonnade with twelve shops along the inner side. The floor of the colonnade was covered with a mosaic of geometric pattern dating from the beginning of the fifth century A. D. and commissioned by a certain Alytarchos. However, judging by the southern walls of shops Nos. 3-8, the colonnade was already in existence during the first century A. D. These shops, roofed with barrel-vaulting, lay at the rear of the colonnade and as the style of construction and frescoe-rests betray, their latest restoration dates to the sixth century A. D. The staircases of shops Nos. 7 and 10 show clearly that there was another storey above the ground floor. It was, however, less in height and consisted of bedrooms called pergulae in Roman times which were used by the owners or shop personnel.* **B 1-4)** *Domus, two-storeyed house of a wealthy family. It lies on the second terrace and is partially supported by the structures of the lower terrace with its shops.* **B 1)** *Peristyle, courtyard surrounded by colonnades of the Ionic order. It was originally built in the first century A. D. but was probably restored after the earthquake in A. D. 37 and altered in the time of Diocletianus around A. D. 300. In this period the whole of the Domus was renovated with colored marble revetments of which only a few have been preserved. The fountain in the southern part of the peristyle was also built in this period of alterations — its pool remains.* **B 2)** *Oikos, hall. At the time of the initial construction in the first century A. D. its roof was supported*

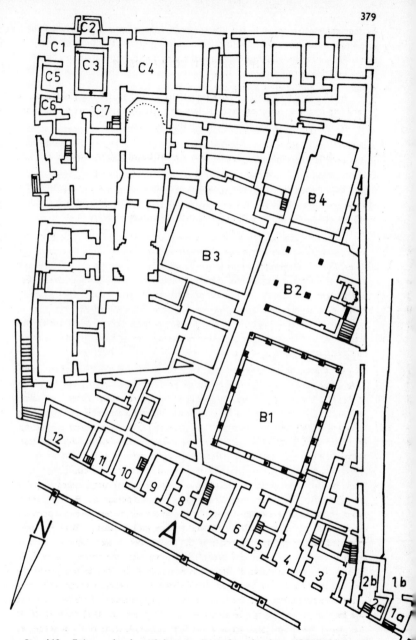

Fig. 169 – Ephesus. Insula with houses, situated on the slopes of Bülbüldağ opposite the temple of Hadrian (see p. 162, Fig. 58, No. 11).

380

by four columns. Located in the western part of the oikos is a niche containing a fountain which was covered with colored marble plates in the time of Diocletianus. Remains of the staircase leading to the story above the peristyle may be seen on the vaulting of this fountain. **B 3)** Cenatorium, dining room, built in the first century A. D. and altered during the reign of Diocletianus, ca. A. D. 300. The doors giving access to the oikos were blocked during these alterations. The cenatorium was again altered after the well known earthquake which occurred in A. D. 358 or 368. **B 4)** The hall south of the oikos which was originally roofed with barrelvaulting, has been identified as a private basilica. During the alterations in the time of Diocletianus, this hall was roofed with groined-vaulting. In the eastern part of the insula and on the second and third terraces there are several houses dating from the early Christian and Byzantine periods, all with entrances opening onto the side-street to the east. Another lies on the third terrace, in the south-eastern corner of the insula (C 1-7) with its entrance leading to the western side-street.

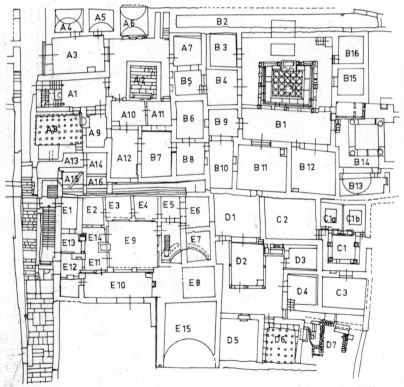

Fig. 170 – Ephesus. Insula with houses located to the west of the insula in Fig. 169.

Fig. 170 – Western insula. So far, in the excavated part of this complex there have been unearthed five luxurious peristyle houses in an excellent state of preservation. Many of the rooms were decorated with frescoes and the art objects found during the excavations are of great importance. All of these houses were provided with running water.

A 1-12) This peristyle house, with 12 rooms on the ground floor and an upper storey, occupies the south-east corner of the insula. It was first built in the first century A. D. but the present plan dates from the second century A. D. after which it underwent further alterations and renovations in the 4th and 5th centuries A. D. The two storey combined provided a habitable surface of about 900 m². **A 1)** Vestibule. A staircase leads from the side-street down to this room. **A 2)** Peristyle, courtyard of the house providing sun and air to the surrounding rooms. Its floor is covered with a mosaic of ornamental pattern. On the south side there is a fountain. The west wall shows two layers of frescoes dating from different periods. Of the older frescoe, painted in the first century A. D., only the figure of an Eros has been preserved. In the overlying frescoe, which dates back to the last quarter of the 2nd century A. D. according to Professor Vetters, are represented pastoral scenes in which can be discerned a harvester, a man with a sack and a man with a basket gathering fruit. **A 3)** A hall richly decorated with mosaics. Originally higher, the present height of the walls reaches 4 meters. On the west wall are represented scenes from a comedy of Menander called Sikyonioi and from the tragedies, Orestes and Iphigenia, of Euripides. The main scene in the upper zone, as recognised by G. Langmann, depicts the combat of Herakles and Acheloos (river god) who are fighting over Deianeira. Professor Vetters describes the scene as follows: Acheloos is about to transform himself into an animal and his left leg has already taken the form of a hissing snake. Herakles is leaning over a youth and Deianeira, in a crouching position, is seizing his other leg. To the left can be seen Iolaos, companion of Herakles, and to the right Ares, who supported Acheloos in this fight according to Pausanias. Professor Vetters dates the painting to the last quarter of the 2nd century A. D. The east and south walls were also painted with frescoes of similar scenes but they have been badly preserved. **A 4-6)** Rooms covered by barrel-vaulting. The frescoes in these rooms, represent figures situated between floral motives. Among the figurative representations are a peacock, a woman in the motive of Ariadne and an Eros with a flower basket on his baek. These are dated by Professor Vetters to later than A. D. 300. In room A 6, there is a triclinium which served as a divan during the summer. **A 8)** Bathroom with bathtub. Pillars 45 cm. high supported the floor and provided space which served to retain the heat produced by a furnace. **A 10-11)** The frescoes of floral arrangements and small Eros-figures in these rooms date from the first century A. D. **A 12)** A room with a mosaic floor dating from the first century A.D. **A 13)** Kitchen. **B 1-16)** Peristyle house in the south-west corner of the western insula. Originally built in the first century A.D., it was a two-storeyed house. Remains of its collapsed walls were found in the peristyle and surrounding rooms and judged by the finds, they were also painted with frescoes. **B 1)** Peristyle with Corinthian columns. The frescoes, depicting two Eros-figures carrying a huge garland, and the mosaic, with Nereide sitting on a hippocampus led by a Triton, are dated by Professor Vetters to the end of the 2nd or beginning of the 3rd century A. D. A glass mosaic which originally adorned the vaulting of the niche was found on the ground in pieces and has now been restored by Mr. and Mrs. David (Vetters, Grabungs-bericht 1969, Wien 1970 pl. 4a, b; 1970 Wien 1971 pl. 23). In it are represented the heads of Ariadne and Dionysus as well as figures of birds within floral orna-ments. Professor Vetters dates it to the end of the 5th or beginning of the 6th century A. D. **B 3-8)** Most of these rooms contain floor mosaics in ornamental pattern and well preserved frescoes consisting mainly of representations of birds. **B 9-10)** The walls of these two rooms are Painted with frescoes depicting standing muses dating from around A. D. 300. **B 11)** In this room have been found a great number of art objects which had fallen from the upper floor. **B 12-16)** Rooms with frescoes painted ca. A. D. 400. Room **B 14** , with a basin in its center, is a kitchen. **C 1-3)** Peristyle house. Originally a two-storeyed house lying to the north of the peristyle house. It was erected in the first century A. D. The walls of all of the rooms are painted with frescoes. **C 1)** Peristyle, courtyard surrounded by rooms. A mosaic depicting the heads of Medusa and Dionysus was found in an excellent state of preservation. Dating to the 3rd century A. D. (?) it lies above another mosaic in geometric pattern which belongs to an earlier period. **C 2)** The frescoes in this room date to around A. D. 300 and represent Apollo and nine muses with the poetess Sappho as the tenth muse. On the south wall can be seen some scenes from Greek tragedies. **C 3)** The floor mosaic, which represents a lion with one paw resting on a bull's-head, is a fine work of art but rather late in style. **D 1-7)** The ground floor of the house, constructed in the first century A. D. is composed of six rooms surrounding the peristyle (No. D2). The upper storey has been comple-tely destroyed. **D 2)** Peristyle. A courtyard with a fountain and frescoes repre-senting the heads of the Spartan philosopher Cheilon (on the left) and Socrates (on the right). These date from the first half of the second century A. D. **D 6)** Private baths. **E 1-15)** Originally a two-storeyed house built in the first century A. D. and lying in the north-eastern corner of the peninsula. **E 9)** Originally the courtyard (peristyle) of this house but later roofed over and used as a hall. **E 10)** A frescoe representing Socrates seated and dating from the first century A. D. was found in this room. It is in an excellent state of preservation and has now been conveyed to the Selçuk Museum. **E 15)** This building, containing an apsis and roofed with barrel-vaulting, measures 9m × 12m in area. It was a private basilica erected in the 2nd century A.D.

The Later Artemision and its Altar:

In the last few years, Anton Bammer has successfully worked on the ruins of the Temple of Artemis and its altar. He has now published his remarkable results (A. Bammer Die Architektur des jüngeren Artemision von Ephesos, Wiesbaden 1972).

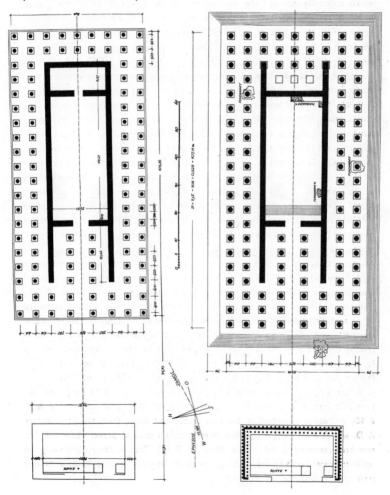

Fig. 171a,b – Ephesus. Temple and altar of Artemis (after Anton Bammer) a) Archaic Artemision. b) Later Artemision.

We regret that we do not have sufficient space in this supplement to deal with the problems discussed in his book. We hope, however, that the graphic reconstructions reproduced here (Figs. 171, 172) will provide some idea of the achievements of their author.

Fig. 172 – Ephesus. Temple of Artemis. Elevation (after Anton Bammer).

The Re-erection of the Celsus Library :

Some of the most remarkable work being done in Ephesus is that which is concerned with the anastylosis of the Celsus library. Almost all of the important architectural elements of the building have been preserved, thus making it possible for the excavators to reconstruct this unique monument in its original form.

Fig. 173 – The Celsus library, the brocken pieces of which have been almost completely reassembled, will be re-erected within two years following the graphic reconstruction which is seen in this drawing by F. Hueber.

EUROMOS

The temple of Zeus at Euromos has now been completely unearthed by Ümit Serdaroğlu. However, during the impression of this third edition we were only able to include the new plan (see p. 246, Fig. 93) but not its relevant text. It is a peripteros of the Corinthian order with 6 by 11 columns. The pronaos is preceded by four columns and in the interior of the cella there is a naiskos.

SUPPLEMENT TO THE BIBLIOGRAPHY

AIZANOI : Hans WEBER, Der Zeus-Tempel von Aezani. Ein Panhellenisches Heiligtum der Kaiserzeit AM 84, 1969, 182-201. Umberto LAFFI, Tempio di Zeus ad Aizanoi (Athenaeum 49, 1971, 2-53).

ALABANDA : Hans LAUTER, Reisenotizen aus Karien. Bonner Jahrb. 171, 1971, 132-149.

ANAMUR : Elisabeth ALFÖLDİ-ROSENBAUM, The Necropolis of Anemurium TTK Ankara 1971.

ANTIOCHIA : G. DOWNEY, Ancient Antioche, Princeton 1963.

APHRODISIAS : Kenan T. ERİM, Aphrodisias Awakened City of Ancient Art, National Geographic, June 1972, 766-791.

ASPENDOS : Hans LAUTER, Die hellenistische Agora von Aspendos, Bonner Jahrb. 170, 1970, 77-101. Heinz GÜPPERS, Getreide-magazin am Forum in Aspendos, Bonner Jahrb. 61, 1961, 25-35.

BOĞAZKÖY: Kurt BITTEL - Peter NEVE, Vorläufiger Bericht über die Ausgrabungen in Boğazköy im Jahre 1969. MDOG 102, 1970, 5-20. Kurt BITTEL, einige ausgewählte Funde, ibid. 21-26. Peter NEVE, Eine hethitische Quellgrotte in Boğazköy, Ist. Mitt. 19/20, 1969/1970, 97-107. — Bericht über die Deutsche Boğazköy-Expedition im Jahre 1970 TAD, 1970, 175-186.

COINS : Hans v. AULOCK, Kleinasiatische Münzen, Jahrb. für Numism. u. Gesch. 19, 1969, 79-88. Kleinasiatische Münzstätten ibid. 20, 1970, 151-159; 21, 1971, 15-23. Frank BROMMER, die Kleinasiatischen Münzen mit Hephaistos, Chiron 2, 1972, 531-544, Pls. 18-29.

DASKYLEION : Ekrem AKURGAL, Reliefs aus Daskyleion, Iranica Antiqua, 6, 1966, 147-156. DUPONT - SOMMER, CRAI, 1966, 12 January, 44-58. Necati DOLUNAY, Istanbul Arkeoloji Müzesi Yıllığı, 15-16, 1966, 1 ff. G.M.A. HANFMANN, BASOR, 184, December 1966, 10-13. F. M. CROSS, ibid. 7-10. M. MELLINK, AJA, 69, 1965, 148. P. BERNARD, RA, 1969, 17-28. X. TEIXIDOR, Bullet. d'Epigraphie Sémitique, Syria, 45, 1964, 375-377, J. M. DENTZER, Reliefs au "Banquet" dans l'Asie Mineure, RA, 1969, 195-224. Henri METZGER, RA, 1967, 7 ff. — L'Antiquités Classique 40, 1971, 505-525. Jürgen BORCHHARDT, Ist Mitt. 18, 1968, 161 ff. Hans MÖBIUS, Zu den Stelen von Daskyleion, AA, 1971, 442-455.

EPHESOS : W. ALZINGER, Ephesos, Ein Rundgang durch die Ruinen, Koska, Berlin-Wien 1972. — Ephesos, Paulys Realencyclopädie. Suppl. XII, 1588-1704. H. WIEGARTZ, Zu den Columnae Caelatae des jüngeren Artemision, Marburger Winckelmann-Programm 1968, 41-73. Anton BAMMER, Beiträge zur ephesischen Architektur, ÖJH 49, 1968-71, 1-40. —Die Architektur des jüngeren Artemision von Ephesos, Franz Steiner Verlag, Wiesbaden 1972, 1-71, pls. 1-12. Kenneth P. OAKLEY, the Diopet of Ephesus, Folklore, 82, 1971, 207-211. Hermann VETTERS, Ephesos Vorläufiger Grabungsbericht 1971, Österreichische Akademie der Wissenschaften Wien 1972, 1-20. — Zum Stockwerkbau in Ephesos, Mélanges Mansel, Ankara 1973, 69-92. Volker Michael STROCKA, Ein ephesisches Urkunden-relief, ÖJH, 1968-71, 4149. Werner JOBST, Griechische Wandinschriften aus dem Hanghaus II in Ephesos, Wien 1972 (ÖAdW) 235-245. H. ENGELMANN, Zum Pollionymphäum in Ephesos, Zeitschrift für Papyrologie und Epigraphik 10, 1973, 89-90.

DIDYMA : Klaus TUCHELT, Didyma, Bericht über die Arbeiten 1969/70, Ist. Mitt. 21, 1971, 45-108. — Die Archaischen Skulpturen von Didyma, Ist. Forschungen 27, Berlin 1970. Weihrelief an die Musen zu einem Votiv aus Didyma, AA, 1972, 87-105. Burkhard FEHR, Zur Geschichte des Apolloheiligtums von Didyma, Marburger Winckelmann-Programm 1971/72, 14-59.

ERYTHRAI : Helmut ENGELMANN und Reinhold MERKELBACH, Die Inschriften von Erythrai und Klazomenai, Rudolf Habelt, Bonn 1972.

GALATIA : Stephen, MITCHELL, A Hadrianic Milestone from Galatia, Zeitschrift für Papyrologie und Epigraphik, 10 1973, 73-74, pl.1. Ferdinand MAIER, Bemerkungen zur sogenannten galatischen Keramik von Boğazköy. Jdl 78, 1963, 218-255.

388

IONIA : H. BÜSSING, Zur Ostfront des polykratischen Hera-Tempels auf Samos, Marburger Winckelmann-Programm 1968, 22-28. Hans WALTER, Frühe samische Gefässe, R. Habelt, Bonn 1968 (Rev. by Coldstream JHS 202-204). Günter KOPCKE, Neue Holzfunde aus dem Heraion von Samos, AM 82, 1967, 100-148, Pls. 45-83. Helmut KYRIELEIS, Orientalische Bronzen aus Samos AA 1969, 166-171. Ulf JANTZEN, Die Bedeutung der Greifenprotomen von Samos, Festschrift für Hans Jantzen, Berlin 1951, 26-29. — "Assurattaschen" von Samos, Antike Kunst 10, 1967, 91-93. HIMMELMANN-WILDSCHÜTZ, Zur Geneleos-Gruppe beim samischen Heraion, Marburger Winckelmann-Programm 1963, 13-17. — Beiträge zur Chronologie der archaischen ostionischen Plastik, Ist. Mitt. 15, 1965. R. HORN, Hellenistische Bildwerke auf Samos, R. Habelt Bonn 1972. Wolf KÖNIGS, Ein ionisches Kapitell aus Samos in Berlin, Forschungen und Berichte 11, 1970, 97-102.

KAPPADOKIA : R. M. BOEHMER, Havuzköy in Ost-Kappadokien AA 1967, 132-141.

KARIA : Günter NEUMANN, Eine neue Karische Inschrift aus Chalketor, Kadmos 8, 1969, 152-157.

KAUNOS : Paavo ROOS, The Rock-Tombs of Caunus, Göteborg 1972.

KILIKIA : Alois MACHATSCHEK, Die Nekropolen und Grabmäler im Gebiet von Elaiussa Sebaste und Korykos. Graz-Wien-Köln 1967. (Öst. Akademie). BEAN-MITFORD Journeys in Rough Cilicia 1964-1968. Graz-Wien-Köln 1970. (Öst. Akademie). Ludwig BUDDE, Antike Mosaiken in Kilikien I (1969) II (1972) Verlag Aurel Bongers Recklinghausen.

KNIDOS : Iris Cornelia LOVE, A preliminary Report of the Excavations, AJA, 76,1972, 393-405.

KÜLTEPE : Kutlu EMRE, Anatolian Lead Figurines and their stone moulds TTK Ankara 1972. Tahsin ÖZGÜÇ, Kültepe and its Vicinity in the Iron Age, TTK. Ankara 1971.

KYME : H. ENGELMANN, Zu einer Inschrift von Kyme, Zeitschrift für Papyrologie und Epigraphik, 10, 1973 87.

LYKIA : Jürgen BORCHHARDT Ein Totengericht in Lykien, Ist. Mitt. 19/20, 1969/70, 187-222.— Das Heroon von Limyra, Grabmal des lykischen Königs Perikles, AA 1970, 353-390. Günter NEUMANN, Neue Funde und Forschungen in Lykien, Jahrbuch der Akademie der Wissenschaften in Göttingen, 1971, 34-49.

MILETOS: Gerhard KLEINER, Stand der Erforschung von Alt-Milet, Ist. Mitt. 19/20, 1969/1970, 113-123. — Das römische Milet, Steiner Verlag, Wiesbaden, 1970. Hanns GABELMANN, Zum Weihgeschenk der Orionsöhne, Marburger Winckelmann-Programm 1964, 1-5. G. HERES, Greifenprotomen aus Milet, Klio 52, 1970, 149-161.

MYRINA: S. MOLLARD-BESQUES, Un atelier de Coroplathe du début du IIe siècle avant J.-C. à Myrina, La Revue du Louvre, Paris, 6, 1964, 299-311. S. BESQUES, Catalogue des figurines et reliefs en terre-cuite grecs, etrusques et romains, Musée du Louvre. Editions des Musées Nationaux, Paris 1971 III (3 vols).

OLBA-DIOKAISAREIA: Christoph BÖRKER, Die Datierung des Zeus-Tempels von Olba-Diokaisareia in Kilikien, AA, 1971, 37-54.

PERGAMON : Esther v. HANSEN, The Attalids of Pergamon, Ithaca and London 1972 (second edition, revised and expanded). German HAFNER, Pergamenische Herrscherbildnisse, Aachener Kunstblätter, Aachen 1971; 154-164. **PERGAMON,** Pergamenische Forschungen I, Gesammelte Aufsätze, W. de Gruyter, Berlin 1972. Klaus STÄHLER, Das unklassische im Telephosfries, Aschendorff, Münster, Westfalen 1966. (PINKWART, GGA 220, 1968, 201-211). Erwin OHLEMUTZ, Die Kulte und Heiligtümer der Götter in Pergamon, Darmstadt 1968. Huberta HERES-VON LITROW, Untersuchungen zur Reliefgestaltung des Telephosfrieses, Forschungen und Berichte 11, 1970, 103-121. Ernst KÜNZL, Die Kelten des Epigonos von Pergamon Würzburg 1971 (Beiträge zur Archäologie. Herausgegeben von Hampe-Hölscher-Simon).

PESSINUS : P. LAMBRECHTS, De Brug, 12, 1970, 280-291; 1970, 259-270; 1971, 253-265; 1972, 266-272. — Documents inédits de Cybèle au Musée d'Eskişehir, (Extrait du : Hommages à Marie Delcourt, Collection Latomus vol. 114, 1970, 211-218, 1971, 253-265). — Les fouilles de Pessinonte: Le temple, L'Antiquité Classique 41, 1972, 156-173. — et R. BOGAERT, Nouvelles données sur l'histoire du christainisme à Pessinonte. Festschrift für Franz Altheim, Berlin 1961, 552-564. M. WAELKENS, Pessinonte et le Gallos, Byzantion 41, 1971, 349-373.

PHRYGIA : O. HAAS, Die phrygischen Sprachdenkmäler, Linguistique Balkanique XI Sofia 1966. — Das Problem der Herkunft der Phryger, Acta Antique Academiae Scientiarum Hungaricae 18, 1970, 31-69. O W. MUSCARELLA, Phrygian or Lydian, JNES, 30, 1971,49-63. G. NEUMANN, Phryger und die Phrygische Sprache, Der Kleine Pauly IV 822-825. W. Wilson CUMMER, Phrygian Roof Tiles in the Burdur Museum, Anadolu 14, 1970, 30-71. C.H. Emilie HASPELS, The Highlands of Phrygia, Sites and Monuments 2 vols., Princeton N. J. 1971. Claude BRIXHE, un ouvrage sur la Langue phrygienne, Revue de Philologie II 1968, 306-319. M. J. MELLINK, Mita, Mushki and Phrygians, Anadolu Araştırmaları (Festschrift für H. Th. Bossert) Istanbul 1965, 317-325. G. L. HUXLEY, Titles of Midas, Greek-Roman-and-Byzantine Studies. 2, 1959 (Cambridge, Massachusetts) 85-99.

SARDIS: G.M.A. HANFMANN, on late Roman and Early Byzantine Portraits from Sardis, Hommages à Marcel Renard, III Collection Latomus, vol. 103, Brussels 1969, 288-295. Andrew RAMAGE, The Fourteenth Campaign at Sardis (1971) BASOR, 206, 1972, 9-39. Crawford H. GREENEWALT, Jr. An exhibitionist from Sardis (Studies presented to George M. A. Hanfmann, von Zabern Mainz 1971, 29-46. — Lydian vases from Western Asia Minor, California Studies in Classical Antiquity I, 1968, 141-154. Andrew R. SEAGER, The building History of the Sardis Synagogue, AJA, 76, 1972, 425-435. John Griffiths PEDLEY, Ancient literary Sources on Sardis, Archaeological Exploration of Sardis, Harvard University Press 1972.

SMYRNA : Georg PETZL, Zwei Inschriften aus Smyrna, Zeitschrift für Papyrologie und Epigraphik 9, 1972, 61-67. Romolo Augusto STACCIOLI, Gli edifici sotterranei dell'agora di Smirne e ancora, sui cripto-portici forensi, Latomus 16, 1957, 275-292.

THRAKIA : Zafer TAŞLIKLIOĞLU, Trakya'da Epigrafya Araştırmaları, Istanbul Edebiyat Fakültesi 1971.

TOPAKLI : Luigi POLACCO, Excavations at Topaklı, preliminary reports, Studi Micenei ed Egeo-Anatolici, Fassicolo Ottavo 1969, 76-84; Fassicolo Decimo , 1969 54-68; Fassicolo XIV, 1971, 7-25 ; Fassicolo XIV 1971 ,27-38.

TROY : Wolfram HOEPFNER, Zum Entwurf des Athenatempels in Ilion, AM 84, 1969, 165-181. H. KÄHLER, Athenatempel in Ilion, Gnomon, 36, 1964, 79 ff. Oğuz EROL, Photo-Geomorphologic Map of the Troy Area, Jeomorfoloji Dergisi 4, 1972, 1-12.

URARTU : Tahsin ÖZGÜÇ, Altıntepe II, Tombs, Storehouse and Ivories TTK. Ankara 1969. R. D. BARNETT, An Urartian Mirror, Festschrift für Bossert Istanbul 1965, 51-54. O. W. MUSCARELLA, Near Eastern Bronzes in the West, Art and Technology, A Symposium on Classical Bronzes, The Mass. Inst. of Technology 1970, 109-128. W. KLEISS, Urartäische Plätze in Iranisch-Azerbaidjan, Ist. Mitt. 18, 1968, 1-44. M. SALVINI, Neue Urartäische Inschriften aus Karmir Blur, Orientalia 36,1967,437-449. Urartäisches epigraphisches Material aus und Umgebung Van (Belleten 37, 1973). Franz HANCAR, Das Urartäische Lebensbaummotiv, Iranica Antiqua VI, 1966, 92-108. I. M. DIAKONOFF, Hurrisch und Urartäisch, München 1971.

XANTHOS : Henri METZGER, Fouilles du Létoon de Xanthos (1966-1969). R. A. 1970, 307-322.

BOOKS ON VARIOUS SUBJECTS

AKARCA, A., Şehir savunmaları TTK Ankara 1972.

AMANDRY, P. Gnomon 41, 1969, 796-802 (Herrmann, Die Kessel der orientalisierenden Zeit).

BAYBURTLUOĞLU, Cevdet, Tekirdağ Kuros'u, Belleten 34, 1970, 347-351.

FIRATLI, Nezih, Uşak Selçikler Kazısı TAD 19, 1970, 109-160.

GRAEVE, Volkmar von, Der Alexander Sarkophag und seine Werkstatt, Ist. Forschungen 28, Berlin 1970.

HARRISON, R. M., Churches and chapels in central Lycia, Anatolian Studies 13, 1963.— Architectural Sculpture in Central Lycia, Anatolian Studies 22, 1972,187-197.

HASE, Friedrich-Wilhelm von, Zum Fragment eines Orientalischen Bronzeflügels aus Vetulonia RM 79, 1972, 155 165.

HOEPFNER, Wolfram, Zum ionischen Kapitell bei Hermogenes und Vitruv, AM, 83, 1968, 213-234.

HÖLSCHER, Fernande, Die Bedeutung Archaischer Tierkampfbilder, Konrad Triltsch Verlag, Würzburg 1972.

HROUDA, Barthel, Vorderasien I, Mesopotamien, Iran und Anatolien (Handbuch der Archäologie) München 1971.

KASPER, Sandor, Eine Nekropole nordwestlich von Soma, AA 1970, 71-85.— Zum grossen Altar der Demeter-Terrasse (Pergamen. Forschungen I Berlin 197).

LAVIOSA, Clelia, Una testa ionica archaica di Museo Arch. di Firenze, Rivista Archeologia Classica 16, 1964, 13-25.

LEONARD, Marie Brian, Braziers in the Bodrum Museum, AJA, 77, 1973, 19 - 25.

MANSEL, Mélanges Mansel, TTK Ankara 1973 (2 vols.).

MARTIN, Roland, Chapitaux ioniques de Thasos, BCH 96, 1972, 303-325.

METZLER, Dieter, Ein Meisterwerk Späntantiker Porträtkunst, AA 1969, 195-203.

MOORTGAT, Anton, Noch einmal zur Datierung des Kapara, Festschrift für Kurt Galling, Tübingen 1970, 211-217.

NIZETTE-GODFROID, J., contribution à l'étude de l'influence du Lion Neo-Hittite sur la constitution du type léonine dans l'art grec Orientalisant, l'Antiquité Classique 41, 1972, 5-48.

NIBBE, Alessandra, The Sea Peoples : A reexamination of the Egyptian Sources Oxford 1972.

NYLANDER, Carl, Ionians in Pasargade, Uppsala 1970.

SEYRIG, Henri, Une déesse anatolienne, Antike Kunst 13, 1970, 76-78.

SPANOS, Peter Z., Untersuchungen über den bei Homer "depas amphikypellon" genannten Gefässtypus, Tübingen 1972.

STROCKA, V. M., Kleinasiatische Klinensarkophag-Deckel, AA 1971, 62-86.

USSISHKIN, David, The date of the Neo-Hittite enclosure at Sakçagözü, BASOR 181, 1966, 15-23. — Observations on some monuments from Carchemish, JNES 26, 1967, 87-92.— Building IV in Hamath and the temples of Solomon and Tell Tayanat, Israel Exploration Journal 16, 1966, 104-110. — On the Dating of some Groups of Reliefs from Carchemish and Til Barsib, Anatolian Studies 18, 1967, 181-192. WEBER, Martha, Die geometrischen Driefusskessel, AM 86, 1971, 12-30.

PLATES

Troy, Fortifications of the sixth settlement. Destroyed about 1240 B. C. Above in the foreground, Tower VIh. In the background Gateway VIS. Below, the wall between Gateway VIS and Tower VIh.

Rock-relief at Ivriz near Ereğli, Konya. King Warpalawas paying homage to the god of fertility.
Neo-Hittite style with Aramaean influence. Second half of the 8th century B. C.

Phrygian round-mouthed jug, found in a tumulus at Gordion. Middle Phrygian style.
About 700 B. C. Archaeological Museum, Ankara.

a. Phrygian cult monument at Midas City near Eskişehir. 6th century B. C.
b. Phrygian cult monument with high relief of Cybele in the niche.
   Near Afyonkarahisar, 6th century B. C.

a. A Lycian tomb on the acropolis at Xanthus. Fourth century B. C.

b. A Lycian rock-tomb at Limyra. Late 4th century B. C.

A Lycian rock-tomb at Antiphellus. Fourth century B. C.

Ivory statuettes found in the foundations of the Artemis Temple in Ephesus. Left, lady with distaff and spindle. Late 7th century B. C. Right, eunuch-priest. Beginning of the 6th century B. C. Archaeological Museum, Istanbul.

a. Priene. Terrace wall of the Athena Temple. Fourth century B. C. In the background to the right, the remains of the propylon. Augustan age. In the foreground, the rear wall of the sacred agora. About 130 B. C.

b. Priene. The remains of the Temple of Zeus. 3rd century B. C.

a. The Alexander Sarcophagus from the royal necropolis at Sidon. Late fourth century B. C. Archaeological Museum, Istanbul.

b. Pergamon. The sanctuary of Demeter. 3rd century B. C.

9

a. Uzuncaburç (Diocaesarea or Olba) near Silifke. Temple of Zeus of the Corinthian order.
    3rd century B. C.
b. Labranda. Andron A. Middle of the 4th century B. C.

a. Didymaion. The three upstanding columns of the second row of the dipteros.
First half of the second century B. C. See also Pls. 68-71.

b. Miletos. In the foreground, the court of the Bouleuterion (175-164 B. C.). In the background,
centre, the remains of the fountain, 2nd century A. D. On the right, the foundations of the
entrance pylon of the South Agora. 2nd century A. D.

11

Aizanoi. Temple of Zeus. Pseudodipteros of 8 by 15 columns of the Ionic order.
Reign of Hadrian (A. D. 117-138).

Miletos. Theatre. Built in the Hellenistic age and rebuilt in Roman times.

13

a. Aphrodisias. Stadium. Roman period.
b. Perge. Stadium. Roman period.

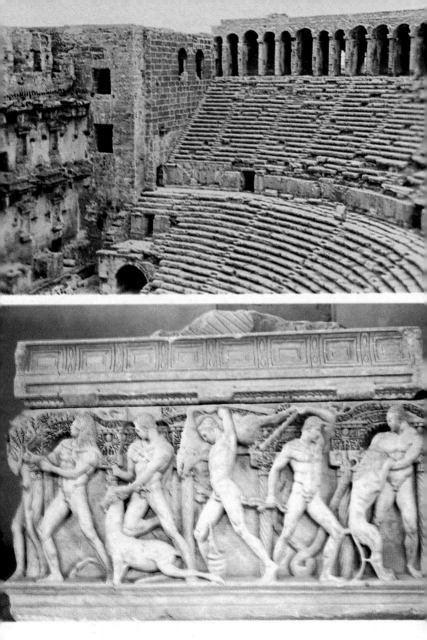

a. Aspendus. The theatre, designed by the architect Zeno, son of Theodorus, during the reign of
   Marcus Aurelius (A. D. 161-180).
b. Columnar sarcophagus found at Yunuslar near Konya. About A. D. 250.
   Archaeological Museum, Konya.

15

a. Nemrud Dağ. West court. Colossal heads of Zeus and Antiochus I of Commagene. About 50 B. C. See also pl. 112.

16

b. Detail of Demeter in the Agora at Izmir. Middle of the 2nd century A. D. See also Pl. 49-51.

Neo-Hittite orthostat relief with a banquet scene, Zincirli. 832-810 B. C. Archaeological Museum, İstanbul.

a. Column-base from Zincirli. Neo-Hittite - Aramaean style with Assyrian influences. Last quarter of the 8th century B. C. Archaeological Museum, İstanbul.

b. Neo-Hittite orthostat relief from Zincirli, 832-810 B. C. Archaeological Museum, İstanbul.

Marble head of a young man from Samos. Archaic Ionic style. 560 B. C.
Archaeological Museum, İstanbul. (Parts of the body are in the Samos Museum).

Graeco - Achaemenid funerary
stele from Daskyleion.
About 400 B. C.
Archaeological Museum, İstanbul.

a. Lycian sarcophagus from the royal necropolis at Sidon. Amazons (?) in chariot hunting a lion. About 400 B. C. Archaeological Museum, İstanbul.

b. Detail from the other side of the same sarcophagus. Men on horseback hunting a wild boar.

21

a. Sarcophagus of the Mourning Women from the royal necropolis at Sidon. About 350 B. C.
Archaeological Museum, İstanbul.

b. Alexander the Great, hunting. Detail from the hunting scene on the Alexander Sarcophagus found in the royal necropolis at Sidon. Late 4th century B. C.
Archaeological Museum, İstanbul.

22

Alexander the Great, fighting. Detail from the battle scene on the Alexander Sarcophagus found in the royal necropolis at Sidon (see pl. 9a). Late 4 th century B. C. Archaeological Museum, İstanbul.

Marble statue of
Alexander the Great by
Menas of Pergamon.
Found in Magnesia a l
Sipylum. Middle of th 2
second century B. C.
Archaeological
Museum, Istanbul.

Marble head of Alexander the Great, found at Pergamon.
First half of the second century B. C. Archaeological Museum, İstanbul.

Marble statue of a young athlete
found at Tralleis (Aydın). Reign of
Augustus (27 B. C. - A. D. 14).
Archaeological Museum, İstanbul.

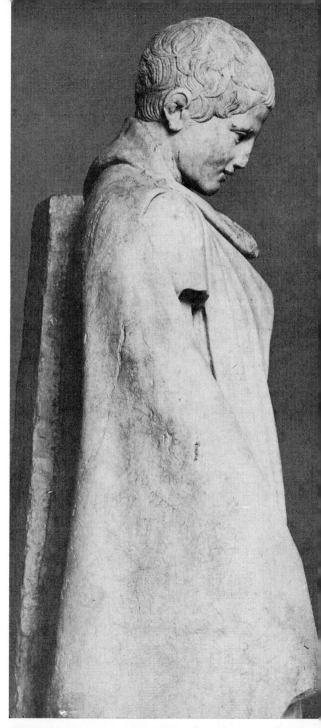

Marble statue of a young
athlete (side view)
found at Tralleis (Aydın).
(27 B. C. - A. D. 14).
Archaeological Museum,
İstanbul.

Marble statue of a young athlete (Detail). Found at Tralleis (Aydın).
Reign of Augustus (27 B. C. - A. D. 14). Archaeological Museum, İstanbul.

Column fragment from the Temple of Hadrian (A. D. 117-138) at Cyzicus. Open - Air Museum at Erdek, near Bandırma.

Fortifications of Assos in the Troad, showing the tower-flanked main gateway (bottom) and a smaller gate (top) of the city, 4th century B. C.

a. Pergamon. Theatre and long terrace, built in the 3rd century B. C. and partly renovated in the Roman period.

b. Pergamon. Theatre terrace with Dionysus Temple (see Pl. 32 and Pl. 35 b). Above, terrace wall of the Temple of Trajan (see Pl. 34a).

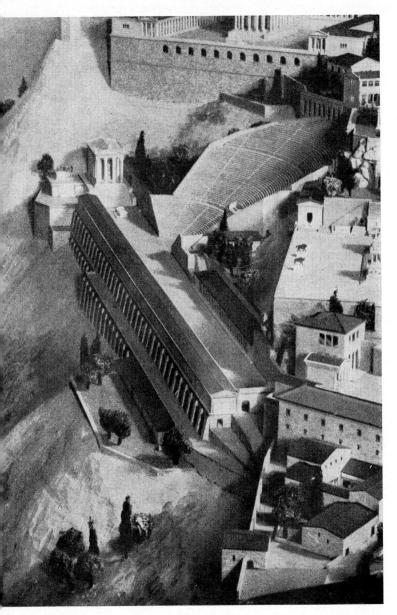

Pergamon. Model of the west part of the citadel. Above, the Temple of Trajan with supporting terrace wall; in the centre, the theatre with the terrace wall and the Dionysus Temple.

a. Pergamon. In the centre, the Temple of Athena, 4th century B.C., with its surrounding colonnades, 2nd century B.C., and the library adjoining the northern colonnade of the Athena Sanctuary, 2nd century B.C. In the background, the palaces of Attalos (on the left) and of Eumenes (on the right).

b. Pergamon. In the centre, the Great Altar of Zeus (see also Pl. 34b). In the background to the right, the Agora, second century B.C.

a. Temple of Trajan (A. D. 98-117) with surrounding colonnades.
b. Great Altar of Pergamon. First half of the second century B. C.

a. Great Altar of Pergamon. The foundations.
b. Temple of Dionysus, built in the second century B. C. and renovated by Caracalla (A.D. 211-217).

a. Pergamon. The upper gymnasium, seen from the west. Built in the Hellenistic age and greatly altered in the Roman period.

b. Pergamon. The same gymnasium, viewed from the south-west.

a. Pergamon. Sanctuary of Demeter. Built in the 3rd century B. C. and partly altered in Roman times.

b. Pergamon. The lower agora. Built in the Hellenistic age and partly altered in the Roman period.

Pergamon. Marble head from the sacred way leading to the Asklepieion.
First half of the 2nd century B. C. Archaeological Museum, Bergama.

a. Pergamon. General view of the Asklepieion.
b. Pergamon. The theatre of the Asklepieion. Roman period.

a. Pergamon. Asklepieion. North colonnade. Roman period (first half of the 2nd century A. D.).
b. Pergamon. Asklepieion. The tunnel leading to the round building. Late 2nd century A. D.

a. Rock-relief of a Hittite King in the Karabel pass, inland from Smyrna. Second half of the 13th century B. C.
b. Hittite rock-relief of a goddess at Akpınar on the north foot of Mt. Sipylos near Manisa. Hittite period, 13th century B. C.
c. Bayraklı (ancient İzmir). Oval house. Mudbrick, about 900 B. C.

41

a. Capital from the Temple of Athena at Bayraklı (Old Smyrna). About 580 B. C.
b. Entrance way and south side of the Temple of Athena at Old Smyrna. About 580 B. C.

a. Ancient coin from Smyrna. Electrum, representing a lion's head. First half of the 6th century B. C. British Museum, London.

b,c. Statue of a lion from Bayındır near İzmir. Sixth century B. C. Archaeological Museum, İzmir.

Marble head of a young man from Keramos. About 540-530 B. C. Archaeological Museum, İzmir.

Group of two statues found at Torbalı, near İzmir. First century B. C. Archaeological
Museum, İzmir.

a. Alexander the Great dreaming under a plane - tree and the two Nemeses (goddesses
   worshipped in Smyrna) bidding him to found the new city of Smyrna on Mt. Pagos.
   Roman coin minted in the reign of Philippus Arabs (A. D. 244-249), von Aulock Collection,
   İstanbul.
b. Agora of İzmir. 2nd century A. D.

Marble head of a young lady found in İzmir. 2nd Century A. D. Archaeological Museum, İzmir.

a. Detail from a marble statue of a young hunter found in Ephesus. 2nd century B. C.
Archaeological Museum, İzmir.

b. Side view of the head in plate 47.

c, d. Marble head of "Aspasia" found at Ephesus. 2nd century A. D.
Archaeological Museum, İzmir.

Marble statues of Poseidon and Demeter, found and still standing in the Agora of Izmir. 2nd century A. D. Demeter was the goddess of corn and Poseidon the god of the sea. The ancient Smyrniotes of the 2nd century A. D., in representing these two deities side by side in their agora, wished perhaps to illustrate that they dominated both the land and the maritime commerce of their time.

49

Marble statue of Poseidon from the group in Plate 49.

Marble statue of Demeter from the group in Pl. 49.

Portrait statue of Flavius Damianus, the sophist, as imperial priest. Found in the west hall of the East Gymnasium at Ephesus. Period of Septimius Severus, about A. D. 200. Archaeological Museum, İzmir.

Portrait statue of a sophist. Found in the "Imperial Hall" of the Vedius Gymnasium.
Time of Septimius Severus, about A. D. 200. Archaeological Museum, İzmir.

Sardıs. Temple of Artemis, seen from the east (above) ad from the west (below). The temple
itself about 300 B. C. The columns of the peristasis surrounding the temple, about
A. D. 150. The capital surmounting the left-hand column in the picture below, 2nd
quarter of the 2nd century B. C

Teos. Temple of Dionysus, ca. 130 B.C. Peripteros of the Ionic order with 6 by 11 columns and stylobate measuring approximately 18.50 x 35.00 m. Built by Hermogenes.

a. Sardis. Marble Ionic capital from the Temple of Artemis. About 300 B. C. Standing on the site.
b. Ephesus. Temple of Hadrian (A. D. 117-138).

a. Ephesus. The Library of Celsus. Aout A. D. 110. Now beeing restored.
b. Ephesus. The Theatre, Built in the Hellenistic age and altered in Roman times.

Artemis Ephesia (detail), dating from the time of Hadrian (A.D. 117-138).
Archaeological Museum, Selçuk (Ephesus).

a. Hierapolis (Pamukkale). Roman baths.
b. Nysa (Sultanhisar). Council Chamber. Roman times.

Aphrodisias. Ruins of the Temple of Aphrodite. Erected in late Hellenistic times (about first century B. C.) and altered in the reign of the Emperor Hadrian (A. D. 117-138).

Aphrodisias. Temple of Aphrodite. Erected in the first century B. C.
Fourteen columns (of the Ionic order) are still standing.

a. Aphrodisias. Columns of the Agora.
b. Aphrodisias. The Stadium (see also Pl. 14a).

Aphrodisias. Aion, the representation of Eternity. Detail from the Zoilos frieze.
First century A. D. Local Musem at Aphrodisias.

a. Alinda. Substructure of Market Building. Hellenistic times.
b. Labranda. Temple of Zeus. Peripteros of the Doric order dating from the middle of the 4th century B. C.

a. Alinda. The east gateway of the theatre.
b. Labranda. Entrance to Andron A. Middle of the 4th century B. C.
c. Labranda. The south wall of Andron A, with windows. Middle of the 4th century B. C.

a. Priene. Street leading up to the Temple of Athena (3rd quarter of the 4th century B. C.). In the centre to the left, the terrace wall of the sanctuary of Athena. In the background, the remains of the Propylon built in the reign of Augustus.

B. Priene. Bouleuterion, or Council Chamber, about 150 B. C.

Priene. The theatre, built in the late 4th century, altered in Hellenistic and Roman times. Above, Prohedria (front row seating, benches of honour). Beginning of the 2nd century B. C. Below, theatre seen through the western parodos (side entrance).

Temple of Didyma. Dipteros of the Ionic order (300 B. C. - 2nd century A. D). Top, view from the southeast. The three columns still standing date from the first half of the 2nd century B. C. Bottom, cella (adyton) and chresmographeion (oracle room), seen from the west. In the foreground, foundations of the Hellenistic naiskos (about 300 B. C.) and remains of earlier naiskoi. The cella walls with griffin frieze date from the first half of the 2nd century B. C. The chresmographeion was built at the beginning of the 3rd century B. C.

Temple of Didyma. Two columns with capitals and architrave are still standing in the northern inner row of the surrounding colonnade of the temple. First half of the 2nd century B. C.

Temple of Didyma. Seventh column base from the south in the eastern outer row of the surrounding colonnade of the temple. Roman period.

Temple of Didyma. Third and fourth column bases from the south in the northern inner row of the surrounding colonnade of the temple. First half of the 2nd century B.C.

Corinthian capital from the Bouleuterion (Council Chamber) of Miletos. About 170 B.C. Standing on the site.

Corinthian capital from the Belevi Mausoleum near Ephesus. Middle of the 3rd century B. C. Standing on the site.

a. Didyma. Medusa head from the frieze of the temple, 2nd century A. D.

b. Miletos. Entrance pylon of the South Agora of Miletos, restored in the Berlin Museum. 2nd century A. D.

a. Alabanda. Bouleuterion (Council Chamber). Late Hellenistic period.
b. Herakleia under Latmus. City gate. Hellenistic period.

Halicarnassus, The newly-found sculptured slab from the frieze of the Mausoleum.
Middle of the 4th century B.C. Archaeological Museum, Bodrum.

Tomb at Mylasa (Milas). Second century A. D.

a. Euromos. Temple of Zeus. Peripteros of 6 by 11 columns of the Corinthian order.
   Middle of the 2nd century A. D.
b. Xanthus. Acropolis. In the background to the right, the Harpy tomb.
   First quarter of the 5th century B. C.

Aizanoi. Temple of Zeus. Pseudodipteros of the Ionic order with 8 by 15 columns.
Reign of Hadrian (A. D. 117-138).

79

Aizanoi. Temple of Zeus. Columns with composite capitals in opisthodomos.
Reign of Hadrian (A. D. 117-138).

Rock cut Phrygian tomb, called Arslantaş. Near Afyonkarahisar. 6th century B. C.

Rock cut Phrygian cult monument, called Arslankaya, with high relief of Kybele, flanked by two lions in the niche. Near Afyonkarahisar. 6th century B. C.

a. Ankara, Temple of Augustus and Roma. Probably erected at the beginning of the reign of Augustus about 25-20 B. C. and restored in its upper parts in later Roman times.

b. Ornaments on the cornice of the cella wall (Roman Imperial period).

c. Ornaments on the wall foot of the opisthodomos (early Augustan period).

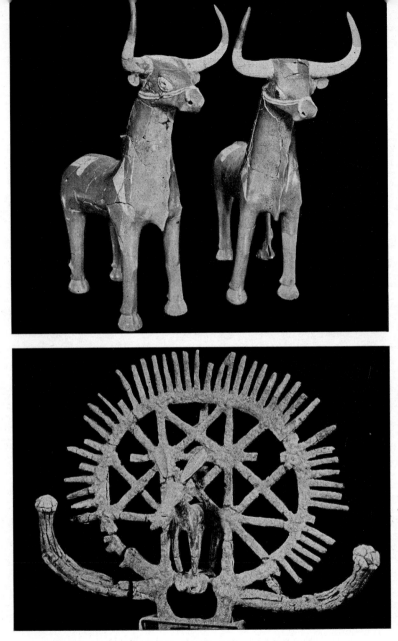

a. Hittite Rhyta (ritual vessels) found at Boğazköy. 14th century B. C. Archaeological Museum, Ankara.

b. Cult standard symbolizing the cosmos. Bronze. Found at Alacahöyük. About 2100-2000 B. C. Archaeological Museum, Ankara.

Cult standard in the form of a bronze stag. Found at Alacahöyük. 2100-2000 B. C.
Archaeological Museum, Ankara.

a. Early Hittite vessel in clay found at Alişar. 17 th century B. C. Ankara Museum.
b. Early Hittite beaker - jug in clay found at Alacahöyük. 17th century B. C. Ankara Museum.
c. Early Hittite jug in clay, found at Kültepe. 18th century B. C. Ankara Museum.
d. Early Hittite vessel in clay, found at Alacahöyük. 17th century B. C. Ankara Museum.

Hattic statuette of a woman, Silver, with gold - plated head and neck.
About 2000 B. C. Archaeological Museum, Ankara.

a. Hittite orthostat reliefs from the city wall of Alacahöyük. 14th century B.C. Archaeological Museum, Ankara.

b. Neo-Hittite orthostat relief, found at Carchemish. Middle Neo-Hittite style. About 750-717 B.C. Archaeological Museum, Ankara.

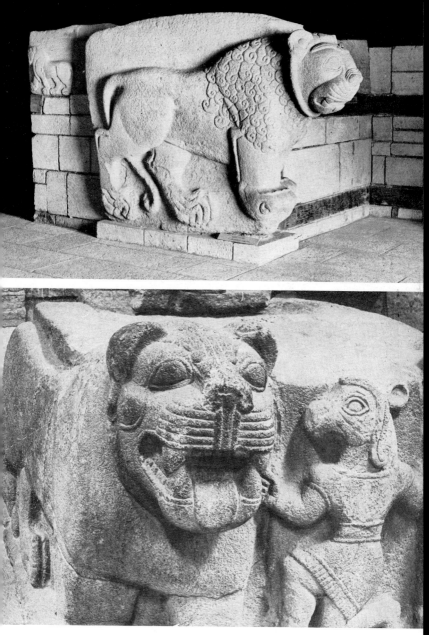

a. Lion from the Gateway at Malatya. Early Neo - Hittite style. About 1050-850 B. C.
   Archaeological Museum. Ankara.
b. Lion base of a statue, found at Carchemish Middle Neo - Hittite style. About 750-717 B. C.
   Archaeological Museum, Ankara.

a. Orthostat relief with lion - hunting scene, found at Malatya. Middle Neo - Hittite style.
   8th century B. C. Archaeological Museum, Ankara.
b. Funerary stele representing a wine merchant with his wife. Found at Maraş.
   Neo-Hittite - Aramaean style. About 700 B. C. Archaeological Museum, Ankara.

Orthostat relief found at Carchemish, representing a war chariot.
Middle Neo - Hittite style. 750-717 B.C. Archaeological Museum, Ankara.

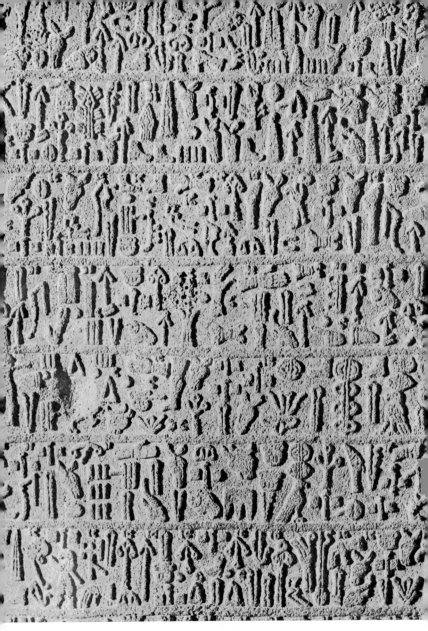

Hieroglyphic monument from Neo-Hittite period. Found at Carchemish. 8th century B. C.

a. Alacahöyük. City-Gate with sphinxes (original) and orthostat reliefs restored in concrete casts. 13th century B. C. The original slabs are in the Archaeological Museum in Ankara (see Pl. 88 a).

b. Boğazköy. Great temple of the Weather - God and the Sun - Goddess of Arinna. Storage jars in the northwest store-rooms. 13th century B. C.

Columnar sarcophagus found at Yunuslar (Pappa Tiberiopolis) near Konya. The front end; the seated man is the dead person; he is represented as a philosopher. See also pl. 15 b. About A. D. 250. Archaeological Museum, Konya.

a. Termessos. Bouleuterion. Hellenistic period.
b. Termessos. Theatre, originally erected in the Hellenistic age, →
   restored in Roman times.

a. Perge. Theatre. Roman period.
b. Perge. Colonnaded street. Roman Period.

Head of Aphrodite. Roman copy, middle of the 2nd century A. D. Found at Perge. Archaeological Museum, Antalya.

a. Perge. Outer Gate. 4th century A. D.
b. Perge. Inner Gate. Hellenistic Period.

a. Side. Temple of Apollo (Temple NI). 2nd half of the 2nd century A. D.
b. Side. Arcades of the theatre. Roman Period.

Aspendus. Theatre, designed by the architect Zeno, son of Theodorus, during the reign of Marcus Aurelius (A. D. 161-180). Dedicated to the gods and to the Imperial House.

Aspendus. Theatre. See also Pl. 15a.

Uzuncaburç, Diocaesarea (Olba). Temple of Zeus in Corinthian style, 3rd century B. C.
a, b. Capitals from the temple. c. General view of the temple.

a. Uzuncaburç, Diocaesarea (Olba). Tychaeum. Second half of the first century A. D.
b. Uzuncaburç, Diocaesarea (Olba). Columns from the colonnaded street. Roman period.

Close - up of the columns seen in Pl. 103 b.

Karatepe near Adana. Orthostat with mother suckling her child.
Neo - Hittite - Phoenician style. about 700 B. C. Open - Air Museum at Karatepe.

Karatepe near Adana. Orthostat relief. Neo-Hittite style, about 700 B. C. Open - Air Museum at Karatepe.

a. Column - base from the temple at Tell Tainat. Assyrian lion - type of the Tiglath - Pileser period used as a Hittite architectural motif. 2nd half of the 8th century B. C. Archaeological Museum, Antakya.

b. Hittite - Aramaean column base from the Bit Hilani at Tell Tainat. 730-700 B. C. Archaeological Museum, Antakya.

Mosaic found at Antiocheia. The Evil Eye. Second century A. D. Archaeological Museum, Antakya.

Huge slab representing a hand - shaking scene between King Mithradates Kallinikos of Commagene and Heracles. Hierotheseion at Arsameia, Commagene. About 50 B. C. Standing on the site.

King Mithradates Kallinikos. Detail from the hand - shaking scene in pl. 109.

Heracles. Detail from the hand-shaking scene in pl. 109.

Nemrud Dağ, west court. Colossal heads of Zeus (in the foreground) and of Antiochus I of Commagene (in the background). About 50 B. C. See also pl. 16 a.

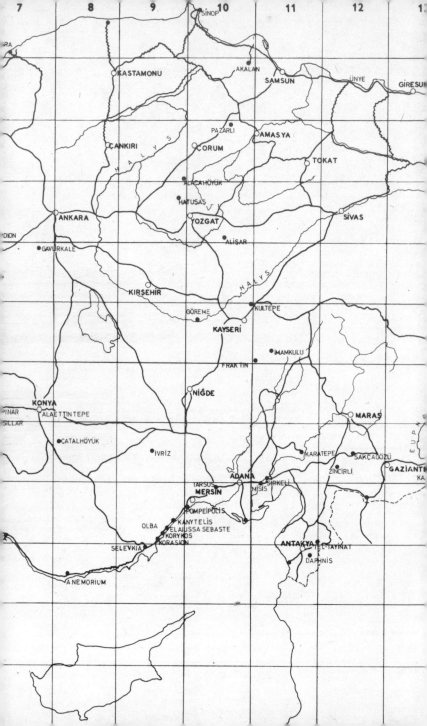